# Positive Development

## From Vicious Circles to Virtuous Cycles
## through Built Environment Design

*Janis Birkeland*

publishing for a sustainable future

London • Sterling, VA

First published by Earthscan in the UK and USA in 2008

ISBN:    978-1-84407-578-2    hardback
         978-1-84407-579-9    paperback

Typeset by Safehouse Creative
Printed and bound in the UK by MPG Books Ltd, Bodmin, Cornwall
Cover design by Rob Watts

For a full list of publications please contact:

**Earthscan**
Dunstan House
14a St Cross Street
London  EC1N 8XA
UK
Tel:  +44 (0)20 7841 1930
Fax:  +44 (0)20 7242 1474
Email:  earthinfo@earthscan.co.uk
Web:  **www.earthscan.co.uk**

22883 Quicksilver Drive, Sterling, VA 20166-2012, USA

Earthscan publishes in association with the International Institute
for Environment and Development

A catalogue record for this book is available from the British Library

Library of Congress Cataloging-in-Publication Data

Birkeland, Janis, 1945-
  Positive development : from vicious circles to virtuous cycles through built environment design /
Janis Birkeland.
    p. cm.
  ISBN 978-1-84407-579-9 (pbk.) -- ISBN 978-1-84407-578-2 (hardback)  1.  Ecological engineering.
2.  Sustainable development. 3.  Sustainable architecture.  I. Title.
  GE350.B58 2008
  628--dc22
                                                                              2008011448

The paper used for this book is FSC-certified.
FSC (the Forest Stewardship Council) is an
international network to promote responsible
management of the world's forests.

**Mixed Sources**
Product group from well-managed
forests and other controlled sources
www.fsc.org  Cert no. SA-COC-1565
© 1996 Forest Stewardship Council

# Positive Development

PRAISE FOR *Positive Development*

'This is a wonderful book that should be on the desk of every architect and planner. It shows how our decisions about the built environment can be a positive contribution to shaping a sustainable future.'
Emeritus Professor Ian Lowe, President, Australian Conservation Foundation

'One of the best books on sustainability I've read in a long time … clear, compelling, and dead on. The challenges of sustainability are fundamentally design problems and Janis Birkeland is a remarkably insightful guide to the transformation. Must reading.'
David Orr, Oberlin College, author of *The Nature of Design* and *Ecological Literacy*

'Birkeland's book takes the next step beyond Ian McHarg's design with nature and Janine Benyus's design like nature. It argues that design *for* nature, or "design for eco-services", is long overdue, and explains how we can do it.'
Hunter Lovins, President and founder of the Natural Capitalism Solutions

'A heralding work of how a positive and innovative design agenda for the built environment, underlined by an uncompromising valuation of ecology and nature's services, can mobilize our efforts in becoming native to the planet.'
Michael Braungart, Professor of Material Flow Management at University Lüneburg, Germany and co-author of *Cradle to Cradle*

'Drawing on her expertise in law, planning and design, Janis Birkeland always has something startling to say. And in an area dominated by so much utopian dreaming, she puts politics as well as careful analysis into sustainability. This book is an unusual, and heartening, combination of the radical and the realistic.'
Clive Hamilton, former Executive Director of The Australia Institute, author of *Growth Fetish* and co-author of *Affluenza*

'While some are beginning to realise that we cannot continue to take resources from, and dump waste freely back on, our planet, there still pervades the notion that *sustainable development* is about minimizing the impacts of these actions. Birkeland convincingly argues that this cannot continue. She then shows us how we can "develop" in a way that replenishes and increases the planet's life-giving services through "Net Positive Design". I urge that this book be read and championed equally by our infrastructure designers as well as those working traditionally with buildings.'
David A. Hood, FIEAust CPEng, Chairman, Australian Green Infrastructure Council

'This book provides a framework for an approach that brings together environmental management, policymaking, planning and sustainable design. It shows how design can increase the ecological base and public estate over pre-development site conditions. It is invaluable not just to designers but to all those whose work impinges on the environment.'
Ken Yeang, Architect, Llewelyn Davies Yeang, UK

'Birkeland is one of the world's leading thinkers on sustainable built environments. In this book she distils her wealth of experience into a very accessible text on how we can achieve net positive development, for urban and regional planning and design.'
The Natural Edge Project, authors of *The Natural Advantage of Nations*

To my ancestors, family and progeny

# Contents

# Figures and Tables

## Figures

## Tables

# Preface

Nature has provided for the infrastructure and basic services to support human life, and has even subsidized our profligate Western lifestyles. Now, however, we have exceeded the Earth's carrying capacity. We have also exhausted the cultural and social viability of many resource-rich, but impoverished countries and colonies around the world. This unilateral relationship between humans and nature must be reversed. Fortunately, urban design and architecture could undo much of the damage of past policies, actions and developments. However, genuine sustainability will require more than social change and ecological 'restoration'. *It will require increasing the total amount of ecosystem goods and services, as well as increasing the health and resilience of the natural environment.* This book contends that the built environment can create the infrastructure, conditions and space for nature to continue its life-support services and self-maintenance functions. Development can provide greater life quality, health, amenity, conviviality and safety for all – without sacrificing resources, money or comfort. For it to do so, however, we need a new approach to the planning, design and management of our built environment. What we will call 'Positive Development' would actually expand the 'ecological base', meaning ecosystem goods and services, natural capital, biodiversity and habitats, ecological health and resilience, and bio-security. It would also expand the 'public estate', meaning the substantive democracy that ultimately depends on equitable access to, and expansion of, the ecological base – the means of survival.

Our current methods for addressing sustainability challenges are shaped by institutional and intellectual frameworks that reflect negative, defensive attitudes towards the environment. Negative impacts are seen as inevitable, so we only aim to slow the pace of environmental destruction. The belief that we have no option but to 'trade off' nature for social and economic gain is deeply engrained. We assume the best that sustainable development can do is provide (short-term) *social* benefits that compensate for long-term *ecological* losses. Traditionally, policymakers and environmental managers have thought they were dealing with sustainable development issues by merely monitoring, measuring, managing and mitigating the predicted negative impacts of future plans, policies and designs. However, creating environments that are socially and ecologically productive requires breaking out of our mental cubicles and undoing what has already been done. Towards that end, this book provides:

- New paradigms and design concepts that enable us to *expand* future options, increase resource security, increase human and ecological health, and improve life quality for all.
- New design criteria, review processes, assessment tools and design methods that shift from narrow 'input–output thinking' to design that *supports* natural systems and communities.
- New approaches to analysis, assessment and management systems that move from mitigating negative impacts to multiplying *positive* ecological and social synergies.
- New approaches to futures planning methods, strategies and incentives that do not just prepare for a grim future, but increase the means of survival and *meaningful* life choices.

A critique of 'best practice' planning, design and management systems forms the basis for new methods and processes to facilitate design and innovation for net Positive Development. We will call this *positive* approach 'SmartMode' (short for Systems Mapping And Re-design Thinking Mode). It is intended to reverse negative attitudes towards the natural and built environment, and provide an analytic framework to help us reverse the impacts of *past* development by design. SmartMode aims to help us leapfrog the intellectual and institutional barriers that are entrenched in the foundations of urban and regional planning, natural resource management, and even 'green' urban design and building. It challenges vestiges of negative thinking in green design criteria, standards, benchmarks, rating tools, reporting systems, planning strategies and design methods. Alternatives to each of these are suggested to help de-couple environmental impacts from economic growth, but also to *add value* to the public estate (at a net economic gain). This may, however, only be possible through community-based initiatives, to which industry and government must contribute, but which they must not control. The suggestions are collated in the last section to provide a generic framework to guide more positive forms of community planning, design and decision-making.

# Acknowledgements

I would like to thank people who have read and commented on parts or all of drafts, including Wendy Rainbird, Joanne Warren-Wilson, Heather Aslin, Konrad Knerr, Sharon Stacy, Stephen Boyden, Robin Tennant-Wood, Richard Mochelle, Shannon Satherly, Christina Renger, Dominique Ness, Cheryl Desha and the team from The Natural Edge project, Ben O'Callaghan and anonymous reviewers at Earthscan. Thanks also to Daniel Thomas for preparing the illustrations and Denise Scott and Deborah Murray for proofing the draft. In addition, I would like to thank the Faculty of Built Environment and Engineering at the Queensland University of Technology for the friendly work environment. In particular, I thank my students who, without exception, have suffered this material over the years with bewildering tolerance and chirpy dispositions. No one is responsible for any aspects of the content or errors but the author.

# Reader's Map

**Boxes**: To assist the reader, this book has a section of boxes on pages 275 to 342, referred to throughout the text, which are intended to provide complementary information, some from specialist contributors.

**Glossary**: Some new terms, or terms used in a special way, are used to help shift from conventional ways of thinking. These are defined at their first usage in the text. A glossary of both conventional and special terms is also provided at the back of the book.

Positive Development requires basic changes at the urban level

| Section A<br>*Urban Level* | Chapter 1<br>Design for<br>Eco-services | Chapter 2<br>The Case for<br>Eco-retrofitting | Chapter 3<br>Sustainable Urban<br>Form |

Basic changes at the urban level require new kinds of planning and design

| Section B<br>*Building Level* | Chapter 4<br>Development<br>Standards and Criteria | Chapter 5<br>Building Rating<br>Tools | Chapter 6<br>Design Methods<br>and Models |

Changes in design and planning need new environmental management concepts

| Section C<br>Management<br>Approaches | Chapter 7<br>Urban Sustainability<br>Assessment | Chapter 8<br>Regional<br>Sustainability Audits | Chapter 9<br>Sustainability<br>Reporting |

Changes in environmental management need new methods and strategies

| Section D<br>Newer<br>Strategies | Chapter 10<br>Futures Thinking<br>Tools | Chapter 11<br>Eco-service Trading<br>Schemes | Chapter 12<br>Bioregional<br>Planning |

New strategies require new approaches to eco-governance

| Section E<br>Eco-<br>governance | Chapter 13<br>Constitution for<br>Eco-governance | Chapter 14<br>Reversing Resource<br>Transfers | Chapter 15<br>The SmartMode<br>Process |

# Introduction

## Sustainability versus Negativity

This introduction explains why sustainability requires that we expand future options through reversible, adaptable, net Positive Development. Positive Development refers to physical development that achieves net positive impacts during its life cycle over pre-development conditions by increasing economic, social *and* ecological capital. Positive Development would not only generate clean energy, air and water, it would leave the ecology better than before development. It would be 'reversible' as well as achieving net positive impacts over its life cycle. No one suggests that buildings should be structurally unsound, yet we still allow buildings that are ecologically unsound. From a whole systems perspective – and one grounded in real life – a building would not be considered 'structurally sound' if it falls down either socially or ecologically. So-called 'green buildings' have begun to address the human environment, but not the ecology. Given the Earth's diminishing biodiversity and carrying capacity, development can only be considered sustainable where it increases natural capital and reduces overall resource flows – as well as meeting conventional sustainable development criteria [Boxes 15 and 22]. Some eco-solutions that improve environmental conditions and create positive multiplier effects through resource reduction and waste reuse already exist. However, they are not yet integrated into our designs and structures.[1] But first, it is important that we are clear about what is meant by 'sustainability' in the context of this book, as the term is often used in different ways in different circles.[2]

Perhaps the first statement of sustainability by a national government was in NEPA, the 1969 US National Environmental Protection Act. Almost four decades ago, the preamble contained the basic issues and ethical mandates that the term sustainability generally implies today. It implied intra-generational and inter-generational equity, resource limits, transborder flows, and the need for transdisciplinarity and participatory decision-making.[3] However, the term 'sustainable development' perhaps first came into common currency among sentient people with the World Conservation Strategy in 1980 (produced by the IUCN/UNEP/WWF, re-published as *Caring for the Earth* in 1991[4]). Like some other early definitions, sustainability was defined as 'improving the quality of human life while living within the carrying capacity of supporting ecosystems'. This definition was a fairly positive one in suggesting we can improve life quality and asserting the importance of carrying capacity and ecosystem health to human survival and life quality. However, another implication contained in this and similar definitions was negative – the suggestion that we could not increase the Earth's carrying capacity and ecological health. We cannot improve upon nature, but we can allow nature to expand.

### But isn't it important to emphasize the limits of resources and nature?

Absolutely. It was important back then. The focus on the limits of nature was necessary to overcome the widespread 'myth-perception' that technological fixes could perpetuate industrial growth for ever, or at least beyond the horizon of current decision-makers' life-spans. By emphasizing the existence of ecological thresholds, these early definitions attempted to *counteract* the false but widespread belief that development could continue 'as usual'. It backfired, however. The soft notion of sustainable development as 'living within limits' was subsequently watered down by the seminal United Nations

*Brundtland Report* (1987).[5] This provided what is now the standard definition: 'development that meets the needs of today without compromising the ability of future generations to meet their own needs'. The *Brundtland Report*, published as *Our Common Future*, presumed that negative impacts could be mitigated through more knowledge and technology, but assumed that the Earth's carrying capacity had not been reached. The *Millennium Ecosystem Assessment Report*, published less than 20 years later (in 2005), made it clear that we have already degraded 60 per cent of the Earth's ecosystems services – including farms, fisheries and forests, and significant biodiversity.[6] What was useful about the definition in *Our Common Future* was that it emphasized the links between the distribution of wealth and environmental problems.

### So was the Brundtland definition an advance over earlier definitions?

In some ways. The problem was that the *Brundtland Report* took for granted that negative impacts and tradeoffs were necessary as "economic growth and development obviously involve changes in the physical ecosystem". "A forest may be depleted in one part of a watershed and extended elsewhere, which is not a bad thing if the exploitation has been planned and the effects on soil erosion rates, water regimes and genetic losses have been taken into account".[7] In other words, the conventional view was that, as long as we 'know what we are doing', we can interfere in natural systems. In reality, we will never fully understand the infinite complexity of nature. Yet the *Brundtland Report* sanctioned the ideas of sustainable yield and 'substitutability' as long as we can assess the impacts. Substitutability is the notion that, if wealth-producing development and industrial infrastructure replaces nature with means of production, future generations can be compensated for the loss of environmental amenity and 'luxuries' like wilderness experiences.[8] The creation of an international document calling for sustainable development as well as social justice was a virtually unparalleled accomplishment. However, it framed the concept of sustainability as 'industrial growth with less impacts'. Oddly, mainstream environmental management and planning has never really challenged the terminal process of offsetting ecological losses with social benefits.

### But isn't industrial growth necessary to meet basic human needs?

Logically, industrial growth cannot meet basic human needs, over the long term, unless it has *net positive* ecological and democratic outcomes. Growth has instead relied on a fanciful 'trickle-down' effect. Not only did the *Brundtland Report* definition allow for substitution, 'needs' were not adequately differentiated from consumer 'preferences'. Humans *need* a healthy natural support system that provides access to the 'means of survival' (land, air, water, soil, food and other ecosystem goods and services) – not just the 'means of production'. While the *Brundtland Report* was an impressive milestone, it marginalized ecology from the mainstream sustainable development debate. It treated nature as only a resource, and framed the sustainability issue as one of resource efficiency and equitable distribution. In other words 'how to divide things up' more fairly. For example, it considered a 3 per cent growth in GDP (Gross Domestic Product) to be essential to achieving social equity and environmental quality. We will see that only design, not accounting, can de-couple economic growth from environmental impacts. According to the CSIRO (Australia's government-supported research body), a 3 per cent growth in Australia's GDP could easily be achieved by mere efficiencies in the construction industry, along with a 10 per cent reduction in construction costs. However, if we continue simply to produce more products more efficiently (sometimes called 'green business'), a 3 per cent growth in GDP could mean a geometric escalation of total resource flows.[9] Our definition of sustainability has therefore created problems by equating it with 'sustainable consumption'. A positive approach to sustainable development would instead make the health, resilience and expansion of the life-support system central to development decisions and economic planning.

## Can we base policy on sustainability goals without a shared definition?

Shared definitions and explicit understandings are indeed important. After all, we should have waited for a definition of the petrochemical economy before rushing headlong into it. But while some researchers have counted over 400 different definitions of sustainability in the literature, there is nonetheless a certain consistency among them. Most definitions simply vary across a spectrum from anthropocentric (human-centred) to ecocentric (ecology-centred). However, they are ultimately compatible when people fully appreciate how human survival and wellbeing depend on the ecological integrity of the planet. The term sustainability has helped to convey the realization that everything we do affects everything else, and that nature is a complex system that is inseparable from society – another complex system. However, sustainability and equality in consumption would not mean much if future generations have nothing, or live in steel cages within concrete jungles that are not of their own making or choosing. True sustainability requires intra- and inter-generational justice and democracy. For future generations to enjoy substantive democracy, they would have to be ensured the same or a greater range of meaningful choices and environments as we have today. So we need a stronger conception of sustainability: *expanding* future options, or at least keeping options open.[10] This suggests that sustainability will require not only behaviour change, but fundamental changes in the way we design our institutions, infrastructure, buildings and decision-making systems – and ultimately even our cultures and religions.

## Hasn't the term 'sustainability' already been co-opted by industrial interests?

Today, as in the 1980s, the complaint is frequently heard that sustainability has been co-opted by government and business to justify development. But sustainable development at the very least still encompasses the idea of the 'triple bottom line', which today often includes a fourth category of 'governance'. That is to say, sustainability has become a shorthand term for expressing the interconnection of environmental, economic and social factors. Before the term sustainability became well-worn, many mistakenly thought environmentalists were only concerned with single issues, not whole systems. The popularization of the term sustainability, by any definition, has also raised the general level of awareness. We have, for instance, largely moved beyond the earlier notion of sustainability as the 'sustainable yield' of forests, rivers or soil resources.[11] Of course, any and every new concept will be captured and twisted to some extent. For example, the term 'sustainable development' has sometimes been interpreted literally to mean 'permanence'. Thus it has been used by some to imply, ironically, that environmentalists fear change. This stereotype may in fact be a negative projection. It is, after all, the status quo that represents social, political and biophysical change at an exponential rate – in the wrong direction. The military-industrial complex anticipated by President Eisenhower in the 1950s, and the 'corporatist' state that took hold in the 1980s, have imposed one, largely irreversible, pathway.[12] Environmentalists are no more fearful or irrational than those who choose to live in a military industrial complex.

## Wouldn't sustainability mean the imposition of 'green' values upon others?

Positive Development does not prescribe a particular aesthetic or set of values. It is the current system that reduces choice and prescribes a narrow range of values. The lack of meaningful choice is manifested in, for example, the reduction of crop varieties and seeds to a fraction of what was available 100 years ago. While industrial farming has led to more products on the shelves, the number of varieties of fruit and vegetables has been greatly reduced. Many competing brands of foods are owned by the same companies and contain very similar ingredients.[13] Likewise, housing seems to be produced by a cookie cutter, where 'choice' pertains to superficial variations in the conspicuous consumption of materials and fixtures. The attempt to rationalize the lack of future choice has become pervasive. For example, some say that major changes have happened over geological time, so climate change and extinctions are 'natural'. In fact, some even argue that militarism is 'natural'. But even *if* these positions are correct, it would not absolve humans of responsibility for the loss of biodiversity, human cultures and ecosystems. This is because sustainability is a matter of ethics and equity (not sunspots, comets, Earth wobbles or communists). Sustainability has always been about fairness among all people in present and future generations. Thus the fact that major catastrophes occurred on the planet even before humans existed does not justify inaction in preventing mass extinction. Material addictions can arguably be satisfied by 'virtual realities' (assuming these realities can someday transcend pornography and violence).[14] But while virtual worlds might reduce the need for some forms of material consumption, high quality public environments may be necessary to reduce conspicuous consumption.

## Isn't sustainability just a concept for the privileged – What about the poor?

The poor are most affected. While non-sustainable or status quo development affects all people, it first impacts upon disadvantaged children, women and the poor generally. Each year, at least three million children under the age of five die due to environment-related diseases. For example:

- Over 200 million children are living in shantytowns
- Over 30 million children are homeless
- Over 500 million children live on less than $1 a day
- Over 30 million children do not have safe drinking water
- Over 30 million children do not have toilets, or other sanitation services like waste collection
- Over 180 million children are in child labour, mostly in non-sustainable resource exploitation

While statistics vary, such shocking figures are widely available and compiled by international agencies such as the World Health Organization.[15] It would not be consistent with the theme of this book to repeat a litany of crises and injustices. However, one cannot dispute that there is a clear pattern. The current path is genocidal. Acts of 'omission' on this scale must be seen as consequences, not just coincidental by-products, of conventional models of economic growth. Inaction in addressing inequities is a deliberate form of action. The current 'solutions' – either to impose Western environmental standards on the developing nations or to lower standards in the developed nations – are not satisfactory.[16] We need design standards that favour higher life quality through low-impact natural systems in *both* sets of countries.

## How can inaction be considered deliberate, since people are not fully aware?

Because we *do* know better. It has long been appreciated that environmental destruction is subsidized.[17] Water is a good indicator of sustainability, for example, as we can only live a few days without it:

- Up to 12 million children under 5 die per year (roughly 33,000 per day) from disease and poor nutrition alone, much of this directly linked to water quality and quantity
- 5 million people a year die from disease caused by contaminated water
- Serious water shortages in 80 countries affect 40 per cent of the world's population[18]

Yet world water consumption is subsidized to the tune of $50 billion a year.[19] Water shortages also involve economic costs for the wider population. For example, a third of the Earth's topsoil and cropland are already ruined, while we have continued to subsidize unsustainable agriculture.[20] These subsidies indirectly contribute to climate change, droughts and floods (which have cost Australia billions in recent years).[21] These systems are not substantively rational and, due to the wealth transfers involved, could be characterized as 'systemic corruption'. In other words public funds or resources are being diverted to serve special interests rather than whole systems change.[22] The public pays for everything in the end, in effect, so corporations, public agencies and politicians should be obliged to put the public interest over special interests. One reason that such systemic corruption continues is our Orwellian culture: positive thinking is (paradoxically) equated with 'see no evil, hear no evil, speak no evil'. An objective analysis of our environmental frameworks, methods and tools will reveal that they are inherently negative. To design better systems, we first need to understand why the old systems do not work. This monumental death and destruction is by design, yet design is still widely regarded as a trivial pursuit. Hence, good design requires critical thinking and self-reflexivity.

## Don't such dire statistics and critical views make environmentalists 'negative'?

Accepting reality is not negative as long as we take action to make things better. Interestingly, environmentalists have been labelled as 'pessimistic', although they invest their time and energy trying to create a better future. It could be argued that it is the dominant paradigm that is pessimistic and negative, because it assumes that we can do nothing about the degradation and diminution of the natural environment – at least not without sacrificing our creature comforts. We have a remarkably negative view of nature and a remarkably positive view of cities. Nature, our life-support system, is still seen as somehow in conflict with human interests and outside of, or even superfluous to, the economy. In contrast, cities are seen as exciting and even aesthetically captivating. Yet, on the whole, cities are dreary cages, set among grimy alleys and congested streets, that are unfit for even battery hens.[23] Urban areas are widely perceived as places where natural systems cannot survive or do not even belong.[24] But through urban 're-design' we could create more healthy, stimulating and beautiful urban living environments that reunite humans and nature. Cities can solve serious ecological and social problems at a net economic gain. Eco-retrofitting of buildings is a low-risk business investment that can be cheaper than doing nothing [Chapter 2]. Eco-retrofitting, here, means modifying (and 'greening') urban areas to improve environmental and human health while reducing resource depletion, degradation and pollution. The aim would be to achieve a 'sustainability standard' – net positive improvements over existing conditions, not just resource efficiency [Chapter 5]. However, financial, environmental and health gains from improving our cities cannot achieve sustainability if total resource flows continue to increase beyond the Earth's carrying capacity. If we are to sustain the economy, then urban development must also restore and expand the ecological base of the surrounding region.

## But is this really 'affordable', even given net resource and financial savings?

The sometimes explicit but largely unconscious view that sustainability is impossible or unaffordable needs to be challenged head on. If biophysical sustainability can be shown to be possible through eco-innovation, there would be no excuse for 'survivalist', zero-sum strategies at either the individual or collective level. Sustainable systems would logically cost far less than our current systems of industrial production. After all, solar power is virtually infinite, many resources are renewable and microbial 'employees' work for free [Box 18]. Positive Development and eco-innovation do not imply more 'technical fixes'. They entail institutional or physical design that improves human and environmental health and whole system efficiency. Eco-innovation often involves the use of natural systems and environments to replace 'unnecessary' machines or products. Models and sources of inspiration for eco-innovation are all around us [Box 3]. If corrective action were taken now, we could avoid cumulative, irreversible negative impacts of industrial (read fossil-fuel-based) systems, which are more costly to correct as time passes. In this context, the idea of the 'limits' to natural resources, paradoxically, can be counter-productive. There are, of course, biophysical limits – and we are certainly exceeding them. But the companion view that negative impacts are an inevitable consequence of development has blinded us to the obvious. We could design development to increase the size, health and resilience of natural systems, while improving human health and life quality. However, instead of 'design', we are still engaging in 'accounting activity': developing tools to mitigate the impacts of change upon development-as-usual. The 'path' to sustainability must therefore start from a new place.

## Just what is sustainability supposed to be then – A 'path' or a 'destination'?

Both and neither. For those with a largely human-centred or 'anthropocentric' orientation, sustainability is seen as a path. Cultures and relationships evolve; hence we should not dictate how future societies will live. For those who take an ecological perspective, however, it is not enough to be on a path, as things they want to protect will soon be gone or extinct. The task for them is to get there, not just make progress.[25] Of course, if that end state were seen as fixed or permanent, it would not be consistent with a complex, evolving, natural world. It would also violate the principle of inter-generational equity. Citizens today and in the future must be able to determine their own lifestyles and habitats, within responsible parameters. To debate whether sustainability is either a path or a destination is 'either-or' thinking. Sustainability requires a complete change of direction, as our intellectual and institutional frameworks are incompatible with sustainability. To achieve sustainability, then, we need new, multiple pathways and destinations: different ideas about where to go and how to get there. Our environmental management processes, tools and methods are misguided and misleading. This is partly because, as we shall see, most of our planning and decision tools have borrowed concepts and constructs from reductions fields, where technocratic frameworks and methods dictate social values and choices. To reverse direction, then, we need to examine our negative development paradigm from the other side of the looking glass. In fact, we need to design our way out of a veritable hall of mirrors.

## So how does design differ from our standard reductionist way of thinking?

Design is an interactive, imaginative process for creating something that has never existed before, such as sustainability. Design provides a means of generating win–win–win solutions. In the dominant decision mode, decisions are made by choices assessed through various kinds of cost–benefit analyses.

These decision tools, infected by outdated politico-economic constructs, are designed to choose between competing interests and existing positions, or make tradeoffs between costs and benefits in a zero sum context. Design can help to reverse this systemic lobotomy. Instead of picking winners and losers, we can expand both social choice and biophysical sustainability by design. There have been many critiques of the dominant economic mode of thinking, so they are not repeated in this book [but see Boxes 42 and 43].[26] However, economic concepts and decision tools should be seen as subsidiary to design, because they cannot, in themselves, create eco-solutions. They can at best provide 'incentives' for better design. As recently as 2007, an Australian federal treasurer said the economy depended on population growth. If so, this means the Australian economy is fundamentally in conflict with sustainability.[27] The economic system is not pre-ordained. It is a designed system. When the design of an economic system militates against the ecology, we need to redesign the system.

## Doesn't sustainability mean balancing economic and environmental goals?

No. Sustainability means the *integration* of social, economic and environmental goals, not interest balancing. In fact, economic 'means' have become the 'ends'. As we will see, the ongoing sacrifice of social and ecological 'ends' by culturally-specific and ecologically flawed 'means' creates vicious circles. So, to summarize:

- **Social sustainability** means future generations must inherit substantive democratic rights and effective control over the means of survival (eg soil, air and water). We can enhance the public estate to enable secure public access to the means of survival – which the preservation of democracy ultimately requires. Decision systems that transfer resources from the poor to the rich cannot remain substantively democratic because power differentials will increase over the long term. If we were serious about sustainability, then, we would design a future in which all people (and other species) have at least the same range of responsible life choices and environmental quality that the 'privileged' on Earth now enjoy. This requires the design of decision systems that can ensure that public resources and means of survival are 'effectively' in public control [Chapter 13].
- **Ecological sustainability** suggests we must create healthier living environments (both built and natural) for everyone – including future generations. Decision systems that encourage the substitution of social or manufactured capital for nature are not sustainable. Given increasing flows and diminishing carrying capacity, development must be designed to expand the ecological base.[28] Urban development can be designed to, in a real sense, *over*-compensate for the impacts of existing development, by increasing our ecological support systems beyond what was there before development occurred. This can be achieved by design that creates the conditions for ecosystems to function in urban development, through 'design for eco-services'.
- **Economic sustainability** depends on social and environmental sustainability. Its reason for being should be to support the society and environment, not the reverse. Economics is not valid if it does not support sustainability. The economy is merely a social construct, while the ecology is the basis of all life. Economic theories and methods are only legitimate to the extent that they implement social and ecological sustainability [Boxes 42 and 43].

## So how do we design built environments that give back more than they take?

To be truly sustainable, the artefacts and mechanisms for natural systems must be replaced by the task of 'design *for* nature'. Where we lack the design capacity to expand the range of substantive life choices available to present and future generations (while preserving wilderness), we need to make development, land-use and resource decisions that are 'reversible'. This can only be achieved by design. We increasingly hear a distinction made between circular (as opposed to linear) metabolisms, or closed loops, where wastes from one process become resources for other processes.[29] McDonough and Braungart have shown that instead of closing loops, we can create no loop designs, where no waste is generated in the first place. We might add to this a third variation: 'direct action' to correct past design failure. This means *physical* design solutions – as opposed to indirect incentive systems that can have unintended consequences.[30] Direct action could be described as a 'reverse linear system'. This more proactive approach is exemplified by earthworms. Worms are linear systems, but they perform in the opposite direction to industrial factories: they turn wastes into resources. Arguably, therefore, worms have evolved to a higher level of 'intelligent design' than human societies, which continue to turn resources into waste. (They are also a good source of food in themselves, although 'wormburgers' have yet to take off.) Worms could thus be said to encapsulate a net Positive Development approach at the micro-level. The following chapters aim to show how this proactive approach could be up-scaled to urban and regional planning and design. A *direct* design approach is intended as an antidote to the 'managerialism' that now dominates environmental planning, management and design.

# SECTION A: REDEFINING THE PROBLEM AND GOALS

# 1
# Design
# for
# Eco-services

## From design for sterility
## to design for fertility

Poor urban design and architecture kills more people each year than terrorism. In just two weeks in Europe, for example, up to 35,000 deaths resulted from the 'urban heat island effect' (which means cities are several degrees hotter than their surroundings).[1] More people reportedly died in one day from heat-related causes than died in the '9/11' attack on the World Trade Center. The design of urban development both externalizes and conceals negative impacts. The rich tapestry of urban life, however stimulating, masks a resource transfer process that:

- Harms human and environmental health
- Destroys our means of survival (the life support system)
- Reduces secure access to food and water
- Reduces public space and natural amenity
- Chains us to the fossil fuel economy
- Transfers wealth from the many to the few
- Generates conflict over land and resources
- Cuts off basic life choices for future generations

These negative impacts are *not* inevitable. Many adverse effects are not a necessary consequence of physical development, or even of economic growth per se. They are a function of 'dumb design', to borrow Sim van der Ryn's term.[2] It is not people themselves, but the systems that they *design* that create excessive waste, ugliness and poisons. From a biological perspective, humans do not produce any more waste or pollution than other animals: about six tons of poo in an average lifetime (which microbes could happily recycle for us). Therefore, on the physical plane at least, sustainability is a design problem. The good news is that since most negative impacts are caused by physical and institutional design, they can be reversed by design. However, few appreciate that the 'built environment' (cities, buildings, landscapes, products) could generate healthy *ecological* conditions, increase the life-support services, reverse the impacts of current systems of development and improve life quality for everyone [Box 15]. This requires design based on positive thinking, not competition.

The idea that development could be net positive seems too good to be true. This is partly because we cannot get to sustainability from where we are. Conventional 'sustainable development' criteria and design tools currently promulgated by planning agencies can not increase overall sustainability [Box 22]. As we will see, some even prohibit eco-solutions. For development to become the solution instead of the problem, it must provide the infrastructure for nature to regenerate, flourish and deliver ecosystem goods and services in perpetuity, through 'design for eco-services' [Box 1]. This is not only possible, but arguably easier than what we are doing now. The only impediment is fear of change itself. In addition, it will be argued, built environment design can also become a lever for social transformation as well as better environmental management.

## How can built environment design drive social transformation?

There are many ways in which the built environment shapes social relationships and could encourage positive interactions. As environmentalists have long argued, equitable and efficient resource allocation would help to reduce many of the underlying causes of social conflict and improve social justice. The built environment, as we will see, can help to improve health, equity, security and amenity. However, it is true that healthy environments, creature comforts and social space alone will not bring about social change. Achieving sustainability (by any definition) will be a complex, multidimensional challenge. It will involve public engagement, debate, education and a new ethic; new forms of governance and conflict resolution; family planning and support; new economic institutions and management frameworks; basic changes in public planning, policies and priorities; and empathy and compassion. All of these are *prerequisites* of the others. Therefore, they all need to progress together in virtuous cycles. We will begin with a broad overview of the issues and how we can begin to *reverse* detrimental resource transfers through Positive Development that:

- Improves human and ecological health, resilience and viability
- Increases natural capital, biodiversity, and ecosystem goods and services
- Increases secure access to food and water
- Enhances urban space for both people and natural processes
- Transforms our infrastructure from fossil fuel-driven to solar-powered
- Helps correct imbalances in power and wealth
- Conserves open space, wilderness and natural resources
- Increases life quality and substantive life choices for present and future generations

## Haven't the environmental professions aimed for Positive Development?

Not at all. As we will see, the impediments to Positive Development are *not* technical or financial. They stem more from the marginalization of design, the polarization of power, closed minds, institutional and intellectual inertia, and so on. The ongoing tradeoffs of environmental and human health for toxic forms of development continue, despite increasing environmental technologies, policies and regulations. This is in part due to the very planning, design and management systems that were created to 'protect' the environment in the first place. Of course, thanks to regulation, progress can be measured in many areas. Air and water are cleaner today in some cities than before. There are even cases where threatened ecosystems and species have had a stay of execution. But we have not begun to address the big picture – the diminution and degradation of the shared, living environment (public estate) and means of survival (ecological base). Our tools still focus attention on symptoms, such as pollution, waste and climate change, rather than on tracing problems to their sources in systems design and correcting these root causes. Thus many efforts to manage environmental problems work to perpetuate them. In some cases, environmental regulation works against 'best practice'.[3] But in other cases, best practice works against eco-innovation.[4] Best practice, in the context of sustainability, is the moral equivalent of 'price fixing'. It sets the bar at what we have done in the past. Our tools turn designers into apprentices of past practices. Moreover, like the Sorcerer's Apprentice, we are too busy keeping up with 'tools of the trade' to question their real efficacy.[5] Consultancies multiply as resource consumption, environmental degradation and total resource flows increase [Chapter 5]. We do not need a more accurate body count in our war with nature. Our basic approach to institutional and physical design and practice must change.

## Why do we need to change our design approach in order to change outcomes?

A new architecture is an *essential* prerequisite of biophysical and social sustainability. The re-design of the built environment will require decision systems and tools that encourage design for diversity, adaptability and genuine reversibility.[6] Material flows and negative impacts are largely a function of the *design* of development itself. It is futile to try to protect the natural environment from the growing 'side effects' of conventional development. In fact, the cumulative impacts of our modest buildings, both upstream and downstream, are monumental. The true scale of impacts is veiled by the omnipresent nature of the 'man-made' environment. Currently, buildings are 'directly' responsible for a major portion of energy consumption, raw materials extraction, toxic landfill, packaging waste and greenhouse gas emissions, along with timber, water and soil depletion, and many human illnesses. In fact, it would be hard to think of any economic, environmental, social or distributional impacts that are not shaped and/or reinforced by the design of development. Problems such as deforestation, climate change, soil depletion, air pollution, water shortages, biodiversity and habitat losses, and pollution *cannot* be reversed or prevented within the current model of development. Further, negative impacts at the source of materials and site of construction are only part of the problem. Dumb design largely determines the *amount* of resources, space and energy consumed by people in the wider environment into the future.

## But isn't the real problem 'consumer behaviour' or poor personal choices?

Currently, we only have limited choices as individuals. The design of infrastructure, building systems and construction processes largely determines the demand upon industry to provide materials and products downstream in the market.[7] That is to say, consumer demand is dwarfed by the 'demand' for natural resources that the design of development itself generates – unnecessarily. Design also dictates the waste and toxins that flow from the production and use of goods and services used in the built environment.[8] In this built environment context, people simply cannot choose truly sustainable lifestyles. They are trapped within non-sustainable environments by both physical and institutional design failure. The potential of behaviour change as a driver of sustainability is limited by the relatively trivial range of consumer items at the end of the industrial supply chain. Design limits the range of substantive choices available to people in the *future* by locking us into manufactured environments that will drive excessive consumption and waste for decades.[9] Design also contributes to social problems by creating environments that generate social segregation, alienation, inequity – ultimately leading to conflict over diminishing space and resources. More immediately, built environments contribute directly and indirectly to human health problems.[10]

## How can built environments be said to reduce health and social equality?

Take indoor air pollution, for example.[11] It is generally greater than that of outdoor air, and can exacerbate other medical conditions like asthma, allergies and multiple chemical sensitivities [Chapter 2].[12] It is caused by a combination of materials that off-gas toxins (such as formaldehyde and volatile organic compounds), outdoor air pollution and a lack of adequate ventilation. Mould is another problem in many regions, both in terms of occupant health and building longevity. In San Francisco, for instance, toxic mould inside walls is becoming a major economic problem, as a direct result of conventional construction materials and components.[13] Mould is less a problem with organic materials, however, as natural materials can in a sense breathe.[14] Also, conventional design reinforces disparities of status and opportunity. Marmot has shown that longevity and health correlate with success and socioeconomic status.[15] The gap between the life expectancy of the poor and the rich is increasing despite higher average wealth in some places. Other factors such as smoking and stress only account for part of this longevity gap. This gap is much greater in the US than in more egalitarian countries such as Sweden.[16] With the diminution of public space and natural amenity in cities, the impacts of poverty on the life quality and lifespans of the poor grow ever greater. This also wastes the intellectual capacity of a significant portion of the human race. We do not count the 'brain waste' of the many potential geniuses in the 'Third World' damaged from malnutrition or social deprivation due to maldevelopment. Indeed, a Martian could be forgiven for thinking we go out of our way to design urban systems that reduce health, equity and longevity.

## If these problems could be reduced by design, why do they still exist?

The legacy of dumb design creates vicious circles. We are surrounded by buildings that have excessive negative impacts, too numerous to list.[17] Perhaps because we are increasingly fixated on small computer, television and phone screens, we do not seem to notice the condition of our urban environments. Some new buildings are now even turning façades into dancing digital screens.[18] Meanwhile, urban development drives the spirals of waste, consumption and pollution that are potential sources of social conflict. As we will see, environmental management methods are not designed to create positive impacts and positive environments. They are only designed to reduce space and energy. Thus many are consigned to live in alleys, public toilets and other 'left over' urban public spaces in a dark world beneath the discotheque of commerce. Again, this is partly because we are taught to believe we cannot improve human relationships or increase living systems in urban areas through built environment design. The idea of creating virtuous cycles that increase nature's carrying capacity – relative to human consumption – is almost never contemplated. Our self-referential 'designed world' reinforces the belief that all development must have negative impacts. These negative assumptions have been entrenched in our environmental management systems, which, in turn, have prevented us from trying to improve human and environmental health through design.

## How could development actually improve human and environmental health?

Built environment design will need to actively contribute to the ecosystem goods and services that constitute the Earth's life-support system. Ecosystem goods and services include:
- Supporting biodiversity
- Disposing of organic wastes
- Sequestering carbon

- Controlling pests and diseases
- Producing food, fibres, pharmaceuticals
- Producing healthy construction materials
- Regulating the local and global climate
- Developing topsoil and maintaining soil fertility
- Producing crops and natural fertilizers
- Heating, cooling and ventilating using the sun
- Preventing soil erosion and sediment loss
- Purifying water and air
- Storing and recycling fresh water and nutrients
- Regulating the chemistry of the atmosphere
- Maintaining habitats for wildlife
- Alleviating floods and managing storm water runoff
- Protecting against UV radiation

## But surely development cannot protect nature or provide such functions?

We will see that development could provide these functions, but it can only do so efficiently if it uses and supports nature itself in the process. It is not sustainable to replace nature with mechanical imitations of nature. 'Eco-services' is short for the 'ecosystem goods and services' provided by natural systems, such as those listed above. But here, the term is used to encompass the idea of ecosystems valued for their *own sake*, not just for their instrumental functions. That is to say, the term eco-services expands the human-centred notion of ecosystem goods and services to include ecology. Our environmental management frameworks treat nature as if it were a collection of dead inputs and outputs [Chapter 4]. We have therefore only been concerned to make production and development more efficient. This means that, at best, we will reduce natural capital and close off future social choices and life quality options 'more efficiently', while nature as a whole diminishes. This is a philosophy worthy of a concentration camp. Instead of adding value, our decision-making methods, processes and design decisions 'balance' off our life-support system for short-term social and economic benefits. Eco-efficiency is a good thing, but it is not good enough.[19]

## How can development be expected to do better than achieve eco-efficiency?

To go beyond eco-efficiency, we need a better understanding of nature as a living thing, not a set of inert inputs and outputs. Eco-efficiency measures are seldom net positive – humans and the ecology are seldom healthier after a development than before it was constructed. Positive Development would thus require design for eco-services. This means changing the basic functions and forms of development itself, so that urban areas can generate natural functions without capital- and resource-intensive industrial systems [Chapter 6]. We cannot continue to simply squeeze more materials out of the environment, squeeze up cities, or squeeze more goods and services out of nature. If we just aim for more efficient materials and production processes, the total flows of resources and wastes attributable to the built environment will continue to increase. If we just compensate for adverse impacts of development elsewhere, we will run out of 'elsewheres'. Thus far, the implicit assumption in development control systems – including 'sustainability assessment' – is that we can simply compensate for, or 'offset', ecological impacts by providing short-term social and economic gains [Chapter 7]. Even though development assessment criteria increasingly call for 'positive contributions to sustainability', virtually none require positive *ecological* impacts. This is because our criteria reflect a tacit belief in the legitimacy of what environmental economists call 'substitution'.

## What is substitution and how does this relate to sustainability?

Substitution means that we can trade off natural capital for social capital. For example, developers may promise a cultural centre and jobs for Aborigines in order to gain approval for a mining development on traditional lands. This may represent an improvement over past practices, but does not replace losses in eco-services, ecology and culture. Today, there are many new eco-service trading schemes that purport to compensate nature as well as investors [Chapter 11]. But this is nothing new: bargaining, payoffs and tradeoffs to 'balance competing interests' in conservation and development have always been part of the planning and development process. To achieve a true 'balance', by contrast, cities would need to perform the services of (for instance) the world's lost forest cover, as well as replace the forests that they use [Chapter 4]. A truly sustainable built environment would therefore require a fundamentally different intellectual 'DNA' for environmental management and design. To move forward, then, it is important to distinguish eco-logical design from what is currently called 'green building' [Box 27]. We are using the term 'Positive Development' to refer to design that reverses the impacts of current systems of development, increases the ecological base and public estate, and improves life quality. This is to be distinguished from green building, which largely aims to reduce negative environmental, economic and social impacts. Positive Development requires capacity building in design. We cannot wait for markets to stimulate better design indirectly.

## Can't consumer choice and market signals bring change toward sustainability?

No. Market signals mean little when sustainable living options – let alone 'green' buildings – are not even on the market. But there is a bright side. Because the design, construction and management of the built environment is *central* to most sustainability issues, it is also a source of eco-solutions. Construction amounts to about half of national capital investment in many countries. It uses roughly half of our resource consumption by weight (over seven tons of materials per person per year).[20] It also consumes about half of our energy.[21] More important, as we noted, building impacts are inseparable from the impacts generally attributed to extraction and manufacturing industries, such as forestry, transport and mining. This means the built environment is arguably not only the biggest driver of consumption, but the largest discretionary area where environmental improvements can be made without life quality sacrifices – apart from the military. It is important to remind ourselves that there is no shortage of money. What the world spends on military activity in three days would solve most of the world's 'environmental problems'.[22] Spending money on peacemaking (eg building local schools) would be more cost-effective. Moreover, re-designing the built environment would create jobs at far less cost per job than the military – but with *positive* spill-over effects on the economy. Eco-retrofitting, and even just 'greening', urban areas to achieve net positive improvements over pre-construction conditions would cost no more than perpetuating ongoing damage. This is especially true since we already provide, maintain and refurbish places almost continuously [Chapter 2].

## Figure 1 Eco-retrofitting example

Any building can be retrofitted to reduce its heating, cooling, lighting and ventilating bill, while cleaning air and water, reducing the urban heat island effect, and producing soil and food.

### How can greening the urban environment provide ecological gains at less cost?

Through design we can not only increase efficiencies, but provide for more responsible, equitable, higher quality lifestyle choices. It is widely accepted that, from a systems perspective, the most efficient way to reduce both costs and environmental impacts in construction or renovation is in the preliminary design stage.[23] This stage predetermines over 90 per cent of impacts. Further, creativity does not *in itself* cost time, money or resources. Many established processes already exist for reducing energy and material flows through development, and these have proven to provide safe and profitable investments. For example, case studies in 'design for environment', 'cleaner production', 'eco-efficiency' and 'design for disassembly' have been widely disseminated.[24] These have achieved 'Factor 4' or greater reductions in materials, energy and waste ('Factor 4' means doubling productivity while halving resource use[25]). Eco-efficiencies can be achieved at all stages of construction as well. In turn, these can generate 'compound' savings upstream and downstream from the construction site.[26] In most cases, however, these green approaches only mitigate the impacts of development through *resource* reduction. Eco-efficiency is improving rapidly, but it has thus far meant more industrial growth at the expense of nature and ecosystems. Eco-efficiency, therefore, can never replace value adding by design [Chapter 6]. We need instead to make life, social and human–ecosystem *relationships* central to planning and design. This would mean a wider range of healthy lifestyles, environments and social connections.

### How does conventional development increase consumption or consumables?

Despite our belated concerns about climate change, we are still seeing the perpetual expansion of consumer 'choices' between products that nobody needs. There is an ever-growing array of cosmetics, candies, cars and contraptions that differ only in 'branding' and packaging. This explosion in often 'disposable' consumer items is reflected in the built environment as well as factory outputs. As Mark Jayne has argued, not only are cities consumers of land, water, energy, raw materials and space, consumption is now the prime organizational feature of cities. In other words, the contemporary city is defined by and through consumption.[27] In the developed world, we are witnessing increasing numbers and sizes of homes, with more space per person – but often less real social space. We have luxurious single-function kitchens along with sumptuous single-function dining rooms increasingly used for heating imported frozen dinners, high in fat and 'food miles'. In Australia, some gardens are now being converted to second outdoor kitchens. Today, what pass for 'green homes' sometimes embody more resources, energy, space, luxury fixtures and features than older models. From an ecological perspective, then, conventional design is still taking us down the wrong pathways. Materialism may help people 'offset' a lack of meaningful relationships in a poorly designed society, but it is ultimately zero sum.[28] Conflict can only increase when a third of the world's population continues to suffer deprivation, malnutrition and brain damage – while their resources and labour, in effect, trickle up to the top percentiles.[29] The design of conventional development increases the disparities and transfers of wealth between countries, regions, classes and sectors.[30]

## How can the built environment contribute to wealth transfers and disparities?

Wealth transfers through conventional development occur on many levels. For example, materials and energy are extracted from the public domain and transformed into private property. In other words, even if not wasted, consumed or disposed of, others lose access to them.[31] So resources are essentially 'privatized' – whether in the control of a government bureaucracy or private corporation.[32] The built environment has become a capital accumulation process that precludes many legitimate needs and interests. For example, many among the younger generation in Western democracies believe that they will be effectively locked out of the housing market. Land, resources and nature are ultimately finite and our current development decisions and designs are largely irreversible. Without systems design change, this is a terminal process. Because the demands of a growing population can no longer be met by acquiring new territories or colonies, industrialized development can be likened to a pyramid scam.[33] Currently, wealth is transferred from rural to urban areas in the 'developed world', and from subsistence communities to trans-national corporations in the 'developing world'. In other words, conventional 'industrialized' development works to transfer materials and energy (the basis of wealth) from poor to rich, nature to development, rural to urban interests, small to big business, and future to present generations [Chapter 14].

## Isn't this blaming development for the results of human apathy and greed?

No. It is a complex systems problem. The design of development has evolved to reflect and reinforce myriad forces and factors. We sometimes attribute systemic injustice to human nature, religion or acts of god. However, since the depletion, degradation and diminution of the public estate are deeply embedded in current patterns of development, they are 'by design'. As noted above, they may not be intentional or even conscious, but they are designed into our systems. Figuratively speaking, we designed a society in accordance with a dualistic paradigm – a heaven and hell, as it were. This dominant Earth-denying paradigm meant that the real meaning of life is seen as 'off the planet'. To make people more obedient, we created palaces for reward and ghettoes for punishment. This negative social control strategy was based on the notion that fear or greed shapes behaviour, an extraordinarily negative and authoritarian legacy. This is perhaps partly why we allow the existence of slums with the excuse that they reflect the sloth of its residents. Fortunately, we now have the collective capacity to re-design our systems of thought to create a heaven on Earth. There is no need to evacuate to Mars. The challenge of designing cheaper, more equitable and more ecologically-sound living spaces would be rewarding on many personal and social levels. If this possibility were widely recognized, people would not feel the need to claw their way to the top of a social hierarchy in order to avoid the depressing living conditions that poverty entails.

## Won't the population explosion negate any net positive design solutions?

To the contrary. In fact, better design is essential for dealing with population issues. Design cannot increase the size of the planet or make people smaller. However, it can improve the quality of life, access to public facilities, security and amenity without additional space or money. Environmentalists have long argued that if everyone were safe and secure as individuals, and/or as members of minority races and religions, there would be less pressure to have children as 'old age insurance' and less pressure on resources. Yet, at the same time, some countries with high living standards are worried about declining human reproduction rates. Incredibly, population growth is still being encouraged in some places, to meet the market system's insatiable demand for ever-expanding consumption – by reproducing consumers. In 2006, the Australia federal treasurer argued that it was the patriotic duty of Australians to have more children to help the economy: 'one for mom, one for dad and one for the country'. Of course, urging people to abstain from having children, to reduce consumption or to redistribute wealth are very difficult messages to sell. Instead of creating ever more disposable products for ever more people to consume, however, we could create more jobs and monetary flows by designing better, healthier environments with positive outcomes for all parties. Development could become a sustainability solution rather than a problem.

## How can we possibly create more jobs with less space and resource flows?

We can, for example, provide more shared public spaces and high-quality recreational, educational and social facilities in ways that increase usable space for people, nature, and ecosystem goods and services. Human and environmental services can be increased without additional resources or 'extra' space, because recreational and productive human functions can occupy the same area as natural systems [Chapter 3]. Moreover, jobs in construction and service provision are a good thing. They are more 'productive' than jobs created by proliferating disposable trinkets, consumer items destined for landfill, or the world's biggest businesses (weapons manufacture and trade in illegal drugs, rare animals and timbers). Too little attention has been paid to the *quality* of jobs in relation to resources consumed. Design and construction that utilize natural systems are less capital- and more talent-intensive than many industrial systems. Design also demands and develops more creative capacity and know-how. Eco-logical design and retrofitting is site-specific and thus challenging, unlike repetitive, mind numbing jobs created by assembly lines or call centres. If we re-designed human habitats to expand the ecological base and public estate and to provide eco-services and environmental amenity, the wealthy might not require material opulence. The loss of material goods would be outweighed by the increase in their personal security and substantive life quality.[34]

## But isn't the re-design of development beyond the reach of poor nations?

Design for eco-services would be of benefit to both over-developed and under-developed nations.

Poorer communities in developing nations, facing immediate threats to survival, have the most to gain from low-cost, low-tech, net Positive Development. Most diseases and injuries in developing nations could be averted through small biophysical interventions and community development programmes in the local area [Box 16]. For example, we know that roughly 6000 children in poor countries die from dirty water each day. Dirty water can be:

- Prevented in the first place by protecting its source in natural systems through, for example, restoring the health, absorptive capacity and resilience of watersheds
- Reduced by development that avoids earth moving, tree clearing or components that involve mining and toxins that seep into groundwater
- Filtered by home-made, low-cost clay and coffee ground filters baked in cow dung or glass cones that use evaporation to extract clean water
- Treated with low-cost, low-tech strategies, like landscape or building systems that utilize the principles of Living Machines to clean water and create useful products[35]

Professional organizations (like appropriate technology societies) and organizations (like Architects sans Frontiers or Engineers without Borders) are working to provide commonsense solutions to social problems resulting from the over-exploitation of resources. Due to vested interests in existing wealth transfer processes, however, many development initiatives in poorer nations are still highly capital- and resource-intensive. A case in point is the Three Gorges Dam in China, a 'single function' use of land and resources that has dislocated hundreds of thousands of poor people and drowned millions of hectares of agricultural land and soil. It may reduce some small floods in the future, but it may also exacerbate bigger ones.[36]

## Are there examples of planning that do not trade-off nature for development?

Yes. There are examples of commonsense modifications to conventional planning and resource management that improve environmental conditions. The city of Curitiba is a well-known example of practical planning that aims to create whole system efficiency and multiple benefits through small-scale, community-based solutions.[37] Curitiba is the capital city of Paran in Brazil and, like most cities in developing nations, it faces problems of poverty, overcrowding, pollution and limited funds. From the early 1960s, under the leadership of Jaime Lerner, the city embarked on a team design effort to address social, economic and environmental problems. Rather than spending on capital-intensive, large-scale engineering projects, they invested in on-ground, people-oriented solutions. Curitiba now has an exceptional public transport system, recycling programmes, increased public parks and community services, revitalized historic districts – and civic pride. Its achievements are celebrated in many sustainability texts and forums. For example:

- **Recycling**: Curitiba's approach to recycling enables the poor to exchange scavenged metal and glass waste for fresh produce. This builds health and safety improvements into the waste solution, while providing supplemental income for the poor.
- **Green space**: Curitiba built housing for squatters in order to relocate them off a floodplain that was subject to periodic flood damage and water contamination. Then it converted the floodplain into public parkland that can manage occasional floods. By reclaiming land for public parks, Curitiba now has more green space per person than other Brazilian cities.
- **Historic preservation**: Curitiba preserved old buildings using transferable development rights (TDRs) [Chapter 11]. This enabled owners of old buildings to use their development rights to build elsewhere or sell these 'unused' rights to others. Historic areas were preserved

in this way, and have since become multi-use tourist destinations.

- **Public transport**: Curitiba created an efficient, fast, accessible and inexpensive bus system. This avoided building a subway that would have served fewer people at higher costs and involved decades of disruption and crippling loan repayments. Today, most travel in Curitiba is by bus, and its citizens use less petrol per capita than other Brazilian cities.
- **Financial rationality**: In a risk-, cost- and profit-sharing arrangement, private companies operate buses and taxis under contract to the city and share the costs of terminal and road maintenance. Before passengers board the bus, they pay for the ride on a loading platform, to save time and assist the disabled. Passengers pay one fare for anywhere in the city, which means poor commuters can afford to work wherever they can get jobs.
- **Services**: Many social and educational services are delivered on 'retired' buses, including health classes, physical activity and dental care. Subsidized goods are also delivered to poor districts on buses converted into little shops. Vegetables are salvaged from farmers who had previously destroyed them to avoid oversupply, or due to mere visual defects.

The Curitiba innovations may be marginal, relative and modest. It is, after all, a 'poor' city. The point is that it proves money is not the barrier to improving urban life quality or equity, or even achieving systems change.

## So where would we begin to create low-cost, ecologically sustainable cities?

We must start with a new conception of sustainable design; one that aims to make cities and buildings eco-productive and socially satisfying as well as eco-efficient. In the past, the design of cities and buildings, like that of factories, treated the surrounding environment as an infinite source of materials and energy and a bottomless sink for toxins and wastes. It could be said that most urban environments were designed on the model of the blue bottle, an Australian jellyfish that sucks up nutrients and sends out toxins through its long, deadly and almost invisible tentacles. 'Externalities' are where a private development or industry directly imposes collateral damage upon society in general, as in the case of pollution from a factory or fertilizer runoff from a farm. They are considered 'external' to the economic framework, but are intrinsic to its design. A city or building could be considered 'impact-neutral', then, only if it were in some kind of 'ecological balance' with its environment or bioregion. However, even impact-neutral cities would still not be sustainable. This is because the ability of natural systems to regenerate and evolve is already greatly impaired.[38] The 'carrying capacity' of nature itself is now inadequate to supply enough services or absorb enough toxins. Nature's productive and assimilative capacity continues to decline.[39] So even if all new development were, by magic, carbon neutral and 'zero waste' from this moment on, cities would still not be sustainable. Just eliminating the externalities of future development would not begin to address the sustainability imperative.

## What would qualify as zero waste and/or sustainable design then?

'True zero waste' would be where all waste generated in the supply chain was prevented or reused, not just 'zero waste to landfill' [Chapter 4]. Similarly, Carbon neutrality would be where total $CO_2$ emissions were at pre-industrial levels. But even true zero waste would not qualify as sustainable. To be truly sustainable, cities must (among many other things) increase nature's immune system and self-healing abilities. We need to increase the Earth's ecological health, habitats and carrying capacity – simply to accommodate existing development and population levels, let alone to protect our life-support systems for the future. We also need to re-design existing development to correct or compensate for the past legacy of inequitable resource transfers. In reality, this can only happen if it does not disturb special interests. That is, the redistribution of resources would have to be achieved in ways that do not threaten anyone's interests. Logically, then, development must make everyone better off (including the rich). We can only achieve this if development *expands* and enhances the ecological base and public estate. In other words, to be ecologically sustainable, cities and buildings must proactively heal the rifts between rich and poor, and between humans and nature. Fortunately, the physical *and* ecological footprint of urban areas can be reduced substantially. Perhaps even our remnant wilderness areas could ultimately be spared if we were to 're-naturalize' our built environment.

## Wouldn't it be easier to just lock up natural areas than to re-design cities?

We cannot protect ecologically sensitive environments or endangered species by putting a fence around wilderness areas. Even now, in Australia, a political party has formed around the goal of greater access to protected environments for 'recreation'. Global warming, 'feral' or invasive species, pollution, and other unpredictable biological or climatic shocks are reducing the prospects for nature's evolutionary forces to recover and replenish themselves.[40] Further, in the context of the resource demands of a growing global population, locking away resources may be physically and politically impossible anyway. Given the increasing numbers of impoverished and displaced peoples, it may also be morally indefensible. In Australia, for example, we have locked up many political and environmental refugees behind barbed wire – and for years – in what are euphemistically called 'detention centres'. Again, this is the philosophy of reward and punishment, and not a positive approach to problem solving. Realistically, wilderness and 'rurban' areas (urban and rural areas considered together) can no longer be regarded as isolated systems [Chapter 8]. To expand the ecological base will require that rurban development be re-conceived as one symbiotic system. Instead, our cities and buildings are, at best, 'machines' for living: an artificial reality that alienates humans from nature. Design for eco-services implies 'gardens for living' that *re-couple* humans and nature, while *de-coupling* negative environmental impacts from economic development. This requires a new design paradigm.

## Would this new design paradigm mean the imposition of a specific aesthetic?

No. The values of diversity and choice can justify pockets of aluminium, steel and glass or 'glam and glitter' [Box 21]. New buildings will always be needed. But there is no excuse for even skyscrapers that are not green, as demonstrated by architect Ken Yeang.[41] Deteriorated central city areas and suburbs can be retrofitted while maintaining the diverse qualities that people like (or, more precisely, that their designers like) [Boxes 5 and 8]. The tendency in green design, however, is towards squeezing up people into hi-tech, albeit eco-efficient, modernist cages. Designers of green buildings are under pressure to prove green buildings do not cost more than conventional ones. Therefore, it is hard for them to provide adequate space for biological and cultural diversity – let alone even 'retail therapy'. Net positive design could increase luxurious living and meaningful lifestyle choices – unless conspicuous consumption is the only criterion for luxury. The ongoing substitution of manufactured for natural capital means that future generations will have to live with the consequences of today's design ideologies and consumer preferences, the by-products of corporate profits and power. By integrating human functions with space for both macro and mini ecosystems and eco-services, natural habitats, nature corridors and so on, cities could serve as 'nature reserves' that nurture endangered species and regenerate indigenous ecosystems. If cities regenerated nature and revived the human spirit, escape to (vestiges of) nature via jammed freeways, or into virtual realities through two-dimensional windows, might be less necessary.

### So why can't we just require 'best practice' green buildings?

Best practice is still not very good. In contrast, passive houses have only about 15–20 per cent of the space heating/cooling requirements of conventional new homes.[42] On a large scale, this would mean a dramatic saving. Resource autonomous homes have been around for ages, but are still scarce.[43] Yet 'best practice' exemplars are seldom even resource autonomous. It must be said, of course, that recent progress in green building represents an advance over past practices. Nonetheless, we cannot achieve biophysical sustainability through what now passes for 'green building'. So far, green buildings only aim to reduce negative social and environmental impacts relative to *standard* buildings [Chapter 5]. The 'greenness' of buildings is usually based on claims such as 'the building will use 40 per cent less fossil-fuel energy and 30 per cent less water than typical buildings of the same kind'. That is, we aim only for 'less bad' designs. Further, many of these buildings support claims such as being 'carbon neutral' by counting offsets. This means that, in reality, such projects have merely included provisions to, for example, reduce the 'need' to drive cars, plant trees to compensate for added carbon emissions or purchase green power to add clean energy to coal-based electricity sources [Chapter 11]. As we will see, we are so busy measuring things that we measure the wrong things. In our obsession for point scoring, we lower the bar and stretch the tape measure in lieu of designing solutions. Indeed, if we labelled cigarettes the way we label buildings, people might start smoking more 'light' cigarettes to get healthier.

### Shouldn't offsets be encouraged in any case to reduce total impacts?

While offsets should certainly be encouraged, it must be understood that they do not reduce existing impacts – let alone constitute net ecological gains [Chapter 11]. Green buildings are better than what might *otherwise* have been built. But without the green building itself, there would be far less fossil fuel, land and water consumption. Sustainability is not just about consuming less in the future. To make a net positive contribution to sustainability, development would need to reverse the social and ecological impacts of past and ongoing development – the existing urban context. So it should not be considered impact neutral to just offset future environmental impacts. Environments for safer, healthier and more convivial social interaction should be a given, not something for which we give 'extra credit'. If we are serious about sustainability, then we would not just add more 'green' buildings to the skyline. The built environment would provide the space and conditions for natural systems to repair and sustain themselves. We could eco-retrofit existing urban development to make cities carry their own weight and create synergistic relationships with their region. The target would be what we will call a 'sustainability standard': net improvement in human *and* ecological health over what would have been the case if the development had not been built [Chapter 5]. Positive Development would, of course, also meet standard triple bottom line criteria, as enunciated in many planning policy documents [Box 22].

### Wouldn't such a high standard be both too costly and too unrealistic?

As suggested earlier, targets that represent incremental improvement over current norms are essentially price fixing. It is well accepted that green buildings need not cost more than 'sick buildings'. In fact, it has been shown that 'dark green' buildings cost less to construct than 'pale green' buildings due to synergies created by integrated design.[44] So there is really no excuse for conventional architecture. But even green buildings, which gradually move the goalposts further, are pointless if we are still on the wrong playing field. New green buildings just reduce the increasing *rate* of environmental degradation in the construction supply chain. Sustainability cannot be achieved within the existing prototype of development. It is a matter of simple arithmetic. Several international government and research organizations, such as the OECD, have warned that we have only a few decades to reduce material and energy flows by 90 per cent (depending on who is counting what). Buildings use about 40 per cent of energy and produce about 40 per cent of greenhouse gases. Half the energy use of new buildings is energy 'embodied' in construction (20 per cent of total energy flows).[45] So even green buildings add more consumption to the equation than they can reduce. Also, only 2–4 per cent of the building stock is new each year. So even if *all* new buildings were green, it would only address a tiny fraction of resource flows (2 per cent of 20 per cent, or 0.4 per cent). If we are to cut back consumption dramatically, therefore, we have to re-design *existing* development. We need a new architecture that increases the social and ecological use of space for less net cost. This would not be difficult.

## Wouldn't design for eco-services entail more space and expense?

Not really. Increasing the ecological base and public estate in urban areas would involve allocating more space to support natural ecosystems, but not at the expense of human functions. Natural systems can actually 'add value' to human activities without any net subtraction of space. This is, again, a matter of design. We are in the habit of segregating spaces, but it is just a bad habit. In rural areas, we can arguably only 'repair and restore' the damage to ecosystems, because we cannot expand the total land area. In urban areas, by contrast, we can increase the horizontal and vertical space and 'edge' for habitats, because we already have multistorey structures, walls, roofs and alleyways that can be retrofitted to generate eco-services.[46] We can also provide more infrastructure and open space for indigenous plants, animals and ecosystems than originally existed through better, multifunctional use, or addition, of decks, atriums and mezzanines [Box 14]. Many eco-services, like air and water cleaning, heating and cooling, soil production, and sewage and greywater purification, can be retrofitted into urban areas at less cost than fossil-fuelled redevelopment or new appliances. If, however, we continue to 'infill' with more sterile structures, we will cut off future social options and biological diversity [Box 4]. Today, many sustainability planning documents call for mixed economic uses, as in urban villages. However, they do *not* call for a mix of human and ecological functions. There are precedents of design for eco-services, however.

## If there are examples of 'design for eco-services', why don't we use them?

There are many existing examples of eco-logical design concepts that use natural systems and provide eco-services. These include vertical wetlands, breathing walls, multifunctional atriums or sunspaces, Living Machines, and solar ponds.[47] However, they are seldom applied in net positive ways [Boxes 3 and 5]. Nor have they been incorporated into the basic structure and fabric of urban areas and buildings. They are still add-ons. This often means unnecessary added costs [Box 4]. By eco-retrofitting our urban areas to better integrate natural with human functions, we can create space for ecosystem functioning and rehabilitation, while simultaneously providing more environmental amenity and space for building occupants and neighbours. For example, when we eliminate cars, we can retrofit our garages as greenhouses. There are methodological reasons for sterile forms of development that must be corrected. Waste, pollution, mal-distribution and unfair allocation of resources have been accepted as an inevitable aspect of progress, because they have co-evolved with the dominant model and methods of development. For example, as we will see, we have regarded space as empty and therefore a waste, so we try to eliminate it rather than use it better. We are in the habit of reducing everything to units of energy or money that can be expressed as numbers [Chapter 3]. This is partly because complex natural systems are currently beyond our comprehension, let alone our ability to create, maintain or measure them. We cannot re-create nature, but we can design *for* nature by creating the infrastructure for natural systems to unfold in their own way.[48]

## Why can't we just design buildings using nature as a model?

An analogy can be used to explain why providing the conditions for eco-services is different from using nature or ecosystems as a model for development. In the healthcare fields we have moved (conceptually at least) from (a) alleviating symptoms to (b) curing illness to (c) preventing disease to (d) programmes to *improve* health over the norm. If we simply design (lifeless) buildings to function 'like' ecosystems, we may design zero waste or closed loop systems. But this approach is stuck in stages (a) to (c). It makes no sense to bank on 'cryogenic' solutions or autonomous space pods to escape unhealthy environments, when we can instead take steps to increase whole system health and longevity. Drawing analogies between buildings and ecosystems, plants or other natural systems can, of course, stimulate innovation. An example of a building technology 'modelled' on nature is natural air-conditioning based on the principles of termite mound construction. Cool air is drawn from a shaded or underground tunnel, and hot air rises through solar chimneys.[49] This principle has been used for centuries in design. The danger of attaching such nature metaphors to modern buildings, however, is that they can make mechanical systems seem greener than they are. Living or working in buildings designed to be mechanical trees or termite mounds might be an improvement over buildings designed as machines for living. They do not, however, allow for increased native biodiversity, habitats, ecosystem functioning or human healing. They replace fertile with sterile systems.

## But isn't eco-logical design often inspired by the imitation of natural systems?

Indeed, natural systems have been an inspiration for building design concepts and eco-innovations. The current leading-edge green design metaphor is to design 'buildings *as* ecosystems'. If buildings were organisms or ecosystems (eg like a tree), they would theoretically be in balance with their surroundings [Chapter 10]. There are a number of excellent books that indirectly suggest how buildings can draw ideas from natural systems, such as *Biomimicry* by Benyus, *Wildsolutions* by Beattie and Erlich and *The New Economy of Nature* by Daily and Ellison.[50] These show how nature could be a model for design. They do not, however, suggest how we might design development to create the infrastructure for increasing nature's goods and services. Nor do they look at the built environment as a lever for systems change. Design for eco-services essentially means expanding the capacity of natural systems to regenerate a deteriorating planet, by integrating ecosystems into existing urban areas and structures. The only way we can create a 'positive' ecological footprint is to design cities so that they not only function like ecosystems, but also enable ecosystems to flourish. Using nature as a model does not necessarily achieve this. So we need to distinguish design for eco-services from what is generally called 'biomimicry'.[51] Design for eco-services implies that we need to design *for* nature (ie design for eco-services), as well as *with* nature (Living Machines) and *like* nature (biomimicry). After all, at the built environment level, hi-tech forms of biomimicry can be less efficient than nature itself.

## Just what is biomimicry and how does it differ from design for eco-services?

Biomimicry looks for solutions in nature. To take a simple example, silk is stronger than steel, so it makes sense to research and apply its secrets. But biomimicry has tended to focus on the design of hi-tech, *patentable* products. Some designs that come under the banner of biomimicry involve high costs, embodied energy and risks (eg new chemicals or genetic engineering).[52] Cities and buildings should indeed draw ideas from nature *and* emulate ecosystems. But in the case of the built environment, accessible and locally available resources are usually more appropriate, because of the amount and scale of materials required in construction. Thus, in the context of market capitalism, biomimicry – when applied to building technology – could perpetuate the current tendency to substitute nature with resource-intensive and often unnecessary products in lieu of passive solar solutions. Also, as currently conceived, biomimicry could continue the trend towards sterilization in lieu of, say, design for fertilization. We need therefore to add a caveat to biomimicry. Regions, cities and buildings should be designed on the model of a whole forest or reef, rather than mimicking spiders, molluscs or blue bottles in isolation from their environments. While low-cost built environment design solutions are already widely available, we still under-design for passive systems and rely on hi-tech solutions [Chapter 6]. The *scale* of the built environment should preclude capital-intensive solutions, whether inspired by biomimicry or not.

## What are some examples of hi-tech solutions that are being promoted?

Most hi-tech innovation is still not directed towards sustainability. Eco-innovation would result in net positive, safe, secure environments that create reversible, adaptable and diverse future options. They would reduce the grounds for conflict over space and resources. Hi-tech, capital-intensive solutions have been favoured at the expense of low-cost design solutions, such as greening the built environment. They generally increase the disparity of wealth and/or power. Recently a TV documentary (supported by NASA) presented five solutions to global warming:

1  **Sunshade**: Firing 16 trillion one-gram glass disks into space to divert the sun's rays. This would take 30 years, cost 4 trillion dollars and give a whole new meaning to flying saucers.
2  **Sulphur blanket**: Firing rockets into the air to put 1 million tonnes of sulphur 25 kilometres into the stratosphere. This could increase acid rain and damage the ozone layer. The inventor argued that we should reverse environmental regulations, which have reduced pollution but increased global warming.
3  **Denser clouds**: Making clouds more reflective by building ships with 10-metre vertical rotors that shoot sea water vapour into the clouds like a spray gun. Salty residue in the water goes into clouds, which makes the clouds denser. We would need 50 ships a year.[53]
4  **Phytoplankton**: Nitrogen-rich urea granules (fertilizer) would nourish the ocean's phytoplankton, which both release oxygen and die and sink to the ocean floor taking $CO_2$ with them. How this would affect the ecological balance of the oceans is not known.
5  **Artificial trees**: Machines that suck up $CO_2$ out of the air which can then be stored under ground. These would look a bit like wind farms dotting the landscape. (The inventor described this as biomimicry.)

## Perhaps such extreme responses are required for our cataclysmic problems?

Such extreme and expensive ideas may be explained partly by the fact that they are potentially proprietary and monopolistic solutions. They can be owned by corporations. Also, substantial public investment will be required to subsidize these radical schemes. Government R&D funding has increasingly prioritized commercialization potential over the public interest, whether or not the innovations bring cost savings to the general public (or rather, commercialization potential is seen as the highest public good).[54] Furthermore, these hi-tech 'solutions' only address symptoms.[55] The same focus on symptoms is sometimes seen in environmental management. Simply legislating carbon neutral buildings and cars, or taking affirmative action to convert cities into Positive Development, would be simpler and less expensive than perpetually addressing symptoms. Low-cost re-design strategies would generate small businesses and employment while replacing our concrete jungles with garden environments. The operational savings of resource conservation and reuse strategies would in fact pay for the capital costs of retrofitting[56] [Chapter 2]. Positive Development would be more equitable and sustainable without reducing anyone's quality of life. There is no extra cost in eco-retrofitting, as we upgrade our physical environments regularly anyway. However, we need to prioritize the implementation of eco-innovations that solve ecological problems and social inequities – rather than creating incentives in hopes the right outcomes will occur on their own [Chapter 14].

## If low-cost eco-solutions already exist, why aren't they being adopted?

Our intellectual paradigms and institutional frameworks, as well as power relationships, are biased in favour of innovations that benefit large corporations and/or bureaucracies. This is at the expense of reinforcing the capacity of nature to support us. The reasons are endemic and ubiquitous. But they all have roots in our development paradigm. Just some of the systems design and adoption issues that subsequent chapters will expand upon, and propose solutions for, are as follows:

- Available low-tech, natural solutions are obstructed by perverse subsidies and a lack of 'full cost pricing'. That means we do not pay the replacement cost of resources. Resource transfers occur through economic mechanisms that obfuscate their long-term consequences (eg externalities, expropriations, perverse subsidies, discounting and privatization).[57] These systemic biases favour innovation in existing industrial construction and production systems (eg investment in 'clean' coal instead of solar energy). While we recognize externalities, we still ignore what we will call 'internalities': where developers extract excessive benefits at no cost from the public estate. Built environment design can benefit the general public without reducing benefits to owners or profits to developers [Chapters 7 and 8].
- Design is marginalized as a mere means of communication and self-expression. It is, however, an *alternative* 'way of thinking' to linear, reductionist kinds of environmental problem solving. Our educational systems have neglected design in favour of accounting skills. Consequently, we seek templates and tools that tend to circumvent and subvert design. Even many 'green' design norms are rules of thumb that avoid innovation and can actually run counter to sustainability in certain sites or contexts. Moreover, design tools largely predict, compare and measure the future impacts of *given* designs, which tend to reinforce failed templates [Chapters 3, 5 and 6].
- The fragmented, competitive nature of the construction industry militates against innovation in whole systems, such as more eco-efficient supply chains [Box 33]. Even tendering and designer selection processes can impede eco-logical design. Widely recognized arrangements

for encouraging innovation, such as partnering, performance contracting, cooperatives and 'charrettes', have been slow to be adopted. Moreover, the trend is towards more mass production of 'engineered' industrial homes and buildings, which are designed to sell more products more cheaply, not to reduce *total* resource flows [Chapters 2 and 6].

- Policies and programmes shift responsibility for action from those best positioned to create large-scale systems solutions (corporations and bureaucracies) to consumers who can only choose from what is 'on the shelf'. Governments prefer indirect incentives where possible, such as complex incentive and trading systems that rely upon markets (ie 'carrots' or greed). Markets tend to generate innovation in product differentiation, not systems change. Further, to avoid accountability, bureaucrats implement complex systems for measuring, monitoring and mitigating negative impacts (ie 'sticks' or punishment). While innovation is sometimes subsidized, what is innovated is left to commercial interests [Chapters 4, 11 and 14]. Deliberate and direct action for sustainability action is required (through, for example, public–private+community partnerships) not just incentives for others to do something.

## Is there a problem with stimulating behavioural change through incentives?

Market-based and other incentive systems can be very effective in bringing about minor changes at the individual level, but major systems change requires *direct* public involvement. This might entail genuine partnering arrangements between government, industry and community in planning, design and action – as opposed to award ceremonies and certificates. In some cases, indirect market-based incentive systems work to impede change by diverting resources from problem solving and opportunity creating to 'displacement activity'. For example, building rating and assessment approaches are high in transaction costs [Chapters 5 and 11]. Thus the reliance on marginal change through incentives, again, reflects the view that negative impacts are an inevitable aspect of development. It is believed that the environment can at best be 'cleaned up', not restored. Hence, this seemingly non-profitable, janitorial function has been left to environmental non-government organizations (NGOs). These must lobby for funds, or address environmental issues on a volunteer basis, such as rehabilitating farmland or planting trees – while land clearing is effectively subsidized elsewhere. At the same time, governments have abdicated basic public responsibilities, functions and infrastructure to markets through various forms of privatization, outsourcing and downsizing, as documented in Ridgeway's *It's All for Sale*.[58] Clearly, then, our environmental management systems and incentives are not addressing the fundamental ethical, democratic and ecological issues underlying sustainability [Chapter 12].

## Surely environmental management processes do not impede sustainability?

No, but they supplant action. Our environmental management systems do not actually prohibit investment in expanding natural capital. Nor do they necessarily prohibit investing creative energy in eco-innovation and eco-retrofitting. However, management methods, processes, conventions and tools (founded on the belief that negative impacts are inevitable) resonate with inertia, displacement and negativity. Thus they make creativity and innovation uptake difficult. Technically and conceptually, the alternative – design for eco-services – is comparatively simple. It would be easy to increase the conditions for eco-services and biodiversity, and provide positive off-site impacts that add value to the ecological base. It would also be more clearly justified, counting the savings we gain from replacing resource-intensive systems with natural ones and the costs of inaction in not doing so. But to enable and implement Positive Development, we also need to re-design both our intellectual 'grey matter' and institutional 'dark matter'. The first step is to recognize that our environmental management frameworks do not support, and often impede, planning, design and management for Positive Development. Some of the problems of environmental management are examined in following chapters. There are common patterns on all levels. For example:

- Environmental management and assessment systems are biased toward new resource-intensive buildings. They do not count the social and environmental costs already embedded in existing development, or the costs of demolition. Assessment tools help us see some kinds of downstream consequences in the environment, but not the broader distributional impacts of development over time. They do not encourage innovation to address distributional and equity issues [Chapters 5, 7 and 8].

- Public reporting and certification systems, as currently undertaken, involve high transaction costs. Governments report trends, not the unsustainable waste, inefficiencies and/or inequities caused by existing systems of development. If we mapped the costs of inaction, innovations might begin to address existing system-wide problems [Chapters 9 and 14].

- Planning starts from where we are now and thus only puts marginal changes on the balance sheets of decision-makers. This conceals how far we are from sustainability [Figure 2]. Even bioregional planning has not developed strategies to implement planning visions in a context of existing vested interests and established industries, as protected by power relationships, institutional barriers and hidden subsidies[59] [Chapter 12].

- Futures planning tools are not designed for eco-innovation, that is, creating something that is new and which works to change the social context in positive directions. They purport either to *prepare* for future contingencies or to *chart* a future game plan, rather than redesign the game itself. They operate from a sectional perspective, rather than in the public interest [Chapter 10].

- Trading schemes have not encouraged innovation to improve existing ecological conditions. In other words, they generally only mitigate future harm. Moreover, they often represent a de facto privatization of the public estate (whether through public or private control) by exempting basic resource allocation decisions from democratic safeguards [Chapter 11].

Figure 2 What we do and do not measure

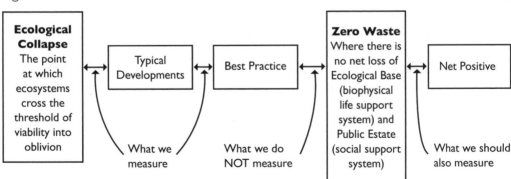

## Then where do we begin to improve environmental management?

The list of places where we could begin the Positive Development process is endless. Chapter 15 outlines some steps to guide action. However, the first and largest step is to challenge the status quo. The status quo is the ongoing, irreversible redistribution and concentration of wealth and power. It is inherently unstable. Thus planning, design and innovation will continue to re-enforce non-sustainable built environments, conceal resource and wealth transfers, and re-distribute wealth through a vertical integration process. This is leading us to increasing 'piratization', where de facto or direct control over public resources is given to special (public or private) interests. An example is the case of bio-piracy.60 Not only have impoverished people around the world lost rights to indigenous medicines, some must now pay for local water or timber that is 'managed' by international corporations, as documented by Maude Caldwell and others.61 The solution is therefore not to foster greater uptake of 'best practice' environmental management processes and decision tools, but to replace and/or supplement them with creative design processes and projects. That is to say, we need to shift from environmental management frameworks that legitimize tradeoffs to those that enable design for ecology and equity. We need to replace incremental targets with action. Ultimately, the full transition to Positive Development will require new forms of design, transdisciplinarity, and a new approach to eco-governance [Chapter 15].

## Does eco-governance differ from conventional environmental management?

'Eco-governance', here, refers to decision structures designed explicitly to suit the nature of ecological and sustainability issues. Eco-governance implies intellectual, institutional and technical systems that respect a diversity of responsible cultures, lifestyles and values – while enhancing the underlying ecological and democratic platforms that make these possible. Our environmental management institutions, regulations and management systems have instead applied old ideas to new environmental issues [Box 49]. Ultimately, it is only the citizenry that can bring about the large-scale, cross-sectoral, whole systems change required, through NGOs in partnership with other sectors.[62] Participation in decision-making and design is essential, though not enough.[63] Civil society will need to re-negotiate the social contract. Business and industry will not adopt substantive due process, which is essential to meaningful public participation, without an eco-sensitive and more democratic constitutional framework [Chapter 13]. New kinds of decision systems are needed that make decision-makers, not just the general public, more accountable. In the case of irreversible decisions, accountability cannot be achieved by electoral defeat or other forms of restitution or retribution after the fact. We need better planning, design and decision principles that can prevent *irreversible* decisions in the first place. A 'constitutional' basis, as well as a transparent, participatory approach to sustainable decision-making and design is necessary [Chapter 13]. The above issues and principles will be teased out in the following chapters to form the basis of SmartMode (Systems Mapping And Re-design Thinking Mode), a process for achieving Positive Development.

# 2
# The Case for Eco-retrofitting

From impact mitigation
to net positive impacts

A major impediment to green building, let alone biophysical sustainability, remains the false belief that responsible design and construction costs more.[1] It is, however, now well established that new green buildings need not cost more than conventional ones, and can cost far less from a life-cycle and societal perspective.[2] Many case studies and reports have demonstrated that investments in building eco-efficiencies can be highly profitable for owners, while reducing externality costs to the public as a whole.[3] Even buildings that have involved a substantial amount of research and development have paid back the extra investment within about 10 years or less, and the payback period is shrinking rapidly.[4] Although far less than 10 per cent of new buildings in the 'developed' nations are 'green', the numbers of green buildings are reputedly increasing by 20 per cent a year in the US.[5] Nonetheless, the rate of uptake of green building strategies and technologies still does not reflect their stunning investment opportunities. We are instead continuing to throw more good money after bad. It is therefore necessary to survey some of the economic and health benefits of retrofitting for owners, builders, developers and the general public.

'Eco-retrofitting' as used here means modifying buildings and/or urban areas to improve overall human and environmental health, and to reduce resource depletion, degradation and pollution – if not expand the ecological base. It implies an integrated and eco-logical design approach, instead of the mere addition of energy-saving equipment. It also implies a planning strategy that considers not just buildings but whole suburbs, cities and urban infrastructure. There are already institutional levers for overcoming impediments to retrofitting. Proposals can be found across the whole spectrum, from small incentive schemes to partnerships or cooperatives for retrofitting entire neighbourhoods.[6] However, it is argued that direct action is required to deliver net positive physical impacts in existing urban environments. The mainstream approach, indirect incentive systems, can have unintended consequences in complex systems.[7] 'Direct action', in this context, means implementing physical design solutions as opposed to indirect incentive systems. Government agencies tend to avoid direct action, partly because they do not obtain recognition for saving resources. Mechanisms are needed to enable government agencies and community groups (as well as industry) to capture some of the credit and financial savings from eco-retrofitting projects.

As new construction is only about two per cent of the total building stock, new green buildings have little impact on the growing rate of resources consumed by development. Moreover, we have seen that new construction necessarily increases overall resource flows despite lower relative operating costs. Given the resource flows embedded in existing development, then, eco-retrofitting is a sustainability imperative. Yet, thus far, little effort has been directed at greening the existing building stock. This is despite the fact that investments in retrofits have been shown to compare favourably with conventional financial investments, such as stocks and bonds.[8] In fact, from a public perspective, eco-retrofitting pays for itself. While retrofitting generally is only undertaken for resource efficiency (at best), net positive eco-retrofitting would aim for whole systems sustainability. Since Positive Development does not yet exist, however, only figures on the benefits and barriers to retrofitting for resource efficiency are available at this time.

### Doesn't eco-retrofitting cost the developer more, even if costing society less?

Retrofitting, as a practice, can cost more initially. But this is largely because there is a cost entailed in shifting from any entrenched 'modus operandi' to more ecologically sound practices. Speed is essential to profitability under current conditions, so change is always problematic. Standard buildings are just as difficult to build, but decades of experience have established routine methods and practices that are hard to dislodge. Retrofitting can also be more complicated than new construction, because it entails dealing with site-specific and unique conditions. This is also because relatively few people are trained in retrofitting. Also, 'green' can cost more if we simply 'add on' energy and water-saving devices to the basic building template. All of these costs can be greatly reduced by eco-logical design. For example, passive solutions (like attached greenhouses) can be integrated with structural design to increase solar heating, cooling and ventilation with no extra costs.[9] But even with 'add on' approaches, the extra expense is soon recovered through reduced operating, maintenance, workers' compensation and personnel costs. This is widely known in eco-logical design circles, yet green building incentive and rating schemes have been slow to address, let alone encourage, eco-retrofitting [Chapter 5]. For example, most green building rating tools still favour new buildings, because they do not weigh in the costs of demolition to make way for new construction. At the same time, not retrofitting is favoured by ignoring the ongoing costs of, and embodied waste in, existing development [Chapters 4 and 7]. In other words, our tools and incentives reinforce systemic biases against retrofitting, while doing little to overcome the inertia of change.[10]

### Wouldn't retrofitting get in the way of a whole new 'sustainable' urban form?

That assumes there is a 'correct' urban form and that we know what it is. There are two main ideological positions regarding what would constitute sustainable urban form. Both advocate sustainable development, but they offer diametrically opposed solutions. Those advocating 'urban consolidation' or 'compact cities' call for more commercial activity and dwellings in inner urban areas. Denser land use would arguably avoid urban expansion, reduce car dependency and revitalize the central business districts. Such densification would entail 'infill' development and/or demolition and reconstruction of neighbourhoods.[11] What we could call the 'urban garden' position, in contrast, calls for dispersed, low-scale, mixed use areas surrounded by greenbelts, and integrated with the natural systems in which such 'satellite' communities would be situated [Box 11]. Neither camp favours 'suburban sprawl' or 'Manhattanization' (as is sometimes suggested by their opposing camp). Both are concerned with how to accommodate a growing population sustainably. Ultimately, of course, neither strategy will work if the growth in population and consumerism remains unchecked. But neither will either strategy work within current approaches to urban design and architecture [Chapter 3]. Green approaches to design will only succeed if they move from their current single-issue focus to a whole systems view of development that addresses the wider regional and ecological context. If the aim is sustainability – ensuring that development decisions today will, at the very least, keep future responsible public options open – we will need to make fundamental changes to land-use planning and design [Chapter 12].

## Isn't it up to the market to determine the choice of urban forms and patterns?

It would appear that the market is doing land-use planning. The market thinks only about maximizing residential units per land area. It is not conserving open spaces required for adaptation to unexpected future social and technological changes. Also, many new green developments are essentially exclusionary. A whole new 'sustainable city' is being developed largely by private investment in Dongtan near Shanghai, China. It is reputedly the biggest single building project in the world.[12] Commissioned in 2005, an early phase should be finished by 2010 for an Expo in Shanghai. It is expected to have 500,000 residents by 2040 and will be self-sufficient in energy, food and water and almost zero $CO_2$ in transport emissions. It will occupy 630 hectares of 'green field' (ie previously undeveloped) agricultural land on an island, connected to the mainland with tunnels and bridges. Linked to Shanghai with a freeway, visitors will park cars outside the city and use public transport and water taxis. There are plans to protect nature preserves on the island. The leading engineering firm, ARUP, promises to 'offset' the greenhouse emissions of its own employees. However, early promotional pictures suggest a technocratic vision of the future: another green 'technology park'. While this impressive project may set a new standard of environmental efficiency, it may also, like other business parks, primarily serve the needs of new industries, such as biotech and software companies and their elite employees. At this stage, this market-driven solution does not look like it will do much to redress the social, economic or environmental problems of existing cities. In the meantime, established cities and cultures around the world are deteriorating.

## If the market fails, can't planners simply regulate for sustainable urban design?

Relying on either business or planning authorities to guide real estate markets has not yet led to overall progress towards sustainable cities. Green spin improves consumer awareness, but can also lull consumers into complacency and consumption. Energy, materials and space consumption and car use per capita continue to grow, while the ecological base and public estate is eroded.[13] Meanwhile, indicators of 'genuine progress' are showing a diminution in public perceptions of their life quality and wellbeing [Box 34]. As Hamilton notes, people are often less happy as material consumption increases.[14] Further, planning legislation has not addressed its contra-ecological legacy. Most cities established plans and policies that shaped development patterns long before sustainability was conceived. Even now that it is often included as a 'fundamental' planning goal, decisions affecting urban land use and density are still made without any real consideration of sustainability [Chapter 12]. In Australia, for example, land release for development continues without regard to the ultimate limits of land, space or urban form. Planning for sustainability is still about mitigating the impacts of market expansion and population growth. In other words, neither the market (business) nor planning (government) sectors has begun to deal seriously with the ultimate implications of their intellectual heritage and internal dynamics in relation to sustainability. That leaves the community.

## If neither sector has succeeded, how do we achieve sustainable cities?

We first need to recognize that we have a design problem. We can neither abandon cities, nor leave them the way they are – due to the waste and operating costs embodied in existing development. About 90 per cent of the stock of extracted materials is now contained in the built environment. We simply cannot replace cities with new ones, due to the material flows and waste that this would entail [Chapter 4]. We could, however, retrofit whole city blocks and suburbs to achieve net Positive Development without demolishing and replacing established areas. This is because even retrofitting for mere energy efficiency alone can pay for itself. Retrofitting would mean employment in design and construction, investments for business and developers, increased occupant productivity and health, and public savings through net reductions in energy use, greenhouse emissions and material flows. In the process of adding social and economic value, we could create eco-productive environments that increase effective open space, biodiversity habitat and nature corridors to ensure 'natural security' and increase future social options. The bottom line is that, from a whole of life and resource flows perspective, eco-retrofitting is essential if cities are to become ecologically self-sufficient and self-sustaining within the limits of natural resources. Yet economists and planners have not designed mechanisms that would allow it to happen – despite its proven financial benefits [Chapter 11]. Moreover, while cities ostensibly offer diversity, opportunity and choice, our planning and design norms have led to mono-cultural and sterile urban environments. We design cities as zoos for people.

## But wouldn't increased nature in cities reduce urban lifestyle choices?

Not at all. In fact, it is construction driven by industrial imperatives that often destroys the variety and diversity that cities have evolved over different periods. Consolidation approaches often betray a 'social engineering' ideology that assumes people should live in a certain way. Eco-retrofitting, in contrast, can preserve and increase difference and diversity, while adding ecological and social value. For example, we can retrofit urban form and buildings to increase land-use intensity in some areas, while increasing total open space and access to natural and urban landscapes. After all, whether more people live in cities, suburbs or rural areas is not the main determinant of the sustainability of the built environment. The driver of choice, conviviality and life quality is the design of development. Through eco-retrofitting, as opposed to bulldozing and densification, citizens could choose more sustainable and diverse lifestyles, either urban or suburban. Retrofitting would also demonstrate the wider lesson that governments, environmentalists and developers can have shared goals and solve environmental problems together, at a profit. This would help to dispel the belief that the environment is in irresolvable conflict with development. However, we need to create the institutional conditions that would enable eco-retrofitting – let alone 'efficiency retrofitting' – to occur. In lieu of a maze of regulations and incentives, governments, in partnership with non-government organizations (NGOs) and businesses, could create exemplars of Positive Development. However, governments have largely resisted such opportunities, seemingly on ideological and territorial grounds.[15]

## If eco-retrofitting is so logical, why haven't governments embraced it?

As we know, governments are slow to act on any sustainability issues, partly because they operate within a short-term political and narrow economic framework. Retrofitting would be more compelling, even to politicians, if our mental balance sheets presented a whole system perspective that made market distortions and the costs of inaction more transparent. That is to say, if the human and natural resource costs of existing development were considered, owners of poorly-designed buildings and development control authorities would have to account for the externality costs that their decisions impose upon society [Chapter 9]. Currently, the externalities of poor building design are, for practical purposes, subsidized. For example, the price of resources does not reflect the environmental, let alone the replacement, costs. The costs of resources are already rising due to increasing scarcity [Boxes 42 and 43]. As these true costs are gradually reflected in their market price, 'savings' in carbon dioxide emissions, materials, energy and water will be increasingly understood as potential 'income' over time. In fact, with 'full cost pricing' (where users pay the replacement cost of resources), the myriad rating tools and costly development control systems would be virtually redundant. In a more perfect world, design would be the first place to which businesses would turn to make profits, not financial speculation.

## Why don't governments just simply require full cost pricing then?

It would appear that governments in liberal societies prefer indirect means or incentives – whether in the form of what are seen as 'positive' subsidies or 'negative' regulations.[16] There may be less friction in handing out money from tax revenue than making consumers pay more for goods or fuels. Of course, incentives have their place. But we do not create incentives for eco-logical design. Our incentives still favour industrial, fossil fuel-based or 'fossilized' solutions over community-based, creative and commonsense actions. The fossil fuel industries receive billions in subsidies despite billions in profits. Green buildings could achieve an even higher financial return if developers or building owners could get 'extra' credit for, or capture the savings in, reduced embodied and operational energy, water, and other human and natural resources. Currently, however, green buildings are still penalized [Chapter 5]. Later we will explore how developers could be given incentives, like tradable credits for resource savings, through existing mechanisms such as 'points' in development control systems, transferable development rights, and so on [Chapter 11]. Since retrofitting could be cheaper than doing nothing, however, it is less a matter of creating incentives than of removing intellectual and institutional impediments and perverse subsidies.

## How can retrofitting existing buildings be cheaper than doing nothing?

They pay for themselves and reduce impacts into the future. Many case studies have demonstrated that the operating energy costs of buildings can easily be reduced by 50–90 per cent through retrofitting. Retrofitting should not be considered an additional cost in the first place, given that buildings are often gutted and renovated on a regular basis anyway. The need for refurbishments is partly because buildings are designed on the basis of 'planned obsolescence'. In fact, large commercial buildings are often designed to be refurbished about every 15 years or so. Also, minor renovations are undertaken every few years to attract or accommodate new tenants.[17] Some even have 'facadectomies', where the façade is replaced just to attract different tenants and higher rents. In other words, buildings are not designed for easy adaptation to market demand, let alone changing social needs. Design for adaptability, disassembly and 'compostability' would at least make these arguably unnecessary changes far less costly. The resource savings gained by retrofitting can quickly pay back the costs and deliver a return on investment year after year thereafter. This is old news. Joseph Romm, in *Cool Business* (1999), documented many instances where a sound return on investment was made in retrofitting projects (several of his examples are discussed below).[18] While whole-of-building retrofits are often better value, even simple improvements with small investments can be highly profitable.

## So what are some examples of simple, low-cost retrofitting that are profitable?

Romm reports that a hospital in Indiana reduced the electricity consumption of its lighting by over 70 per cent just by improving the lighting system, for an annual saving of over $100,000. The upgrade cost $85,000, so the payback period was less than a year. In other words, the construction costs were fully recovered in a year through the energy savings alone. In addition, the retrofits had 'free' benefits to the public, preventing emissions of 1500 tons of carbon dioxide, 13 tons of sulphur dioxide and 6 tons of nitrogen oxides each year thereafter. So simple upgrades of lighting alone can pay for themselves in a year or two and, after that initial payback period, they provide an ongoing annual return. Money saved is money earned. But integrated retrofitting generally has more financial gain in relation to the initial cost than isolated efficiency measures such as just better lighting. The more comprehensive the retrofit, the better the return in either retrofitting or new construction. This is because piecemeal and add-on approaches tend to be sub-optimal. For example, efficient lighting and fixtures can cost more initially but last longer. Similarly, LCD monitors cost more initially than cathode ray tubes, but they use less electricity and do not heat their environments as much as the latter. As companies become more experienced, costs come down. An integrated approach is almost always more cost-effective than addressing one system, like lighting, in isolation.

## Just why is integrated retrofitting better value than small efficiency measures?

Whole building retrofits combine several systems to reduce resource usage synergistically. For example, Romm cites a commercial office in Portland that upgraded its lighting, roof insulation, windows and HVAC system to reduce energy consumption by 61 per cent – saving $130,000 per year. Better lighting combined with efficient windows and insulation can allow for smaller heating, ventilating and cooling systems. This can mean significant savings in capital, operational and maintenance costs, and even save valuable space. Better glazing and lighting systems can reduce the electricity usage of offices dramatically. However, increasing natural lighting through building design modifications, such as better glazing, light-shelves and light-wells, can be even more cost-effective. Once installed, these features require little electricity and involve relatively little maintenance. Facilities management is also a vital component of a whole building approach. An energy management control system that optimizes energy usage can ensure significant savings through more efficient operations and lower maintenance over time [Box 20]. The improved health and safety features associated with integrated retrofits can have even greater economic benefits than those gained from resource savings. Health and safety is increasingly understood as cost-effective in the long term.

## How would retrofits improve the health and safety of building occupants?

Green design features measurably reduce absenteeism and sickness. The World Health Organisation found that a third of new buildings in the developed world generate complaints of 'sick building syndrome'. Some buildings have been deemed uninhabitable and even unsalvageable shortly after construction, due to adverse health impacts. In fact, some have been vacated and demolished after only a few years. Looking at this in a positive way, healthy buildings could reduce a nation's medical costs significantly. In fact, improvements to the built environment are one of the most economical forms of 'preventative medicine'.[19] But opportunities to make positive improvements and cost savings are often ignored. Some years ago, an Australian study found that 62 per cent of occupants of 228 low-rise offices in suburban Melbourne and 72 per cent of occupants of 511 Commonwealth Government offices considered the air in their buildings to be unacceptably stuffy. Although the potential cost savings were calculated and documented by financial experts, few of these buildings were upgraded. Such lost opportunities are often concealed by administrative systems that separate capital and operational budgets. Further, the trend is for government agencies to become building tenants. Therefore they are less likely to set an example by ecological retrofitting. Another factor is the tendency to measure only the negatives. We focus on the adverse health and performance effects associated with poor lighting and indoor air quality, rather than assigning figures to the positive effects of good design [Chapter 4]. However, evidence is mounting that good air quality and lighting can measurably improve occupant health as well as reduce illnesses.

## Even if retrofits can improve public health, why should companies pay for it?

Businesses can save substantial sums while simultaneously contributing to public health. Improved lighting and comfort through natural ventilation, daylighting and amenities (such as atriums, skylights, courtyards and interior fountains) have produced quantifiable reductions in sick leave, absenteeism and workers' compensation claims.[20] In fact, the US Centre for Health Systems and Design, among others, has shown that viewing plants and outdoor gardens in hospitals reduces stress, use of pain relief medication, recovery time and surgical complications. And similar benefits are found in terms of the stress levels and health of workers in offices. Romm found that, while a renovated manufacturing plant in California saved 60 per cent on energy costs, it reduced absenteeism by 45 per cent – which generated a far greater return on investment than the energy savings. Similarly, when a manufacturer in Georgia moved into a daylit building, workers' compensation cases dropped from 20 to under 1 per year. However, the biggest financial benefit of green buildings is not in reduced sick days (a negative), but in increased worker productivity (a positive). Because salaries are the biggest cost in many businesses, the financial savings from happy, productive employees is far greater than that gained from energy savings, or even reduced health related expenses. Happy people tend to move in positive cycles.

## How can we tell if eco-retrofitting can really improve worker productivity?

Daylighting, thermal comfort, air quality, ventilation, and the ability of workers to adjust their own lighting, temperature and airflow conditions have been shown to lead to measurable productivity improvements.[21] For example, according to Romm, Lockheed's daylit energy-efficient engineering facility in California saved up to $400,000 a year on energy bills, but also increased productivity by 15 per cent.[22] Significant (although variable) correlations between school test performance and fresh air supply have also been established. One study showed students in daylit schools (with no glare) out-performed those in non-daylit schools by 20 per cent or more on standardized tests.[23] An analysis by Carnegie Mellon's Centre for Building Performance and Diagnostics showed improved lighting would add $370,000 to the first cost of a typical workplace but save $680,000 in energy use and other reduced operating costs.[24] The productivity benefit, however, could be up to $14.6 million. The City of Melbourne, Australia, made a large investment in achieving a world's best practice standard in its new Council House Two (CH2) building. Technologies included external shower towers, solar stacks, water mining from city sewers, co-generation, wind turbines and chilled ceiling beams. Despite added research and building costs, the city council anticipates a payback period of 8 to 10 years, using a modest estimate for savings in health and productivity. Better yet, the 60L building in Melbourne showed how to retrofit a building. In such cases, even so-called 'mistakes' are constructive as they provide valuable lessons. Moreover, on top of reduced sickness and increased productivity, green buildings have even been shown to increase retail sales.

## How can retrofitting possibly be said to measurably increase retail sales?

Wal-Mart discovered the relationship between sales and daylighting when it built a store that had daylighting on only half of its roof. To cut costs during construction, Romm reports, Wal-Mart only put skylights in half the roof and left the rest without daylighting. Register activity soon showed that sales per square foot, or 'sales pressure', were significantly higher for departments located in the daylit half of the store. Moreover, many employees requested to be moved to the daylit side. Similarly, a study of 73 stores of a California chain found daylighting increased sales by 1–6 per cent, which was far more than energy cost savings.[25] But perhaps the main financial benefit of retrofits is that they are a safe, low-risk investment with a high rate of return. Commercial real estate is bought on the basis of a 10-year return on investment, and most case studies indicate that energy upgrades of existing buildings have a payback period of less than 10 years. A 2003 study indicated that the extra costs of new green buildings was only about 2 per cent on average in California, due to capacity building in green design and construction.[26] And that figure is rapidly going down. Further, corporate investment is reimbursed many times over through a range of wider benefits (see below). The reduced costs achievable through 'capacity building' in green design and materials will translate to retrofitting projects as well. But eco-retrofitting programmes and practices need to consider issues surrounding the recycling of materials as well.

## Would using recycled materials in new buildings avoid the need to retrofit?

No. The trend towards increased reuse of old materials in new construction is a positive one, of course. This trend is due in part to the internet, which can connect builders to recycled materials near the job site. But while important, recycling in construction still has many practical impediments and costs:

- Construction requires timely delivery of materials from nearby areas, as transport costs and impacts can make the recycling of heavy or bulky construction materials too expensive in some cases. This adds risk.
- Many products are not easily deconstructed and reused [Box 6]. For example, aluminium-framed windows, in many cases, cannot practically be removed from brickwork without breaking them. Bricks in many regions now use binders that prevent their reuse, so such bricks are simply crushed and used as rubble, ie 'downcycled' [Chapter 14].
- Sometimes the demolition of an old building is unexpectedly delayed, so the materials are not available when planned for and needed at the new construction site.
- When parts of old buildings are reused or recycled, there is still a lot of embodied waste that ends up in landfill when the rest of the buildings are demolished. Materials sometimes entail toxins, waste and losses of energy in reprocessing. Chemicals in conventional building materials and furnishings off-gas toxins (largely due to petrochemical components in vinyl flooring, PVC pipes, plastics, resins, binders, paints, etc).

To have low life-cycle impacts, of course, eco-logical design principles must apply to material selection, use, and ongoing procurement and modifications, as well as to solar heating, cooling and ventilating, whether in new or retrofitted construction. Even retrofits need to be adaptable.

## What about 'design for deconstruction' so building components can be reused?

Under current urban planning and design patterns, construction and demolition waste will remain a major source of toxic landfill – even with far more reuse or recycling of building components. Until the 1980s or so, older conventional buildings had many components as well as insulation materials containing asbestos (it was allowed in some products in Australia until 2003). Asbestos is still found in many buildings, and its toxic fibres are released in demolition, renovation and fires. Hence renovation, as well as demolition, of durable buildings usually requires licensed asbestos removalists. However, eco-retrofitting that 'encapsulates' old buildings (especially where asbestos is involved) could, in some cases, be better than deconstruction and recycling materials that are harmful during production, occupation, demolition or deconstruction. Historic buildings have been preserved by, in essence, adding a new interior. For example, a new concrete floor was poured into an old city hall building in Portland, Oregon, to level out the warped floors. This created a base for new interior walls that encased the old walls. This method contributed to high insulation levels, as well as the building's longevity as a landmark, and avoided some of the environmental and human health costs of demolition and new construction. So reusable, replaceable components can make sense, but sometimes encasing old buildings in compostable, healthy interior skins may be better. Alternatively, eco-retrofitting buildings with demountable and reversible Green Scaffolding exterior skins can increase building longevity, reduce the negative impacts of existing development, and increase design quality and choice – without wasting materials and energy [Box 5].

## Figure 3 Eco-retrofitting example

In this hypothetical case, the building is massive in embodied energy, and impractical to demolish due to its central business location. However, it is considered an eyesore and has outlived its practical functions. Green Scaffolding could be applied, using a horizontal triangular truss. This encloses a duct to circulate air from hot to cold areas of the building in winter and cold to hot sides in summer, aided by solar fans.

In hot weather, the greenhouse terrarium windows vent to the outside. The heat is also expelled from the Trombe wall, assisted by wind generators. In cool weather, heat is circulated by the horizontal truss duct. The heat is fed into and stored in a 'Trombe wall' (in this case a rock mesh in the module). We can call this a 'reverse' Trombe wall, as it is added to a section of the building that has no windows. The Trombe wall storage can feed into the existing centralized system. Alternatively, heat can be directly vented into the room.

Planters are alternated with the terrariums to alleviate the heat sink effect and articulate the façade. They are electronically shaded, and sprayed with water pipes hidden in the triangular ducting. The planters are accessible through the terrariums, but sensors will guide a plant maintenance system to reduce the need for manual gardening. Water for the plants could be collected on the roof. This building is in a humid climate, so evaporative cooling and roof water collection are limited. In this case, plastic canopies on the roof would collect water from the air while providing some additional shading.

## Don't some green building designers already use double-skin exteriors?

Conventional double-skin buildings only address heating and cooling needs. They also create ecologically 'negative' spaces between the glazed surfaces. They increase the urban heat sink. Also, curtain glass is hard to repair. Green Scaffolding, in contrast, can increase building longevity by providing weather or earthquake reinforcement, reducing impacts of flooding, terrorist attacks and strong winds. If properly designed, it could also reduce the risks of some building parts being dislodged during strong storms, or of tree limbs damaging the core structure (a problem that often causes native tree removal in Australia as they are inclined to drop limbs). They also create ecologically useful (as opposed to dead) spaces. Electronic sensors can regulate environmental controls like shade cloths and reflectors to increase or decrease light and heat as required by plants in side the skins. We have horticultural science that can design seedless watermelons, fartless beans and square tomatoes. If they can design plants to suit the convenience of industry, doubtless they can also guide the design of suitable urban environments for plants and even protein. In some countries, people eat guinea pigs among many other small sources of protein. One could even grow small, relatively happy animals, fish and poultry in parts of the building envelope [Figure 10].[27] There are now urban farm structures that have whole floors allocated to animals as well as plants.[28] Urban community farms are also mushrooming in many places. However, we should distinguish nature 'as food' from nature 'as ecology'.

## What is appropriate for buildings where we want to preserve the façade?

The external façade of historic buildings can be preserved by internal Green Scaffolding. Space frames of steel and cable can reinforce masonry buildings and reduce the potential damage from earthquakes or structural deterioration [Figure 4]. Some older buildings would not survive otherwise, as they would cost too much to maintain, heat and air-condition, and so on. Internal Green Scaffolding can generate natural air-conditioning and insulation, as does the exterior Green Scaffolding. In winter, these structures could trap warm air between the exterior glazed skin and the original wall. In summer, warm air could be exhausted out using wind syphoning or solar chimneys, where hot air rises and pressure differentials move air. Therefore, Green Scaffolding can be used as:

- Walls for new buildings
- To retrofit old exterior walls
- To increase the longevity and use of heritage buildings
- As free standing green space frames in parks and other public spaces to create semi-indoor spaces and nature habitats

All of the above structures can serve multiple human and ecological functions. For example, large space frames defining a public plaza could also be combined with sprays of recirculated water to cool the urban area in heat waves. While there are few on-ground examples, the MFO Park in Zurich provides a limited forerunner of what is possible.

## Figure 4 Eco-retrofitting historic buildings

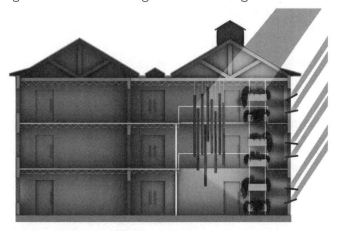

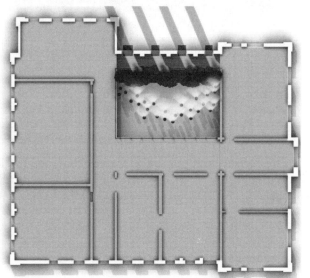

In the case of an older building in need of renovation and structural reinforcement, we can add a vertical landscape to the interior while reinforcing the old structure with an internal scaffold. In this example, to improve natural air circulation, natural light and air quality, an interior atrium is created. This creates a U-shaped interior where air is drawn from the office spaces and out through a new solar stack. The section shows light from a new roof skylight directed into the atrium. The light bounces off a suspended shiny pipe sculpture, which we will call a 'green chandelier'. The pipes that are further from the skylight bounce light down to the lower parts of the planting wall. The round shape of the pipes helps to diffuse the light. The pipes would be controlled electronically to adjust to the changing position of the sun during the day and in different seasons. They can be arranged to block direct light in the surrounding mezzanines or let more light deeper into the interior.

The section also shows how light from the windows is directed into the atrium with light shelves. The planting wall can clean the air and provide some food. In this example, a catwalk allows people to service the plants.

## What is the investment potential of retrofitting commercial buildings?

Enormous. There is a growing supply of aged or underused buildings that are in need of maintenance and upgrading. The (non-environmental) refurbishment industry, with its huge material consumption, is growing at a faster rate than new construction in many regions. In fact, in developed nations about a third of building construction activity can be attributed to renovation. Building renovation and demolition accounts for 91 per cent of the construction and demolition debris generated each year, while new construction accounts for only 9 per cent.[29] Much of this kind of refurbishment is driven by a desire to attract new tenants, by interior design trends, and by the perceived need to outclass business competitors. That is, it has not been driven by efficiency, let alone sustainability. Yet each renovation project offers a potential high-yield, low-risk eco-retrofitting opportunity. Where energy savings can pay off the loan for the upgrade, a return on investment is assured. A US research project, for example, found that businesses could expect to achieve a saving of US$1/ft² of floor space per month with whole-building retrofits. This means financial benefits for the local community as well through job creation and economic multiplier effects. Retrofitting a percentage of the urban office stock would have a significant effect on the local economy.[30] The retrofitting of urban buildings is beginning to happen on its own, as developers gradually begin to appreciate the potential profits involved. In the US, investors can now buy securities in retrofitting. Likewise, it would be relatively easy to develop programmes to stimulate the eco-retrofitting of suburban homes as well, to make them 'resource autonomous' or even net positive.

## Just what is resource autonomy and how do we achieve this?

Resource autonomous homes and buildings are possible, as Robert and Brenda Vale and others have demonstrated.[31] Resource autonomous buildings are those that do not require off-site sources of water or energy. They treat any unavoidable pollution or waste on-site, and use environmentally-friendly, healthy materials (eg rammed earth instead of fired brick). However, resource autonomous homes generally just aim to produce more energy than they consume, as opposed to making a positive contribution to the ecology. Some resource autonomous homes could constitute Positive Development if they also created significant positive off-site and/or on-site ecological and social gains. Due to undeveloped land area on suburban blocks, there is space for individualized, low-tech, site-specific eco-retrofitting solutions like sunspaces and conservatories, garden composting, rainwater collection systems, plants to clean the air and composting toilets.[32] Existing suburbs also have adequate space for immediate action to generate positive impacts, such as water and soil remediation for nearby land, or more extensive biodiversity habitats on the site than existed before development. Yet there has been virtually no attempt to increase the ecology in the suburbs. Also, most green design has been at the building scale. There has been less effort at greening whole neighbourhoods. Eco-sanitation systems, like wetlands or Living Machines, are usually most practical at the neighbourhood scale, as such systems require ongoing and reliable management. Merely increasing residential density with green buildings could preclude land uses that provide eco-services beyond the needs of the individual homes.[33]

## What is the investment potential of retrofitting domestic construction?

Retrofitting can be achieved at no cost to owners, and at a profit to contractors. Mere improvements to the existing housing stock with 'off-the-shelf' technology could reduce annual energy consumption dramatically. A 90 per cent reduction in home energy costs is possible through good design.[34] Let us assume a 30 per cent reduction in energy usage for half of the detached dwellings in a town of, say, 50,000. A residential retrofit programme could save/earn the town several million dollars a year. Therefore the costs of retrofitting could be recouped from home energy savings over, say, 10 to 20 years.[35] Refurbishments are needed as the housing stock ages anyway. Retrofitting could increase the longevity of the housing stock, as we saw in the case of urban buildings. While it may be easier to build new energy-efficient homes, we must include the environmental impacts of construction and demolition, not just operation. About 44 per cent of landfill in some areas is composed of construction and demolition waste (the amount varies by region), and most construction waste still has toxic components. In 2005, the UK initiated a programme to increase the demolition of homes from 20,000 to 80,000 per year in order to replace them with more energy-efficient buildings. The added pollution, resource flows and waste that this demolition and replacement activity entails should be deducted – not to mention the ecological waste [Chapter 4]. These new buildings are not ecologically sustainable, only energy-efficient, and therefore occupy space, use funds and entail 'opportunity costs' (ie lost opportunities). The up-front investment in new buildings could instead be used to retrofit far more buildings far more quickly, while retaining a sense of community and place.

## But what about the 'up-front' cost of retrofitting – can it be reduced?

One of the biggest impediments to retrofitting is the up-front cost – despite the fact that it constitutes a sound and ethical investment [Box 37]. At the domestic scale, for example, an up-front investment of a few thousand dollars in a solar hot water heater compares favourably with investing that amount of money in a savings account. However, many people feel that they do not have 'spare money' to invest (or save) in the first place. Also, developers usually do not have to pay the operational costs of the building, as they pass these costs on to the future building owners and renters. Therefore, they are usually only concerned with keeping construction costs down, and have little incentive to invest in energy efficiency. But there are many ways of addressing this. For example:

- More councils could legislate for mandatory disclosure of the building's energy rating to potential buyers or renters, as is done in some places.[36]
- Councils can create development incentives, such as allowing the addition of a second floor dwelling unit if, and only if, the addition converts both units into 'resource autonomous' dwellings or better [Box 8].[37]
- Mortgage schemes could be modified to encourage retrofits. Favourable mortgage rate programmes already exist in some places for new energy efficient homes.
- Stamp duty could be reduced in proportion to a building's energy efficiency.

Unfortunately, the fact that retrofitting could pay for itself while reducing public externality costs does not always impress people who are concerned only with short-term costs and profits. Oddly, some even treat the payback period as a disincentive.

## Surely a payback would be the biggest incentive for eco-retrofitting?

Due to negative thinking, the payback period is often regarded as if it were a bad thing. Many people forget that, once paid off, the savings from passive solar design and eco-technologies are effectively 'income'. There is virtually no financial risk. The payback time on residential properties can be just a few months or years, making what Richard Heede called 'home made money'.[38] In fact, a study conducted for the US Environmental Protection Agency, back in 1998, showed that, on average, homeowners recover their investments in upgrades regardless of how long after they remain in the home. The property value increases immediately and, on average, covers the builder's upgrade costs.[39] This is partly because purchasers are willing to pay more for an energy-efficient home as an investment – a trend which should increase. In Canberra, where homes that are advertised for sale must publish their energy rating, researchers have found strengthening trends between house prices and energy ratings.[40] Paradoxically, while most people will not buy products where the payback period is deemed 'too long', as in the case of solar panels, they will buy excessively expensive cars for which there is no payback whatsoever.[41] As the personal 'brag value' to be gained from investments in eco-logical design increases, awareness of sustainability issues will also grow. Nonetheless, people still need money to invest in the first place, at least if governments remain unwilling to put systems in place to finance significant retrofitting programmes or to reduce hidden subsidies to new homes.

## So how do we overcome this problem of covering up-front costs?

'Performance contracting' is one way of eliminating this problem. This is where the service providers themselves meet the costs of the retrofit. The providers then recoup their costs through the resource savings over time.[42] This approach can reduce or even eliminate the up-front capital costs of the work to the home or building owner. The owner pays little or nothing up-front (which could be negotiable) and later inherits a reduced energy bill. Because the construction costs are paid for from the operational costs of the building, this approach is in a sense self-funding, generates its own clients, and makes money.[43] A partnership can be formed between the building owner and the energy service contractor (who is also the performance contractor) to ensure a win–win–win relationship.[44] Energy service companies (ESCOs) have been installing energy-efficient equipment at no cost to building owners through such arrangements for some time. The problem is that performance contracting tends to 'cherry pick' the easy bits like energy-efficient lighting to make easier profits. If the 'income' from energy saving equipment is skimmed off the top, it will be harder to finance whole-of-building improvements later, when society finally appreciates the urgency. As a community, we could use performance contracting principles to subsidize a whole-of-building or whole-of-suburb design approach.[45] But to achieve an integrated approach to retrofitting whole buildings, suburbs or cities, we will probably need collaborative institutional structures that include government, industry and community – such as partnering and alliancing.[46]

## What are partnering and alliancing and what assistance can they provide?

'Partnering' is a working relationship where the parties involved in designing, managing and constructing a development (ie builders, owners, designers and specialists) agree to work as a team throughout the construction process to improve both public and private outcomes.[47] They share the benefits of savings and innovations, but also the liabilities for errors, waste or delays. This avoids the adversarial relationship that often surrounds the 'contract variation' process, wherein one party can profit from another's error by charging extra. Comparisons of similar projects constructed under conventional and partnering processes have demonstrated that partnering generally leads to better outcomes in terms of quality and cost.[48] Partnering is a management concept, however, and care needs to be taken to ensure that there is no confusion with other contractual responsibilities.[49] While partnering refers to an agreement on managing a particular project, strategic alliances generally refer to ongoing partnering relationships. Experience is accumulating in performance contracting, partnering and alliancing. This experience can be scaled up to tackle major urban sustainability challenges. New forms of tendering and selection processes will also be needed to promote the new transdisciplinary relationships that sustainability will entail. For example, sustainable design will require teams that include biologists and chemists, in addition to building or engineering professionals [Box 3]. Qualification-based selection could help to allow the entry of new talent and new kinds of teams into the market.

## What is qualification-based selection and how does it differ from the norm?

Designers are still often commissioned on a competitive fee basis. Fee-based tenders tend to drive down costs, but also reduce the quality of services and design. Common means of cutting costs in order to be more competitive are the use of standard design templates, reduced research and innovation, and lower investment in staff training. In a qualification-based selection arrangement, by contrast, the designer is selected before a final fee is negotiated. If design services cannot be brought within the budget, negotiations can then be undertaken with the next best qualified designers. Qualification-based selection enables an interactive relationship between clients and designers at an early stage in developing eco-logical design solutions. It allows designers to educate the client about whole-of-life costing and benefits of investing in design. It also enables designers to develop basic design options in close consultation with the client.[50] Due to such industry initiatives as partnering, performance contracting and qualification-based selection, change is gradually beginning to happen on its own. These (relatively) new practices, if adequately supported, would also create employment and training in retrofitting and capture economies of scale. But time is of the essence. Government action could bring about the transformation much more quickly through up-skilling and education. Government assistance in large-scale retrofit programmes could facilitate a more direct and immediate conversion to ecologically sustainable materials, methods and products. However, government may not act without community pressure.

## Can't the private sector achieve this more quickly, given the potential profits?

The private sector is moving quickly towards greener building, but not towards eco-retrofitting. Dubai, for example, is virtually a new city. It is experiencing almost incomprehensible growth with little consideration for the environment. In fact, development in Dubai is reshaping the seas to 'terraform' a whole new network of artificial islands that increase the shoreline – and hence prospective property values. The skyline is now a series of skyscrapers rising out of a moonscape. At a recent construction industry conference, a developer of a major project in Dubai proudly spoke of the joy of creating the world's tallest buildings. When asked about their extraordinary environmental impacts, he suggested that it was up to the market to develop the innovations required. The private sector, in other words, will pay a fleet of structural engineers to work out how to build the world's tallest buildings; meanwhile, their impacts are left to other markets to clean up. While we create super-tall buildings in the faith that their environmental problems will eventually be mitigated, safe and fail-proof technologies for modest buildings sit on the shelf. As we saw in the case of the new Chinese 'ecocity' of Dongtan, the primary demand driver appears to be business investment. An essential role of government is to provide public goods and services where the market fails. Such goods and services surely include a viable life-support system and preventative healthcare for its citizens. The market fails in this area because it cannot design whole systems solutions and ensure the best design concepts prevail. In fact, despite some impressive green business initiatives, market competition activity frequently operates as a barrier to sustainable development. Often, for example, new green products and services are obstructed by special interests already established in the marketplace.[51]

## If we cannot rely on the private sector, can we rely instead on governments?

No. Both public and private sectors have had adequate opportunities to create sustainable environments on their own. Few people in government or industry have any training in the nexus between natural and social sciences and eco-logical design. Society as a whole does not take design seriously, and even many designers are still dismissive of eco-logical design. Further, design is difficult for those schooled in linear-reductionist thinking. What is sometimes called 'systems design' often only considers energy efficiency without requiring that the upstream source of energy be renewable. Similarly, government programmes have been tailored to address specific goals in isolation from others, such as water efficiency, reduction in greenhouse emissions or lower construction waste to landfill. Sustainability will require the ability to achieve multiple goals simultaneously through systems re-design: changing the basic functions and forms of development systems. Governments could support structural arrangements like cooperatives, public–private+community partnerships and transdisciplinary design teams to collaborate in eco-retrofitting homes and residential areas. Local NGOs could be instrumental in convincing residents and governments to buy into the idea. By instituting retrofitting programmes that target whole districts, local NGOs (in partnership with industry and governments) could help bring about whole-systems efficiencies that none of these sectors have been able to achieve on their own.[52] However, as noted earlier, governments have favoured indirect economic incentives over 'direct action'. Traditionally, Western democracies have tried not to interfere in the market for philosophical reasons. Also, direct action involves assuming *visible* risks and responsibilities.

## Isn't it rational for governments to use incentives to avoid the risks of action?

Incentives systems avoid risks to governments, but they are not very strategic. This is because the costs to government (and therefore the public) of indirect environmental protection programmes are highly visible. Monitoring and enforcement costs of incentive programmes, for example, have been at the expense of both government and industry. These costs are subsequently passed on to the taxpayer and/or consumer. Because the costs impact upon all parties – and are highly visible – regulations tend to be resented by all sectors [Box 49]. Similarly, the benefits of indirect environmental programmes are diffuse and not easily measured. Therefore they are not readily attributable to the government agency that initiated them. Further, the benefits of sound but indirect environmental improvements do not always materialize within the term of politicians anyway. To add insult to injury, if an agency achieves its goals, it may be disbanded or amalgamated into other departments. This negative reinforcement can lead to a blend of risk avoidance and costly self-promotion by government departments.[53] Many agencies spend a fortune on brochures, billboards and award certificates to celebrate what is essentially routine – just as many businesses take credit for environmental improvements that are already, or about to be, legally required. If we want real progress, therefore, government agencies should create incentives for themselves – not just for private business in the hope that sustainable outcomes may follow. If governments were willing to take the initiative, they could also take credit for the long-term, system-wide benefits of direct design solutions.[54]

## Don't we reward agencies for improving environmental conditions?

Good performance by government agencies needs to be rewarded through budgetary systems or other means, as they are seldom directly rewarded in the polls. However it may be organized, government agencies should be able to recoup some of the savings they achieve. If governments engaged in a form of performance contracting and partnering, a portion of the savings could accrue to the government agency that successfully initiates and runs the programme. For example, their budgets could be increased in proportion to the resource savings. A 'snowball effect' would then be possible, whereby the returns from eco-solutions are 'rolled over' into more intractable rehabilitation cases, where payback periods are too long for the private sector to get involved. Government might then be motivated to increase the uptake of systems design solutions in ways that are visible, measurable and have a clear return on investment for all partners. They should be able to demonstrate whole systems savings and positive multiplier effects in relation to government investment. The measure of 'performance' in the public sector, however, is not savings of human and natural resources. Instead, performance measures are usually based on trends in somewhat arbitrary and remote impacts. This is convenient, as there are always excuses for general trends. We need systems of analysis that factor in the costs of government 'inaction' – instead of just predicting the adverse environmental impacts of future private actions or charting general trends [Chapter 9].

## How can resource savings be linked or credited to government departments?

It is extremely hard to link 'indirect' market-based incentives to outcomes due to intervening factors. Savings generated by government agencies are easier to demonstrate where there is direct government action. For example, some large public utilities have applied what we could call the 'direct action principle' by providing free or low-cost energy-efficient light bulbs. The cost of this energy-saving programme can be recovered from customers' energy bills, or from the avoided expense of constructing and financing major infrastructure developments like dams or power plants. Similarly, Australia has recently required incandescent light bulbs to be phased out in three years. Other countries are already following this example. While this is 'regulatory', the savings achieved are direct, measurable, tangible and visible. Ultimately, the costs are spread across society. Some states in the US have made arrangements for providing grants or low interest loans for industry to hire environmental management firms on a performance-contracting basis to make factory complexes more eco-efficient.[55] Consequently, there are a growing number of independent advisory or consultancy services that develop environmental management plans (for which ISO standards exist) to improve production processes and product design. However, their brief has been to create efficiencies within the firm or clusters of firms. They seldom look at whole supply chains and service delivery systems [Box 33].[56] Government action could widen the scope of analysis to address the ecological sustainability of a whole industry, product range, housing sector, city or region [Box 51].[57]

## How can retrofitting programmes bring about whole systems sustainability?

Sustainable settlements will eventually require retrofitting on a whole-of-region scale [Chapter 12]. We can continue to expend vast resources on measuring and mitigating impacts, arguing over how much longer we can maintain the status quo before total systems collapse, or whether global warming is natural or man-made. Alternatively, we can proactively improve the health of the urban ecology and increase its social and biological diversity now. Eco-retrofitting lends itself to both incremental and immediate 'action learning'. If systems re-design is too intimidating, we can begin on a small scale to replace our deteriorating water, sewage and energy infrastructure with natural systems that combine economic and social functions with eco-services. There are already partial precedents where communities have initiated re-design projects on their own. For instance, some resident groups in urban blocks have removed their rear yard fences to create a commons. They not only gain access to more space, they are able to keep an eye out for each other's children. Other resident groups have turned existing clusters of homes into 'co-housing' communities with many shared resources.[58] A whole-of-suburb retrofit would implement wider options, like the reclamation of road space for public uses other than private cars, as proposed by Ted Trainer.[59] There are initial organizational, educational and administrative costs involved in setting up an eco-retrofitting programme, of course. Due to the transaction costs involved in dealing with individual homeowners, and the need for economies of scale, faster change may require public–private+community partnerships or cooperatives. Using performance contracting and partnering principles, such programmes could be designed to operate on a cost-neutral (or at least relatively economical) basis over time.

Figure 5 Levels of eco-retrofitting

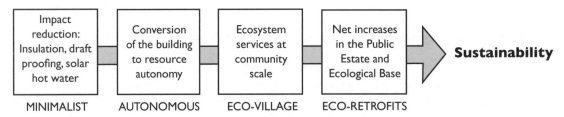

| Impact reduction: Insulation, draft proofing, solar hot water | Conversion of the building to resource autonomy | Ecosystem services at community scale | Net increases in the Public Estate and Ecological Base | Sustainability |
| MINIMALIST | AUTONOMOUS | ECO-VILLAGE | ECO-RETROFITS | |

## What kinds of stimuli could accelerate such retrofitting programmes?

The appropriate stimuli for direct action would depend on the scale of the eco-retrofitting programme. There are a range of strategies and eco-solutions available [Figure 5]. A carrot for homeowners to consider individual retrofits would be free household audits and schematic design options, with estimations of their relative pay-back periods.[60] Homeowners would be advised of options ranging from minor improvements through to whole-home retrofits, or even joint projects with residents of a whole neighbourhood through an existing progress association. For example:

- A minimalist option might include insulation, draught-proofing and solar hot water heaters. The full cost of this 'lowest' level of retrofit could be recovered from the energy savings of the homeowner over, say, five years. As mentioned earlier, however, incremental and marginal approaches can lead to 'cherry picking'.
- The next level, a resource-autonomous option (again independent of external sources of water, electricity and sewage treatment) would involve a combination of passive solar heating, cooling and ventilation, photovoltaics, roof water collection and greywater treatment, xeriscape gardens, arbours, atriums, greenhouse windows, and so on. It might only aim for a payback of 10 to 20 years.
- At an even larger scale, existing suburbs could be converted to resource autonomy or better.[61] This could be supported by credits for 'ecological space' that could be sold or traded to developers [Chapter 3 and 11].
- Finally, cities could be retrofitted to have net positive impacts on the region. Generally, we have only tried to predict and accommodate growth, rather than transform cities.

Funding or investment priorities to develop such programmes and/or partnerships would need to be established with a clear hierarchy of eco-innovations, as provided later [Chapter 14].

## How would we measure and pay for such performance contracts?

There are many ways of tailoring performance contracting to given situations. If auditing and reporting on the annual energy and water consumption of all buildings were required, governments would be better placed to create appropriate eco-retrofitting programmes. There are already many precedents for building audits. We have noted that in the UK required all commercial buildings to report on annual energy use.[62] The ABGR and NABERS rating schemes in Australia provide templates for measuring some of the performance issues of existing buildings.[63] Performance contracting requires targets relative to a standard benchmark, and an independent measurement of operational performance. In minimalist retrofits, the benchmark could simply be the 'previous' operational performance as indicated by the energy and water bills. In this case, the performance contractor can recover the difference between the previous higher energy bill and subsequent lower bill. To move towards net Positive Development, however, we would need to weigh in the benefits of adding value to the public estate, in relation to the costs of inaction – not just improvements relative to 'standard' buildings [Box 44]. The benchmark for eco-retrofitting projects should therefore be a 'sustainability standard' – net positive improvements over pre-development ecological, as well as social and economic, conditions. How cities and buildings could contribute to the ecological, social and economic viability of the surrounding area will be explored in following chapters.

## So how would we start to go about making Positive Development happen?

We have seen that eco-retrofitting, if done properly, could solve many environmental problems at no extra cost. In some cases, it could be profitable for all interests. There are many systems impediments, however [Box 7]. In this chapter we have focused on building delivery systems, such as conventional tendering and designer selection processes, that can conflict with eco-logical design goals. Simple institutional mechanisms for overcoming impediments to eco-retrofitting have been proposed in the literature, such as partnering, quality-based selection and performance contracting. What is now called the 'third sector' (businesses that recycle their profits into public good projects), new forms of public–private+community partnerships and cooperatives, have some potential to generate demonstrations of Positive Development. However, we need to go further and create mechanisms at government, community and industry levels that can roll over the financial savings from eco-retrofitting projects into other net positive projects. First, however, we need to be aware of the systemic biases against sustainable development that occur at the levels of design criteria, tools and methods, and management (in assessment and reporting processes), and at intellectual and paradigmatic levels. In all these areas, we need to move from a managerial to a design orientation. In the next chapter, we will explore some ideological biases in urban planning and design that currently stand in the way of the transition to net Positive Development.

# 3
# Sustainable Urban Form

## From spatial minimization to spatial amplification

Despite the increasing sophistication of systems thinking in urban planning literature, vestiges of linear-reductionist and single-issue approaches remain.[1] For example, discussions of sustainable urban form often assume there must be an ideal shape, such as compact *or* dispersed, vertical *or* horizontal. The dominant view is still that increasing urban residential density, often called 'urban consolidation', is a *universal* urban sustainability solution.[2] The mismatch between this single issue approach and the complex nature of the urban environment can lead to erroneous policies and indicators. For example, the only indicator pertaining to urban development in a Canberra sustainability plan was 'the amount of new development within 15 kilometres of the city core'. This was regardless of how much total development occurred outside the city, or whether future development was ecologically sound.[3] Thus, new non-sustainable buildings, infrastructure and materials would signify progress toward sustainability, as long as growth occurred within 15 kilometres of the city core. One might have thought that, in a sustainability plan, urban population would depend more on such things as carrying capacity and renewable sources of energy and water (ie the extent to which water, soil and energy supply are replenished naturally).

It may be advisable to increase urban residential density or average density in some places to, say, accommodate environmental refugees. However, compact urban form in itself is no indicator of, or shortcut to, sustainability.[4] Densified urban living can be far less sustainable than dispersed settlements, depending on their respective designs. Given current designs, however, *neither* approach is sustainable. Consolidation, if seen as a virtue in itself, can obscure and limit other potentially more cost-effective, eco-efficient strategies for reducing net environmental impacts and improving urban life quality. The densification approach exemplifies the dominant linear-reductionist mode of thinking, which has eclipsed other problem-solving paradigms and methods. In fact, the major alternative framework – design – is generally regarded as a separate activity outside of legitimate problem-solving processes [Box 10]. To achieve sustainable urban environments, we need a new understanding of design as an alternative way of thinking and problem solving that is better suited to deal with open urban systems.[5]

## How are urban systems 'open' and why is design better suited for this?

Cities are fully dependent on their wider region and nature itself. They are not closed systems, or 'islands in themselves'. Yet due to our reductionist intellectual heritage, most policy and planning initiatives still treat urban and rural areas in isolation. We still design urban systems as if their design does not affect rural areas and vice versa. Both urban and regional developments have externalized negative impacts on the other. What goes around comes around. For instance, urban construction waste contains toxic materials that leach from rural landfills (or via floods) into water systems. These eventually re-visit urban residents in the form of polluted water. Conversely, expensive and toxic agricultural chemicals drain into soils and rivers causing, for example, the excessive growth of algae. These chemicals, over time, damage the region's farm productivity as well as its ecological productivity. They also make cities more 'import dependent' for their food supplies. Consolidation proposals tend to assume impacts will be reduced if cities occupy less space, even though they still use their regions as 'sources and sinks'. We have said that sustainability requires cities to reimburse and support their bioregions. Only systems re-design can do this. Positive environmental flows can be increased (and adverse flows reduced) by better urban design, not by reductionist analyses alone.

## Can't reductionist analyses treat cities and regions as open systems?

If so, it has apparently not happened yet. The process of creating synergistic and symbiotic relationships between urban and rural areas could start by examining environmental flows through a whole region. However, we also need to go well beyond the present reductionist preoccupation with energy flows. Energy is fundamental, but it cannot capture the essence of things like space, life quality and living ecosystems. We tend to reduce everything to energy. For example, we see space in negative terms as something that just consumes or wastes energy. Therefore, we try to minimize and zone spaces in buildings and urban areas to reduce 'wasted' space. This is similar to the view that river water allowed to flow to the sea, rather than used for production, is 'wasted'. However, it is public space, not small computer-filled cubicles, that creates the 'human energy' and social vitality of cities. To increase the social and natural functions of cities, then, we need to increase the indoor and outdoor space for natural systems – not reduce it. Space does not cost extra, or use much embodied or operating energy, if we frame it and use it cleverly. We can begin by increasing the public estate in urban areas to provide for ecosystem rehabilitation and expansion, while creating better environments for its human inhabitants. This can be achieved in ways that are compatible with the economic priority of maximizing rentable spaces. So improving the ecological and human health of cities need not entail the geographic expansion of urban areas as a whole.

## Would consolidation work against such eco-logical design improvements?

Not necessarily, but retaining the principles of 'diverse' space would probably entail the least risk. However, the dominant planning approach is to increase mixed commercial and private uses to the exclusion of eco-services. We should not confuse 'intensification' of human activity with 'densification' of private spaces and economic functions. The problem is that the design of consolidation proposals are usually approached in a reductionist way. Here, the term 'reductionist' refers to the way urban studies often focus on limited variables or use key variables as 'surrogates' for whole classes of phenomena. That is to say, they conflate many issues under one concept such as 'density'. Analyses will always involve some reduction, but problems arise when the focus is too superficial (like aerial views), or too narrow (like single issue perspectives). These lenses tend to obscure other important issues. For example, because transport in general is a major cause of greenhouse gas emissions, and private cars constitute a slightly bigger portion of emissions than trucks, truck transport is often ignored. Yet, as we will discuss, the impacts of trucks are usually greater per vehicle (and even in total, depending on urban design). Also, systems design factors that affect the amount of truck transport can be very different from those factors affecting car transport. Efforts to reduce the total impact of transportation, by influencing car use through higher residential density, may increase trucking. In other words, more trucking may be necessary to bring products, services and food into high density areas. Similarly, if our approaches are too 'linear', or start from one solution, we may overlook means to reduce trucking or increase public transport. Urban food production and compostable building materials could, for example, reduce truck transport in and out of cities, while also reducing the need to drive to suburban supermarkets for food.

## How is the dominant approach to urban sustainability 'linear'?

The term 'linear' here refers to the way that urban studies often make causal, sequential links from one factor to another. Cities are complex systems requiring a whole systems perspective – one integrated with the regional ecological context.[6] We need to consider the effects of increased residential density on the other multiple-use values of cities, including biodiversity, ecosystem services, a sense of place and community identity.[7] By proceeding in an iterative but specific goal-oriented approach (eg increasing density), linear analysis can lose sight of important elements down the track, such as access to food, energy and water [Box 10]. For instance, because reduced car travel corresponds loosely with compact urban form, it is generally assumed that increasing residential density will automatically increase urban sustainability, so we proceed down that track. But there are too many intervening variables and contextual factors to make a direct link between increased residential density and sustainability. Thus, even when the goal is 'sustainability', the term is often evoked to justify non-sustainable development that actually increases social, economic and environmental problems. We have seen that, where more urban infill development is desirable, such infill is often poorly conceived from a whole systems standpoint [Box 12]. Infill often increases total material flows, creates private enclaves, and reduces the ecological base and urban amenities. A view that marginalizes the *ecology* is simply not a whole systems view, and does not address the nature of complex problems.

## Do eco-logical design 'outcomes' differ from linear-reductionist outcomes?

So far design, like other fields, has been influenced by the dominant linear-reductionist paradigm. Nonetheless, in design the whole is always bigger than the sum of the parts. Arguably, design is inherently better suited to deal with complexity. A design approach tries to create synergies among all legitimate needs and issues, and to create positive multiplier effects [Box 2]. Design could therefore be seen as the 'opposite' of the dominant linear-reductionist mode. The latter focuses on a key element (like energy reduction) and works systematically and iteratively in a conveyor-belt fashion. Ideally, however, urban design and architecture aims for:

- A synthesis of many different kinds of physical elements (spaces, structures, materials, forms, etc)
- An improvement of contextual factors through each development (social, economic, ecological, functional, cultural, etc)
- The achievement of the widest range of objectives to add value to the environment, society and economy

In other words, design means blending a wide combination of ingredients to achieve many different objectives at once. Linear-reductionist choices tend to impose a particular solution that future generations will have to adapt to. Eco-logical *design* outcomes would be adaptable and reversible, and keep future options open. The fact that dominant approaches to planning, urban design and architecture have sometimes been theorized and practised in a linear-reductionist manner does not reflect on their *potential* as problem-solving and opportunity-creating processes.

## What has been the result of the linear-reductionist approach to planning?

The dominant approach to urban sustainability has focused on density and form. In particular, it has focused on increasing *residential density* through the manipulation of land uses and zoning, although "it is not yet clear exactly which forms are preferable".[8] The emphasis on form itself reflects a social engineering approach to physical design. The bulk of the literature takes a single issue, aerial perspective, which, in turn, risks the imposition of simplified physical templates. Trying to bring more residents into the city, while allowing more shopping and recreation facilities in the suburbs, has created a vicious circle. Densification policies can have outcomes not unlike the monolithic and mono-cultural design solutions following WWII that caused so many urban problems in the first place [Chapter 12]. Densification can cut off options and inhibit the potential of multifunctional natural spaces that could help alleviate urban social and environmental problems. A fundamental problem is that residential density, by whatever reductionist measures (eg population or dwellings per hectare or floor area per person), is not a good measure of sustainability. It is true, of course, that the population density of existing cities often roughly correlates with accessibility to facilities and the reduction of private car use.[9] In fact, there are examples of dense urban living where relatively strong social bonds and security can be found, despite poverty and unemployment. One such case is the (largely single storey) eco-village of Yoff in Senegal. Most agree that this village, with no room for cars, works relatively well.[10] There are, however, many countervailing examples of high-density urban areas that are characterized by social breakdown, high crime rates and poor health – despite relatively high levels of wealth.

## What is the critical variable in urban sustainability, if not increased density?

Design. Assuming local and global carrying capacity were adequate to support an increased population density, a whole suite of policies must be designed and implemented to ensure that increased density does not impact on other sustainable development objectives, such as urban open space, health and safety, water and resource security. To be sustainable, infill development must be carried out in a way that is ecologically and socially constructive and synergistic. Accommodating the myriad biophysical and social needs of an increased population, using less overall space, requires multiple use of space for *both* natural and social functions and more shared space. Denser living arrangements require a corresponding increase in a city's 'ecological base' and more public spaces, facilities and environmental amenities, or the 'public estate'. Densification advocates often assume that increased residential density will create wider access to urban facilities simply because they could be in closer proximity. However, cities have also been described as 'food deserts' where inner city residents have only small corner grocers and fast food facilities, as larger supermarkets continue to move to the suburbs.[11] Also, infill development too often results in privatizing urban space into commercial facilities or residential uses that enclose and segregate open spaces.[12] Sustainable form and space would instead increase carrying capacity *and* reduce the overall demand for construction materials, food transport, land and fossil fuels created by *past* – not just future – development.

## Can we create incentives for business that replace the need for planning?

The line between the public and private sectors has become ever more blurred. It is increasingly a false dichotomy. A 'direct' positive design approach that provides for basic needs, rights and preferences will generally work better than either the managerial (public) or market-based (private) approaches that now dominate policymaking [Chapter 13]. Economic incentives appeal to greed by offering private benefits. Good design appeals to community building by offering shared benefits. In today's society, people cannot be expected to change behaviour unless it brings them money and status, *or* a higher quality of life provided by design. So if we are to ask people of all incomes to have a smaller *physical* footprint (ie use less land per person) and a smaller *ecological* footprint (ie reduce resource consumption and environmental impacts per person), we need good public facilities that expand their *effective* living area and enable responsible lifestyle choices. Currently, environmental managers and planners emphasize the importance of equitable access to urban services (often referred to as 'accessibility'). Yet urban policies deprive the urban poor of usable space, resources and environmental amenities. This is partly due to an increasing reliance on private developers to provide public infrastructure, both social and physical. Equity and accessibility are not enhanced by enclosure and privatization.[13] Environmental managers tend to measure the rate that resource stocks are decreasing or growth is increasing, but not who benefits from both forms of resource transfers [Box 48]. Social impact assessment looks at who suffers from development, but not at 'excessive' gains made at the expense of the general public (unjust enrichment). We also need to consider what we might call 'negative space': the conversion of (public) non-renewable resources and natural capital to private development and use. Measuring negative space (the converse of the public estate) would take into account the distributional costs of the alienation of natural capital, land and ecosystem goods and services in geographical and spatial terms [Chapter 15].

## Has planning contributed to negative space and, if so, why and how?

Absolutely. This is partly because there has been little analysis of how people feel about life in dense, high-rise developments, because this does not lend itself to linear-reductionist research norms.[14] Conventional planning and urban design approaches (as opposed to transdisciplinary ones) have been limited by a narrow conception of the 'tools of the trade'. These tools are land-use policy, regulation and design *control* – as opposed to social and ecological value *adding*. By and large, density has been seen as the solution, because land-use regulation has been the major means of implementing planning policy. Density, after all, is something at least notionally in the control of planners. Thus planners use density to try to reduce energy and fuel consumption. Some problems of using land-use regulation to control density are:

- Land-use controls or other forms of regulation, and even market measures such as taxes and trading schemes, transfer wealth or benefits directly or indirectly. While some individuals benefit from high-density developments, many others get only leftover 'dead' spaces: dark alleys, tiny side yards and treeless plazas.
- Many new green field suburbs have extremely small blocks for detached dwellings (eg in Australia). This mean that trees cannot be planted to reduce the urban heat island effect, there is inadequate space for food production and environmental amenities are sacrificed.[15]
- Regulation will often be resisted because it aims to reduce production or consumption. Accordingly, it constrains both suppliers and consumers, and can create 'losers'. Positive Development would stimulate good behaviour – not simply prohibit bad behaviour [Box 2].

- Land-use planning often proves to be an expensive, long-term process, and market responses to land-use controls are uncertain at best. Planning history shows that many unanticipated market factors can intervene over time to subvert the intended outcomes.[16]
- Even well-targeted land-use policies can be effectively overruled by the actions of other functional departments in government, such as treasury or transportation departments with different agendas (not to mention politicians in the lead up to elections).
- Land-use regulations only set a framework for development. Major public and private sector investment is still required for their implementation. Private investment down the track cannot be guaranteed, as it is largely driven by speculation.

Value-adding to the public estate through *design* should attract less resistance from industry than regulatory or even market-based measures [Box 49].[17] It also allows for more creativity and flexibility on the part of industry.

## Aren't market signals the 'quickest' way to change investment activity?

Not always. Take the example of traffic congestion. There are two common disincentives to individual car travel: market instruments that increase costs and planning instruments that create inconvenience to drivers. Both are slow to have an impact. Meanwhile, car ownership, use and congestion are increasing. Research indicates it can take many years for people to respond to market signals.[18] The OECD has previously suggested a progressively increasing fuel tax to reduce driving. This would certainly be better than 'no action'. However, it would not internalize the full social and environmental costs of cars and roads, and hence there would still be a hidden subsidy. As noted by Mark Diesendorf, subsidies to road and car parking in Australia are estimated at over AU$2000 million per year.[19] Moreover, while economic instruments may be necessary components, they can be just as difficult to enact and as expensive to administer as regulations, from a whole systems perspective [Chapter 11]. 'User pays' systems that internalize the *full* social costs of car transport would respect 'consumer preferences' while creating a more direct incentive. But accommodation of consumer preferences also requires public transport to be available and affordable to the blind, disabled, elderly, young or other groups with restricted choices. That is to say, everyone's needs and preferences should be considered, not 'averaged out', as the market tends to do. Low-cost taxi systems for the disabled could, for example, provide this objective more cheaply and quickly overall than buses alone. Good design considers the diversity of users, whereas the market often ignores the needs of minorities.[20]

## Can design really be an alternative to both regulations and incentives?

Yes. Trying to change producer and/or consumer behaviour through incentives or regulations suggests we do not know what *to* do, only what people should *not* do. Relying on land-use regulation (constraints) has distracted planning theorists from value-adding by design. They have not developed tools to help figure out what affirmative actions to take. Direct action to enable and demonstrate better design and delivery of ecologically sound living environments could have a much bigger system-wide impact on reducing energy and resource consumption than incentives and regulations.[21] Eco-retrofitting would be easier and quicker to implement than land-use controls because, as we saw, it can be profitable, self-operating and implemented immediately. In any case, urban land-use policies designed to increase residential density would still depend on eco-logical design to achieve on-ground sustainable results and market success. Instead of building capacity in design, however, we are still instituting complex regulatory and market-based incentives that often impede capacity building in design [Chapter 5]. Similarly, most demonstration projects aim only at incremental targets or 'best practice'. So we have the worst of both worlds: suburbs are expanding but are losing their environmental and social amenity through densification, loss of public space and failure to maximize passive solar design. Many new suburbs are reducing open public space while increasing embodied energy and building size. Hence they increase the urban ecological footprint and total material flows, while reducing their potential for adaptation.

## Wouldn't suburbs waste space, materials and energy even if retrofitted?

In the short term, at least, suburbs offer the potential for immediate adaptation and 'intensification' without reducing open space. Low-density suburbs could easily be retrofitted to be resource autonomous, while fostering more biodiversity, a greater sense of community and healthier lifestyles. For example, we have seen that homes and suburbs could add units with very little additional land coverage [Box 9]. The point is that space 'minimization' is not necessarily space 'optimization'. In fact, low and medium density housing can be lower in energy and materials consumption per person than large, compact apartment blocks. Small dwellings in large apartment blocks that occupy a small area of land can create far greater resource consumption and ecological damage than large dwellings occupying a larger area. This is because energy and material usage depends on design, materials and factors like shared public space.[22] But when comparing the costs of new housing versus retrofitting, planners generally only look at operating and/or embodied energy. 'Operating energy' is that used to heat and cool buildings and operate lights and equipment. 'Embodied energy' is that used in the production and transport of materials and construction. The latter is relatively small and more complicated to estimate, so it has largely been ignored. However, passive solar and renewable energy sources would eliminate the need for much of the operating energy of buildings [Box 25]. Embodied energy would be more significant than operating energy if we used passive solar design. However, other forms of waste also need to be factored in at each stage of production and use, not just energy and water.

## Isn't fuel consumption always greater in 'spread out' suburbs than in cities?

Perhaps, but this is due to the lack of past investment in public transport, not lack of demand. Roads entail huge amounts of embodied energy and space in both cities and suburbs. Even 'eco-villages' often have unnecessary private driveways and parking spaces, due to poor planning or the residents' desire for gardens and privacy. In buildings, however, embodied energy depends more on design than land area. Some researchers have assumed that apartment buildings and detached housing have about the same embodied energy on a 'square metre' basis – given 'typical' construction materials and methods. However, a higher portion of smaller dwellings are allocated to high-embodied energy items like bathrooms and kitchens.[23] Detached dwellings may use more space and materials per person because of larger average living space per person. However, these can be resource autonomous by using low-impact materials, natural waste treatment and solar energy sources. Although sometimes providing little floor area per occupant, apartment blocks can be surprisingly wasteful of space and materials per person and per square metre. This is because they tend to use materials with high embodied energy, and have expansive parking lots or garages, security lighting, high-maintenance equipment, elevators and large heating plants. Compact living can also create relatively unhealthy or even unsafe living conditions. Again, space itself does not embody energy, only the structure that frames it. For example, a large tent has less embodied energy than a small concrete bunker. It is because of the nature of conventional design and materials that space correlates with high energy use. It is not the building 'type' per se – apartment blocks, single-family homes or mixed-use 'urban villages' – but the design, materials and use of space that matters. In any case, a market economy requires consumer choice, which can best be accommodated in a variety of low-impact living arrangements and building types.

## Isn't urban consolidation ultimately the only way to stop sprawl though?

To work well, consolidation requires eco-logical design. Some dense urban developments actually consume more land area than some lower density counterparts due to poor site planning (eg wasteful parking and road layouts). The real problem is that the dominant 'solution', consolidation, is still based on designing for the car instead of enhancing the ecology and community. In other words, the solution is seen as making it more *inconvenient* for cars.[24] The focus on reducing distances through densification to the exclusion of other criteria (eg environmental goods, services and ecosystems, healthy materials, and urban agriculture) leads us to neglect making cities more self-sufficient, safe and secure. For example, one of the premises underlying arguments for compact urban form is that making car travel less necessary or convenient will reduce total fuel consumption. But this excludes from consideration:

- Effects on other kinds of transport, such as an increase in trucking for bringing in food supplies and materials, and the difficulty of adding bus lanes
- Requirements for other land uses, such as recreational facilities (even sports fields) and large markets that urban residents may want to drive to
- Other drivers of fuel consumption, such as the mechanical heating, cooling and ventilating required by high-density construction
- Other factors that are exacerbated by densification, such as the urban heat island and wind tunnel effects, overshadowing and pollution

The sad reality that cars will rule in a market economy, tempered by the potential for fuel cell cars or electric cars, and other improvements[25]

## But wasn't it cars that created urban sprawl in the first place?

Yes. Suburbs were 'designed' for cars, and the problem should not be understated. Roads take up about a third of urban land.[26] The post-World War II spread of Australian cities was estimated to exceed a million hectares and cost several billion dollars annually.[27] In America, more people now live in suburbs than cities – despite the publicity that was given to the problems of sprawl in the 1960s. But overall, cities as a whole only occupy about two per cent of land, so their ecological footprint is a bigger problem than their geographical spread [Chapter 8]. Suburban sprawl was a result of many kinds of design, not just that relating to cars. As John Thackara put it: "sprawl is the result of zoning laws designed by legislators, low-density buildings designed by developers, marketing strategies designed by ad agencies, tax breaks designed by economists, credit lines designed by banks, geomatics designed by retailers, data-mining software designed by hamburger chains, and automobiles designed by car designers."[28]

While compact cities may arguably increase the efficient use of fossil fuels for transport, they can also compete for space with 'free' passive solar energy or even solar cells. The source of energy is more important than the amount. There is an almost infinite amount of solar energy available for building heating, cooling and ventilating, although this has been made difficult to capture by past planning and design decisions.[29] Fossil fuels, on the other hand, are finite, costly and harmful at each stage of production, however efficiently they may be used, as detailed by Hermann Scheer.[30] The compound and cumulative impacts of hi-tech petrochemical forms of design are often not anticipated or intended [Box 26]. For example, catalytic converters reduce car emissions, but the palladium needed in their production generates acid rain. Low-tech can be far less risky.

## But isn't increased density the best way to reduce driving anyway?

An influential 1989 study found that a high residential density correlated with reduced travel in 37 cities around the world.[31] There are problems, however, with studying the relationship between transport and residential density in terms of energy – in isolation from the life-support system as a whole. If we begin with the proposition that land-use change is the solution, we get very different outcomes than if we support and build upon the ecological base. In other words, using energy as a sole basis for comparing models of urban form can lead to policies that are ecologically counter-productive. And just as land-use controls are problematic tools for tackling car dependency, they can distract us from more 'direct' and immediate solutions – like providing a good bus system [Chapter 1]. In addition to the general problems with planning by regulation listed above, land-use controls involve many indirect administrative costs. They require staffing to administer financial incentives, approval processes, regulatory revision and monitoring. Outcomes per investment dollar required to increase density could be relatively poor in contrast to encouraging central and/or suburban revitalization through retrofitting for increased environmental amenity and public transport. Moreover, removing subsidies to private cars would be quicker than urban consolidation via land-use controls. While a fraction of money spent on bus systems is usually recouped through fares, provision for cars still generally receives far more subsidies than public transport.[32] The costs of subsidies to public transport compared to those of cars and trucks are rarely calculated, let alone made public. It took decades to get climate change on the agenda for public debate. The idea of eliminating perverse subsidies for cars and fossil fuels is seldom put on the table.[33]

## Even if cars remain subsidized, wouldn't higher density reduce driving?

The emphasis on 'densification' through land-use planning to encourage a reduction in personal car usage does not appear to work well. But the debate has helped to keep eco-retrofitting off the agenda. Changing land uses or encouraging infill development to shorten car trips would not be as quick or cost-effective in the short term as making homes more resource autonomous. Figures vary but, for example, the residential sector in Canberra accounts for over 46 per cent of Canberra's greenhouse gas emissions, whereas transport fuels account for 26 per cent. Therefore, retrofitting for passive solar or at least plugging leaks would make sense.[34] Further, less than a third of car trips are to work, so land-use planning to make home and work closer could have a limited impact.[35] Moreover, 'stop and start' traffic due to congestion causes additional pollution (except in the case of hybrid cars). This is not to de-emphasize the car problem. But in the meantime, it would be quick and easy to implement simple energy saving measures such as draft proofing, insulation, external shading devices, solar water heating, and plugging energy and water leaks. Eco-retrofitting homes could save resources, reduce emissions and create jobs while we deal with the political impasse created by a history of subsidies to the car industry. Nonetheless, the concept of retrofitting buildings and suburbs still receives little interest or response. Again, this is partly because even some environmentalists tend to reduce everything to *energy* while ignoring other fundamentals like 'ecological waste' [Chapter 4].

## Surely energy consumption is the key measure of urban sustainability?

Not really. One of the most influential people to link systems thinking and ecology was Howard T. Odum, who did so by using energy as a unifying element of analysis.[36] This was an impressive step forward. But subsequent analyses by 'sorcerer's apprentices' have consequently marginalized other dimensions (like 'life' itself). Reducing everything to one element, like energy, can bar ecological solutions that accommodate living things. Of course, some of the ecological costs of development are represented by energy figures. For example, the amount of fuel used to produce a material or product, and the distance from the site of material production to the construction project, can be roughly accounted for in embodied energy calculations. But other aspects and impacts of materials and use of space are not. Embodied energy does not, for example, fully capture the source of fuels and materials (ie whether solar or petrochemical). Nor can it fully represent all the ecological impacts at the source of materials extraction and construction that are *site-specific* (such as toxic waste, threats to endangered species, or topsoil disruption leading to erosion and loss of carbon sequestration). In life-cycle analyses and some rating tools, figures are added in to represent the destruction of habitat, based on 'expert opinion' or other devices. But these still leave out the time and space for natural ecosystems to recover and evolve. Reductionist approaches that aim to reduce everything to one element cause the omission of other system-wide issues. A simple example is that of passenger car travel, which is only one part of road transport (let alone the urban system) [Box 10].

## Isn't passenger car transport a good surrogate for all road transport?

Reductions in car travel through encouraging denser urban residential development could be cancelled out by increases in truck transport, not to mention air travel and so on. In the absence of urban agriculture, food needs to be transported into a city and distributed everywhere.[37] Truck transport has different 'demand drivers' than cars. Trucking is driven by necessity, while much car travel is discretionary – based on convenience, time and choice. The role of car owner preferences cannot be overestimated. A reduction in car dependency through more compact urban form would still be subject to myriad individual preferences that often have more to do with status, a desire for privacy and other things besides avoiding congestion. In fact, in dense urban environments, the car often serves as a 'cone of silence' where drivers can escape the crowds. Some people in major cities commute very long distances – up to three hours a day – to live in a better neighbourhood and bigger homes. While greater urban residential density corresponds roughly with reduced car travel for convenience shopping and commuting, this does not hold true for other kinds of individual choices. Residents of inner city areas often drive to the periphery for recreation and contact with nature, for example. Moreover, increasing densities will not encourage people to use public transport if a good service does not exist. So the focus on cars has obscured the fact that overall impacts of trucks can be both greater than that of cars and easier to influence.

## What are some impacts of trucking, as opposed to passenger car transport?

Car transport is generally the largest transport sector in terms of fuel and energy consumption, but only slightly more than trucking. The greenhouse gas emissions of trucks are also only slightly less in total than those of cars, but more per vehicle. As trucking is usually a matter of commercial necessity, it can also be more predictable than passenger car travel. Therefore, truck transport could be more directly influenced by design, incentives or regulations. Trucking with fuel cell engines is reputedly relatively efficient.[38] In fact, some trucking and bus fleets are already converting to hybrid engines, as they benefit from economies of scale. Total fuel consumption by trucks may be lower *or* higher in a given place or point in time than those of cars. However, truck transport creates more road damage, seed dispersal and diesel emissions, which are high in particulates. Increased residential density could preclude land-use functions that reduce trucking, such as urban farming, local compostable materials, passive solar design, conservatories, rainwater collection systems and Living Machines. These require appropriate forms of space, scale and management systems to operate efficiently. While eco-service functions can be integrated with human activity in virtually any development, it is more costly and difficult in denser environments. Composting toilets (that do not require piped water), for example, are impractical in high-rise buildings [Box 13]. So we need to look at the urban environment as a designed system, rather than a background for human activity.

## Has the linear-reductionist approach 'backgrounded' environmental design?

To a large extent. By ignoring built environment design – which currently traps us in energy-intensive production systems, processes and materials – 'upstream' levers for reducing energy, greenhouse and other impacts through planning and design were overlooked. There were many other reasons for this, of course, including how we *frame* policy issues. For example, energy and greenhouse gases were seen as products of primary industry rather than design. Therefore, environmental management initially focused on primary industry, like agriculture, forestry and manufacturing. Construction was thought of as a 'secondary' industry, so its impacts were presumed to be secondary.[39] In reality, the material and energy flows through 'primary' industries are shaped by the 'demand' for materials and products. And, as we have seen, demand is largely determined by design. For example, much of the greenhouse gas emissions attributed to transport are due to materials mined and transported for construction and/or demolition. Because we have considered the design of development as 'a given', however, we have tried to reduce the impacts of extraction and manufacturing at one end and consumer behaviour at the other end [Chapter 1]. Another example of how framing issues shapes results is that the conventional greenhouse 'pie chart' usually breaks down into commercial, residential, manufacturing and other slices. The effect of this is that the built environment is divided among different categories, and hence marginalized. In other words, by dividing the built environment into different wedges, it does not appear as a huge generator of greenhouse gases, or material and energy flows, and their accompanying waste and pollution, in other sectors. This, in turn, conceals areas where improvements can easily be made through changes to design and construction systems.[40] Design has great potential to reduce energy and greenhouse gas emissions in all wedges of the greenhouse gas 'pie'.

## But isn't transport reduction still the best way to lower greenhouse impacts?

It is essential that all sectors reduce greenhouse gas impacts, but transport is a relatively small contributor to greenhouse gas totals. While 70 per cent of roads are in cities, only 5 to 10 per cent of greenhouse gas emissions are attributed to road transport globally. The *production* of cars is reportedly a bigger contributor of greenhouse gas emissions than driving. Car ownership is not necessarily reduced by fewer car trips. Encouraging less driving while maintaining a fossil-fuel driven automobile industry is hypocritical. Likewise, measures of energy and greenhouse gases greatly underestimate the benefits of public space or treat it as a negative. Public open space not only allows ecological and environmental benefits, it can create more social space and interaction, as seen in Curitiba [Chapter 1]. So policies driven by energy reduction – instead of conversion to solar energy – can lead to inadequate solutions in terms of social vitality, quality of life and public health. Reducing the energy and greenhouse gas emissions of transport by densification would not come to terms with the problems of urbanization, or increase overall urban life quality. Efficiency is not a good surrogate for environmental quality or ecological health. Fossilized sources of energy and materials in buildings create a large portion of the chemical toxins and allergens in the indoor environment. The impact of dense living on health is still downplayed. Indoor pollution is usually many times greater than outdoor pollution, due to the fact that outdoor pollution seeps into buildings while petrochemical materials off-gas toxins in poorly ventilated buildings. Environmental quality requires the improvement of health, not a reduction in illness. This requires space for plants to clean and cool the urban air.

## Wouldn't reducing car travel greatly improve the health of city dwellers?

Indeed, some research has found that compact cities perform best in terms of fuel efficiency, carbon dioxide emissions, and pollutant emissions of, for example, VOCs, NOx, CO, $SO_2$ and smog. Other studies, however, have linked compact urban form to increased air pollution and respiratory disease, especially that associated with fine particle concentrations. Therefore one cannot separate out the influence of building design and materials, and the amount of green space, from these health statistics. If people are exposed to more pollution by walking than taking a train or car, as is often the case, it is not reasonable to ask them to walk. Of course, councils could have lower registration fees for hybrid cars and even lower fees for cars that do not use petrol. However, *indirect* economic instruments aimed at encouraging more 'efficient' engines do not differentiate electric or fuel cell operated engines from fossil fuel operated engines. Marginal improvements in engines operating on fossil fuels can only mitigate the 'measured' impacts of conventional cars. Direct actions that force the re-design of cars, buildings and public transport systems, in contrast, could greatly reduce greenhouse gas emissions, energy consumption and pollution. For example, super-efficient and light weight 'hypercars', electric cars and fuel cell buses could reduce greenhouse gas emissions quicker than either land-use controls or indirect economic incentives.[41] Their adoption would be aided more quickly by the removal of fossil fuel subsidies than by land-use densification. Nonetheless, the life-cycle and public costs of new hypercars are rarely, if ever, compared to conventional cars. Only fuel efficiency has been presented in the media, and cheaper fuel (and more guilt) is presented as the answer.

## If cars are fuel-efficient, or emissions-free, will that eliminate the problem?

No. We probably cannot wean people off their cars, but designing zero emission cars is not solving the problem. Not only are emissions entailed in the manufacture of new hypercars, they have *not* been designed to reduce the impacts of accidents. In Australia, for example, there are 350 deaths a year resulting from car accidents in a population of just over 20 million. We design cars to reduce damage to the car body and its passengers. We do not design cars to reduce their impacts on the cars and passengers that they hit. A more positive design approach would be to design cars that also reduce damage to other cars, pedestrians and cyclists. Although urban sprawl was partly caused by design for the convenience of cars, the solution is not simply to design for the inconvenience of cars. Cities must instead be designed *for* people and nature.[42] Discouraging car usage by creating congestion, while subsidizing cars, has created a vicious circle. Car owners pay about a quarter of the full *public* cost of cars, which includes fossil fuel consumption, premature deaths, medical costs and other forms of collateral damage.[43] As long as we do not have adequate public transportation alternatives, costly, long-term land-use planning strategies will not address excessive car usage, let alone car production and ownership. Good planning would instead make it more convenient, safe, quick and pleasant to take public transport, use bikes or walk.

## What is the starting point for increasing urban sustainability, then?

The starting point should be the ecological base and public estate, not a given 'solution' [Chapter 15]. Residential density as a 'solution' can lead to overly compact development patterns that close off future options by reducing the natural life-support system and future (responsible) social choice. Due to changing land values, increasing urban density often occurs at the expense of open space and the future adaptability that space provides. If central city living is overly 'compact', people and businesses may choose, in a free society, to relocate where they can access more open space and environmental quality. To compete with outer regions, where land tends to be cheaper, urban development cannot afford to sacrifice natural amenity. Communities are now increasingly voting to re-acquire land for parks and open space, as public appreciation of its social and economic value grows. The Trust for Public Lands in the US has collected many analyses of how open space increases property values and saves the community money overall.[44] 'Intensification', or introducing multiple uses by integrating *nature* in existing urban areas, would be a better indicator of sustainability than 'densification' (ie compact living with more mixed *economic* uses). Economic methods are now better able to assess some of the economic value of nature and eco-services, so there is now less excuse for just measuring distances and density [Boxes 42 and 43].

## Isn't more residential density still a good way to increase sustainability?

Density is not a good indicator in isolation from other variables. In fact, densification can indicate less sustainability. Density is not an accurate indicator because, first, it does not recognize the need to accommodate different lifestyle choices and diverse family styles. An investment in value-adding design and spatial options that improve health, life quality and resource efficiency can make inner city living more attractive. Exciting design features are more easily achieved by the diverse use of space, rather than the multiplication of uniform cells. Second, density is easy to measure, but not easy to measure meaningfully. For example, students sometimes overcrowd in shared housing, while more single people are tending to occupy bigger homes. While average space per person is increasing, that factor in itself does not cause sprawl. Poor design causes sprawl. Third, densification can reduce living space, natural goods, services and amenity, while also increasing total resource flows. Increasing 'dwellings per hectare' or 'new buildings in the central business district' can increase materials and energy consumption per person, per building and in total. It can also, again, reduce potential adaptability to climate change by restricting passive solar heating and cooling, which requires space and solar access. So while the contemporary suburban model is non-sustainable, the negative impacts of both cities and suburbs could be increased by densification. Eco-retrofitting would be a more direct solution that avoids the risk of policies that have unpredictable results.

## Do existing suburbs have the potential for low-cost eco-retrofitting actions?

Yes, either with or without more density. Suburban or rural development now entails a great deal of waste, such as duplication in infrastructure and services. Many suburbanites have their own lawnmowers, boats and washing machines, which they use infrequently. Also, suburbanites are generally more dependent on cars than urbanites. Multi-family urban dwellings, condominiums and co-housing can achieve some resource savings through shared cars, building services and landscaping, common facilities, and saved construction materials. For example, common walls and floors can reduce the need for materials and insulation. Compared to the resource-autonomous suburban model, however, replacing suburbs with apartment blocks or condominiums can have greater resource flows due to the (likely) use of conventional infrastructure (eg sewerage, electricity, drainage and parking structures). In established urban areas, capital and resource intensive infrastructure is usually necessary and entails high ongoing operational and maintenance costs. Construction and transport costs are much higher in urban areas due to the inflexible nature of the existing inner city areas. Alternative technologies are available in either context but, generally, urban re-development is more difficult and expensive. The space in suburbs, in contrast, offers unique opportunities for low-cost retrofitting for food, water and energy self-sufficiency through *intensification* – rather than densification – of land uses.

## Is food, water or energy self-sufficiency a realistic goal in suburban areas?

Some suburban blocks may be too small for self-sufficiency in food production, especially in places like Australia where soils are poor. However, domestic food and garden waste can be turned into soil nutrients. Roof, deck and wall greenhouses can provide planting shelves. Truck transport or 'food miles' can be reduced by more 'edible landscapes' or urban food production at different scales, such as balconies, community gardens or de-commissioned roads. 'Permaculture'-inspired arrangements can enable each dwelling or housing complex to operate as a self-contained domestic production plant – if not also a supply of food, clean air and water for neighbouring homes.[45] We can call such areas 'ecological space' – indoor or outdoor areas that are designed to provide eco-services. Ecological space could save public resources by natural air and water cleansing; natural heating, cooling and ventilating, providing habitats for native species, and even increasing resource security without using additional space. The addition of ecological spaces in existing suburbs could support the ecological regeneration of cities. We will later see how ecological space can serve as a measure of positive impacts. Further, as domestic solar hot water and space heating require little roof area per household, energy independence in suburban areas is quite feasible [Box 9]. Suburbs offer space for renewable energy systems to support the inner city, such as neighbourhood-scale electricity production, using renewable sources such as wind or sun. Solar disks, for example, are efficient at the neighbourhood scale and take little land area [Box 18].[46] They can be situated in pocket parks or community gardens or on existing infrastructure, without reducing usable open space.[47]

## Isn't renewable energy more expensive at the local scale of production?

It can be. Scale is a fundamental determinant of whole systems efficiency [Box 14]. Domestic-scale sewage and electricity production tend not to be cost efficient, but neighbourhood-scale energy production can be more efficient than large-scale projects. Centralized sewage and energy systems can also have greater environmental impacts. For example, hydroelectric power may be efficient to operate, but dam construction involves extensive resource flows in mining and transport. The associated 'land-morphing' destroys habitats, ecosystems and soil. It is therefore important to reduce the demand for electricity by designing buildings, transport and other systems to consume far less energy but, more importantly, to avoid fossil fuel plants and dams. Photovoltaic cells, which generate electricity from the sun, will soon be economical for private homes and buildings – notwithstanding the long history of subsidies to centralized, or fossil forms of energy production.[48] Many towns, states and countries already have rebates for solar cells and/or net metering, where people are paid extra for the energy they put back into the grid. This is because their decision-makers recognize that solar and wind power save the community money and increase their economic security. Since energy and materials are used in the production of solar cells, however, it is important that passive solar energy be maximized first. Until solar technologies improve, some 'non-solar' energy in cities may still be required. However, there is generally no excuse for the use of fossil fuels in heating, cooling and ventilating buildings, given their adverse impacts throughout their supply chain.[49] Buildings should, at the very least, use direct solar energy for heating, cooling and ventilation.

## Wouldn't solar design encourage 'sprawl' for access to renewable energy?

It should not. For example, the sun need not hit walls for heat to be collected. Roofs are excellent for capturing solar energy for heating, cooling and ventilating. In the suburbs, there are immediate opportunities to increase both the land-use *mix* and residential *density* – while adding ecological values and functions to the built environment [Box 11]. These opportunities could be lost with conventional approaches to urban and suburban infill development. The same issue arises with access to wind. While wind power is one of the most efficient centralized forms of energy production, distributing electricity over long distances reduces efficiency. Of course, centralized urban wind energy production can be impeded by the effects of buildings, hills and trees. However, there are now very lightweight, low-embodied energy wind generators that can more than cover their own cost and ecological waste over time [Box 17]. Just as the source of energy is more important than the amount, the *use* of space is more important than the amount used. While space is inherently limited, minimalist segregated spaces for isolated functions can be more wasteful than large spaces, as they tend to exclude *both* human and natural values. By maximizing the ecological space per person (ie infrastructure for eco-services), we can enhance adaptability and social and natural capital, and reduce total consumption. Both high-density urban building and suburban developments could be eco-retrofitted for ecological space without waiting for land-use or real estate markets to change. So instead of replacing existing housing with units, for example, we could retrofit for shared housing, or convert some existing rooms to bio-productive greenhouse spaces (perhaps aided by fibre-optic lighting in some cases).[50] In contrast, conventional urban design, by reducing energy independence, reduces 'natural security'.

## How does conventional urban design reduce 'natural security'?

Many of our cities, in both 'developing' and 'developed' nations, segregate people from the means of survival, such as healthy soil and food and clean water and air. When someone plugs up the conduits that supply these fundamental resources, people suffer (as seen in Palestine, Lebanon, etc). Political terrorists can easily detect 'systems design errors' in places where people lack access to the means of survival. In fact, studies found that the Twin Towers in New York collapsed in part because of the nature of its very 'efficient' structural design system.[51] Most skyscrapers around the world have similar vulnerabilities, despite differing structural details. Moreover, there is virtually no tall building that could withstand every earthquake, whereas low-density structures can be earthquake-proofed with wire or even low-cost variations on Green Scaffolding. The 'Quake Safe', for example, is a frame made from string, bamboo and wire that is retrofitted into an existing adobe house or incorporated into a new earth-walled house for structural protection against earthquakes.[52] Eco-logical design could also reduce the causes of conflict and militaristic approaches that restrict personal freedoms, life quality and genuine security. Design does not by itself redistribute wealth, of course, but it can better distribute the things in life that were meant to be free. Through sustainable design, the community can enjoy environmental amenities created by eco-logical design at no extra cost to the developer. However, most design professionals have still not embraced a whole system or ecological perspective. Even worse, some mainstream planners, environmental managers and engineers still generally relegate design to cosmetic treatment that comes after the basic industrial infrastructure is established.

## Why don't all urban planning professionals embrace systems design?

Perhaps this is because, in order to develop a 'credible' theoretical base, the design professions have borrowed frameworks and concepts from other linear-reductionist fields [Chapter 12]. These fields tend to marginalize design by conceiving it as a *means* of communication and expression, rather than as a different *kind* of thinking. This is reflected not only in the planning literature, but also in built form itself. Urban design has often been less about achieving social, economic and ecological objectives than about creating a sense of 'urbanity'.[53] In fact, architecture can feed materialism and drive consumption. For example, design journals describe how the building user's senses may be manipulated, such as encouraging shopping through store design that generates visual 'noise' and excitement.[54] The dictates of style and commercialism, as well as industrial systems of production and construction, go some way towards explaining why most modern cities look alike, despite completely different climatic, geological and ecological zones.[55] 'One size fits all' thinking, narrow design objectives, and the desire to impress fellow professionals and critics are found even in green building design [Chapter 6]. In contrast, Positive Development would prioritize the diversity and equitable distribution of environmental quality and amenity over feats of engineering.[56]

## How can spatial design provide an equitable distribution of benefits?

Equity and sense of community are more about environmental amenity than access to shopping.[57] The research into the relationship between compact form and equity has had inconsistent findings, so drawing a connection between social equity and compact form is problematic. The advocacy of compact cities has often been based on the qualities of dynamic European inner cities, but the urban cultures may be very different. The fact that some correlations exist does not necessarily mean that one factor has caused the other. For example, in Australia, cities were relatively equitable in the past, and were not the product of consolidation policies. In established high-density European communities, strong social bonds and networks may have developed for many reasons unrelated to dense living arrangements. Furthermore, what worked at one time or place may not apply in another era, culture or context. Increasing residential density in a new inner city area is not likely to create a sense of community. Urban design need not only be site specific, then, it needs to be adaptive. While living for a few months in a beautiful medieval village in Spain, the author found that residents had many complaints about their picturesque and fairly equitable and cohesive community. It was a cold stone environment without gardens, and many preferred to move to the surrounding, admittedly 'ugly', modern city just to obtain more sunlight and space. Further, density did not reduce car usage. Residents rebelled against parking restrictions, so the cobblestone streets were choked with cars. A direct design approach would mean implementing immediate improvements to urban life quality, ecology and equity that accommodates changing needs and preferences – not controls that attempt to change preferences.

## Can we address equity and access issues while increasing urban density?

Some research has indicated that compact cities do *not* necessarily promote greater on-ground access or equity. The benefits of high-density urban areas are often counterbalanced by negative equity effects. 'Mixed uses' in central urban areas are widely considered to have 'positive' equity impacts, but the research is inconclusive, and it would be hard to separate out other contributing variables.[58] Re-urbanization and re-development of derelict land or buildings – called intensification – has generally been associated with increased equity. However, this could be partly due to the optimism and opportunity that tends to accompany any physical re-generation. Further, research data based on existing conditions and relationships tends to reinforce options that already exist, rather than encourage the exploration of new design strategies. In one study, the *negative* aspects of compact urban living were found to be (in descending order of importance) less domestic living space, lack of affordable housing, poor access to green space, increased crime levels and a higher death rate from respiratory disease. The *positive* aspects were found to be (also in descending order of importance) improved public transport use, lower death rate from mental illness and reduced social segregation. We could design new options that capture these good qualities, without the bad, through design. This can be done with or without increasing density.

## Can we improve the wellbeing of the poor in relative terms by design?

Yes. Design can at least improve the relative position of the poor by improved public amenity (in the absence of economic solutions). For example, we could redirect investment to public spaces and land uses that both rich and poor people can feel comfortable using, rather than providing more luxurious units. Remedial measures – greater scope for walking and cycling, better job opportunities for the lower skilled, and better access to facilities – could be achieved in low- and/or high-density environments. Once again, instead of creating shorter work–home distances to encourage people to 'walk for their health' in polluted and congested environments, or cycle on dangerous, congested streets, we could create more places to exercise that are safe and attractive in their own right. The design, size, variety and quality of the public estate offer more direct, low-risk means of increasing equity, access and quality of life quality than density. In practice, consolidation usually means design that divides, privatizes and zones space into separate spaces and properties. It seldom adds value to the public estate. It uses space inefficiently from an ecological perspective, and can prevent future development options, wildlife habitats, nature corridors and access to public facilities. Tall buildings, for example, reduce solar access and create wind tunnel effects over a large area, even when the skyscrapers are green.[59] Instead of focusing on density, we could look at the amount of ecological, social, spatial and solar resources we can add by more clever use of space. To do this, we need different criteria [Box 15].

## How would increases in such spatial resources be measured?

Space is generally measured in reductionist, non-qualitative terms, such as dwellings per hectare, or square metres per person. These figures are often used as 'sustainability indicators', regardless of whether or not new development is sustainable. Yet people cannot even seem to agree on whether more space per person or less space per person is an indicator of sustainability. The aim of design should *not* be simply to reduce space per person. The aim should be to reduce resource consumption per person – while increasing accessible social and ecological space, amenity and ecosystem services, and solar resources. Green open space (both internal and external to buildings) has been largely overlooked as a means of accommodating the ecological, social and economic needs of urban residents. Designs can provide for social purposes while supporting ecosystems and their services in *existing* urban areas. Ecological space, the effective ecological area provided in a building or development, would be easy to measure. We cannot measure ecosystems, but we can use surrogates, such as square metres or ecological space per person, floor area allocated to the provision of eco-services, and so on. Ecological space is a measure of *positive* impacts. It is almost the opposite of the 'ecological footprint', which is a measure of *negative* impacts that can only be reduced. The inclusion of ecological space in private development could be a condition of construction or renovation, or provision of development credit. Planning provisions have long required public amenities in exchange for development privileges, such as public plazas or roof gardens for climate mitigation, so this would not be difficult.[60]

## So where do we begin to increase and manage ecological spaces?

Urban designers should investigate means of supporting the region's ecology by considering both natural and functional flows between regions and cities [Chapter 8]. It is widely held that the heterogeneity and diverse scale of the urban 'greenscape' (eg trees, indigenous domestic gardens and public parks) and connectivity of urban ecosystems (eg through nature corridors and micro-habitats) are essential to maintain biodiversity. Open spaces are also essential to provide the flexibility to meet changing (public and private) land-use requirements over time. Open spaces that are part of major private developments have usually only been 'decorative'.[61] There are many 'brown field' sites – contaminated and virtually abandoned urban land – that can be, and are being, rehabilitated through (public) urban forestry or (private) bioremediation. Of course, remediation by itself is not net positive, especially if the sites are converted to non-sustainable development later on. This will require the inclusion of biologists and ecologists earlier in urban planning, design and management.[62] We do not have a profession that protects urban ecosystems from the invasion of ferals, disease, fire and other threats to biodiversity. Yet we have many professions built around the repair and maintenance of conventional fossil fuel-based equipment and machines. Ecological space will mean employing scientists in the positive task of increasing the health of ecosystems, instead of trying to determine when species and ecosystems will cross the threshold into oblivion.

## Where would this different conception of space lead to?

We have said that urban areas themselves must become ecologically self-sustaining and eco-productive. Eco-retrofitting is possible, feasible and necessary. However, we need to go beyond a linear-reductionist analysis – which reduces space and even living things to units of energy. Design is an alternative way of thinking that can provide an antidote to excessive reductionism. It fosters synergy, synthesis, symbiosis and synchronicity among otherwise conflicting criteria and values. The next section looks at how we might transform conventional design criteria, processes and practices towards ecologically sensitive ends. We will begin by re-considering the conventional views of nature, environmental impacts and waste, and how these work against sustainable development, let alone Positive Development.

# SECTION B: CRITIQUE OF METHODS, TOOLS AND PROCESSES IN BUILDING DESIGN

# 4
# Development Standards and Criteria

## From 'designed waste' to zero waste

The previous chapters form a background for a discussion on the new design concepts, standards and methods that the next few chapters explore. We have said that, in the context of the increasing rates of resource depletion and degradation, the built environment must do more than reverse the negative impacts of future land use and development. What are currently regarded as 'ecological' design goals, criteria and concepts are not geared towards improving whole systems health, only reducing collateral damage. Consequently, our design processes have not evolved to foster the creativity and imagination required for true sustainability. An entirely new standard is required:

- It is not enough to re-design products or buildings. Every new design should contribute to the conversion of the industrial system in which it is embedded (eg construction, farming or forestry). Each design can leverage system-wide changes aimed towards true zero waste.
- It is not enough to eliminate waste and toxins. Each design should help to reduce the total flow of materials and energy throughout development. The built environment can be converted to a living landscape that restores, detoxifies and expands the ecological base.
- It is not enough to restore environmental quality. A design could expand usable public urban open space, contact with nature, food production, resource security, biodiversity, and ecosystem goods and services. In other words, it can add value to the public estate.
- It is not enough to make incremental improvements that slow the accelerating spiral towards ecosystem collapse. Development can be adaptable, reversible, and provide future generations with an expanded range of substantive life choices and future social options.

'True zero waste' would mean the elimination of all avoidable waste throughout the supply chain: from the source of extraction and production to recycling and disposal.[1] Positive Development would go beyond even true zero waste by generating positive impacts, both on-site and off-site, over its life cycle, increase economic, social *and* ecological capital, and improve human and ecosystem health. Instead of design that exaggerates differentials of wealth, Positive Development would increase equity [Chapter 14]. We will begin by exploring the dominant conceptions of 'waste' and 'limits of nature', and how these militate against efforts to reduce the rate of ecocide. Then we will look at what we will call 'designed waste': the avoidable duplication, disposability, planned obsolescence and wasteful end purposes to which resources are put by virtue of their design.[2] To eliminate or reduce designed waste, we need new forms of analysis that make 'waste' visible, expose biases against sustainability and front-load design. Conventional development approval processes focus on predicting the amount of known impacts in the future. They still exclude many uncertain future, long-term and cumulative impacts. To address this, our concepts of waste can be expanded to account for the waste 'embodied' in development and 'ecological waste' – the time, space and effort required to restore the source of materials in nature.

## Why is waste an important issue, and how does design affect waste?

Environmental management initially focused on pollution, rather than 'non-toxic' waste. But both forms of waste created by construction and demolition result in significant negative impacts.[3] For example, construction, renovation and demolition waste can account for up to 80 per cent of landfill by weight and up to 44 per cent by volume – some of it leaching toxic chemicals. Further, up to 50 per cent of 'packaging' waste has been attributed to construction.[4] Such waste and inefficiency also costs money. For example, the Australian government's research organization, CSIRO (Commonwealth Scientific and Industrial Research Organisation), estimates that efficiencies in the construction industry could create a 10 per cent reduction in construction costs and lead to a 3 per cent growth in GDP.[5] While construction represents only around 10 per cent of GDP, its design largely determines the amount of *upstream* resource consumption and emissions in mining, forestry, transport and manufacturing. Waste has generally been regarded as a problem that emerges at the end of the pipe. However, waste is 'designed in' long before products reach the construction site or building user. For instance, only 5 to 15 per cent of a tree ends up in wood products, with the conversion of logs to structural timber being roughly 30 per cent. This means the specification of more efficient products like 'radial sawn timbers' can generate 'compound savings' upstream in the forest.[6] But upstream waste figures do not reflect how the design of environments and artefacts can lock society into patterns of consumption *downstream* that perpetuate waste for decades.

## Doesn't waste depend more on behaviour than systems design?

There is nothing inevitable about waste. If it can be used as a resource for productive purposes, it is arguably no longer 'waste'. As Bill McDonough has observed, there is no waste in nature, because 'waste = food'.[7] Waste is instead produced by the *systems* that humans design, especially industrialized, fossil fuel-driven construction, manufacturing, transport and agriculture. The built environment has been estimated at three billion tons per annum, or over 40 per cent of materials worldwide.[8] To get an idea of the scale of waste involved, the UK construction industry annually consumes more than 400 million tons of materials and generates over 100 million tons of waste, with around 30 million tons ending up as construction waste going straight to landfill.[9] Construction and demolition waste in the US has been estimated at over twice that amount.[10] Clearly, we need to move beyond 'reduce, reuse and recycle' to a major 'rethink' of the end products of design.[11] Our design methods, concepts and criteria need to catch up with the growing perception that all waste is harmful, not just the poisons, like mercury and dioxins, that are accumulating in the food chain, the environment and human body.[12] For example, as Hardin Tibbs noted, carbon dioxide is a naturally occurring compound, but in the quantities that are being released, it can alter our climate, sea levels and biodiversity, and therefore wreak havoc on the economy.[13] A zero waste economy will thus require radically different kinds of building prototypes, urban design principles and policies.

## Aren't there already zero waste programmes that address these issues?

There are growing numbers of government jurisdictions that have 'zero waste' policies. Canberra was reputedly the first city to adopt such a policy, but has quietly dropped this goal. New Zealand as a nation now has a zero waste policy. However, when governments talk about zero waste, they just mean 'no waste to landfill'. But landfill represents a small fraction of waste: about 6 per cent of materials used in resource extraction and production reach the consumer. Most of this is disposed of within a few months of purchase.[14] Some argue that 'true' zero waste, let alone Positive Development, is impossible due to 'entropy'. However, in a realistic timescale (say, during the period that humans have been on Earth), social and environmental 'disorder' have been due to physical and institutional design, not entropy. The sun will not run out of energy for the foreseeable future. In any case, we are currently closer to 100 per cent waste than 0 per cent waste. The rubbery use of the term 'zero waste' as waste to landfill also reinforces the concept of waste as something that only occurs during production or after a product is purchased. While consumption and design issues are inseparable, the focus on consumer behaviour implies that society has to change behaviour first. This has provided a good excuse for buck-passing by industry and inaction by regulators. But consumers do not design the systems that result in waste, toxins and inequity [Box 19]. They can opt to have fewer possessions, boycott specific products or even have fewer children, but they cannot 'choose' products that have not yet been designed. In fact, they have little say over what is on the shelf, how it got there or what fashions will come down the pipeline next year. After all, consumers demand services, not waste.

## Does this mean that recycling approaches are a waste of time?

Absolutely not. Although post-consumer waste recycling is an 'end-of-pipe' approach, its economic value should not be underestimated. For example, the California recycling and waste management industry accounts for 85,000 jobs, generates $4 billion in salaries and sales, and produces $10 billion worth of goods and services annually. In one year the industry saves enough energy to power 1.4 million California homes, reduces water pollution by 27,047 tons, saves 14 million trees, reduces air pollution by 165,142 tons and reduces greenhouse gas emissions equivalent to removing 3.8 million cars from the road.[15] In the built environment, the opportunities for resource savings are also impressive. Recycling creates jobs and profits, and saves money and resources, while reducing public hazards and business risks.[16] Many waste audit tools, waste training programmes, model waste reduction contracts, and waste management plans, guidelines and strategies are now available to aid councils, designers and builders in generating efficiencies during construction.[17] Nonetheless, most recycling programmes address only post-consumer waste, a tiny fraction of the waste entailed in materials extraction and processing products. While economical, recycling has little impact on total resource flows. Likewise, 'cleaner production' and 'eco-efficiency' processes aim only to reduce waste and toxins, not net resource consumption.[18] Hence, these processes only slow the rate of toxins accumulating in the environment. The future success of recycling will depend upon front-of-pipe strategies such as financing, product design, collection and processing infrastructure, and end-markets [Box 50]. We can 'close loops' in the construction industry by ensuring construction by-products are converted to resources and not wastes. But we also need to develop building prototypes that use far fewer materials and energy in relation to the functions and services that they provide. Fortunately, the design professions are in a privileged position to reduce resource consumption and create meaningful consumer choices. We may not be able to control how people use buildings or products, but we can design them so that conservation comes naturally and creates a higher quality of life.

### Why aren't existing construction waste management practices adequate?

Most waste minimization strategies in construction are about 'process improvements' to a non-sustainable development prototype. While important, they often favour compliance activity, or 'ticking the boxes', over systems transformation through design. Take for example the experience of an environmental manager at a large university. His curiosity was piqued by the amount of waste that was leaving a building renovation site on campus, given that he knew the local council had approved their waste management plan. When he checked with the council, their 'plan' was to *not* recycle glass, brick, aluminium or, for that matter, anything else. The builders were in total compliance with their plan. Design thinking, as opposed to process-oriented strategies, is more likely to assist in making the quantum leaps required. Some well-known eco-design strategies include design for disassembly, for the environment, for maintenance and for adaptability.[19] These are well documented but, unfortunately, still under-utilized. There are also some institutional mechanisms that could help stimulate better design on the part of industry. 'Extended producer responsibility' laws, for example, are beginning to be enacted around the world.[20] These laws require producers to take back products at the end of their useful life and recycle them. James Greyson has also offered the idea of 'precycling'.[21] In this model, premiums would be paid by significant producers according to the risk that their products will end up as waste. Here, products that are more likely to become a new resource for other industries would attract a lower premium. Such systems design concepts are beginning to shift attention and funding from waste disposal to prevention.

### Can't firms just compensate in some other way for their waste impacts?

Sustainability requires, among other things, that our natural life-support systems are not depleted, degraded or distributed inequitably over the long term [Introduction].[22] The current model of development is destroying the life-support system, while cutting off future democratic and lifestyle options. There has, however, been significant progress in recent years towards compensating for, or 'offsetting', negative impacts [Chapter 7]. One of the more progressive examples is Wal-Mart's commitment to preserve land equal to its ecological footprint to compensate for the land it has consumed and sprawl it has encouraged (130,000 acres).[23] Offsets are ultimately *not* sustainable, however, as they do not reverse the impacts of previous development [Chapter 11]. Likewise, if we plant trees to offset our individual carbon offsets, we will not be offsetting the ongoing tree clearing elsewhere. As all manufacturing and construction processes generally involve some degree of waste, it would be necessary to compensate for the time and space it takes to regenerate land at the source of extraction as well. Simply reserving some land that might otherwise be developed someday is not a net gain. Moreover, as resources diminish and land becomes scarcer over time, there will be growing political pressure to re-allocate that land to development. In some places, governments are buying back land virtually given away to industrial interests in the past. At the same time, as James Ridgeway documents, there are also increasing moves to open up more public reserves to private exploitation.[24] A vicious circle of negative resource transfers dwarfs tokenistic offsets.

### Can we really expect more than the protection of remaining natural areas?

Yes, if we realize that the built environment is one area where we could 'de-couple' economic growth from negative environmental impacts. For example, according to the CSIRO, Australia spends AU$100 billion a year on infrastructure, and much of this on *aging* structures like bridges, sewerage and water systems.[25] A 10 per cent cut in ongoing infrastructure costs through mere efficiencies was estimated to be equivalent to 3 per cent GDP growth. Meanwhile, we are leaving older urban areas to deteriorate to the point where it appears 'cheaper' to demolish rather than revitalize them. There are many ways in which our project assessment and review processes favour new development over eco-retrofitting. A basic one is that the standard for *new* construction is so low. A 'sustainability standard' would mean that development is better ecologically and socially after construction than before. If all development were expected to increase appropriate ecosystems and habitats, for example, development on green field sites would have to enhance the ecological health of its site and/ or region. Similarly, if we counted embodied waste, eco-retrofitting would be understood to cost less and involve less resource flows than new development. The use of 'unspoiled' land would be seen as a privilege, not a right. Another basic reason our conceptual frameworks favour new construction is that they conceal our dependence on the ecological base. For example, our economic models represent environmental impacts as external to the economy. We still see nature as the opposite of human development – if not a threat to civilization.[26] Not surprisingly, then, current environmental management and planning systems allow development to trade off natural for artificial environments. Positive Development will therefore require new institutional and intellectual constructs. One of these is a new understanding of how waste is embedded in built environment design and construction.

## How should we understand the problem of waste in existing development?

New criteria and design concepts are proposed to help shift the institutional bias against sustainability and lift the bar for eco-logical design. Designed waste, again, is waste caused by dumb design.[27] Forms of designed waste include 'embodied waste' and 'ecological waste', which are defined below. Our design and assessment tools conceal total resource flows and waste that are continuing to build up in the environment by, for example, comparing the energy consumed in new buildings to 'typical', more energy guzzling, buildings [Chapter 5]. But energy is only a small part of the waste embodied in development. A new green building may use less energy than the norm, yet add to the total embodied and operating energy – and other impacts – of the city as a whole. Most cities and buildings have been designed as if they had an infinite supply of water, air, energy and sewage services perpetually available through pipes and wires – a one way 'umbilical cord'. Even 'dark green' development usually only aims to create self-contained (or 'autonomous') structures. These segregate space and replace natural systems with mechanical ones. At the same time, we regard 'empty' urban space as 'waste'. This is because space is viewed primarily in terms of its effect on energy consumption, and usually only in terms of increased transport or heating required to service spaces [Chapter 3]. If we assess ecological space, then, it would help to reverse these tendencies. Natural spaces in urban areas can support the bioregion, increase the net use of space, and add to the vitality and health of cities.

## But haven't we moved beyond the umbilical cord conception of nature?

In some circles, this *linear* view of resources has been replaced by a *metabolic* model, which conveys two-way flows, or 'closed loops'. This is an improvement over the umbilical cord, but it can reinforce input–output thinking. As we shall see, even a closed loop framework can create mental 'visors'. For example, if what goes in must equal what comes out, we will not try to increase positive outputs or create surplus benefits. Let us start by looking briefly at some benefits and limitations of metabolic analyses [Chapter 8]. In biology, metabolism refers to the total chemical reactions by which an organism, cells of an organism or a whole ecosystem, transforms energy, maintains tissues and reproduces itself.[28] Biological systems have inputs and outputs, but not waste *per se*, as everything is reused in the ecosystem. Hence ecosystems are, in a sense, true zero waste. Like biological organisms and ecosystems, cities (or industrial plants, farms and regions) have inputs and outputs that are dependent upon the wider environment.[29] Metabolic studies, however, show that cities are not sustainable. Cities treat the natural environment as a limitless faucet and sewer. As currently designed, urban and industrial systems create one-way flows of resources and wealth from nature to development. So analogies to biological metabolism enable us to assess how eco-effective our 'man-made' designs are. They can help us to measure how far we are from true zero waste. However, the metabolic analogy, like our traditional models, does not depict nature as conceivably net positive.

## So does the metabolism concept provide a good model for development?

Not the way we currently apply the concept of metabolism to industrial and urban systems. Environmentalists worked hard to convince people that there are limits to natural resources – as of course there are. In so doing, however, they have inadvertently contributed to the belief that nature, and our relationship with nature, is always zero sum. Even though the concept of 'metabolism' has proven useful in thinking holistically about urban and industrial systems, it can limit our imagination. With the inherited emphasis on negative impacts, for example, we have primarily used metabolic studies to compare what goes into a system and what comes out. So when used as a basis for design, the aim has consequently been just to reduce or recycle waste (eg industrial ecology). This metabolic metaphor emphasizes the lean, mean attributes of nature or its ultimate limits. But instead of visualizing nature as a competitive struggle, we could just as easily depict it as moving towards ever more complexity, variety and *abundance* (in between cataclysms of course). For example, nature produces enormous surpluses that can be captured without destroying ecosystems. And nature works virtually for free if treated well. It can even supply billions of microscopic unpaid workers on demand. Thus our 'social Darwinist' conception of nature prevents us from conceiving of built environments that are 'ecologically positive'. Metabolism may inspire the design of relatively no-waste development systems – but not systems that *add value* to the human and natural environment.

## If nature were seen as cornucopian, wouldn't that create unrealistic optimism?

It would be more constructive than our present conception. Our view of nature encourages unhealthy 'survivalist' attitudes. Biological systems are harsh and unforgiving in some respects, but they can *also* be seen as net positive. For example, fish produce thousands of eggs so that some will survive. 'Surpluses' are an integral part of their survival strategy. So nature is both mean and generous. In fact, productive natural systems were largely able to replace the goods that were extracted for human use – until the last few thousand years. Since then, societies that overpopulated and/or overexploited their environment have collapsed. Early humans and other species generally 'cropped' nature without clearing it. Elephants and gorillas, for example, often follow a circuit to allow natural systems to recover from their grazing. However, systems analogous to grazing should not be confused with 'sustainable'. Sustainable development has yet to be invented. 'Sustainable yield' is often code for 'how much we can extract from the environment' via industrialized systems, aided by chemicals and technology. Carrying capacity has usually been defined as the population of humans or other species that a natural area can support, without reducing its ability to support that species into the future. In a sense, therefore, carrying capacity has been conceived of as the 'interest'. As environmentalists have long pointed out, however, we are now living off the capital rather than the interest. What has not been appreciated is that it is now necessary to increase natural capital, not just live within limits. The central insight offered by this book, then, is that urban development could *create* natural capital: a 'surplus' of renewable resources provided by natural systems – plants, soil, air, water, food and fibres.

## Doesn't metabolism offer a 'positive' metaphor to inspire creating surpluses?

Not as applied. The metabolism analogy reflects our negative conception of 'sustainability' – development that 'does not *reduce* the capacity of future generations to meet their *needs*'. This definition does not inspire the design of cities and buildings that create environmental surpluses. A change in paradigms is required to help environmental managers step outside the negative space bubble shaped by inherited metaphors, models and methods. If we study everything in an input–output (zero sum) framework, we will inadvertently exclude ideas and phenomena that do not fit, such as 'design'. Metabolic models can therefore work to impede the idea of Positive Development by emphasizing closed loops and limits. Some environmentalists use a metabolic metaphor when they argue that ecosystems, like reefs and rainforests, are to a large extent self-sufficient, self-maintaining and self-regulating. Unlike most cities and industries, ecosystems such as rainforests do not really externalize waste and toxins as, in a sense, they are 'in balance' with their biophysical context. If no waste systems are therefore possible, humans should be able to design zero waste systems of development. Thus, they argue, buildings, cities and industries should be designed as if they were ecosystems that are 'resource autonomous'. This means that unavoidable waste (unused outputs) and operations would be re-used as a resource elsewhere. This is still largely input–output or zero sum thinking. If instead we realize that urban areas can increase ecological space, we might not keep trying to squeeze more outputs from the hinterland using more industrial inputs. For example, urban areas could even produce soil. Interestingly, soil used to be a limiting factor, but aquaponics now allows plants to grown in water fertilized by fish.

## Just how does the metabolism analogy reflect input–output thinking?

Take the case of urban and/or industrial ecology (also called 'industrial symbiosis') for example. These models aim to create efficiencies and recycling between systems.[30] Industrial ecology aims to establish links among different industries so that one industry's waste becomes another's resource.[31] Industries can also share utility infrastructure for energy production, water and wastewater treatment. Industrial ecology evolved without government initiatives or incentives because it made good business sense. It is now being picked up by major industries with government support in Australia and around the world (eg the Centre of Excellence in Cleaner Production at Curtin University of Technology and the Centre for Sustainable Resource Processing).[32] The Kwinana Industrial area in Western Australia has established industrial symbiosis projects among heavy minerals processing and chemical industries.[33] Another industrial symbiosis project in Wagga Wagga, New South Wales, integrates secondary industries to capitalize on recycling opportunities including co-generation (recycled heat), water recycling, nutrient capture, and mining of valuable trace minerals (such as potassium from wool scours using natural bioconversion systems) [Box 47]. The resulting clean water and organic fertilizer is being utilized on an adjacent farm. In other words waste is being converted to useful materials or products. But interpreting nature through an input–output or eco-efficiency framework can nonetheless be limiting.

## What is limiting about input–output thinking in an industrial ecology context?

Industrial ecology does not reduce pressure on living environments for the initial demand for raw materials.[34] Input–output thinking is certainly better than faith in a magic umbilical cord. However, the fields of industrial and urban ecology have thus far concentrated on 'closing loops' within industries or sectors. In practice, metabolic analysis often just results in industrial plants being co-located so that waste from one industry can be more easily transported to others [Box 32]. Of course, this input–output thinking has led to some conceptual advances. Over time, industrial ecologists have sought ways to close loops on an increasing scale and even between sectors. For example, as above, the conglomeration of manufacturing industries in Wagga Wagga are remediating the landscape, while closing loops between agriculture and manufacturing sectors. Closed loops in production plants, equipment and processes can make an enormous difference in resource consumption per unit or product. However, this approach is essentially recycling. We must both *reverse* the imprint of existing development *and* increase the ecological base. Eco-retrofitting cities to provide surplus eco-services (like clean energy) would be the logical place to start. Peter Droege has recently outlined the many ways that cities can generate renewable energy.[35] We have over 15,000 times more solar energy than humans need for all industrial systems of development.[36] Australia has enough wind (not to mention waves) to provide all its energy needs. Solar energy could be used to increase natural capital and carrying capacity, while creating healthy urban living environments. But we also need cities to regenerate ecosystems, not just services. And we will not achieve this until our environmental management systems regard nature as a living ecosystem, as opposed to a collection of resources, and see the built environment as a means to expand nature.

## Would seeing nature as alive and cornucopian support behaviour change?

Yes. Our view of nature is a projection of ourselves and therefore also shapes our behaviour. Where nature and its services are seen as limited, it seems natural to fight over rapidly disappearing resources. If we project social Darwinist ideas onto nature, there is little to stop us from continuing to grab and hoard resources and to ignore the plight of less fortunate species, classes, races, regions or religions. Our industrial system initially created wealth but, in the context of the diminishing natural capital and space it has caused, there are winners and growing number of losers. Wealth trickles up through the myriad capillaries of capitalism. Today, many powerful organizations are extracting the natural 'capital and interest' from poorer regions of the world.[37] This is not good karma. For example, chemicals banned in the US have been sold overseas, recycled and returned in the guise of treated products in a vicious 'circle of poison'.[38] But if we realize that we can increase the carrying capacity of nature without creating hardships at either end of the social order, then there is no justification for the prevalent survivalist or zero sum ideology. If development were re-conceived as potentially 'net positive', we might invest in activities that make everyone better off. Designing cities that are healthy, safe and pleasant for everyone also reduces the need for defensive design and expenditure, like security guards and gated communities. In the given 'closed' intellectual frameworks, defensive design appears to make sense. In contrast, the belief that we can increase the ecological base and substantive democracy while living off the interest would turn the spotlight on institutional structures that systematically transfer land, wealth and resources from the many to the few [Chapter 14].

## Can development occur without concentrating wealth or destroying nature?

As our eco-logical design capacity improves, we could systematically replace industrial with 'natural' production processes. The way to create net Positive Development is to re-design industry, agriculture and construction systems to increase the space, infrastructure and conditions for the essential goods, services and system self-maintenance functions that can be provided by nature. Ecologically self-sufficient, regenerative cities would reduce pressure on our diminishing wilderness and at least 'buy time' until we are able to preserve and expand nature reserves as well. This means designing buildings that serve as bioconversion facilities, produce materials, *and* increase ecosystems and habitats. We have discussed how built environments can easily be retrofitted to integrate vertical wetlands and Living Machines, fungi and earthworm bioconversion 'soil factories', butterfly and frog breeding terrariums, or even hamster and fish farms [Box 3]. Such functions have only been applied within development in tentative, piecemeal ways, but they provide design precedents. For example, the 60L Building in Melbourne, Australia, which integrates a Living Machine and other eco-design concepts into a building retrofit, provides a good laboratory for study (despite some minor glitches).[39] Perhaps there are no net positive buildings yet, but they would be just as easy to design as negative ones.[40]

## Even if buildings can be net positive, could whole cities ever be net positive?

Many existing eco-solutions can be applied at the urban, as well as the building, level. For example we can look at some water-sensitive design strategies that can be easily achieved at the domestic, urban and regional scales [Box 13].[41] But these have not been well integrated with social and economic functions thus far. This is partly due to urban design and architecture traditions that, in the name of efficiency, try to minimize the space allocated for each separate function [Chapter 6]. At the urban scale, design for eco-services could create more interesting and varied urban living environments and spaces, without increasing the net consumption of land. The integrated, multiple use of spatial resources in buildings and cities for both social and ecological functions could help avoid the ongoing sacrifice of environmental amenities and the expansion of urban areas. For example, there are a range of options for framing space with low-cost organic materials, such as some designs by Shigeru Ban.[42] Likewise, we saw how green space frames can support a wide range of ecological functions in public streets or parks, such as free standing Green Scaffolding [Box 4].[43] By eco-retrofitting urban parks, streets and buildings to create multiple (biological and social) land uses with reversible, low-impact structures, we can increase opportunities for food production, social interaction and income generating activities at the same time. But sustainability will also require that all human systems, even manufacturing processes, are eventually re-designed to restore, regenerate and improve human and ecological health in all respects.

## Even if whole cities could be net positive, how can this apply to manufacturing?

There have been impressive eco-efficiency advances in production, even if the documentation of these resource savings sometimes exaggerates their on-ground achievements. Arguably, perhaps, the only manufacturing systems that can produce a surplus of environmental goods and services will be at the bacterial level. Bacteria can be reproduced as needed, and are fed by the process of doing their work. This can be a net positive system, as a surplus of workers is created to meet the supply of waste itself, and laying such workers off does not cause discontent or social dislocation. Of course, resource-efficient technological innovation at the micro-level is increasing at a geometric rate in many areas, such as nanotechnology and biotechnology – for better or worse. In these cases, however, the criterion is primarily profitability, which often means (financial and natural) capital accumulation and zero sum resources transfers. Yet many financially sound operations already turn ecological negatives into positives, in the sense that they run on what would otherwise be environmentally harmful waste. Some industrial processes not only eliminate toxins from the environment, but also produce healthy 'surplus' products for sale. For example, toxic sludge and abattoir waste can be converted to fertilizer and water, and then delivered to farms [Box 50]. John and Nancy Jack Todd's Oceanarks projects have demonstrated that positive production methods can go beyond remediation, making the human and natural environment healthier, while producing useful products for the economy out of waste. This could be seen as a virtuous cycle, not just a closed loop.[44]

## So are there on-ground examples of net positive production systems?

Yes. One example is the Burlington Eco-park in Vermont in the US. There, waste is blended with manure from organic poultry operations, injected with the spawn of mushrooms and put into bags that grow several crops of (non-toxic) mushrooms.[45] The end product goes into bins to produce earthworms, which are then blended with duckweed to feed the fish that are growing in Living Machines. (Again, these are ecosystems of micro-organisms that convert wastewater, sewage and toxins into clean water and soil and/or fish.) Worm eggs are left behind to hatch and continue to produce fertilizer and compost. In winter, this material grows crops. In spring, it is sold as worm castings and compost. Such 'manure-facturing' processes could happen in a suburban environment or on an urban scale as well. In another Oceanarks project in a Chinese village, scenic tourist walkways over what were once open sewage canals have been combined with Living Machines that clean the water. This adds value to the urban landscape and provides tourism potential for the community as well.[46] To begin to change direction, we need to put these net positive systems into production on a large scale in urban and regional development systems. However, as many in the construction fields now accept, the building industry has tended to resist ecological modernization until very recently. The community will need to take action and enlist government support, if the problem of ongoing waste and toxins embodied in the built environment is to be addressed [Chapter 2].

## Is the construction industry beginning to take on board industrial ecology?

We are a long way from construction ecology.[47] Waste minimization strategies in the building sector aim only to reduce or recycle the extra waste caused by the project itself, not pre-existing or off-site waste. The main activities where resource efficiencies and recycling are currently practised are:

- In construction: modular and prefabricated systems, dimensions for standard material sizes, detailed construction documentation, and specifying recycled materials
- In demolition: design for deconstruction, reuse and retrofitting
- In operation: design for maintenance and renovation; design for adaptability and flexibility

Our building science tools enable us to *substitute* better industrial materials and technologies for worse ones, by estimating life-cycle impacts. But this generally leads to only marginal reductions in impacts. As we have seen, closing loops, increasing resource efficiency or reusing waste generated by conventional design does not in itself reduce the ecological impacts upstream caused by mining, agriculture or forestry. Likewise, processes like geo-sequestration and incineration only slow the accumulation of impacts and disruption of habitats. They only deal with part of the emissions or solid wastes after they are produced. Further, every time something is recycled there is a loss of material and energy. Nonetheless, they can be important in a mix of pragmatic steps. What is missing from the suite of responsible waste management practices is the pre-construction phase, such as design that uses less total materials and energy, sourced in ways that are far less damaging to habitats and yet serve more functions. To increase the health and resilience of the ecological base and generate positive off-site social and ecological impacts, both eco-efficiency and eco-logical design are needed.

## Just what is the difference between eco-efficient and eco-logical?

Eco-efficient design and production processes reduce resource consumption per unit of material or per product, but not total consumption over time.[48] Resource flows are continuing to increase despite the impressive efficiency gains made in recent years.[49] One reason is that industries do *not* increase efficiencies in order to sell fewer products. The efficiencies might lead either to lower prices to capture more of the market or, conversely, to increased profit margins. This does not, however, reduce the increasing number of unnecessary or luxury items in the marketplace that we do not really need. For example, there was no demand for electronic pets until they were designed and marketed.[50] Designers therefore need to think eco-logically and consider the waste embodied in product *purposes* and building *prototypes* themselves. For example, designers often:

- Design more efficient lawnmowers, rather than plant native grasses or ground covers that would eliminate mowing
- Design more efficient kitchen appliances, yet supply extravagant, material-intensive kitchens for ordering in pizzas or microwaving processed food
- Create demand for air-conditioners by designing spaces that overheat, or by under-designing for passive solar cooling capability
- Create better paints that emit less VOCs and other toxins, but use paint where it is not necessary

Waste caused by design can best be reversed by design. To eliminate waste through planning, design, decision-making and assessment systems, then, we need new concepts for understanding designed waste. A three-pronged approach to designing waste out of the system would help bring a greater appreciation of the 'opportunity cost' of poor design:

**Step 1**  Think seriously about 'designed waste', or the relationship between waste and design

**Step 2**  Develop new concepts like 'ecological waste' that take into account the *living* dimension, not just inputs and outputs of resources

**Step 3**  Assess and prioritize innovations and investments in terms of their potential to improve ecosystem health

## What is meant by the first step, awareness of designed waste?

As a society, we need to appreciate the role of design in generating excessive waste and toxins. The following factors contribute to designed waste, or waste that is 'designed into' our industrial and construction systems:

- Products are often designed for wasteful purposes or redundancy
- A small fraction of materials used in production ends up in products
- Many products are designed for planned obsolescence and/or disposal
- Much of what is bought is surplus to need, including extra cars and homes
- Reused materials and goods are mostly 'down-cycled' to lower uses
- Packaging can be resource intensive (and require us to buy ten bolts when we need one)

- A small fraction of waste is diverted from landfill, and even less is recycled
- Many products combine materials which then cannot be recycled economically
- The means of survival (natural capital and eco-services) are being laid to waste
- Efficiencies in one area are counterbalanced by the 'rebound effect'

## What is the rebound effect and what do we do about it?

The rebound effect is where consumers save resources and therefore money, but then turn around and spend the extra money on carbon-rich or conspicuous consumption.[51] For example, people who save money due to investing in energy efficiency may then spend that money on an overseas holiday via jet plane, instead of rolling it over into more efficiency measures. The rebound effect can probably only be addressed by designing built environments that create a rich range of low-impact choices. Environmental solutions that rely on altruistic and responsible behaviour can never be foolproof. Overall, most innovation is still aimed at increasing consumption.[52] Business does not create new products or designs to reduce their net sales.[53] Design approaches that make responsible living 'cool', like one firm's stylish but 'compostable' shoes, are therefore more likely to succeed than approaches that require sacrifices. Style influences behaviour, so by defining what is *cool* through design, we can begin to reduce our ecological footprints. At this stage in our development, *cool* still often means adding an extra Prius to the existing fleet [Box 54]. Instead, however, good design can be a means of reducing the need for retail therapy in the first place. A comfortable and beautiful built environment can substitute for personal consumption and material goods. Of course, designers are seldom taught to substitute low-impact, high-quality environments for high impact consumables. They are seldom taught to seek the optimal relationship between durability, flexibility and adaptability – let alone to consider concepts like reversibility, compostability or edibility. Designers of materials, components, sites and buildings must learn to consider how to accommodate and stimulate responsible change in human needs and preferences.

## What does the second step – ecological waste analysis – entail?

Step 2 addresses the need for new ways of understanding, assessing and measuring waste. As a society, we undervalue nature's tangible 'products' that provide the means of survival, such as energy, water, space, soil, materials and amenity. But we also undervalue biodiversity and ecosystems – or nature for its own sake. Since, as a society, we do not value nature as a living ecosystem, we do not seriously consider waste at the ecological level.[54] If nature is just a resource, more efficient use is all that matters. Instead of supporting ecosystems, biodiversity and habitats, our methods aim only to reduce pressure on the environment in general. So when we assess environmental impacts, it is in terms of inputs of raw materials or outputs of pollution. In life-cycle assessments, again, we add in numbers (often based on the values of experts) to represent negative impacts during resource extraction, demolition and final disposal. However, we seldom, if ever, take into account the time and space needed to restore the ecology. To design for ecological health and resilience, we need to consider what we can call 'ecological waste'. Ecological waste is the loss of ecosystems and encompasses the space, time and cost of replacing them. For example, we would consider the whole forest ecosystem, not just the biomass. Ecological waste (a negative measure) could be seen as the converse of ecological space (a positive measure). We can identify three different levels of thinking about designed waste in the built environment. These are illustrated in the following sections by timber, trees and forests.

## 1 MFA and LCA

'Material flows' analysis (MFA) and/or life-cycle analysis (LCA), applied to waste, would aim to reduce the amount of timber going to landfill or discarded prematurely. Such a best practice approach would consider cumulative waste and efficiency in extraction, production, delivery and construction, and/or the longevity of the product. MFA has an advantage over tools based on LCA for these purposes, because adding in a value to represent the loss of a natural resource in input–output equations treats waste as a mere 'externality'. Such losses and impacts need to be seen as intrinsic to the design, which is better expressed by MFA. However, tracing the material flows in the timber supply chain does not usually consider the element of *time*: the product life-cycle and the life-cycle of the tree.

## 2 Embodied waste analysis

Embodied waste analysis would include embodied materials as well as energy and water. Embodied waste (the converse of efficiency) would be aimed primarily at making resource transfers more visible [Chapter 14]. Those who would take this view of waste would aim beyond reducing cumulative waste, increasing efficiency or increasing the amount of the tree embodied in final products. Metaphorically speaking, embodied waste is the hole in the doughnut. Figure 6 depicts the timber captured in finished products (the doughnut) to that which is wasted or 'down-cycled' in the production of a timber product (the doughnut hole). One can reduce the size of the hole, or turn the donut holes into positives. In other words, we can have our doughnut and eat it too. The assessment would consider the life span of the resource, not just the product – the time it takes to replace the trees. In the case of timber, then, embodied waste analysis might take into account:

- Timber volume
- Percentage of the forest captured in permanent products
- Rotation period or replacement time of the trees
- Public costs entailed in forest management and regrowth
- Life span of the products

While we know that the preservation and enhancement of the ecological base is essential to achieve sustainability, we largely ignore it. We have not acquired the data or the processing tools to measure it. Instead of trying to model nature (which again is impossible), we can use nature as a model.[55] But we should also try to ensure that the product purpose is also ecologically responsible. We do not need to wait for data and computer programs in order to consider the end use of the product. Embodied waste analysis would only look at the trees as a resource. It would not determine the highest ecological use of the timber, or weigh in the re-generation time and space required to recover the ecosystems from which the timber was extracted. Therefore, embodied waste would constitute only a subset of the ecological waste.

## 3 Ecological waste analysis

Ecological waste analysis would count the costs of restoring the whole ecosystem. It would consider the resource base as a *living* system. Depending on the scale of the project, it would notionally or quantitatively measure the effects on the life-support system, future social options, and the equitable distribution of the means of survival and quality of life. In other words, it would 'weigh in' the replacement cost, time and value of the forest as an ecosystem, not just the trees or timber contained in them (Figure 7). This would challenge the conventional approach of trading off competing interests in forest products by converting good farmland to tree plantations, instead of using degraded land.[56] There is no human material or non-material need that requires ecological waste.

## Figure 6 Material flows of trees in timber production ('doughnut model')

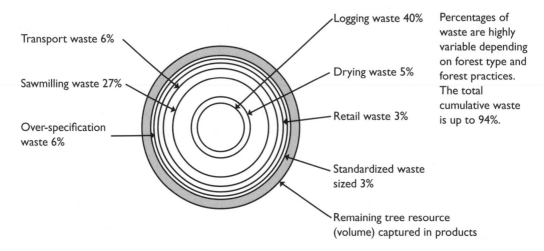

Transport waste 6%

Sawmilling waste 27%

Over-specification
waste 6%

Logging waste 40%

Drying waste 5%

Retail waste 3%

Standardized waste
sized 3%

Remaining tree resource
(volume) captured in products

Percentages of
waste are highly
variable depending
on forest type and
forest practices.
The total
cumulative waste
is up to 94%.

Cumulative – compounded – waste through the supply chain does not consider the life span of the timber product or the replacement cost, space and time required to replace the tree or forest, let alone to restore the ecology.

## Figure 7 Ecological waste of forests in timber production

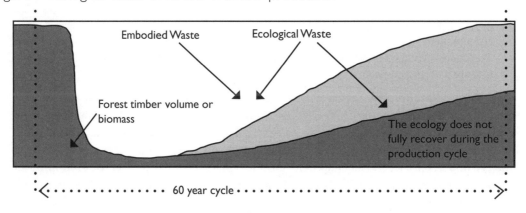

Embodied Waste

Ecological Waste

Forest timber volume or
biomass

The ecology does not
fully recover during the
production cycle

<......... 60 year cycle ..........................>

### What would the idea of ecological waste contribute to our awareness?

Sustainability demands an analysis in which the ecology is central, since it is the basis of human existence. Figure 7 is intended to communicate the idea that biomass may recover during the production cycle, but not the ecology. The concept of ecological waste is intended to help account for the health of the life-support system itself. Embodied waste could be recovered over the production cycle of the forest, as the trees grow to maturity. However, apart from a few heirloom objects, the whole forest, with its creatures and habitats, virtually 'goes to waste', because the production cycle is shorter than the period in which the forest ecosystem can regenerate. In some regions, the forest may not regenerate as a healthy ecological system approximating the original variety of tree ages, species and biodiversity for centuries. This means the ecological base is 'in deficit' for a much longer period than the life-cycle of a typical wood product or timber building or even the 'crop rotation' period. The embodied waste of timber in a clear-felled native forest can arguably be reduced by planting and maintaining mixed species and mixed use plantations, but such plantations still cannot replace the ecological base, with its complete set of eco-services. Truly sustainable resource-allocation decisions would consider the time it takes ecosystems to recover to something equivalent to their original state.

## Wouldn't reducing ecological waste be detrimental to the economy?

Not if we define economic progress in terms of human development and life quality, as some ecological economists have tried to do.[57] In any case, assessment systems only provide information and guidance. They do not make decisions or generate design solutions. Decision-makers and the general public may, of course, continue to choose designed waste over eco-logical design, either deliberately or unthinkingly. But while 'design' creates something that does not yet exist, assessing and 'choosing' among options is often a matter of the elimination of 'less bad' options. Thus, for example, selective forestry or plantations grown on degraded land for timber products might generate less ecological waste than clear-felling and mining native forests for woodchips. Decision-makers can continue to ignore critical sustainability issues such as time, space, living ecosystems, and the wealth transfers entailed in allocating land and resources to development. Nonetheless, the public has a 'right to know' what is happening. After all, basic democratic rights are inextricably linked with the control of and access to the means of survival, much of which is determined by land-use and development control decisions. Decision systems that ignore ecological waste also ignore the loss of the means of survival (ecological base) and the loss of substantive democracy (public estate) that result from the linear and unilateral pattern of resource transfers over time. It is apparent that analyses of waste that treat resources as inert materials will not preserve nature over the long term.

## What would a new conception of ecological waste bring to current analyses?

We can use a simple example. An ecological waste analysis on whether to build a nuclear power plant would put a value on time, space, ecosystem functioning and end purposes, along with the other impacts and issues like reliability of uranium supplies, nuclear proliferation, etc.[58] An ecological waste analysis for a nuclear power plant would quantify:

- The opportunity costs of storing spent fuel rods for thousands of years (ie what could have been done instead).
- The land area or space that uranium mining and waste storage would alienate from other purposes over thousands of years.
- The time required for the ecology to restore itself as complex and resilient ecosystems.
- The effective commissioned life span before the plant becomes a contaminated liability, which is only about 50 years (the costs of decommissioning nuclear power plants have generally been left to taxpayers).
- The purposes to which the uranium will be put (eg weapons) as well as the alternative means of achieving those ends (eg peacemaking).

Environmentalists consider these things, but they are not integral to the balance sheets, and they are often excluded from the debate because they are ostensibly 'unquantifiable'.

## Don't assessment tools consider time, cost and value already in some way?

Generally our assessment tools are designed to predict the future damage our plans and designs will do to the environment [Chapter 5 and 7]. For this reason, we often largely ignore or undervalue past ongoing damage caused by the existing built environment. We generally only count the additional costs from this point on – not the cumulative ongoing costs of existing development systems. In other words, as we shall see, development assessment and even sustainability assessment processes have been highly selective. They do not weigh in the costs of inaction or lost opportunity costs of poor design. Moreover, as snapshots in time, LCAs focus on inputs and outputs at the system boundaries [Chapter 8]. Selective measurements of waste therefore distract us from addressing fundamental truths:

- Costs and impacts of existing development are non-sustainable
- Resources required to replace existing development with 'green' buildings are too great

Even if we could sustainably harvest enough materials, water and energy to replace the existing building stock with new green buildings, we would only be reducing *relative* operating energy, and perhaps some embodied energy. The resource flows and ecological costs of new green construction would leave us further from sustainability than we are now. For example, councils usually ignore the waste of energy due to allowing existing development to remain as it is. Councils also seldom consider the environmental costs of demolition because 'a clean slate' is accepted as the baseline. Since project assessment and approval systems undervalue or ignore the ecological waste entailed in demolition and new construction, these tools favour new development over eco-retrofitting. We need to invest more creativity and imagination into eco-retrofitting to generate healthier air, water, soil and biota, often without wasting existing infrastructure where possible.

## So our views of waste can actually discriminate against eco-retrofitting?

If we do not measure something, we often leave it out. For example, our assessment tools still focus on the 'operating' energy that will be used by the building after construction [Chapter 5]. This is because operating energy has been much greater than 'embodied energy' (energy used in construction), which is hard to measure. However, with passive solar design and solar electricity generation, we could virtually eliminate operating energy, using free solar energy for heating, cooling and ventilating. Instead, due to our limited views of waste, we have tended to support hi-tech solutions to low-tech problems, like more efficient air-conditioners. But such perceptions are rooted in more fundamental economic structures. For example, due to market distortions (like undervalued natural resources), developers have little incentive to address the impacts of existing development. Reusing existing structures can save substantial sums (generally over 30 per cent). Developers are seldom asked to consider the environmental costs of demolition. They generally only consider the private costs of retrofitting as against the private costs of new development. It is often easier to simply knock down buildings and use well-rehearsed industrial construction processes. After all, few people are trained in retrofitting and there is little private benefit in building capacity when natural resources are so cheap. There is little public pressure to preserve basic building structures, except in the case of heritage buildings. Further, developers currently only pay for waste to landfill, not embodied waste. Development approval systems ignore the 'opportunity cost': the on-site and off-site externalities imposed by the *existing* urban context that a retrofit could address. They do not, for example, weigh in the costs of maintaining the built environment 'as is', relative to the cost of correcting and improving it (over time). Governments could remove the institutional biases against eco-retrofitting, or ensure new development compensates for the waste caused by *previous* development through remediation projects. Instead, they just require development proposals to offset their additional new impacts.

## Does this mean our views of waste get in the way of Positive Development?

If we just add up the costs and benefits of environmental change from this point on, we do not design for whole systems improvements. Assessments are used as a basis for approving development proposals whenever and wherever they are put on the table by willing investors [Chapter 7]. Remarkably, the benefits of a development still *only* need to be deemed to outweigh the costs. The project need not contribute positively to sustainability objectives or reduce existing impacts in the environment. Approval is generally assured if a project is 'less unsustainable' than conventional buildings. In theory, the market should be able to close loops on its own, as eco-efficiency improvements to existing processes and products are inherently cost-effective on a level playing field. But in this institutional context, it cannot. We could, however, reverse the process of market-driven, government-subsidized innovation that ignores the ongoing public costs of development. For example, planners could:

- Identify problems and waste in the existing environment that developers can address through eco-retrofitting
- Determine positive low-risk development opportunities for innovators and investors to invest in
- Allocate public investment to stimulating eco-innovations that can replace resource-intensive machines and products with natural systems

Our development approval systems discriminate against sustainability, because they do not consider the ecology (let alone the 'solar system'). Therefore they do not consider the foundational complex system, nature, upon which all else is built.

## Why can't we just require the externalities to be internalized?

Internalizing usually just means paying (a portion of) the immediate economic costs of negative impacts. In other words 'internalizing', in the conventional usage, is not the opposite of externalizing. Even if private industry 'internalized' public costs, as green economists propose, this would not repair the damage. Nor would it compensate the public for the goods and services that benefit developers – such as environmental quality and transport systems that bring the employees, clients and customers to their business. Over time, environmental management systems have effectively facilitated the transfer of public goods and resources (eg land, water and forests) to private interests. We can consider these transfers 'internalities', as they are the converse of externalities. These benefits are left out of assessments. This happens through both direct and indirect forms of institutional design [Chapter 14]. In other words:

- Externalities include indirect transfers that result from allowing toxins and waste to accumulate in nature and diminish the ecosystem viability of the ecological base
- Internalities include political policies that allow public resources and space to be used for private purposes and profits in a way that diminishes the public estate

An example of internalities is where public goods and services are effectively privatized through environmental management systems that allocate 'rights' in pollution, water ownership, and so on [Chapter 11]. The privatization of resources appears more 'efficient' than it really is when the analytical framework does not take into account the loss and opportunity cost or long-term ecological viability. Our environment is being shaped to fit an economic model and decision process that not only devalues natural resources, but treats them as inert. If we considered the cumulative privatization of environmental benefits (as well as the distribution of negative impacts), and its effect on the ecological base and public estate over time, we would at least make the loss of ecosystems more 'visible' [Box 52].

## Don't we include the value of eco-services in environmental valuation?

Sometimes. But economists have considered eco-services in a non-ecological, anthropocentric way. Moreover, economists' tools *discount* the future to compensate for inflation and the fact that people are generally willing to pay more for something now than for something they can only enjoy in the future. In a 'legitimate' sustainability assessment, we would need to count the ecological damage (and hopefully ecological enhancement) in real time – not discount it. The idea of an 'ecological factor' (the opposite of a discount rate) has been suggested by some to take into account the fact that society will increasingly value the natural environment as it becomes more scarce. This, of course, would be a fairly arbitrary (market determined) number, however, as it could not reflect the reality of *unknown* ecological thresholds. So even if an ecological factor were used in sustainability assessments, it would not have meaning in an ecological context [Boxes 42 and 43]. The concept of ecological waste, in contrast, provides a means of measuring the relative depletion of the ecological base over time. To begin to reverse the downward ecological spiral, we also need to weigh in the costs of inaction, which is in fact negative – not neutral. But we also need to value positive impacts. We could measure and reward design for development that *adds value* to natural systems or surrounding development.

## If ecological waste measures negatives, how do we measure positives?

It would actually be easier to measure positive impacts than negative ones. Environmental management has focused on quantifying the unquantifiable: negative impacts in a complex system. But the fact that complex systems cannot be predicted or measured is what makes them 'complex systems'. And even if it were possible, the measurement of complex systems would be too costly and unreliable, because we would have to trace all interactions between the environment and humans and their imprint on an unpredictable future. Consider, for example, the synergistic effects between immune systems and toxins over time. These complex relationships can change unpredictably due to exogenous forces and variables. There can also be interactions between immune systems and the (roughly 1000) new chemicals that are added to the environment each year without testing. On the other hand, when we *add value* to the ecological base, we do not have to trace things through permutations. There is no reason to trace health 'improvements' in the air, water, soil and people. We need only be certain that conditions will be better than before, and that we do not use chemicals or components with unknown or irreversible effects. That is to say, we do not need to estimate interactions with impaired immune systems if we are not contributing to further impairment. The issue therefore becomes 'which net Positive Development projects should the public (or private) sector invest in for best overall results?' [Chapter 14].

## How do we decide how much, and which, development to invest in then?

One of the roles of planners should be to determine the best public and private investments to achieve net Positive Development most effectively. Some planners have promulgated basic green design guidelines, but they have not developed and disseminated methods to ensure that development contributes positive on- and off-site impacts. Instead of encouraging 'positive' actions that we know are safe, effective and economical (such as eco-retrofitting), our environmental management systems seek ever more specialized ways of quantifying the risks of inherently dangerous activities – much of this at public expense. We have traditionally made planning and design decisions according to what is the least bad land-use option, or the best design alternative for which there are current investors. Then we implement complex regulations, incentives and tools to encourage developers and designers to reduce waste and mitigate negative impacts at the margins. Proposals are not assessed so that they can be rejected; they are assessed so that these activities and associated risks can be mitigated and approved. Paying consultants to measure the damage of a building proposal relative to standard buildings will seldom, if ever, result in significant net improvements to pre-existing conditions.

## How do we avoid ecological waste and opportunity cost of poor design?

Greening the old prototype or constructing less wastefully is relatively trivial, given the 'opportunity cost' of unsustainable built environment design. There is a simpler and quicker way to improve the standard of development than a proliferation of decision and design aids: front-loading design. To foster eco-logical design, we could require designers and/or developers to consider eco-retrofitting and eco-innovation options and describe these investigations in an 'eco-design report', as discussed in the following chapter. A hierarchy of eco-innovation, to guide investment, is provided in Chapter 14. However, the basic message that has emerged from the above conversation is that built environment design could not only provide positive on- and off-site impacts, it could create a 'surplus' of eco-services and ecosystems, often at no extra cost. Next, we will review what we are doing instead of design.

# 5
# Building
# Rating Tools

From best practice to a
sustainability standard

The technical advances and industry uptake of building rating schemes and assessment tools are both growing rapidly.[1] Despite this impressive growth, however, they are still used in only a small portion of buildings.[2] These building assessment and rating tools each have heuristic value. They also serve as a means of demonstrating compliance with local regulations and standards. However, they tend to promote 'best practice' instead of a sustainability standard. In effect, they encourage incremental approaches, marginal thinking and 'tradeoffs'. They also tend to supplant design thinking with managerial 'displacement activity', by requiring developers/designers to invest human and financial resources in measuring, monitoring, mitigating and managing negative impacts, instead of design.[3] While many of these tools apply 'whole of life-cycle' accounting, their analytical framework is essentially reductionist, data-intensive, aggregative and sequential. Like environmental impact assessments, they evaluate a design 'retrospectively', rather than helping us design something completely new [Chapter 7]. Thus they prioritize bean counting over design, accounting over accountability, and prediction over performance.

Of course, creativity can still occur through tentative, incremental, accountancy-oriented activities – but it is not likely. It is even less likely that underlying norms and assumptions will be challenged in the process. Designers should be encouraged to think about maximizing positives and to imagine new 'possibilities' – not 'impossibilities' like predicting collateral damage in a complex system. There is no harm in advancing our ability to estimate the number of beans in a jar.[4] However, it not the kind of interactive, outcomes-oriented, collaborative design processes that stimulate synergies and syntheses. Measuring the predicted impacts of a proposed development relative to standard ones keeps the finish line close to the starting block. It does not mean we go any faster. The question should be 'How can we achieve a genuinely sustainable building?' – not how to measure how much less bad it may be. Eco-logical design tools should instead help designers 'think outside the box' to create reversible land-use planning and net positive, adaptable designs, materials, forms and other win–win–win solutions.

## So how do we think outside the box to create reversible building design?

To move toward sustainability, a building, city or settlement should improve its biophysical context – well beyond the building, product or the 'box' as defined by the investment. Buildings should be seen as an opportunity to create positive environments that remedy some of the deficiencies of surrounding development. Improving the ecological conditions of the site and wider region will require a new approach to planning, design and assessment: one that looks beyond the inputs and outputs of the region, the building envelope, and components and/or materials. Designers need to look at total environmental flows through the existing or proposed development [Chapter 6]. At the same time, they need to look at flows between the development and the surrounding region and natural environment [Chapter 8]. To build capacity in design for sustainability, then, we need *design* tools that:

- Analyse and identify specific economic, social and ecological problems in the urban and regional context that development can correct through positive on-site and off-site impacts
- Facilitate collaborative processes that encourage creativity and innovation in design for eco-services aimed at value adding to the public estate and ecological base

Here we will review some of the conceptual and practical problems of rating tools and project review and approval processes. Then we will look at a proposal for front-loading the design and planning process. This is intended to drive self-education in eco-innovation, reduce compliance costs and reward those who create positive impacts. It should also help us to focus on creating better futures, by being less retrospective and more future oriented.

## How are rating tools retrospective rather than future oriented?

To assess or rate something, it has to exist – at the very least in the mind. Creating a sustainable built environment is not a hi-tech problem. However, we need to create something that does not yet exist. Instead of waiting for experts to tell us how much further we can go before we cross over thresholds, we could simply take action to reverse direction. The growing raft of complex rating tools obscure the very idea that we could reverse ecological decline through design.[5] They also do little for paradigm shifts or capacity building in design. We noted how poor systems design is *inbuilt*, so simply improving producer and consumer education, values and behaviour will not sustain our threatened life-support systems [Chapter 1]. At the same time, tools that make 'design' a specialized technocratic process, instead of a creative one, tend to dis-empower the citizenry. A sustainable future will require aligning our human-designed systems of development (ie built and institutional infrastructure) with local, regional and global ecosystems. This will also require capacity building in eco-logical design. Most building assessment tools simply measure the 'generalized' future impacts of a building typology or material. They do not facilitate consideration of the ecological and social context, and how it can be improved by design. Because we lack methods to assist design innovations that prevent, reverse or replace negative with positive impacts in development, however, our increasingly sophisticated toys are often called 'design tools' by default. This has caused some to overlook the fact that we lack tools that foster ecological design.[6] Tools that evaluate building *forms* appear to inform design, but do so based on conventional building typologies, not ecological functions. Moreover, if we only have technical, predictive tools, we will not develop our creative skills, only our technical capacity.

## Why can't 'predictive' rating tools also serve as 'design' tools?

Predictive tools are, paradoxically, not future oriented. Rather, they are 'accountancy-based' and retrospective in orientation. They measure the *predicted* impacts of a design, technology or material. So before using the tools, developers and designers already have an investment of time, effort and ego in a proposal or prototype. Therefore, while they may be happy to fine-tune the design, they will not want to start over from scratch. The tools, in fact, almost demand conventional designs. The emphasis on measuring the predicted impacts of a proposed design therefore eclipses creative processes that are directed at generating *new* design concepts or strategies. Of course, design requires 'assessment' in order to both help us understand where existing systems have gone wrong and to evaluate technical aspects of alternatives. However, the tools need to be relevant to the nature of sustainability.[7] Measurement is important, but only if we measure the right things. Sustainable alternatives to standard construction, like earth buildings, have been penalized since the introduction of rating tools through a lack of sustainability research and benchmarking, flawed calculations, and misinformation.[8] Tools also create vested interests in consultancies to assess negative environmental risks and impacts. There would, after all, be little need to trace the myriad negative repercussions of development in a complex natural system if we eliminated them altogether by design.

## Is there a problem with consultancies specializing in applying rating tools?

A raft of consultancies seems to emerge with each new variation in environmental impact assessment tools, because most are proprietary. More jobs in environmental planning and management are, of course, a good thing. However, building assessment tools tend to focus on problems for which there are already solutions. They also tend to make the norm the reference point, instead of the ecology. The fundamental 'design' assumptions underlying many consultants' tools are not very transparent. Users must simply trust the ecological validity of the processes. Knowledge about *how* environmental impacts are measured needs to be transparent because all tools embody assumptions. Often even public domain tools do not explain their implicit assumptions.[9] Further, private consultancies often want to create and protect intellectual property. This means that methods used in measuring impacts tend to be ever more complex and inaccessible to the general public. Consultants' tools sometimes even privatize information through 'commercial in confidence' claims. Thus, without knowing it, environmental managers and consultants may implement methods that are inconsistent with, and even create barriers to, sustainability. By analogy, as Mary O'Brien has pointed out, thousands of pages of analyses were written about the risks, impacts and life-cycle costs of organo-chlorines in paper manufacture – when non-toxic paper bleaching alternatives were already available.[10] Finally, tools shape design. The basic design strategies are also, in essence, being usurped by programme designers and tool applicators, who are often neither ecologists nor designers.

## Surely building rating tools identify problems and improve design, though?

To an extent, of course. New rating tools can assess the relative advantages of alternatives, such as what happens if we add ventilation, thermal mass, insulation or better windows. But designers already know about these options anyway. Besides, the tools cannot yet tell us categorically what combination of passive solar devices would be optimal or cheapest in a given situation. We do not trust what we could call 'ecological intuition' (the mind drawing upon experience), because we do not believe that humans can really be in tune with nature. Yet very early architecture, based on observation and experience (eg the Sumerian civilization), applied very ecologically-sophisticated design. Today, design is seen as (and often is) the application of a style to a standard building typology. One reason that eco-logical design is still considered an 'added' cost or luxury is that developers choose to invest time, energy and money to have a building design rated. This creates a vicious circle, where the rating tool is the beginning and end of design. Applying environmental impact assessments or building rating tools to large commercial buildings can cost over a hundred thousand dollars. Tools sometimes provide points for innovation, but this is usually 'innovation for its own sake'. Imagine if more of that effort were invested in better design (imagination) in the first place. The time and energy that tools require to be devoted to predicting and measuring 'collateral damage' takes human energy away from creative efforts to find alternatives that avoid the damage altogether. These methods reflect and reinforce the obsession with quantification and formulas for compliance that dominated twentieth century environmental management generally.

## Does this mean rating tools don't acknowledge and reward good design?

Currently, most rating tools reward predictions of performance – based on computer models laden with hidden assumptions. 'Stars', certificates and other awards could instead be based on post-occupancy evaluation, or even the factual evidence provided by energy and water meters. That is, on achievement instead of predictions.[11] There has been little follow-up after certificates are awarded to check post-occupancy performance. We seldom check the comfort of the users, the actual mechanical performance or means to improve upon the performance that has been achieved. It may make sense to give awards to actors for convincing performances. It does not make sense to award developers for hiring consultants that can provide the most convincing assurances that the building will perform well. Designers used to be regarded as 'synthesizers' who could grasp the complex relationships in the construction process. Modern architecture, however, has seen a gradual devolution of responsibility to other professions, such as project managers and, more recently, tool programmers and building rating assessors. It will be interesting to see if new digital tools are used to recapture the position of designers or further depose them [Box 23]. The marginalization of design has occurred partly because design skills are not required for 'pruning' costs and cutting corners. Quantity surveyors have been external to the design process, so when tenders come in too high, designs are sometimes altered by non-designers after the fact. If we wanted to foster good design, we would reward net positive impacts and value for money – not the impoverishment of our surroundings. We could give 'minus' stars to developments that are less than resource autonomous.

## So, in a sense, rating tools penalize good design and reward bad design?

In a way. Designers do not usually aim for a surplus of social or natural capital or an improvement in human and environmental health, partly because it goes unrewarded. In some respects, the process treats developers of green buildings like criminals. To stretch the analogy somewhat, incentives are generally limited to reduced costs or expedited approval processes (commuted sentences) or offsets like transferable development rights (plea bargaining). When developers take the initiative to 'do the right thing', we actually make them pay extra to prove their 'innocence'. They have to earn certificates to display on their green buildings. While offenders in the criminal system can get credit for 'community service', developers are not encouraged to provide community service by creating positive off-site impacts. In contrast, developers of conventional buildings that vandalize the environment get off without penalty. The externalities (damage to the public estate) and internalities (embezzled funds) are not recovered. The general public (victims of crime) are not compensated.

We simply require EIAs (such as victim impact statements), which bureaucracies process at public expense. We assume there were 'mitigating circumstances' in the case of conventional developers (ie 'the market made me do it'). We do little about impact prevention through investing in design education and training (rehabilitation). In short, environmental vandalism is normalized and green building is still treated as if it were deviant - a vicious circle that works against systems change.

## Surely rating tools will gradually lead to systems design change?

Rating tools tend to reproduce the conventional design morphology. Because assessment tools reinforce the type of buildings that the tools were based on in the first place, they favour easily measured 'add on' technologies over new integrated design solutions. Yet we have seen that an entirely different kind of urban form and infrastructure is required if buildings are to enable nature to function and sustain and repair itself, let alone expand.[12] Most tools would have difficulty measuring Green Scaffolding or Green Space Walls before construction, for example [Box 44]. Consequently most designers would abandon the idea. Yet common sense, and perhaps even the laws of thermodynamics, suggests that we cannot continue to replace 'free' natural systems with costly, resource-intensive structures. Nor can we afford to rehabilitate natural or social systems after they are degraded and desecrated. In contrast, it would not be difficult to develop planning and design tools that reward developers for designs that add value to the public estate by, for example, creating incentives for ecological space and infrastructure [Chapter 11].[13] Nonetheless, our tools and processes do not encourage us to modify the basic form and design templates of cities, buildings and landscapes. Our templates are anti-ecological. So until our rating and assessment tools change, we cannot blame developers for using the wrong templates.

## Can we really blame rating tools for perpetuating old design templates?

Yes. Computer programs will eventually be able to deal with radical changes to conventional building forms and materials. Currently they still lack adequate data and much of this may be 'commercial in confidence' [Box 23]. Measurements have therefore favoured generic industrial materials for which data are readily available. But buildings today shape our development options tomorrow. Therefore solutions that marginally improve upon a non-sustainable development and favour industrial materials with high embodied waste can actually be *counter*-productive. Even if more eco-efficient than the norm, such buildings still cut off future options, constrict future rights and fail to provide freedom from future harm, such as climate change. Currently, as long as impacts do not exceed those of the norm, there is no incentive to experiment, innovate or re-examine basic design concepts. A building is seen as a winner if it is the 'biggest loser', even if it is detrimental to building users and whole systems health overall. Hence, eco-logical design methods and assessment tools need to be devised that look at value-adding to the community, bioregion and planet. They could respect and foster life, not just resource efficiencies. Front-loading design is necessary to add ecological value. Good design can have a much better 'rate of return' than counting things after the fact.[14]

## Why don't assessment tools encourage the front-loading of design?

Again, the 'reference points' for our existing tools are *conventional* building forms, spaces and materials. Some of our methods of analysis tell us how far we are from home, and others tell us how far we are from ecological collapse. But they do not measure how far we are from sustainability [see

Figure 2, page 21. While tools may increase awareness of our 'numerical' dependency on nature, they deny our 'spiritual' connection, and treat nature as a material resource only. They conceal the fact that we are not yet dealing with remediation – let alone creating positive impacts. Moreover, tools aimed at measuring the inputs and outputs of the parts do not convey their internal transformations and contextual relationships. By developing design methods and assessment tools that map resource flows through the site and urban context, we could find deficiencies of existing development that a design could aim to reverse or ameliorate [Chapter 6]. Similarly, by mapping the biodiversity of the (pre-existing) site and region, we could ensure that development enhances urban nature corridors and microhabitats to help restore and revitalize the bioregion [Chapter 8]. Such site and/or regional ecological analyses would also assist designers in improving their ecological consciousness. But instead of encouraging designers to draw symbiotically upon the free services of nature, our tools encourage the use of universal engineering solutions that disregard the 'glocal' ecology (ie the global and local combined).

## Haven't good results been delivered through universal engineering solutions?

Yes and no. Good design questions end purposes. The industrial engineering approach is often accompanied by a perceived need to reduce everything to numbers, or energy equivalents, for efficiency and accounting purposes.[15] This marginalizes positive impacts, which concepts like 'happiness indicators' and ecological space try to convey [Box 34]. (By analogy, technology itself does not cause war, but it makes efficient annihilation normal.) An overemphasis on numbers reinforces the bias towards mechanistic over fluid design. For example, assessment tools often employ arbitrary 'rules of thumb' that replace creative, synergistic thinking [Chapter 6]. Given their engineering orientation, rating tools tend to prioritize technical fixes that embellish the box, and detract attention from fundamental systems health and environmental flows. In Australia, the NatHERS tool discriminated against eco-logical design by not adequately accounting for the effect of airflows on comfort levels, while the newer AccuRate tool (reputedly) overcompensates for natural ventilation.[16] It does not account for the variable effects of wind on interior air flows. Even when actual buildings are tested, the individual experience of comfort depends on many complex factors. Moreover, many tools reduce things to *one* number for comparing different buildings on different sites with different functions (below). To avoid energy-efficient but sub-optimal building technologies that substitute nature with mechanical equipment, we need assessment concepts, criteria and processes that foster innovative design for specific, *unique* contexts, sites and functions: diversity not uniformity.

## Do quantitative approaches really militate against diverse natural systems?

Arguably yes. Many tools are based on life-cycle analysis (LCA), which aggregates the impacts at each step in the production process. Building rating tools based on LCA help us to quantify impacts at each separate stage of the life of the project, to reduce materials, energy, and emissions or waste. This is a very useful way to improve upon an existing process, or help us to make choices between existing products. But this reductionist framework tends to segregate factors that are inseparable, such as human and environmental health.[17] Such a framework also diverts attention from *total* stocks and flows of materials and energy. It instead encourages adherence to given design templates derived from typical walls, roofs and/or boxes. Complicated processes for comparing and aggregating components of buildings can themselves obscure opportunities for creating more equitable environments and whole system synergies [Box 31]. For example, the author has seen many debates about whether bricks or concrete walls, or wool or cellulous insulation, have more adverse impacts. Being focused on either/or comparisons, people forget to consider organic materials or other forms of insulation combined with living walls or vertical wetlands. Conversely, when people measure the resource efficiency of double skins, they forget to measure their contribution to the urban heat island effect. Although natural systems are variable and hard to predict, measure and compare, they are easy to adapt after construction if they fail to perform well. For example, we can easily adjust the thermal mass, insulation or shading of low-cost organic materials.

## How do we ensure LCA-based tools work to support whole systems design?

To do so, designers need to be aware of the assumptions and values embedded in the design of the tools. We have already mentioned how formulas begin with standard buildings conceived as boxes and discriminate against natural systems. Another example is that LCA uses 'normalization' processes to put entirely incommensurate impacts on the same scale, such as biodiversity impacts and global warming. This is in order to assign numbers for comparison purposes. Some incommensurable issues in life-cycle considerations include:

- Sources, including how (eg mining or herbicides used) and where (eg valuable habitats)
- Species and ecosystems affected (eg stream flow and quality)
- Renewable fuels and materials (eg growth rate of timber)
- Impacts of production (eg life-system costs and impacts on workers)
- Energy used (eg transport of products and workers)
- Longevity (eg reusability and composting)
- Machinery and fuels involved in production (eg upstream fossil fuels)
- Toxins and chemicals (eg global warming and worker health)
- Operating energy and efficiency (eg insulation value)
- Companion products that may be used (eg toxic components)
- Mitigation (eg ecological restoration)
- Reuse and disposal (eg landfill and incineration)
- Management systems (in the forest and the factory)

Incommensurables lead to tradeoffs. Tradeoffs are thus 'designed in' to most decision and design tools. They are an indicator of sub-optimal solutions – not whole systems rationality.

## Isn't it important to determine which factors have the biggest impacts?

Of course. By determining what portion of net impacts the product, process or material constitutes, those with the greatest impacts can be reduced. But trying to reduce the impact or efficiency of each variable in a conventional building does not encourage new design prototypes that support and enhance nature itself. Furthermore, to assign numbers and compare them, these incommensurate, unquantifiable variables need to be reduced to numbers. While expert opinion is often used to determine the relative weightings, 'expertise' reflects the application of established views (which still undervalue nature). One becomes an expert only when one's views are accepted by the mainstream. Moreover, the view of many professionals and academics is that if they cannot apply their tool to a problem, the problem is not relevant to their work. So a problem that does not submit to LCA will not be studied by LCA experts. Moreover, if it does not have immediate business potential, the research to improve these aspects of LCA may not even be funded. Re-design to expand substantive choice and future options will not happen where the methodologies, institutions and processes evolve within an unsustainable social order [Chapter 13]. So we will still need to foster ecologically and socially sound systems of design processes and governance that ensure that important issues – like environmental justice and ecological gain – do not fall through cracks.

## How could LCA tools work against environmental justice?

LCA generally treats each stage of production as a box with inputs and outputs. Whereas embodied energy analysis looks at impacts upstream, and impact assessment looks at impacts downstream, LCA purports to look both upstream and downstream. However, the basic conceptual visors created by measuring inputs and outputs sequentially are seldom if ever questioned [Chapter 6]. In contrast, the first eco-logical design questions might be:

- Do we *need* the product or building, or is there some other way of providing the service?
- Does it improve environmental justice?
- Is the proposed project the best use of the land and human resources?

In practice, LCA can actually be a contradiction in terms. At a conference the author attended on LCA in Arlington, Virginia, for example, a Department of Defence delegate proudly presented its 'green bomb'. It was claimed to be clean and efficient in all stages of its production. At the end of its 'life-cycle', disposal or landfill would not even be an issue. In fact, the green bomb could be said to give a whole new meaning to the term 'zero waste'. Not counting the military, conventional development, with its fossil fuel and chemical dependency, is arguably the biggest contributor to the increasing rate of resource consumption, waste and pollution from a whole system perspective. Yet LCA reduces the built environment to myriad little parts. These tools are designed and applied to look at one element, such as a building or component, in isolation from its social and ecological context. The existence of complex tools also creates the illusion that total impacts are being reduced. Things appear to be 'under control' by technocrats, who are therefore assumed to be accountable.

## Surely the thinking of environmental managers is more sophisticated now?

Perhaps, but when an accounting tool is used, there is pressure to tick all the boxes, in spite of limited information. For example, the author has heard LCA professionals express the view that if the impacts are *not* known, they should not be added in, as that would create inaccuracies. Thus, remarkably, some LCAs have even left out a figure for a suspected toxin because their bio-toxic effects are not yet clear. The toxins that are excluded to avoid 'inaccuracy' can, however, have multiplier effects that nullify the validity of the whole analysis. This could lead to the use of a new product or material with unknown risks. While LCA tools are rapidly expanding their databases, they cannot capture every element – let alone their interactions. It would be better to avoid the use of any questionable chemicals altogether in accordance with the 'precautionary principle'. But precaution is still not positive, or proactive [Chapter 12]. The problem is the narrow, linear-reductionist framework of environmental governance and policymaking that prioritizes mitigation over transformation. For example, at time of writing, state and federal governments in Australia awarded AU$150 million in subsidies to a 'clean coal' (ie less dirty coal) project in Victoria. It will purportedly save 30 per cent on greenhouse emissions and 50 per cent on cooling water compared to other coal production projects. It will, however, only bring 'brown' coal up to the standard of black coal. This protectionism is often the rule. Subsidies for research and development support for fossil fuels is AU$153 million a year in Australia.[18] The newly elected Labor Government has promised AU$500 million to 'clean coal'.[19] Instead, that amount of money could have been spent on systems transformation: converting to solar resources and clean energy to save lives and money.

## Do these decision tools actually impede systems transformation though?

To the extent that they create the impression we are doing anything, yes. We have noted that assessment systems begin with existing, familiar design patterns and materials for which data is easily obtained. Consequently, tool designers (and their computer programs) may overvalue factors for which they have data and hence downplay ecological factors. Even basic materials like earth, straw and stone are highly variable and not proprietary, so less data is available. It is not in large industry's interests to encourage decentralized construction technologies. Thus, for example, the lack of data in a data-based system can create a bias against organic materials. More construction materials are, of course, being added to LCA and building rating tools each year. Nonetheless, the relative value of 'compostable', organic materials in terms of site-specific and/or whole systems health is difficult to measure. Because of the extensive data on recyclable steel, in contrast, it may be easier to specify and apply rating tools to steel structures than to use recycled, cellulose-based structures [Box 21]. Yet cellulose structures can span distances as great as steel, and are likely to have far lower life-cycle impacts. An example is the Japan Pavilion in Expo 2000, Hannover, Germany, which used a timber lattice structure to span a huge area.[20] In short, the focus on what is easily measured (such as conventional industrial materials) can distract attention from exploring new, healthier energy sources and resources.

## So do data-driven processes actually work against eco-logical design?

Often. Some rating tools give more points for reducing the use of a material than avoiding it altogether. Other tools give more points for using harmful materials that have recycled content than using none at all. In at least one rating tool, adding 'extra' sustainably harvested timber – even surplus to requirements – could increase the number of stars that the building earns. In other words, the tool can encourage more resource consumption. While reductionist tools have an important role to fill, they still tend to replace, rather than support, design. Data-intensive processes work against design to the extent that they are not *subsidiary* to design. These processes cultivate society's bean-counting skills, but do not build capacity in eco-logical design. An illustration of data-induced myopia is the comparison of the impacts of paper versus Styrofoam coffee cups. In debates over which container is worse, few stop to realize that the production of coffee has arguably far more negative social and environmental impacts than either kind of cup (ie thinking outside the cup). Even fewer stop to consider what implications this may have for environmental policy and systems design solutions. Cutting back on drinking coffee would not convert coffee production to organic farming or eliminate child slavery in coffee production. Further, given the range of variables, it would be hard to assess which is more harmful: disposable cups from centralized commercial coffee shop machines or smaller high-pressure coffee machines for each staff coffee room. In other words, linear-reductionist frameworks focus attention on the products while more 'needs' are simultaneously being created by the market. Moreover, the data itself can be misleading.

## How can objective, data-based processes be misleading in themselves?

Design criteria and indicators, for example, being based on available and easily accessed data, do not always correspond directly to sustainability goals. Most data has been collected for other isolated purposes in industry, academic and government spheres, not sustainability. Given that the dominant public policy is still growth, governments have traditionally collected information that is relevant to business growth. A lot of data on materials is only available from manufacturers, so the data can even be questionable in some cases. Likewise, the data may not be appropriate to the *context* in which the design is being developed. For example, some kinds of data have historically been collected in zip codes or political districts rather than, say, at the bioregional level. Reliance upon an approach that appears scientific or objective, because it is quantitative, can discriminate against designs that do not fit the standard equations or computer programs. Natural systems are hard to measure, and some technicians would rather just deal with things they can measure. As we saw in the case of some planning approaches, some tools and standards reduce everything to energy. This is a poor surrogate for space, time and the health-giving functions of nature.

## Can't we support the use of natural systems within a reductionist framework?

Theoretically, perhaps, but it does not seem to happen. By prioritizing 'number crunching' over design, we may overlook potential new uses of natural systems, or even uses for talented designers. We know, for example, that passive solar design can avoid fossil fuel systems in the first place. Nonetheless, many engineers prefer unopenable windows in order to facilitate calculations of system or greenhouse gas performance.[21] This is despite the fact that air-conditioning systems account for a substantial portion of electricity use, $CO_2$ emissions and poor indoor air quality. Natural ventilation is difficult to predict and measure, but it can greatly reduce indoor air pollution in certain locations. Yet many tools do not even count air quality. Some tools have actually favoured larger homes despite their embodied waste, because the space-to-envelope ratio is more efficient. These and other glitches are slowly being addressed. However, new design prototypes which are not suited to the application of rating tools may be derided by those who have to figure out how to measure them. To encourage innovation and facilitate new means of satisfying human and ecosystem needs, again, we need to front-load design. Instead, if other jurisdictions have sustainability assessment processes and tools, councils often feel pressure to 'keep up with the Joneses' and divert staff resources to selecting or developing tools. The possession of tools becomes the benchmark for (or symbol of) sustainability.

## Why is it important to front-load systems design and innovation?

Front-loading design is important because, as we well know, most negative impacts and costs are determined at the schematic design stage. For example, to be cost- and eco-effective, natural ventilation, passive solar cooling, and air cleansing with planting walls and the like need to be designed into the basic building or retrofit concept from the outset. To front-load design, we need new standards and design processes, and less burdensome assessment systems to stimulate creativity. The proposed sustainability standard (below) would lift the bar by requiring a new development to constitute an improvement over the original conditions on-site. In other words, to achieve a sustainability standard, a development would leave the ecological conditions better after, than before, development. To create an *extra* incentive, the standard could be relaxed for eco-retrofits so that they simply need to reverse the negative impacts of the previous development. Development approval need not require that the sustainability standard be met, of course. But the concept would signal a priority on eco-logical design processes over compliance activity. Once a conventional design is conceived, or templates applied, it is usually too late. If developers/designers had to report on what they are doing against a sustainability standard, it would refocus development proponents on creative solutions. This could be achieved by what we can call an 'eco-design reporting' process.

## How would an eco-design reporting process differ from standard approaches?

An eco-design reporting process would, at a minimum, require a systematic exploration of leading-edge, eco-logical design options. The eco-design report would document efforts that the designers have undertaken to make the development contribute improvements to the urban context. That is, it would require proponents to report on the eco-solutions they have investigated in relation to net positive design criteria [Box 15]. If such options were rejected, the eco-design report would have to explain why. If the design did not achieve net positive impacts in key areas (eg water, soil, biota, air and human health), the eco-design report would need to demonstrate that this was not yet feasible and affordable in the given situation. It would thus encourage the good faith attempt to achieve Positive Development. Designers may not achieve a sustainability standard, but they would have at least undertaken a systematic exploration of, if not immersion in, eco-logical design. This would, in turn, drive continuous learning and upgrading of skills.

## But don't we need measurable benchmarks for sustainability assessment?

In this new design review process, the baseline would be the pre-existing site or building conditions, rather than estimates of negative impacts of standard buildings performing the same functions.[22] This 'ecological benchmark' recognizes that every site is different and every building project has different functions in relation to surrounding development. Seeking improvements over pre-development conditions would favour retrofitting and remediation projects, but it would also encourage net positive initiatives. One way to meet the standard would be to restore the health of the environment *beyond* the site boundaries – for which there is currently little or no incentive. If, for example, a surrounding area is a 'brown field' or contaminated site, or a run-down sewage treatment facility or abattoir, the new development could convert the waste from these neighbouring areas into a useful or marketable resource. As we have seen, bioconversion is being achieved in industrial ecology projects. There is no reason why it cannot be achieved in urban development [Boxes 32 and 47]. The requirement that eco-logical design strategies be explored would also make the designer think about finding better energy *sources*, rather than just specifying more efficient fossil fuel equipment. Instead of measuring the potential reductions in energy consumption compared to that of a typical building, *any* use of fossil fuels would have to be justified. Thus the eco-design report would help to avoid the existing bias against passive solar design by making it necessary to justify the *source* of energy, whether from fossil or solar resources. If the proponents argued that 'the payback period of solar resources is too high', they would have to show that the payback period of fossil fuel resources is lower.

## Wouldn't this process be just as onerous to apply as rating tools?

It should be less onerous. As is the case in existing impact assessment processes, the amount of detail that is appropriate in an eco-design report would depend on the scale and complexity of the project. In either case, for example, if the project was likely to be resource intensive, a consideration of ecological waste could be required. In the end, the degree of scientific analysis required for the eco-design report would be a matter for the local community and government. However, we would be saving *human* resources, time and energy by not measuring the wrong things. For example, as we saw earlier, the focus of current tools is on 'operating energy' (the energy used to operate a building after construction). This has devalued passive solar design. We invest heavily in tools to predict operating energy – which the electricity meter would read anyway. Operating energy is currently about four to ten times greater than embodied energy over the life of a typical building.[23] However, this is only because most buildings are not designed for passive solar heating, cooling and ventilating. In sunny Australia, for example, only about 3 per cent of homes are reported to employ passive solar design. If buildings took advantage of passive/active solar technology, operating costs would be negligible. In other words, there would be little need for rating tools which emphasize 'operating' energy if we used passive solar design. With full cost pricing of energy and materials, embodied energy would become even more significant.

Figure 8 Diagram of the sustainability standard

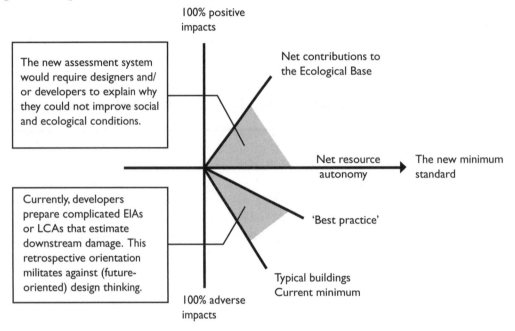

## But doesn't the embodied energy of passive solar buildings cost extra?

With good design, it should cost less, as there tends to be more embodied energy in hi-tech equipment and industrial materials. The eco-design report would also shift the burden of proof from assessors to designers or project proponents, who are in the best position to avoid impacts in the first place. We have seen that the tendency is to starve the design process while adding ever more complex bureaucracy, technology and compliance activity. Yet this activity does not make project proponents re-examine their own untested assumptions, such as 'sustainable design costs more'. Environmental impact assessments and rating tools track the extremely complex negative impacts of fossil fuels, rather than explain how they cannot be avoided.[24] By avoiding or reversing impacts, and improving human and ecosystem health, designers could reduce assessment and reporting costs. Eco-design reports would be less costly than rating tools and conventional assessment processes in that they would not require outsourcing to specialist consultants. Since the work and expense incurred in reporting would be greater for projects that are more harmful, the costs would shift to those who do not attempt sustainable design for a change.

## What would be the role of government in the eco-design reporting process?

Currently, in most places, proposals that meet a minimum standard are automatically approved. In contrast, eco-design reports would enable public sector assessors to suggest alternative, more creative solutions. At present, the focus on individual buildings and their components limits our ability to rethink buildings and urban form, and their functions, in relation to their ecological and regional context. Planners could facilitate net Positive Development by mapping:

- The costs of existing systems (ie past, present and 'opportunity' costs)
- The costs of inaction (ie future costs that will result from not eco-retrofitting)

This would help to identify deficiencies that a new or retrofitted development could correct. However, to work towards a resource balance between a city and its context at any scale (eg bioregion or ecoregion), positive environments would need to *over*-compensate for any unavoidable impacts of the proposed development. By identifying regional 'surpluses', planners can ensure buildings are designed for, say, the incorporation of the most suitable sources of energy and materials for the given location [Chapter 4]. Planners can also identify materials with potentially positive social and environmental impacts. For example, the production of sustainably-farmed biobased materials could contribute to rural revitalization (or reimbursement) as well as healthier urban environments.[25] In this process, planners can also help to identify leverage points where modifications can generate constructive ripple effects throughout the region, or what Lerner calls 'urban acupuncture' [Chapter 1].

## But don't we need building rating tools and, if so, how do we improve them?

Building rating tools need to transcend the dominant environmental paradigm that holds that all development must inevitably have net negative impacts. Based on inputs and outputs, their 'design DNA' is aimed squarely at marginal improvements to an unsustainable building prototype. To summarize the points above, building rating tools could be re-designed to move from:

- **Retrospective analysis to future-oriented design**: The analysis of the predicted impacts of a proposed design can reinforce old forms and patterns of development at the expense of forward-looking processes that seek to value add and create new synergies.
- **Impact reduction to impact reversal**: The emphasis on mitigating negative impacts can be at the expense of eco-innovations that seek to improve social and ecological conditions through positive off-site and on-site impacts and health improvement.
- **Building on templates to changing underlying concepts**: Tools that encourage incremental modifications to conventional building templates can delay or prevent the re-design of basic infrastructure, spaces and forms that would increase the ecological base.
- **Universal engineering to natural systems solutions**: The perceived need to reduce everything to numbers can lead to mechanistic approaches that exclude the ecology, because natural systems defy simplistic measures (being complex systems).
- **Aggregating impacts to mapping flows**: Analyses that aggregate measurements to get a point value can obscure the potential for whole systems efficiencies to positively affect total resource flows by creating synergies among systems on different scales or levels.
- **Sequential and segmented processes to integrated ones**: The focus of LCA-based analyses on inputs and outputs of processes at separate stages during the construction process can encourage sub-optimal changes at the expense of rationalizing the whole supply chain.

- **Data-driven indicators to implementing change**: Overvaluing factors that we have data for can come at the expense of mapping systems dynamics to find better means of meeting needs or new 'leverage points' for positive ripple effects throughout the system.
- **An individual project to a contextual perspective**: The focus on the efficiency of individual buildings and their components can be at the expense of rethinking buildings in relation to their context to improve social, structural and ecological deficiencies of the urban area.
- **Fossil fuel reduction to a shift to solar resources**: The emphasis on energy reduction (through efficient use of fossil fuels) distracts attention from means to convert to healthier *sources* of energy and tends to lead to 'under-design' of passive solar systems.
- **Reducing space to value adding space**: Pseudo-efficiency and cost reduction through zoning and minimizing spaces in buildings can come at the expense of optimizing spatial resources by simultaneously accommodating human activity and viable ecosystems.
- **Reductionist accounting to design reporting**: Reductionist analysis can lead to tradeoffs between positive and negative factors at the expense of holistic design processes that explore wider options with the aim of increasing social, natural and economic capital.

Analytical processes to help front-load design are further developed in subsequent chapters. We will next look at design methods that would assist in visualizing total environmental flows, as opposed to just quantifying inputs and outputs.

# 6
# Design
# Methods

From eco-efficient
to eco-productive
buildings

We have discussed how greening the built environmental can provide many opportunities for triple bottom line and sustainability gains at no additional cost. Nonetheless, the construction industry is widely recognized as trailing behind most other sectors in green initiatives and outcomes.[1] Over the years, studies by government, academic, community and industry groups have identified technical and institutional barriers to the uptake of eco-logical design principles and practices in both renovations and new buildings [Box 7]. A host of new institutional arrangements and incentives have been put forward to address some of these impediments, such as performance contracting, green procurement, partnering, building rating tools, reduced mortgages for green buildings, and so on. However, greening the built environment will require more than attention to production and consumption drivers in the building supply chain. And a new architecture will require new design methods.

There have been many green demonstration projects that show how improvements can be made within the ambit of traditional, tried and tested, passive solar design. Many of these, however, just graft passive solar design techniques onto the basic house template. The rationale is that people supposedly prefer what is already on the market. In a few cases, some have tried to go further and integrate sustainable principles into the fabric of the development.[2] For example, the Village Homes development in Davis, California, has received much attention over the past 40 years as a demonstration of integrated passive solar housing, water sensitive landscaping and environmental amenity. Yet the example was not followed in the suburbs that sprung up around it. Today, the property values in Village Homes are significantly higher than the 'houses on steroids' in the adjacent suburbs. Such passive solar homes do not cost more to build. They are in high demand because they provide a high quality of life and status.[3]

Given the available technical and institutional solutions, a major barrier to sustainable design would appear to be the lack of design capacity. Although passive solar design concepts and improved design processes have been around for a long time, they have not been adopted by the majority of designers or developers. Of course, most buildings are not designed by architects – it is generally accepted that only around 5 per cent are designed by architects. 'Green' designers cannot be expected to drive change through the design fields and construction industry on their own. They still have only a niche market at present and it is hard enough for them to get 'light green' designs appreciated. Further, there is a countervailing force to more capacity building in environmentally sensitive design: the growing number of mass-produced project homes and factory-produced prefabricated structures.[4] The overriding objective in the design of these has not been sustainability; rather, it is the minimization of price and installation time. Nonetheless, whether one-off custom design, robotically constructed buildings, 'Dot Com' and modular homes, or even urban villages, examples of even light green design are still rare.

## Why hasn't green, let alone sustainable, design caught on yet on a large scale?

It was suggested earlier that one of the reasons for the persistence of old design models is 'input–output' thinking. Even green design reflects this dominant reductionist form of problem solving [Chapter 3]. The implicit goal in design has been mere 'eco-efficiency', through optimizing energy, air and water inputs and outputs at the building envelope. This does not encourage re-thinking design purposes or adding value to ecological and social goods and services.[5] That is to say, mere eco-efficiency gains are not likely to enhance the conditions for whole system sustainability. Designers – and we are all designers – need to question our own tacit assumptions.[6] Here we will examine the lack of whole systems thinking still apparent in 'green' building design, due to:

- Vestiges of conventional design methods
- The old industrial frameworks in which buildings are produced
- Unquestioned dogma about durability and efficiency

Then a new design method will be proposed. It challenges the focus on the building envelope in both light green and non-green design typologies. This alternative 'flows approach', inherent in design for eco-services, would integrate ecosystems into the building structure itself. The concepts of ecological space, Green Scaffolding, Green Space Walls, provide examples of how this can be achieved.

## Besides rating tools, what has been done to promote green building design?

There have been many green building workshops and think-tanks for built environment professionals. However, they seem to always get stuck at the 'identification of barriers and weaknesses' stage. It is easy to get bogged down in the impediments facing green designers. The author has convened courses and workshops aimed at trying to leapfrog from 'light green' to deep sustainability through built environment design.[7] One of these workshops (in 2003), for example, consisted primarily of green building practitioners, selected for their expertise and advocacy of eco-logical design. The task before them was to explore new strategies to foster deep green design and eco-retrofitting, and find opportunities for real change in the construction industry. The express purpose was to go beyond standard notions of green design, and avoid 're-inventing the wheel' or listing impediments. Several devices were employed to try to start from where other green building workshops tend to leave off. One such strategy was having potential 'solutions' to debate. These included:

- Articulation of a new paradigm: design that reverses the environmental impacts of existing development and increases natural capital and biodiversity (ie Positive Development)
- Possible incentive schemes to implement the eco-retrofitting of suburbs, utilizing design teams and performance contracting, etc

- Group critiques of proposed eco-retrofitting technologies (such as the Solar Core, the reverse Trombe wall, greenhouse terrariums, and integrated sprinklers from water tanks in homes and landscapes for cooling and fire mitigation, landscaping, etc)

## Did the idea of skipping impediments and focusing on implementation work?

Actually, no. The assumption was that best practice is as 'green' as we can hope for in the given socio-political climate. The proposition introduced at the beginning – that the bar for green design could be raised to a 'sustainability standard' – was ignored. Instead, the conversation centred around why the standard light green model was not more widely adopted. This was understandable, of course, as the expert participants had made huge personal sacrifices in trying to get 'light green' accepted. Green designers are still generally viewed as either radical fringe or 'boutique'. They face an uphill battle to get their work adopted in an era of mass-produced suburbs. In this context, designers cannot be expected to push the boundaries further. On the other hand, the educational and incentive programmes of government will not progress to a more ecological level if ecology is not on the agenda of leading green design professionals. As we noted earlier, even if all buildings were green by today's 'best practice' standard, such green cities and suburbs would not be sustainable. Strategies to implement 'greener' buildings are gradually making more headway, but they do not target the fundamental issue: the lack of sound eco-logical design premises and models in the first place. To design sustainable environments, then, ecological designers need to challenge their field's 'best practice' design precepts, processes and products – not set the bar at the height of their comfort zone.

## Did the conclusions of the workshop participants support this view?

The consensus of the participants was that, while there were many impediments to the uptake of eco-logical design, the 'lack of public awareness' was the biggest issue. This popular view translates roughly into 'the problem is other people'. Most workshops that aim at furthering the sustainable development agenda seem to end up as tacit 'buck passing' sessions:

- Architects say they cannot do things differently because clients and builders lack environmental concern or awareness
- Builders say they have to do what the designers and clients tell them to do, and designers make lots of 'practical' mistakes (ie do not follow convention)
- Developers say they have to follow the market, but virtually no resource autonomous homes exist in the market
- Clients say they cannot find architects or builders that can deliver truly green but low-cost buildings, and that many actually discourage their client's green ambitions
- Educators say, to quote an architecture department head, "We will teach sustainable design when the profession (ie accreditation panels) demands it"

In this vicious circle, *other* people in government, community or business organizations will always need to change first.

## Surely green designers recognize that they have to take the initiative?

Green designers are generally beleaguered, like other environmentalists. Even now that most people accept the idea of climate change, no one is saying 'greenies' might also be right about other things as well. Deep green designers are few in number and have few resources in comparison with large development firms. Yet they are expected to do for free what large firms with huge budgets refuse to do until others 'prove' to them that change is painless and profitable. Many green building non-government organizations (NGOs) have formed to educate the industry and increase demand for green buildings, but they tend to serve their members' business interests. Their primary aim is therefore raising consumer awareness and demand for existing products – not deep social, structural and institutional transformation or paradigm shifts. Of several strategies canvassed by the workshop participants, therefore, the preferred option was to tap local, state and federal funding programmes. Getting funds for a demonstration case study to educate people was deemed the best way to proceed, whether that meant a private home that opened to the public periodically or a permanent display home. The strategy adopted was to develop a business plan to convince government of the merits of financing a green demonstration project. However, the funding of a green home would be unlikely, given that this was hardly a new idea. 'Best practice' retrofitted homes are already displayed in popular, annual 'solar home tours' around Australia and presumably elsewhere.

## So what's wrong with the current best practice approach to green design?

Green design is still aimed at making conventional design more energy efficient, rather than sustainable.[8] We have already flagged some examples of basic principles and practices that do little to further eco-logical design:

- **Resource minimization**: A bias towards 'standard' passive solar design templates with minimalist use of natural systems can limit design experimentation and eco-innovation, and lead to design approaches that are not responsive to local ecosystems or cultures.
- **Single function spaces**: A priority on space minimization can lead to the single function use of space enclosed by rigid boxes that reduce the opportunity for biological landscaping, ecological functions and eco-services to be integrated with the structure itself.
- **Durability**: The belief that permanence is always a virtue, even in relatively temporary residential construction, can lead to reduced adaptability and reversibility (eg concrete slab and steel instead of compostable, organic, easily modified materials or composites).
- **Densification**: Contemporary approaches to infill development and land-use planning tend to privatize and alienate urban space, and de-nature the urban environment. Cities and buildings could (figuratively) serve as oases, rather than deserts.

We noted above that eco-logical design would, on a level playing field, be more eco-efficient than standard construction. This is because it utilizes 'free' natural systems and reduces the social and environmental costs of development. Nonetheless, there is little use of passive solar design, let alone design for eco-services, in contemporary building design. At best, we aim for only 'optimal' (ie minimal) use of passive solar design.

## Wouldn't 'minimal' passive solar design be cheaper and more 'efficient'?

No. Most 'green' buildings are *under-designed* for passive solar energy. Consequently, such buildings need backup equipment, which makes green design seem more expensive. Yet we have seen that there is a *surplus* of sunlight hitting the Earth (thousands of times more than humans need). A surplus means that, to a reasonable extent, solar energy can be exploited for human use without harming natural systems [Chapter 4]. But instead, we are using fossil fuels many thousands of times faster than they are produced. Operating the existing built environment constitutes about 20 per cent of fossil fuel use, much of which could be avoided by eco-retrofitting. From a systems perspective, therefore, it makes no sense to use fossil fuels in heating, cooling and ventilating buildings [Box 22]. Passive solar design can fulfil these functions more cheaply and efficiently. Thus, for example, once installed, light shelves, light wells and shade cloths can avoid glare while bouncing natural light deep into space without any electricity. Solar stacks, Solar Cores and reverse Trombe walls provide heating, cooling and ventilating at little or no operating cost. In short, minimalist 'optimizing' of solar design can create sub-optimal results and make solar design appear more expensive than it need be.

## Why are many green buildings under-designed for passive solar gains?

There are several reasons for this. First, the dominant view is still that only energy conservation features that have a short payback period are justifiable. Fossil fuel-based systems are not required to meet this payback criterion, of course, because 'standard' equipment is viewed as the norm. That is, first, the cost of fossil fuel systems is not seen as 'extra'. However, mechanical equipment requires regular maintenance and often needs replacement during the life of the building. Second, solar technologies have always had to compete with fossil fuels on a sloped playing field, because fossil fuels are under-priced, due to subsidies and perverse incentives.[9] Moreover, their externalities like global warming and militarism are not weighed in. The ecological waste that fossil fuels entail is usually ignored altogether [Chapter 4]. Third, engineers are generally trained to optimize things, and not use anything 'extra' – yet some benefits outweigh their costs and have a return on investment. Fourth, there is a tendency in analyses to reduce nature to a 'dead' resource. Thus, for example, the '30 the Bond' building in Sydney is an exemplar of energy efficiency. It encased a landmark natural rock in glass for thermal mass. However, while exploiting this natural attribute of the site, it removed the feature from the public estate – much like turning a moose into a moose head trophy. We probably cannot over-employ 'free' solar design and natural features – as long as the ecological waste is minimized. Sunspaces, atriums, planting walls, Green Scaffolding, Green Space Walls, the Solar Core and reverse Trombe walls can all use materials and structures with relatively little embodied waste.

## Still, wouldn't it be wasteful to over-utilize passive solar systems?

Minimalist passive solar design generally only averages out daily (diurnal) temperature swings. This means that conventional passive solar homes will be too hot during heatwaves and too cold during 'coldwaves'. Therefore, 'light green' buildings will require backup mechanical heating and cooling systems. In fact, many sets of green criteria and indicators in moderate climates assume the need for non-renewable energy systems. But this extra mechanical equipment could be avoided altogether in many cases if passive solar design were not seen as 'extra'. For example, there are many homes in extreme climates that are comfortable year round without mechanical heating or cooling. If well designed, insulation, glass or rock thermal mass adds little to overall cost and impacts. Likewise, shade cloths can be designed to create a cooling effect by generating air movement as well as shading. This is especially the case where a source of cool air can be created, like a shaded garden pool. Water (from rainwater tanks) can drip over planted wire screens for evaporative cooling and even fire mitigation. In areas like Australia, where many homes do not have central heating, passive solar retrofitting would be easier to implement than in countries where there is already a huge investment in centralized heating systems. Nonetheless, this opportunity for energy and greenhouse gas reduction is being lost by new Australian homes. They are being designed to require air-conditioning, which makes them vulnerable to energy 'brown outs' and ongoing maintenance costs. Not only that, passive solar concepts are also applied in an overly standardized way.

## What is wrong with a standardized approach to passive solar design?

Good design is always 'site-specific' as each ecosystem and microclimate, and each urban site and context, is biophysically unique. However, textbook passive solar templates are often superimposed on different sites and situations. This results from many causes, such as a lack of imagination, time pressures, the demands of industrialized construction systems, and so on. But another reason for the 'one size fits all' approach is the international style of architecture that grew out of the Bauhaus.[10] This 'International Style' has been credited by some for the 'mutually assured destruction' between modern buildings and the environment in the 20th century. Although some early proponents of the movement were conservationists, many of their disciples were more frugal with forms than with natural resources. The tacit belief that 'ideal forms' can be applied across the board infected the dominant approach to energy-efficient design.[11] As a result, green building has sometimes been taught as if it were a 'style', composed of certain kinds of hard-edged forms and features. The countervailing approach to the 'nuts and bolts' or technocratic style – the 'nuts and berries' or hippy style – in contrast, stererotyped passive solar design as 'mud brick igloos'.[12]

## Was this because the 'International Style' was what consumers wanted?

Consumers, or future building users, are seldom really asked. They are just given 'choices' among existing norms. Further, there are few options for them to choose from. (There are exceptions, of course, such as the 'organic' ING building, which was the outcome of user participation in design.[13]) It is widely assumed that most consumers either want their home to look like all the others on the block, or to look stunningly different. Of course, passive solar design could meet either aim. However, fashionable and passive solar design have tended to be seen as mutually exclusive. Standardized passive solar design strategies, while climate-sensitive, often work against local ecosystems and cultures in the same way that the International Style failed to respect regional cultural traditions.[14] There are passive solar design templates for each climatic zone that are optimal from an energy-efficiency standpoint. However, these templates seldom respect the site's ecosystems and biodiversity. Design templates work against the exploration of creative, site-specific solutions that would, for example, provide habitats for native flora and fauna. As a case in point, 'slab on ground' construction is often considered the 'bottom line' in temperate climates in Australia – regardless of the site, slope, landscape, biodiversity or soil productivity. But if we valued the soil as necessary to our survival, we would hesitate to bury it alive. We could instead consider having vertical thermal mass in walls to allow the Earth and its micro-organisms to breathe, absorb runoff, grow plants and produce soil, and just 'be'.[15] Adequate insulation for ground floors can be made from recycled styrofoam, strawbale, and so on.[16]

## Doesn't standardization make adoption of passive solar design easier?

To some extent, standardization could increase adoption by developers of mass-produced homes. At the same time, however, it contributes to the devaluation of design and diversity itself. Also, as a result of these templates, a suite of negative stereotypes regarding passive solar design have emerged. These further impede its adoption. Many of the 'excuses' for not applying eco-logical design principles may stem from boredom inspired by the replication of standardized passive solar design templates. This is a criticism that has been levied against the BedZed project in London, for example.[17] The idea that green design is 'boring' could partly be attributed to the unimaginative solar design templates that are presented in educational materials. Several architecture teachers have explained their resistance to green design to the author by saying passive solar design is 'ugly'. One could see this as a failure of design ability among architecture teachers. Conversely, this could be because so many people *not* trained in architecture design passive solar homes, due to a vacuum caused by the architecture profession [Box 25]. It should be emphasized that the rebuttal to nearly all the stereotypes would be that 'it all depends on the design'. That is, the problem is not the solar design principles themselves, but poor application. In addition to a lack of design imagination, there is a failure to optimize space for the needs of both humans and nature. But this is essential where space is increasingly scarce and costly.

## Why is it essential to use space for both natural systems and human functions?

The emphasis of (conventional) urban design has been on social engineering, managerial processes and mechanical efficiency.[18] Thus, as we have seen, urban consolidation has often been undertaken in a manner that eradicates nature from buildings and cities [Chapter 3]. The creation of 'dead space' (lifeless or privatized space) in so-called green planning and design is due partly to the confusion between:

- A city's *spatial footprint* (land area) and
- A city's *ecological footprint* (total area required to support its material and energy consumption)

Since urban space is at a premium in dense urban areas, the norm is still to 'zone' buildings – as well as cities – to achieve minimal interior and exterior spaces for each function and human activity. Ostensibly, the aim is to reduce energy consumption and greenhouse emissions in energy intensive functions like transport or the heating and cooling of buildings. But these aims are not necessarily achieved by smaller, specialized or single-function spaces. On the other hand, large high-rise buildings with open plan flexible interiors also manage to create 'dead' office spaces with stuffy, polluted air. At the same time, the zoning or separation of social and environmental functions tends to exclude or choke off natural systems. Few buildings are designed to support plant life – the 'canaries' in our urban 'coal mines'.[19] Likewise, outdoor urban spaces are usually designed wastefully because they are used only as decorative backdrops. Urban landscaping often seems to be merely embalming fluid for dead architectural forms. Through the multi-functional use of space, however, we can create positive synergies between social and biological functions, while using resources more efficiently from a whole systems perspective.

## Can we increase services while reducing the ecological and physical footprint?

Yes. However, spaces in urban areas are increasingly allocated to private consumption, not public services.[20] This is partly due to land values, but also partly because vacant land is perceived to be 'wasted' space that should be converted to private indoor uses. We have mentioned some ways of increasing the space available for functioning ecosystems in buildings and cities that *neither* increase 'sprawl' or 'Manhattanization' *nor* reduce economic and social activity. Design for eco-services can complement either high-density or low-density living. Again, we can:

- Increase the use of spaces over streets, or on façades and roofs, by adding green space frames that combine ecological, climatic, aesthetic and practical functions [Box 4].
- Eco-retrofit low-rise buildings so that there is more 'ground area' on-site than existed prior to construction by integrating planters with roofs, atriums or balconies, etc.[21]

- Design buildings so that the landscape flows through the ground level (eg using vertical thermal mass or Trombe walls, etc, to capture and distribute heat or coolness).
- Integrate Living Machines and vertical wetlands with both indoor and outdoor areas that serve additional social functions as well, such as meeting, recreation and eating places.[22]
- Convert some suburban streets to public uses (other than driving and parking), such as food production, gardens or skate parks where homes are accessed by, say, shared golf carts.[23]
- Create incentives for owners of urban buildings to contribute to nature corridors planned by ecologists (eg roof gardens or suburban roads covered by space frame gardens).
- Retrofit existing suburbs in a way that increases the number of dwellings without significantly reducing land area, such as adding second floor units [Box 8].
- Retrofit public parks to provide more ecosystem goods and services, such as climate mitigation and fire prevention using structures like green space frames.

In addition to questioning our implicit assumptions about space, we need to question our assumptions about durability. Some building and product designers believe that new but 'durable' buildings are more sustainable than retrofitted ones, even if the latter use recycled materials.[24]

### Don't durable buildings avoid the complexities of recycling and retrofitting?

In general, long-lasting products and buildings can be a virtue. But there are many factors that contribute to a tension between permanence and reversibility. For example, many people will wish to modify their homes to express themselves, or meet changing needs as they age, rather than leave their neighbourhoods. Many who have to move for specialized jobs will want to personalize their new homes. On the other hand, some architects appear to want the homes they design to remain unchanged forever, as humble monuments. But durable designs are not necessarily more sustainable. For example, durability usually means the use of mined 'industrial' materials like concrete, steel and aluminium, which are high in embodied water and energy.[25] The reasoning behind durable buildings is that they will have lower impacts if those impacts are *amortized* over the predicted life-cycle of production, occupancy and demolition. But that is not a lower impact in absolute terms. Moreover, we may amortize negative impacts over the life of the building but ignore how long it takes to restore the environment after 'durable' materials are wrenched from it [Chapter 4]. Organic materials are generally low in embodied energy compared to materials 'mined' from the Earth's crust. In fact, durable materials can be less durable than organic ones.[26] Nature moves. Organic structures such as strawbale and earth often last longer than industrial ones, as they move and settle with the earth over time.[27] Both organic and durable materials can crack or become unstable, and organic structures can often be easier to repair. Recently a concrete and steel central freeway in Brisbane, Australia, was closed for months simply because of a hairline crack.

### Even so, surely organic materials can't last as long as durable mined materials?

Buildings are seldom demolished because they lack durable materials as such. They are demolished because durable materials either fail or lack functional adaptability. In New Zealand, Britain and Australia, for example, 'durable' commercial buildings last only about 50 years, in the US about 35, and in Japan about 20, due to changing land uses.[28] This is not because they are too soft and fluid. In Australia, durable buildings are often imploded to make way for changing owner needs, long before the end of their structural life span, due to market demands or land-use trends. Also, durable buildings do not always respond well to constantly changing technologies, occupant needs and social trends [Box 8]. But design for durability is problematic in terms of social sustainability as well. Durable buildings limit future living options and interactive responses to demographic, lifestyle and value changes. So the mainstream goal of replacing old, leaky buildings with durable 'green' ones needs to be questioned. Recycling and/or reuse of components and materials is seen by many as an alternative to durable buildings. However, even if durable building parts and fixtures are reusable, the basic building templates may change, making such components redundant.

## But doesn't recycling materials have more negative impacts than re-use?

Often recycling has re-manufacturing impacts. But many of the current negative impacts of recycling relate directly to design and could easily be reduced or avoided. Organic or healthy materials in building components, office fixtures and furnishings could greatly reduce resource extraction impacts, toxic emissions and water usage over the many inevitable renovations. Organic materials, such as earth, or 'bio-based' materials from plants, use fewer petrochemicals components in construction. As such, they are generally better for human health, and healthier workplace environments have been shown to attract and retain renters [Chapter 2]. So even from an economic standpoint, the status quo industrialized approach to refurbishment and recycling is questionable. After all, virtually all products made from petrochemicals can be replaced by industrial (non-hallucinogenic) hemp or other bio-based materials.[29] Such plant-based materials, at least in interior building products and furnishings, could greatly reduce the health impacts related to indoor air pollution (estimated at around US$400 billion per year in America).[30] Healthier, bio-based materials also lend themselves to more interesting and adaptable designs, of which there are many inspiring examples.[31] They would also give people more choice and variety over time [Box 54]. Hence compostable building materials and reversible designs may be more sustainable than recyclable but mined components – especially in office fitouts that are replaced on a regular basis. Currently, we are not really able to measure and compare basic options, like re-use versus recycling. This is because we measure costs of alternatives within the constraints of *existing* commercial circumstances. We need to compare the costs of cities to their bioregion as a whole in both cases, not just the costs of the increments.

## Would durable structures be more sustainable, from a whole systems view?

Paradoxically, it is in a sense the longevity of poor design and durable materials that has meant decades of unnecessary energy usage with toxins accumulating in the built environment. Because of changing contextual forces (economic, social and technological), durable incremental change tends to create rigid cages that preclude future options. In fact, one of the reasons that we have not provided housing for the world's poor is that we tend to assume they need 'conventional' development. (Or perhaps it is because that is all we now have to export.) We saw already how old earthen structures in the third world could be retrofitted with low-cost wire technologies to reduce earthquake damage. Similarly, low-tech forms of Green Scaffolding could be used to reinforce buildings in developed nations.[32] New and eco-retrofitted buildings using organic or biobased materials for non-structural elements could also increase their life expectancy through greater adaptability.[33] The use of compostable materials would at least increase society's capacity to reverse dumb development decisions later. In other words, it makes more sense to have adaptable design with reversible consequences than to make incremental decisions with permanent consequences. One way to support 'reversible' land use and development would be to legislate to prohibit the construction materials from being sent to landfill or incinerated at any stage of construction (resource extraction, construction, occupancy and demolition). Compostable materials sourced from solar energy sources, such as sustainable farming and forestry, would then be preferred.

## Even if healthier materials are used, don't they still end up in landfill?

Yes, because we still usually take everything to landfill and mix it together. Little attention has thus far been paid to reducing the negative impacts of office renovations – whether materials are healthy and compostable or durable but reusable. The monetary and material flows through conventional renovation activity can be higher, overall, than that of new construction. For example, the design of modular office layout systems usually leads to a complete gutting and reconstruction of interiors for new tenants. Moreover, even green renovation activity is usually undertaken with a view only to efficiency, not to improving health.[34] As in new construction, little thought is given to the ecological efficacy of the designs – let alone the resource flows and waste embedded in renovations. In addition to the often toxic office fit-outs, tons of office furnishings are transported at great expense to landfill sites, where their toxic components gradually seep into the soil and water. As Graham Treloar has observed, there can be more adverse energy and health impacts from furniture and carpets than from the building itself over its life-cycle.[35] The transport of office waste to landfill could also be reduced by office layout systems composed of organic, non-toxic materials. At the end of their life spans, these materials could be ground up on the construction site and composted in urban parks, or sold as mulch and fertilizer to local gardeners. Building fixtures, furnishings and carpets are, nonetheless, generally regarded as a separate and marginal issue in green building. But just as both the car and its fuel have impacts, so both the building and its contents have impacts.

## Aren't there health problems associated with organic materials as well?

There can indeed be health risks with most materials. This is another reason that design is always case specific. Radon, for example, can be found in earth construction as well as in concrete. It is a colourless, odourless gas produced by the radioactive decay of the element radium. It can be found anywhere because it becomes dissolved in water. But although radon must be considered in using earth walls or concrete basements in some regions, its emissions can be reduced through simple design strategies.[36] Similarly, earth that is suitable for pressed earth walls construction can be found in most places.[37] However, care must be taken to ensure the soil has not been contaminated with toxic waste, sheep dip, asbestos or other toxins from prior human activities. Bio-based materials can also have problems.[38] Many particleboards are still bound together with formaldehyde – even though safer, non-toxic compounds are now available (eg masonite or strawboard). Of course, agriculturally-based fibre materials are only sustainable relative to mineral-based materials if they are derived from sustainable agricultural systems and processes.[39] Also, crops used for any purpose extract minerals from soils, which need replenishment.[40] Generally, though, organic or solar materials are better than mined ones for non-structural uses, from a life-cycle and health perspective. However, there has been relatively little investigation of the potential problems associated with, or benefits of, organic materials.[41] This may be partly because most research goes into industrial materials, as they are proprietary. This bias will only change when we begin to count the waste embedded in conventional industrial systems and/or the public costs of existing systems of development – rather than seeing them as a neutral baseline [Chapter 7].

## Wouldn't prefabricated buildings make more sense than compostable ones?

Prefabricated units could conceivably contribute to value-adding and positive impacts in urban areas, but *not* under existing planning, design and delivery systems. Currently, most prefabricated homes and buildings have few redeeming ecological or social features. Further, they are not tailored to the biophysical context of particular sites. Plans for kit homes and modularized industrial architecture have been around for decades, but can now be purchased on the web. This has been accompanied by 'Dot Com' architecture, where plans can be individualized through an interactive 'design' process between the purchaser and designer over the internet.[42] Whether prefabricated buildings advance or derail the trend towards greener buildings will not depend on their materials and energy consumption alone. It will also depend on whether the infrastructure for eco-services, such as ecological space, is incorporated into the resulting buildings and/or cluster developments. So far, even 'environmentally conscious' Dot Com designs have a tendency to perpetuate design concepts, materials and processes that are largely incompatible with deep sustainability principles. As in the case of conventional green design, green Dot Com designs do not increase the ecological base or public estate. Often, for example, modular houses are squeezed close together to save land and money. And, because they are essentially 'boxes' connected by roads, they can replicate the existing environmental defects of conventional suburbs.

## Wouldn't sustainability be served by housing more people more cheaply?

No one could object to more inexpensive housing – in combination with policies for achieving sustainable population levels, of course. Prefabricated homes have the *potential* to house more people more cheaply, depending on the externalities of their production. However, current models of prefabricated housing are high in embodied energy, so their system-wide costs are high. Prefabricated industrial structures also have the danger of becoming like the car industry, where, historically, entrenched special interests have stifled innovation. For decades, corporate power diverted resources away from public transport and blocked innovation in energy-efficient cars.[43] In return, we received a (superficially) wide array of car bodies within a very limited range of substantive design choices. If it was not for the work of environmental NGOs, we might not have real choices today, like electric fuel cell or hybrid cars. For example, the Rocky Mountain Institute ideas for hybrid cars were widely published, rather than patented, in order to drive competition.[44] New modular homes are also likely to create more pressure to demolish existing homes, rather than retrofit them, based on the argument that new homes are more efficient and affordable. After all, many of the externalities of resource extraction and landfill are still excluded from the analyses [Chapter 8]. While reducing construction costs to the owner, the long-term costs of conventional approaches to urban space and urban form must be paid for by the taxpaying public eventually.

## Is there an ecologically sound but practical form of prefabricated buildings?

As suggested earlier, a more cost-efficient means of reducing sprawl, energy consumption and greenhouse emissions might be to retrofit the suburbs, rather than replace existing homes with new energy-efficient modular buildings. But if prefabricated buildings eventually prevail over site-specific retrofitting, they could be used in ways that reduce net land coverage and resource flows. Prefabricated structures could also be constructed off the ground and combined with greenhouses for heating, cooling and ventilating and for food production. Or resource autonomous, prefabricated greenhouse units could be added on top of existing suburban, single-storey houses. The Habitat

67 development in Montreal, for example, provides an interesting model for prefabricated units. Based on Lego blocks, the design created private spaces and gardens by stacking units up in an irregular, perpendicular fashion.[45] But although site planning and design modifications can ameliorate their impacts, prefabricated buildings will be contra-ecological unless deep sustainability principles are incorporated in their design, materials and production systems. Basic patterns 'designed into' new technologies and production processes today can shape and restrict future design options. For example, standardized construction methods have thus far reflected the design legacy of the International Style, rather than new eco-logical solutions.

## Can't standardized construction allow ecological principles to be built in?

Possibly, but this is not likely because, again, eco-logical design is site-specific. Moreover, in commercial development, 'robotic' architecture is in the pipeline. This is where buildings are virtually 'squeezed out of a tube', according to a computer program. This could be better or worse for the environment. The prognosis is grim, however, given the current lack of ecological considerations in industrial design and construction generally. However, the *potential* for more efficient and interactive design and construction is still there. Computer-aided design already reduces the time (and hence cost) of drafting and construction. It can also eliminate the need for complex and costly 'hard copy' plans. Builders can refer to 3D computer drawings on-site, and designers can make modifications in one area without causing unanticipated problems elsewhere in a complex plan. But deep sustainability considerations will need to enter the basic pre-programming phase, where irreversible decisions are made. Work has begun in this area [Box 23]. But while green engineers and architects may be involved in program design, they are statistically unlikely to be ecologically astute. So many basic decisions may be pre-determined by the imperatives of new profit-driven technologies, rather than the public interest. Despite recent public pressure, construction processes have never been ecologically motivated. Due to the enormous investments in land, plant and equipment, they are most likely to remain driven by economies of scale and standardization. Positive Development therefore requires a fundamental break from business-as-usual.

## So how do we shift from standard design to eco-logical design?

The author's experience in teaching architecture suggests change will not come about unless different design methods are introduced. It is difficult to compare and contrast design methods, as the design process is often quite subjective, individualistic and personal. Most designers have well-established personal work habits, if not explicit design strategies. Yet there is surprisingly little published in the area of actual design thinking.[46] This may be partly because the design process is difficult to articulate. Also, some designers may like to retain some mystery or mystique, or to conceal the lack thereof. Generalizations can nonetheless be offered for purposes of opening up the topic of design method for wider discussion. First, conventional design has been driven by stylistic and industrial norms, as a review of design journals would readily confirm. That is to say, buildings are designed of, for and by the industrial system, and modified by the imperatives of current fashion. The broad trend in green design has thus been towards 'greening' the International Style.[47] However, green buildings could meet the demands of industrial production without reflecting industrial values. Second, many architecture schools still tend to emphasize image, graphics or sculptural elements (eg shape, line, form and axes). In many student exhibitions, 'artistic expression' seems to be elevated over whole systems or ecological considerations. And high art has often been equated with 'other worldliness'.

## Can't eco-logical design be integrated with artistic and sculptural qualities?

Absolutely. All good designers could integrate ecological functions with sculptural forms. They could blend exciting 'modern' forms with 'ancient' passive solar and eco-logical design principles, or vice versa. As we said, both ecologically and structurally sound development are essential for public health and safety. Therefore, ecological standards should be no more voluntary than structural or safety standards. But often, when taught, eco-logical design principles tend to be presented as optional. The author was once told by the head of an architecture department that teaching ecological design could limit the career opportunities of those who might wish to do other kinds of architecture and would not know how. Also, passive solar design is often taught as part of the 'mechanical equipment of buildings' stream, in a way that largely appeals to more mechanically-minded students, and is then forgotten in the design studio. In some schools, passive design principles are treated as token technical issues to be squeezed into the curriculum – *neither* as high art, nor as a basic 'bottom line'. In other words, the artistic and experiential aspects of design are given more importance, and ecological elements are seen as mere technologies. So although skylights, atria and other features could create exciting sculptural features, they are usually just optional mechanical 'add ons'. And when the design cost exceeds the budget, 'add ons' are the first to be cut by project managers. Exceeding the budget is almost inevitable, due to the exclusion of quantity surveyors and builders from the design process, among other things. However, the design method itself also relegates ecological considerations to secondary status.

## How can green design methods marginalize ecological considerations?

There appear to be two typical approaches to design from the author's observations: the 'inside–out' or *human*-centred method and the 'outside–in' or *resource*-centred method [Box 24]. These two basic approaches are not mutually exclusive, of course. However, due to the tendency to address problems in a linear sequential (although iterative) way, most designers start from one direction or the other. Those that prioritize the individual building 'user' tend to start the design process from the inside. They often begin with a bubble diagram that translates into a two-dimensional floor plan (which is then extruded into three dimensions). This approach emphasizes the manipulation of natural and built systems to achieve a comfortable and productive environment for the occupants. This is similar to ergonomics in product design, where design is matched to the needs of people, particularly human characteristics and behaviours (rather than social and ecological interdependencies).[48] Human factors, such as privacy or even spatial hierarchy (eg more prestigious spaces for executives), often drive the inside–out approach. Designers then 'add value' through things like *unusual* interior spaces, shapes or 'journeys' that aim to affect the sensory experience of the user. To impress the user, they may try to create 'wow' experiences.

## So how does the outside–in approach differ from the inside–out approach?

The outside–in approach tends to emphasize building forms over interior spaces, although better designers aim for both, of course. Those that prioritize exterior environmental factors often start from the building site and context (although sometimes starting with two-dimensional cross-sections and projecting these into three dimensions). Urban design considerations include the relationships between the project and other urban functions, such as pedestrian and traffic access, public spaces, and symbolic forms or features that might distinguish the project. Such considerations result in an emphasis on the exterior shape (or style), which can be modified to accommodate interior spatial requirements. These may then be reconciled with environmental factors impacting on the site (eg sun or overshadowing, noise, pollution, security and privacy, or wind and fire prevention). The resulting building skin is then modified to achieve an optimal combination of human comfort factors, such as heat, light, ventilation, views, air and noise (ie not the ecology). Those concerned with building form will tend to massage a building design to impress the general public or spectators, more than the building users. Value adding within this outside–in approach often appears through such visible statements as public art and impressive entrances or plazas, which can constitute positive social and cultural amenities. Both approaches thus often *add* personal and/or social value, but still only 'mitigate' environmental impacts and forces. The inside–out method is really the flipside of the outside–in method, and the results are not too dissimilar.

## So just what difference in outcomes do these approaches have?

The inside–out approach takes the perspective of the user, and the outside–in approach takes the perspective of the external observer. While neither is exclusive, of course, it is often obvious which approach has been prioritized. For example, an office building with an interior, windowless office space can result from a priority on the building shape as seen from the outside (outside–in design). Buildings with windows that reflect heat and glare on neighbours can result from a priority on creating exciting interior spaces and views (inside–out). Both methods tend to be concerned primarily with the building envelope. Whether designers work from the inside out or outside in, they meet at the building skin, so to speak. This, of course, oversimplifies the process. Any design process will be informed by diagrams, checklists, site analyses and other studies, in addition to the client's 'design brief'. But the process is often one of trading off space for quality materials, shapes and fixtures. The activities, physical requirements and spaces needed to accommodate the 'brief' will be arranged on the site plan. The spaces will be reconciled with the allowable floor area, set back, height and other city planning restrictions. The specification of optimal floor space considered necessary for each function or activity already establishes a mindset that assumes spaces need to be divided up. When functional activity is constrained by space reduction, and minimalism is seen as a virtue, then natural amenities and eco-services are inevitably sacrificed. Designers usually add economic, social or 'environmental' value (or triple bottom line considerations), but virtually none aim to add net positive ecological gains. Green design is thus still tokenistic.

## So these two approaches are seen in green as well as in conventional building?

Yes. The inside–out approach mitigates environmental impacts on the user and the outside–in approach mitigates environmental impacts on the building. Green design today likes to compare a building envelope to a 'skin'. The inside–out green design approach tends to focus on environmental forces affecting the user's skin, or human comfort. The outside–in approach tends to focus on environmental forces acting on the building skin. Both conventional and green design approaches thus arguably reflect input–output thinking. That is, figuratively speaking, both draw a boundary around the design problem, and then find ways to mitigate impacts or forces impinging upon the human and/ or building skin. Although thinking outside or inside the box comes fairly naturally to most green designers, both inside–out and outside–in approaches can create mental visors. Just as in LCA, if we focus on the inputs and outputs, we will draw boundaries around a problem, and thus concentrate on mitigating environmental impacts of inputs and outputs. In other words, environmental factors are perceived as *impacts* on users or *forces* on the buildings that must be manipulated, mitigated and controlled. This negative mindset means that we are not inclined to think of:

- Turning those forces around for advantage (eg creating and storing additional cooling potential versus just preventing excessive heat)
- Increasing environmental flows (eg generating additional oxygen and warmth or coolness) versus sealing off and heating smaller spaces
- Generating off-site positive environmental impacts to create ecological gain for the community versus adding social offsets to compensate for ecological losses

### Is the outside–in or inside–out better suited for value-adding ecological space?

They are probably about the same. We noted that traditional design can concentrate on the inputs and outputs at the building envelope or 'box'.[49] In passive solar design, input–output thinking is manifested in many instances in the reliance on passive solar design 'cross-sections'. That is, the passive solar diagrams typically used to explain thermal heat gain, loss and storage in materials and walls are understood and conveyed by cross-sections of walls, floors, ceilings and glass: the envelope. In turn, these diagrams (showing forces entering, exiting or warming up the box, depending on its shape, mass, insulation, etc) are often the starting point from which passive solar design begins. Many passive solar buildings, in fact, often seem to simply extrude two-dimensional passive solar diagrams into three dimensions. A cross-section of an 'efficient box' is generated to fit the spatial requirements of the client and planning requirements of the local authority. The elements are optimized for economic, social and environmental efficiency, tradeoffs are made, and the resulting green envelope is modified to meet the dictates of style. Then, once again, a quantity surveyor or tendering process confirms that the building is over budget and the green bits are excised from the plan

### Can't design templates based on input–output thinking stimulate good design?

Good design generally results from synthesis, synergy and symbiosis, supported – but not driven – by a linear-reductionist analysis and iterative process. If there is such a thing as an ecological intuition, many design schools teach students to be counterintuitive. Of course, input–output thinking has provided many useful insights when applied to environmental and other challenges. It led to tools, like LCA, which help us to understand, measure and mitigate negative impacts [Chapter 5]. However, any pattern of analysis that is seen as 'all-encompassing' or 'the solution' will confine our thinking and eventually lead to blinds spots, or what we could call the Sorcerer's Apprentice syndrome. Like our other tools of environmental management, the input–output approach in building design breaks problems down into forces or impacts at the boundary. This also reflects and reinforces a negative view of nature. The environment, in design, has been implicitly perceived as a constraint or threat, and buildings have often been described as 'shelters' from a hostile nature. The focus on 'negatives' limits opportunities for 'positive' thinking. Since forces or factors are conceived as acting at the building envelope (or castle wall), green design solutions are often a response to threats. Therefore, the building becomes a mix of *defensive* strategies (eg shading, insulation, and sound and visual barriers). As suggested earlier, better design would come from affirmatively supporting nature by providing the infrastructure and space for nature to support us.

Figure 9 'Outside–in' and 'inside–out' approaches to design and assessment

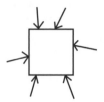  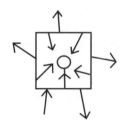

| Outside–in: analysis of negative environmental factors impacting on the building envelope (resource-centred). | Inside–out: analysis of negative environmental factors impacting on the building user (human-centred). | Impact assessment: analysis of negative environmental impacts of the building on the environment and/or humans. |

The environment has been represented by negative threats or forces that need to be mitigated by buildings, and more recently, forces created by the building upon the environment that need to be mitigated. That is, the perception that green design must control environmental forces on the building or user is simply the reverse of building impact assessment. This could be re-conceived as environmental flows with surpluses that could be captured for human use, if not unduly interrupted by development.

### How does this 'defensive' approach contrast with Positive Development?

In the defensive approach that reflects the dominant environmental management paradigm, the impacts of the environment on the building or its occupants are 'predicted and mitigated'. This is partly because the building will be evaluated according to its potential impacts on the environment (through rating tools, impact assessment, etc). If they are concentrating on environmental forces affecting the building site and occupants, designers will only try to reduce the impacts of the building upon the occupants and/or community. When in a defensive design mode, one does not try to improve ecological or human health or conditions beyond the site boundaries – even when altruistic design costs nothing extra. Thus input–output thinking in green design could be seen as the other side of the impact assessment 'coin' [Figure 9]. Both approaches are defensive. Even when designers claim to create buildings that are 'like ecosystems', the result is more like the life-support systems in hospitals, if not cryogenic capsules. The built environment needs to broaden its scope and provide life-support for ecosystems (the hospital) as well as species (patients), so to speak. Our buildings reflect the idea that we can support humans in a hostile atmosphere – as if we were in a spaceship. Yet there is no reason why buildings could not also create the infrastructure for ecosystems to flourish.

### So how do we begin to think outside the building envelope when designing?

A flows approach would help get away from the standard reliance on cross-sections, floor plans or envelopes. It would help us to think beyond inputs and outputs at system boundaries. Whereas input–output thinking concentrates the mind on the building envelope, a flows approach would look at opportunities for design to add functions and values *beyond* the site boundaries: 'pushing the envelope' as it were. By focusing on the building envelope, some green designs – like conventional design – create a sense of separation between the human and the natural environment. This reinforces the false belief that humans can be independent of nature, the life-support system. This in turn limits our capacity to perceive new alternatives that would break down the physical and metaphorical division between humans and nature. A flows approach draws into question the very nature of the building envelope.[50] So we might instead incorporate ecological space in indoor and outdoor areas – and in the envelope itself [Figure 10]. A building could be more like a space frame that combines space for ecosystems and biodiversity with walkways, balconies and other social space, while serving the many other practical functions of the building skin [Box 4]. Design for eco-services, as partially exemplified by Green Space Walls and Green Scaffolding, challenges the nature–society barrier. Such proposed structural concepts are potentially compatible with any style, and can be retrofitted into virtually any building.

## Figure 10 Sample Green Space Wall image

The Green Space Wall is a set of demountable modules that would vary depending on the orientation of the wall as well as functional purposes. It would create an internal microclimate that not only helps to heat, cool and ventilate the building, but produces clean energy, air, water and soil. The modules support a range of visual and ecological functions, from gardens to butterfly breeding to food production (similar to the retrofitting version, Green Scaffolding). The modules are supported (off the ground) by a structural system which is integrated with solar stacks, ventilation systems and light-weight wind generators. In this example of a sustainability education centre, the floor plates are narrow, and wrap around internal courtyards, forming a diversity of virtual pathways to sustainability.

### But don't some green designers already try to create 'living buildings'?

If they were living buildings, they would be largely invisible. Given that architecture is regarded as a 'visual art', *invisibility* is generally not the image sought by designers. Blending in with the environment might also be resisted as a challenge to the 'monumental' self-image of some architects. Green Space Walls challenge the billboard or huge computer screen model that is emerging today. Remember, most building designers are under intense external and internal pressure to impress the architectural fraternity. A building shape and façade may score points in design competitions by incorporating eco-logical design principles, but the building must 'show off'. It is the building shape, or sculptural and stylish façade, that wins awards.[51] But passive design could be sculpturally exciting, even though relatively invisible, and challenge the nature–human divide through the *integration* of the structure with ecological space [Figure 10]. New intermediate spaces (eg half indoor, half outdoor) could be retrofitted to add many human/ecological health improvement functions. They could help to transform existing buildings into 'gardens for living', as opposed to 'machines for living'. This requires a new approach to space, however.

## Doesn't space cost money, even if human and natural functions are integrated?

Currently, our ways of enclosing space are resource and capital intensive. If natural systems are uninterrupted and integral with building functions, they should not cost more. Space does not actually cost money: it is the real estate, structure, layout and materials enclosing space that add costs. After all, the embodied energy of a balloon is not reduced by letting its air out. Enclosing space, in itself, need not be detrimental. The environmental impacts result from the transfer of land from ecosystems to development, and the embodied waste in the structures crushing the land and so on. Of course, developers lose money if they do not maximize units per area. If we combined ecological space with development, however, it would increase market values. Developers might then compete for spatial qualities, not material riches. Yet creative multi-functional use of space has not been used as a tool of eco-logical design. Ecological space is rare, to the extent it exists at all. Although architecture is fundamentally concerned with space, environmental issues have been narrowly couched in a pollution and energy-efficiency framework which green designers have adopted. While other resource issues, like $CO_2$ and water, have taken on more importance, materials are often maximized for purposes like thermal mass and durability, not to mention achieving a palatial image. In other words, designers use 'space' ostentatiously to impress either users (inside–out) or the general public (outside–in), or eliminate it to save energy.

## What would be the advantage of a flows approach and how do we proceed?

If we just look at current conditions, any project that appears 'relatively' harmless is deemed good enough. Mapping the resource flows through an existing facility in a retrofit, or the site of a new building in relation to the surrounds, can enable ecological issues and past impacts to be identified and addressed. Similarly, mapping environmental flows through the wider site context, both before urbanization and at present, can enable the designer to see ways in which the development can support the urban ecology and bioregion. The focus on environmental flows could help shift the emphasis from assessing the impacts of (conventional) alternatives to using and enhancing the free services of natural systems for human purposes. Design for eco-services would foster urban ecosystem functions, as well as 'surplus' ecosystem goods and services. By comparing the bio-physical impacts of existing development to pre-development or natural conditions, ideas for restoration and enhancement may be stimulated (ie biomimicry on a regional scale). To develop a systems mapping re-design method (SmartMode), then, we need new systems of analysis that establish the ecological baseline, or what we will call ecological transformation (ET) analysis. We also need to analyse resource transfers and their effect on the public estate, which we will call resource transfer (RT) analysis. But first, issues pertaining to project analysis, sustainability assessment and environmental reporting are taken up in the following section. They show the need to move from an input–output to a flows approach at the policy level as well.

# SECTION C: CRITIQUE OF METHODS, TOOLS AND PROCESSES IN ENVIRONMENTAL MANAGEMENT

# 7
# Urban Sustainability Assessment

From predicting
negative impacts to
adding value

There is a growing diversity of assessment methods and approval processes designed to assist councils in predicting and mitigating the adverse impacts of developments within a triple bottom line framework.[1] The trend is towards assessing projects, plans and programmes using a broader geographic scale, time frame and scope of analysis. Due to the internet, there is also rapid dissemination and cross-fertilization between jurisdictions and organizations on procedures, indicators and targets, which are then tailored to meet local concerns.[2]

Given the growth and diversity of methods, therefore, we need a generic typology to compare and discuss them. For our purposes, assessment methods can be classified by whether they audit actual performance or predict future impacts.

### Present (actual) performance

Methods for *auditing* the actual performance of an existing operation, organization or development include:

- **Environmental audits** of buildings, designed to diagnose and improve the environmental performance of existing developments (but usually just energy or lighting) [Chapter 8].
- **Specification tools** to assist specifiers in selecting the best product or building component that is available, and to educate designers [Boxes 28 and 29].
- **Environmental reporting systems**, which assist business and industry in improving the environmental efficiency of their management and operations [Box 36].
- **Ecologically sustainable development reporting**, which should report on positive actions taken, but usually just charts trends against broad indicators [Box 35 and Chapter 9].
- **Regional sustainability audits**, which look at ecological impacts and inefficiencies of existing development patterns, such as material flows analysis (MFA) and ecological footprint (EF) analysis [Chapter 8].

### Future (predicted) impacts

Methods for *predicting* the performance of a design concept or plan for a proposed policy, programme or development include:

- **Risk assessment**, which aims to predict and avoid financial and/or ecological threats that might arise from policies, actions or developments
- **Building energy rating tools**, which predict the future resource consumption of proposed developments (especially energy and water) compared to 'typical' buildings [Chapter 5]
- **Sustainability assessment**, which predicts the future impacts of plans, decisions, actions or development proposals against triple-bottom-line criteria [Chapter 7]

The distinction between predicted and actual performance is not always exclusive, of course. It is important to distinguish between them. This is because there is sometimes a tendency to find problems that suit our preferred tools. Prediction is often used where auditing would be more appropriate, as we saw in the case of building rating tools that award stars for predicted performance that may not materialize. Processes are needed that precede and support design in order not only to front-load design, but to re-set design priorities. This chapter focuses on how we plan, while chapter 12 looks at how we should plan.

## Has impact assessment improved environmental decision-making overall?

Certainly. We have come a long way since the early 1970s, when environmental impact assessment processes (EIAs) were introduced and adopted in many countries around the world.[3] In the post-war period, when planners determined an area was rundown it was essentially earmarked for bulldozing and 'redevelopment', with infamous results. Although EIAs were only intended to discipline the decision-making process, rather than to actually protect the environment, they created a wedge into the hegemony of government authorities. EIAs did not stop government agencies and developers from continuing to replace 'unruly' natural systems with capital- and resource-intensive infrastructure and development projects. They did, however, make people in built environment professions more aware of the environmental and social consequences of development. Further, EIAs shifted the organizational culture by necessitating more government staff being drawn from different disciplines, such as chemistry and biology. They also exposed bureaucracies to direct public oversight through more inclusive information processes. These changes, in turn, contributed to a greater appreciation of the legitimacy of different values, stakeholder preferences and types of knowledge. More important, there is now more scepticism of scientific expertise. It became apparent, for example, that some scientists could be found to support virtually any position. So today, there is less public patience with obfuscation and/or volumes of confusing data that had become institutionalized with EIAs. The overall outcome has been a growing demand for more transparent and accessible analyses and more democratic decision processes in planning.

## Has public involvement in planning and assessment affected outcomes?

To an extent. EIAs almost never stop proposed developments. However, increasing public engagement in project approvals generated by assessment processes has made more people aware of the externalities and subsidies entailed in development.[4] Simultaneously, it has made them aware that many fundamental decisions impacting upon the environment are still outside the public purview. Special interests whose power transcends governments will always control the outcomes of any major resource allocation decisions. Issues of fundamental importance on the whole systems level, such as whether to develop nuclear power, are still usurped by power politics.[5] Once a 'green light' for nuclear power is decided by cabinet, for instance, EIAs will be conducted on the technicalities of individual nuclear plant proposals only, not the concept itself or their alternatives. In total, EIAs have cost untold sums of money, but have resulted in few significant modifications to development proposals – even where many citizens believe the projects would create an environmental catastrophe. On the other hand, participatory processes and requirements to prepare EIAs have discouraged some proposals from being developed in the first place, and these outcomes are not generally reported.[6] Unfortunately, however, EIAs were not very well integrated with design. Thus, while beneficial in many ways, they were costly in relation to benefits.

## Could developers benefit from such costly impact assessment processes?

Developers increasingly understood that assessment processes could lead to economic benefits through greater efficiencies in development. Thus EIAs contributed to a gradual acceptance on the part of development interests of greater public oversight of design. Instead of seeing these studies as a necessary burden, they are becoming an integral part of business planning today. In fact, some developers now go 'beyond compliance' and actively market their firm's ecological sensitivities.[7] They realize that EIAs can demonstrate 'good will' on the part of industry, much like corporate environmental management and reporting processes [Chapter 9]. Green measures are increasingly incorporated in development approvals through various kinds of point systems. However, a proposal that evinces any green development measures at all tends to be approved, despite overall environmental harm ('it is the thought that counts'). So while many architecture firms now market 'green credentials', what passes for sustainable development is often conventional development with green features.[8] The EIA process does identify project alternatives, but the alternatives explored are usually mitigation measures. So far, assessment processes do not take basic alternatives seriously.[9] The initial design concept usually remains the same. There is a need for processes that step back and consider fundamental *sustainability* considerations, such as the best ecological use of land.

## Why would developers be interested in identifying the best use of land?

They would not be. That is why we need planners, ecologists and others involved. Developers usually look for the best site for a given type of project from an economic perspective, whether a fast food outlet or apartment block. Alternative kinds of land uses for a particular site are seldom on the table, even if the assessment addresses the 'no development' option. Starting with a given project and looking for the best economic location is quite different from trying to optimize the ecological and other potential public good values and functions of the site. Project proponents, of course, have no reason to try to find better land uses for a particular site, let alone the best ecological use. This is one of the roles of government master plans. Currently, however, even 'sustainable' master plans start with how to accommodate growth with fewer impacts, instead of starting from how to enhance the ecological base [Chapter 12]. Planners promulgate criteria and indicators for certain land uses (eg office, residential or commercial), and the market determines the site according to land availability and price. Sometimes, planners may provide site analyses and site-specific criteria for prime development sites.[10] Logically, a sustainability assessment (SA) process would determine the best land uses (since master plans and zoning schemes seldom do), in order to optimize social and ecological factors.[11] However, SAs tend to be just EIAs with a triple-bottom-line framework.[12]

## So just how do SAs differ from EIAs then?

In theory, but not yet in practice, SAs are meant to apply to all decisions in project development. Sometimes they are even meant to apply to 'whole of government' decision-making.[13] The idea is that all areas and agencies of government should weigh all policies, organizational structures, decisions and actions against sustainability principles – not just a final project, plan or design. Thus SAs have brought about some theoretical improvements over EIAs.[14] However, despite their wider scope and technical advances, SAs still retain the basic intellectual construct underlying EIAs: the emphasis on predicting and mitigating impacts upon the status quo. Consequently, they help us to choose the least bad option, but not to transform whole systems or create healthy, 'living' environments. As currently framed, therefore, SAs cannot adequately guide us towards net Positive Development, let alone stimulate the design of positive impacts. Instead of front-loading creative processes, SAs can even reinforce the defensive, negative impact mentality described in previous chapters. This is because projects qualify as exemplary if they merely offset *irreversible* ecological losses with short-term social and economic benefits. Again, substitution and tradeoffs do not satisfy the concept of sustainability used in this text: expanding future options and natural security [Introduction]. So far, then, SAs have merely broken the ice on the subject of sustainability.

## Why aren't these assessment methods adequate to achieve sustainability?

Like other environmental management tools, SA methods still reflect the idea that we can only mitigate impacts and reduce risks. Because we cannot assess something until there is a design concept, any resulting changes will tend to be at the margins. SAs examine alternatives for realizing certain private investment goals. There is little evidence that they require examination of options to invest in reversing the impacts of existing development, or in generating positive off-site impacts. Further, assessment methods are geared for measuring and mitigating *future* damage from a retrospective orientation. Accounting activities can buttress a non-unsustainable prototype of development against fundamental design change. Throughout environmental management, the vast majority of resources in sustainability are still invested in initiating, applying or modifying assessment processes, criteria and indicators themselves. Changing the prefix from environmental to sustainability does not change the outcome. More time and effort appears to go into developing means of assessing future projects than in addressing existing system design problems. So while there is nothing wrong with impact and risk assessment *per se*, they can cause designers, developers and local authorities to ignore problems that could be fixed. The focus on future actions or projects also distracts public debate away from existing inequities [Box 48]. Assessment methods should therefore be re-designed to find ways to be more proactive and direct: to improve existing urban areas through new or retrofitted development and encourage whole systems thinking or innovation.

## Why haven't SA processes been used to encourage net Positive Development?

There are many reasons. One is that most planning processes, including what is called sustainability assessment, respond to private initiatives. When planners proactively invite development proposals to, say, encourage urban revitalization, it is still usually to promote 'growth'. Neither public nor private development is undertaken to increase the urban ecology. SAs are designed to assess *new* development, and this creates a vacuum (which nature abhors). Assessment processes do not look at what we can do to address the urban problems and damage that has already been created. Thus, for example, few eco-retrofitting proposals are on the table, despite the benefits for developers, government and community [Chapter 2]. Also, assessment processes place development issues in an 'interest balancing' framework rather than a net positive one. Offsets legitimize additional impacts. Similarly, because current assessment methods *aggregate* externalities or impacts, they create the impression that the negative impacts on each individual citizen would be small if a project were approved, but would mean huge losses for the individual developer if not approved. Another reason that SA processes do not encourage Positive Development is that, in a market economy, planners find it easier to implement development controls, guidelines and tick-the-box processes than to conceive and devise on-ground whole systems improvements. Instead of just assessing impacts, governments could assist developers to identify net positive investment opportunities [Chapter 14].

### Can't consultants identify positive criteria and opportunities for developers?

Not at present. Consultancies generally apply their methods to specific tasks of benefit to their patrons. They make profits by replicating a standard idea or process, not by solving unique problems that affect the whole community. Individually, some make very positive contributions, but most consulting amounts to the repeated application of brand methods. On the one hand, consultants cannot represent the public interest. On the other, planners get little encouragement from civil society to do more planning in the public interest. There is also little public appreciation of the benefits of planning in the first place. The widespread, detailed, analytical activity performed by private consultants, checked and ticked off by public planners, can also lull people into believing that sophisticated activities are being undertaken. This is especially the case where SAs purport to be 'comprehensive' and sustainable, giving the impression that the problems of development are being addressed. In reality, assessment processes are still applied to relatively few proposals, and mostly only address pollution and energy impacts. Hence, even many environmentalists incorrectly assume that sustainability issues would be addressed *if only* these methods were more widely adopted over more project proposals and more layers of policymaking. Just as we saw at the building scale, then, environmental assessment displaces creative processes with book-keeping. If there are no methods or resources to directly stimulate systems re-design at the urban scale, it is very unlikely to occur.

### But surely impact assessment cannot actually impede systems re-design?

EIAs and SAs were developed for project approval purposes. They were not intended to design better futures. They were only to make decision-makers more aware, in the belief that good information would lead to good outcomes. Over time, these project review and assessment activities – measuring, mitigating and monitoring – have eclipsed planning processes that might have evolved to design sustainable futures.[15] Instead, project approval systems, supported by EIAs or SAs, have been taken to be almost synonymous with 'environmental protection'. As long as there is a planning process that takes environmental issues into account, environmental issues must be under control. In effect, development control 'writ large' has suppressed sustainability planning. Moreover, both development control and advance planning tend to respond to and accommodate the market. To the extent that 'comprehensive' planning exists, it is still largely concerned with promoting growth, even where lip service is paid to conserving nature. Also, its approach to the environment still reflects its origins in zoning: keeping development off landslide areas or flood plains, or encouraging more growth in certain areas like central business districts. There are, of course, also ongoing efforts to physically improve and revitalize existing urban areas. However, these tend to be limited to promoting infill development, mitigated by public investment in a shrinking public estate. Investment in better streetscapes – with sidewalk cafes, street trees, signage and bus shelters – supports business in the outdated belief that business 'growth' will then solve all our other problems.

## Has the character of comprehensive planning today changed?

Today, the focus is on developing better *assessment* criteria, guidelines and indicators by which to measure private proposals, and sometimes even government performance. But this performance orientation is not new, as sometimes implied. In San Francisco among other places, for example, a set of broad policies were developed in the 1960s to ensure urban design, environmental, social, transport and other considerations were taken into account in new development. These were adopted by San Francisco's legislative body, so that staff were able to implement these relatively 'subjective' criteria in a design review process. This enabled an interactive approach to design review, where staff could suggest to developers means by which the criteria could be better met.[16] At the same time, urban design guidelines for *specific* sites were prepared to ensure developers were aware of the range of applicable design criteria that projects should meet before the design process began. Planners could then assist or discourage the siting and/or basic design of proposals through a variety of informal but relatively open and flexible means. If there was an impasse, developers, as well as community groups, could take the matter to a discretionary review hearing. Today, we are increasingly trying to replace *engagement* by reducing things to formulas, 'point' systems, or web-based forms. These processes only encourage 'best practice' (ie professional price-fixing). In point systems, for example, there is still little indication of how projects can improve existing urban environments or conform to regional carrying capacity. Planners need erasers as well as rulers.

## Can't generic performance criteria or point systems ensure positive impacts?

Not really. In Australia, for example, some cities have developed sets of standard indicators to set minimum criteria for the design of different kinds of development, such as office, commercial or housing projects. In some jurisdictions in Australia, developers are given an extensive list of criteria out of which they must earn only, say, 60 out of 100 points. This flexibility avoids potential conflicts between the generic criteria and the functional objectives or site conditions of the project. While obtaining 60 points is relatively easy, this list provides options or ideas for consideration that might 'enhance' a development from environmental, urban design or other perspectives. In some cases, council planners might try to revitalize a socially and economically disadvantaged area by encouraging the development of an eco-industrial park nearby. The promulgation of guidelines for eco-industrial parks then provides a 'signal' that proposals for such developments are encouraged.[17] Planners might also designate sites that would be beneficial to developers simply because, for instance, the location is or can be serviced by trains or public transport. Guidelines for 'buildings types' are not sufficient, however [Box 22]. First, projects are reliant on developers initiating proposals. Second, the criteria are nearly always environmental (ie human comfort), not ecological. Even enlightened zoning and green design guidelines do not encourage positive ecological improvements.

## But aren't such criteria the only way we can encourage sustainable land uses?

They may encourage sustainable land uses if they are based on whole systems criteria such as carrying capacity [Chapter 12]. Attracting green development is an improvement over what was sometimes called 'proactive' planning in the 1980s. Back then, planners tried to attract *any* development to the municipality to promote economic development. But zoning and incentives still start from the 'type' of development – they are based on anticipating economic trends, like technology parks. They do not start with the health and wellbeing of humans, nature and land. Development control guidelines and indicators sometimes pay lip service to the value of 'ecosystem integrity', or the ability of natural systems to maintain themselves. However, they do not seek increases to the ecological base or space that would increase ecosystem integrity. SA systems are beginning to call for 'contributions to sustainability' (or similar phrases). But to the extent that they associate terms like positive gain, adaptability, cultural diversity and biodiversity with conventional urban development, they are 'greenwash'. Eco-services need to be integrated into actual physical infrastructure, to support indigenous species and enhance human and ecosystem health through design. When only 60 out of 100 design points need to be achieved, developers have little incentive to do their best. Cities can gradually increase the number of points in 'boom' periods. However, developments built to low initial specifications or points will be there for a long time. Conventional design is irreversible, so the 'opportunity cost' of ordinary development is incalculable.

## But surely planning criteria could simply call for net Positive Development?

Positive Development represents a paradigm shift, and thus requires *proactive* re-development initiatives to lead the way. To the extent that money and effort are invested in bureaucratic processes, the choice between optional policies, projects or plans is likely to be made on the basis of opportunities presented. The choice made will minimize risks to business-as-usual. The 'least change' to the current paradigm that appears to meet policy directives will usually be preferred. Assessment by government agencies leans towards convention – that which is easily predicted by business, planning and other tools. Because innovative eco-logical design is virtually non-existent, it is therefore seen as inherently risky (hence another vicious circle). Without *direct* government initiatives and signals, private investment is unlikely to be directed at improving urban social and environmental conditions – let alone increasing the ecological base. At best, it will aim for greater eco-efficiency. This is partly because impact assessments do not 'weigh in' the benefits of natural systems. Nor do they put a value on their potential to *replace* high-maintenance, capital-intensive urban infrastructure with natural systems. At all levels of environmental management, the economic and social gains still only need to outweigh the ecological losses. Thus, while SA has potential, it so far has only extended the EIA process. Approvals are still based on relativity, not sustainability, and usually allow tradeoffs.

## Why and how do SAs allow tradeoffs of ecological losses for social gain?

The EIA process has its conceptual roots in cost–benefit analysis, the dominant model of decision-making available back then. The idea of tradeoffs is intrinsic to the cost–benefit decision framework. Initially, EIAs couched analyses in terms of whether the net *economic* benefits outweighed the net *environmental* costs. Many early impact assessments counted the economic benefits of proposed developments, but not the economic costs of externalities to the public. They also balanced environmental costs against financial benefits in 'person years', not in ecological time. Even when the economic costs of environmental damage were gradually recognized, the scales were weighted towards economic benefits. EIAs not only downplayed the economic costs of environmental disruptions, they downplayed the economic benefits of an undisturbed environment. Many decision processes, in effect, still do this. A development that created jobs and commerce would appear to be an 'improvement' over the status quo – despite what were considered 'inevitable' environmental impacts. At the time, the idea of creating net positive ecological improvements was inconceivable. Therefore, people could not ask more of a development than that the gains offset some of the public costs. Gradually, means were developed for offsetting negative impacts by transferring some costs to developers, called 'exactions'. Exactions, or impact fees, are offsets negotiated or legislated from developers by councils in exchange for development approval [Box 30]. Examples of exactions would be the requirement that suburbs provide their own services or public parks, or that commercial buildings provide public plazas or day-care facilities.

## So what's wrong with exactions to offset environmental and social impacts?

The problem is that exactions enable more growth with more negative impacts overall, without reducing total resource flows or fixing the environmental problems created by existing development. Moreover, short-term social benefits and long-term ecological costs are not commensurate in any way. Ecological values have completely different metrics than social ones. No-one really knows how to measure either, let alone how to compare them because, once again, both society and nature are complex, interactive systems [Box 41]. In any case, we almost always 'discount' the future, subjectively if not formally [Box 42]. Tradeoffs or exactions are also subject to the values of planners and to the planners' power relative to developers and their political associates. In seeking concessions from more powerful developers in a cost–benefit context, planners would not think of requiring net positive environments. Also, the idea of a design approach that uses and enhances natural systems (rather than choosing the lesser of evils) is outside the traditional planning paradigm, let alone the cost–benefit framework. The exclusion of natural systems from the design repertoire is exacerbated by the division of planning and urban design. Land-use planning did not evolve within a design paradigm. The origins of planning were in 'zoning', the division of land uses into single function areas to avoid nuisances (ie noise, smells and dirt). Therefore, as we shall see, planning decision tools (influenced by business administration and operations research) were designed to allocate land and compare and choose options – not to conform to, or expand, carrying capacity [Chapter 12].

## Could sustainability assessments simply 'not' give any credit for tradeoffs?

Tradeoffs are integral to the triple bottom line (TBL) approach, as well as to cost–benefit frameworks. SAs purport to include sustainability within the EIA framework. But a TBL approach *either* separates social, economic and ecological values *or* puts them in one list on the grounds that they are inseparable. Paradoxically, either approach is 'additive'. That is, values in these three areas are treated as more or less equal and can be traded off to achieve a total 'score' (whether or not translated into numbers). Given the fundamental (false) premise that the ecological base of cities cannot be increased, one can sacrifice ecological for social values if the total positive benefits seem great enough relative to the negatives. In practice, therefore, the implicit SA 'standard', like that of EIAs, is *still* essentially whether the economic benefits outweigh the environmental benefits. SA will not foster net Positive Development until there is a widespread recognition that:

- The ecological base or life-support system is the bottom line, not competing values and interests
- Development can create the conditions by which urban areas can contribute to the ecological base and public estate

A process that assumes we can offset negative environmental impacts with positive social impacts in a cost–benefit framework also reinforces the biases against eco-retrofitting.

## But surely SAs would favour eco-retrofitting over new developments?

No. SAs are applied to development proposals and usually do not compare new buildings to eco-retrofitting alternatives. If they did, the costs of maintaining urban areas and buildings and suburbs would probably not be considered in the assessments anyway. Existing development needs ongoing investment in upgrades and revitalization. Yet relatively little attention has been paid to measuring the maintenance costs of new developments, let alone the environmental impacts of maintenance and renovations in the future. The resource costs entailed in maintaining old ('fossil fuelled') urban areas in their present condition, or the waste entailed in demolition, seldom appear in the balance sheets. Therefore new development seems better value than retrofitting. When a proposed development is assessed, the future negative impacts on the urban environment are considered, of course. Things like increased congestion and wind tunnel effects can be marginal, however, in comparison to total urban resource flows. Assessments may look at the relative incremental social and economic impacts of new or retrofitted development on its surrounds. They seldom if ever compare the ecological health of the whole urban area before and after construction. A true sustainability assessment would assess the pre-existing and ongoing social and environmental impacts in the surrounding urban area, to see what urban conditions can be improved by the project. It would not just determine whether the additional harm of a proposal appeared to be 'acceptable'.

## How could planners assess the urban context along with project proposals?

They would compare what the urban ecology and eco-services would be like before and after the proposed development [Box 38]. Failure to look at the health of a whole area is one reason why new shopping malls were allowed on prime agricultural land outside of central business districts, to the detriment of inner city commercial areas. The decisions only considered the future costs and benefits that might be caused by a particular new development – as if the existing urban context were cost-free or impact-neutral. The social, economic and environmental costs of maintaining or decommissioning the old shopping areas or business districts were not really factored in. Nor were the effects of the new regional shopping malls on total resource flows in or through cities assessed. Consequently, many inner city commercial areas have been subjected to a vicious circle of social and economic deterioration, while continuing to leak greenhouse gases, energy and pollutants. Analyses that help us to predict and measure negative impacts and their ramifications do not help us to identify areas where we can reduce resource flows through either eco-retrofitting or urban acupuncture. Planners must stimulate investment in eco-retrofitting – the market cannot address design failure on its own. Today, SAs continue the tradition of examining proposals within small systems boundaries in a case-by-case framework. This framework reinforces the biases against eco-retrofitting.

## Why does a case-by-case framework create biases against eco-retrofitting?

The potential of new development to correct existing problems in the urban environment is limited by the reactive, incremental framework of SAs. Proposed projects only need to be 'greener' than alternative proposals. There would need to be a competing proposal to retrofit the old commercial district on the table at the same time for it to be compared to the above regional shopping area. Today there is a growing *rhetorical* appreciation of the need to consider development proposals in the context of cumulative and regional impacts. This is growing due partly to the fact that green field sites are increasingly limited. The fact that farmland has been displaced by regional shopping centres, for example, is beginning to bite into food productivity. In many cases, however, development of green field sites is deemed 'sustainable' if there are enough social benefits or green building features thrown in.[18] Ironically, green field developments have also been favoured by accounting that expands the range of ways to offset ecological losses. For example, green field developments can claim offsets of negative impacts by purchasing 'green power' elsewhere, rather than designing zero carbon buildings. Gradually, a 'looser' range of offsets has been accepted in order to justify development approvals. Green power, which essentially charges people extra for clean energy, penalizes users of clean energy sources and removes the guilt from users of subsidized, dirty energy. We could remove perverse incentives such as green power and simply require users of 'dirty' energy to pay relatively more, at least over time (costs could be passed onto consumers uniformly and fairly through cross-subsidies). On a green field site, no *ecological* compensation is required, only *social* compensation, because we cannot increase the carrying capacity of natural environments.

## Isn't environmental preservation really up to voters, not planners?

Voting usually comes too late for the environment, let alone for the voters. Many communities still assume that if they allow their resources and amenity to be exploited, they will still be able to enjoy nature reserves in other regions. This is a variation on the 'tragedy of the commons' (a vicious circle).[19] On the other hand, as noted earlier, there is a growing public willingness to approve bonds to buy back urban open space and reserves.[20] But there are also countervailing forces at work. For example, many local governments can still increase their tax base by allowing green field development within their boundaries. As land gets scarcer, property values go up. The cost of housing, in turn, puts pressure on politicians and planners to open up more land for development (another vicious circle). As recently as 2006, the (then) Australian Prime Minister urged states to release more land for more suburbs on green field sites which, again, councils cannot afford to service because they do not consider the option of resource autonomous homes.[21] He did so, hopefully unintentionally, while cutting the ribbon on an urban eco-village. In addition, the best land in terms of ecology is usually allocated to development first, as it often has the best views and other environmental amenities. The remaining land has fewer natural values to protect, so has less appeal to public protection.[22] Thus, despite the consumer demand for urban open space, regional parks and wilderness areas, the development of relatively natural areas will continue until they are eventually gone. The public debate increasingly centres on which nature reserves are most expendable – rather than how to protect them.

## Surely in a democracy, such choices are up to society, even if unwise?

Cutting off the choices of future generations through an incremental resource allocation and wealth concentration process is not democratic. Further, the outcomes are not a result of direct or deliberate public decision-making, because the cumulative loss of the public estate is concealed by EIAs or SAs. They examine proposals in terms of what seems the best development option available at a given point in time. Impact assessments only present options that currently have financial backing, not what might otherwise have been proposed in different economic circumstances. This process does not provide a genuine opportunity for voters to make a considered choice. It only responds to relative pressure. Moreover, the fact of a case-by-case framework in itself will divert thought away from increasing options. With each incremental project approval, we are making irreversible 'planning' decisions that cut off future options: 'one more green field development cannot hurt'. The increasingly complex development assessment framework means that few intellectual, financial and institutional resources are directed at fixing market, political and design failure [Chapter 14]. Because the opportunity cost is ignored, community engagement is often limited to visual design aspects of particular developments. People are usually only notified if a development proposal is going to affect their property anyway. This limited view reflects the influence of the Pareto Optimum on decision-making frameworks. That is to say, we only try to ensure that no-one is unduly harmed, or that the tradeoffs are not so negative as to constitute an injustice.

## Shouldn't only those directly affected be considered in assessment processes?

Good design would leave everyone better off than before, a decision rule that we will call the 'Green Optimum' [Chapter 9]. After all, sustainability is about preserving the rights of future as well as present generations. They are also 'stakeholders' in planning decisions. Offset systems allow current residents to, in effect, 'negotiate' compensation. Thus the immediate beneficiaries of development determine acceptable levels of environmental impacts and reductions in the public estate that future generations will have to bear. Despite community input, developers can win support for controversial development by, in effect, 'buying off' the local community. For example, Alaska receives about 85 per cent of its revenue from oil royalties, so parochial forms of 'democracy' are not likely to prevent the granting of oil rights to wilderness areas. The fact that local or even aboriginal people decide what will compensate for the damage to their environment and loss of resource stocks or cultural heritage does not constitute sustainable decision-making. Compensating current beneficiaries for future generations' access to natural resources does not create net positive outcomes. An ecologically terminal process, over time, violates the rights of future generations to the means of survival. Further, by allowing the alienation of green field sites and wilderness areas to development, incremental approvals implicitly assume that we are still operating well within ecological thresholds. But even if the development is relatively short lived, it changes an ecologically sensitive site for all time. Instead of allowing offsets for the harm we are going to do in the future, then, sustainability would require that we reverse and/or offset the harm we have already done [Chapter 11].

## What about just requiring 'extra' positive offsets or exactions?

It would not be enough. We also have to move towards increasing future options and responsible choices, which are rapidly disappearing in the built and natural environment. Exactions or impact fees generally do not cover the direct costs of development to civil society. They only reduce the public costs of providing services to private development, such as the costs to a city of providing piped services to new suburbs or shopping malls. This means that developers may be required to provide some of the services that governments used to provide wholly at public expense to encourage growth. This approach can only offset negatives, not increase positives. Where such impact fees are negotiated, the outcome will depend on the relative power of the parties represented at the table – usually just staff and developers.[23] The point at which public benefits appear to outweigh the costs will depend on precedents, the media and changing power relationships – not the ecological base. Planners have been losing power since the 1970s (at least in some English-speaking democracies), with the move towards smaller government.[24] Thus if a city council got more concessions from a developer than they had managed to obtain in recent years, the benefits would be deemed to outweigh the costs. Planners cannot push for too much, as the developers might react politically or through the courts. They must, of course, simultaneously placate the community for the same reasons. This is what is usually meant by the 'balance' between conservation and development. We balance off more of the public estate each year to 'resolve' conflict by appeasing current stakeholders.

## Don't exactions and approval processes impose penalties on the developer?

The public pays for everything in the end, regardless of who pays up-front. Planning is generally misconceived as a financial imposition and a constraint on the market. In fact, however, exactions can conceal some of the public costs of conventional development. Even though the financial costs to the taxpayer are reduced by exactions, the ecological costs of conventional development never disappear. Taxpayers, in a sense, pay government agencies to mitigate the externalities of development. Moreover, assessment methods fail to weigh in the positive impacts accruing to the developer from the general public or public sector investment (whether from dams, sewage treatment, highways or telecommunications systems). This is what we have called 'internalities'. Direct benefits to developers can include land capability analyses, land remediation, infrastructure and service provision to the site. There are indirect services by planners as well. For example, planners often provide free expertise and advice to developers. Council staff and officials also act as intermediaries, resolving conflicting rights and keeping community objectors away from the developer. Planning is a safety valve for reducing the impacts of social discontent at the lowest cost to business. Thus planning transfers some private costs to the public (ie externalizes costs), but planning also transfers public benefits to private developers (ie internalizes benefits).

## Surely development fees at least pay for the contributions of planners?

If development fees for processing applications and exactions covered the benefits provided to development by the public sector, planning agencies would operate on a cost-neutral basis. So, again, government subsidizes private development through planning services provided with taxpayers' funds. This is not necessarily a bad thing. But since we already subsidize conventional development, why not subsidize net Positive Development instead? Planning could at least ensure that the taxpayers' indirect costs are appropriate or proportional to the benefits the general public receives. This would require tracing both internalities and externalities – who gains as well as who loses over the long term. Our assessment and rating tool suggests that we are improving with each 'greener' development. But planning inevitably transfers wealth by allocating land and resources. Planning methods do not map, or assign numbers to, these resource transfers. In effect, therefore, these methods 'invisibilize' resource transfers [Chapter 14]. Planning should register non-sustainable, inequitable, resource transfer processes over time, so that we can track our growing distance from sustainability. At the very least, planning could make subsidies and internalities far more visible. Rather than just assessing and mitigating development proposals that arise from the market, then, public planning could proactively seek public and/or private investment opportunities that reverse externalities, reduce disparities of wealth and generate win–win–win outcomes.

## What are some public costs that planning currently does not make visible?

Let us take the above example of the new regional shopping mall. Even if the developers pay for the roads, each customer must drive further to get to the mall (a cost to the general public). Net fuel consumption is a cost to society as a whole, even though distributed over large numbers of people whose incremental costs may seem negligible. Meanwhile, inner city residents may increasingly be left with only fast food outlets (ie a 'food desert'). The new shopping centre may remove valuable farmland from production for decades, if not permanently, due to pollution. Even if the developer and future owners pay very high rates for the land, this may not compensate for the (priceless) permanent alienation of biophysical and spatial resources. The costs of food production will rise, and ecosystems will be lost or degraded by land clearing and toxins. There are also social implications in the alienation of land. Due to the rising cost of increasingly scarce land, young people who do not inherit property or wealth may effectively be left landless. Yet even the assessment of social impacts generally begins from the status quo. When the existing distribution of wealth and amenity is the reference point, historical inequities embodied in the built environment (and entrenched by economic systems) are accepted as a value-neutral baseline. This vicious circle repeats itself with each development decision. This would be reversed by assessing development proposals by how much closer they would bring us to equality and sustainability [Figure 2, page 21].

## How does treating the social status quo as a neutral baseline affect design?

First, building incrementally on the status quo limits options to those that fit into the existing system. We saw earlier how it is hard to get radically new designs approved as they cannot easily be assessed [Chapter 5]. Conventional developments need only 'not make things worse' or 'not make poor people poorer' (Pareto Optimum). Second, assessment methods perpetuate physical inequities along with social ones if they do not consider resource (wealth) transfers, the impacts of existing development and the costs of inaction. By starting from where we are now, EIAs and SAs tend to treat net economic and environmental impacts as if they were distributed equally. New development that merely reinforces the current distribution of wealth and resources is not seen as 'inequitable'. For example, in Australia, the response to global warming by both major political parties has been the continuation of coal-fired electricity. This is because decisions do not count past, present and future health costs, the costs of subsidies to fossil fuels, and the resulting control of resources and political influence.[25] Consequently, we are currently committing huge sums to maintaining and modernizing the coal industry through 'cleaner' processes and geo-sequestration [Chapter 11]. It would be cheaper from a whole systems perspective to phase coal out, pension off the workers, managers and executives, and convert to clean power. But increased coal mining is not seen as making things much worse. Regardless of whatever is the best 'plan' for the future, however, the only real decision criterion has been whether investors are present or not. This causes us to ignore the wider context: the ongoing costs of past 'bad decisions'.

## How do planning studies ignore the ongoing costs of past decisions?

Planning assessments can be very 'selective' in choosing whether to consider the sunk cost or not (ie money already invested in existing systems and developments). As noted above, we do *not* consider the resources that were invested in a town's central business district when we approve a regional shopping centre that will lead to the town's economic and social deterioration. But we *do* consider the sunk cost in coal-fired power plants when deciding to invest huge sums in geo-sequestration research and development (a risky public investment) and starving funding for renewable energy (a safe public investment). We seldom count the public funds already spent in cleaning up the externalities of fossil fuel and nuclear sources of energy, but we do count the public funds already invested in solar energy. It is often argued that we cannot change to solar energy because of the infrastructure and jobs (sunk cost) already allocated to fossil fuels. Throwing good money after bad is not the way to a sustainable future. We therefore need to put the costs of inaction and sunk costs on the same page. There are already numerous studies that go a long way towards quantifying perverse subsidies of existing development, or sustainability audits.[26] Some studies assess the impacts of existing patterns of development in terms of their ecological footprints.[27] Others assess the impact of countries, cities and regions in terms of their 'material stocks and flows'.[28] However, these generally do not show transfers of ownership and control of resources, or internalities, let alone 'unjust enrichment' [Chapter 8].

## Wouldn't measuring existing impacts be as complex as predicting future ones?

Not at all. It would be relatively straightforward. One might suppose that considering the resource transfers and costs of inaction embedded in existing development could lead to the same problems of data collection and incommensurable measurements as is the case in assessing predicted negative impacts. However, it is much easier to measure impacts of existing systems than to predict changes in complex systems in the future. Hidden subsidies and transfers of public and private costs and/or benefits need not always be measured in great detail to see that there is a largely irreversible transfer of resources, wealth and power between people, sectors, regions or nations. Moreover, to create positive impacts, we need not inventory and quantify each and every impact. As we saw in the case of building rating tools, positive impacts using natural systems only need be an improvement over prior site conditions. In Positive Development, the primary issue would be 'What changes might improve human and environmental health, and reverse negative impacts caused by existing development?'. If an action or development makes *everyone* better off (hopefully even including other species), we do not need risk analyses. We only need to make an investment in Positive Development relatively more attractive than investment in harmful projects. Once we determine an area where we can make positive impacts at no net cost, as in eco-retrofitting, measurement becomes subsidiary to eco-innovation. We can simply set priorities and create programmes to implement them – in other words to 'plan' in a constructive way. Again, there is nothing wrong with impact and risk assessment *per se*. The problem is that we are spending 90 per cent of our effort on 10 per cent of the problem.

## So how do we proceed to implement some or all of these suggestions?

Some of the problems of project assessment that have been retained in sustainability assessment can be overcome by integrating 'impact prediction' with processes for auditing impacts of existing areas. The confusion, in practice, of prediction and auditing activity has meant that, while we may reduce the ecological harm we plan to do, we do not use development as a lever for reducing impacts already created. Planners could analyse defects in the design of the surrounding development and region to determine design objectives for new development. For example, an assessment of a new commercial building in an urban area should consider the negative impacts of surrounding development that could be ameliorated or reversed by a new building. Likewise, an assessment of a proposed regional shopping centre should consider how to support or modify existing shopping areas and public transport patterns. But major project assessments should *also* map de facto cumulative resource transfers by conducting what we have called resource transfer (RT) analysis. This would map the transfer of resources over time (from poor to rich, rural to urban, public to private, etc), in order to identify inequities that a new development or policy might help to reverse.[29] This might help build political momentum to address the inequitable resource transfers that are obfuscated by traditional (ostensibly neutral) planning analyses and incremental perspectives. Having seen how development assessment and control processes often fail to examine wider ethical and ecological relationships, the next step in developing SmartMode is to look at regional auditing methods.

# 8
# Regional Sustainability Audits

## From invisible to transparent resource transfers

The term 'assessment', as distinct from 'audit', has been used above to refer to methods that predict and measure negative impacts of *proposed* developments, plans or policies. We saw how assessment methods at the level of individual projects can perpetuate non-sustainable prototypes, as in the case of building rating tools and development control processes. To guide better design, Chapter 6 suggested a comparison of the ecology of existing development to indigenous site conditions (ET analysis). Chapter 7 introduced the idea of a sustainability audit of the surrounding urban area to indicate ways that a development could improve existing social and environmental conditions (RT analysis). This chapter looks at sustainability 'auditing' tools for assessing the *performance* of existing development, such as the ecological footprint (EF) analysis and the material flows analysis (MFA). However, it adds the element of ethics to assessment and looks primarily at the regional level. Audits of business and government organizations are discussed in Chapter 9 and include urban sustainability indicators, state of environment reporting, ecologically sustainable development reporting and corporate reporting.

It is suggested that MFAs can be more 'diagnostic' than EF analysis. That is, MFAs can trace wastes and imbalances in resource flows back to their causes – as well as total stocks or trends in consumption per capita or per area. So, for example, an MFA would show that household waste contributes a relatively small portion of total waste compared to upstream mining, extraction and production. A household EF would not offer this perspective. By tracking resource flows through the bioregion, audits could help us to find new ways to close, eliminate or reverse resource loops. They could help to link the design of cities, buildings and infrastructure with the wider urban, regional and natural environment and resource base.[1] EF studies tend to capture broad trends in average consumption (eg by income or family size), but conceal who benefits and who loses from existing patterns of land-use and resource allocation. But MFAs can also be myopic in terms of ethics and distributional justice, of course. When MFAs only examine stocks and flows of materials and energy, they can conceal the transfer of control over land and resources: the 'means of survival'. Like EF analysis, they do not indicate who wins and who loses over time. In other words, flows analyses, like input–output analyses, can be applied in a linear-reductionist framework. We will therefore look at how MFAs can be applied in a more positive, proactive and ethics-based design framework to generate positive impacts and increase environmental flows [Box 31].

## Why is it that audits don't tell us who loses or gains control over time?

Curiously, *financial* audits can tell us who benefits at whose expense, whereas *sustainability* audits do not. They sometimes consider externalities (the private costs that are dispersed over the general public), but not internalities. Historically, growth itself has generally been seen as an adequate public benefit to compensate for externalities. To guide sustainability, we need to:

- Audit trends in the access to, and control over, land and resources in time and place – from nature to development, from poor to rich, and from public to private
- Audit 'internalities' as well – the disproportionate public benefits that are captured and privatized by private interests and which can constitute unjust enrichment

The concept of unjust enrichment can be used to draw attention to cases where excessive benefits or profits are gained at the public expense.[2] Cost–benefit analyses can (ostensibly) measure the losses of social and ecological capital against economic gains. However, they do not capture the transfer of excessive benefits to developers or irreversible losses to the environment. RT analysis would put auditing in a time and space context. The proposed modifications to assessment and auditing tools to support systems re-design form part of SmartMode. SmartMode aims to combine ethically informed *design* thinking with auditing processes in a constitutional framework, to drive institutional change [Chapter 13]. The aim is to assist in making planning, design and decision-making more relevant to fundamental sustainability issues, which requires ethics and creativity, as well as eco-efficiency.

## What measurement methods are used in regional sustainability audits?

Currently, the best known regional auditing method that considers equity issues is EF analysis.[3] The EF is "the area of productive land and water (ecosystems) which is required to produce the resources consumed, and to assimilate the wastes produced, by a given population ... wherever on Earth that land may be located".[4] This is calculated by converting fossil fuel consumption, air pollution and other impacts into 'equivalent' units of land or ocean areas, in addition to the land actually occupied by the development. The EF concept makes the environmental consequences of poor systems design more easily grasped by the public. It was an important advance over previous ways of conceptualizing environmental problems, because it related resource consumption to land area. Economic analyses, by contrast, are largely ethereal and often ignore biophysical realities (ie the life support system). By linking consumption and production to the spatial dimension, EF analysis helps to bring home the reality there are critical *spatial* as well as total resource limits to growth. It shows that if all people lived like those of us in well-off nations, we would need several planets. Interestingly, EF analysis has been used to compare the impacts of eco-tourism in relation not only to other forms of tourism, but also to staying at home: that is, behaviour change as opposed to behaviour-as-usual.[5] Eco-tourism can have lower impacts than staying at home. This suggests people can reduce their overall footprint while having a good time.

## How does EF analysis deal with problems of inequitable consumption?

EF analysis shows that people in the industrialized world are, in effect, eliminating far more of the world's means of survival (land and water equivalence) than 'Third World' countries. EF analysis is useful for visualizing the problem of over-consumption. It is also able to portray the often inverse relationship between population size and per capita consumption. As environmentalists have long pointed out, children from wealthy nations can consume over 400 times more than an average child from an impoverished nation.[6] This deflates the common position that population growth in poor nations is *the* problem – a view that may have helped some to ignore systematic genocide in Africa. Both consumption and population are critical issues in all countries, but in different respects. On the one hand, poverty drives environmental destruction, such as land clearing and poaching for food. On the other hand, over-consumption in some nations is made possible by poverty in other places, for example the exploitation of cheap foreign resources and labour. It also helps to communicate the idea that urban land use has a significant relationship to regional carrying capacity, and that humans as a whole are using more resources than the Earth can sustain. So EF analysis conveys the importance of *inequitable* consumption of resources in reducing increasing total global resource consumption.

## Does EF analysis point to 'solutions' to the global inequities it exposes?

Not directly. The EF is an abstracted and generalized measure of *negative* impacts. It converts completely incommensurate issues, like air pollution and timber consumption, to a common factor. That factor, however, is 'tangible'. Land or carrying capacity is more concrete than rubbery concepts like willingness to pay, satisfaction or money, which are subject to inflation and political spin-doctoring. For example, we can print more money, which would affect the value of money, but not necessarily relative happiness [Box 34]. The tensions in relationships between consumption, population, land area and carrying capacity depend on the specific biophysical and socio-political context. Solutions therefore also depend on that site-specific context. Further, the EF does not measure what is arguably the most fundamental equity issue in sustainability. Specifically, that access to the means of survival is being transferred from civil society and placed in the control of private corporate interests and bureaucracies. We have noted that, over time, this tends to close off future social options and democratic choice. An EF analysis may communicate that water is being consumed at an unsustainable rate, but *not* how much water has been allocated to private (corporate or bureaucratic) control. It does not register how, in many parts of the world, water is being sold out from under the poor, who now cannot afford what was once a widely accessible means of survival.[7] In recent years, for example, many farmers have committed suicide in public protest over the loss of their water and/or land.[8]

## Isn't it enough that EFs reveal disparities of wealth and resource control?

No. EF analysis certainly highlights inequities in existing conditions, but we already know that there are great disparities in wealth, access and power. The issue is how to redistribute resources and amenities in win–win–win ways that minimize the *causes* of social dislocation and further conflict. In some cases EF analysis, like other tools, can be used to support preconceived solutions. For instance, some EF studies of Western cities have classified the consumption of household products by factors like family type, size, land occupied and income bracket. But when smaller families occupy more land area, it does not mean they necessarily alienate land from future ecological functions. So the ecological and geographical footprint are sometimes confused. This confusion appears to be because certain EF studies were based on the *preconceived* notion that sprawl was the big issue. Therefore, reducing 'effective' land area per person (urban consolidation) was the 'solution' [Chapter 3]. The fact that small families sometimes use more space than large ones could lead to strange conclusions. For example, the author heard a conference speaker argue that polygamy is more ecologically responsible than traditional family units because we need to share (private) space. According to him, promiscuous lifestyles are apparently more sustainable.[9] People's effect on material flows may also depend more on the *type* of products they consume and from where they are sourced (eg 'food miles').[10] The focus on families and individuals in some EF studies derives from a dominant problem description: that reducing resource consumption is a matter of individual behaviour, not systems. This deflects attention from, say, large corporations with vested interests in continued net resource consumption. Gains from squeezing people into smaller 'shoes' may be cancelled out by the increasing number of luxury shoes for the wealthy.

## How do we avoid the consumption of redundant luxury products?

Tools such as EF analysis foster environmental awareness among the educated. But if misapplied, they can reinforce buck passing or 'blame games'. This is one way some large industries and bureaucracies avoid change. For example, some fossil fuel interests spawned arguments about the causes and measurements of global warming for years. Some got bogged down in whether climate change was 'natural' or not – when we could not afford biodiversity, financial and other losses in any case. Likewise, large company ads managed to divert issues surrounding the fossil fuel supply chain towards individual behaviour. For example, the spotlight on plastic bags distracts attention from oil spills. Because environmental issues are presented in terms of individual consumption, environmentalists have been portrayed as people that want to 'tell others how to live'. The concept of 'environmental space', proposed by the environmental organization Friends of the Earth in the 1990s, starts from a somewhat different place. It estimates the sustainable use of resources such as timber and oil, or allowable greenhouse gas emissions, and divides that by the world population. This measures how far an individual, city or nation is from sustainable consumption. It is a form of absolute sustainability standard, as opposed to a relative one. To calculate environmental space, one only has to work out the stocks of resources – not calculate all the flows at each stage of production or regional boundary. (A similar approach is now being championed by an organization called Contraction and Convergence).[11]

## Can these analyses measure positive directions as well as negative ones?

The notion of a 'positive EF' is a contradiction in terms, since EF aggregates negative impacts. But we could, of course, measure net reductions in negative impacts over time. In fact, Denmark has supposedly reduced its footprint. But a 'less' negative footprint is not a positive one. Using the term 'positive' to mean 'less negative' could create the impression that progress is being made when we are merely reducing the *rate* of accelerating ecological decline. Environmental space and ecological footprints aid the realization that the existing global order is non-sustainable. However, these concepts have *not* been very effective in encouraging on-ground change. Some of the world's poor want a bigger share and, evidently, some of the rich do too. If some among the very rich see the rest of the world as a threat to their comfort levels, or their 'birthright' to a certain level of consumerism, some will want to pull up the ladder, or just look the other way. We might ask 'Do CEOs really work 400 times harder per hour than average employees?'. Would they be as productive if they did their own maintenance work like filing, cleaning and photocopying? Yet, as we have noted, solutions must be to everyone's advantage, including the rich – or disparities of wealth and power will continue to create conflict and reduce future options. On an overpopulated planet, sustainability requires reversing the growing inequities in the distribution of land and spatial resources, materials and energy. It is widely held, after all, that a fairer distribution of wealth is one of the few things that can help to curb population growth.[12]

## How would we get people to cut back their footprint or environmental space?

Footprints, environmental rucksacks and/or environmental space analyses all suggest that 'overdeveloped' countries like America, Australia, Canada and England need to cut back consumption and/or reduce their populations. As a society, we could at least cut back our footprint where it is painless to do so. This can be achieved by good design, more eco-efficiency and quality public space. Over-consuming countries can afford the innovations and environments that reduce consumption and material flows. They could provide more *responsible* consumer choices, rather than asking average citizens to either reduce their quality of life or accept bigger risks from hi-tech solutions. Simple, equitable ways of reducing consumption have been kept off the agenda, such as full cost pricing and/or capping maximum incomes. These do not require extensive investment in measuring consumption by variables that are inappropriate or complex to track, control or change. For example, people over a certain total net income could allocate the excess to charities, non-government organizations or research foundations of their choice. Wealthy people could create their own philanthropies, as some do now, if they wish to invest in social and environmental issues that reflect their personal values. This would avoid draconian measures like rationing, which might otherwise become necessary one day. Change will only occur if everyone is ensured of a higher quality of life. High quality public space could reduce the need for private consumption.

## How can we reverse the disparities of wealth through better design?

Whether or not we eventually choose to design an eco-logically rational economic system, we could at least improve the 'effective' distribution of wealth and quality of life through increased environmental amenity. At present, some people enjoy several palatial homes around the world, which they visit by private jet. Meanwhile, environmental refugees cannot even obtain decent tents. We can begin to counteract the negative impacts of wealth disparities and urbanization through the creation of public spaces that improve urban living, health and wellbeing. Replacing ongoing construction with design for eco-services would cost less than what we are now doing. The trend is in the opposite direction, however. We are moving away from whole systems improvements towards 'defensive design': social enclaves and even 'gated communities' for protection *from* the disgruntled. This privatization not only removes spatial resources from civil society, it reduces our opportunities to erase design errors in the future. Shared access to increased natural public resources, space and amenity is efficient, and can bring relative improvements to the lives of the poor without sacrifice by the rich. The evidence suggests that the power elite, as a whole, will not support fairness, equity and social justice unless and until sustainability benefits them. Positive Development could improve life quality well beyond what can be obtained through defensive design. MFA could help us find opportunities for Positive Development if 'modernized' to take into account ecology and ethics.

## Could MFA really assist in finding opportunities to create positive impacts?

It offers at least one advantage. MFA can be more 'place specific'. Tracing resource flows can help identify the distributional implications of existing development systems, so that design can work to reverse these problems. An MFA traces a substance or material throughout a system, production process or supply chain. This contrasts with methods such as life-cycle assessment (LCA), which, as we have seen, attempts to aggregate the inputs and outputs of all separate activities in the production, use and disposal of a product. The difference between LCA and MFA is largely one of focus: MFA follows particular substances (eg water, phosphorus, cellulose or cadmium) through human and/or natural systems. It shows changes that the substance undergoes from its origin in nature to its final disposal or reuse [Chapter 8]. But MFA could combine information about the transformation of materials (design) with input–output analyses (quantities). Although MFA has not yet really been used as a design aid, it has potential. To design a life form, after all, you would start with metabolism. Similarly, to design a living building, you would start with securing sustainable sources of energy and food.[13] To design a living city, we have to create mutually beneficial relations with surrounding ecosystems. Fortresses do not work well in a siege.

## How could mapping flows assist in improving whole systems?

Mapping an urban area in the wider systems context can identify waste in whole systems, not just component parts or stages of production. It can also identify financially profitable means of converting wastes to resources through cyclical processes. Some simple examples include:

- **Sewage**: Conventional sewage systems use electricity to pump wastewater and to oxidize the organic material. Then additional electricity and oxygen is used in aeration basins. The processes convert oxygen into millions of tons of $CO_2$. Bricks can entombe solids from industrial effluent waste and even sewage sludge, up to about 25 per cent of the fired bricks. The process kills the microbes. But this is, of course, an 'end-of-pipe' industrial solution. It is paradoxical that nutrients have become a source of pollution in our 'modern' form of industrial development. Instead, we could adopt a more 'rhizomatic' approach. Organic waste could be captured and used in gardens or agriculture, as in the city-to-soil project [Box 50]. Since the 1970s, in fact, some tree farms have been irrigated by nutrient-rich wastewater from sewage plants to produce timber and sequester $CO_2$.
- **Cement**: Building products are a major source of embodied energy, groundwater pollution and water consumption, from the production of components in factories through to construction waste to landfill. Portland cement embodies water and accounts for about 90 per cent of $CO_2$ emissions from concrete. If magnesium carbonate is used instead, it would soak up $CO_2$, according to materials expert John Harrison.[14] Portland cement uses huge amounts of energy to roast the calcium carbonate to make the 'clinker' that generates 7 per cent of total global $CO_2$ emissions (a ton of cement = a ton of $CO_2$). Likewise, titanium dioxide can be painted on existing urban surfaces to oxidize a range of air pollutants other than $CO_2$ (although it has negative impacts in production).

## If this is profitable, why doesn't private development do this on its own?

It does. However, private businesses will often pick the lowest hanging fruit and leave the rest to rot. This means the profits from eco-efficiencies fail to subsidize less profitable efficiencies. Therefore, the solutions chosen by the private sector are often sub-optimal. For example, consider the enormous 'wastes' from the wood chipping of native forests in Tasmania. An industry might decide to use woodchips or milling waste as an alternative to fossil fuels in electricity generation ('pyrolysis'), or as biomass for methane production. This can save money and offset negative impacts. Generally, it would not be net positive, however. Burning woodchips generates greenhouse gases and wastes organic materials that could be used for bio-productive purposes like growing food, while sequestering greenhouse gases for a while. Thinking in somewhat wider circles, it might make sense to add value by composting the chips with appropriate additives to create soil conditioners for remediating agricultural areas near the forestry operations. But from a whole systems view, these remedial uses for woodchips might delay the transformation from mining native forests to practising eco-forestry.[15] Currently, for example, Tasmania's wilderness areas are still being woodchipped for pulp. That is, they are not even used for timber. As opportunities for eco-efficiencies captured by the market are often sub-optimal, regional planners are needed to guide investment towards positive, whole systems solutions [Chapter 14].

## Are there urban and regional metabolism studies that guide investment?

Metabolic studies have been around for some decades.[16] However, like many other environmental management methods, they are often still at the 'problem description' phase.[17] MFA has been used to calculate the stocks and flows of natural and manufactured resources flowing through a city, farm, region or country. A growing number of researchers in several countries have used MFAs at local, regional and national levels to analyse social, economic and environmental problems.[18] Stephen Boyden was one of the first to conduct an on-ground metabolic analysis of an urban system, by tracing the material flows in and out of Hong Kong in the 1960s.[19] As outlined by Boyden, MFAs have three components:

1   **Inputs:** At the urban scale, disruption to ecosystems result from impacts related to metabolic inputs, such as the harvesting of vegetation for food, timber and fibres (causing soil erosion, salinization, disruption of nutrient cycles, loss of biodiversity and the progressive colonization of the natural world).

2   **Outputs:** Chemical pollution is associated mainly with metabolic outputs, causing acid rain, contamination of rivers with nitrogen and phosphorus, greenhouse emissions and ozone depletion, and the release of an increasing number of toxic substances into the biosphere.

3   **Transformation** (internal metabolism): Energy and resource consumption are particularly associated with internal metabolism in transportation systems, infrastructure and facilities, consumerism, heating and air-conditioning buildings, and recycling products.

In practice, however, metabolic analyses have tended to measure and describe the inputs and outputs of cities, factories and regions. For example, looking at farm inputs and outputs made us aware of the impacts of fertilizers, but not of the loss of soil fertility flows over time. As in LCA, this can lead to a preoccupation with data collection and processing that operates to supplant 'design thinking'. It is the *internal* metabolism that offers the best guidance for systems re-design or transformation. Through the design of systems that convert what would otherwise be waste materials into bio-productive products and waste, we could reduce inputs and outputs more dramatically than through efficiency measures.

## Couldn't LCA do the same things as MFA?

Again, LCA focuses on inputs and outputs, rather than flows and transformations. It aggregates inputs and outputs in a highly detailed way. It is difficult to undertake LCA for complex developments, let alone the total impacts of sectors or regions. This is because it separates components or processes that are in turn composed of many other substances, sources and processes. Aggregation involves highly complex quantification processes. LCA is therefore more suitable for determining the *relative* efficiency of different products, production systems and minor variations. For example, LCA (or MFA) can trace energy inputs through each step in timber extraction, processing, manufacturing, transport and the construction process to its final resting place in, say, the stud in a wall. This is excellent for creating efficiencies at each stage, but does not encourage better wall framing systems. Thus, as we saw, it is good for comparing and selecting among existing materials, processes and designs, but less useful for *new* ways of avoiding waste through entirely new services, products, processes or even supply chain structures. A flows analysis is better suited to help us find opportunities for innovation, although it too is not sufficient [Chapter 14]. We often fail to apply the most suitable mix of methods for addressing an issue or, again, pick issues that a given method can address. Both have their place.[20] LCA encourages a submarine view and MFA encourages a helicopter view. But as we will see, SmartMode aims to apply ecological and ethical prisms to these analyses.

## What is the practical value of MFA to sustainability then?

We can go beyond the calculation of waste at each point in the product cycle (ie input–output studies) to map the actual systems and processes that feed into and support the cycle (ie systems analyses). Such maps can facilitate *innovation* in both strategies and designs. That is to say, detecting losses in flows of materials and energy through and between urban, industrial and/or regional areas can indicate opportunities to generate resource savings, which is effectively 'income'. Presently, eco-designers have to do their own research with limited tools. While the EF facilitates environmental awareness, and LCA facilitates efficiency, MFA could facilitate relevant innovation and collaboration by providing an overview of the stocks, flows and cumulative waste of large-scale systems that can be diverted and/or converted into energy or useful materials. Thus:

- Business and industry could use MFA to help develop new products, processes, services and business strategies
- Municipal governments could use MFA to identify leverage points where direct actions may have fundamental system-wide benefits to the community
- Federal governments could use MFA to identify import-replacement products or more resource-efficient public services
- Regional governments or catchment authorities could use MFA to find means to make regions more self-sufficient

Moreover, MFA lends itself to communicating basic information about resource flows in simple visual maps.[21] Transdisciplinarity is a key element of innovation.[22] MFA can assist communication across many research disciplines and professional languages involved in sustainability issues. Finally, MFA could provide another basis for evaluating innovations, once conceived. It can help to determine the best use of the best type of resources for the best purposes, or even be used to re-examine a supply chain for areas of lost opportunities.

## How can a flows analysis help to create innovation in a supply chain?

Let's use timber as an example. Historically, environmental managers tended to focus on the extraction of timber at one end of the supply chain, or construction waste at the other. Thus, there was less attention to innovation, or potential value-adding along the various stages of a log's life-cycle through new design and construction practices. The total waste of timber in building construction is generally increased by things like standardized timber lengths and surfacing dimensions [Figure 6]. Designers (as specifiers), builders (as customers) and society as a whole are all effectively paying for the wasted offcuts and so on. Designers can, of course, increase project savings by:

- Developing plans that employ standard timber lengths
- Specifying and ordering exact lengths
- Designing more timber-efficient framing systems
- Considering the replacement of some timber with earth wall and/or bio-based materials

However, it is important that designers do not just adjust to an inherently wasteful system by working within industry conventions. As interested parties, they could influence the suppliers' practices upstream and encourage cooperative behaviour downstream. For example, agreements can be sought between all key participants in the construction process to identify and to reduce all sources of waste collectively (ie 'partnering'). In other words, to design optimal solutions, MFA can help us find out *where* and *how much* waste occurs. Of course, we also need to discover *why* it occurs, and whether this is due to consumer behaviour, management failure, institutional structures, or physical and intellectual infrastructures. This is what we will call institutional design (ID) analysis, which will be introduced later.

## Does this mean MFA can be used to discover 'new' problems to address?

Yes. For example, tracing the flow of critical materials and substances through systems could enable us to identify areas of 'impending' resource pollution or depletion – even before we might otherwise predict them. In this way, MFA could support more proactive planning: identifying new problems before they have measurable impacts, such as toxins gradually accumulating in ground water, or toxic dust accumulating downwind from mining operations. Because flows analysis is grounded in specific regions, we could proactively address problems created by past development by, for example, 'mining wastes'. Unexpected insights can emerge when helicopter and submarine views are combined. For example, MFA was applied to the river system running through the Australian Capital Territory (ACT). Our researcher, Robert Dyball, discovered that the isolated data compiled by the numerous government instrumentalities concerned with water management in the region did not add up.[23] Apparently none of these agencies had yet mapped and quantified the whole water system. The various authorities were only 'responsible' for isolated sections of the river. Water had been treated as inputs and outputs, not as a whole hydrological and ecological system (the umbilical cord view of nature). This may be partly why, despite awareness of an impending water quantity and quality crisis in the region, virtually nothing was done to 'drought-proof' Australia until it appeared that the drought might never break. So whereas input–output thinking does not tend to inspire vision or action, auditing stocks and flows at different scales could encourage innovation [Box 39].

## So does MFA meet all the criteria for a sustainability auditing method?

No. The potential of flows analyses as an aid to equitable distribution does not appear to have been realized. Again, a key value of MFA is that it can look at both place and materials, so it can link resource consumption to the specific region and its unique natural systems. So, MFA could be used to support the re-design of basic systems of production or construction. It could help map the transfers and transformations of energy and materials within a development or city, and those between that development or city and the wider ecology. We have suggested that tracing and quantifying flows of key materials as they move from their sources in nature, through urban, industrial and regional areas, and back to the natural systems in which they are embedded would support eco-logical design. However, MFA would not necessarily support the design of socially equitable and ecologically sound environments and institutions. This is partly because MFAs have tended to be conducted within the conventional linear-reductionist framework. Further, the solutions suggested in most MFA studies have tended towards recycling initiatives, not re-design. In other words, MFA has been used to reduce or re-use waste, but not to improve relations between natural areas and 'rurban' development (let alone between people). Environmental thinking needs to move beyond closing loops to creating virtuous cycles.

## So how could we describe the current stage in environmental thinking?

There have been significant additions to our approach to environmental management that shows progress towards systems design thinking.[24] Environmentalists have developed ever wider conceptual frameworks for addressing vicious circles, which could be summarized as:

- Whole of pipe: 'design for environment'
- Whole of product: 'no pipe design'
- Whole of business: 'cradle to cradle'
- Whole of industry: 'industrial metabolism'
- Whole of city: 'urban metabolism'
- Whole of region: 'material flows'
- Whole of government: 'eco-governance'
- Whole of economy: 'solar economy'

However, we have not yet developed many ways of adding value to the ecology and society. By focusing on future negative impacts, we overlook existing urban sustainability problems that could be easily corrected. To achieve Positive Development, we need a comprehensive framework of analysis to support eco-logical design in both innovations and environments. SmartMode aims to integrate analysis with design. It would link resource stocks and flows to the ecological base (ET analysis), and examine how institutions have transferred wealth and resource control (ID analysis), and how this reduces equitable distribution and access to the means of survival (RT analysis). This would provide a basis to guide systems re-design to reverse existing negatives and create positive gains.

## How could SmartMode assist in value-adding as well as in reducing flows?

SmartMode can help us examine space and spatial relationships (not just boundary conditions), and factor in time (not just energy). By drawing upon MFA and other analyses, it could help identify means to generate positive off-site impacts. So far, our LCA and MFA methods have visualized cities, rural and natural systems as separate sectors. Thus their inputs and outputs can only be reduced by closing loops between them [Box 39]. To design sustainable cities or regions, rurban and natural areas need to be seen as one complex system. Rurban systems must be not only relatively self-sufficient in the production of clean air, water and soil, but also supportive of the ecology and eco-productivity of natural areas. That is, to ensure resource security, we need to increase urban eco-services, biodiversity, wildlife corridors and habitats through cities to support the bioregions. There is an evolving trend towards value adding, but it has left out nature [Chapter 14]. We can add environmental and social value to cities and regions simultaneously. For example, we could increase regional economic sustainability *and* revitalize rural communities by sourcing building products from agricultural 'surpluses' or bio-based materials.[25]  At the end of their life, such lightweight materials could be composted to support urban agriculture and ecological landscaping.  Conversely, urban green waste can be composted and sent to farms at less cost to city councils than sending it to landfill [Box 50].

## But if MFA can help find ways to value-add, do we still need design?

We cannot significantly reduce the demand for resource extraction through mining, forestry, farming or 'primary' industry unless we change our ways (means and ends) of producing food and designing shelter.  Our development systems must provide not only for basic human physical needs, equity and social satisfaction, but also for nature.  We saw how the design of buildings, farming structures, and systems of construction and production are fundamental *upstream* drivers of material and energy flows throughout the development system.  But they also determine the future quality of land uses and eco-services *downstream* (such as water quality, soil productivity, erosion, salinity and flood control).[26]  To achieve urban and regional sustainability, therefore, both construction and farming sectors need to be reconceived and re-designed as integral to the natural environment.  It is not enough to reduce impacts on nature by efficiency, recycling and reuse.  Cleaner production and resource efficiency in the farm, forest, fishery or factory will not be sufficient – unless and until they are designed to actually *increase* natural capital.  Both urban and agricultural development therefore need to be re-designed as suppliers of 'surplus' eco-services [Chapter 1].  For example, we can re-design farms to provide the eco-services of carbon sequestration, wind energy production, biodiversity protection, catchment management and other eco-services [Chapter 11].  We can re-design cities to increase urban agriculture, mitigate climate change, and reduce transport between rural and urban areas.[27]  If governments and industry refuse to act, community groups could set the example by designing (cost-neutral) eco-retrofits that save resources and turn urban dead spaces into eco-productive spaces.

## If virtuous cycles are possible, why are we stuck in vicious circles?

Because of institutional design, politics is about competing interests, deals and tradeoffs, not designing win–win–win solutions.  Political and bureaucratic processes favour general policies that place constituent group interests over direct action to solve problems.  This coincidentally avoids accountability, as well as obtaining patronage and a kind of social pension upon retirement (known as the 'revolving door' between government and industry).  Privatization creates powerful supporters for decision-makers, and outsourcing avoids responsibility for basic service provision (and sometimes civil rights).  Recently, for example, the (then) Australian Federal Government denied compensation to a citizen who was erroneously locked up in a detention centre for illegal immigrants for 10 months.  The Government argued that since it had privatized this function, it was not responsible.[28]  In terms of *financial* balance sheets, of course, private management appears more efficient.  This is because ecological rationality and social justice issues are left to governments (ie externalized by the private sector).  Of course, neither public nor private sectors necessarily manage resources more wisely or poorly than the other.  The difference is this: the more resources that special interests gain control over, the more power they have to determine future prices and resource allocation decisions outside of the democratic process [Chapter 13].  Yet the long-term effects on access to and control over the means of survival are not even in the public discourse.  In Australia, renewable energy solutions have been kept off the shelves.[29]  Many Americans and Australians complain about the price of fuel, yet few complain that their tax dollar subsidizes the fossil fuel industry and ecological destruction.

A framework that concentrates on a narrow range of negative impacts hides private gains made at public expense. Measurement of impacts can sometimes be difficult but, surprisingly, measurement of internalities (unjust enrichment) would be relatively easy.

## So why do we not analyse externalities and unjust enrichment?

The public is aware of generalized externalities, and the fact that some gain benefits at the expense of the community. But talk of 'externalities' can be vague and almost synonymous with pollution or collateral damage. Our generalized problem descriptions – population, global warming, over-consumption, ecological footprint and so on – represent everyone as equally responsible and equally harmed, at least within a given region, class, nation or other category. But the costs and benefits of environmental damage are not experienced equally.[30] Carbon footprint calculators can tell us our individual contribution, but all individuals combined account for only about 10 per cent of emissions. These calculators do not link resource transfers to the acquisition of power, wealth and other benefits that accrue to those who are more capable of reducing externalities. Environmental management has been studiously apolitical. And apolitical, in this context, amounts to actively supporting the status quo. It is easier to blame an anonymous 'other': aggregations of people like suburbanites or the rich as a class. Yet in a project approval setting, the interests of an individual developer appear much greater than the interests of a community, because the losses to the individuals in the community are relatively small. That is to say, the loss to the community is aggregated and distributed uniformly over the population, so people appear to have little to lose individually (eg only an increased 'statistical' chance of cancer). In contrast, any extra gains (unjust enrichment) to the developer are not counted. Yet the losses of expected profits that the developer would forego if the project were not approved are often tacitly considered. This parallels the frequent expression of sympathy for a rich man who goes to jail as he 'has so much to lose'. There is no sympathy for 'common criminals' who have little to lose.

## How would the concept of unjust enrichment help to correct externalities?

Immediate physical harm can lead to legal action with possible compensation and even punishment. However, there is no limit on how much profit can be made at the long-term expense of the community – unless there is also *financial* impropriety. This is ironic, because people can be compensated for financial losses. While externalities refer to the transfer of private costs to the public, again, we are using the term 'internalities' to refer to the inequitable transfer of public benefits to private developers. Vicious circles are maintained by 'internalities' or excessive profits that result from externalities, or excessive pollution. Some inequitable resource transfers might reduce environmental impacts in the short term, but they eventually militate against sustainability. So we need to consider other balance sheets, such as the changing balance between the general public and those with escalating power and control over the public estate. If we want to find cost-effective eco-solutions that make everyone better off, we need auditing methods that make the resource transfers embedded in existing or proposed development *transparent*. One way to do this, then, is to recognize the 'unjust enrichment' that occurs through inequitable resource transfers. This is, in fact, a legal term which refers to people who receive an inordinate benefit at the expense of others.[31] In that context, unjust enrichment is a remedy or measure of damage; it is not a crime or misdemeanour in itself. But it can serve as a concept to guide planning and decision-making. It has a precedent in the concept of 'betterment' in planning (like capital gains). In planning, however, betterment usually refers to increases in land or property value due to public planning regulations, not the lack thereof.

## How can the concept of 'unjust enrichment' be used in decision-making?

We need to recognize that the ecological base is ultimately the main source of wealth. Of course, material resources, space, human talent and labour are also necessary. However, if the ecological base is consumed, then no one can acquire wealth, no matter how clever they are or how hard they work.[32] There is a negative misperception that wealth creation results from the innate superiority of individuals – a view often favoured by the successful. This helps some to whitewash the fact that a few hundred individuals in the world now have as much wealth as millions of the world's poor. If a developer or corporation makes a fortune from destroying public amenities or shortening life spans, they are 'unjustly enriched'. For example, a large construction company in Australia used asbestos for a couple of decades after it was banned. This was about 100 years after it was known to cause serious harm. The company was ultimately required to pay compensation, but avoided doing so for years. This was strategic, as the compensable 'damage' to the workers (paradoxically) can disappear when they die. The award amount created a fund to support future victims, but did not cover the unjust enrichment (profits) obtained by years of deliberately putting people at risk. Until we limit personal and corporate profits, and measure damages to the environment and people in terms of unjust enrichment, sustainability will remain an end-of-pipe dream.

## But haven't our decision tools looked at equity as well as efficiencies?

Some purport to. However, our decision tools emerged from a cost–benefit framework that 'balances the interests' in future actions in a pluralist (versus public good) framework [Chapter 12]. Had our tools emerged in a whole system, public interest framework, the internalities, cumulative resource transfers, costs of inaction and double standards would have been more apparent. In a development issue, of course, all parties appeal to public values and make claims about relative costs and benefits to the public. However, the accumulation of wealth and power – which both determines, and flows from, land-use and development decisions – is not debated. If researchers mapped the resource transfers of *existing* systems of development (materials, space, energy, wealth and/or power) and how they shaped environmental quality in terms of equity, there would be a basis for public debate [Box 48]. Instead, the status quo, with its radical and accelerating concentration of wealth, is treated as if it were the 'natural order'. Using the status quo as the benchmark thus obfuscates power relationships. We have seen how sustainability auditing, as well as other environmental management methods, are selective in what they measure. They validate and reinforce the existing costs, inequities and decision-making influences already embedded in the industrial systems of development by 'normalizing' them. After that, environmental planning and management can only ensure the impacts are not so great that they cause social conflict that can destabilize the given order.[33]

## What are some examples of how we ignore the costs of contextual systems?

We saw earlier how 'sustainable' transport plans often fail to compare the net impacts of cars to sustainable transport options.[34] Instead, they compare the costs of change to the incremental costs that would be incurred from this point on by continuing to provide more infrastructure for cars. Although the information is available, the negative impacts of *existing* car-oriented transport systems are often not counted. Nor are they included in public debate. Similarly, assessments of solar technologies often still do not weigh in past and present resource transfers and subsidies to fossil fuel industries. Or, even worse, they count these costs as 'an investment' that would be lost if we moved to more sustainable systems [Chapter 7]. Social impact assessments examine which groups may benefit or lose from a proposed programme or project, but it is usually in relation to what they had to begin with (how poor or rich they were).[35] By ignoring the distributional impacts of *existing* conditions in a regional analysis, we only see how much worse off people will be. Because our assessment and auditing methods only measure change from where we are, they do not consider reduced social options over time. Further, they do not look at the unjust enrichment of individuals. As means of survival are privatized in corporate or state bureaucracies, there is a gradual loss of democratic rights. Examining internalities as well as externalities would help to reveal the problems created by the concentration of wealth.

## But how would we assess how transfers impact on sustainability?

We have said that keeping future options open, or increasing them, is the essence of sustainability. Therefore, a major issue in sustainability auditing should be the adverse effects of existing systems on future options, social choice and substantive democracy over time. To examine the resource transfers that have already resulted from urban development and interventions in the natural environment, we could, for example, measure 'negative space' [Chapter 3]. This would reflect some of the distributional costs and benefits resulting from the alienation of natural capital, land, and ecosystem goods and services. Instead of just measuring the rate of decrease in natural capital stocks, then, we could look at the conversion of (public) space to private control. Negative space would be a measure of the reduction of access to the public estate, through the privatization of space or 'enclosure'. By mapping resource transfers and existing inequities, and their spatial consequences, we have another basis for eco-retrofitting: to redress existing impediments to universal health and quality of life. The reduction of dead (lifeless) space or negative (privatized) space would be one indicator of design quality [Chapter 6]. By identifying resource transfers and the institutional structures that have caused social and environmental imbalances, we can find opportunities to reverse them through net Positive Development [Box 53].

## Would SmartMode therefore replace LCA and MFA as planning analyses?

Quantitative analyses cannot design for us. In SmartMode, such quantitative tools are therefore subsidiary to design. Only through design can we increase the ecological base and public estate, and create 'reversible' developments. A design-oriented approach (value-adding) is needed along with flows analysis (system efficiency) and input–output analysis (resource efficiency). LCA and MFA could serve as 'support tools' for eco-innovation and eco-retrofitting. There is no shortage of things to audit or measure that are still largely omitted by researchers:

- Overall flows through development generally, such as detoxification of the environment
- The costs of inaction due to not addressing the impacts of existing development
- Internalities and inequities already embodied in the built environment
- The degree to which existing buildings fall short of resource autonomy
- The negative economic impacts of *existing* urban areas
- The opportunity cost of land alienated from future public purposes (negative space)
- Dead space (space that excludes nature or bio-productive ecosystems)
- The amount of ecological space added (per person or square metre)
- The highest ecological use of specific areas of land and value of existing natural systems
- The public purpose of proposed land uses (eg whether a cigarette factory or a public park)
- The time it takes renewable resources and ecosystems to regenerate (ecological waste)

- Relative environmental impacts of the surrounding area before and after construction
- The opportunity cost of poor design (eg irreversible planning decisions)
- Unjust enrichment from planning decisions (ie 'per capitalist' as well as 'per capita')

## How do we find the causes of these resource transfers?

The linear transfer of the means of survival (from rural to urban, from nature to development, from poor to rich, and from public to private) tend to be the critical ones in terms of sustainability. They irreversibly close off future democratic and ecological options. To find direct and positive actions that can reverse the consequences of resources transfers, we can begin by looking at mechanisms by which they occur (ie ID analysis). Some mechanisms by which resource transfers result in vicious circles are technological and engineering conventions; institutional decision processes and regulations; economic valuation frameworks; and urban planning and design precepts. For example:

- **Technological conventions**: Resource-intensive infrastructure and technologies often 'intervene' in natural systems to reduce natural capital and natural life-support systems. These create vicious circles. For example, dams produce energy but drown soil and ecosystems. Roads disturb habitats and migration patterns. Air-conditioning systems have caused many tropical houses to be insulated and made airtight. These, in turn, make cities dependent on centralized energy production, and vulnerable to brown outs or black outs – such that more dams or power stations are needed. Likewise, engineering conventions such as storm water pipes (in lieu of water-sensitive urban design) reduce environmental flows and increase urban floods. Centralized industrial systems that place the means of survival in the control of a few create technological dependency and make urbanites vulnerable to terrorism or extreme climate events.
- **Institutional mechanisms** often 'expropriate' previously held rights or options. Laws, regulations or processes that reduce or transfer freedoms, property or resources from the public domain to, say, corporations, individuals or government bureaucracies at below replacement cost are examples of this. Gated communities and private ocean fronts reduce public space physically, and deprive others of environmental health and amenity. Enclosure and privatization could be seen as forms of expropriation. Again, since power parallels resource control, inequitable wealth transfers lead to power imbalances that, in turn, affect future resource allocation decisions and even decision systems (eg trading systems in lieu of regulations).
- **Economic frameworks** transfer wealth by treating externalities (where the private costs of development are shifted to the general public) and internalities (inordinate benefits received by special interests at the expense of the general public). Environmental impacts are exacerbated by economic conventions such as 'discounting' [Box 43]. While assessing internalities and externalities could assist our understanding, the economic concepts themselves make environmental damage seem 'collateral'. Currently, internalities and externalities are intrinsic to the design of the economic system. The past use of the term 'market failure' itself implies that we are not responsible for the inability of the economic system to meet the growing demand for environmental protection and public health.
- **Planning and design precepts** are 'redistributive' and can therefore have negative *or* positive outcomes. Planning decisions have tended to create inequities, as land and development approvals have been allocated on a first come, first served basis. Ecologically insensitive

planning and design can also re-distribute environmental amenities indirectly, such as where a view is gained by blocking others' views, or access to sunlight is removed by a tall building. While planning systems try to balance rights, this has been done in an unbalanced framework that ignores unjust enrichment and only determines if public *costs* are too excessive (addressed to some extent by the concept of 'betterment' or capital gains tax). A 'balance' between conservation and development should mean ecological restoration, not reserving bits of the remaining public estate each time the rest of it is allocated to development.

## How would such institutional analyses help us create positive outcomes?

It is important to understand how inequitable resource transfers and costs, through all these interconnected channels, become embedded in the built environment. The above examples can be viewed as 'negative', because they work against future life quality options and democratic choice. If we accept these systems, we can only debate how to re-distribute what is left over. However, these institutional mechanisms do highlight areas where we can reverse, replace or re-design non-sustainable systems [Boxes 52 and 53]. So, by mapping such resource transfers, we can get a more balanced view of the consequences of the dominant approach to planning and development than the 'selective' balance sheets created by our current assessment and auditing methods. Chapter 14 looks at how to turn negative resource transfers into positive ones, and Chapter 15 outlines a generic process for action and investment in Positive Development. In the following section, we will examine several 'best practice' planning and management methods for their potential to contribute to whole systems improvements. But first, we will look at how we can improve upon current means to chart progress and evaluate performance through sustainability reporting.

# 9
# Sustainability Reporting

From environmental
accounting to
management
accountability

For our purposes, the defining characteristic of environmental and/or sustainability reporting is that it measures the management and operational performance of an organization. Whereas assessment and auditing tools are concerned with the performance of physical structures, products or production systems, reporting is intended to aid self-assessment and operational improvement. Some methods touched on here are corporate environmental reporting (CeR), state of environment (SoE) reporting, and ecologically sustainable development (ESD) reporting. Government and corporate environmental management systems and corporate reporting are increasingly seen as *de rigueur*.[1] The focus of this chapter is on public sector reporting.[2] Over the last decade, many local councils have developed sustainability reporting processes in order to present 'report cards' to their communities. Reporting can be mandated, but it is usually voluntary and thus, some feel, often driven by public relations. Yet reporting can provide guidance on decisions, policies and priorities, as well as grade performance retrospectively, so it is useful even if the individuals responsible have moved on.

The general approach is to select targets and periodically measure relevant indicators to track changes in impacts on ecosystems, human health and life quality. There are now myriad sets of indicators for physical, chemical, biological or socioeconomic phenomena. Some types of indicators include environmental quality indicators (EQIs), urban sustainability indicators (USIs) and genuine progress indicators (GPIs). Many local governments have now created their own indicators to reflect local citizen participation and priorities. Government agencies are even beginning to apply sustainability principles to the design of decision systems as well as organizational performance. Most frequently, however, urban sustainability indicators lack reference to the regional ecological context, such as endangered ecosystems. There needs to be more work in integrating structures and decision frameworks with sustainability goals, establishing creative policymaking or eco-innovation processes, and tracing outcomes to specific actions. So the questions are whether reporting can:

- Integrate sustainability considerations into decision-making
- Align actions, decision structures and budgets with sustainability principles

- Make government and industry genuinely more accountable
- Encourage *direct action* on sustainability issues
- Improve the performance and culture of management

## Has sustainability reporting improved the culture of organizations?

Perhaps slowly. Some have argued that the rhetoric of reporting is not matched by tangible outcomes. However, gradual improvements in organizational culture and awareness appear to percolate up through organizations that engage in environmental management systems and reporting. Reporting encourages a more positive, proactive orientation among business, government and community organization in general. Just as EIAs increased awareness of the negative impacts of development, environmental reporting has expanded our appreciation of potential efficiencies. Businesses and government agencies that undertake reporting for compliance and public relations reasons later realize that reporting can help to improve their 'bottom line'. Many firms have achieved significant costs savings through eco-efficiencies and organizational improvements, which can also result in greater worker productivity or health. There is now growing support from business and industry for legislative action to enforce corporate reporting. This could ensure a more level planning field among firms.[3] To move beyond compliance and public relations activity to proactive improvement, however, reporting might need to encourage organizations to influence change across industries. For example, reports might include a section on collaborative initiatives with community groups and other industries: horizontally (same industries), vertically (the supply chain), and diagonally (other industries and community).

## Has reporting improved public sector accountability and performance?

Public reporting is less straightforward than corporate reporting, as government bodies are responsible for more than eco-efficiencies.[4] Private firms can focus on doing what they do best, while government agencies do not always know what they should be doing. Therefore they tend to report on general trends. USIs are sometimes a compilation of broad principles or rubbery value statements that cannot easily be tracked.[5] The problem with charting trends is that it is difficult to determine if changes in the environment are actually due to government policies. There are myriad intervening factors, unpredictable variables and exogenous forces acting in an open urban system. When environmental reporting focuses on symptoms or downstream impacts in the environment, this tends to reflect more on the resilience and adaptability of the environment (ie nature's ability to cope) than on the organization's management performance.[6] Theoretically, measuring and monitoring changes in the environment should help determine what actions to take. However, there is little evidence that ESD reporting shapes public policy, increases human accountability or builds design capacity. When ESD reporting was introduced, it generally meant more accounting activity, rather than direct actions to enhance sustainability. In the public sector, then, management should be measured by 'affirmative actions': steps the agencies have taken to *improve* environmental conditions. Direct actions and their effects would be easier to assess than exogenous changes in the environment. By reporting on positive and direct actions themselves, accountability would also be more transparent. Urban issues also need to be reported in their regional context. ESD reporting has also been weak at linkages between urban agencies and regions.

## Why should urban sustainability reports have a regional perspective?

Urban sustainability reports often list isolated changes (inputs and outputs) of flows at the urban boundary. If treated as separate from the *bioregion*, they cannot reflect the significance of urban policy on the region, and vice versa. As long as goods and services are on the shelf, urban consumers will believe they can acquire those products into the foreseeable future. There will be general confidence that the linear 'umbilical cord' will continue to ensure a flow from outside the urban borders. A case in point was a draft 'strategic' plan for a town in the Australian Capital Territory (ACT).[7] Only two 'sustainability issues' were considered in the plan's sustainability section: water and sewerage. The plan said that there was adequate water and sewerage infrastructure in and out of the city. Hence, sustainability was not a problem. The apparent assumption was that the city could continue to turn on faucets and flush toilets in perpetuity. Shortly thereafter, the ACT experienced water shortages and became drought affected. Since humans can only live without water for a few days, the lack of a plan for a secure source of water was not very 'strategic'. The author pointed this out, but the planning consultant said it would be inappropriate to raise the issue, as it had not arisen in the focus groups that he ran. If planners do not raise these issues, we can hardly expect citizen focus groups to be concerned about the sustainability of fundamental resources. Of course, this also reflects the tacit priority on economic issues over resource management in sustainability plans. The concern is often with inputs and outputs: ensuring supply is matched by consumption.

## Isn't sustainability now better integrated with local government planning?

There is a growing effort in some countries to incorporate sustainability goals across the 'whole of government' to inform all levels of decision-making in all departments, or at least to pay lip service to the idea. Even some treasury departments are beginning to grapple with, at least, a triple-bottom-line approach.[8] But the emphasis has been on adding more rows in balance sheets, not tangible action. There is little reporting on what organizations are actually doing to change themselves. The mere fact of using scorecards conveniently conveys the message that a council or firm is performing responsibly – regardless of tangible outcomes. But it also entails more book-keeping activity. Staff need to be diverted to this work from elsewhere. Moreover, attempts to integrate staff, or to spread sustainability considerations across government, have not always ensured the cooperation of other departments. This is partly because agencies often see reporting as another costly compliance activity that should only pertain to departments with a specific environmental mandate. Also, targets and benchmarks could even reveal inadequacies that such government departments might prefer not to publicize.

## Don't targets ensure that continuous improvement will occur?

In a political world, targets may often be used speciously. For example, the former Australian Government would not sign the Kyoto agreement, but simultaneously claimed to be meeting its Kyoto target (which allowed an *increase* in greenhouse gas emissions and credit for *not* clearing more land). Also, if reporting is to serve as a means to back up claims of continuous improvement, great care must be taken in the selection of indicators. Indicators must be easy to measure, inexpensive and likely to show improvements over time. So a lot of energy and time goes into their selection.[9] If targets and indicators prove to be too difficult to achieve, a jurisdiction must change its targets. This takes time and money away from fixing problems. In one case experienced by the author, for example, a whole new greenhouse plan was prepared because the earlier one had targets that later appeared too difficult to meet. The development of indicators can thus supplant efforts to discover new strategies and actions to increase sustainability. The tendency is to select abstract indicators of trends, rather than look for specific areas of waste and inefficiency that could be turned into resources. But if data about consumption trends had been enough to stimulate public demand for change, people would have acted long ago. Why jump out of a spa before the water boils?

## Is this really why such general indicators and targets are used in reporting?

Not entirely. The idea of sustainability is still new to many people in government. It tends to be equated with being more holistic. Holistic is taken to mean including a wider range of social and environmental considerations in what remain largely financially driven decisions. Government agencies often feel the need to be as comprehensive and general as possible (with 'spin'). But it is also convenient that comprehensive indicators cannot be linked very directly to the performance of specific political parties, urban managers or decision-makers. Tracking general trends in the environment is like reporting on the weather: no one can really be held accountable for the accuracy of the predictions, let alone the weather (ie nature). The result is that changes in the environment are often reported as if commentating on a spectator sport, the weather or the market. These are things we can try to influence, but cannot control. While money can be made by gambling on change (eg predicting options markets and the results of horse races), little sustainability gains occur without *direct* investment in eco-solutions. Priorities for public investment are currently more a result of pressure-group demand than research to identify where the largest resource flows can be most effectively addressed [Chapter 14]. 'Research' in the political sphere seems to be more about manipulating, anticipating and/or controlling opinion about business-as-usual than about determining priority actions to make everyone better off. 'Public education' is often about promoting government policies after the fact.[10]

## Doesn't reporting indicate where financial resources should be invested?

Reporting that is based on general indicators requires a lot of investment in tracking trends that could instead be invested in eco-solutions. Even when 'sustainability offices' or environmental departments invest in reports, or even ecological footprint analyses, it does not mean their findings will be translated into policies that are specifically aimed at positive action. Most planning and sustainability agencies are still preoccupied with increasing development with less negative impacts. Identifying opportunities for Positive Development could be seen as exposing these departments or agencies to political risk. To target positive action, public investment would need to be informed by an assessment of both the costs of current inefficiencies and waste in urban development and the cumulative costs of inaction. Reporting should guide the elimination of existing problems, not just monitor what is essentially market activity and its impacts. We are not responsible for nature's ability to cope, but we are responsible for interfering in its ability to do so. Tracking trends that are subject to exogenous forces does not encourage policy innovation or accountability as, again, trends are usually only remotely related to (politically inspired) actions and policies. Managers could instead be acknowledged for fixing specific problems already existing in urban development. 'Costs of inaction' (CI) analysis would give a better baseline for measuring management performance than 'how much worse things may be in a year from now'. It would also make decision-makers more accountable, both individually and collectively.

## Does SoE reporting link human actions and policies to sustainability?

In theory, yes. The pressure–state–response (PSR) model that underpins state of environment reporting in Australia, and some other OECD countries, purports to link indicators back to human behaviour or performance [Box 35]. The PSR model provides a means for monitoring actions and changes that occur in *response* to human actions. The idea is that human activities put 'pressure' on the environment that alters its state. The changed state then calls for new responses that, in turn, put a new pressure on the environment, and so on. This iterative analysis aims to draw attention to 'causes' as well as 'impacts'. It also increases public awareness of the complexities involved in social and environmental interactions over time. Because it is difficult to monitor environmental impacts, however, SoE reports tend to be more managerialist than heuristic. They document past decisions and predict further problems by projecting past impacts into the future. SoE reports seldom concentrate on positive actions undertaken by all departments to fix the cumulative costs of externalities or make tangible progress towards sustainability. This would go beyond establishing new sustainability offices. (A parallel form of managerialism can be found in academia, where performance is increasingly measured by the amount of measurements that academics undertake on behalf of management.) Direct positive actions would be relatively easy to measure because they can be linked to their direct outcomes – such as resource savings. But in practice, reporting seldom makes a connection between impacts and policy development or decision-making.[11] Not only are the links between indicators and real world cause and effects weak, they are seldom directly referred to while making decisions.

## Aren't environmental reports and indicators used in decision-making?

Few decision-makers actually *read* SoE reports, let alone refer to them in making decisions.[12] They do not have the time or interest in reading volumes of environmental facts, figures and trends. Also, people in government do not want negative information to be widely circulated, as it could reflect on the governing party's performance, as well as their personal personal performance. For example, the author was present when a federal environmental agency was deciding how to announce and disseminate an SoE report – given that it was *not* a good news story. The author suggested its potential for raising environmental awareness be used as a positive message. However, the decision was later made to downplay the very existence of the report – despite the enormous costs involved in its production. Moreover, although SoE reports largely only measure environmental problems, they can have the effect of lulling people into the assumption that something is being done. The author has heard government decision-makers say that 'we should wait until the next report before acting in case things are improving'. That is, why would we want to make things better if they are not getting worse. Further, while SoEs are a useful, objective source of information, they can also create the impression that the decision framework and process itself is objective, rational and responsive to environmental issues. This fosters and reinforces an unrealistic and idealized view of decision-making. Treating decision-making as an objective process can lead to criticisms being dismissed out-of-hand as 'subjective'.

## How do SoE reports support or reflect an idealized view of decision-making?

Environmental auditing, valuation and reporting tend to be couched in the 'rational man' model. This holds that better information automatically leads to better decisions – so all we need is more information. However, most decision-makers think politically. This is partly how they came to occupy decision-making (political) positions in the first place. 'Real life' decision-making processes are characterized by bargaining, deals and tradeoffs. In this culture, personal and political interests can become confused, and expedience can prevail over substance. In financial areas, where there is a money trail, we have many safeguards against the misuse of funds, bribery and undue influence on decision-making, even if they may be difficult to enforce. It is accepted that corruption occurs, and we have legal mechanisms for policing this. However, in land-use and development arenas, despite the enormous potential for corruption, there is a tendency to regard decision-makers as objective, scientific and acting in the public interest [Chapter 12]. Decision processes seldom require 'reasoned' opinions for major development decisions, except in the case of appeals to environmental courts. Written decisions could avoid appeals in some cases. In other cases, they would make appeals more useful in improving performance. Although our *financial* audits, in theory, tell us where money goes, our *environmental* auditing methods and indicators obscure who gains at whose expense. Yet unlike financial transactions, resource allocation and land development decisions are largely irreversible. Again, we can print more money to provide restitution or compensate victims in the case of financial fraud, but we cannot print more land and resources. Given this irreversibility and potential for inequitable resource transfers, there is all the more reason for 'due process' and transparency in land-use and environmental decisions.

## So why doesn't reporting provide genuine transparency and objectivity?

The ostensible 'objectivity' of land-use and environmental decision-making reinforces the tendency to accept existing resource stocks and ecological conditions as the benchmark. Quantitative reporting defines the issue as 'how efficiently resources are being used', not who gains or loses. Apolitical, public engagement in government reporting and quality control is not deemed necessary. Transfers of public resources to private interests are not an issue, as long as resources are used efficiently and individuals are not immediately and measurably harmed. But the real sustainability issue would be the *purpose* to which finite land and resources are allocated. Reporting addresses impacts and actions in terms of general categories (eg land, air, water). It is not so good at addressing local opportunities for positive action [Chapter 14]. Further, as we saw in other areas of environmental management, resource consumption is often aggregated (ie total consumption of a particular resource) and/or divided by population (ie per capita consumption). This conceals which needs are being met, and which people or sectors are accumulating control of resources and power. A diminution of total resources may not, for example, reveal a growing disparity of wealth and an incremental loss of democratic control over, or access to, the means of survival. Transfers of resource control can be even more irreversible in terms of democracy than the fact of diminishing resources. If, for example, control over public land is granted through forestry concessions or mining rights, the public can theoretically extend the life of those resources by reducing consumption. In other words, in theory (only) the public can express their preferences for environmental protection by their 'unwillingness' to use the mined materials. But future generations may lack the decision-making power to reverse those public land and resources decisions.

## Why don't we report on resource transfers as well as resource stocks?

Perhaps this is for the same reasons that other environmental management methods ignore ethical issues. It would be politically awkward for government-funded SoE reports to show transfers of wealth or control over the means of survival. Few want to draw attention to issues that might 'rock the boat'.[13] Planning has automatically allocated public resources to private development at a rate that does not cause excessive voter or civil discontent (ie planning could be said to function like a toilet stopcock). Also, to appear 'objective', decision aids, models and analyses must be abstract and detached from political issues. Thus analyses and decisions are unlikely to take into account effects on power relationships over the long term. The design of 'objective' analyses reflects the past unwillingness of researchers, on the whole, to accept responsibility for the social and environmental consequences of their work. To be seen as objective, environmental scientists, in practice, also need to appear apolitical.[14] Many espouse the view that by providing 'objective' methods, decision-makers will act on information in objective ways. By subscribing to the myth that they have a more pristine and detached perspective, researchers do not have to account for the political outcomes of these tools.[15] This creates a vicious circle. This may seem overly cynical, but one can only imagine the reaction a scientist or academic would receive for developing a reporting methodology that mapped wealth transfers through discretionary planning decisions over time.

## Surely not all scientists and consultants support the status quo?

Not at all. However, scientific integrity is compromised by a growing privatization of information. Scientific methods, models, tools and data are increasingly applied by private consultants under commercial-in-confidence provisions. Consultants, even more than scientists, cannot afford to offend clients and need to appear 'credible'. But credibility is often code for supporting the status quo. Therefore consultants usually present ostensibly value-neutral, apolitical analyses that recommend little or no basic change. So while reporting creates jobs for environmental scientists, it also creates vested interests in 'passive' kinds of methods, measurement and reporting frameworks that do not challenge business-as-usual [Chapter 7]. After all, if old tools addressed environmental problems, we would have solved them by now. In short:

- Scientists are not 'scientific' unless they are apolitical
- Consultants must say what their clients want to hear
- Politicians need to cover up or down play problems
- Planners feel they need to accommodate the market
- Designers are segregated from science and politics

There is a gap here. There is no mainstream field of enquiry or decision sphere concerned with the costs of inaction and/or growing differentials of wealth and power [Chapter 13]. Hence reporting has not yet done much to make decision-makers accountable.

## Is this to suggest that technical research is influenced by power relationships?

This is old news. As we saw, in Australia, 'clean coal' (an oxymoron) research has been well funded, while renewable energy – though proven to work – continues to receive relatively little funding. A major portion of government funding in Australia is instead going into geo-sequestration for removing and storing a percentage of the $CO_2$ emitted in energy production. 'Geo-sequestration' means piping carbon from fossil fuels back into the ground, where it will remain for a couple of hundred years or so. The amount of money spent on geo-sequestration would have funded solar cells on thousands of homes in Australia. This would have greatly reduced the need for power plants, and greatly reduced the cost of the solar cells through economies of scale. Geo-sequestration may be a financial as well as physical 'black hole'. Pensioning off fossil fuel industries and coal miners might be justifiable on social justice terms alone (ie to reduce the pain of change). But geo-sequestration can also prolong the transition to a solar economy. By fostering the 'sustainability of fossil fuels', geo-sequestration perpetuates the transfers of public funds to 'fossilized' forms of development that damage health, while increasing resource consumption and disparities of wealth. It also directs public funds away from things like eco-retrofitting which could improve public and ecosystem health and distribute environmental benefits to a greater number. Allocating resources to the industrial processes that cause global warming – instead of investing in well-known, low-risk solutions – can only be explained by the *past* accumulation of power through resource control and resulting concentration of wealth. As resource and wealth are transferred to private interests, the public gradually loses effective control over both resource distribution and consumption.

## Can't we have sustainable development in spite of a concentration of wealth?

No. Regulation of industry becomes more difficult as corporate power becomes more concentrated (and located offshore). It is no coincidence that we have to rely more and more on voluntary self-regulation by industry. Not only do average citizens lose decision-making power, however, they can also lose meaningful choices about how they live. For example, if totally artificial cells are more profitable than healthy garden environments, everyone but the rich will live in cells. If inter-and intra-generational equity are genuine considerations, therefore, a basic social indicator should be control over the means of survival. This is quite different from 'willingness to pay' for goods one needs to survive on, but cannot afford [Box 34]. In the environmental sphere, inaction means supporting a pyramidal resource transfer process that is irreversibly cutting off future options, and therefore rendering our democratic system impotent. Environmentalists, perceived as rocking the boat, are often seen as a threat to the given social order. Yet the status quo is not stable or unchanging. It is a whirlpool of change. The status quo is a radical re-distribution system, so non-action has radical outcomes. Opportunities for reversing ecological damage or improving substantive democracy in relation to the environment are being reduced daily. Through their inaction in addressing sustainability and disparities of wealth, decision-makers are transferring wealth (surreptitiously or perhaps unwittingly) from the general public (their 'employer') to special interests (their mates or 'class') for personal, even though usually *indirect*, gain (like membership of a 'club').[16] This is a form of systemic corruption.

## Can we hold decision-makers accountable where there is no personal benefit?

Why not? Modern managers are skilled at making 'hard' decisions concerning the livelihoods of others, so their performance should be accountable as well. Society as a whole does not yet appreciate the need for a resilient ecological base, so environmental reporting has had little impact as yet. However, most societies accept *democracy* as a fundamental need and right. If our auditing and reporting methods associated ecology with democracy more directly, people might understand the long-term implications for democracy of wealth transfers. Thus our reporting methods could examine the causes and outcomes of resource flows and transfers in terms of how they affect future democracy and human rights (eg supported by RT, EW and ET analyses). Assessing the social and environmental 'costs of inaction' in sustainability reporting would be a step towards making decision-makers and managers more accountable. In the private sphere, corporate directors are increasingly held accountable for environmental crimes, such as the illegal dumping of toxic waste. However, no one is really accountable for inaction in preventing the production of toxic waste in the first place. Perhaps this 'proactive' form of accountability can only happen through an emphasis on *rewards* for positive improvements. Governments and industry may not readily accept accountability for failure, but they might accept recognition for success. Thus to measure management performance, treasury departments need to develop the capacity to link resource *savings* to specific sustainability initiatives. Likewise, treasuries should be accountable for inaction in this regard. The recognition for resource savings might lead managers in government to take steps that would begin to reverse resource flows and re-distribute environmental costs and benefits. After all, Positive Development, as has been argued, should not constitute a threat to anyone.

## Wouldn't reversing past resource flows mean withdrawing existing privileges?

We have talked about how positive actions towards sustainability need not be at any group's or individual's expense. Imbalances and inequities could be addressed by employing different decision rules. Currently, probably the most basic decision rule is the Pareto Optimum, which is implicit in most decision tools. It is a fundamental principle of economics which says a decision is good if it makes individuals better off without harming others. In a finite world, however, this can lead to zero sum outcomes over time. It rationalizes individuals' acquiring wealth, which in turn leads to the production of status symbols to satisfy the competitive, conspicuous consumption of the few (ie designed waste). It does not, in practice, recognize that the 'demand' for products and structures with excessive embodied energy for the few means a reduction in 'supply' of basic needs for the world's poor. Impacts on the other side of the world seem to be remote and distant consequences. In a shrinking world, however, the Pareto Optimum has outlived its shelf-life. Sustainability requires affirmative actions that make everyone better off without harming individuals. We have called this decision rule the Green Optimum.[17] Instead of making an organization or individual better off relative to others, the Green Optimum acknowledges that we can make everyone better off by direct actions and positive policies that increase the ecological base and public estate. The Green Optimum provides a way of illuminating the 'opportunity cost' of conventional decision-making and design.

## What difference would it make to shift from a Pareto to a Green Optimum?

Our current approach is to sit back and wait for private interests to propose developments, or encourage private investment through public infrastructure provision. We could instead *proactively* identify and implement actions that make the whole community better off. There are many readily-available decentralized technologies that increase energy independence and resource security while saving society as a whole resources, health costs and so on [Box 3]. The public planning sector could therefore at least identify 'good' investments for the market: direct actions that benefit everyone and have a good return for investors [Chapter 2]. In the short term, proactive planning and policymaking is required to determine opportunities for net Positive Development which the private sector can undertake. To encourage this, reports could do more to give professional bodies, government agencies and/or individuals credit for positive direct action or programmes that reverse inequities and generate savings. Currently, however, the public sector does not really have incentives, 'tradable' credits or rewards for correcting environmental damage. Some argue that the profit motive is the only viable incentive. But if competition is a virtue, why is it not being enlisted in the cause of the public good, or being applied to the public sector?

## So why don't we measure the costs of inaction and savings of direct action?

Sustainability reporting, like other forms of environmental management, tends to compare trends in resource consumption from the time that a reporting process is initiated. Accepting the existing urban or regional environment as the reporting baseline means decision-makers in government and industry are not expected to correct *existing* problems. By starting from current conditions, as we have seen, inaction does not appear to be making things much worse. Unless indicators reflect specific eco-services already lost or in need of repair, it will be hard to find ways to increase ecological carrying capacity. We have seen that framing the existing situation as 'normal' can work to conceal the ongoing cumulative transfer of land and resources. Because indicators generally only track improving or worsening conditions from the initial start of reporting, they often draw attention to environmental stresses or ecological crises when it is too late. The sustainability standard, proposed earlier, would measure how far we are from sustainability, not just from the time we began assessing and reporting [Chapter 5]. Comparing an existing urban environment to the ecological conditions that existed before development (ET analysis) would ground reporting in biophysical reality, rather than variables and relativities that are suspended in the ether. A higher standard would better reflect the benefits of positive actions over inaction.

## How would measuring positive impacts and savings encourage change?

If we report actions and the savings they achieve, we encourage action. If we only report broad trends in negative impacts, we will only watch in horror. A focus on impacts of existing development and costs of inaction, including future impacts on democracy and choice, would help change the emphasis from mitigating future change to fixing existing problems (although both are important). Positive Development would increase future options and return development to more natural conditions, guided by the ecological context. Instead of investing in public relations, taking action and reporting on resulting positive impacts would also make responsible councils and firms look better. While we are getting better at tracking stocks and flows of materials, species and the like, reporting is currently like learning to carry out a more accurate 'stock-take' of supplies in a depression. The great US Depression of the 1930s was addressed by creating jobs that had long-term benefits for society – not by measuring how fast we were emptying the shelves. To stretch the analogy, we are trading off our resource stocks while gambling on the continued ability of nature to replenish the supplies – an attitude which has been described elsewhere as a 'cargo cult'.[18] In short, to improve reporting, we need to measure different things, in different ways, based on different starting points. But we also need new indicators of what should be re-designed.

## So what kinds of design indicators would be more proactive?

We need design-oriented indicators that suggest where things need fixing. For example:

- **Single function spaces**: Single function spaces in urban development are indicators of wasted opportunities to improve human and environmental health by integrating social and ecological space (eg Green Scaffolding or converting garages to greenhouses).
- **Energy leakages**: Urban areas that are emitting heat can be detected and mapped using GIS (eg using infrared radiation). Eco-retrofitting programmes could address these leaks at little or no net cost (as is happening in the US).
- **Toxic work relations**: Toxic work environments indicate that the planning organization or

government agency is not likely to be meeting meaningful goals or engaging in creative strategies. Reporting seldom reflects human productivity.

- **Climate change**: Flood and damage can be reduced, as in Curitiba, by urban lakes and other positive landscaping amenities (rather than collapsible dikes as in New Orleans). Green Scaffolding could protect many existing urban areas from wind, flood, extreme heat or fire and earthquakes.
- **Tradeoffs**: Tradeoffs are an indicator of bad design, as good design is inherently about creating synergies. Tradeoffs are usually only required to appease competing interests or buttress the established social infrastructure.
- **Waste**: There is systems re-design potential wherever there is waste, as any unavoidable waste can theoretically be turned into a productive resource. A caveat is that the uses of waste can sometimes be anti-ecological.
- **Inequity or low wages**: A product that is produced with low wages, or child labour, effectively transfers wealth, and an increasing concentration of wealth is an indicator of unjust enrichment (eg golden handshakes to CEOs even when their companies' profits sink).

Unlike typical urban sustainability indicators, the above symptoms are not measures of 'trends', but systems design problems that point to places where we can create positive economic activity that is creates efficiency gains or long-term savings. In other words, indicators should relate to building society's ability to improve, or adapt to biophysical reality, rather than nature's ability to cope with society [Chapter 14]. New kinds of indicators developed by environmental economists over recent decades could play a part in developing more relevant sustainability measures.

## How can economic indicators and measures be relevant to sustainability?

Environmental indicators are still trumped by economic ones. We have been too busy predicting the rate of environmental decline – how much longer the environment will be able to adapt to society – to re-design our systems of planning and policymaking around meaningful measures. There have, however, been many comprehensive critiques of the main government indicator, gross domestic product (GDP).[19] GDP measures market activity or material consumption – rather than human wellbeing or sustainability. Despite its known problems, it is still the dominant indicator of 'progress'. In fact, ironically, GDP is often used within sustainability reporting. When 'ESD reporting' was introduced in Australia, for example, it meant moving to a 'triple bottom line'. So economic concepts were added on top of environmental and social indicators, ostensibly in keeping with sustainability principles. This often meant colonization of environmental efforts by an economic mindset. In a parallel process, sustainability and economic personnel were integrated into the same government divisions, ostensibly to support the concept of a whole-of-government approach. The adoption of the 'triple bottom line' in government circles and the integration of financial and environmental analysts sounds positive. It suggests mutual learning and problem solving. However, it has often meant the re-colonization of environmental agency staff and programmes by the dominant economic ideology. The use of GDP is one way that environmental programmes lose their potential to create genuine progress.

## Can indicators like GDP actually impede progress toward sustainability?

Yes. Many environmental economists have critiqued GDP as failing to measure 'genuine progress'. Because it only measures market transactions, for example, GDP does not measure the loss of eco-services or waste of natural resources. Nature is not a commodity that is bought and sold in markets. Further, GDP does not distinguish between activities in the market that are good for ecological and human health and those that cause harm. Any activity or product that is produced for sale is deemed to *add* to national wellbeing. Tsunamis, earthquakes, wars and oil spills can increase GDP. GDP can 'go up' even when our stock of resources is reduced and when unemployment and poverty are increased. Further, because GDP does not count things outside the market, as environmental economists have shown, it devalues the contributions of the family, such as volunteer work, housework, and care for the disabled and the elderly. Some have noted that GDP goes up if a family eats out and goes down if a man marries his housekeeper.[20] 'Defensive expenditure' – such as money spent cleaning up pollution, protecting oneself from crime, moving to avoid congestion and noise, or setting up 'pollution permitting' authorities – is considered 'positive' in GDP terms. In other words, GDP creates vicious circles where negatives are counted as positives.

## What can we do about the problems caused by economic indicators?

Over the last two decades, many ecological economists have argued for new economic indicators to replace GDP at the national level. The Human Development Index (HDI), for example, is a measure of human wellbeing based on various standard of living indicators, especially child welfare. Similarly, genuine progress indicators (GPIs) attempt to treat triple-bottom-line criteria more equally.[21] The need for this is buttressed by research that has demonstrated that quality of life has been falling despite economic 'growth' as measured by GDP [Box 34]. Since the mid 1970s, statistics on GDP and social wellbeing have diverged. That is, wealth no longer correlates well with happiness. This is partly because, in developed nations, health is influenced more by income 'distribution' than material wealth, and disparities of wealth are increasing [Chapter 1]. The psychological and social consequences of living in an inequitable society also affect life quality and wellbeing.[22] Some countries are moving in the direction of life quality indicators, such as Norway and Tibet.[23] But despite the fact that GPI indicators correspond better than GDP with the real world, the uptake of GPI has been slow. Among the many reasons for this is that mainstream economists have been able to ignore the critiques of GDP due to their hegemony on political influence. Another reason for the slow uptake of GPI is that it can be complex and technical (in parallel with rating and assessment tools). One cannot yet pull GPI figures off the shelf for built environment issues.[24] Therefore GPI are not generally used in environmental management, let alone in development assessment. And to the extent they are used, they are inadequate to reflect distributive justice. This is partly because GPI emphasize not what is happening to the ecology and democracy but how people feel about it.

## Could genuine progress indicators register things like resource transfers?

Not likely. Indicators of relative wealth or happiness do not fully capture changes in the ownership or control of resources that will prevent or enable genuine social choice, freedom and independence in the future. Measures of individual wellbeing and happiness are subjective and do not fully register basic values like the benefits of environmental health and amenity and a high quality, accessible public estate. Further, GPI does not assess wealth transfers from poor and rich, public to private interests, rural to urban, natural to artificial, and so on. This is because people are not necessarily aware of these transfers, despite a correlation between unhappiness and disparities of wealth. Also, happiness can be temporarily achieved by 'cake and circuses'. GPIs do not show us how environmental decisions re-distribute wealth. They only register how this indirectly affects people's attitudes and awareness.

This reinforces other environmental management methods that conceal resource transfers within a narrow incremental and relative framework. For example, GDP could go up if an entrance fee is levied in a national park or an oceanfront is alienated to private development. GPI might instead record this as a negative – but only if people are not happy about it. Therefore one could assert that people are happy about the cumulative effects of 'enclosure' of the public estate, or a loss of future democratic choice – if they are happy in general, otherwise preoccupied or too stressed to worry about it. People with knowledge of fundamental systems dynamics are not necessarily unhappy. Early childhood experiences and genetics also play a part in attitudes. Finally, GPIs cannot, on their own, reflect the central element of sustainability – keeping future options open.

## So how can we develop indicators that aid deep sustainability considerations?

Indicators of whole systems health must relate to the ecological base and public estate. Most indicators focus on single issues or measurable impacts in separate environmental media like air, soil or water. There are growing attempts to integrate indicators with actual *planning* – as opposed to assessment, auditing and reporting processes – at least in rhetoric. For example, indicators have been integrated into management plans at all levels, such as farm plans, catchment plans and local council plans. This means that they could become a guide to action, rather than a retrospective assessment of performance. There are also many indicators that reflect impacts on the health of ecosystems. However, in the case of biodiversity, for example, the overall health of the system can be concealed by looking at certain 'keystone' species. Thus, by the time they are threatened, it is too late. To ensure select species survive, we need to restore the whole food chain, by expanding ecosystems that support the complex network of other species upon which they depend. In other words, a 'rhizomatic approach'.[25] A sustainability standard (with guidelines and prototypes for inspiration) therefore provides a better handle for built environment design. Sustainability indicators should assess either how far we are from sustainability (using RT, EW and CI analyses) or identify areas of design failure [Chapter 14]. If urban and rural developments are to provide eco-services and address inequities, we need not only to consider how to generate and measure positive improvements, but how to ensure their *ongoing* management.

## Can reporting be used to ensure ongoing management improvements?

To improve performance in design over time and throughout the whole life-cycle, there must be management systems in place that ensure developer or manufacturer responsibility for ongoing positive action. In environmental management systems, 'continuous improvement' is an established principle. But in the built environment context, developers' or producers' accountability often ends with project approval or product sales. The concept of continuous improvement through ongoing management, monitoring and 'verification' (comparing actual to predicted impacts) is gradually being introduced into development approvals. It has long been recognized that there is a need to reassess projects after construction to check the accuracy of predictions and ensure compliance with development conditions. This has seldom been a budgetary priority, of course. There is also a growing trend towards 'extended producer responsibility' (EPR), or 'product stewardship'. This requires manufacturers to take back products at the end of their life or be responsible for their disposal. This approach fosters the implementation of 'design for disassembly', and 'deconstruction and reuse', as opposed to just reprocessing discarded products as raw materials [Box 6]. It would be hard to 'take back' buildings, after their useful life span, for many reasons. There are nonetheless ways of addressing continuous improvement of buildings.

## How can the idea of continuous improvement be applied to buildings?

In the case of a development, the responsibility of developers usually ends with the sale of the buildings. Developers would find it onerous to have responsibility, and hence liability, over the full life of the development. It would also be difficult to require building owners to retrofit or even integrate eco-innovations into the building in the future, when new technologies or standards become mainstream. There is some movement in the direction of extending the responsibility of building owners, however, such as requiring that the energy performance of buildings be reported each year. There are also now building rating tools that measure building performance in areas beyond energy and greenhouse – to at least consider the ecological dimension which could be incorporated in reporting (such as NABERS in Australia).[26] Reporting could also be extended to buildings using post-occupancy evaluation (POE). POEs can look at occupant satisfaction and/or the operational performance of buildings. The field of POE is *not* new, but has yet to be utilized in most project specifications or tendering processes. Facilities managers are, or could be, positioned to improve buildings over time – at least where these pay for themselves in resource savings. A new kind of facilities management is needed to deliver more sustainable or healthier goods and services in developments when eco-technologies become available (and/or become more competitive) in the future. For purposes of rewards and incentives, we can also measure the environmental quantity and quality of the air, soil, water, sewage treatment and energy when it leaves the building.

## But won't facilities managers continue to rely on mechanical systems?

Perhaps, if they are not retrained. Facilities managers of the future will need training in biology and ecology as well as mechanical equipment. Facilities managers will prefer to manage mechanical systems if they are only trained to operate conventional (fossilized) equipment. However, these systems are high-maintenance [Box 20]. Eventually, the maintenance and operational savings provided by natural systems will be seen as a potential financial asset. Eco-development will eventually be more self-maintaining and cheaper to correct or adapt than projects relying on mechanized systems. POE and extended developer responsibility via facilities management will therefore gradually favour eco-retrofitting using natural systems rather than industrial heating, cooling and ventilating. Already in some programmes, money saved by energy and water efficiency are put in a separate fund and rolled over into further eco-efficiency improvements.[27] Facilities managers could be encouraged to upgrade buildings, using funds raised from energy and water efficiency savings over time, or an eco-retrofitting bank [Chapter 11]. This approach has been used in energy upgrades, but could also be applied to eco-retrofitting that increases ecological space in the urban environment. To make reporting more than a public relations opportunity, government agencies should be allowed to internalize some of the savings achieved, or even savings accruing to the general public indirectly, and 'roll over' these funds to expand their future sustainability programmes. Likewise, if a progress association decided to install, say, solar cell-powered street lamps to increase neighbourhood security, the association could receive the monetary equivalent of a portion of the policing and energy costs that would otherwise have been incurred (or as negotiated).

## If reporting does not always ensure improvement, where do we go from here?

In sustainability reporting, as in other environmental management methods, the focus has been on tracking and quantifying trends and/or predicting future impacts. It has been suggested that it might be more useful if reporting showed progress towards identifying and addressing the opportunity costs of poor design and the costs of inaction. Ironically, while the assessment, auditing and reporting methods examined in this section involve prediction (or, more accurately, projections of trends), they are still essentially 'retrospective' in orientation. They are focused primarily on measuring and reporting negative impacts of given operations in complex open systems. They also focus on promulgating 'best practice', rather than social transformation. In effect, we have concentrated on tracking changes in the resilience and capacity of nature, rather than the eco-effectiveness of human-designed systems and their management. We need to re-direct more efforts towards analysing the systems design failures that could be addressed through innovation and design. In the next section, we will look at innovation, planning and implementation strategies that might enable us to create a more sustainable future. The approaches to be examined are futures thinking tools, trading systems and bioregional planning. They have little directly in common, except for their apparent *future* orientation and the fact that they are not concerned primarily with quantifying the unquantifiable, but instead with implementing change. However, the question is whether they can help us design better futures, or simply prepare for futures that have been pre-determined by our institutions, ideas and tools.

# SECTION D:
# CRITIQUE OF TRENDS, IN STRATEGIES, INCENTIVES AND PLANNING

# 10
# Futures Thinking Tools

From predicting the unpredictable to expanding future options

This chapter looks at some better known futures thinking tools and planning decision aids, such as roadmapping, futures wheels, mind mapping and scenario planning. These are now complemented by many computer-aided mapping tools on the internet that can facilitate workshopping and innovation.[1] Here 'futures tools' refer to planning aids designed to help us achieve future goals. They purport to take into account myriad factors like interdependency, complexity, unknown variables, and multiple stakeholders' values and interests. Unlike most environmental management tools, they are geared primarily towards anticipating and preparing for future *contingencies*. That is, they can help to select alternative strategies or actions that will avoid or mitigate risks, factors or forces that might impede progress towards a given goal or project, such as getting a new product on the market or implementing an organizational agenda. Many such tools involve *forecasting* future market and scientific forces that may affect an organization or impede its goals. They set out to predict contingent forces in order to develop strategies. They help organizations manoeuvre around risks and threats to prepare for, or negotiate their way through, possible futures. This is despite the recognition that, in any forecasting methods, there are uncertainties that can alter these predictions and preparations almost beyond recognition. Thus we could say:

- Traditional planning tools seek to 'control the uncontrollable'
- Assessment tools seek to 'predict the unpredictable'
- Life-cycle assessment tools try to 'quantify the unquantifiable'
- Futures tools help us to 'expect the unexpected'

These tools start from a given playing field and analyse the consequences of available alternative actions – primarily in terms of negative impacts or risks to the decision-maker. Strangely enough, we have done little to mitigate *environmental* risks, such as climate change, in spite of so many available environmental management, planning and design tools designed to mitigate impacts. The discourse in environmental management is now changing towards 'adaptation'. But this often refers to defensive design (like flood barriers) – not even mitigation. Thus some futures thinking tools could be said to be 'defensive'. A conceptual framework that makes threats and negative impacts seem inevitable also makes them somehow acceptable, as if they are part of the scenery. Tools applied in a defensive way can lead to defensive design outcomes. Hence, ironically, these futures tools can work to reinforce business-as-usual, rather than whole systems re-design. In fact, by focusing on how to achieve a given goal in a given context, futures tools can also militate against sustainability itself. Despite major differences, then, futures thinking tools could be said to reflect the same kind of negative thinking as the methods we have already visited. Futures tools are not designed to 'expand future options' or carrying capacity, only to find pathways. They are thinking aids, but not design tools.

## Why aren't futures tools designed to enable us to expand future options?

This is partly because futures tools take the perspective of the individual, agency or firm – rather than the perspective of society at large or the wider public interest. This orientation may enhance the position of an organization or product in the market, but it is not the best framework for designing a better future for everyone. If our strategies are inherently about maximizing one's position in a given context, a self-fulfilling prophesy is created. A zero sum world is normalized. While futures thinking tools are goal-directed and future-oriented, they can promote 'win–lose' strategies in a context of uncertainty and change. In the culture of business, the dominant view of the world is that of a game where the objective is winning by outsmarting the competition. It has been said that competition is like swimming among sharks: you only have to out-swim the person next to you. But this also means you do not have to help anyone else. Design that is driven by the aim of making existing processes more lean and mean will tend to eliminate the risk of competitors, not risks to society (as in the new, cheap 'Nano' car promoted in India). As we will see, futures tools do not suffice, on their own, for inventing new directions and new futures. We need to develop futures thinking processes that recognize the systems problems found in existing development, and identify opportunities found in natural systems, so we can design systems and environments that can:

- Correct the ecological imbalances and social inequities of current systems
- Increase the resilience, adaptability and productiveness of human and natural systems
- Make everyone better off (with the poor at least proportionately better off)
- Expand future options and equitable control over, and access to, the means of survival

Roadmapping is an example of a futures thinking process that is geared towards progressing the goals of an organization, rather than changing the context.

## What is roadmapping and how can it be used to serve sustainability goals?

Roadmapping does not purport to be a sustainability tool as such, but it is increasingly applied to sustainability issues. A roadmap enables us to select the best path from where we are *now* to an intended destination. That end-point could be sustainability or other environmental objectives. It might, for example, be a map for implementing a technology or goal, such as a water management regime or water efficiency measures. Roadmapping involves deciding which routes should be taken, which intersections crossed, what milestones reached, and in what sequence the water regime should be changed. By charting a network of tasks and events to be undertaken in a logical order, we can avoid detours or roadblocks that might otherwise delay the completion of the journey. Thus roadmapping is designed to find the most cost-, impact- or time-efficient pathway to an end-point in a *given* context. Suppose the goal were to get a new green product on the market quickly, for example. We would map the research and development projects, tests and approvals that will be required along the way. Then we would estimate the time between nodes and assign probabilities to different pathways. To ensure little time is lost waiting for other parties to complete steps, we would chart the interdependencies and sequences of the tasks required. The aim is not to improve the political situation, but to optimize one's position in that system by, for example, using market-based incentives. As a form of strategic planning, then, it can help the adoption of a systems design. However, its potential to help us expand future options is questionable.

## What do roadmaps look like and how do they help us make decisions?

A roadmap could begin by identifying key action nodes. These nodes in the road network may be other organizations that need to take certain steps, or decisions by others that may impact on one's progress towards a given goal. The roadmap provides a chart of chosen milestones and linkages between them, with a description of their relevant attributes and uncertainties. The assigned attributes can be qualitative and/or quantitative, and may include the probabilities that the events will occur. Generally, the nodes and numbers are supplied by teams of experts, who rely to a large extent on subjective knowledge and experience in anticipating the future. The criteria for the nodes, links and destinations should therefore be explicit. This helps to plan 'when, where and what' to invest in project implementation. Critical 'intersections' can be identified which, to stretch the metaphor, may lead to:

- Shortcuts (eg joining with partners)
- Detours (eg avoiding competitors)
- Rocky uphill stretches (eg knowing strengths and weaknesses)
- Key challenges along the way (eg obtaining permits or patents)

In short, roadmapping is a predictive exercise aimed at determining factors and forces that may influence preparatory strategies, actions and their timing. Roadmapping, then, is less a learning tool or design tool than a sophisticated, pictorial representation of strategic planning.[2] A distinction between technology and science roadmapping is sometimes made.[3] Both technology roadmapping and science roadmapping are goal oriented, but differ in the types of goals they aim for.

## How do science and technology roadmapping differ in terms of goals?

Technology roadmapping usually has a specific goal in mind, like advancing a specific production technology. Science roadmapping has generally been applied to advance a whole field, research programme or area of potential discovery. In 'pure' research and innovation, after all, the exact destinations or research outcomes cannot and should not be always fully anticipated beforehand. The goal of a science roadmap process could, for example, be to improve the field of sustainability research in general. That is, it can highlight gaps in research or the need to create links between different scientific disciplines or 'silos', in order to foster more innovation. Interestingly, students of the evolution of scientific knowledge have found that many of the necessary events that had to occur before the adoption of a new system (eg patents, scientific discoveries) actually happened coincidentally, not by planning and mapping. Non-mission-related events occurring elsewhere aided other areas of scientific progress by serendipity. Yet this is one of the benefits that trans-disciplinary cross-fertilization can foster. This also raises the distinction that is often made between 'push' and 'pull' forms of roadmapping to stimulate innovation.[4] 'Push' often refers to investment (or environmental taxes) by governments in innovation, or 'supply', such as grants. 'Pull' refers to market incentives or policies that create 'demand', such as the requirement that industry source a percentage of its power from renewables.[5]

## Which strategies, pull or push, are best suited for fostering eco-innovations?

Pushing an innovation agenda or pulling specific types of innovations can both be part of a roadmap aimed at reaching a target, such as the decarbonization of industry. For example, a roadmap could find the quickest route to 'pull' eco-innovations onto the market, such as a carbon tax or full-cost pricing. Alternatively, a science roadmap could assist a research plan, or find steps required to solve a technical problem in order to 'push' a scientific agenda, such as sponsoring renewable energy incubators. Investment in 'directed' research has generally been found to lead to adoption more quickly than 'undirected' research. Applied science is therefore seen as more effective in fostering new scientific advances (despite the serendipity factor noted above). However, most environmental policy seems to be directed at creating market incentives that favour high-tech (patentable) *products* over the application of natural *solutions*. That is to say, the goal is a pre-established one. In this case, roadmapping can only help identify when and where resources might be applied at particular intersections to create shortcuts along the route to the desired end-point. But where the end-point is a new 'higher order' one – like democracy, equity and ecology – we need to create new kinds of *contexts* altogether. This requires the design of new kinds of institutions and biophysical environments: not just push or pull, but direct transformation. And, again, transformation requires design. In roadmapping, however, the design or innovation process itself is generally a 'black box'. There is relatively little in the academic literature on understanding or creating the conditions for creativity itself, other than through encouraging cooperative processes among experts.

## Would just creating the environment for creativity ensure good outcomes?

No. We have said that sustainability is a design problem, but that efforts to define sustainability have been shaped by old ways of thinking. Old ways of thinking either impose (ideologically based) visions of how people should live, or apply methods that lead to a certain kind of future through their own internal logic. But as discussed earlier, we do not really know what sustainability will look like. Imposing a specific vision of society would not be consistent with sustainability. Sustainability is about expanding options and social equity, not implementing a particular ideology [Introduction]. After all, a particular conception of sustainability in a particular time and place is likely to be idiosyncratic or even ill-conceived. Design for sustainability therefore implies the intellectual, institutional and physical infrastructure that can create reversible, diverse and adaptable decisions, environments and eco-technologies. Roadmapping is designed to get to a preconceived goal within existing parameters, not to rethink the goal itself or to ensure more goals are met through design that creates synergies. It examines the forces likely to impact on, say, product development or organizational advancement in a given context. A sustainability planning process would be less concerned with expediting the emergence of new technology through market or regulatory levers. It would be more concerned with determining what kind of technological, behavioural or institutional strategies will provide levers of influence from a whole systems – ecological and democratic – perspective. A better approach would be analyses that identify leverage points (or acupuncture) for systems re-design, such as RT, EW, ET, and CI analyses introduced earlier.

## Can roadmapping be used in finding levers for systems change?

The ultimate aim of planning for sustainability – expanding positive options – is substantively different from roadmapping, which aims to get us from A to B. However, a sustainable planning process might employ a roadmapping exercise to commercialize an eco-innovation or implement an eco-retrofitting programme that has already resulted from a collaborative systems design process (eg SmartMode). In other words, roadmapping can be used for charting the decision nodes or impacts of future actions after we have imagined eco-solutions. A more appropriate metaphor for design thinking might be a river: a fluid, natural system, rather than a road. A road is an instrumental, static, linear, hard infrastructure created by bulldozers. It could be said that strategic thinking is like a car trying to avoid potholes or fallen trees on a road to a known destination. Design thinking is like a river, creating new contours by working with the landscape [Figure 11]. To find actions that would improve the health of a river, we have said, we can compare current conditions to those that existed originally and examine upstream and downstream blockages or diversions (ET analysis). In turn, we can identify the sources of barriers to healthier flows and link them back to human interventions, such as capital-intensive infrastructure and technology, institutional mechanisms and economic frameworks (ID analysis).

## Figure 11 Roadmap versus river metaphor

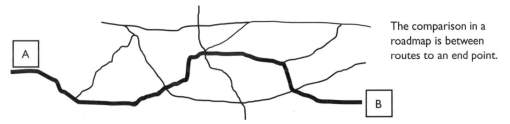

The comparison in a roadmap is between routes to an end point.

If we used a river rather than a road metaphor, we might think to: re-design past upstream human interventions (dams, weirs, irrigation) that have impeded environmental flows, rather than engineer the river: design our boats to use wind and currents, rather than engines; enjoy the tranquility of the natural environment, rather than fight the current, etc.

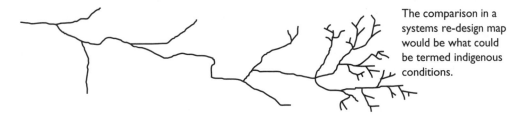

The comparison in a systems re-design map would be what could be termed indigenous conditions.

By fostering a wider range of options that increase natural capital and reverse impacts, social choice would be greater than before. Roadmaps aim to find the shortest or quickest route rather than creating the best experiential journey, so to speak.

## So how would mapping contextual issues help improve futures thinking?

We can look for ways of increasing environmental flows by tracing resource flows and transfers, expropriations and externalities back to their sources in human-designed systems. We tend to get preoccupied with threats and barriers to plans, policies, programmes and products. Examining environmental flows in their original ecological state (ET analysis) would not just help us to assess how far we are from sustainability. It could also help us gain inspiration from nature (ie biomimicry), and identify opportunities to tap into, and amplify, the free services and surpluses that nature can provide. After that, roadmapping can be used to chart the future exogenous variables that can be anticipated, modified or manipulated to advance the resulting solutions. In other words, a roadmap seeks a faster route, not a different vehicle. The political vehicle of choice – market solutions – is now taken to be mandatory. Yet the market often does not correspond well to biophysical realities [Box 42]. Despite decades of critiques from many perspectives, there has been little effort by mainstream economists to alter their frameworks, or even to consider the brave new worlds that markets are shaping. And sustainability roadmaps tend to obey market or consumer trends. We need processes that help to create more responsible consumer trends in the first place [Box 54]. We must therefore create the biophysical and institutional infrastructure that would encourage people to make sustainable choices.

## How can we use roadmapping to create the conditions for sustainability?

Science roadmapping may look at how a discipline, institution or research programme can be modified to progress a scientific field, or research outcomes in general. So, theoretically, it could look at how to progress towards sustainability. However, the direction society takes is still left to technologies, bureaucracies or markets to determine. Innovations are judged by the invisible hand, not by their potential to improve whole systems. Roadmapping processes have been geared towards fostering any technology that has 'acceptable' levels of risk by (figuratively speaking) creating warning signs, sirens or passing lanes. Democratic or participatory processes involving lay citizens are seldom part of roadmapping exercises, because the implicit value is *efficiency* of means to given ends. Likewise, innovations are seldom assessed by their social value and contribution to democracy. The future democratic consequences of decision systems are not analysed. For example, the decision to allow irradiated or genetically engineered foods has implications for democracy. It could mean corporations are taking ownership of the whole food chain.[6] This could reduce future democratic choice irreversibly. Similarly, roadmapping could easily lead to trends that are in ultimate conflict with ecological integrity. For example, science roadmapping tends to favour actions or investments that are measurable (in numbers) or profitable (in money) in the short term to justify each strategic investment. Due to its internal logic, then, values like equity and health and other whole systems issues may be allocated a lower priority where they conflict with efficiency. The point is that all tools have embedded assumptions, and tools from the world of business have little to do with the ethical nature of sustainability issues.

## But would ethics and altruism really be a realistic alternative anyway?

Not in the current win–lose 'dominant paradigm'. Here, altruism is seen as irrational, and incidental beneficiaries are seen as 'free riders', or burdens rather than benefits. Sustainability decision tools should enable us to shift from win–lose thinking to positive design thinking. An alternative approach would be to start from fundamental sustainability principles to develop strategies for determining and implementing positive contributions to whole systems health. This means investing human resources in the design of eco-governance or constitutional approaches that advance 'non-negotiable' values like sustainability. Future democracy – or the ability to have genuine input in decisions on what really matters – requires a biophysical environment that is reversible, diverse and adaptable and keeps future options open. Making people free from harm and healthier would entail both 'substantive' and 'procedural' due process [Chapter 13]. Some would argue that current decision-making is democratic because present generations have, in a sense, chosen a non-sustainable world. But the notion that people voted and therefore endorsed the destruction of their life-support system is of course nonsense. Substantive democracy would instead mean that such basic irreversible decisions would actually be debated and voted upon. Decisions would flow from deliberative processes, not from an invisible hand operating under the table. Substantive democracy would also mean that one group, generation or country could not make terminal decisions for other groups, generations or countries (eg biotechnology or human cloning). We simply do not have institutions or tools that are designed to deal with such higher order issues like sustainability.

## Why can't roadmapping deal with higher order issues like sustainability?

Roadmapping and other design and decision aids that we have examined thus far cannot address higher order issues because they are largely strategic tools that help us to *chose* by comparing costs and benefits, not to *create* new physical and institutional environments [Chapter 12]. Roadmapping or other tools could, of course, be applied within a broader sustainability framework. This will not happen on its own, however. The problem can be illustrated by a US Department of Energy roadmapping exercise aimed at identifying the research and development needed to foster carbon sequestration.[7] Sustainability roadmaps must start from sustainability basics. For example, the study did not ask 'How do the proposed technologies and strategies work to enhance the whole systems health of the community and ecology?'. It did not ask 'Will geo-sequestration keep future options open or will it, instead, perpetuate a reliance on fossil fuels?'. Nor did it consider the risks of continuing in a fossil fuel pathway. After all, we cannot begin to sequester all the $CO_2$ that is currently being emitted. While fossil fuels must eventually run out, that fact will not alter their ongoing legacy. As Hermann Scheer has documented, the fossil fuel supply chain underpins modern society. Yet it is harmful at all stages of production, delivery and consumption, and is one of the biggest threats to world democracy and peace.[8] The roadmapping exercise (like assessment, auditing and reporting methods) avoided the fundamental sustainability issue by starting from the status quo, not sustainability. Yet simultaneously it also implicitly counted the previous sunk cost (prior investment) in existing coal-fired power plants.

## Surely the case study examined the whole range of issues and alternatives?

Only within a limited range of parameters. The tacit premise was apparently that the solutions would need to be large-scale industrial processes, presumably to suit established investment institutions. Therefore even the kinds of 'bio-absorption' alternatives that were selected for investigation in the study would require further investment in the fossil fuel system. This, in effect, would take investment away from low-tech, adaptive, eco-economical strategies that were not included in the balance sheet. Nor were creative, decentralized financial mechanisms considered. Further, the study indicated that geo-sequestration is dependent on several basic scientific discoveries in numerous fields that may not materialize. It did not therefore even represent a 'precautionary' or risk-averse strategy, but was rather a proposal for further subsidies to industrial systems. In effect, such studies minimize the risks to previous investments. They protect the sunk cost in fossil fuels, despite the fact that it is not usually considered wise for businesses to count the sunk cost in their decisions. The study did not look for the best way to source and generate power. One could only conclude, then, that the tacit objective of the roadmap was to find the best way to support existing industrial interests to preserve the fossil fuel system. If we instead start with threshold questions concerning sustainability, we might not direct so much talent, energy and money to driving in the same vicious circles.

## How do we approach these threshold sustainability questions then?

A sustainable research and design process would ask whether something should be done in the first place – *before* analysing choices about how to do it. That is, before investing enormous public resources in comparing alternative geo-sequestration pathways, we should ask 'What is the best and cheapest way to reduce or eliminate carbon emissions?'. A study that asks 'How do we mitigate further emissions?' can justify more emissions. As mentioned above, if geo-sequestration offered a means of pensioning off fossilized industries, it may have some transitional value. However, the effect will be to extend the longevity of harmful activities. Meanwhile, rumours of oil shortages can be used to manipulate prices and open up wilderness areas to exploit gas, oil or coal deposits. This roadmap to geo-sequestration also exemplifies the problem of defining things as 'best practice'. A pulp mill recently conditionally approved in Tasmania has been justified as being world's best practice. The Federal Government based its support on its Chief Scientist's investigation. In preparing his report, however, the Chief Scientist was not allowed to consider issues in the jurisdiction of the Tasmania State Government, such as air pollution. His brief was to determine the probable impacts of dioxins, and other effects like noise, in the marine environment (which could not really be assessed in his estimation). We will not know the effects on endangered species until they are measurable, when it is too late to mitigate them. The proposed mill could threaten the viability of other 'green' industries in the region, such as vineyards and fisheries, for which Tasmania was building a good reputation.

## But wouldn't roadmapping at least find the best pathway to sustainability?

Not necessarily from a whole systems perspective. For example, another study in Australia found that geo-sequestration would eventually result in carbon sequestration at a much cheaper rate 'per ton of carbon sequestered' than carbon trading.[9] A few years later, however, after millions were committed to industrial geo-sequestration research, estimates put the cost of geo-sequestration much higher than tree planting, to achieve the same sequestration levels. This disparity might have been intuitively obvious from a systems perspective, but we often rely on data generated by those who are not trained to think in whole systems. Research into the quickest route to geo-sequestration can drain resources, and postpone the implementation of tried-and-true, positive eco-solutions. Fossil fuel based technologies, in contrast, take years to get on line and further entrench the hydrocarbon economy. Hi-tech solutions are unlikely to be as economical as 'free' natural systems that do not produce $CO_2$ in the first place. Geo-sequestration can never be net positive as it cannot capture all $CO_2$ emissions, let alone reverse the build up of $CO_2$ in the environment. So it will do little to mitigate the impacts of climate change. Sustainability requires that we establish systems that reverse impacts of existing systems, and expand the existing range of sustainable life choices and biodiversity – which geo-sequestration cannot do.

## Could we just conduct a roadmap of wider sustainability issues?

This is unlikely, as we always seem to start with a solution in mind. For example, there was a roadmap of water issues in Australia that began with the proposition that we need to have market-based solutions for dealing with water issues.[10] This was despite the fact that, when water trading was first implemented a decade before in Australia, it failed because water was over-allocated. And now water rights for the environment will need to be bought back with public funds. The environment was given a lesser allocation than it needed, because ecological carrying capacity was undervalued. The water roadmap reflected tacit acceptance of the idea that environmental services are 'substitutable'. It did not really consider restoring environmental flows to original conditions, even though this might ultimately be the most efficient, cost-effective alternative. Collective action in the public interest is not seen as a realistic option as, supposedly, the market works its magic through competitive individualism. This follows the planning mantra that if we have the 'process' right – currently market-based vehicles – we do not have to design sustainable pathways or new destinations. If we are on the right road, so to speak, we assume we can put the car on cruise control. Conveniently, if an automated system happens to picks winners and losers, it must be 'apolitical' by definition. After all, markets and trading mechanisms do not 'think', and therefore cannot collude. It is a matter of faith that a system for making the best tradeoffs is embedded in the market-based trading process [Box 41]. That is, the market appears to make the political tradeoffs for us apolitically. The danger is that an agenda that cannot be achieved through the market, such as sustainability, will ultimately be stalled or sacrificed.

### Then what processes can support such systems re-design exercises?

There are a number of mapping devices that could assist brainstorming and design activities to diagnose and intervene in poorly designed human systems. They can be applied to varying levels of complexity, and include impact wheels and mind mapping processes. They derive from the initial 'futures wheel' of the early 1970s.[11] Previously, these tools have focused on mapping negative impacts. After all, we live in a man-made world that must now be further 'managed', and we still do not know what we are doing. Given our ecological ignorance, the low-risk option would be to increase natural security by ecological restoration and enhancement. We need a more positive mapping process to support this. By mapping positives instead of negatives, such maps could be used to find ways of facilitating ecological restoration and community revitalization. Impact maps have been used to support design charrettes, and could be reversed to support positive actions.[12] Impact maps could also be used to trace cause and effect relationships back to their initial origins. In the urban context, for example, there has been a movement to expose and restore urban streams that have been covered by concrete.[13] Mapping the improvements that would flow from this could serve as a kind of micro-model for correcting the mistakes of past design. Mapping of landscape changes over time has also been used to guide rural landscaping interventions in restoring natural water flows and soil retention – to reverse the past impacts of 'terraforming', pipes, dams and other interventions. By creating a positive impact wheel, we can identify and amplify the positive impacts that could be achieved in, say, restoring more natural water flows.

### So just how are 'impact mapping' exercises generally conducted?

In the typical 'futures wheel', the key activity, trend, issue or idea is written in the 'hub' on a whiteboard. Their impacts are identified in a brainstorming session and lines are drawn to primary impacts. More lines or 'spokes' are then drawn from each of these primary impacts to their secondary impacts, and circles are drawn around those impacts. Then the process is repeated for tertiary impacts and so on. These sets of impacts create concentric circles around the hub. Of course, impacts are not really primary or 'tertiary', as they are all cumulative and interconnected. Because impact wheels divide impacts up into separate factors, they can simplify things too much. The 'mind map' is a variation that attempts to express more complex relationships. In mind maps, the extent of the connections between impacts at different levels can be mapped by, for example, double and triple arrows. A variation on these mapping techniques divides impacts up into categories, such as cultural, psychological, economic and technological, between the spokes. There are even three-dimensional versions to supposedly enable a better understanding of historic forces, and current and future consequences. However, there is a tendency in workshops to make comprehensive lists of needs (noise) and impediments (earplugs). Wrapping up all issues in a ball, or 'dung beetling', does not always get participants past the initial problem description that brought them together in the first place [Chapter 6]. By analogy, comprehensive planners can tend to try to include every issue in policy plans, but seldom go beyond statements of comprehensive values to identify specific *new* actions. After all, if we stick to comfortable old problem descriptions we will not find new solutions.

### How do we get around that aspect of impact mapping or futures wheels?

Mind maps or diagrams, like policy plans, are good starting points to identify issues and generate ideas but, too often, they become end-points in themselves. The focus is still on negatives. Reversing the impact map can help us focus on means to identify and reduce the initial causes of problems in a more 'rhizomatic' design approach [Figure 11]. But we could go further and use it to look for means to create positive impacts and synergies. The resulting diagrams could also be used to communicate the positive impacts of design interventions. For example, mapping all the positive functions that an atrium in a building could perform could lead to new design elements that add multiple benefits. It could justify the inclusion of (low-cost) space for ecosystem services to a building owner who might otherwise see it as just an added cost. Further, we can identify past and present resource *transfers* which have reduced social equity, future democracy, and ecological and human health – whether they occurred through market, physical or institutional design failure. So the SmartMode approach should help refocus the process to designing actions to *reverse* these resource transfers, as well as identifying key variables or actions that will have positive ripple effects on these systems. Strategies and actions can then be partially compared and assessed by the number of positive, synergistic impacts.

Figure 12 Futures or impact wheel reversed to explore positive impacts

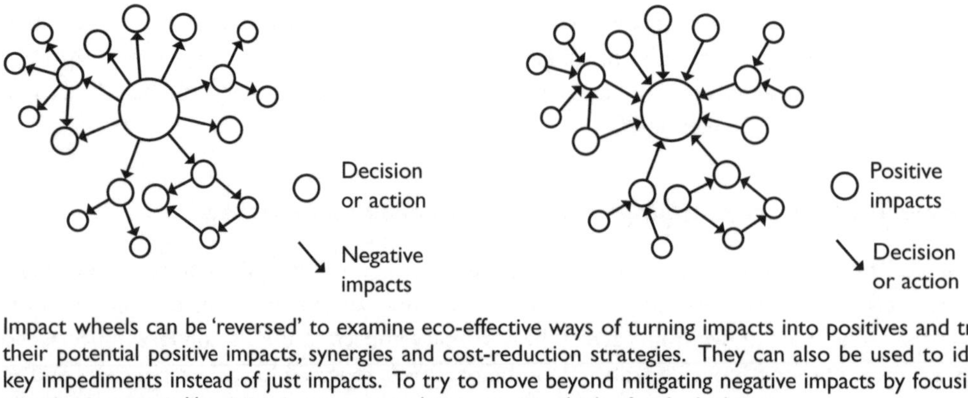

Decision or action

Negative impacts

Positive impacts

Decision or action

Impact wheels can be 'reversed' to examine eco-effective ways of turning impacts into positives and tracing their potential positive impacts, synergies and cost-reduction strategies. They can also be used to identify key impediments instead of just impacts. To try to move beyond mitigating negative impacts by focusing on negative impacts is like sitting in a corner and trying not to think of pink elephants.

## Just how do we convert 'impact mapping' into positive design ideas?

As in the case of other environmental management processes we have reviewed, mapping processes should focus more on flows than just inputs and outputs, and focus more on positive potentials than just negative trends. Take, for example, a simple systems map of soil degradation issues in Australia [Figure 13]. By tracing factors and their connections in soil degradation, it became apparent that soil 'structure' was a key factor in virtually all impacts.[14] This facilitated further analysis of the relationship of soil structure to other environmental problems and identified it as a potential leverage point. If we then reverse the map – drawing it with soil structure in the centre – it can assist in finding interconnections and synergies to generate positive impacts. In other words, since damage to soil structure is a negative consequence of many actions, strategies that improve soil structure directly could have positive spill-over effects on a whole range of other issues. Flows analyses suggest that there may not be enough organic material to fertilize soil, given the losses of topsoil worldwide from industrial agriculture and desertification (and salinity in some areas). However, low-cost organic solutions have also been proposed to improve soil health. Aquaponics, where fish fertilize the water, could possibly assist food production in areas of poor soil. Likewise, proposals have been generated to reverse impacts by developing mechanisms for delivering treated urban organic wastes to rural areas, or using compost locally to increase urban food production [Box 50].[15] Ultimately, such a mapping process suggests that cities will need to produce soils as well as food, to counteract past topsoil losses in the bioregions.

Figure 13 Soil degradation impact wheel[16]

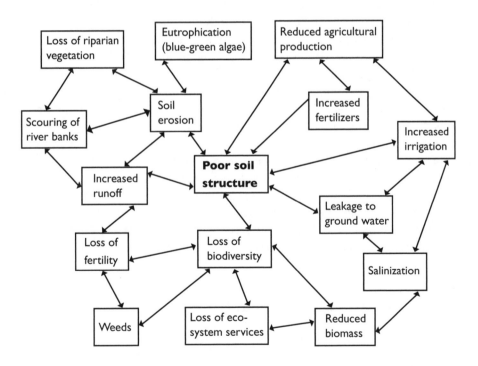

By reversing this negative impact wheel, we may identify programmes that enhance soil structure directly and have positive system wide spill-over effects.

**But can positive impact mapping help us find large-scale eco-solutions?**

Mapping can be an aid to moving towards closing loops and/or creating synergies in ever-wider circles [Box 39]. An example is provided by an initiative of Zero Waste Australia in collaboration with the Asian Network of Organic Recyclers. Australia is a nutrient-poor nation and Japan is, in a sense, suffering from nutrient overload. Japan imports much of its food from Australia and, with it, embodied nutrients. A simple mapping of nutrient (resource) flows shows that there is a net flow of nutrients out of Australia. This growing nutrient imbalance exacerbates other environmental problems in Australia as well. Boats shipping produce to Japan come back empty, so their hulls are filled with bilge water, which is then dumped in Australian waters. This bilge water contains foreign organisms that have caused ecological havoc in Australia's marine ecosystems. Zero Waste Australia therefore proposed treating organic nutrients through bioconversion processes in Japan. The sterilized liquid compost would be shipped from Japan to rural Australia in the hulls of boats. This would simultaneously eliminate the need for the harmful foreign ballast water that is contaminating Australian waters and increase soil health in Australia.[17] As well as identifying solutions, however, we need to anticipate and avoid 'adverse feedback' loops, where a 'solution' in one context can inadvertently become a problem in another context. Scenario planning purports to look at the consequences of actions and policies, in relation to future changing contexts.

**So just what is scenario planning, and when should it be used?**

We have seen that many future thinking methods are concerned with predicting future risks or determining the best route to a selected future. Scenario planning instead helps us understand what may happen if we continue on the same path or choose another one, by comparing the future consequences of policy options.[18] It is therefore perhaps more useful in choosing alternative pathways than for creating new outcomes or expanding future options. There have been many analyses that have explored alternative futures that would result from different energy policies. Perhaps the best known are two studies by Meadows et al, the first in 1972, the second decades later.[19] These showed the need for long-term planning. An example of scenario planning applied to the built environment is MetroQuest [Box 38], which relates planning alternatives to the future biophysical effects they will have on the region, in order to communicate to people how decisions made today will affect their life quality and space tomorrow in tangible ways. In scenario planning, generally, the first step is to identify the central area of concern. For example, the key issue may be the energy needs of the nation, community or private firm. The second step is to identify key variables in the external environment that can intervene in actions or policy directions in the future. Third, alternative pathways are selected for analysis, including the business-as-usual. Contextual forces, key decision-makers, and changing social and environmental conditions that may, in turn, affect these intervening variables need also be considered.

**How are contextual forces and conditions factored into scenarios?**

Cultural or latent values will affect the parameters of the scenarios. Scenario planning asks 'What if?' questions to anticipate and prepare for problems that may occur in the context of *alternative* future situations, trends or likely events (political, social, technological, etc). Values underlying the scenarios should be explicit, as hidden agendas and world views can influence outcomes.[20] The capacity of an organization to adapt to change is also an issue. Existing organizational cultures (such as, perhaps, the more calcified among planning authorities) may, for instance, be unable to deal with sustainability issues in scenario planning. Conversely, NGOs advocating sustainability may have to deal with internal and external forces that sabotage change. For example, former executives of a large paper company boasted on TV that they paid employees to infiltrate green groups in Australia to destabilize them and try to destroy their reputation with the public and politicians. Scenario planning for sustainability needs to look at such strange contingencies. It takes into account capacity, threats, weaknesses, barriers and responses – which all involve a self-assessment and an understanding of the political context. Nonetheless, scenario planning for sustainability (like roadmapping) is about forecasting the likely consequences of decisions, policies or actions in a changing but given context, not re-designing the context itself.

## So can scenario planning be used as a means of keeping options open?

Not as such, because it is not designed for creating conditions that expand future options. Theoretically, of course, if aimed at sustainability goals, scenario planning could contribute to healthier policies. In the past, we have relied on alternative technologies materializing, such as means to store nuclear power, instead of creating the infrastructure to make low-risk energy alternatives work better in a *variety* of possible scenarios. Scenario processes geared towards sustainability could arguably test the relative viability of various means of diversification or expanding options. But instead, scenarios have tended to be used to scare people away from certain pathways – whether such studies advocate green or industrial solutions (again, this resonates the idea that people are motivated by fear or greed) [Chapter 1]. A sustainability approach, focused on creating positive environments, would *not* put most of its resources into doomsday scenarios. Instead of comparing end-points of different energy systems, a positive approach would expand social, environmental and economic opportunities [Box 45]. That is, policy analysts and strategic planners would apply scenarios to assist in looking at 'what could be', not just what may occur.

Figure 14 Scenario and least cost planning[21]

**Scenario Planning**

The present

End point 1
End point 2
End point 3
End point 4
End point 5

Scenario planning anticipates/predicts ends that will result from alternatives (means, politics, actions, investments).

**Least cost Planning**

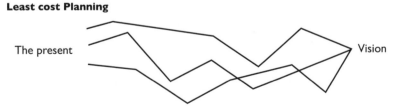

The present                                                    Vision

Least cost planning maps and compares alternatives (means, politics, actions, investments) to achieve a specific desired end or goal. Where a specific goal is clear, least cost planning can be used to select the best route to get there, but it is less suited to sustainability where the goal is to expand options.

## What other futures tools might enable us to expand future options then?

'Back-casting' is a popular term in sustainability circles.[22] It is almost the reverse of scenario planning. Scenario planning compares given pathways, based on predicted risks, to see where we will end up. Back-casting is like 'least cost planning' in that it starts with a defined goal or end-point, and seeks the best way to get there [Figure 14]. The application of these target-oriented tools becomes very complicated, however, if the target cannot be defined. An expansion of options, ecosystems and environments in a constantly changing context is hard to model. Since nature has lost some of its capacity to adjust to human activity due to ongoing market and government interventions, we need planning processes for adapting and conforming society's physical and social systems to the constraints and opportunities presented by natural systems and/or carrying capacity. As noted earlier, in an increasingly unpredictable climate, the safest strategy is to increase the range of responsible social options, habitats and biodiversity – not to define a target and eliminate or abandon other options. This can be achieved by systems that actively encourage low-risk eco-innovations to create adaptable, diverse and reversible environments that increase the ecological base and public estate. Sustainability is not just a target to think backwards from. Sustainability must be the foundational element of the constitution for governance and decision-making itself. To achieve this, we can design new planning, decision and management systems that enable people to envisage and design better futures, not just survive.

## Won't people choose poor goals despite sustainable decision structures?

People can make poor choices, but we would have a better chance of good decisions if we invested more in design, instead of putting all our energy into targets and indicators. It is generally held that planners and decision-makers should not pre-empt or predetermine the basic goals and choices of a participatory democracy. As argued above, however, our decision systems, due to their inherent biases, already do exactly that. By choosing the best alternative amongst those that are currently available, or already on the social radar (by whatever criteria), future options are limited by current thinking and market-driven consumer preferences. In this context, the setting of targets can lock in the future and foreclose options. For example, we saw how, in the name of urban consolidation, many non-sustainable, compact suburbs are built that share the worse aspects of both sprawl and consolidation [Chapter 3]. Likewise, society did not choose a fossil fuel path or demand excessively wasteful systems of production and consumption. These complex systems evolved because structures were not in place to prevent unchecked access and control of public resources by special interests over time [Chapter 13]. Since then, there has been an ongoing, and generally zero sum, competition among conflicting interests to make the fossil fuel system 'work better' for either special interests or the public interest, depending on the swing of the political pendulum. The issue is not 'public versus private' control, of course, as both government agencies and corporations can and do abuse power. As we will see, the issue is the lack of substantive and procedural due process in environmental policymaking, planning and design that has shaped the range of trivial pursuits currently called market 'choice'.

## Why can't futures thinking tools simply aim to make everyone better off?

The above futures thinking tools are mainly designed to choose means to get products and processes onto the market, advance the position of an organization in the market place, or choose a course of action in a given socio-political context. To re-design systems, products and environments would require planning systems that enable the *design* of eco-solutions, not tools for making choices. Like many other decision aids, futures thinking tools tend to reflect the competitive values inherent in 'game theory'. Those who see the world as a game (a pinball or poker machine writ large) aim to gain some advantage, score points, or get somewhere with less costs and risks. A competitive, negative and defensive framework has evolved that perpetuates zero sum outcomes. Given the existing inequitable context, sustainability requires correcting the slope of the playing field so it is less biased towards special interests and more biased towards whole-of-society benefits. We need to re-design the game board itself. This means we need new frameworks (such as SmartMode) to help us understand how the game is rigged, and how to re-design it so that everybody wins – including future generations and other species. Futures tools and other 'soft technologies' can be used in combination with sustainable decision frameworks, but only if we bear in mind the hidden assumptions embedded in their design. It is important to apply them strategically, not routinely or formalistically. But before looking at planning and decision-making systems that may be more suitable for sustainability, we will examine the prevalent strategy for implementing change: environmental trading systems.

# 11
# Eco-service Trading Schemes

## From emissions tradeoffs to eco-service credits

This chapter considers the potential value and limitations of the trend towards providing credits for human activities that create environmental goods and services.[1] Since the 1970s, the 'market' has been increasingly advocated as a panacea for all environmental problems. Various kinds of exchange mechanisms have been developed and applied to address a range of development impacts, such as air and water pollution, carbon emissions, allowable building envelopes, and habitat destruction. More recently, carbon trading has been widely promoted as the solution to global warming. Carbon trading, in effect, means an industry can emit carbon if it reduces carbon emissions elsewhere. Carbon becomes a currency. Artificial property rights are created in environmental 'goods' (eg carbon sequestration) or 'bads' (eg pollution emissions). In order to trade the goods and services of nature, they must be treated as separate from their natural context. By attaching a value to these rights, they become commodities and can be sold or traded. Exchange mechanisms create a 'license to pollute', or a right to use a certain amount of water or air up to a limit or 'cap'. In this way, a market is created without the actual ownership of the land, air or water changing hands. In other words, industries can buy, or receive allocations to, the right to continue to generate (or generate more) environmental damage.

Industries that own a right to pollute can trade any unused right below the allowable amount. To reduce environmental harm over time, an 'exchange rate' is usually imposed. This means that the amount of allowable pollution or resource consumption can be reduced each time a transaction occurs or, alternatively, each year or two. This offsets some of the future damage that would otherwise be done. It also gives industries an incentive to clean up their act. By introducing cleaner production methods, buying out another factory and closing it down, or going out of production, an industry can then sell these 'unused' rights to another. So environmental impact mitigation is achieved over time, relatively or absolutely. With active trading, the exchange rate will result in lower waste or pollution. But because the reductions in the cap or exchange rate are essentially set through the political process, they have generally not been adequate. The main aim of trading systems has been to achieve emissions reductions where it is easiest and cheapest for industry to do so. Environmental trading could reduce emissions, and pay for the restoration of rural ecological systems. However, so far, trading has not been applied to achieve net gains, especially in urban areas. Despite the rhetoric, offsets only reduce impacts in one part of the system, by allowing more negative impacts in another.

## Are trading systems better than environmental regulations overall?

Markets in environmental goods or bads may have the same ultimate effect as regulations. However, they enable more flexibility in meeting target reductions. The virtue is that reductions in negative impacts can occur with minimum disruption to the economy as a whole. Trading protects the system, but could slowly work to change it. As currently conceived, however, trading schemes cannot achieve Positive Development. Like other environmental management systems, they are designed to reduce future negative impacts, not past mistakes. In fact, trading systems could delay the necessary transition from fossil to solar resources that is a prerequisite for social and biophysical sustainability. With regard to global warming, for example, carbon trading systems still prioritize tradeoffs, or compensation for ecological destruction. Offsets are a bit like 'indulgences' that the Catholic Church dispensed for people who could afford to have their sins absolved. They do not ensure the most important forms of action or mitigation are undertaken first. Offsets are better than nothing, but they can postpone the transfer of public investment from *indirect* incentives to *direct* eco-solutions. Credit systems should reward only actual reductions in the impacts of existing conditions. So we should ask:

- Could eco-service trading systems be modified to require a net increase in the ecological base?
- Could they encourage development decisions and designs that are reversible and/or reverse past damage?

## What were the origins of environmental trading systems?

The idea of trading in environmental goods (or bads) has been around for a long time. An early precedent was 'transferable development rights' (TDRs), which have been used in urban planning since the 1960s. This is where city planning regulations allow developers to exceed the allowable floor area or height limits on another property as compensation where development rights were restricted by a new regulation, such as the creation of a historic district. Alternatively, the property owners can be permitted to sell the floor area elsewhere that they would have been entitled to develop 'but for' new planning regulations. This enables planners to reduce development rights in a particular area in order to implement urban design policies, such as height limits, without undue repercussions. Planning provisions can also allow developers to obtain permission to exceed the normal height limit in certain locations if they provide publicly beneficial land uses, such as day-care facilities or public plazas. Similarly, developers seeking approval to build new suburbs can be permitted to provide parks, infrastructure or facilities to offset some of the public costs of roads, water and sewage services. Of course, TDRs were not aimed at improving the ecological health of the urban environment. Ecological sustainability was scarcely contemplated when concepts of trading development and/or environmental rights were created. TDRs did, however, enable environmental amenity to be included in the urban environment with less resistance than is often engendered by regulations.

## Why do we use trading instead of just requiring known eco-solutions?

Due to the influence of the dominant market ideology, and the prominence of economists and accountants, the priority has been to use markets to address virtually any problem. Our academic fields, professional cultures and decision systems have not evolved to equip us to 'design' problems out of the system in the first place. Therefore we compensate for the collateral damage of economic activity with indirect incentive systems. This may also be another example of the subtle preference for mechanisms that shift responsibility from managers and decision-makers to producers and consumers. To solve environmental problems through the market, however, we ordinarily need to be able to put a monetary value on eco-services. This is like placing a monetary value on life. Before trading schemes were conceived, the challenge for ecological economists was to translate environmental issues into measurable entities. The author has heard several economists state that 'if something cannot be measured, it does not exist'. Similarly, some environmental managers state that 'if something cannot be measured, it cannot be managed'. However, eco-services cannot be given a 'meaningful' quantitative value as, once again, we cannot measure complex systems. Since we cannot measure nature, by that logic it does not exist [Box 42]. Nor does 'society' exist for that matter, as the former UK Prime Minister Margaret Thatcher famously proclaimed. Therefore, economists have developed a range of devices for measuring eco-services indirectly. Perhaps the simplest is to measure what it would cost to provide similar functions through industrial systems instead.

## If eco-services do not have quantitative values, how can we trade them?

Trading schemes cleverly avoid the problem of measurement by using the market to set the price. Incentives and trading systems, in a sense, avoid the measurement of eco-services. So trading schemes for carbon reduction or sequestration have been designed and implemented despite the fact that there is still scientific debate about how much carbon is (or can be) sequestered in the trees and soils of different ecosystems as they vary so dramatically.[2] As forests become more stressed by lack of water, for example, they begin to give out more carbon dioxide. This can accelerate the warming of the climate which, in turn, increases the release of carbon dioxide from the soil and oceans in a deleterious feedback loop. If we cannot be sure of the net effect of sequestration (a positive eco-service), we cannot know its value. We can only measure the economic impacts. Eco-services have economic value, of course, but numbers or dollars cannot really capture the value of life, because it is infinite. Al Gore's film *An Inconvenient Truth* showed a droll Powerpoint slide purportedly used by 'global warming sceptics'. It puts the Earth on one side of a scale and a bar of gold on another and asks us to 'choose'. Nonetheless, the economic value of eco-services to humanity in general was calculated by some environmental economists back in 1997. They estimated the value of the Earth's ecosystem services at $33 trillion, which exceeded the economic contribution of all human activity at the time (the GDP was estimated at $18 trillion).[3] And this estimate did not count many essential eco-services, such as the cycling of *essential* nutrients through the system.[4] Nature's economy is bigger than man's.

## Doesn't putting a price on eco-services help to preserve them?

It can, but it also diminishes nature's true value. Some have made the observation that eco-services are essential to life itself, so putting a dollar value on them is an inherently flawed – though a well-intended – exercise. That is, while US$33 trillion was a big number at the time, it seriously underestimated infinity.[5] If life on Earth is only worth trillions, then given the growing divide between rich and poor, and the privatization of the means of survival, a single individual or corporation may soon be able to buy the Earth in its entirety. In some cases, the financial worth of eco-services becomes greater as they become more scarce, so poachers or corporations with control over scarce resources would stand to gain by increasing their scarcity. We have seen this already in reduced numbers of seed varieties and endangered species. The value of private access to rare animals goes up when they are more endangered, so there is no incentive to make such species commonplace. For example, before the recent conflicts in Uganda, Rwanda and Democratic Republic of Congo, gorillas were visited by tourist parties. The natural habitat itself was effectively converted into a zoo. Having come to trust humans, many gorillas were later slaughtered by militants in Uganda. Moreover, valuing eco-services can lead to negative tradeoffs. If a firm wants to continue polluting, for instance, it can buy forests and commit to not chopping them down in the future. However, there is no net gain where the forests already exist. Likewise, in the case of restoring 'degraded farmland' to forests, these lands existed *as forest* until the recent past. In come countries, a commitment not to chop forests down can be rescinded when circumstances or governments change. We have seen something similar in the case of international commitments to ban commercial exploitation of whales. On the bright side, however, the growing commercial interest in eco-service trading is having some positive spin-offs. It shows that, in some cases, simply leaving ecosystems alone can be profitable.

## How can leaving ecosystems alone be more profitable than exploiting them?

It is increasingly recognized that eco-services reduce risks, save money and create wealth for business, industry and government. More progressive industries are therefore recognizing that ecosystems can provide more value through their ongoing services than as items of one-off consumption. Whereas eco-retrofitting urban areas can cost less than doing nothing, leaving regional ecosystems intact can earn more than exploiting them. Ecosystems like forests, wetlands and reefs provide essential services to society that can have a higher value as intact eco-productive systems than as consumption items. For instance, it is now widely appreciated that forest catchments automatically purify water, prevent floods and landslides, control insects, and so on. Nature can provide these goods and services at less cost than resource-intensive engineering systems, such as mechanical water purification and sewage treatment. After the 1927 flooding of the Mississippi, for example, engineering structures were built to try to control future floods. These levees made the great 1993 Mississippi flood far worse than it would otherwise have been, as more catastrophic floods result when higher levees are breached. After that, hundreds of millions of dollars were spent moving towns, removing engineering works from the Mississippi floodplain, and restoring natural environmental flows. Generally, however, the old engineering approach is still replicated around the world. New Orleans, for example, is being redeveloped on parts of the same flood-prone land (as were some Australian towns after floods). The new levees may be higher and homes may be built above ground level, but we are still tempting fate. This is especially the case given the unpredictable effects of climate change.

## Wasn't the case of New Orleans just a matter of bad governance?

Perhaps. The New Orleans fiasco was a matter of political failure in that there were many unheeded warnings that flooding was almost inevitable, yet nothing was done.[6] Regardless of whether this inaction was due to political priorities, ignorance, racism or ideology, the New Orleans story does indeed raise broader issues of environmental governance. Many consider the essence of environmental issues to be the transfer of private costs of development onto the general public, or 'externalities'.

However, in an era of 'small government' and privatization, governments are outsourcing more basic responsibilities in the other direction. That is, more of the public costs of environmental protection are being externalized to the private sector and NGOs [Figure 15]. Governments are not investing in environmental restoration, as they once did, during Roosevelt's New Deal, for instance. They increasingly rely on private interests and markets – and unpaid volunteer and citizen groups – to manage the environment.[7] However, private industry can simply choose *not* to act – with impunity. They have no electoral mandate to take responsibility or positive action. Business contracts can be breached, at least if there is appropriate financial restitution. But when the social contract is breached, and environments are destroyed, there can be no restitution. For example, a US telecom company received government funding for upgrading their systems to broadband, and simply did not carry out their obligations. They ignored the public regulators. The CEO returned an enormous profit for the shareholders by short-changing services and delivery, and was rewarded by roughly a billion dollars in total for his services. His 'inaction', in effect, transferred wealth from consumers to shareholders, while the public paid for government regulators to try to enforce the original agreements.

Figure 15 Brokering resource transfers

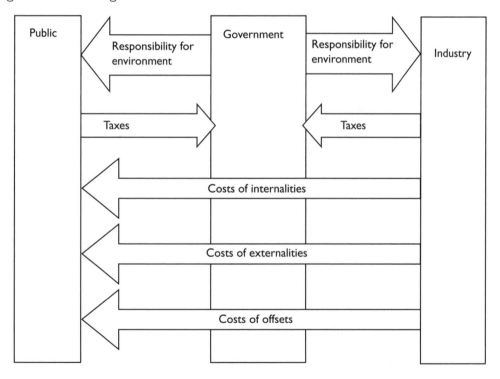

Small government 'down-sources' responsibility for environmental management to NGOs through small grants, and 'out-sources' responsibility to industry through insurance, incentives and other mechanisms. Offsets are in a sense taxes for pollution that bypass government. Government is therefore increasingly a broker rather than a service provider. It mediates resource transfers between the community and industry. Governments can still influence the amount of internalities (public benefits transferred to special interests) and externalities (private costs shifted onto public) of development.

**But don't trading systems ensure private industry will perform their duties?**

In a world where private industry can challenge environmental laws as barriers to trade, large incentives are needed to encourage the fulfilment of ethical responsibilities. Trading adds opportunities for speculation on an international scale. Reducing public spending on environmental management by shifting responsibility to the private sector through trading systems may appear cheap. However, it is not a cure for having let industry shift these externalities onto civil society in the first place. As the costs of floods, hurricanes, droughts and rising sea-levels take their toll, 'small governments' are having to fall back on the military to deal with large-scale environmental disasters (eg New Orleans). In the public sector vacuum left by market-dominated solutions, paradoxically, private insurance companies are becoming the de facto environmental standard-setting bodies. They are increasingly refusing to ensure risky projects on business grounds. The United Nations Environment Program and reinsurer Munich Re calculated that, by 2050, the negative effects of global warming may cost the global economy US$300 billion a year. This cost estimate was increased dramatically by the 2007 Stern Report in the UK and may increase yet again as information about climate change grows.[8] While insurance companies can stop risky projects, however, they are not structured to provide ecological restoration – let alone Positive Development. It may be quicker and cheaper from a whole systems perspective to regulate against bad development, rather than rely on its ultimate lack of profitability. However, we also need systems to facilitate good design in the first place. Both ecological preservation and eco-retrofitting currently have to compete with development that does not have to carry its own weight (let alone its ecological waste).

**Can the value of eco-services justify public or private ecological preservation?**

The challenge is justifying the cost of ecological restoration in a particular market system, as opposed to an ecologically rational economy. The 'cost avoided' by eco-services is one way to justify environmental preservation in the given context. New urban buildings and infrastructure could work to restore eco-services while eliminating the costs of mechanical equipment, such as heating and air-conditioning. At the regional scale, the value of eco-services has been estimated by comparing the cost of preserving a watershed to that of avoiding the cost of alternative engineering structures. An often cited early example of valuing eco-services was New York City's Catskill watershed. Development in the watershed had begun to contaminate the City's water supplies, so it was necessary to either repair the watershed or build an expensive filtration plant. At the time, the new plant would have cost about $8 billion, with annual operating costs of about $300 million. In contrast, restoration of the watershed would cost under $2 billion and involve relatively little maintenance and operating costs. The city chose eco-restoration and catchment protection on financial grounds. A similar decision was made by the city of Melbourne in Australia. There are also examples of communities acting to protect and restore ecosystem services, without waiting for government or industry to do cost–benefit analyses. They have recognized the intrinsic and 'multiple-bottom-line' values of nature.

**Why and how would communities restore eco-services on their own?**

Many people understand that the amenity provided by the surrounding natural environment is essential to the quality of life, not just property values. Improvements to individual homes and landscapes mean little if the wider environment is deteriorating. Gated communities are no protection in an environment under siege by drought, storms, disease and floods. This realization has driven communities not only to take on obstructionist industries and bureaucracies, but even to reverse past and proposed resource-intensive infrastructure projects. In Napa, California, as described by Geoffrey Heal, some resident groups sought for years to restore the natural flow of the river that once glided through the region and town centre. As with the case of the Mississippi, structures designed to suppress natural flows were causing floods to be more expensive and dangerous when they inevitably breached the engineered boundaries. To remedy this, the community had to obtain widespread support for the removal of structures that had been constructed by the Army Corps of Engineers. Three hundred people had to be persuaded to relocate their homes and businesses from the floodplain. Nonetheless, in the end, they managed to turn a "stagnant urban bathtub" into a living river with wetlands, natural habitats and trails for hikers.[9] There are also many cases where even private companies have deemed the economic value of eco-services to be worth the funding of ecological restoration projects.

## How can ecological restoration be worth the cost to business or government?

One of the first businesses to appreciate the value of ecological restoration to the financial bottom line was Perrier, the French bottled water company. They realized that pesticides and fertilizers from farms in their watershed were posing a threat to their business and source of clean water. In 1990, the company had to pull its bottles off the shelves when benzene, a carcinogen, was found in the water. Instead of relocating to a more pristine environment that might later also be under threat from new development, they invested millions in purchasing land around the springs. They also signed contracts to guarantee more environmentally benign practices from farmers already operating in the catchment.[10] And even national governments are capable of recognizing the value of eco-services. Costa Rica, for example, initiated a programme where landowners received compensation for regenerating and maintaining the forests on their property. This created jobs for local people and was paid for by a tax on fossil fuels. In one of those rare examples of a virtuous cycle, money gained from taxing negative activities was invested in positive activities. Costa Rica recognized the diverse ecosystem services that flow from forested lands, such as carbon sequestration, watershed protection, biodiversity resources and eco-tourism. Daily and Ellison call Costa Rica's approach "paying mother nature to multi-task". It showed it can pay financially for governments to generate positive ecological impacts, or at least restore ecosystems.

## Then why don't we have more of these examples of virtuous cycles?

We can trace this back to the underlying notions that 'we can only mitigate impacts', and that 'nature unused is wasted'. For example, in the Australian debate about dealing with the water shortage, the concern has been expressed that 'if it is just a drought, rather than global warming, we may be wasting money on water efficiency measures'. This was despite the fact that natural flows have not been sustained. As we saw, in some parts of Australia, because the amount of water allocated exceeded the supply, and extreme drought followed, the public now has to 'buy back' water. In Queensland, water was reserved for the environment before the rest of it was allocated. However, the needs of the environment cannot be known in advance of climate change. The then Federal Government responded to the water crisis with a ten billion dollar initiative. Three billion dollars of taxpayers' funds was intended to be used to buy back over-allocated water. Such actions may enable some farmers to exit the industry who could not survive financially because they did not receive their allocation in dry years. If the funding goes ahead, six billion dollars will be invested in hardware for more efficient irrigation water. Irrigation has often been wasteful, but more efficient systems are being developed. For example, an irrigation cooperative in Coleambally, Australia, reportedly achieved 90 per cent efficiencies. This will not, however, restore or enhance the river ecosystems or pension off those who lose out. With recent rains in Australia (at the time of writing) the need to increase environmental flows may be forgotten until the next drought.

### Surely it is only fair to buy back resources that private parties now 'own'?

True. Private parties should not be disadvantaged by the past mistakes of governments. However, in many cases, these resources were not really earned or paid for. In many places, people and companies were given land grants on the condition that they cleared the land. Many forests were virtually given to industry in exchange for their exploitation of resources.[11] The idea, of course, was that this would generate economic growth. But increasingly, governments have spent millions buying back 'rights' to resources that were given away at below market cost.[12] In a sense, then, the public is now paying a ransom for the 'things in life that were meant to be free'. These private grants to large companies, such as forest concessions or water rights, are often not considered reversible, especially in the case of large-scale operations. Yet while development decisions are usually irreversible ecologically, past preservation decisions have proven to be politically *reversible*. When political pressure is great enough, the cork pops, and protected ecosystems are allocated to development. Clearly, people should receive restitution for private costs or losses incurred directly due to changing rules – but not for 'lost expectations'. Nonetheless, there are precedents for using trading to protect and restore nature, not just reward speculation and privilege.

### Could trading systems be used to protect species as well as resources?

Yes, there are some cases where trading systems have been used to protect species. For example, the US introduced a trading scheme to protect endangered species in 2003. An even earlier precedent was a tradable quota on Alaskan halibut, established in 1995 to protect the fishing stock. It enabled some fishermen to exit the business by selling their unused quotas to others, who were then better positioned to invest in bigger boats and get more fish. Similarly, in Zimbabwe, tribal people were given property rights over animals, so they could auction quotas of animals to the highest bidders (ie Western hunters) for the right to shoot them for sport. The profit from hunters was then shared, so they had *less* motivation to kill the animals that invaded their gardens. This contrasts with the approach in Kenya, where a paramilitary force was marshalled to combat poachers. Both these market and militant approaches were reputedly reasonably effective. One of the author's students suggested a third hybrid model, where tribal communities could auction rights to rich Western hunters to shoot the poachers. This is not that big a stretch, given that much modern warfare is now outsourced to private sector corporate mercenaries.[13] Governments already pay private companies to shoot people, and arms manufacturers are well positioned to broker this system. (The ultimate market-based solution to the escalating costs of militarism would be to sell rights to shoot people, or give out free tickets to heaven.)

### What about using trading systems to protect the habitats of species then?

Protecting the habitats that species depend on is more difficult. Since ecological values cannot be separated from the land, habitat protection and restoration schemes are not tradable as such. However, government, NGOs or industry can, say, pay farmers for credits earned by restoring and managing land for native vegetation. In the US, there was some objection to programmes that pay farmers to take land out of production, due to the work ethic. However, paying farmers to convert degraded land to natural habitat and to manage ferals, disease, fire hazards, etc can also foster both rural revitalization and land regeneration, so it is a good investment for governments. Such programmes could arguably even result in an increase in carrying capacity. The Victorian BushTender scheme in Australia set the value of beneficial ecosystems restored by farmers through auctions. An auction assures a viable market value by definition; that is, a willing buyer and seller. But habitat protection is somewhat complicated by the fact that ecosystems are open systems. Waterways, for example, have many upstream sources of pollution, degradation and diminution. The idea of creating a type of trading system to protect ecosystems was used to protect wetlands as early as 1972. The US Clean Water Act required developers who destroyed a wetland to restore or conserve another wetland area elsewhere. On the face of it, restoring one ecosystem to compensate for damaging another sounds 'balanced', but this is not necessarily so.

## Couldn't wetlands trading be net positive if it increased the total area?

If that worked, perhaps. In fact, an exchange rate was applied so that two new hectares of wetland had to be restored or created for each hectare destroyed. But this was not very successful in ecological terms. From an ecological perspective, each wetland is unique, irreplaceable and wedded to a particular location. For example, the destroyed wetland may have an – as yet unidentified – endangered species that the new area does not. Similarly, a new artificially created ecosystem is not very likely to evolve into a healthy, resilient ecology. In any case, the wetlands provision of the Clean Water Act was ineffective in preserving the total area of wetlands. Wetlands continued to disappear at an alarming rate. In 1995, to improve the situation, private wetland restoration banks were allowed to buy and restore wetlands. Developers who needed 'points' to obtain development approvals could then buy wetland credits from organizations specializing in wetland restoration. This reduced the difficulties of enforcement and monitoring and worked better than the previous system in reducing the rate of wetland destruction. However, even if some of these new 'artificial wetlands' survive, they are seldom as ecologically sound as the ones they replaced.[14] A sustainable trading scheme would require that the health, resilience and scale of whole systems were increased to the pre-development level of biodiversity and ecosystem viability. Trading systems are beginning to make ecological restoration possible, but this is mostly through exactions for damage elsewhere.

## If they enable ecological restoration, what is wrong with trading systems?

So far, these systems allow *additional* urban environmental impacts in the future, in exchange for remediation of natural areas. For example, in parts of the US, a developer can exceed the height limits or floor area ratios defined by planning code requirements in the city if he pays for credits to organizations or banks that are remediating degraded farmland. The ecological restoration (informed by regional ET analysis) is valuable work that attracts investors. However, this offsetting system does not recognize that the impacts of the *additional* urban development are felt in the region. For example, urban development contributes to global warming, which impacts upon the restored landscapes. Also, the demands by urban residents will stay the same or increase. That is, the functions that were provided by the degraded farmland, such as crops, meat or milk production – that did the ecological damage in the first place – will go elsewhere. They will continue their impacts. Again, this is because, in trading systems as well as in other areas of environmental management, *post*-development conditions are used as the baseline. Credits are based on the improved ecosystem functioning beyond the initial damaged state. Arguably, one cannot restore natural areas beyond original conditions, even if their eco-services increase. This presumes that we can improve upon 4 billion years of evolution in the creation of complex living systems. We have to redesign urban systems, not offset or shift around their impacts. As long as developers can buy credits, however, they will not deal with systems re-design.

## Could trading systems result in sustainability if applied widely enough?

Not in themselves. Trading systems, as currently conceived, may achieve offsets that reduce the additional negative impacts of an industry or new development. However, slowing environmental destruction cannot achieve sustainability. A case in point is sulphur dioxide trading. It was established in 1990 and reduced US sulphur emissions by 37 per cent. This was lauded as a great success because it reduced emissions for less money than predicted. However, while it was effective in reducing emissions cheaply, it did nothing to restore the lakes and forests damaged by acid rain. Similarly, a mining operation may do things to assist a local (or aboriginal) community development, if only for 'good will'. But this will not compensate nature for the damage. Aboriginals, after all, are not nature. Of course, an industry should certainly get some sort of credit for such compensatory, if only peripheral, activities. Presumably though, they already get a benefit, or industries would not make such investments in good will in the first place. Development approval systems that allow developers to provide transient, one-off social benefits in exchange for reducing the *rate* of destruction of the life-support system are not an indicator of a higher civilization. The sustainability issue in, say, mining for jewellery should not be how much compensation or offsets (or in some cases even bribes) can be negotiated by the local community from a mining company.[15] We are beginning to recycle precious metals from mobile phones into jewellery. However, the issue is whether we should be pushing so much jewellery – with its wasteful purposes and excessive ecological waste – onto the market in the first place.

## So are trading systems perpetuating systems that are going the wrong way?

If there is *not* a net reduction in total resource flows, an increase in ecosystem health and resilience, and greater ecological carrying capacity, the system is not contributing to sustainability. Exchange mechanisms could, of course, require net positive improvements over existing conditions. But this is not yet the case. Currently, companies establish plantations (often on prime agricultural land), or buy the sequestration credits of a forest to compensate for carbon emissions that they will generate elsewhere. The idea is that the forests will continue to provide carbon sequestration. But either humans or nature can reduce the value of these assets overnight. Whole stands of forests that have received carbon credits in Western Australia are dying. Bonds, insurance and replacement plans have their limitations. Also, carbon trading basically only looks at one of the eco-services of forests (sequestration), not the value of whole ecosystems and other eco-services, such as water purification, habitat protection, soil production and erosion control. Thus, remarkably, carbon sequestration has also been used as an argument for clear-felling forests. In fact, timber 'harvesting' has been promoted by some as better than retaining old growth forests, on the grounds that wood products sequester carbon – at least until landfilled or burned.[16] A PhD study recently showed that the timber sequestered in housing in Victoria equated to taking 80,000 cars off the road.[17] But this does not really account for the ecological waste (loss of ecosystem integrity and resilience) in production forestry [Chapter 4]. Markets and trading systems cannot design; they only create incentives. If costs can be cut elsewhere, market incentives will not design ecological waste out of a production system. In some instances, then, trading systems could be considered 'positively negative'.

## Just how could trading systems be 'positively negative' in this context?

Using offsets to justify *production* forestry for the single purpose of carbon sequestration does not protect old growth forests containing ecological systems with multiple values. The production argument is that young forests sequester carbon at a greater rate than aging forests. Mature and old growth forests are considered, at best, to be carbon neutral, because the carbon fixed in photosynthesis is the equivalent of the carbon released in respiration. This supports the claim that when no net carbon fixation gains are made by a mature or old growth forest, they should be turned into products. Recent scientific studies have shown, however, that native forests can sequester more carbon than production forestry.[18] Moreover, in some types of forests, most of the carbon may actually be stored in the forest floor anyway.[19] In Australia's sensitive land, topsoil is lost under forestry practices that, in effect, plough up the soil. Although tree *planting* is being encouraged by carbon trading, *clearing* is still proceeding at an increasing rate in the Amazon basin and even wealthy places like Australia. The net effects on climate change from tree clearing in the Amazon may nullify the tree planting for credits used to justify increasing emissions – a vicious circle. Australia, for example, claimed to have met its Kyoto target (it did not sign the Protocol) which would allow a net increase in greenhouse emissions of 8 per cent achieved by merely 'slowing' the rate of tree clearing. This meant increased coal-fired electricity production was justified at the expense of the long-suffering Australian agricultural sector. There is arguably not enough fertile land to support the amount of forests required to offset existing Australian coal-fired power stations, given the need to accommodate other land uses. Over all, then, carbon trading has not been net positive.

## Isn't carbon trading still a low cost and efficient activity overall?

It is effective for reducing the 'growing rate' of emission more cheaply, but only for the industries involved. It is not necessarily cheaper for society as a whole. The fastest solution to environmental problems can be cheaper in the long term. As we saw earlier, trading schemes transfer public goods to private interests without determining the value of the eco-services. A price on carbon emissions may be recommended by scientists, but it is mediated by politics. Rights to public resources are allocated to the private sector without it having to pay the full costs of the land surface. This can indirectly increase the wealth of those positioned to acquire rights cheaply and in turn secure their future political influence. Also, if a company emits carbon in manufacturing on the grounds they have purchased carbon credits in another nation's forests, there can be enforcement issues and costs. If the forest is subsequently harvested or destroyed by fire or disease, liability for replanting forests can be resolved with legal instruments. However, payment for carbon credits in politically unstable or corrupt governments may not benefit the local indigenous population that may have relied on the forest goods and services for their subsistence. Conceivably, resources that indigenous people draw from forests could be indirectly expropriated without compensation where a forest is preserved. On top of that, little is being done about illegal logging in 'third world' countries. Companies do not like being undercut by illegal logging of tropical forests, but market forces are not good at stopping cheap products, regardless of their source. Preventing illegal logging requires direct action by governments. In the end, we cannot really know if social injustices resulting from trading schemes outweigh the 'presumed' environmental gain, as it is a self-referential system [Chapter 15].

## In any case, aren't trading systems better than regulations overall?

Markets are not independent; they cannot really operate outside a regulatory framework.[20] Trading systems only work where there is a regulatory framework that sets a cap, and a means of reducing the cap. These amounts are established through a political process and involve at least de facto regulatory 'negotiation'. It is the regulation that is actually achieving the reduction. The market only makes the transactions. Ultimately, of course, it is the market that sets the monetary value of the credits. For example, the EU began selling carbon credits a few years ago. This meant a windfall for the big energy producers who were given free credits (as was perhaps deemed necessary to get them to accept the new system). Increasing demand for energy led to an inflation of permit prices. In fact, through market mechanisms, the cost of carbon credits can actually exceed the cost of the coal. In the case of Southern California's emissions trading scheme, for example, the skyrocketing carbon prices led to a return to a regulatory scheme of penalties and pollution control requirements. Trading schemes can also create windfalls and speculative profits. Yet, at the same time, they do not avoid transaction costs. The costs of implementation are not eliminated; they are just more dispersed and less *visible* than the costs of regulations. Trading systems can still involve a lot of regulatory, monitoring and enforcement costs, and often legal processes. Trading mechanisms should not conceal the costs to government that are ultimately paid for by the taxpayer [Box 41].

## If consumers pay in the end anyway, why are trading systems preferred?

Industry is justifiably more comfortable with flexible systems that enable a choice of responses. The caps on trading schemes create commercial imperatives, but industry can meet them through various strategies that take into account their unique business risks and opportunities. Moreover, industries can benefit several times over from trading schemes. They:

- Do not forego any of the commercial benefits flowing from the externalities they created in the past when establishing their market power and competitive advantage
- Capture the value of the credits which, in some cases, are even allocated to polluting industries for free (as in the EU carbon trading programme)
- Are able to make economic gains just from credit inflation or price increases, as energy and resources become more scarce
- Have new opportunities for 'creative' activity, for example where brokering and speculation enables wealth creation without any real production (eg the case of Enron)
- Are able to create wealth 'out of thin air' without buying the resource base itself (ie land, air or water);
- Can, in effect, obtain 'indulgences' for extra waste and pollution;
- Gain control of the productive functions of the ecological base and thus remove public options, as we become more vulnerable to environmental change.

In the 1970s, the early days of environmental regulation, some firms invested more resources in avoiding compliance, by opposing legislation in court, than it would have cost to install the required environmental technologies. A parallel risk attaches to market-based solutions. Middlemen may invest their creative energy in finding ways to exploit the new schemes, instead of achieving the spirit of the legislation.

## So how can we enlist eco-service trading to generate net positive gain?

We can start by making distinctions between what we can call 'eco-service' credit schemes as opposed to 'emissions trading' schemes. An eco-service can be said to refer to a *positive* service of nature, as opposed to a pollutant caused by human systems. $CO_2$ could be seen as an emission to be 'reduced' because, again at the scale it is being absorbed into the atmosphere and oceans, it threatens the world's ecosystems and ultimately humans. However, $CO_2$ *sequestration* is a 'surrogate' for a positive eco-service ordinarily provided by nature: that of a stable climate. Traditional emissions trading systems 'rewarded' industry for reducing pollution. In contrast, eco-service credit systems could reward industry for creating *positive* ecological impacts. Thus, for example, trees play an essential role in natural cycles, so increasing the total area of healthy 'native' forests creates a more stable climate. Reducing the rate of forest clearing or turning native forests into plantations does *not* create a more stable climate. So again, if we want a 'balance' between conservation and development, it would mean at least restoring the ecologically-suitable tree cover that existed several hundred years ago. A more practical approach might be eco-service credit systems that 'over-compensate' for existing ecological problems by value-adding to the ecology. Ironically, carbon trading systems are being used to justify new sources of fossil fuel energy. Instead of just mitigating the harm new projects will do (ie just reducing *future* $CO_2$ emissions), then, we need to compensate for the harm that excess $CO_2$ in the air and oceans is already doing. Cities could begin to play the role of the forests they replaced, but not by adding 'mechanical trees'.

## Could eco-service credits compensate for past development, realistically?

Unlike emissions trading, eco-service credit systems could create the conditions for positive environmental impacts in the built environment that compensate psychologically for past damage. Earlier environmental management systems required, in effect, only *financial* compensation for environmental damage. The various kinds of fines, fees, royalties and charges were intended to create incentives for modernization by transferring some externality costs back to producers. This was in accordance with the 'polluter pays' principle, which holds that, if producers have to pay for pollution, they will reduce it to improve their bottom line. Financial compensation for physical damage, in a sense, converts emissions to a monetary value. The 'polluter pays' principle assumes that money and ecology are somehow commensurate or, at least, that we can internalize environmental impacts through fiscal means. Emissions trading systems therefore represented an advance over financial compensation. They required some *physical* reductions at the home plant or at other plants. However, carbon and emissions trading also allow industries to compensate for their ongoing and future carbon emissions by physical offsets elsewhere. A reduction in future emissions cannot be considered an eco-service. Likewise, sequestering a portion of additional carbon emissions after they are produced by a power plant is not net positive. Emissions trading systems therefore create imposts upon industry, but only slow down ecological degradation [Box 41]. Regarding eco-services as 'commodities' to be effectively owned and traded by private interests does little to encourage Positive Development. However, as we will see, the 'space' for eco-services in urban areas itself could be traded.

## Can't financial incentives that reduce negative impacts lead to positive ones?

Not likely. Because corporations can offset impacts through operations in other countries, trading can also increase the incentive to acquire resources cheaply from poor countries. Power imbalances between the first and third world set the market value of resources. Commodities can be privatized and/or consumed as long as there is a willing buyer (eg an international corporation) and willing seller (eg a weak, poor government). In some cases, trading schemes could, therefore, facilitate wealth transfers from poor to rich. Effective ownership of natural capital can be alienated to special interests with no ties to the country. So it is important that we distinguish negative *offsets* from positive *credits*. Emissions trading that allowed some to gain wealth by doing less harm was buttressed by the belief that pollution control costs extra and reduces productivity, goods and services. But we now know that this is untrue, at least in a whole systems perspective. Our institutional and intellectual frameworks need to keep up with our growing awareness of our interdependency with nature. A distinction between eco-service offset schemes and eco-service credit schemes would help to change the vocabulary that currently confuses mitigating future impacts with reducing existing impacts. Eco-service credit schemes should ensure credits can only be gained by creating new or improved forms of production or development that increase natural capital and carrying capacity. In short, an eco-service *credit* scheme would require net positive improvements over current conditions, not the reduction of damage as yet to be done.

## Just how can trading systems be used to generate positive physical impacts?

By decoupling economic growth from ecological destruction. This could be partly achieved by a two-tiered incentive scheme: actions that undo the damage of previous development would generally get more points; actions that offset emissions of ongoing activity by the particular firm or industry would get less points. That is, we can make a distinction between:

- Eco-service *offset* schemes requiring physical offsets, such as new (hopefully viable) forests and wetlands. Mechanisms like wetlands banks or ecosystem service banks may be able to create artificial wetlands that eventually become viable, eco-productive ecosystems where land is currently degraded.
- Eco-service *credit* systems requiring positive actions that reduce the negative impacts of *past* development or repair damaged ecosystems. Credits would only be given for positive actions like ecological restoration in rural areas by farmers, or eco-retrofitting of cities by developers. Net positive outcomes could, however, be achieved by outcomes and actions that have positive effects on other sites.

Development can be designed to overcompensate physically for existing problems by increasing actual eco-services and the ecosystems that provide them (ie forests, reefs and wetlands).[21] But an 'incentive' to solve environmental problems is not a solution in itself. In some cases, systems that enable firms to profit from reducing designed waste may slow the rate of ecological destruction. In other cases, as we have seen, they may also slow the transformation to sustainable systems. We need to ensure that trading systems do not have the effect of privatizing the means of survival in exchange for reducing future harm (a kind of systemic extortion).

## How could eco-service 'credit' systems be transformative then?

The invisible hand is not a magic wand. The public still needs to act, and they may need to bypass government and industry, or partner with them, to do so. Eco-service credit schemes should not be allowed to eclipse or delay direct action by communities to implement available eco-solutions. Governments must ensure that developments do not receive credits unless they are designed to advance sustainability, through a net increase in natural and social capital. Thus, for example, industry should *not* be able to continue to emit carbon by simply buying rights for the sequestration capacity of a forest and its soil – unless that forest is managed for *multiple* eco-service values in perpetuity. Likewise, industry should *not* be able to invest in new coal-fired power stations by simply piping a portion of the new carbon emissions in a hole (ie geo-sequestration). We cannot reduce the total rate of carbon emissions by sweeping some of them under the carpet. Geo-sequestration would increase emissions overall, even though more modern plants would replace existing ones (with high embodied energy costs). The role of government should not just be 'quality control', but to improve upon proposals through mechanisms like the eco-design reporting process [Chapter 5].

## Table 1 Typology of environmental trading systems

| | Conventional regulation | Conventional emissions trading | Conventional eco-service trading | Proposed eco-service credits |
|---|---|---|---|---|
| **Type of compensation for damage** | Fiscal penalty: Penalizes some negative impacts of future development | Fiscal incentive: Creates a competitive advantage through impact reduction | Physical offsets: Offset negative impacts with reductions that can be elsewhere | Physical positives: add positive impacts as well as reducing negatives (off- and on-site) |
| **Theoretical underpinning of scheme** | Polluter pays for damage in order to balance costs and benefits | Creates interest in reducing pollution (eg phasing out old production plants) | Reduces cost of impact reduction, but transfers resources to producers | Restores natural systems and increases the ecological base |
| **Objective and/or outcomes** | Requires end-of-pipe controls – technology forcing | Reduces rate of future harm through cleaner production | Reduces ongoing and/or future harm in total | Reduces present, future and past harm |
| **Type of action promoted by scheme** | End-of-pipe measures shift toxins to other media | Measures reduce emissions under a cap at the plant or other factory | Reduces the rate of damage by substitution or offsetting impacts | Motivates direct action by public and private sectors for credits |
| **Tools used to achieve aims** | Licences, fines, fees, inspections | Reductions in 'licensed pollution' over time | Offsets (eg carbon sequestration) anywhere | Ecological space, ecological waste, net metering, etc |

## So what would the criteria for an eco-service credit system be?

At a minimum, to earn eco-service *credits*, a project or development should:

- Be net positive. For example, a carbon credit scheme should only allow credits for the substitution of fossil fuels by ecologically responsible sources of energy (eg solar or wind power). Again, complex trading schemes that create incentives to reduce – rather than replace – fossil fuels delay the conversion to solar resources.
- Be 're-distributive'. For example, by enabling farmers to obtain tradable credits for eco-services such as water, air and soil improvements, carbon sequestration, wind power, and increased habitats and biodiversity, we could also foster the revitalization of declining rural economies.
- Create actual *improvements* to the ecological base and/or public estate. Credits should not be given for the 'substitution' of social, built or manufacturing capital for natural systems, as these do not increase eco-services.

An eco-service credit system would encourage direct actions by the government or community.[22]

Market mechanisms tend to divert funds from potential direct actions, such as loans to install solar systems or the re-design of particular industries. Savings accrued from direct actions could be rolled over into a fund for ecological restoration programmes.[23] An eco-service credit system should contribute to sustainability without transferring wealth from poor to rich, resources from public to private interests, and so on. Instead of spending money on complex incentives, governments could instead invest in win–win–win eco-solutions that make everyone better off, or provide credits to government and non-government organizations that do.

## Don't we need to know that benefits of direct actions will outweigh the costs?

Not if the eco-solutions are a good investment for private developers or public agencies, and work to improve social and ecological values. In that case, the only issue is one of investment priorities [Chapter 14]. We have seen that it is not difficult to establish that a building does not use toxic materials, and makes the environment and people healthier. Improvements in, say, air or water quality from its entering to its exiting the building are easy to verify. Natural systems (using plants, natural light and air movement) seldom hurt, and sometimes even strengthen human health and immune systems. In many cases, of course, we need to measure the predicted ecological (as opposed to environmental) gain before construction occurs, for project approval purposes. To do so, we can employ emerging technologies like bioacoustic measurements.[24] Alternatively, we can simply establish a surrogate for increases in the amount of biota, indigenous species and habitat in a development – beyond what the site could support before construction. Again, surrogates are used because we cannot actually measure complex natural systems. Ecological space provides one such surrogate and is easy to measure [Chapter 3]. Thus, increases in natural capital in urban areas could be achieved by assigning credits for infrastructure that supports potentially self-managing ecosystems and eco-services in the built environment. Credits for ecological space could be allocated through existing building rating tools or TDR schemes. Or, one could simply add 'points' for ecological space in standard development review and approval processes.

## Wouldn't space for biological systems compete with economic functions?

We have seen that space can be designed for multiple social, economic and ecological functions [Chapter 1]. Atriums or sunspaces can actually expand the usable home or office space at little or no extra cost, as they envelop, heat and cool space cheaply. Attached greenhouses can serve environmental, social and economic functions. Interior spaces can be integrated with light wells and vertical landscapes that clean the air and water. Garages or even spare attic spaces can be converted to greenhouses. So instead of reducing usable floor area, ecological space can add usable space, amenity and market value to existing buildings. As we have noted, wind power and solar disks do not take space from other productive activity in urban or rural areas. A simple, low-cost incentive to encourage ecological space in retrofitting would be to allow exemptions from building envelope restrictions for sunspaces that provide ecosystem services. That is, we could allow functional solariums and greenhouse spaces in rear or side yards where this does not interfere with the amenity of neighbouring properties.[25] This could be extended to large buildings by allowing floor area, set back or height limit exemptions in exchange for the provision of ecological space. There are many 'dead spaces' in urban areas where the opportunity to generate passive solar heating, cooling and ventilating could be achieved with concomitant increases in ecological space. There are also dead spaces in the interior of many homes that could be converted to energy capture and storage (as in the Solar Core) [Box 9].

## Can we also create 'extra' financial incentives to promote ecological space?

Yes. Incentives like exemptions to planning provisions for sunspaces would increase ecological and environmental values without added resource-intensive infrastructure – and with very little increase in land coverage or public infrastructure. There is a constant turnover of properties and, just as many people renovate homes for resale, businesses could develop a specialization in eco-retrofitting homes for resale. We could create additional incentives by enabling 'non-owners' to develop ecological space in cities, suburbs and buildings. This would be achieved by de-coupling space from land area and buildings (similar to mining rights, TDRs and carbon trading systems). Thus, for example, homeowners could sell the right to develop part of their property (eg yard or roof) for urban food or solar electricity production purposes. This could be seen as a 'reverse TDR', as people would acquire the right to use another's building, property or infrastructure, either through purchase or a percentage of profits. Added income to homeowners from the use of their property for eco-productive activity by others could enable elderly residents to stay in their homes longer – as more and more are choosing to do. Grants or trading systems that reward eco-retrofitting for ecological space could be implemented by 'eco-retrofitting banks' that sell points or credits to developers who need them to obtain development approvals. Similarly, as mentioned earlier, mortgage systems can offer incentives for eco-retrofitting that increases the ecological base of cities, just as they are now sometimes used to reward people for energy-efficient homes.[26]

## How would ecological space be quantified for TDR or trading purposes?

There are various ways of quantifying this. Since ecosystems defy measurement, all we need to do is select relevant 'surrogates'. *Passive* solar heating, cooling and ventilating, for example, are eco-services provided by nature (sun, wind, etc). It is easy to measure the financial benefits of eco-services in building design. We can, for example:

- Read the energy and water meter (instead of predicting performance).
- Measure the costs and risks of mechanical air-conditioning equipment that is avoided. A factor that should be considered is that eco-services need not entail risks. We do not calculate the risks of explosions of fossil fuel systems (eg gas), and we do not calculate the risks of 'brown outs' of centralized electricity eg coal).
- Measure the square metres allocated to things such as vertical landscapes, or the amount of productive soil that the building infrastructure supports in roofs, decks, ground floor, balconies, atriums or green walls.
- Measure the health of the air, water and soil that comes out of the building or neighbourhood relative to their quality before they entered the building or neighbourhood. Community or individual biological water-treatment systems already require ongoing testing for public health reasons. Testing improvement in water, indoor air or soil quality is not onerous either. Soil samples of the mechanical properties of development sites have long been required for structural engineering purposes. There are already many kinds of soil testing services that measure the biological health and carbon content of the soil (although some argue the science is not settled).[27]

## How would we ensure the ecosystems receiving credits actually survive?

It is true that the soil, plants and biota – or even the infrastructure that supports them – could be neglected or later removed by tenants or future owners. However, monitoring and enforcement is an issue in all development approvals. This problem is not any different to that of established building rating and development approval schemes. Monitoring developments for adherence to conditional approvals or other planning regulations has been a weak point in most development control authorities. The energy efficiency and environmental impact predictions that form the basis for the approval, rating or awards can be highly inaccurate in the first place. Also, the equipment may simply not be installed or implemented after the rating is received [Box 20]. There is little third party verification or post-occupancy evaluation as yet. Further, tenants' future behaviour can nullify an energy and water efficient design in any case. In the case of eco-services, however, the design criteria can ensure that only actual *infrastructure* for ecosystem services counts, not intentions or plans. After all, if one has already invested in internal or external infrastructure to support eco-services, they or a subsequent tenant are likely to want to maintain it, if only for the amenity value. Of course, planters on exterior walls and roofs must be provided with shade, light and water. In fact, all living things must be designed for. While eco-services are theoretically self-managing and self-repairing, a degree of maintenance would be required when ecosystems are integrated with the built environment.

### How can we ensure that building-integrated ecosystems are maintained?

All physical infrastructure needs periodic maintenance. Fossil fuel-based systems are generally more expensive to maintain than natural systems. Nonetheless, we generally accept these conventional costs as given and do not deduct them. One way to ensure that points gained through conventional green rating schemes and ecological space are legitimate and maintained over time is to put systems in place for post-occupancy evaluation and 'green' facilities management. Facilities managers are currently not rewarded for improving buildings, let alone increasing their eco-productivity [Chapter 9]. To assist the shift from measuring nature's ability to cope with human interference to measuring responsible human management, we need a new profession of facilities managers that have ecological training. We have noted that it is easier to measure improvements than the negative ramifications of harmful systems and designs in unknown future climatic and ecological conditions. It is also easier to reward positive actions that managers take than figuring out just how irresponsible we can allow developers and designers to be before environmental costs to the public outweigh the financial benefits to the developer, require fixing at public expense or are simply too late to address.

### What would provide adequate incentives for such a shift in our approach?

It has been argued throughout this book that nature can be allowed to maintain itself, but also to provide 'surplus' eco-services. This would be new in human history, so it requires a fundamental shift. The problems of food, water and global warming are essential to national security as well as to human survival. It is odd, therefore, that we do not rely on the market system for national security, but we rely on markets to provide 'natural security'. Of course, the idea that value-adding costs more may often be true when we are trying to mitigate negative impacts. We have seen how marginal thinking and markets discourage the idea of zero waste. They can also work to reinforce the mindset that we gain more by being frugal with positive actions. We need to overcome the belief in the 'law of diminishing returns' as applied to improving the built environment. The tendency toward marginal thinking and reliance on marginal market mechanisms can also work against positive forms of competition. Presently, cities can only compete to be the most sustainable by having a relatively less negative ecological footprint. In such cases, the outcomes would usually be more a function of historic coincidence than of affirmative actions anyway, despite impressive efforts to 'green' some cities, such as Chicago. If, on the other hand, we recognized the possibility of positive impacts, we might instead begin to compete towards positive goals, such as the greatest amount of new ecological space per capita each year. Of course, there are many other systemic reasons why the institution of planning, in its broadest sense, has only aimed to mitigate the externalities of development at the margins. Therefore, we need to examine some basic paradigmatic and process problems within planning itself. Next we briefly critique traditional planning thought and bioregional reforms, with a view to how urban and regional planning could be made more relevant to sustainability.

# 12
# Bioregional Planning

From choosing among current options to designing futures

Land-use planning is central to a sustainable future. Land-use decisions change the environment for all time and are often not ecologically reversible. This is partly because traditional planning methods and practices did not engage seriously with sustainability.[1] Planning was initially instituted to protect public health and hygiene by, in effect, replacing nature with engineering infrastructure. Over time, planning methods evolved that channel us into predicting problems and choosing pathways or prototypes – none of which have been sustainable. 'Predicting' usually means projecting current trends. 'Choosing' usually means eliminating alternatives among presently available options. The concept of intergenerational equity has no meaning if development decisions lock future generations into unsustainable living patterns. The alternative, we have said, is 'designing' to expand future options. Given the ongoing reduction of natural carrying capacity, urban development must be re-designed to support, catalyse and re-generate the region. We can do this through reversible, adaptable, diverse Positive Development, which provides for 'ecological infrastructure' at the building, community and regional scales. However, this also requires new planning methods, which are the subject of this chapter.

The same patterns have emerged again and again in our Cook's Tour of environmental management methods. Environmental management is designed to predict the negative impacts of future developments (assessment and rating tools), compare risks of future policies (risk assessment, scenario planning), prepare for contingencies (roadmapping), and/or offset future harmful activities (trading mechanisms), and so on. These and other methods purport to deal with 'wicked problems' in a complex environment. However, they do so in a manner that contradicts the very nature of complexity. Because design has been subsumed by the dominant planning paradigm, we miss opportunities to create net positive (win–win–win) outcomes that counteract the impacts of past resource transfers. We only try to do better from this point on, or shift various forms of taxes onto harmful products and developments. Positive Development would reverse the linear resource flows between humans and nature, rich and poor, urban and rural, etc – not trade things off.

To achieve this, planning must be converted to a form of 'eco-governance'. This would mean the design of intellectual, institutional and technical systems that respect a diversity of responsible cultures, lifestyles and values, yet protect the underlying ecological and democratic platforms that make these possible. Bioregionalism is a possible contender. It aims to design place-based, participatory systems of governance that synchronize with the natural ecology of the region. But can bioregionalism:

- Address the gradual loss of public decision-making oversight and influence resulting from ongoing resource transfers (eg globalization and privatization)?
- Offer a pro-active framework that can tackle problems in the existing built environment?
- Help us move from 'choosing' among current options to 'designing' environments that increase future options?

## What were the origins of environmental planning and management?

Environmental planning had somewhat bipolar roots in science (nature conservation) and business administration (urban development). There are few urban ecologists, or professionals trained to address the complex interface between humans and nature, let alone between cities and regions. While environmental planners applied their concepts and methods to nature (not cities), urban planners applied their concepts and methods to cities (not nature). Environmental planners dealt with how downstream ecosystems respond to changing human pressures, not how cities caused them. City planners dealt with social – not ecological – carrying capacity. As a new profession, environmental management was concerned with being rigorous, objective, scientific and strategic (ie professional). So when addressing new ecological issues, environmental managers applied the available 'scientific' tools and frameworks for predicting risks. The scientific process is predictive, as hypotheses need to be created and tested or disproven.[2] Therefore, much effort in environmental management went into predicting and modelling nature, to estimate ecological thresholds and extinction rates. Improving our predictions of the risks of imminent disaster did not slow the rate of decline, however. The protection, restoration and expansion of the remaining life-support system was left to conservation authorities. In the urban planning context, many tools for prediction could really just 'project' past trends. Planners anticipated whether we needed more apartments or fewer schools or private dwellings by tracking population growth and demographic patterns (ie human behaviour). They tended to choose strategies for accommodating growth with the least damage to current systems and interests. This owes partly to the fact that some influential models of urban decision-making were borrowed from those of business administration and operations research, which drew, in turn, upon military strategy. Business and military strategy is about anticipating risks and making choices among competing interests. So, to cut a long story short, urban decision theories that underlie our planning and policymaking tools evolved to distinguish and compare options or pathways, so we can choose between them.

## On what basis does urban planning choose among competing interests?

In the 1960s, planning adopted a 'pluralist' political theory. This essentially adapted the market metaphor to planning.[3] This was intended to be an antidote to the centralized, top–down, 'socialistic' urban redevelopment of the post-war period.[4] Pluralism could be seen as 'bottom–up'. However, interest group competition can lead to top–down power relationships over time. Winners emerge from among competing proposals, interests, policies and options. Competition, like choosing, is not a framework for designing a wider range of possibilities. Pluralist struggle is about winning out over other people or groups, not including the widest range of people and views. Of course, pluralist planning has descriptive value, as the dualistic, 'either/or' thinking that characterizes interest group politics has been an integral part of day-to-day planning practice. Development control often involves negotiating and bargaining with developers and/or mediating between developers and community groups. Thus a mantra among many planners has been 'planning is politics – it is all about making tradeoffs'. Planners can, of course, require that developments include public uses or amenities. But in so doing, they are often in the position of supplicants, trying to extract concessions from developers and politicians. In this situation, planners are unlikely to challenge existing patterns of infrastructure, resource allocation and wealth transfers. Competition and tradeoffs can, of course, help to resolve short-term conflicts over land use and development. In general, though, compromise and offsets resolve planning conflicts at the expense of the public estate and ecological base.

## Surely planners understand the interdependency of nature and society?

Indeed, and many planners have long understood that they must deal with multiple goals and wicked problems that emerge from our past lack of appreciation of interdependency.[5] It has not been appreciated, however, that the basis of business decision-making – choosing – was *incompatible* with 'planning for sustainability' or expanding substantive choices. There is now a resurgence of the idea that there is a public good – not just competing individual or pluralist 'interests' to choose among.[6] The green movement was partly founded on the understanding that the public estate and ecological base is one interdependent whole. It is not just a compilation of resources to be allocated among petitioners by those wielding King Solomon's sword. By using decision tools that entrench a process of *choosing*, however subtle, planning theorists contributed to a development context that incrementally reduced future social choices. This reductionist conceptual framework (with its simplified ideas of decision-making and the decision-maker and its set of tacit values) arguably impedes ecological modernization. Participation and collaboration in planning provided a channel for taking into account and accommodating differing interests. However, so-called 'bottom–up', participatory planning processes do not, in themselves, protect social diversity and biodiversity. Irreversible decisions, even though made incrementally and with community engagement, do not avoid ecological risks. Nor do they erase past mistakes.

## Don't incrementalist choices reduce the risks of irreversible mistakes?

Not really. Owing partly to planning theory's derivation in business and operations research, the concern has been with risk or change management. This focus on control is a different mindset than that required to proactively design safe, resilient environments. In practice, even a 'precautionary' strategy, in a context of accelerating change, usually results in choosing actions that mitigate impacts upon the status quo.[7] Planning requires an understanding of future risks, of course. But the precautionary principle puts risks in a negative, balancing framework. The principle often reads 'we should not use a lack of scientific evidence as an excuse for inaction in addressing an environmental problem'. Several negatives do not make a positive. It is not affirmative to say that a particular excuse for inaction should no longer suffice, which has been the position of some countries with regard to climate change, for example. While it purports to shift the burden of proof, the precautionary principle does *not* say we should act to improve conditions even when there is no threat. Generally, in the built environment context, the precautionary principle is only applied, if at all, incrementally in response to a proposal for a development or innovation. Planning could have evolved to be positive, rather than precautionary. It could have aimed to implement diverse risk-free pathways and environments with tried and tested eco-solutions [Box 15]. But instead, it accepted conventional forms of growth and tried to manage the social consequences.

## Why did planning for 'growth' not have net positive outcomes?

Pluralist planning challenged the bulldozer approach of post-WWII comprehensive planning which had tried to wipe the slate clean to impose a vision of modernity. The belief in industrial growth as being synonymous with progress is widely known as the 'dominant paradigm'. The underlying conceptual framework contains assumptions about what are deemed to be:

- 'Essential' or inborn human characteristics (eg rational)
- 'Natural' social relationships (eg competitive)[8]

Because this patriarchal conception of the human was couched in the dominant, self-referential framework, one end of the spectrum of human characteristics was taken to be a universal model of man. Despite being applied to *public* planning issues with multiple goals, the implicit viewpoint in this dominant paradigm was that of a self-interested individual or firm. Much theoretical concern was invested in determining what the 'rational man' would do when confronted with complex opportunities and obstacles in a social Darwinist environment [Chapter 4]. This decision model contained an implicit and sometimes explicit goal of progress as 'independence from nature'. Man was meant to achieve a man-made or virtual reality: to rise above the 'primordial slime' (or even escape the planet). The goal of business growth (profit) was largely invisible (part of the wallpaper) in planning, because profits were almost synonymous with progress. Since growth was above and beyond debate, the only issues left for debate were operational ones. That is, decision-making methods were directed at how best to get to a pre-existing goal (growth). Given the presumption of rationality, the public decision-makers' own countervailing goals of optimizing their personal careers, situation and power in a given political context was likewise made *invisible*. It did not fit the rational man model, so it was not included in the analyses.[9] Likewise, the subjective needs of ordinary citizens that did not fit the mould (women, minority races, children and the elderly) were backgrounded in this postwar vision of modernity. It was this rationalist construct that pluralist and incremental planning meant to address.

## How did planning learn to deal with multiple needs and risk of change then?

The theoretical break with 'rationalist' planning came with systems metaphors and incremental adaptive management. Incrementalism was introduced in the planning literature by Davidoff in 1962.[10] Incrementalist approaches to decision-making basically meant taking small steps to avoid big risks. By the 1970s, planning theorists realized they were dealing with open systems, and increasingly saw planning as one way of making incremental decisions in a context of uncertainty.[11] Systems concepts like cybernetics, where decisions are based on feedback systems, came into vogue.[12] Terms such as 'feedback', 'iterative' and 'cybernetic' imbued planning with a whole systems approach. Nonetheless, this new planning theory left out the ecology – the foundational system. In some cases, planning theory treated ecology as an abstraction that could be represented by energy alone. In other cases, planning literature regarded ecology as merely environmental amenity for people. Adaptive management suited the new (partial) systems image. Adaptive management refers to making *experimental* management steps, checking their feedback signals and impacts, and then revising strategies accordingly.[13] However progressive in theory, incremental adaptive approaches were transplanted into the dominant 'change management' framework. Incremental, adaptive, participatory planning continued to dislocate established and viable human communities and ecosystems. Thus it had on-ground results not dissimilar to the large-scale redevelopment programmes of the post-WWII period that it theoretically deposed.

## Does participatory planning balance development and community interests?

Participatory design processes have often been useful in resolving conflicts. There is little evidence, however, that they have succeeded in creating more sustainable systems designs. This is partly because participation has been largely interest group struggle, when the reality is a disparity of power. The history of community participation in some observers' view has often been one of manipulation – a contest between the gullible and the duplicitous – even if some win and lose 'less' than they otherwise might have.[14] In a paradigm of interest group competition or pluralist struggle, community participation will not shift planning from 'interest balancing' to 'value-adding'.[15] Planning has been about the reduction of interests or values into separate components to distinguish, compare and select winners and/or compromises. The more recent trends towards charrettes and partnerships between business, industry and community, discussed earlier, may have more potential to make the transition to a design paradigm. Design, again, is imagining and creating something that has never existed before. But as long as we view decision-making as choosing, bargaining and compromising, we marginalize the idea of 'design'. Design thinking is about the coalescence of interests and ideas, not compromise or 'balancing' powerful financial interests against disparate and dispersed individual interests.[16] Collaborative frameworks help to create an *environment* that fosters design, instead of comparing and eliminating competing options.

## Does this mean a framework designed for choosing actually impedes design?

Yes. A planning framework based exclusively on choosing impedes creativity. In conventional frameworks, debate is over a given range of alternative actions, design formulas or even ideological positions that are put on the table by sectoral and special interests. Rather than foster collaborative design from the ground up, conventional participatory planning frameworks foment debate over competing positions or land uses or alternative proposals. Bringing more players to a poker table, when the elements of a sustainable future are not yet 'on the cards', will not change the nature of the game.[17] Thus many planning decisions still result from choices that unfold over time due to market trends that are driven by *opportunism*, not open, creative design processes. Writ large, our planning system means land-use decisions eventually 'prune' or cut off other branches at the end of a 'decision tree', which leads us further 'out on a limb' [Box 45]. Just as we cannot get the best developments through case-by-case approval processes, we cannot get to the best land use by a process of debating only those development options presented by competing interest groups. The alternative is collaboration among 'disinterested' groups, such as not-for-profit environmental or public interest organizations, that start from a common ground of sustainability. Where interests are not yet vested, people can be more open, creative and accommodating in respecting and supporting diversity [Chapter 15].

## How could land-use planning processes aim to create more diversity?

To torture the above tree metaphor a bit further, we can create more diversity by *splicing* on more branches [Box 45]. We have said that replacing trees with buildings designed 'like trees' does not create habitat, biodiversity or eco-services. However, we can increase the range and diversity of (metaphorical) 'trees' in the long term by creating the infrastructure and systems conditions that improve whole systems health. Urban planning and design, again, should create the conditions for natural systems to function. By analogy, fostering the conditions for bacteria that have symbiotic relations with root systems is the way to achieve true bottom–up planning. In contrast to this rhizomatic approach, incremental processes are like selective breeding or pruning, which can create urban morphologies that are too specialized and non-adaptive. Instead of mitigating the impacts of development after the design stage, planning can enhance the opportunities for ecosystems within the structure of urban development. By 'splicing' on new branches or infrastructure for eco-services, planning could enrich the eco-productivity and diversity of life. This requires planning for the functional integration of nature and natural systems, along with reversible, adaptable and compostable design. We need to design *for* nature, not just *with* nature. Environmental management and planning must be re-designed to foster the 'growth' of carrying capacity. For example, dumping abandoned car frames in oceans may not be the best use of past waste, but it can create the infrastructure for coral reefs and their ecosystems to develop, and provide habitats for species threatened by coral bleaching and sea-level rises in other areas.[18] (Similarly, shading corals may be expensive, but perhaps we cannot afford *not* to protect the economic and other values of reefs.)

### Don't we still need to resolve competing interests in land through planning?

True. Most conflicts over land could be said to result from poor planning due to our lack of understanding of ecology. Once there are conflicts or competing proposals, however, planning requires processes that can resolve them.[19] Where there are developers and community groups with radically opposed positions, there is usually an alternative design solution that can satisfy both parties. Environmental mediation works by bringing opposing parties around a table and focusing on a site plan or area map – not on their initial positions.[20] By engaging in creative and fun activity, erstwhile opponents stop worrying about winning or losing, and begin coming up with ideas that add value. This can be virtually the opposite of 'work'. Ideas tend to *flow* from the free exploration of ideas and collaborative, interactive processes [Figure 11].[21] Design comes from free 'play' – rather than work, struggle and competition.[22] By value-adding or splicing, rather than trading off or pruning, design can replace win–lose struggles by virtuous circles of cooperative conflict-prevention processes. So good design can find ways to meet the legitimate needs and interests of all parties. A partial prototype for positive planning blossomed for a short time in the 1960s in the US. The 'advocacy planning' process was not entirely dissimilar to what is now called 'action research', except it was more activistic and change-oriented.[23] Advocacy planning began from the public interest and fostered design through cross-sectional collaboration and participation.[24] Designers and planners worked *with* the disadvantaged, rather than workshopping or managing them. As a part of the 'war on poverty', however, most advocacy planning organizations were, ironically, starved out of existence within a decade.[25]

### So how is advocacy planning different from incremental adaptive planning?

Both incremental action and adaptive management imply experimentation and iterative reassessment based on feedback. There is no doubt that these are important strategies in a mix of planning methods. In practice, however, incrementalism meant choosing among the claims of competing interests case-by-case. It did not mean looking *behind* these claims to find alternative designs that meet whole systems needs. We are increasingly applying the rhetoric of adaptive management to new projects, instead of implementing known and safe solutions creatively to fix existing development problems. Adaptive management is an experimental approach that is appropriate for *unknowns*. It is for scientists to explore unknowns; it is for environmental planners and managers to implement known, positive solutions. Terms like 'iterative, incremental and adaptive' have an ecological ring to them, but they do not mean 'reversible'. Despite its theoretical claims, incremental adaptive management is also used as an excuse for procrastination in implementing eco-solutions and developing reversible structures. It could be seen as a case of 'theory justifying inaction'. The built environment requires re-envisioning and re-designing reversible, net positive environments, not defensive adaptation and mitigation of existing templates. For example, the current response to greenhouse gas emissions is somewhat negative and defensive: to 'adapt' to symptoms rather than address causes (on the grounds that 'it is too late'). Just as a belief in markets allows us to avoid 'seeing' equity issues, a belief in incrementalism allows us to avoid 'doing', or investing in affirmative action.

### Can planning and decision theories really become excuses for inaction?

In theory, the individual decision-maker, trying to 'muddle' his way through a pinball machine of obstacles and opportunities, makes choices on the run by what was called a 'satisficing' process.[26] This means doing what is good enough or expedient. However, in reality, risk minimization and opportunism have often been critical decision factors in the bureaucratic context. Inaction appears to be the safest personal survival strategy in a defensive organizational culture. Creating diversions or displacement activity (eg calling for another study) can do a lot to make an individual or department appear productive. Failing that, a scattergun approach can be used – aiming for *any* 'runs on the board' where opportunities arise, to appear productive or obtain measurable performance outcomes. Setting incremental targets – instead of incremental actions – also works to advantage where one does not want to take affirmative steps. Such bureaucratic survival strategies are not necessarily undertaken on a conscious level. Nonetheless, they do presuppose that we can continue on the same basic trajectory. Incremental adaptive change management approaches are most appropriate when we want to reduce the threats of current trends upon the status quo or our jobs. Like other environmental management methods, they start from where we are now. But this works only if we are already headed in the right direction. An incremental decision process only makes small errors at a time, case-by-case. Nonetheless, it shapes the future as irreversibly as master planning. By inaction, it pre-determines, but does not design, the future.

### What's wrong with incremental adaptive planning pre-determining the future?

Creating the infrastructure for nature and society to heal themselves requires affirmative action in design and implementation. The rise of incrementalist planning theory was partly because of the need for planning to appear more relevant to the market. In the dominant ideology, government is not supposed to 'intervene in the market'. Only the market is allowed to intervene in governance.[27] But while the market could be a driver of resource efficiency – given the right regulatory framework and signals – it cannot *create* sustainability. Likewise, an incremental planning system that is paramorphic with the market cannot protect and increase the public estate and ecological base. Incrementalism therefore encourages people to accept the given environment and structures of power as the base line. In other words, current power relationships are accepted as the natural order. In this 'pragmatic' framework, past cumulative resource transfers that have created vested interests are not on the table. Thus, currently, planning minimizes the inequitable outcomes of an inherited power structure that society did not consciously design, or even agree to. We will not try to design a better system of eco-governance, however, if we are given to believe there are only two models to choose from: the market or bureaucracy [Chapter 13]. In both these systems, the more fundamental ethical issues underpinning sustainability are out of bounds. Thus, for example, what is now called 'planning for sustainability' is often just the greening of development control criteria. However, planning could be designed to help society envision 'what could be'.

## So are there models for planning systems that could address ethical issues?

This will require a decision arena where the ethical issues surrounding resource transfers can be made transparent, debated and resolved, as discussed in the next chapter. However, at a more modest scale, bioregional planning perhaps provides a model to build upon.[28] It aims to establish structures of governance and planning processes that can create better futures through collective community processes.[29] It is an emerging field that is based on the view that land-use planning and natural resource management should be re-structured at a bioregional scale, and along natural – rather than political – boundaries. The premise of bioregional planning is that human cultures co-evolved with nature and that they are, and will always be, interdependent. Economic, social and environmental institutions therefore need to be designed to align with, and correspond to, the bioregion. According to bioregionalism, human settlements, agriculture, manufacturing, urban infrastructures, construction and other systems of development should be transformed to function within the limits of the carrying capacity of each particular bioregion. To achieve this, systems of production and consumption would be largely 'closed loop' systems, where waste is avoided or used as a resource in another process [Box 39]. In other words, according to bioregionalists, it is not enough that human systems become more eco-efficient. They should also conform to the unique biophysical *and* cultural characteristics of the region.

## Where did bioregional planning come from and has it had any impact?

Bioregional planning emerged from 'bioregionalism', a social movement which developed in the 1970s, although it had much earlier philosophical roots.[30] Bioregionalism implies maintenance of regional and cultural diversity. Each region offers different resources and, consequently, unique opportunities for specialized, ecologically-suitable crops, industries, products and services. If bioregionalism were implemented, therefore, the culture, economy, architecture and products of different regions would gradually regain their distinctive regional qualities. They would reflect both the region's natural environment and indigenous culture. Bioregionalism also implies a degree of local autonomy. Regions would be relatively self-contained and self-sufficient from an ecological perspective. Opinions vary among bioregionalists on the extent to which trade among regions is desirable. However, it is fair to say that bioregionalism is *not* compatible with corporate globalization. Also, if politics and planning emerge from the region, there would be no one universal planning template. So bioregional planning requires new processes, structures and methods that can identify and celebrate the special constraints, diversity and unique opportunities offered by different bioregions.

## What does this diversity mean for planning processes in actual practice?

Decision-making structures and processes, as well as lifestyles, would vary according to the local ecological and cultural context. Some general principles would apply universally, however. For example, planning processes would prioritize lay citizen input. Bioregionalists hold that since local traditions evolved in relation to unique natural conditions, local people, especially those who work the land, often maintain a deeper understanding of their regions than central authorities or professional planners [Box 45]. While local residents generally have the best knowledge of local environmental and social issues, however, they often lack 'ecological literacy'. Studies indicate that children know many more corporate logos than native plants and animals in their bioregion.[31] So, in reality, many local inhabitants are not really in touch with their ecological home. Bioregional planning is therefore concerned with creating processes that encourage people to learn to reconnect with, and 'reinhabit', the bioregion. By 'living in place' and coming to understand the local ecology, people would presumably make better decisions regarding land use and development. Both participatory planning and environmental education, therefore, are integral parts of bioregionalism. Consequently, bioregional planning has sometimes been less about the transition to sustainable systems, and more a vehicle for environmental education through participation.[32]

## Isn't participation already an essential element of most planning systems?

Participation is an issue that seems to reinvent itself every few years. As suggested earlier, that 'bottom–up' planning systems can have very different consequences, depending on whether they are in a competitive or a collaborative context. This was a major planning concern in America in the 1960s, when urban advocacy planning emerged. Planners, architects and other professionals worked with community groups to develop community plans and sometimes 'counter-plans' in opposition to major re-development proposals. Like advocacy planning, bioregionalism attempts to take participation in planning to a new level of community empowerment, well beyond consultation, surveys or other user preference studies. People are expected to participate in hands-on planning exercises, such as conducting inventories of local species and habitats. Citizen mapping exercises, where people draw maps of how they 'experience' their local areas, are one of the ways of eliciting what is meaningful to local citizens about their existing environments. Charrettes are also increasingly popular in obtaining wide input from the community and setting goals for a community or region.[33] While bioregional processes make people more aware of their ecological home, they also aim to enable communities to *envision* better futures. Bioregionalism goes beyond the advocacy model, which merely tried to reduce the impacts of capitalism. Bioregionalism also aims for the creation of appropriate systems of eco-governance. It recognizes that genuinely democratic processes require substantive due process, not just participation in procedures [Chapter 13].

## What has been the actual on-ground outcome of bioregional planning?

The influence of bioregional planning has been reflected in the establishment of catchment management authorities in Australia, Canada and the US. The term 'bioregion' has now become part of the standard vocabulary of planners and environmental managers. For instance, a planning conference on national planning was convened by a professional planning institute in Australia in 1995.[34] But in the government adaptation of bioregionalism, there has also been a growing emphasis on volunteerism. In Australia, for example, there have been organizations like LandCare, WaterWatch, BushCare and WasteWise. These enlist communities to work together (virtually for free or for small grants) to reduce the environmental impacts of business-as-usual agriculture and industry. This has been viewed by some participants as a form of 'volunteerany'.[35] In some cases, it is what we could call 'bottom–down' planning – exacting more work from the already overworked. While many farmers are ecologically sensitive, they lack the time and resources to deal with the cumulative consequences of the limited choices they have in the marketplace. Transitioning to somewhat more sustainable systems, such as agroforestry, requires investment funds they may not have. At the same time, they have to compete with large investment management funds. When businesses contribute to environmental protection and/or eco-efficiency, such activities are usually tax deductible. Of course, it is sensible to compensate business for reducing impacts. However, we should not ask the community and farmers to clean up the impacts of past development systems for little or no compensation.

## What processes are advocated by bioregionalists to fix this imbalance?

In bioregionalism, participation would begin with deciding how decisions should be made. After all, decision frameworks, to a large extent, influence the decisions themselves. Exactly how decision-making processes should be institutionalized would vary according to the regional context and culture. However, there are some shared and well-established processes in bioregional planning processes that would apply in most cases. These include:

- Engaging local people in identifying and affirming the unique ecological and socio-cultural qualities that it is important to preserve
- Determining what significant characteristics should form the basis for setting the boundaries of the regional decision-making unit
- Making inventories of the habitats and biodiversity elements that are especially important to the native ecology, as well as those that are threatened
- Developing decision-making structures, as well as systems of production and settlement patterns, that are responsive to the region's unique cultural and biophysical characteristics

Apart from establishing new regional boundaries of study, engagement and action, the underlying principles and practices of bioregionalism have not been widely implemented in 'mainstream' bioregional planning. Perhaps this is because bioregionalism is conveniently 'bottom–up' (which, as we suggested, can effectively be 'bottom–down'). Bottom–up planning assumes the people currently on top are in the way and will move over. However, they will remain in the way until they are re-educated. The education of managers could be called 'top–up' planning.[36] Paradoxically, the community (the so-called 'bottom' in the participatory planning framework) will have to re-educate the 'top' (government and industry) from *above*.

## Have these bioregional processes been adopted by government planning?

Yes. Auditing and planning at a bioregional *scale* is perhaps the main influence of bioregionalism upon mainstream planning. The idea of engagement, planning and decision-making at the regional level requires information to be collected and analysed on a regional basis. Previously, data was collected according to political jurisdictions, business needs or convenience (eg postcodes), not in relation to bioregions. Further, there was little data on biodiversity. Drawing upon the enormous advances in technologies for mapping regions, such as GIS, geographic mapping was undertaken to begin to fill this gap, mostly in relation to specific issues like biodiversity conservation.[37] Inventories of regional resources and land uses were subsequently conducted (including the continental shelf). Thus far, however, land has not been inventoried for the potential *alternative* resources of, say, a new carbohydrate or solar economy (eg biomass fuels or biobased materials for construction).[38] Rather, inventories of resources have been dominated by the search for standard industrial processes that can be attracted to a region. Even catchment management authorities in Australia have been accused of favouring entrenched development interests, rather than changing the nature of development to make it more ecological. Decision-making at the regional scale will not, by itself, change the dominant paradigm of development. Nor will it change the nature of pluralist politics with its short-term horizons.

## Wouldn't the change to regional planning influence paradigms and politics?

Despite the creation of catchment-level planning authorities, the zero sum nature of traditional politics – picking winners and losers – does not necessarily change. Participation still happens largely through interest group struggle rather than, say, community engagement through collective design processes. The idea of larger-scale bioregional boundaries has been taken on board, however. Since natural regions and social decision-making jurisdictions are meant to be 'aligned' in bioregional planning, it is increasingly considered *de rigour* to define regions by natural boundaries. This may explain a preoccupation with defining regional boundaries. There has been a prolonged and distracting debate in the bioregional literature over how to determine the boundaries of regions.[39] Unfortunately, such a debate can tend to emphasize 'form over function'. It is generally held that the determination of bioregional boundaries should be guided primarily by 'edges' between natural regions with different vegetation, climates or topography. A variety of criteria for determining edges have been suggested, such as:

- The 'biotic shift' (ie the percentage change in species of flora and fauna from one region to another)
- Watersheds (ie catchments or groupings of catchment areas)
- Cultural patterns, as indigenous people have retained knowledge and practices that evolved with their bioregion[40]

Of course, the focus on edges and regional boundaries is in conflict with the understanding that bioregions and ecosystems, as well as cultural systems, overlap.[41]

## How does bioregional planning deal with overlapping ecological boundaries?

Regions have generally been seen as 'nested', such that 'bioregions' (eg a catchment) sit inside a 'biome', which is an ecological community such as grasslands or wetlands. These, in turn, sit inside a 'georegion', which is a geological region such as a range of mountains or discrete section of coast. Categories may include 'ecoregions', such as an island or desert region.[42] This may have stemmed from the idea that there are 'nested hierarchies' in nature. More recently, the concept of a 'mosaic' of overlapping areas of different sizes has taken hold, recognizing that natural boundaries are permeable, fluid and changing over time.[43] Nonetheless, bioregional planning has often emphasized defining static boundaries or mosaic patterns, instead of prioritizing ways in which different land uses can support each other. Too much emphasis can be placed on how to fit nature into a spatial taxonomy or concept of 'hierarchy' in conformity with traditional reductionist models. Our models of nature will always fall short, especially when based on preconceived abstractions or concepts borrowed from other fields. The concern should be less on typologies, metaphors and tools, and more on designing human systems that are zero waste or net positive at some scale – whether buildings, settlements or biomes.

## Once we define our nested, overlapping or amorphous boundaries, what next?

The second step in bioregional planning is usually to make an 'inventory' of both biotic and abiotic resources. To do so, planners draw on the local knowledge of residents and the natural history of the region, including traditional Aboriginal knowledge. Information on flora and fauna, climate, landforms, human ecology, resource potential, existing settlement patterns, demographics and so on is combined to create a 'directory' of the bioregion. Given the inertia of institutionalization, however, bioregional planning has yet to get much beyond information collection in many places. Nonetheless, the analysis of the resource inventory and carrying capacity of the bioregion could provide the material basis for re-designing systems of production and construction in order to increase regional self-reliance and low-impact reversible development systems. Bioregionalism has tended to stop at this stage. It is recommended, therefore, that some form of resource transfer (RT) analysis be added to bioregional planning. This would provide an analysis of the inefficiencies, waste or losses due to past and ongoing resource flows and wealth transfers in the region. Mapping biodiversity, calculating carrying capacity and/or ecological footprints, and disseminating environmental literacy and education will not protect the environment if entrenched patterns of resource transfers are continuing to deplete them.

## Why analyse existing resource flows instead of just seeking improvements?

If we want to make a region more sustainable, we need to reverse linear flows to restore and enhance ecosystems. The existing physical and economic infrastructure reinforces these negative flows. Hands-on activities like inventories and biodiversity surveys by local residents can, of course, foster an awareness of our interdependency with nature. But such inventories only tell us where we are now. As such, they are not sufficient to motivate behaviour change. By tracing transfers of resources and wealth, from rural to urban areas, natural to negative space, poor to rich, and so on, citizens can become informed as to the true ecological/economic 'trade balance' of their region or sector. That is, mapping the redistributive impacts that past government and industry policies are having on the region could make people aware of how their interests are affected over time. In this way, people can appreciate what may have been lost through a 'trickle up' vertical integration process, not just what 'may' happen in the future. This knowledge, currently concealed, could eventually translate into political pressure. It might also show the need for specific economic responses like regional import substitution.

## Hasn't information about growing disparities been around a long time?

Yes. And, clearly, complaints about perverse subsidies have not motivated decision-makers to implement options that might re-balance the ongoing transfer of public resources to special interests. But we have seen how, in environmental management and planning, means of exposing resource transfers appear to have been studiously avoided. Certainly, the aim of politics is not whole systems rationality. Therefore one response from environmentalists has been to advocate eco-innovations that might bypass the monopoly enjoyed by industrial magnates and their 'gatekeepers' or politicians. Specific innovations in certain technological areas, like low-cost solar cells, fuel cells or thermal chips, may indeed achieve this. But to contribute to the health of the region, we need processes that stimulate constructive institutional change as well as product substitution. After all, ecologically insensitive human interference in complex ecological processes at the regional scale took millions of years to evolve. Built environment planning and design are eliminating these living systems overnight. The removal of universal access to soil, water and food interferes in their ability to meet local human needs self-sufficiently. To reverse this would entail environments (not just widgets) that create net positive synergies between the built environment and nature, urban and regional systems, and so on. One place to start, again, would be ecological transformation (ET) analysis. In regional areas, ET analyses are already informing ecological restoration projects, often beginning with the re-creation of the hydrological system.[44] However, there is little evidence of ET analysis informing urban planning and design.

## But how can comparing original and current conditions lead to systems design?

To look for planning solutions that can counteract problems of existing development, we can map how past physical interventions in natural and social systems have led to current biophysical and social disorder. Diagnostic and creative stages need not necessarily occur in a set order, of course. By analysing a human-designed system relative to its 'natural context', however, some previously unrecognized opportunities for biomimicry may come into relief. For example, we saw how man-made interventions in river systems for irrigation and flood control in Australia have led to major disruptions of 'environmental flows'. This has, in turn, contributed to floods, droughts, salinity, erosion, the loss of habitats and ecosystems, and so on. Substantial work has been invested in proposals to improve irrigation- and water-management efficiency. Some of the proposals in Australia have included:

- Piping water from one drought-ridden area to another where the drought is 'worse'
- Diverting a river from a wet region to a dry one that would mix different river ecosystems
- Moving farmers to tropical regions, where there is lots of water
- Creating storage dams upstream with a network of pipes, so that water could be released in times of drought

The aim in some instances has been to open up new areas for agriculture – not for ecological rationality or restoration. None of these 'solutions' really treat water as a critical part of the system, let alone the ecological base. There appears to be little interest in how such human interventions created the problems in the first place.

## Wouldn't efficient use of water automatically support the ecology?

Yes and no. By way of example, the Pratt Report on water efficiency in Australia (2004) identified 1,334,000 megalitres per year of unaccounted or lost water flows. It showed that a $824 million investment in infrastructure to save water would translate into $293 million per year of additional farm-gate production income, and $421 million of new capital investment opportunities in production enterprises, which could lead to a $245 million boost to regional income and 4500 new jobs.[45] It was claimed that piping water to upstream storage areas for later agricultural uses would create efficiencies and leave enough water for the environment. However, a precedent was the Snowy Mountains electricity scheme in Australia, which replaced a river with pipes and killed a whole river ecosystem. Communities downstream lost more water than they could afford to. Proposals to circulate water through pipes rather than through landscape forms are attractive to economical rationalists. Where water is piped, it can be 'privatized'. Pipes also enable (private or public) enterprises to control the future supply of water. The privatization of the basic means of survival is seldom a 'reversible' decision because, again, the concentration of economic power through control of basic needs (food and water) leads to political power.[46] The risks of privatized water pipes in a 'free' market also include a loss of resource security, equity, eco-efficiency and even national security. In many parts of the world, the poor cannot afford water where water systems have been privatized.[47] Therefore piping water – the industrial solution – could have irreversible impacts on our democratic systems and security as well. Ownership is one means of stimulating investment, but it often occurs at the cost of giving away public assets at below cost. We should not pay plumbers by giving them the tap and sink. Mechanistic approaches that start from where we are now, without reference to the initial ecological state and equity considerations, seldom lead to synergistic, 'reversible' solutions.

## Isn't it simply too late to restore natural systems?

We could think in terms of gradually, but systematically, replacing engineering structures with natural systems that were previously replaced by engineering structures. In some places, like California, serious consideration is being given to 'unplugging' certain dams and letting rivers return to original flows. This is not just romanticism. Increasingly, people are realizing that a return to natural conditions would be more economical and efficient from a whole systems perspective. Other alternatives to privatizing and/or piping water include design concepts like the 'chain-of-ponds', a water restoration approach for drought-ridden Australia. This concept, developed by Australian farmer Peter Andrews, was based on the study of ecological systems that preceded the advent of Western agriculture [Box 46].[48] By creating a series of ponds off the main river, flooding, loss of topsoil and other problems caused by interventions in the natural flow of rivers have been reversed. The approach creates synergistic effects in the environment that pipelines do not, such as purifying water, increasing biodiversity and habitat, and reducing floods. The system works as a Living Machine, but on a landscape scale. It may only be suitable for certain landscapes, however. An earlier advocate of using natural systems was Ian McCarg, who looked at solutions for a wide range of conditions. Back in the 1960s, he developed landscape design concepts based on the biophysical characteristics of regions. He looked to the original landscape and ecosystem functions for inspiration in his seminal *Design with Nature*.[49]

## How would this apply to urban bioregional planning in built-up areas?

The advantage of the urban context is that, unlike natural areas, cities could increase overall carrying capacity over pre-development conditions. This would require *neither* the kind of large-scale, socially-disruptive re-development associated with post-war planning *nor* the abdication of planning to incremental approvals of (least bad) market-driven development. After all, the ownership of buildings is constantly being transferred, and buildings constantly upgraded and re-sold. So eco-retrofitting can occur as opportunities arise. Buildings, their façades and roofs, and the spaces between them can be 'churned' through an eco-retrofitting programme as they become ready for refurbishment, in a virtuous circle. But again, sustainable design solutions will not become mainstream until the political ramifications of current accounting methods are made transparent. Putting alternatives on an equal footing would not be difficult, but it is seldom done. The capital budgets of maintaining large buildings or universities are enormous and expensive refurbishments are periodically undertaken. Such 'deferred maintenance' of unsustainable development is not worth the long-term cost, but we discount the future. Due partly to current accounting methods, however, decision-makers seldom consider investments that would reduce maintenance costs by using natural systems. In a sustainability analysis, we should at least put the status quo system and the proposed alternatives on the same page. Instead of the 'sunk cost' in vast industrial infrastructure, we would compare the relative costs of the status quo and eco-logical design alternatives *as if* neither were yet in place, and consider what each would cost to maintain in the long run.

## What sort of analyses would inform these kinds of choices?

We need to look directly at resource flows (erosion, energy, soil nutrients, farmers leaving the land, etc) and the institutional and physical systems designs that result in wealth transfers. Otherwise, we will not design policies and eco-solutions that reverse these flows, let alone create net ecological gain. Bioregional planning analyses therefore need to examine environmental flows and resource transfers on a deeper level. Using water as an example, research to support a bioregional approach might include a mapping of several kinds of system 'design failure'. For example:

- **Physical design failure**: Map changes that have occurred in the hydrological system due to technology (pipes and dams) or planning (land-use change), using ecological transformation (ET) analysis.
- **Market failure**: Map negative linear and inequitable wealth transfers of past interventions between and within bioregions, using resource transfer (RT) analysis.
- **Legislative failure**: Map water rights transfers that have caused waste or reductions in environmental flows that have resulted from resource allocation and consumption systems (eg water rights legislation) using institutional design (ID) analysis.
- **Management failure**: Examine 'unjust enrichment', or benefits accrued from transfers of natural to financial capital that are disproportionate to their contribution to the community, using cost of inaction (CI) analysis.

Currently, we do not compare the eco-effectiveness of industrialized system of dams and pipes to hi-tech (eg efficient irrigation) or low-tech (eg 'natural sequence farming') alternatives in terms of losses of health, choice, security, ecology and opportunity (ie past cumulative impacts).

## Why doesn't planning put alternatives on a level playing field already?

We do not have a planning *arena* where we can debate the best investment options for improving whole systems health [Chapter 13]. Investment usually comes from private commercial interests – or pressure from them for public investment. Public funds are later used to clean up the environmental messes that some enterprises have left behind.[50] We have seen that positive design solutions do not require a quantification of synergies and symbioses if an investment will pay for itself. But currently there is no forum for deciding the best investments to improve systems conditions – whether sourced from the private or public sector or partnerships. Planning seems to be stuck in negative debates over the amount of negative externalities that should be allowed from activities like coal-fired electricity generation, new green field suburbs and road building in wilderness areas. (Nor do we have 'glocal' debates about investing in peacemaking instead of military 'solutions', an omission that may nullify the utility of all planning). In short, bioregional planning inventories do not identify ongoing flows embedded in the status quo, the costs of inaction, or means to invent, prioritize, design and implement proposals for direct positive action. Hence a central function of planning should be to identify priority areas for eco-innovation and eco-retrofitting [Chapter 14]. We sometimes evaluate programmes according to triple-bottom-line frameworks, but priorities are determined by interest group politics.

## Surely we have means to measure the appropriateness of public priorities?

Yes, but not in terms of ecological improvement. Our ways of evaluating investment are highly reductionist measures of outputs against inputs. For example, the Landcare programme in Australia was designed, in theory, to empower farming communities to make improvements to the land. This sounds like positive and direct action, or at least remediation. The performance indicators of the investment in the program, however, were things like 'metres of fences installed' (ie bandaids), not positive outcomes for people and nature. Many Australian farmers have since been forced to leave their ancestors' lands. The programme did not address the basic causes of farmers going bankrupt, or means of increasing soil fertility. However, there is now a public inquiry in Australia to analyse why large grocery chains have been increasing the price of farm goods with relatively little benefit to farmers. But this is studied in a monetary framework only. The whole community suffers when, despite higher profit margins on food in the grocery store, no one pays the full costs of mining soil nutrients. In other words, we have hidden the resource and wealth transfers by reductionist methods of measurement. Instead of measuring fences, for instance, we could measure the:

- Relative number of farmers who are still 'unwillingly' abandoning their farms (whereas most economists focus on 'willingness' to pay)
- Relative soil health and productivity resulting from Landcare projects
- Relative biodiversity after Landcare compared to recent and pre-farming conditions
- Relative results of surveys of farmers using genuine progress indicators
- Relative capacity of a farm to continue to be productive, or whether particular land might be more productive if returned to natural habitat

Such measurements may occasionally be undertaken ad hoc by researchers but are seldom, if ever, part of a holistic planning framework that encourages public engagement and debate on ethical and ecological issues. The next chapter explores structural principles that could assist in creating decision-making systems that are compatible with the fundamental ethical and democratic nature of sustainability issues.

# SECTION E:
# A FRAMEWORK FOR ECO-GOVERNANCE AND MANAGEMENT

# 13
# Constitution for Eco-governance

## From interest balancing to ethical frameworks

It has been argued that our decision systems and support tools do not suit the nature of sustainability issues. Common patterns were seen in development standards and criteria, rating tools, design methods, development assessment, auditing and reporting methods, futures tools, trading systems, and bioregional planning. Some recurring themes among these decision systems and tools are that they prioritize:

- Choosing over design
- Efficiency over ecology
- Technical over ethical issues
- Mitigation over direct action
- Assessing future over ongoing impacts
- Incremental targets over affirmative actions
- Offsets over value-adding

We have seen that sustainability is not just one among many optional values in a zero sum competition of ideas. A sustainable society will not happen unless it is achieved in a manner that makes everyone better off. This requires not only environmental quality, but opportunity for a diversity of responsible lifestyle choices and perpetual, secure access to the means of survival. In a context of diminishing political and social choice, substantive democracy will require greater respect for diversity and basic human rights, as well as acceptance of new responsibilities. This, in turn, requires a new form of development that improves the health and wellbeing of, and relationships between, human and natural systems, and eliminates the inequitable impacts and resource transfers that are embedded in *existing* development. At the same time, any attempt to impose a particular belief system or set of values would be authoritarian and inconsistent with diversity. Thus, a *constitution* of sustainability principles is proposed that couches ecological issues in terms of long-standing and widely-shared precepts of human rights and responsibilities, rather than in a particular ethic.

## What would a new 'constitution' for environmental decision-making involve?

A constitutional approach means that the decision structures and processes would be designed to fit the nature of sustainability issues. These are essentially ethical in nature.[1] It has been argued in previous chapters that a major ethical issue in sustainability is the cumulative and irreversible transfer of power, wealth, resources and space through conventional development. Our resource allocation and management systems are not designed to address this. A sustainable environmental planning system would aim to prevent inequitable resource transfers in the first place, and make existing environmental conditions more equitable. The US Constitution can provide a (somewhat dated) model, if only to show that eco-governance is compatible with traditional conservative values. It has many structural devices built in to avoid the accumulation of power. However, it was designed at a time when land and resources were still seen as infinite.[2] An anthropocentric framework, as used here, may have more potential to gain wider acceptance. Such a framework can accommodate eco-centric values if humans are understood as dependent upon nature. An anthropocentric framework, focused on democracy, requires a caveat, however. Problems gradually emerge to the extent that physical and institutional designs do not respect the reality that the natural environment is a living ecosystem of which humans are inextricably a part.

## Would a constitutional approach differ from ordinary mission statements?

Most urban sustainability plans start from a statement of values and principles or mission statements. These are often (triple bottom line) statements of volition, sometimes followed by politically achievable goals. In other words a wish list supporting what seems feasible in the given socio-political context at the time. A sustainability constitution, in contrast, means decision rules, methods and processes would be founded on essentially 'non-negotiable' *ethical* principles. Constitutions provide the basis upon which more specific decision-making systems are built. Sustainable policies and decisions would need to be justified in relation to these explicit sustainability premises and principles. The suggestion of writing and/or adopting new constitutions is usually tossed into the 'too hard' basket.[3] However, the founders of the US Constitution managed without the internet or computers to aid in their communications. Also, it can be easier for a community, region or nation to negotiate principles that are fundamental and universal than case-specific decisions that threaten people's immediate or vested interests. Once there is agreement on general principles, it is then easier to gain acceptance of more specific policies and programmes flowing from the agreed Constitution.

## How can environmental decision systems be based on ethical principles?

If agencies and organizations took their sustainability mission statements seriously, the decision systems themselves would be designed to address the kinds of fundamental ethical issues that are prerequisites to sustainability. Our larger-scale decision-making spheres, such as the political, market and legal arenas, each have clear functions and virtues. However, they are not designed to help us align our resource allocation systems with social and ecological sustainability imperatives. The underlying causes of environmental problems, such as fossil fuel dependency, population growth, poverty, habitat destruction, militarism, sexism, colonialism and religious dogma, cannot be resolved within an economic rationalist edifice, competitive individualist politics or even a positivist science framework.[4] Nonetheless, the fundamental issues about life itself and our future have been left to the market and political arenas, which are power-based, competitive and/or conflictual forms of decision-making (ie 'might is right'). We do not have a decision arena that can deal with what is perhaps the most fundamental conflict today – the conflict between humans and nature that our human-designed institutions have helped to create. This basic conflict is now contributing to other escalating resource distribution conflicts among humans. As the life-support system disintegrates, global conflict over resources promises to bring even more human misery (if not nuclear annihilation). A futures-oriented planning 'sphere' is needed to deal with ethical issues and conflict resolution underlying environmental destruction, again, by increasing future options for all.

## How exactly is environmental destruction linked to human oppression?

Most forms of human oppression occur at the expense of the environment. Power is obtained through the acquisition, exploitation and consumption of and competition for social and natural resources.[5] It is increased by reducing others' access to resources. Warfare is the extreme example, but there have been countless deliberate actions by governments and industries that have had outcomes damaging to both human and environmental health. For example, replacing indigenous food sources harvested by women with cash crop plantations farmed by men, or replacing breast milk with expensive formulas, has tended to dispossess communities of their control over the sources of sustenance and self-sufficiency. Further, colonialism, sexism, racism and so on are often fostered to manipulate and maintain control over populations politically. That is, the intellectual and emotional justifications for oppression (expressed through phenomena like racism, sexism and patriotism) are often cultivated for political gain. They are *means* through which power is sought, maintained and abused.[6] Prejudice, for example, has a 'chicken and egg' relationship with the manipulation of public opinion for corporate or political purposes. To get past such pervasive 'smoke screens', still dominating the news media, we need more in-depth community engagement in ethical issues as well as more equitable resource-allocation systems.

## Can institutional design reduce the manipulation of public opinion?

Our systems of governance still reflect the industrial growth paradigm. They encourage the exploitation of land and natural resources.[7] Power is ultimately derived from the control of natural resources. Given blank cheques in exchange for resource exploitation over time, some companies grew to become powerful lobbies that could manipulate public values and opinions.[8] Therefore sound environmental management is of the essence in preventing the abuse of power and manipulation of fear and insecurity. Despite often the best intentions, most systems of governance only mitigate the social conflict created by externalities, by ensuring benefits 'trickle down' to the disadvantaged. Yet the concentration of wealth continues to grow. We have seen that environmental management and planning systems conceal the mechanisms by which the growing disparity in the distribution of wealth and accumulation of power are perpetuated. In this way, planning supports disparities and ultimately, therefore, conflict. Environmental and planning laws have been added on incrementally, as some would say, in response to sporadic public 'noise'. However, ad hoc laws do not constitute a system of eco-governance. To counteract the imbalance of power, the government system itself must be *modernized* to recognize the centrality of environmental ethics in attaining and preserving distributional justice. We need to develop a collective, future-oriented process of imagining, thinking, debating and problem-solving within a set of agreed superordinate sustainability principles. In other words, a new planning sphere.[9]

## Why can't existing constitutional structures prevent the abuse of power?

The American system of governance was based on ethical principles, such as human rights, substantive and procedural due process, and equality – even if just among white men. Checks and balances were built into the system to prevent the accumulation and abuse of power. The problem is that this system of governance was designed and developed when few people realized that natural resources were finite in an industrial society. They were not even aware of ecological issues. In fact, nature has often been seen as a threat, not a necessity. So while the American Constitution was explicitly designed to prevent the abuse of power, it also reflected the assumption that there was no limit to resource consumption. It manifested a frontier ethic.[10] After all, at the time it was designed, the greatest threats to human liberties were from monarchs, not climate change, tribal terrorism or nuclear war. Large bureaucracies and powerful international corporate interests were scarcely on the scene. The system design focus was therefore to prevent the abuse of power by those with hereditary positions. Consequently, the system of governance allocated resources as if they were infinite. Over time, these 'first come, first served' decisions generated unequal access to, and control of, natural resources. This, in turn, led to unequal power relationships and excessive corporate power. Unchecked power inevitably leads to injustice and conflict over time.

## How was the US Constitution designed to prevent the abuse of power?

The US Constitution largely prevented an imbalance of power from developing by dividing powers into government branches. This was to create 'checks and balances'. First, power was divided vertically through state and federal jurisdictions. Second, decision-making power was also divided horizontally into legislative, judicial and executive functions. Third, an upper and a lower legislative body were created to represent people by both geography and numbers, and to create a 'house of review' to check legislation. By creating checks and balances, it was intended that one branch of government could not become too powerful. In this way, the same individual or agency could not be the lawmaker, policeman, judge and executioner – which had been a common complaint about various monarchs. Among the virtues of this model is that it reminds people in any organization that they are performing a role with clear duties and responsibilities, as opposed to running a private club. Nonetheless, large resource-allocation decisions have often been made in 'corporatist' decision frameworks, which can appear to be like private clubs (see below). These legislative, judicial and executive branches were also given different functions, venues, personnel, methods of appointment, decision-making processes and so on. Their operating principles were designed to align with the different roles and functions of these decision spheres.

## Why use different decision-making processes in the different branches?

Different types of issues require suitable types of analyses, forums and processes. Decisions affecting the environment occur in all these arenas, of course, and sometimes simultaneously, depending on the issue and circumstances:

- *Judicial* processes are designed for deciding cases and controversies *after* the fact, where interests are already vested. In theory, both sides are able to advocate their position competitively under adversarial procedural rules, so that all relevant issues are raised.
- *Legislative* processes are designed for resolving conflicts *before* they occur. They also establish policies to guide the future resolution of controversies that keep arising. As

representatives, politicians are deemed capable of looking after people's rights, and sorting out conflicting interests among them.

- *Executive* processes are designed for implementing policy and are administrative in character. They are designed for efficiency and for accessing specialist expertise as required, though sometimes executive effectiveness is in conflict with accountability.

## Has the division of decision-making to create checks and balances worked?

Not surprisingly, it has proved impossible in practice to separate these functions and procedures completely. However, it established norms for, and disciplined, decision-making processes to a large extent. The American constitutional structure thus still arguably stands as a model for preventing the abuse of power.[11] Its design acknowledges that decision processes should fit the nature of the problem, and that checks and balances are always needed, as unchecked power will eventually be abused. It also institutionalized the concept of 'due process'. Due process does not just mean a 'fair go'. It has both a substantive and a procedural dimension. This means that twisting rules legally to obtain unfair results is not acceptable. But the division of powers and creation of different types of decision-making systems amount primarily to conceptual and procedural *restraints* on bad behaviour. Restraints do not encourage good behaviour. Moreover, they do little to redress past (legal or illegal) exercises of power that have created historic and social inequities. They also do little to address the lack of accountability for government inaction in the face of serious ecological problems. In other words, government systems create a framework through which power and resources are distributed, but do not stimulate positive actions in themselves. Government, and its component decision structures (eg judicial, executive and legislative), should be understood as a resource-allocation and conflict-resolution system writ large. Hence, like environmental management, planning and design, then, our larger-scale frameworks of governance need ecological modernization.[12]

## Why haven't checks and balances prevented an imbalance of power?

The checks and balances did not prevent the emergence of large bureaucracies or corporations that combine de facto legislative, judicial and administrative powers. The mission of large government bureaucracies (eg the US Bureau of Land Management) was to exploit environmental resources. Given the dominant belief that industrial growth was the purpose of human existence, this made sense. In a changing context, constitutional precepts, laws and policymaking procedures (initially intended to ensure social justice and resolve conflicts) can gradually evolve into systems that allow unequal access to, and eventual control of, natural resource-allocation decisions. In all levels of decision-making, institutional and intellectual biases in favour of the powerful develop, creating vicious circles. If the underlying structure allows undue political influence, ad hoc environmental laws cannot overcome a tendency towards the division, consumption and destruction of the public estate. So we need to 'design in' mechanisms that ensure environmental decision-making prevents the alienation of the means of survival to special (corporate or government) interests. This is not to say that centralized bureaucratic and/or corporate structures are problems in themselves, necessarily. But whether natural resources are controlled by bureaucracies, corporations or corporatist combinations, constant vigilance and structural safeguards are required.

## So how do we avoid imposing one group's ethics or beliefs on others?

The constitution should be based on shared democratic principles, so that it does not favour one set of values. However, life itself, has intrinsic value. It is generally accepted that people tend to value freedom, even though they do not always see the relationship between freedom and the ecology. While few may embrace the genuine sustainability that this book advocates, democracy is almost universally understood and valued. Thus sustainability can be couched in a democratic framework. One example of a set of widely-shared democratic principles is the Earth Charter. This is a fundamental statement of values developed over a multi-year worldwide, cross-cultural, international and participatory process.[13] It recognized that it is imperative to commit to global responsibility. Two of its principles are pertinent here:

- Ensure that economic activities and institutions at all levels provide human development in an equitable and sustainable manner (Section III, paragraph10)
- Strengthen democratic institutions at all levels, and provide transparency and accountancy in governance, inclusive participation in decision-making, and access to justice (Section IV, paragraph 13)

Such basic concepts of governance are almost universally acceptable, at least among people not in a position to abuse power over others. Given that safeguards for democracy and preventing the abuse of government power were fundamental to its design, we can build upon the American model. And, if we can build on established principles, ecological modernization cannot be said to be too radical or too hard.

## What are some safeguards that can prevent power imbalances over time?

One safeguard was the Bill of Rights. 'Rights', of course, imply mutual respect and responsibilities. Having basic rights and access to fair processes makes a difference in the culture of civil society, as safeguards like free speech make people more 'open', secure and honest.[14] Decisions are less likely to be conducted behind closed doors if those affected can assert their rights to natural justice and due process. Safeguards corrode over time, however. For example, to promote business, the legislatures and courts granted corporations the rights and protections accorded to individuals. This greatly altered the nature of democracy over time. Another example of relevance to resource allocation is how a principle like the private ownership of land can be affected by a changing context. Initially, the private ownership of land ensured individuals had independent means of survival.[15] This right made sense when the frontier seemed limitless, as everyone could – in theory – acquire land if they worked hard. As available land is reduced, however, those who do not inherit property, or otherwise become wealthy, can be effectively shut out of the property market. With property, vast amounts of power can be acquired by a relatively few individuals or businesses. Without property, the ability to acquire life quality and resource security is compromised. This makes people vulnerable to changing economic circumstances (eg urban renters can be subject to rents that are disproportionate to wages). So a provision designed to safeguard people can gradually became a source of unequal power relationships. Another safeguard was elections to ensure decision-making accountability. However, elections cannot hold decision-makers accountable with regard to sustainability issues, as the voting cycle is too short compared to environmental impacts.[16]

## Could a constitution really protect the right to a sustainable future?

No, but it is probably a precondition. The American Constitution was not designed to protect environmental rights or the rights of future generations to a sustainable environment.[17] It was based primarily on 'freedom to' do things, rather than 'freedom from' the actions of others that cause environmental harm. Nor were democratic processes intended to protect the public from corporate or bureaucratic interference in substantive democracy. It viewed private property and individualism, not the commons and community, as the basis of liberty. Thus, the Constitution required the State to do no harm with respect to the rights of citizens. It did not require the state or citizens to *do good* or protect the ecological base and public estate, human and ecosystem health, and so on. The State could placate demands and resolve conflict in the short term by dividing up resources. Politicians could enhance their position by giving away natural resources. So again, the common good or public interest was left largely to individuals, charities and, later, not-for-profit organizations. It is unlikely that environmental groups would ever be able to buy up all natural habitats to protect ecosystems from unwise bureaucratic decisions or individual and corporate excesses. So although the US Constitution was designed to prevent the abuse of power by the State through structural means, it is clearly insufficient in today's circumstances.

## How do decision-making structures change despite good constitutions?

Constitutional provisions that restrain the accumulation of government power did not prevent corporations from gaining undue influence over resource-allocation decisions. Corporations could become a force for sustainability, but this is not likely when they operate above governments (through, for example, the WTO). They are not subject to enforceable ethical precepts of relevance to sustainability [Box 37]. In a supply-driven economy, consumer abstinence is a lot to ask for, whereas consumer demand for environmental quality is not likely to be met. Many studies, over the last two decades at least, document the transfer of public resources to private corporate interests at below cost. For example, as Robert Repetto noted some 20 years ago, logging companies are clear-felling public land at a net loss to the taxpayer. Sometimes timber has been auctioned off to logging companies for less than the transaction costs of preparing for the auction. Moreover, the sale of timber does not cover the cost of managing the forest. And the proceeds do not cover the replacement cost of the resources (ie natural capital) – which businesses would ordinarily have to provide in the case of manufacturing capital. This squandering of resources and expropriation still continues in many countries through the active complicity of governments.[18] Perhaps only a global system of eco-governance can prevent current levels of resource expropriation.

## Can't regulations and economic instruments prevent resource expropriation?

In theory, but they are not doing so. Regulatory and market-based instruments have scarcely addressed the problem of 'perverse subsidies', let alone ecological waste [Chapter 4]. Studies have documented perverse subsidies worth over $650 billion world wide to prop up natural resource-intensive industries and activities (logging, farming, fishing, mining, oil drilling, livestock grazing, energy consumption and cars), the equivalent of 9 per cent of government revenue. Subsidies at the global level include $40 billion to forestry, $54 billion to fisheries and $300 billion to fossil fuel/nuclear energy.[19] Relatively little is spent on environmentally protective subsidies, such as soil or wetlands conservation. Many more subsidies still go to fossil fuels than solar power.[20] Because perverse subsidies occur under the active gaze of government agencies, and over many decades, they should be seen as systemic – not coincidental. The fact that they continue to exist is an indicator that governments are not really accountable to the general public. And if they are not, the institutional system needs re-design. Natural resources – the means of survival – are being depleted, polluted and privatized by taxpayer's 'representatives'. Hence it cannot be said that the taxpayer's long-term interests are being represented. If decision systems erode the rights and security that a constitution was intended to protect (let alone sustainability), it should be seen as 'institutional corruption'.[21]

## Surely 'inanimate' market or government mechanisms cannot be corrupt?

Systems that transfer wealth in ways that benefit the few far more than the many, and militate against sustainable resource consumption, cannot be said to be in the best interests of the ultimate 'employer' in a democracy: the citizenry. There are, of course, many extraneous reasons for perverse subsidies, including the fact that the market often creates price efficiency at the expense of efficient resource usage. And, of course, some consequences of government decisions are simply unintended. But systems that transfer public assets to special interests at below cost are not ecologically rational. Environmental governance is often corrupt in the conventional, financial sense as well. The sad saga of the Aral Sea illustrates this level of conspicuous corruption. The Aral Sea has virtually dried up due to the syphoning-off of upstream water supplies, largely for rice growing. It is reputedly a case of financial corruption, as money collected to protect the sea was (allegedly) pocketed for other purposes.[22] But it is also a case of systemic corruption, as the previous Soviet government essentially 'piratized' the lake by diverting its water for some favoured regions at the expense of others. Similarly, government complicity in essentially illegal and unsustainable logging of tropical forests is still rife in many 'biodiversity hotspots' around the world. Most resource transfers are more subtle. Of course, there are many systemic reasons why governments have permitted disenfranchisement, piratization, perverse subsidies, unjust enrichment and the abuse of power to continue – if not increase.

## Why have some democratic systems allowed systemic corruption to evolve?

One reason for this is deeply entrenched in the dominant worldview. When our current decision systems were designed, the 'founders' were concerned only with two dimensions: individuals and the state. The environment and its natural resources (the third dimension) were considered only as property, because nature was seen as an endless supply of resources and space. Thus private property was meant to ensure people had access to the means of survival as well as to promote growth and trade. The significance of the existence and integrity of the natural environment to the protection of individual rights, social justice and survival was not appreciated. The links between freedom and access to the means of survival (which, back then, was ensured by land ownership) were a formative part of the Western Frontier societies. However, as noted above, the links between human oppression and environmental destruction were not understood, or were simply ignored. The irony is that, because the design of our Western systems of government overlooked the centrality of the environment to security and freedom, they could not continue to balance power relations between individuals, groups and society as a whole. There cannot be equal opportunity where the environment, the basis of survival, can be divided up and accumulated. Over time, therefore, the first come, first served approach to land allocation creates environmental injustices. As a system, it cannot be sustained.

## But don't regulations constrain resource exploitation and injustice?

Yes, but many regulations and environmental management systems are out-dated. Environmental management systems generally only create friction on the rate of resource consumption. They do not alter its inevitability [Box 49]. We also need to remember that the mechanisms by which power is theoretically constrained – through 'checks and balances' – do not fully apply to basic resource allocation decisions. Instead, many large resource allocation decisions are actually made through 'corporatist' decision-making. This is where governments negotiate policies and their implementation with leading business and industry organizations. For example, the Crossroads Project – developed behind closed doors – laid out a blueprint for an economic rationalist Australian society. The adoption of this meta-policy was not a matter of public discourse, yet was fundamental in shaping Australia's future. Somewhat ironically, the corporatist model was adopted and implemented by a Labor Party Prime Minister (ie the left wing.) One of the problems with corporatism has been that the 'environment' is not fully represented in the negotiations and/or its representatives are out of their depth on someone else's game board. Sometimes the negotiations include environmental organizations, but case studies and first-hand accounts have indicated that the rug is pulled out from under public interest representatives at some point. It is, of course, important to bring all parties to the same table for mutual education and communication. There cannot, however, be meaningful participation without genuine 'due process' provisions that protect weaker parties from power games.

## Don't corporatist decision-making processes help to build bridges?

Except for public interest groups, the parties at the table (industry and ex officio representatives of statutory authorities, cabinet, unions, etc) generally have a direct interest in resource allocation and exploitation for their political survival. Their agenda is to obtain access to natural (and other) resources for their constituents. Of course, the aim of the representatives of environmental organizations is environmental protection. However, in interest group politics, the issue is how to *allocate* or divide up resources (eg between conservation and development). Sustainability – the expansion of future options – is in direct opposition to the nature of corporatist decision-making. Corporatism was never voted upon by the general public or their representatives. In fact, in Australia, the basic decision-making offices of government (eg Cabinet and the Prime Minister) – let alone corporatist resource allocation – were not even anticipated or mentioned in the Constitution. Both the official government system in Australia (ie rule by convention) and corporatism (ie rule by collusion) were the outcome of the interplay of power relationships over time. They were not the outcome of deliberative and democratic institutional design to create a secure, healthy and equitable future. Arguably, then, public–private+community partnerships and cooperatives have more potential than corporatism to address sustainability issues through direct action. In any case, they can be more open than political parties facing elections or public–private partnerships sheltered by 'commercial in confidence' provisions.

## Are public–private partnerships an alternative to corporatist decision-making?

They are not always very dissimilar. However, partnerships are more project-oriented than policy-oriented. They could be a means of implementing net positive projects that demonstrate the potential of development to improve existing social and ecological conditions. A cross-cultural, cross-sectoral approach is necessary if industry and government are going to increase the public estate, instead of 'pork-barrelling'. However, public–private partnerships have thus far tended to exclude the community. In fact, such conventional partnerships raise the risk of ad hoc corporatism. Even if partnerships are inclusive of community representatives, corporatist processes will often determine the major decisions: what, when and where land and resources are allocated or developed. Partnerships only have the potential to be transformative if they include the community *and* have adequate procedural and substantive safeguards.[23] The 'third sector', or businesses which reinvest their profits into social goals, is also beginning to rise to the occasion. While cooperatives, third-sector businesses and public–private+community partnerships could be a vehicle for creating exemplars of sustainability, however, sustainability also ultimately requires social transformation. As many involved in social change generally agree, paradigm shifts and value change require face-to-face, interactive learning, which can only be achieved through collaborative projects. Thus a new public arena for dialogue, debate and collective action concerning ethical issues is needed that can support both conflict resolution and social transformation.

## So how do we start to design a new ethics-based decision sphere?

First, as exemplified by the above discussion, we can start by assessing the structural pluses and minuses of our existing systems of governance. Even though sustainability was not understood when democratic systems of governance were first designed, our inherited constitutional decision spheres can perform vital functions:[24]

- The market arena is designed for price and distributional efficiency (although it is not efficient in terms of resource optimization). It could resolve competing interests between individuals, and distribute private 'wants' and 'preferences' efficiently.
- The political policymaking arena is designed to allocate resources, although usually based on picking winners and losers. It could resolve competing demands of different interest groups by implementing programmes that would increase natural capital, rather than divide it up.
- The political law-making arena is designed to resolve conflicting interests over resources (although often based more on power than need). It could resolve future conflicts between humans and nature by replacing constraints and incentives with positive actions.
- The legal arena is designed for settling disputes that have already materialized, although based more on past rules than new responsibilities. It resolves conflicts when it is too late for preventative legislation, and can also police systems of checks and balances.

In practice, of course, these distinctions are largely conceptual. For example 'wants' created by the market are often protected as basic rights or needs in the political system. But this framework also reveals a fundamental *gap* in our basic structure of governance.

## So what is this fundamental gap in the basic structure of governance?

The gap is this. The sustainability imperative cannot be met by our present market, state or legal institutions. There is no decision-making arena that can *adequately*:

- Resolve competing interests between society and nature over the long term (by adaptive, proactive design as opposed to incentives and constraints)
- Resolve the ethical issues inherent in sustainability (intra- and inter-generational equity, the rights of other species to exist, etc)
- Ensure that the means of survival and basic needs (including emotional and culturally based needs) are protected, enhanced and accessible to all

The reason that existing decision spheres cannot fulfil these functions is that each requires ecologically sustainable land use and development. While individual planners may do their best, conventional planning evolved as a mere administrative appendage of state and local governments (which are the levels responsible for land use in Australia and the US). We have already seen that our project-assessment and futures-planning methods are anachronistic and fundamentally incompatible with sustainability [Chapter 12]. Therefore, a new planning sphere should be grafted onto our existing constitutional model, like the cerebral cortex was grafted onto our reptilian brain.[25]

## Figure 16 Tripartite model of eco-governance

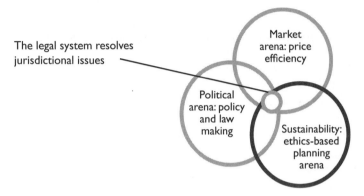

The legal system resolves jurisdictional issues

Market arena: price efficiency

Political arena: policy and law making

Sustainability: ethics-based planning arena

To improve systems health and create positive relationships, we should try to create more equitable relationships between individuals, society and nature. There are currently three types of conflict resolution areas which resolve conflicts among differing interests. This new model would add an ethics-based planning sphere. In the proposed model of eco-governance, the highest court would be the arbiter of jurisdictional disputes, as it is now.

## Can't current planning systems simply be modified to address sustainability?

Not likely. The nature of the planning system would have to be radically different from what planning is now. It is essential, of course, that ecological modernization occur in each decision arena – as well as in the professions and academic disciplines – so that they can all address sustainability issues [Figure 16]. The judicial sphere is not included in this typology because it largely deals with conflicts after the fact, not future decisions. Although legal decisions create precedents for the resolution of future conflicts, these can, in effect, be overturned by the legislature (and vice versa). To summarize this typology, there are three dimensions of conflict prevention: the conflicts between individuals, between individuals and society, and between individuals, society and nature [Table 2]. These conflict areas tend to involve different interests, respectively wants, rights and needs. These interests in turn correspond to different criteria or standards of decision-making, respectively equity, efficiency and ethics. These criteria suggest different processes (eg trading, negotiating, and debate and dialogue). These in turn suggest different kinds of decision arenas, respectively markets, electoral politics – and a missing arena. The proposed constitutional model therefore adds to the state and market spheres a new sphere for resource allocation and conflict resolution: a sustainability/planning sphere. This would also provide a forum for active community engagement, mutual learning, and identifying and implementing Positive Development projects. The new tripartite framework is based on each sphere's function in meeting different interests and resolving conflicts, specifically:

- Rights/responsibility – the state
- Wants and preferences – the market
- Basic social, emotional, spiritual and bio-physical needs, or sustainability – a new planning sphere

Table 2 Tripartite model of eco-governance

| Dimensions | Interests | Key value | Processes | Arena |
|---|---|---|---|---|
| Individuals | Wants/preferences | Efficiency | Trade/exchange | Market sphere |
| Individuals/society | Relative rights/stakes | Equity | Vote/negotiate | Political sphere |
| Individuals/society nature | Needs/responsibilities | Ethic of care | Collaborative design | **New planning sphere** |

## Is it necessary to create a new decision-making sphere for sustainability issues?

Environmental issues today are fundamentally matters of ethics, and these concern collective responsibilities – not individual rights (politics) and personal preferences (markets). They involve decisions as to how we, as a society, should live and what constitutes our responsibility to future generations, other species, ecosystems, ethnic groups, cultures and so on. These ethical issues cannot be resolved by achieving equal rights in consumption or efficient distribution of goods and services alone. This is because things can be 'equal', but still be 'unfair' and/or unsustainable. That is, resources could be divided up equally, but this would not in itself stop the destruction of the ecological base and public estate. The fact that an appropriate sphere for environmental decision-making does not yet exist is one reason why we got the planet into so much trouble in the first place. Each of our existing decision arenas and planning systems is designed for dividing things up – not for increasing the means of survival and quality of life. Each of our decision frameworks and tools is designed for choosing (comparing and selecting), not expanding future options. Progress towards sustainability has also been stymied by this binary (or non-design) form of thinking. For example, the diversionary debate over whether the market (business) or state (bureaucracy) is best suited to solve the environmental crisis has blocked debate over creative alternatives. A tripartite model would, in itself, help to dislodge the conventional dualistic public–private or state–market choice and associated 'blame games'.

## How does the conventional state–market model create blame games?

The dualistic public–private or state–market model has masked the fact that both the state and market prioritize individual wants over collective rights, and rights over responsibilities. The dichotomy directs our attention to superficial debates: who should decide, or where decisions should occur. The debate has been largely over which side of the coin can be trusted with our future: the private or public sector. Given the amalgamation of corporate and state interests, this is a false dichotomy.[26] Those advocating private enterprise characterize the public sector with terms like 'bureaucratic', and associate the private sector with terms like 'entrepreneurial'. Those advocating a stronger public sector characterize the private sector with terms like 'capitalistic', and associate the public sector with terms like 'equity and accessibility'. The real issue is not the respective morality of bureaucratic and corporate players, however. The issue is which decisions should be made, and what decision-making structures and processes are most suitable for the nature of those decisions. So a new decision sphere could help us escape the vicious circles caused by this dualistic thinking and the false choices that they create. Sustainability is too important to be left to the markets or political arena, which have proven inadequate to the task. For the community to take responsibility, a new sphere will need to be created, in which collective decision-making processes and methods are tailored to the ethical dimensions of environmental issues.

## Isn't it too much trouble to restructure or add a new decision arena?

On the contrary. What we are doing now is too hard, but for the fact that we have been doing it all our lives. Besides, over the past few decades, managers in government, corporations and universities have embarked on major restructuring processes almost continuously (known as 'managerialism'). Some cynics suggest that the drivers are largely personal agendas, like consolidating control, re-branding or downsizing the organization. A new planning sphere, in contrast, would be designed to contend with issues like human survival – issues that have fallen through the cracks in most organizational restructures. 'Add-on' institutions, like sustainable development advisory groups or sustainability commissioners, have had little tangible success. Nor has the mere expansion of existing state and regional planning systems sufficed. These only serve to muddle accountability. The new model would clarify the system of governance by realigning rights, wants and needs with the appropriate type of decision-making structures and processes – a democratic state, the market and sustainability planning. The new mandate would be to prevent conflict by expanding future options. Planning would be reconceived as a community-building and ethics-based process for determining collective social, economic and environmental goals in the long-term public interest. Therefore planners, with varied training, would help communities identify and prioritize public investments that have net positive impacts (aided by ET, RT, CI and/or EW analyses). They would not just open up suburban land or infill urban spaces to appease consumers and/or producers.

## So would this new configuration change the roles of the other spheres?

Somewhat. The reconfiguration would involve 'tweaking' so that these spheres also support sustainability. This means that the functions of the existing decision arenas would need to be re-clarified in terms of their role in achieving sustainability and conflict prevention:

- **The market system** can reconcile individual demands, preferences and choices with production and distribution systems. It can be good at providing for the efficient delivery of material goods and services to meet consumer demand by facilitating efficient 'exchanges' (at least compared to, say, state capitalism). While it claims to 'balance' supply and demand, powerful individuals, corporations and oligopolies have acquired sufficient power to control both [Box 49]. Producers seem able to create unnecessary and insatiable 'needs' through the media and other marketing channels. Further, in spite of the efforts of ecological economists, the market still treats environmental goods and services – the very basis of the entire economy – as if they were free, or else just commodities to be bought and sold. Seen as a conflict-resolution system, though, the market could help to avoid or resolve conflicts among individuals through informal bargaining and exchange processes. It cannot deal with underlying ethical issues, however.

- **The political system**, seen as a conflict-resolution system, was designed to restrict state interference in the rights of individuals. It was also designed to restrict individual interference in the rights of other individuals, groups or society as a whole. Of course, it is important to ensure representative democracy does not evolve into 'selective representation', as some interests are more politically influential than others (through limits on campaign funding etc). Further, political mechanisms are not an appropriate means to resolve basic sustainability issues, because these are ethical in nature, not distributive. Once again, even *if* the political process resulted in more equal decisions and outcomes, democracy in dividing up public goods and consuming them is not sustainable. There has, of course, been a lot of work in the area of ecological democracy, but this has not entered mainstream political debates. Moreover, sometimes terms like ecological democracy are confused with conventional 'environmental management'.[27] Like the market, the political arena has not yet dealt successfully with sustainability issues.

- **The legal system** is not presently designed to address issues concerning environmental and public 'goods', as most of its basic concepts and procedures derive from property rights concepts or other antiquarian precedents. Case law has been slow to evolve public law principles suited to sustainability issues. It has a retrospective orientation and requires problems to have 'ripened' before they can be addressed. So legislation is needed. Nonetheless, the courts are equipped to resolve disputes that result from jurisdictional conflicts. Thus they could sort out territorial issues arising from the updated roles of the other resource-allocation arenas. The highest court could be the final arbiter of disputes over interpretations regarding the ecological modernization of the constitutional framework.

## Would the planning sphere become 'conventional' planning writ large?

There is indeed a danger of this. Without new methods and tools, planning will continue to simply manage public distress over the impacts of conventional development. Arguably, conceptual principles and tools could be implemented without the development of a new planning sphere. However, the current attempts at ecological modernization within the existing system of governance do not seem to be working. Examples of these contemporary approaches are as follows: integrating sustainability into decision-making across the whole of government; relying on greening of business and industry through technological efficiency; and promoting innovation and new green technology.

- **Integration in government**: Efforts to introduce whole-of-government reform, where all departments are encouraged to integrate sustainability into their processes, do not really dislodge existing power relationships. Each branch of government and each department must modernize, but this will not happen by osmosis. People with environmental values are more likely to be eclipsed by the values of those that inhabit nearby dominant-paradigm cubicles. Denial and resistance to change is a powerful force. Without fundamental systems re-design, mere re-badging will continue to occur.
- **Efficiency in industry**: The call for a 'new industrial revolution' through radical resource efficiency will hopefully inspire a positive self-fulfilling prophesy. But conventional industry will not easily give up its home advantage and compete on level ground with new environmental businesses.[28] Unless existing planning controls, commercialization criteria and government subsidies change dramatically, innovation in the construction industry will further entrench, not transform, our development system.
- **Innovation**: While there are many tools that can support creativity and innovation, they were not designed for sustainability.[29] Creative-thinking stimulators help us think outside the box. However, the main focus of innovation tools and processes has been on developing new processes, products or services to compete with, or leapfrog, old ones. On the whole, most current innovations do not reduce total production, consumption and resource flows.[30] We need better criteria for investment [Chapter 14].

## Why hasn't environmental planning been able to modernize itself over time?

There are many reasons for the incoherence of environmental planning in contemporary society. One of these is that planners who are concerned with conservation, or even sustainability, have operated within the paradigm framed by industrial development interests. Those representing industrial development have sought greater access to cheaper labour, transport and resources, and more consumers and consumption per capita. All of these demands contribute to a greater throughput of materials and energy. Those representing conservation interests have only managed to create systems that reduce the negative inputs and outputs. Reducing the inputs (materials and energy) by taxing resource extraction, or reducing the outputs (pollution and waste) by using indirect regulatory or market incentives, cannot convert an industrial system to an eco-logical economy [Box 49]. Moreover, setting taxes or caps on resource extraction and production will please *neither* producers (lobbyists) *nor* consumers (voters). Thus many view environmental regulation as 'negative', despite some good outcomes overall. The problem with regulation is that while it can limit bad behaviour and require more efficient goods and services, the restriction of bad behaviour does not create good behaviour or outcomes. The alternative, or more accurately the companion, to environmental regulation and incentives would be ecologically and ethically principled planning and design.[31] We have said, however, that planning has not identified opportunities for positive outcomes. The next chapter therefore explores means that planning (at any level of governance) could begin to identify and prioritize positive actions.

# 14
# Reversing Resource Transfers

From pyramidal to
positive resource
distribution

There have been great efficiency gains in some areas, which have mitigated the impacts of growing resource flows and disparities of wealth. By comparing components through input–output analyses, we can make plastic bottles thinner, make more efficient air-conditioners, and increase the yield of crops relative to the cost of chemicals. But as a society, we still seldom ask whether we actually need more plastic bottles, fossil fuel heating and cooling, or chemical fertilizers. The emphasis on reducing consumption trends can instil the false impression that we have a demand-driven economy. Our supply-driven production systems put candy in front of people and then ask them to abstain. We have neglected the ecology and failed to appreciate the ability of built environment design to value-add social and environmental benefits. Input–output thinking means other design relationships tend to be neglected, such as the nexus between functions, materials, space and context. Instead of escapism, what we really want from products and buildings are comfort, conviviality, convenience, quality of life, love and laughter. Buildings – energy-guzzling glass, steel, concrete and aluminium cubicle containers – may not be the best way of achieving these qualities.

Our methods and tools have not helped us to design net positive buildings or balanced environmental flows between cities and regions. We have seen the need for design tools and processes that instead help us re-conceive development (cities, buildings, farms and factories, infrastructure) in relation to each other, development, the bioregion and the life-support system. Systems design must better address social sustainability as well, not just a more fair distribution of pollution. Design should counterbalance or reverse inequitable resource transfers – in ways that make everyone better off. To do this, we have said, planning analysis tools are needed that, among other things:

- Identify social, environmental and ecological problems and inequities in *existing* development (resource transfers, internalities, costs of inaction and so on)
- Track the transfer of resources through development and land-use allocation, including the transfer of space from public to private uses
- Help find ways in which 'rurban' development could improve upon these conditions (design

for eco-services) and restore environmental flows (eg river restoration, nature corridors and biodiversity habitats)

- Provide a framework for prioritizing public and/or private investments in eco-innovations to turn vicious circles into virtuous cycles

In this chapter, we will outline a conceptual framework to guide methods to map resource flows and transfers, assess the effectiveness of planning policies, and prioritize investment in Positive Development.

## How can flows analyses assess the effectiveness of planning policies?

Flows analyses could be used to calculate 'embodied waste' over time. That is to say, losses in total underground water supplies, fossil fuels, soil fertility, and so on [Chapter 4]. By tracking resource flows through a city over time, we can also assess the effectiveness of urban planning policies on resource flows and inequities. For example, one of the author's students tracked major 'sustainable' policy initiatives in Canberra against consumption (water and energy) and wastes (greenhouse gases) over time [Box 40]. He discovered that there was no discernable correlation between sustainability plans and policy initiatives and the actual flows of water and energy and greenhouse emissions. The initiatives had generally not counteracted the increase in total consumption relative to population growth, let alone reduced or reversed the absolute rates of flows. But, as we have said, sustainability requires a broader perspective than eco-effectiveness of proposals in relation to the current conditions. We also need to track how far we are from sustainability, by relating back to the original pre-development conditions (ET analysis). Measuring how far we are from sustainability also requires economic and social benchmarks: a consideration of who is obtaining the benefits and burdens of resource transfers from nature to development, poor to rich, public to private, future to present, etc (RT analysis). Environmental management tools fail to adequately compare the costs of inaction (CI analysis) or the long-term consequences of linear flows (ID analysis). Public investment could be directed at correcting these imbalances, but planning has largely let the market set investment priorities.

## Can't linear resource transfers be made more efficient in any case?

Only if we also reverse past negative flows. Throughout most of history, urban areas have enjoyed linear wealth transfers from their tributaries, and linear resource flows from natural systems to human populations. We know that if we give little or nothing back to nature, our urban and industrial systems will eventually crash. We can trace how urban systems drain soil fertility and water from rural areas. Yet environmental planning and management still usually deals with rurban areas, national and global flows, and human and natural systems in isolation. As long as our analyses separate urban, rural and ecological issues and focus on linear inputs and outputs, our solutions will be (literally) end-of-pipe. More efficient irrigation systems, showerheads and low flush toilets, for example, reduce but do not reverse environmental impacts. Instead of re-designing the rurban operations that cause the runoff, erosion, waste and reduced environmental flows in the first place, we create more dams, pipelines and desalination plants. While end-of-pipe solutions are ultimately terminal, of course, they can be an important part of the mix. Clever, small changes downstream can reduce flows upstream, through 'compounding'.[1] In Australia, however, our major river system, the Murray Darling Basin, is (at time of writing) unable to provide any water to some irrigators, so greater efficiency is a moot point.[2] The separation of environmental studies by sector and jurisdiction, as well as social and ecological issues, leads to separate and sectoral policy responses. This has meant that potential synergies, or win–win–win initiatives, have often been opposed by 'competing' regional interests (eg farmers versus city dwellers), because they are in competition for funding and political priorities.

## How do we turn linear rural–urban resource flows into symbiotic ones?

This requires the integration of science, humanities and design in a process we are calling SmartMode. We have suggested that a flows analysis can help sectoral interests appreciate their shared interests in better regional systems design. For example, it can demonstrate that linear resource flows are not sustainable (socially, economically or ecologically) for either urban or rural interests. It can show current inequities and imbalances, identify 'new' ecological problems before their impacts are felt, and measure the effectiveness of solutions [Box 31]. But flows analyses alone cannot tell us how to increase ecological health and to 'design' regional and urban systems as one symbiotic system. On the other hand, terminal resource flows, as indicators of design failure, are also a good indicator of economic opportunities. We have seen that even waste can be reduced and recycled, while generating profits and reducing some relative impacts of existing systems of development. Theoretically, in a market economy, this level of eco-innovation should happen *without* the need for government subsidies. This is because reuse and recycling are inherently more efficient than industrial mechanisms where materials must initially be extracted from nature. The opportunities for private companies should therefore be enough to drive marginal systems improvements. But while markets should drive efficiencies, they often simply shift benefits and burdens. As we saw, developer exactions, whether in city planning or eco-service trading systems, still allow increased negative impacts overall [Chapter 11]. This is still the case in carbon trading as well.

## So which can best drive systems transformation: planning or the market?

Some advocates of markets argue that pollution creates a market for pollution-reduction technology, so markets can solve the problems that they create. However, in a market system, things have to be pretty bad before it is 'profitable' to clean them up. Until then, the taxpayer pays most of the costs for medical care and pollution control (another vicious cycle). From a glance at the shelves of most shops, there still appear to be more ecologically harmful or inherently wasteful products being generated than positive ones. Take, for example, the proliferation of processed high sugar, high fat foods. These have created a new market in 'low fat' products. Yet high sugar, high fat products are also still multiplying. Likewise, the market on its own will never regenerate a city beyond the condition that existed before harmful development systems were created in the first place. Nor will the market ever support a reduction in population and/or consumption. Efficiency measures can be restorative of ecosystems by removing some of the causes of damage, but they will only be net positive by accident (or to attract higher prices). In the meantime, many 'efficient' innovations can be suboptimal. Many inventions are still anti-ecological and can, in effect, delay the transition to whole systems improvements. The most efficient design from the perspective of a business seeking a market advantage may mean more investment in a largely dysfunctional system. We can only create Positive Development by *design*. The public therefore needs to set priorities and guide public, if not private, investment in systems re-design.

## But why do we need the public to set priorities, since eco-innovation pays?

Some conventional industrial-scale waste management industries have developed a vested interest in waste. Some of these have even opposed innovations that would reduce waste, because (within a myopic perspective) waste is their source of income.[3] Similarly, many would argue that the construction industry as a whole has avoided change, even though ecological modernization would be in its own rational collective interest. Public investment may be necessary to overcome systemic impediments to eco-retrofitting. However, priorities need to be set if we are to stretch our design goals beyond recycling and restoration. Stretch goals are intended to encourage ecological and social value-adding, not just getting across a line. Therefore it is important to make distinctions in terms of the *scale* of positive impacts. Incremental *stages* in achieving stretch goals would be far better than continuing to set incremental (ie minimalist) *targets*. For example, savings from small energy-efficient improvements can be rolled over into larger projects. Likewise, a recycling opportunity may just pick 'low-hanging fruit', yet have more economic and resource value to the community as a whole, because of its ripple effects on a larger scale. St Vincent de Paul in Eugene, Oregon, has created hundreds of jobs and resource savings through myriad small, but innovative, recycling projects. They have also used the income from recycling to build low-income homes and establish other programmes that improve the community as a whole. St Vincent has been able to do this with little government support, because waste does not cost much and there is a lot of it. They had the flexibility to evolve and adapt, without becoming dependent on particular waste streams. And they have continuously looked for new loops to close. Due to this 'snowballing' approach, and the total scale of these 'waste to value' projects, they have had a significant positive impact on the local economy. Thus, many small actions in the third sector and cross-sectoral partnerships can have a big impact overall.

## Haven't we said there are problems with relying on markets though?

Yes, the exceptions prove the rule. We will run out of low hanging fruit. Besides, the market is the mother of 'product differentiation', not innovation for positive systems change. The public sector should act to correct market failure by assessing and supporting research and development in terms of their *transformative* potential. The likely financial success of private commercial ventures should not be the primary concern of innovation programmes. Presently, however, governments are not structured to provide leadership in sustainability or to foster net positive market activity. In fact, governments often fund private companies to do research based on its commercial potential, rather than the public good. The results become privatized information or 'commercial in confidence'. Instead of increasing competition and dissemination, then, government funding often provides private access to, and control of, information and innovation. When governments pick winners and losers through trading systems, grants or regulations, these public funds are sometimes ultimately used to exclude potential competitors. Where market potential is a criterion, government grants and subsidies often tacitly prioritize low-risk innovations that fit into existing systems, rather than transform them. So potentially, 'ineffective' businesses can be set up at public expense while precluding eco-effective ones. For example, in Australia, targets were set in 1997 that required the sourcing of 2 per cent of energy from renewable sources. This provided an incentive to implement renewable energy plants such as wind power. But the (then) government subsequently withheld further support for renewable energy. One of the grounds was that the incentive was resulting in generators for wind power being imported from cheap overseas sources. The priority was apparently on stimulating innovation for the sake of innovation, with little regard for economic, social and environmental outcomes for Australia as a whole.

## How do we avoid innovation that does not have positive outcomes for all?

A key function of a new planning sphere should be to help set public priorities for investment in sustainability research, eco-innovation and even academic problem solving. But it is essential to ensure that government support does not translate into de facto commercial monopolies that can later prevent competition. The saga of how the car industry resisted energy efficiency innovations for decades is well known. Billions of dollars were invested not in energy efficiency improvements but in automobile 'fashion' research and development. Also, given an existing physical configuration of land-use and transportation systems, the most commercial solution in the current situation may not be the most efficient from a long-term perspective (such as the new, cheap 'Nano' car being promoted in India). That is, the potential spectrum of eco-solutions that are given serious consideration will be limited to those products or building types that fit the industrial, rather than the ecological, order. This, in turn, can impede transformation to sustainable systems. For example, large buildings – as currently designed – need very complex air-conditioning systems. Consequently, these systems require a range of specialists in design, manufacturing, sales, distribution, installation, commissioning and maintenance. This creates vested interests in existing industrial systems. With an ever-increasing array of complex air-conditioning systems, more things can go wrong, and specialist parts may be hard to find [Box 20]. This also creates the need for regulatory, education and training programmes to meet the demands of these businesses, which further entrenches current construction norms. This past investment is perpetuating unsustainable vicious circles and creating more industry resistance to change. The challenge of eco-logical design is therefore to fit into existing institutional and physical systems – while working to transform them.

## How can we break these vicious circles and change to sustainable systems?

A hierarchy of eco-solutions could assist in guiding public investment towards programmes that re-direct jobs, energy and innovation towards whole systems improvements (below). Through a hierarchy of eco-solutions, planning or the public sector generally, could assist the identification and implementation of new business opportunities according to their potential to drive systems re-design. Currently, when an industry or government procurement office chooses a product, it can refer to green purchasing guidelines, product or building rating systems, and/or specification tools. These estimate the negative impacts of alternative products, designs or materials [Box 30]. They generally rank products by how little harm they do within the existing system of development; they do not expose the whole system impacts (eg a living wall requires maintenance, but so do other walls). Certification and labelling systems are effective in providing consumer information about products that are on the market.[4] However, they do relatively little to encourage new products that might transform whole systems. This is because such tools do not identify public needs that private and/or public sector investment could target through innovation. For example, we sometimes rank different timber by how responsibly managed the forest was.[5] This, of course, is important [Box 36]. But we are putting more sustainable timber into excessively large suburban homes, while ignoring the needs of the homeless. Also, green labels do not protect good products from political activity, subterfuge or espionage from competitors that still feel threatened by higher standards.[6] Conventional products still have a home court advantage. At the very least, then, we need better forms of ethical technology assessment.[7]

## What could government do to encourage positive whole systems change?

Instead of protecting established interests, the public sector could stimulate investment in eco-innovation. For instance, it could conduct sustainability audits of existing development, supply chains or factories to identify opportunities for savings. The public sector could also help to find ways of implementing large-scale uptake of existing, eco-effective innovations. If development approvals were based on the best, rather than the 'first off the starting block', competition would be over net positive contributions to sustainability. The present decision system is too often pyramidal and exclusionary, as development depends on the concentration of wealth. In a competition over positive contributions, any firm or developer would be able to shift to more eco-logical designs (although some industries would need to diversify, such as cigarette, gun and drug companies which the free market now favours). A hierarchy, from remedial to positive, and from narrow to whole systems solutions, could assist in ranking grants and subsidies, start up funding, offer awards, and so on. We can distinguish six levels of eco-solutions (presented below), with the first being the *least* positive and the sixth being the *most* positive. The spectrum is based on both the nature and scale of transformation likely to be generated. The categories overlap, but provide a rough scale between marginal change and systems transformation. If this fails, and we cannot get governments to undertake polices and programmes that enhance the ecological base and public estate, then, as individuals, we can work through NGOs or third sector businesses. If that is too difficult for some people, they can at least ensure that their personal investment goes towards ethical investment funds. These limit funding to businesses that are at least *relatively* ecologically, socially and economically sound [Box 37].

## So how could eco-solutions be ranked in terms of their whole system impacts?

The following sections present a hierarchy of eco-innovations.

### Level 1 – Cleaner production

This level includes new designs, products or production systems that may increase resource flows overall, but do so at less negative impact per unit than the norm. This level reduces the relative impacts of *future* actions.

For example, geo-sequestration (which captures and buries some of the emissions from oil and possibly coal production) could arguably qualify as a (low) level 1 action. However, it creates risks which must be considered. In 1980, sudden leakage of $CO_2$ from Lake Nyos, in Cameroon, killed 1700 people by asphyxiation. $CO_2$ also causes acidification of groundwater. It also does not capture all the $CO_2$ produced at the plant and it can only address a fraction of total $CO_2$ emissions. Further, it only reduces some impacts. It does not reduce radical terraforming and the production of toxins entailed in mining. In the case of coal (as opposed to oil) production, it is only applicable to new plants, not retrofitting, so it increases embodied waste as well. It is only better than continuing to build very dirty industries. Thus public funding in this category could be next to counterproductive.

### Level 2 – Recycling and 'down-cycling'

This level is where the innovation reduces the impacts of waste from *ongoing* processes or activities, through reuse or reassembly. While recycling can reduce resource flows dramatically, there is usually some waste, and a reduction of use value or down-cycling.[8]

An example of addressing problems of ongoing waste is mattress recycling. Until recently, old mattresses were dumped, partly because 'reuse' involved health issues. But in some places today, they are reconstructed with replacement materials, while old components and materials are reprocessed. However, the term 'recycled' can be misleading. For example, recycled steel takes a quarter of the energy of ordinary steel to produce, but 'recycled steel' may only have 25 per cent recycled steel content. Likewise, recycling aluminium soft drinks cans is not as good as drinking water from a glass. Using waste timber from milling processes to power the plant or equipment (or 'co-generation') could be considered 'down-cycling' if there are better uses for the organic cellulose. This, again, would depend on the viability of options, such as using a solar thermal power system instead [Box 18]. Recycling 'pays', so loans should be adequate to fund the transition to recycling systems. The efficiencies that recycling provide should make them competitive on their own, especially once full cost pricing is instituted, or perverse subsidies are eliminated.

## Level 3 – Closing loops and 'up-cycling'

This level requires actions that reduce the impacts of *past* development, as well as ongoing and future impacts. Closing loops is where a new innovation or activity reduces toxins or waste already in the environment, such as drawing methane from an old landfill site. Up-cycling means using what would otherwise be waste, while creating a higher economic use.

For example, whereas down-cycling would be turning bricks into road base, up-cycling would be re-using the bricks in a 'reverse Trombe wall' or living walls to contribute to both ecological and human functions. Industrial ecology projects, which close loops among existing industries, could amount to either up-cycling or down-cycling. For example, turning used wooden pallets into designer furniture instead of fire wood can be considered up-cycling. However, the profitable product may only be of higher value monetary – which is often the case in conspicuous consumption items. Thus converting waste products to refugee shelters (up-cycling) could be distinguished from converting waste into trinkets that do not meet basic needs (or down-cycling). Closed loop processes do not necessarily meet basic needs, nor do they usually achieve zero waste. Yet there are cases where the poor have created jobs for themselves by, for example, converting waste magazines or Coke cans into jewellery or art works [Boxes 16 and 54]. This improves their financial condition, while increasing social justice.

## Level 4 – Zero waste and 'no loop design'

This refers to innovations where waste is *designed out* of a past, ongoing or future system entirely (notwithstanding entropy). This is what McDonough and Braungart call 'no loop systems'.[9] No loop design is that which does not require recycling processes. For example, chopsticks and bowls can be made edible, or bricks can be made interlocking and therefore totally reusable.

Even if the system involves deconstructing and reconstructing products, a process could still be considered zero waste if it eliminates an ongoing *past* problem. For example, millions of tyres are still stockpiled around the world. An Australian 'backyard inventor' found a way to *deconstruct* used tyres, and reuse all the materials in a range of new products.[10] There is virtually no waste as all parts are used and can produce high value products. The inventiveness was in working out how to deconstruct these technically-sophisticated tyre parts – which tyre manufacturers, with billions in profits, apparently could not do. This could convert huge stockpiles of waste to raw materials for a range of other possible positive uses, undoing some of the past damage. (Worldwide, an estimated 1.2 billion waste tyres are generated every year.) Given the scale of the problem the eco-innovation addresses, therefore, it has potential to make change on a significant scale.

### Level 5 – Eco-cycling

Eco-cycling is introduced here to distinguish up-cycling that contributes to human and ecological health (ie net positive) from up-cycling that may still increase total resource flows or even encourage conspicuous consumption. That is, closing loops can be down-cycling, up-cycling or eco-cycling.

In addition to cleaning up a past problem, eco-cycling would also provide a public good. The Living Machine may best illustrate eco-cycling. Again, the Living Machine is a natural bioconversion process, where ecosystems of micro-organisms, usually in a sequence of transparent vats, treat sewage or wastewater, and grow food or fish. Living Machines can work at a neighbourhood, city or regional scale, while serving as landscape features and eco-tourist education facilities.[11] They convert an unhealthy pollutant into healthy foods and products, such as the conversion of abattoir pollution to farm fertilizer, or turning urban food and plant waste into compost. They are arguably 'reverse linear systems' that turn negatives into positives.

### Level 6 – Net positive

Innovations at this highest level improve whole systems health; that is, beyond the level of the product, building or city. Net positive would be eco-cycling that generates public goods as well as products with human and ecological health benefits. It applies to both physical or institutional design.

**Net Positive Development** not only helps to transform its urban context (socially, economically and environmentally), but also:

- Increases the ecological base (natural capital, eco-services, biodiversity, carrying capacity, natural security, etc) through design for eco-services
- Increases the public estate (access to life quality and the means of survival)

Eco-retrofitting can be net positive, as it can create positive public benefits beyond the original pre-development site conditions and boundaries. (Note that rural systems can arguably be restored up to – but not beyond – original ecological conditions, so the term 'eco-restoration' is more appropriate in the rural context.)

**Net positive systems** need not be physical development. An institutional eco-solution can create a lever for net positive gains at a whole systems scale, such as improvements in the supply or delivery of services, programmes, policies, products or other eco-innovations that convert cities, regions and nations from a fossil economy to a solar one. A transition to a 'solar economy' would, for example, help the ecological transformation of society as a whole and perhaps contribute to world peace and ecological security (through decentralization of power, universal access to the means of survival, etc). This category would enable urban, regional, state and/or national governments to compete in developing institutional means to promote Positive Development.

## But how would we begin to design reversible development?

New concepts are usually required to dislodge old patterns of thought, habit and design methods. Considerations like designed waste, the rebound effect, design for disassembly, hierarchies of eco-innovation and so on can therefore play a part. The new analytical prisms that have been suggested, such as ET, RT, CI and EW analyses, are also supportive of eco-logical design. The hierarchy of eco-innovations would prioritize investment in research and designs that reverse the resource transfers that are causing social inequities and resource imbalances in the first place. We have said that the transfers of resources that are most critical to sustainability over the long term are arguably those that alienate land, resources and space to special interest control and decision-making (whether in the public or private sector). Eco-services and access to resources are shrinking through the gradual transfer of land and resource control to corporate interests, as they operate above governments. Privatization is not necessarily bad in itself, but such resource transfers and tradeoffs have not been subject to meaningful public oversight and accountability. We saw how environmental management, to an extent, can legitimize 'piracy' and unjust enrichment through 'selective' measurements and methods. The problem is even more conspicuous in the 'developing' world where, for example, some companies with access to minerals or oil rights in rainforests have destroyed whole rainforests and their populations' livelihoods, despite impact assessments. In the 'developed' world, by contrast, the alienation of the means of survival to special interests tends to be through more incremental and less visible processes. This is all the more reason why planning must take into account resource transfers in terms of their influence on future decisions and democratic decision processes.

## What are the resource transfers that will most affect future decisions?

We can select four among a seamless web of interconnected transfer processes that are largely irreversible, and therefore foreclose future options. As such, they are most relevant to sustainability:

1   From public to private interests (loss of future collective control)
2   From poor to wealthy (loss of individual self-determination)
3   From future to present generations (loss of future social choice and adaptive capacity)
4   From environment to development (loss of natural capital and ecosystem resilience)

The diagram in Box 52 shows four spheres of critical resource or wealth transfers via interrelated mechanisms. These socio-political and physical mechanisms can be direct or indirect, intentional or unintentional. These transfers can result in negative impacts through either:

•   Direct, physical design (externalities and internalities) or
•   Indirect transfers through the 'design' of institutional and economic mechanisms (expropriations, privatization and 'piratization')

We do not yet count all the *direct* negative impacts of design. We have not even begun to count *indirect* mechanisms (wealth by stealth). Because urban planners do not analyse existing systems in terms of resource transfers, there is little accountability for the gradual loss of urban amenity or wilderness.

## Surely we already hold industry accountable for externalities by now?

Negligent environmental practices of industrial manufacturing have gradually come under scrutiny (and some company CEOs have gone to jail). However, while designers and developers can be held accountable for structural flaws that caused buildings to collapse, they are not held accountable for slow damage to public health, let alone sustainability, through poor design. Yet more people die from non-sustainable development than from falling buildings. Other indirect institutional systems that have the effect of transferring wealth are sometimes totally immune from scrutiny. This is partly because our frameworks and concepts have tended to 'invisibilize' the idea of a public interest. We saw how the idea of a public good has been reduced to an atomistic conception of democracy as overlapping, pluralist interest-group struggle [Chapter 12].[12] Civil society is becoming an apparition. Simultaneously, corporations, regarded as 'fictional individuals', are given the status and rights of individuals in law in many cases.[13] Corporations can now even sue nations for imposing environmental standards that are deemed to restrain their opportunities to trade.[14] Civil society, in contrast, often lacks 'standing' to object to private actions that damage public health or threaten democratic rights over the long term.[15] For example, individuals and corporations can be held to account for toxic torts if these harm individuals measurably and excessively. However, they can still reduce the life spans and future options of an anonymous future 'public' with impunity.[16] The rights of millions of individuals can thus be outweighed by the rights of one fictional individual.

## But surely we hold corporations accountable for negligence?

We tend to ignore negligent behaviour if nature intervenes. When individuals are negligent, they can be held accountable for consequences to others, despite the unexpected intervention of people or objects. A series of repercussions that flow from one's negligent action may not alleviate one's responsibility if the intervening factors are man-made objects or variable human characteristics. For example, if one negligently causes an object to roll, causing a blind person to be injured, one may be deemed liable. However, if one's negligence has indirect impacts on the natural environment, which in turn causes downstream harm to people, the results can be quite different in practice. Intervening natural systems are often implicitly attributed to 'acts of God'. For instance, if hills are denuded by developers or foresters and this results in landslides or floods years later, individuals, governments and corporations may escape liability. We saw how many farmers have lost their livelihoods because water was not managed properly and more water rights were allocated than existed. The (then) Australian Prime Minister announced that people should 'pray for rain' – as if it were due to an act of God instead of the 'inaction' of governments and officials. (Another example of nature being blamed was the recent destruction of 30,000 homes by hot mudflows caused by drilling in Java.) Corporations often argue that nature's unwarranted response to our interventions breaks the chain of human accountability.[17] Remote downstream consequences in a complex system are not yet considered an adequate basis for limiting 'freedom to' generate wealth, let alone increasing 'freedom from' harm by others.

## Is that because it is too hard to anticipate and measure collateral damage?

Partly. But it is also because our environmental analysis frameworks are highly selective. Even though human health impacts were the initial reason for the creation of environmental protection laws and agencies, we under-estimate these cumulative impacts. It is difficult to measure incremental, cumulative negative impacts in a complex open system. However, internalities or unjust enrichment would be easy to measure: we could use the existing tax system to rectify these imbalances. We have chosen not to measure the inordinate benefits that a private organization receives due to, say, the past investment in economic growth made by governments. We never 'call in the loans', so to speak. Moreover, public infrastructure is often sold off below cost, under the guise of more efficient management. When negative impacts result from privatization, it is too late ecologically, and too difficult politically, to reverse the decision. This is despite the fact that the long-term effects of unjust enrichment could, in some instances, be greater than some of the externalities. When oil rights in a rainforest, a coastal area or wetlands are allocated, these decisions create enormous financial gains for a few, and close off future options for the many. We have seen that the ideologies that underlie the design of institutional mechanisms can bias outcomes. However, design of planning institutions themselves can actually work as transfer mechanisms.

## How can the design of planning institutions foster resource transfers?

All institutional mechanisms transfer resources. These include regulatory regimes, legislative structures, taxes, subsidies, and other sorts of incentives, doctrines and policies. Their design will tend to favour either the general public interest or special interests. There is a tendency, however, not to look at the outcomes of the design of the institutional systems that allocate resources. Systems are seen as neutral. Of course, there are regulatory impact assessments that analyse the economic costs and benefits of regulations. However, these assessments generally only compare costs and benefits within an economic framework. They set a monetary value on the lives lost or saved by environmental regulations. We also need to examine the long-term consequences of planning systems, to determine if they are making a contribution to more sustainable outcomes (as in ID analysis). Instead, as we have seen, planning agencies develop mission statements, lists of criteria and complex project assessment mechanisms. The problem with the view that 'if the process is right, the outcome will be right' is that it is an attempt at procedural automation. It avoids responsibility for substantive outcomes. Thus the response to 'that is unfair' is often 'but that is our system' (ie the system is accepted as a given).[18] We need to assess our planning systems themselves. It would be a relatively easy research task to see if planning and decision mechanisms are, in effect, transferring resources over time from public to private interests, poor to rich, future to present generations and nature to development.

## How do decision systems transfer resources from public to private?

A key question is not whether resources are controlled primarily in the public or private sector, but what checks and balances there are over the power to influence outcomes. Again, it is the *differentials* in power that shape future decisions, as power is a function of ownership or control of basic resources. Either government agencies and/or corporations can effectively privatize or 'piratize' natural capital through the absence of substantively democratic processes [Chapter 13]. Outsourcing to consultants (privatizing information) or trading systems (privatizing ecosystem goods and services) appear superficially to be merely administrative expediencies or means to implement policies. They are judged only by how well their internal aims are met, not their long-term consequences for social and ecological sustainability. This is because systems outcomes cannot be predicted and assessed without examining the transfer of resources from public to private control over time. It is partly this *lack* of critical, institutional analysis and open, democratic processes that has facilitated expropriations in the past (where resources are extracted from the public domain at below replacement cost). Control of the basic means of survival – whether in a bureaucracy or corporation – is not easily reversed. Unchecked control over resources will tend to increase the disparity of rich and poor and the loss of substantive democracy in a vicious spiral.

## Just how do institutions transfer resources from poor to rich?

Market-based systems are based on the assumption that markets will lead to the most efficient outcomes. But even if markets lead to lower prices and more efficient consumption, it does not mean a fair *distribution* of environmental values and amenities are assured over time. For example, if water is privatized, efficiencies may result – once water is so scarce that the cost is high enough. But by then it may be too late to save the environmental flows of water. And it can also mean some will be able to waste water while others must go without. Those who can pay can waste. Market-based environmental management tools do not address this kind of market failure. Wealth transfers also occur through:

- Specific conceptual tools or mechanisms like 'discounting', where future values are reduced to present values in analyses.
- Political decisions, deals and favours where ecological issues are seen as not especially relevant, and planning or environmental management advice is not deemed warranted.[19] Many kinds of political decisions have implications for both land use and sustainability, yet do not involve planners at all.
- Legislation where wealth is effectively transferred without the direct allocation of land or resources.[20] For example, mineral rights and trading systems create 'rights' to resources that separate the value from the land or water. Therefore, decisions are made without debate over the best use of the resources.

Infrastructure planning and physical design can compensate for some political and market failure by providing more public facilities and amenities. This would at least ensure that the poor have access to social or natural services, facilities and/or amenities [Box 48]. Even low-cost public facilities, such as parks, community education and urban gardens, can be somewhat re-distributive if they are suitable for access and use by *both* rich and poor. Improving the urban environment would be a relatively inexpensive way of reducing both the negative health, safety and life-quality impacts on the urban poor and the need for defensive expenditure by the rich. That is, the impacts of these negative transfers on life quality can be mitigated, if not reversed, by eco-retrofitting (without harming those who have the power to block Positive Development).

## How do institutions transfer resources from future to present?

We have emphasized how land-use decisions today determine the amount of resources, space and lifestyle options available in the future. Use of non-renewable fossil resources, 'terra-forming' through mining and the destruction of native forests are examples of resource decisions that change the ecology for all time and affect future power relationships. The design of development has not only changed the biophysical context irreversibly, it has created many artificial, unhealthy and constricting environments. These interventions in ecosystem functioning have reduced the carrying capacity and resilience of nature as well as reducing the quality of life. Some ways of reversing this pattern are to design development to:

- Be more reversible (design for disassembly, deconstruction, off-ground construction, low embodied energy, Green Space Walls and Green Scaffolding)
- Generate 'surplus' eco-services and create wider choices of responsible living arrangements (ie design for eco-services) [Box 15]
- Apply a hierarchy of eco-innovations, and the Green Optimum decision rule, to encourage investment in whole systems eco-efficiencies that make everyone better off

## And how do institutions transfer resources from nature to development?

The transfer of control from future to present generations occurs through the conversion of nature to fossil fuel-driven, industrialized forms of development. Industrial forms of design, to an extent, were guided by the values entrenched in, and perpetuated by, professional institutions. The past consequences of industrial interventions in natural systems have reduced eco-services and biodiversity, as well as human health and equity. We have seen how planning could counteract this tendency to substitute natural capital with machinery and equipment. ET analysis can provide clues for reinstituting natural systems that improve existing conditions and life quality. Some precedents we have noted are:

- Planning could start from the optimal ecological use of land and regenerate the urban ecology. For instance, many streams and rivers in urban areas have already been 'daylit', or uncovered and allowed to re-generate.[21]
- Natural sequence farming, which mimics natural landscapes in certain catchments, can successfully restore the soil structure, moisture and fertility of degraded farmland in some catchments (the 'emerald necklace' is an earlier precedent).[22]
- Eco-retrofitting with eco-roofs, Green Scaffolding and so on could reverse the loss of the ecological base and create habitats and nature corridors through urban areas [Box 15].

## Where do we begin to make the shift from vicious circles to virtuous cycles?

Creating planning systems that actively seek opportunities for Positive Development would reverse the 'negativity' of contemporary environmental politics, principles, plans, policies, programmes, procedures and prototypes. With the above redefinition of 'environmental impacts' as 'systems design problems' we, as a society, become accountable for the consequences of our behaviour. With this insight, it also becomes self-evident that problems created by design can be fixed by design. When we recognize that sustainability is a design problem, the possibility that future options could be increased without tradeoffs or additional costs becomes clearer. This is possible through eco-retrofitting our cities to expand the commons and natural environment in urban areas. It has been argued throughout this book that *direct action* through design is needed to make the paradigm shift required. However, incentives systems could be better designed as well. Instead of, for example, giving star ratings to buildings that are less bad, we can assign negative stars to existing buildings that are less than resource autonomous and/or give credit for creating positive off-site impacts and eco-services. Every new or retrofitted development should be able to make positive contributions to future generations, nature and ecosystems, the poor, and the general public. In fact, systems re-design is possible in every sphere. The four resource transfer areas identified by the diagrams and tables in Boxes 52 and 53 indicate priority areas where we can take actions in accordance with the Green Optimum. For example:

- **Economic sphere**: Wealth transfers from poor to rich (facilitated by mechanisms such as 'piratization', perverse subsidies and discounting) can be addressed by eco-innovations that decouple economic growth from environmental impacts through eco-retrofitting programmes, etc.
- **Planning sphere**: Transfers from future to present (eg loss of future social options and life quality) through conventional development can be addressed by planning processes that seek the highest ecological use of land and expand future options.
- **Government sphere**: Transfers of power from public to private (eg privatization of resource control) can be addressed by a constitution for decision-making based on deep sustainability principles, due process and community engagement.
- **Physical design**: Impact transfers (eg pollution and waste) from nature to industrial development can be addressed by the integration of natural systems into the built environment, the conversion of wastes to resources, and reversible, adaptable design.

## Given new criteria for eco-innovations, where do we get the design ideas?

If the environmental costs of the status quo outweigh the environmental benefits, then it makes sense to invest in fixing things now, rather than later. There is currently an excess of venture capital. Alternatively, we could divert both funds and manpower from the military towards constructive purposes. There is no shortage of work to be done or people to do it. There are millions of poor people seeking employment in most regions of the world and thousands of square miles of dreary, dilapidated structures in urban areas in both 'developed' and 'developing' nations to be upgraded. 'Charity' and 'aid' are somewhat politically unpopular, as is spending on healthcare, the environment and education (judging by how tax money is spent). However, eco-retrofitting would save society resources and money, and leave the urban poor better off than they are now – without aid or money being directly allocated to the poor. This could be done, for example, through a form of international performance contracting supported by an eco-service credit (as opposed to offset) trading scheme [Chapter 11]. Small loans to people in poor nations have proven remarkably successful as well.[23] To identify potential projects on different scales, indicators of 'design failure' can be used. The main indicator of poor systems design, of course, is what is often called market failure. Again, the term 'market failure' implies that no one is responsible. However, when the hand of the market is invisible, it is usually in the cookie jar. Market failure is a subset of political failure. Both are manifestations of poor systems design [Figure 17].

Figure 17 Design failure

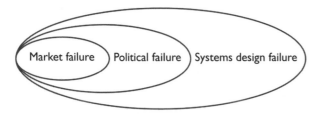

## Why does design failure continue despite our untapped human potential?

We have touched on some of the reasons for design failure throughout this book. Among these are that we rely on the private sector to provide public goods, we rely on the market to correct market failure and we rely on bean counters to correct design failure. When these approaches do not work, we assume we need more investment in these failed approaches. Because the reasons for design failure are system-wide and integral to our way of thinking, the reasons could be described in many different ways. However, some themes we have identified are:

- If we do not believe we can make net positive design impacts, we will not try. We will not take direct action to fix things, we will only try to mitigate the damage of status quo systems with the least change to the status quo.
- If we do not take design seriously, we will not develop design capacity, let alone create a place for 'opportunity creating' in environmental problem-solving. We will continue to ignore the opportunity cost of poor design and the public benefits of good design.
- If we do not believe inaction or non-decision is culpable, or we do not believe that governments should take direct action for whole systems improvements, bureaucracies will

continue to pass the buck ('non-decision' is just another form of decision).

- If we believe that markets are magical, we will not examine their long-term and whole-system outcomes, or make people accountable for outcomes – or even make the market work more fairly (eg through full cost pricing of resources).

Thus how we describe problems and define reasons for the perpetuation of deleterious resource transfers will affect our solutions or cause us to go round and round in vicious circles.

## How do we reconstruct such problem definitions to create positive solutions?

Let us examine the reasons just listed – the lack of a design culture, avoidance of direct action, failure to implement full cost pricing and failure to consider opportunity costs.

### Design

An alternative to total reliance on the market is design and innovation. Of course, design solutions must work within the given political context and market system. They must also fit into the existing physical configuration of land-use and transportation systems. This is a challenge. In this context, what appears the cheapest design solution in the market – because it fits the suboptimal systems context – is often not very efficient from an ecological and long-term perspective. Good design cannot only help to transform society, it can add value to the ecology. The market cannot do this: it only adds commercial clutter, glam and glitter. The market is not 'lean and mean' in terms of products, materials and waste. There is no reason to increase efficiency – or to change the modus operandi – if one is doing well through cheaper access to resources, transport and labour, the elimination of competition, and/or the transfer of risks and impacts to others [Box 49].

### Direct action

Governments are not supposed to 'intervene' in the market, today's 'altar to the human spirit'. Therefore producers and consumers currently use complex and costly institutional incentive mechanisms to encourage behaviour change. Of course, indirect incentives and regulations are both part of the mix of available solutions, and should be used where ecologically rational and cost effective. However, both types of (positive and negative) incentives have unpredictable consequences, due to the potential for many intervening forces. There is really no reason for governments not to take direct action to fix problems using existing eco-logical design solutions. The only reason not to save resources and money by design is blind obedience to an ideology that created the problems in the first place (a vicious circle).

### Full cost pricing

Means of making the economy more rational from a whole systems perspective have been proposed by ecological economists (and largely ignored by mainstream economists). Full cost pricing is often presented as a solution. It certainly makes sense, and could replace many costly regulatory and incentives schemes. However, it has not yet been politically feasible due, apparently, to things like fear on the part of politicians of raising costs to consumers. Somehow it seems easier to subsidize rainwater tanks or photovoltaic cells than to charge more for water or energy. Regulations and incentives create jobs in bureaucracies for overseeing compliance activity (or designing web-based forms) to disseminate transaction costs. Design solutions, in the meantime, could create new green businesses while solving problems created by, among other things, the lack of full cost pricing.

**Opportunity cost**

In analysing the relative costs and benefits of proposed developments, the opportunity cost should be a central consideration. Most land-use development is irreversible, so the optimal use of land from an ecological as well as social perspective is critical. Similarly, the costs of inaction to improve existing development can be higher than the costs of action. But planning should also identify ecological and social problems that can be solved by development. That is, we should look at potential 'opportunity gains' as well as 'opportunity costs'. Some oppose development in general, and some oppose the environment in general, but environmental mediation by design has shown that the two groups can find common ground to create win–win–win outcomes. NGOs, partnerships and third sector businesses can act without waiting for governments.

Chapter 15 partially summarizes the preceding chapters and outlines a process for approaching the design of net Positive Development through community-led planning.

# 15
# The SmartMode Process

## From technocratic to integrated planning and design

We have seen that our environmental management planning and decision-making methods and processes virtually all reflect a fatalistic belief – that the built and natural environments are inevitably in a zero sum relationship. This has led to the use of tradeoffs for externalizing conflict away from development planning and control systems. We cannot predict negative impacts in a complex environmental and social system, but we can find opportunities to take direct action to increase the urban ecology. We cannot eliminate poverty in a market system entirely, but we can give everyone a higher quality of life. Change will not come from the market and political arenas simply because it would be rational, however. Our discussion has shown that there is a vacuum created by government and industry structures. It would appear that only the community sector can catalyse change is the community. NGOs could begin by creating exemplars of net Positive Development, in partnership with government and industry. This chapter provides some guidance to this process. Some principles, concepts, procedures and criteria for a more *positive* community-based, opportunity-creating approach have been identified. We have looked at:

- Eco-solutions using natural systems that can increase both the ecological base and public estate
- Environmental planning, design and management methods and tools that can assist in the transition from negative to positive actions
- Structural principles and organizational forms that planning for sustainability and eco-governance would entail

To reverse the negative approach in environmental management, planning and design, we have developed a positive approach, called SmartMode. The SmartMode process attempts to integrate innovation with development, and design with planning. It aims to turn development into a sustainability solution that generates net positive improvements over past ecological, social and economic conditions. The SmartMode process could be applied by a community group, a cooperative, a public–private+community partnership, or a new planning sphere. This chapter reviews some steps and concepts in the SmartMode process that can help to bypass intellectual and institutional barriers to change through direct action for Positive Development. The basic steps are:

1 Establish common ground on sustainability concepts
2 Adopt a constitution for decision-making
3 Articulate project objectives and criteria
4 Conduct forensic audits for new information
5 Consider 'how and what' to trace and measure
6 Select appropriate methods and tools
7 Develop planning information, concepts and strategies
8 Develop design strategies
9 Apply self-assessment
10 Apply external assessment
11 Ensure relevant measurements
12 Assess accountability and performance

We have noted that planning, design and decision systems should be tailored to the nature of the problem, context and specific issues at hand. Therefore the SmartMode approach is a checklist of considerations or reference points, not a prescriptive process. The above steps could occur simultaneously or in a different order, and so on. The following outline is *not* comprehensive and is *not* meant to stand alone. However, it summarizes many of the principles articulated in the book. This '12 step programme' for recovery from addiction to negative thinking and fatalism is meant to be flexible and adaptable. Positive Development projects can be seen as 'baby steps', changing behaviour by working together to change systems through big or little, but manageable, direct actions.

## Step 1: Establish Common Ground on Sustainability Concepts

The first stage in the SmartMode process involves making assumptions and values explicit, and agreeing on goals, ground-rules and processes. This investment in communication is to avoid costly misunderstandings or crossed wires later on. Key issues are put on the table at the outset. These include people's conceptions of sustainability: differing values, goals, problem definitions and terminology. We saw that most planning and futures thinking tools try to be value neutral (or 'positivist') and valueless (or 'post-modern'), which only protects the status quo from introspection. The status quo means increasing polarization of wealth and irreversible ecological decline and ultimately, some would argue, genocide. So Positive Development is, in contrast, a substantively rational goal. The debate should thus focus on different means and priorities to achieve sustainability, not partisan values or interests. Sustainability should be the point of departure, not something to be re-invented.

### Definition of sustainability [Introduction]

If a project team or community group is serious about working for sustainability, they will adopt a strong definition similar to that presented in this book – preserving and expanding future options. Without this fundamental paradigm shift to a sustainability standard, we will only continue to take 'less bad' steps in the wrong direction. This would not be worth an NGO's time. The strong definition of sustainability recognizes that nature is a living ecosystem – not a set of inputs and outputs. The alternative – the economists' notion of 'substitution' of natural capital and environments by manufactured or built capital – denies future generations meaningful choices. Substitution in physical development has meant the replacement of fertile, life-giving environments with sterile boxes (however uniquely shaped). Further, democratic processes become impotent over time if resources and land are alienated through non-sustainable allocation and distribution systems. Physical development must secure universal access to the means of survival. Otherwise future generations will lose any meaningful say about the means of survival – let alone their quality of life. If we leave future generations 'ecologically bankrupt', they cannot choose to create a sustainable society, as the decision will come too late.

### Open values and goals

Once the 'non-negotiable' bottom line is understood, and true ecological and social sustainability is agreed on, it is necessary to arrive at a mutual understanding of different points of view regarding planning goals and design objectives. It is *not* necessary to share philosophical beliefs, political positions or lifestyle choices in order to agree on basic design criteria and solutions. However, differing perspectives and potential differences in tastes, values or preferences can be signalled from the outset and accommodated through design. The aim is not to agree, but to find design solutions that satisfy all interests. Negotiating, bargaining and tradeoff frameworks lead to 'them versus us' attitudes. Design, in contrast, has the unique 'potential' to satisfy all interests, if people participate in good faith. If the ethical bases of processes are explicit and are agreed, it will help to avoid power games or backroom deals. A fundamental decision principle is that actions must aim to make the public as a whole better off, without causing either unjust enrichment or harm to others (the Green Optimum). If this does not materialize, our decision frameworks will continue to offset negatives with mitigation measures, not improvements.

### Collaboration and inclusion

The design process should be undertaken with the confidence that win–win–win solutions can be reached. In participatory design teams, whether cross-sector (eg government–business–community, or rural–urban) or cross-disciplinary (eg professional–academic–lay citizen), it is important to make all decisions in the open. A common pattern in conventional design processes is 'performance anxiety'. When group members lack confidence, they may unconsciously undermine the process or project. Collaborative design and charrette-type processes help to bypass insecurities by sharing initiative, talent and action. Also, where environmental and development interests may conflict, it is necessary to avoid hidden agendas. Participants should therefore agree to bring any concerns to meetings for open discussion and resolution, and to discuss any relevant ex-camera discussions. A memorandum of understanding (MOU) should set out the contribution that each participant will make. There should also be the 'right of veto' if it can be shown that any final design solutions or proposed actions are not 'fair' to any legitimate public interests.

### Common terminology

Language is critical to social change. Language enforces the status quo automatically by confining creative thinking and positive action to established concepts. An extensive set of new terms has therefore been suggested in the belief that paradigm shifts are facilitated by – or even require – a new language [Glossary]. Of course, any new term will always be co-opted over time, just as the term 'sustainability' itself is often used to dress up business-as-usual. Terms and concepts will also get absorbed and watered down by dominant paradigm forces. For example, we saw that sustainability in the built environment fields came to mean social sustainability, as *ecological* sustainability was implicitly assumed to be impossible. Hence the ecology continues to be traded off for relatively short-term social gains. New and/or explicitly defined terms help to ensure that concepts are understood by all and there is just one working definition among participants.

### Problem definition and identification [Chapter 1]

We have seen how problem descriptions and method of analysis can constrain the range of solutions to preconceived goals. If our problem definitions were correct, our problems would have been solved long ago. It is therefore a useful exercise to see how participants define the key issues. For example, the 'problem' is often defined as, say, to build a five-star building, reduce waste to landfill or develop indicators for green field development. But these problem definitions already presuppose the mitigation of the outcomes of conventional practices – not re-design. Such narrow conceptions of the problem circumscribe thinking to marginal changes *within* the building, waste stream or suburb. Such solutions could therefore have ill-considered side-effects. Rather than beginning with a development proposal and making it better, the SmartMode process starts 'outside the box' with the contextual issues. It looks for opportunities to reverse inequities, imbalances or waste caused by existing systems of development and design. We can start with a general problem (identified, say, by RT analysis, as below) and design a public initiative to address it that generates positive ripple effects in the surrounding area.

After achieving a shared understanding of Positive Development and an agreement on basic problem definitions, decision rules, project and purposes, a 'constitution' of fundamental rights and responsibilities should be developed and/or adopted, as below.

## Step 2: Adopt a Constitution for Decision-Making

Step 1 was intended to ensure participants have an understanding of biophysical sustainability and its integral relationship to design. This second step aims to ensure an understanding of the democratic dimension of sustainability and its integral relationship to design. Design has the capacity to transcend value and ideology conflicts. In a collaborative design process, however, it is essential to have substantive due process (fair outcomes) and procedural due process (fair rules of engagement) [Chapter 13]. This is true whether the undertaking is at the neighbourhood planning level or the international level. There can be no genuine community participation without due process protections. Otherwise the process can be subverted, or the agenda changed midstream, by the more powerful parties. This often happens.

### Substantive due process principles [Chapter 13]

Substantive due process principles can be framed in terms of the rights and responsibilities of the parties. The right to sustainability and genuine democracy means *freedom from* harm to health and safety. This includes freedom from a gradual erosion of environmental quality over time. For instance, people should not be deemed to have agreed to have their rights eroded just because their 'vote' for a political party or personality has that ultimate effect. In essence, the current social order protects the *freedom to* occupy and exploit the public estate, as long as individuals are not unduly harmed (the Pareto Optimum). Thus, we have seen that:

- Small doses of carcinogens are sometimes portrayed as acceptable as long as they are not lethal and we cannot measure the extent to which they will 'shorten' life spans
- Poverty is treated as if it were acceptable because it is not an immediate cause of death, at least when nature intervenes (eg as in Bangladesh or New Orleans floods)

With any set of rights, 'responsibilities' are implied. The Earth Charter can serve as a guide, because it has acquired legitimacy through an extensive process of community engagement and participation in different nations and at the international level. Some of the 'substantive' decision principles that were discussed in the text could become elements of a constitution for Positive Development. For example:

- Sustainability is a basic human right for all, not a 'value' to be weighed along with other preferences. 'Freedom from' harm does not mean 'freedom to' seek disproportionate benefits from community and nature.
- All actions, decisions and design should aim to make everyone better off by improving society's current and future condition, through interventions in existing systems of development to generate positive effects in the surrounding area.
- Direct action and/or investment should be undertaken to improve the eco-effectiveness of systems. Relying on complex incentive schemes to get others to act is uncertain, and often means tradeoffs or wealth transfers without net positive gains.
- A sustainability standard is required, as incremental improvements upon existing trends often reinforce non-sustainable templates. While incremental 'actions' are often necessary, incremental 'standards' impede innovation.
- Natural and national security should be increased by replacing fossil with renewable fuels, as fossil fuels threaten the sustainability of democracy and the life-support system itself.

### Procedural due process principles [Chapter 13]

If everyone has an inviolate right to sustainability and genuine democracy, all people should have 'standing' to object to unfair processes and outcomes – whether affecting themselves, other communities, future generations or perhaps even other species. Remarkably, most legal systems only allow immediate stakeholders the right to object to environmental decisions that will affect their future democratic and constitutional rights. Again, neither the agenda nor 'rules of the game' should be changed midstream without consensus. Meetings should not become a ratification of partisan ex-camera deals. A written agreement to abide by due process principles and attribute sources of ideas or work is an indicator of good will. On smaller projects, a constitution for decision-making might appear as a memorandum of understanding (MOU) between project partners. On larger projects, the constitution would be part of a formal contract. Thus some considerations are that:

- Participatory democracy and substantive public engagement in development planning, design and decisions, and subsequent management, require that pre-agreed due process principles are built into project development and operations.
- Transparency includes the requirement that group members report any 'ex-camera' negotiations or discussions aimed at influencing decisions. Reasons for controversial design and planning decisions should also be in writing and contestable.
- Collaborative design processes (eg charrettes) can prevent future conflict, and provide creative contributions, while including a broad range of diverse input from a cross-section of interests, not restricted to the immediate stakeholders.
- Participants should have the right of veto if it can be shown that a design proposal violates agreed sustainability principles. Good design should be able to meet almost any legitimate objections within a sustainability framework.
- A sustainability ombudsman should be included in the planning and design process, as financial stakeholders cannot adequately represent future generations in decisions affecting the means of survival (eg even indigenous or green groups can be 'bought off').

### Ground rules for investments [Chapter 2]

The purpose of public-oriented projects is to make society better off (the Green Optimum).

Therefore, public–private+community partnerships should be considered as vehicles for the design and implementation of a project. Agreements must ensure that business and government agencies cannot highjack the project after others have contributed labour and time. This requires some kind of formal cost-, risk- and profit-sharing. The partnership should also be structured to prevent 'unjust enrichment'. Once the agreed benefits and/or profits are distributed to the partnership members (community, business, government), extra profits should be re-invested in other Positive Developments. Some financially-related matters that should be sorted out early are:

- Consideration of performance contracting, where a partnership would provide energy-efficiency services at little or no cost to clients and recover their costs and profits from the reduced energy, water or sewage bills.
- Agreement at the outset that parties to a partnership should receive a portion of the benefits of cost savings after costs are recovered, and/or that some of these savings be put into a separate fund to be rolled over to fund other eco-retrofitting projects.
- NGOs ensuring protection of their intellectual property, as often conventional community participation is inadvertently used to transfer intellectual capital by government agencies without remuneration.
- Linking designer's fees, credits or awards to post-occupancy sustainability indicators, perhaps on a sliding scale (or a percentage of fee withheld). Designer's fees are usually tied to construction costs without much incentive for design achievement.
- Programme, action, policy and strategic prioritization of tried and tested, cost-effective eco-solutions that avoid negative impacts should be considered before hi-tech solutions, capital-intensive approaches are adopted.

## Partnering tools [Chapter 2]

Each sector has its own universe of agendas, values and frameworks. Partnering (where parties work collaboratively and share responsibility for innovations and errors) can help bridge the public–private, community–government and sectional divides. There are many books and websites that provide workshop tools and guidance on participatory planning processes and cooperative enterprises, so these are not canvassed here. Instead, the focus should *not* be on 'What if?' or 'Yes, but'. It should be on 'Why not?' Partnerships should consider the life-cycle of the project and:

- Help to avoid an adversarial culture of development versus conservation. Partnering agreements should be written (or contractual) so that parties cannot change the agenda, or charge extra where another has made mistakes.
- Build in commissioning and ongoing facilities management practices from the outset to ensure ontinuous improvement in health standards and ongoing ecological modernization. This requires the involvement of biologists in facilities management.
- Consider qualification-based selection of a design team (wherein the fee is negotiated after the designer is chosen). This facilitates collaboration between designers and clients and can promote mutual education on sustainable design issues.
- Specify a sustainability standard in the architectural brief and contracts. That is, require designs to be net positive and improve off-site systems (social, psychological and biological) health. Where this is not achieved, the process should allow others to challenge the design.
- Establish a design reporting process to ensure that eco-logical solutions are considered from the outset, and that the partnering process leads to mutual education (below), not just another administrative process.

## Step 3: Articulate Project Objectives and Criteria

Once decision principles, processes and rules are agreed upon, specific project goals can be set. For convenience, some sample goals are repeated here under separate physical and social headings. The design brief should ensure that such goals are not to be traded off. Economic goals are not included here, as financial interests have adequate means to look after themselves. Further, economics and accounting tools are too often seen as ends in themselves, rather than means. (As we have said, such tools are only legitimate to the extent that they serve broader social and environmental goals.) For present purposes, the economic question is only to determine if Positive Development is a relatively good investment. The broader issue is whether there are better ways of solving problems in the existing built environment from a whole systems perspective.

### Biophysical design goals [Chapter 1]

Project planning and design goals tend to be at either end of a spectrum between very general performance statements that give no real guidance and prescriptive design solutions that, if applied categorically, can turn out to be wrong in a particular context. The definition of sustainability used in this book has suggested the following basic goals for biophysical development. For convenience, the criteria in Box 15 are repeated here. They can devolve into more specific goals related to the planning area or project. The project should:

- Exceed 'resource autonomy' (ie self-sufficient energy production, water and waste treatment), creating positive on-site and off-site impacts that increase the ecological base and resource security by integrating natural systems with development.
- Increase conditions for eco-services in cities (ie provide conditions and space for the production of healthy food, air, water and soils through natural systems) to improve the ecological viability and self-sufficiency of the surrounding areas.
- Actively restore and increase natural habitats and biodiversity (variety of genes, species and/ or ecosystems) by design that accommodates, and provides habitats for, appropriate indigenous species – rather than just 'mimicking' ecosystems.
- Reduce land coverage while increasing natural capital in buildings and development by creating 'ecological space', or the multi-functional use of space for human and natural functions, such as offices in atriums (or vice versa) that clean the water and air.
- Plan, design and manage development to proactively improve human and environmental health – not just reduce toxins (eg provide opportunities for social interaction, exercise, semi-outdoor spaces and healthy food production).
- Consider replacing resource and capital-intensive machines with natural microbes that work for 'free'. (For patented microbes it should have to be established that no natural life-form can feasibly achieve the same function.)
- Where appropriate, use organic, compostable, adaptable and renewable resources and materials instead of mined (high embodied waste) materials. Ensure bio-based materials are grown sustainably and avoid toxic binders, solvents and so on.
- Increase natural and national security, avoidance of fossil fuel dependency, decentralized energy, and urban food production. Urban areas should be eco-productive and self-sufficient in order to cope with civil emergencies, severe weather events and so on.
- Maximize passive solar heating, cooling and ventilating systems, as these are more efficient than fossil fuels in embodied and operating energy, waste, water, and materials. Ensure solar design is not 'under-designed', as it often is.

## Social design goals [Chapter 1]

Most planning processes state broad social goals that are very general so that, while no one can disagree with them, there is no commitment to specific action. Targets that are really policy statements are often not taken seriously ('encourage more education', 'reduce crime', etc). The definition of sustainability used here suggests the following general design goals for social wellbeing, equity and choice. As with the above biophysical goals and process principles, social goals will vary according to the specific area and situation, and should be translated into more specific goals that are relevant to particular communities. Such goals should:

- Be based on an analysis of the inequities of the existing surrounding area or city, through mapping of resource transfers, conducting needs surveys, and equity mapping or assessment of the accessibility of green space, public facilities and so on.
- Designed to expand responsible future options and social choice, recognizing that legitimate values and needs can change over time – instead of making irreversible (even if incremental) choices that future generations will have to live with.
- Generate positive off-site impacts to correct social and economic deficiencies of the surrounding environment (eg reduce the urban heat island effect, provide day-care and playgrounds, landscape nearby areas).
- Begin from the public interest and ecology to ensure that everyone (the entire public) is left better off. Ensure access and use of built environments by disabled people and the elderly through 'design for adaptability', 'design for accessibility', and so on.
- Identify community-wide needs (public health, welfare, equity, safety, etc) as central criteria. Develop explicit criteria for wider community values (economic, cultural and psychological) – not just specific 'client' needs.
- Re-examine concepts of 'personal needs' through active engagement in participatory design processes. Maximize dedicated public spaces for social interaction, sense of community and sense of place (as well as safety and health requirements and so on).

## Step 4: Conduct Forensic Audits

Once the organizational matters and broad goals are agreed, the community group, or public–private+community partnership, can begin to identify priority areas for Positive Development or eco-innovation projects. Various auditing processes can be requested from governments to acquire information and inspiration upon which to base projects and designs (that is if governments become service providers). A forensic audit can identify significant unilateral transfers of human and natural resources (RT analysis), trace these impacts back to causes (ID analysis), compare current to initial bioregional conditions (ET analysis), and determine the ongoing costs of current development (CI analysis). Mapping these flows – notionally or quantitatively, depending on the scale of the project – will assist in determining priorities for direct positive action.

These analyses can be simply workshop thinking tools or large-scale research exercises. In either case, cross-disciplinary and cross-sector workshops can help at various stages to identify critical elements, flows, system boundaries, and key social and natural resource issues. This fourth step should precede the selection of decision and innovation tools (below), as these often conceal contextual issues, and limit parameters to 'the known'. For example, we have seen how most tools confuse the environmental with the ecological dimension. Thus the SmartMode process identifies systems or environments that can be improved before selecting specific decision tools that help to select among variables.

### Identify linear resource flows and waste [Chapter 8]

If there are limited resources (eg of time, money or staff), a simple waste analysis can be undertaken by private firms, communities or public agencies. The identification of linear flows undertaken as a separate exercise can be a shortcut to finding eco-efficiencies that will create a return on investment. For example, local councils or industries might find a supply of low-cost local materials or, conversely, customers for discards.

- An abridged version of an MFA and/or LCA of, say, a region, farm or city, may uncover significant inefficiencies. These expose places where loops can be closed or even utilize the past build up of waste, toxins and so on.
- Equity mapping could expose areas where a pattern of unilateral choices has disadvantaged some, and where we could, say, create jobs in retrofitting or creating public amenities to reduce inequities.

Small-scale audits should not stop at 'picking the lowest fruit', however. For entrepreneurial purposes, looking for areas of waste, and assessing inputs and outputs, may be sufficient for purposes of saving money or reducing pollution through eco-efficiencies. Such projects could, however, conflict with whole systems eco-solutions. The following analyses can help to identify whole systems issues that Positive Development projects can address.

### Question key flows [Chapter 9]

MFAs can identify flows of materials and energy but seldom, if ever, do they look at emotional and social resources, let alone the ecology (again, nature as a living, as opposed to a dead, resource). An exception here may be instructive. An Australian charity found people eager to go from homeless shelters in cities to work on farms where there was a labour shortage. Many of these 'no hopers' later found rural jobs with their new skills. So their resources were utilized, but in a way that they felt benefited them. Of course, not every aspect of complex systems can be traced and analysed, however, so it is necessary to select key stocks and flows. Some examples of flows that might be considered include:

- Basic materials (cement)
- Elements (phosphorus)
- Dust (toxins, microbes)
- Wealth (money)
- Substances (water)
- Pollination (partner plants and insects)
- Food (nutrients)
- Energy (embodied, operational)
- Space (volume)
- Timber (on public or private land)
- Migration
- Time (effort)

### Ecological transformation (ET) analysis [Chapter 10]

Given diminished carrying capacity, mass extinctions and biodiversity losses, land-use planning decisions should begin from the best ecological use of the land. Paradoxically, forward thinking requires looking back to original ecological benchmarks. Mapping indigenous conditions can provide insights into better future land use or non-use. We usually just start from the present situation. Where such analyses are used, they usually measure progress from the current (degraded) condition, so any project that appears 'relatively' harmless is good enough. Instead, by comparing the biophysical impacts of existing development to pre-developed or natural conditions, specific ideas for eco-restoration and eco-retrofitting may also be inspired (ie biomimicry on a regional scale). ET analysis would, among other things:

- Map the original biodiversity of the bioregion to ensure that new or retrofitted developments contribute to the restoration of appropriate ecological communities, as well as enhancing environmental flows in general.
- Determine the optimal use of land and preserve areas for positive ecological functions in urban areas – as opposed to just keeping development off unstable or flood-prone land, or only protecting ecosystems where land is unsuitable for development.
- To set planning targets that are net positive, compare environmental flows in existing development to initial, indigenous conditions. That is, use the original ecology as the baseline – not relative standards, like improvements over 'typical' buildings.

## Resource transfer (RT) analysis [Chapter 8]

Decision tools have not encompassed issues of democracy and distribution – the growing concentration of decision-making power and political influence. Planning analyses have been largely descriptive of existing conditions and general goals, and ignore transfers of wealth and resources over time. When we look at 'environmental injustice' (eg the distribution of pollution), we usually ignore unjust enrichment. Again, inequitable control of land, space and resources will ultimately lead to the abuse of power. Constructive thinking, paradoxically, requires criticism and introspection. By exposing the transfers of land and resources that have occurred over time, the political momentum may be generated to reverse the increasing disparities of wealth. RT analysis would among other things:

- Map cumulative wealth transfers, such as poor to rich, rural to urban, nature to development, and future to present – rather than just aggregating negative impacts or diminishing stocks of resources [Boxes 52 and 53].
- Look at unjust enrichment, not just which groups benefit and which groups lose in relation to each other. In the past, social impact analysis has tended not to look at internalities, and has focused on the poverty half the equation.
- Map de facto transfers of public spaces to negative space – the inappropriate conversion of common areas to private corporate use and control (eg enclosure). Dead space offers opportunities to increase the urban ecology and public estate.

## Institutional design (ID) analysis [Chapter 9]

Inequitable resource transfers are inextricably linked with resource-allocation structures and processes. Despite statistics about the cumulative losses of natural capital, these losses are seldom traced through the resource-allocation processes and land-use systems that underlie them. They are seen instead as an inevitable by-product of any kind of progress. It can be pointless to fix problems if the initial causes remain. By tracing differentials of power, influence and resource flows to changes in legal and regulatory systems – and environmental management policies, regulations and incentives in particular – we may be able to invent corrective mechanisms. An awareness of the failings of our current institutional systems can help us avoid repeating the familiar patterns of unilateral resource transfers. ID analysis would aim to ensure that:

- Institutional mechanisms do not 'expropriate' previous rights or options (eg laws, regulations or processes that reduce rights or access to means of survival).

- Economic frameworks do not transfer wealth through inequitable *externalities* (where costs are transferred by private interests to the general public) or *internalities* (where inordinate benefits are received by a few at the expense of the general public).
- Redistributive planning and design precepts do not have negative outcomes for the wider public. If there is no limit on resource acquisition (or at least what was once called 'betterment' in planning), disparities of wealth will increase.
- Market-based mechanisms are not used without considering the long-term consequences. Price is currently the key driver of efficiency, but prices, thus far, have not reflected the true value of resources, and full cost pricing has been avoided.
- Technological conventions do not 'intervene' in natural systems and reduce natural capital, life-support systems and eco-services. Past forms of industrial technology have not been efficient from a whole systems (ie ecological) view.

Citizen bioregional mapping exercises can be useful in identifying the significant historical origins of negative resource transfers and fostering understanding of the causes of interventions in natural systems through human-designed infrastructure and institutions.

### Costs of inaction (CI) analysis [Chapter 7]

To create a more positive problem-identifying and opportunity-creating approach to planning and design, we need to identify the ongoing costs of designed waste that eco-retrofitting and eco-innovation could address. CI analysis can also be used to prioritize problems to address, and to put eco-retrofitting projects on an equal footing in cost–benefit type considerations. CI analysis would consider such matters as the following:

- It is often argued that we cannot change to solar energy because of the infrastructure and jobs already allocated to fossil fuels; that is, we consider the sunk cost when deciding to invest in fossil fuel research and development (a risky public investment).
- We seldom count the public funds already spent in cleaning up the externalities of fossil fuel and nuclear sources of energy, but we do count the public funds already invested in solar energy as a negative, even though solar energy avoids many of the externalities of fossil fuels.
- Impact assessments do not 'weigh in' the relative benefits of natural systems and their potential to replace high-maintenance, capital-intensive urban infrastructure. Approvals are still based on relativity, not sustainability.
- On a pristine site, no ecological 'compensation' is required, only social compensation, because we cannot increase the carrying capacity of nature. Also, green field development can, in some cases, make it easier to claim 'offsets' (such as locating near public transport).
- Existing development control and rating tools are biased towards green field development because they ignore embodied waste. Using criteria based on new buildings will favour new buildings.

## Step 5: Consider 'How and What' to Trace and Measure

For comprehensive 'rurban' and 'glocal' planning purposes, identifying waste, linear flows or imbalances in inputs or outputs is not adequate. A complete regional planning exercise or audit requires questioning basic planning assumptions. A SmartMode approach would therefore make the assumptions of a study explicit, and question the determination of any systems boundaries or parameters. Such questions hopefully provide a 'reality check'.

## Question assumptions [Chapter 4]

We tend to limit analyses by excluding long-term social and environmental consequences that appear ambiguous. The impacts of planning policies on the concentration of wealth have generally been seen as too 'remote' to include in analyses. This is despite the fact that they are an inevitable consequence of planning and other resource-allocation processes. What is excluded is as important to think about as what is included:

- Because we reduce everything to energy and/or money, we have devalued time, space and human resources. Hence we ignore ecological waste – the time and space it takes to recover the resource base – not to mention 'brain waste' (lost human resources and talent).
- The focus on mitigating impacts of standard buildings and products has meant that we have largely ignored the inefficiencies of the development supply chain (eg resource extraction) and building life-cycle (eg maintenance) that are driven by design.

## Question 'system' boundaries [Chapter 8]

As we know, in nature and society there are no real boundaries. To conduct a quantitative analysis, however, it is usually necessary to determine the key parameters, relevant scope and boundaries of the project area. Yet boundary definitions can obscure recognition of some causal issues. Community–expert workshops, focus groups and charrettes can assist in determining boundaries, salient issues, flows, parameters, obstructions and limits. A couple of examples are:

- Catchment planning often just looks at one part of a river system, whereas the supply of water to the catchment is affected by development elsewhere (eg global warming, tree clearing, salination, and terraforming through mining and infrastructure).
- Sciences often look at a problem from a disciplinary base. (For example, salinity is shaped by rock formations, as well as by the water table and other geographic, tree and climatic phenomena. Therefore, physical barriers to salinity have sometimes failed.)

The assumption has been that the boundaries must coincide. The boundaries of the region, industry or material to be analysed may have very different kinds of parameters (eg a bioregion versus a river system). Therefore various maps in a regional audit may not need to have the same boundaries. Comparing maps of different orders and scales (social, economic and environmental) can be of heuristic value by exposing both contrasts and parallels. Different maps might include:

- A geographical area (eg industrial system, region, river system)
- Critical social issues (eg access to space, concentration of wealth)
- Specific material or energy flows in relation to their source in nature
- Changes to ecological conditions (eg biodiversity) over time due to development
- Privatization of basic resources over time
- Reduction of the public estate (or increase of negative space) over time
- Waste or other impacts in the supply chain
- The impediments to change (eg lack of public transport)

## Question 'project' boundaries [Chapter 2]

Rather than a development 'site' becoming a boundary for design, a development project should become a leverage point for disseminating sustainable design throughout the wider area. Buildings can be re-conceptualized in relation to environmental flows through cities and regions. For example:

- The neighbours of the site (and potential objectors) could be consulted regarding their future needs and interests with respect to the preferred site. Their active collaboration could be enlisted. This would also foster design and sustainability education.

- The boundaries of the building itself should be questioned. For example, we have seen that roofs and walls can become ecosystems (terrariums, aviaries and/or aquariums) that produce clean air, water and soil as well as heating, cooling and ventilating.
- The site boundaries should be questioned. To increase housing, for instance, we can eco-retrofit existing buildings, or convert some suburbs into more intense co-housing developments, where some facilities and garden areas are shared.
- Ensure the development creates the widest variety of positive off-site impacts (eg reducing the heat island effect, generating cool breezes, creating nature corridors, recycling water from nearby buildings, and/or providing habitat for endangered birds, butterflies, frogs, etc.

## Step 6: Select Appropriate Methods and Tools

### Appropriate tools [Chapter 10]

It is important to select appropriate analytical tools and decision aids that align with the contextual issues and critical flows identified in the above processes. We need to be aware of the pros, cons and limitations of available methods. Community groups or partnerships need to ensure that government agencies conduct studies relevant to sustainability, and also that appropriate methods are used. These tools are subsidiary, however, and should not be allowed to supplant design processes. In the selection and/or design of analytical tools, some considerations include:

- LCA assesses the efficiency by which resources are used, but can tend to limit solutions to incremental design improvements. It can be too complicated for complex systems problems. It can also influence design by reducing living nature to inputs and outputs.
- MFA can help to identify the scale and ramifications of waste. However, it has not yet been used to chart transfers of resources, land or space among sectors, classes, regions or special interests. Where applied as an input–output method, it can lose its potential as a systems thinking tool.
- Futures thinking tools can assist group design processes. However, these tools are geared towards enhancing a group's relative position in a given context, rather than re-designing the development context to make all parties better off.
- GPIs, unlike GDP, may record externalities, defensive expenditure and loss of natural capital as 'negatives', but they do not record the loss of substantive democracy, the public estate or the ecological base over time. They are mainly useful for perceptions and preferences.
- EF analysis links consumption to land, carrying capacity and global equity issues. It conveys the spatial and resource limits of development. In practice, however, it tends to focus on aggregate consumption, as if it were evenly distributed among groups of people.
- EIA methods predict the collateral damage of designs in order to mitigate or offset the future risks that the project will create. However, they do not assist in adding ecological value, or in guaranteeing performance and ongoing improvements in built environments.

The above tools can be seen as potential subsets of SmartMode, as they are subsidiary to *design* for democracy and ecology. SmartMode starts from the perspective of improving public 'health and wellbeing' and works to change the underlying physical and social structures that prevent whole systems health. It is analogous to focusing on healthy food instead of dieting.

**Avoid biases [Chapter 7]**

Traditionally, citizens can challenge facts and decisions, but not the underlying methodological biases. Since planning tools have been derived from non-ecologically-based disciplines, they tend to create a bias against sustainability. Whether we measure more or less is not the issue: it is the double standards in what we measure. Examples of some of the biases we have discussed include the following:

- Cumulative losses of rights and resources have usually been expressed in 'per capita', rather than 'per capitalist', terms. This conceals the distribution of the benefits and burdens of resource transfers between the general public and special interests.
- Standard building equipment is not required to payback its embodied energy, as it is viewed as the norm. The cost of fossil fuel systems is not seen as 'extra', yet mechanical equipment requires regular maintenance, repair or replacement.
- Currently, those who are attempting green buildings are penalized by extra costs. Similarly, many 'green energy' programmes subsidize fossil fuels instead of encouraging conversion to solar energy. The costs should be shifted to those engaged in harmful activities.
- Environmental assessments have traditionally downplayed the economic costs of environmental damage. At the same time, the economic benefits of an undisturbed environment have generally not been assigned numbers.

Our tools need to be redesigned to balance the:

- Relative reduction of negative impacts and risks *with* positive ecological and social gains.
- Economic costs of green development *with* the economic benefits of a healthy environment.
- Improvement of fossil fuel equipment *with* the improvement of passive systems.
- Greening of new construction *with* the greening of existing development or eco-retrofitting.
- Energy efficiency measures *with* the expansion of ecosystems and resource conservation.
- Capacity building in reductionist analyses *with* creative design processes.
- Costs of time in financial terms *with* the costs of restoring ecosystems or ecological time.
- Equitable distribution of pollution *with* the access to open space and the means of survival.

**Question indicators [Chapter 9]**

A SmartMode approach looks for problems in existing development or organizations that can be directly targeted by investments in physical design solutions. It avoids indirect policies and unpredictable incentives when simple net positive solutions can be used instead. Systems improvements can be made before a problem is even 'measurable'. Indicators of poor system design could sometimes be more useful than broad, sweeping trends in the environment generally. They may help dislodge the obsession with trends in 'pollution' and their implications for human health (the outcome of design) to the exclusion of biophysical design itself. Conversely, when biophysical design is considered, the implications for ecological and democratic outcomes are often not. As we have seen, there are indicators of bad design on all levels:

- Single function spaces in urban development are often an indicator of wasted opportunity to improve human and environmental health.
- A product that must be produced with child labour or slavery is an indicator of poor systems design (eg some monocultural coffee plantations).
- An increasing concentration of wealth is an indicator of unjust enrichment (eg golden handshakes and parachutes to CEOs even when their company's profits sink).
- Toxic working relations are an indicator of ineffective management, low productivity, and an environment that impedes creativity and innovation.

## Step 7: Develop Planning Information, Concepts and Strategies

Having conducted forensic analyses, explored assumptions, and selected methods and tools, the next step is to ensure planning research, principles, processes and strategies remain relevant to sustainability issues. Planning and decision-making has not been self-reflective, in part due to instrumental conditioning in the professions (where unthinking behaviours are rewarded, like mice in a maze). For a while, planners called themselves proactive if they tried to attract any industry to a region. Today, they are increasingly trying to attract green business and industry through, for example, eco-industrial parks. While this is an improvement, planners need also to focus on correcting existing social and ecological deficiencies.

### Planning research and information [Chapter 12]

Currently, planners decide what data to collect and what to consult the community on. Instead, communities could ask planners to provide information that would help to identify fundamental sustainability needs that development could address. Planners should be 'answerable' to community groups acting in the public interest to progress specific Positive Developments. Planners could provide maps of relevant information to the community to inspire eco-innovation and eco-retrofitting:

- Prioritize whole systems efficiency through solutions that use natural systems in lieu of industrial ones, where possible, to avoid replacing natural with artificial environments and to reverse the use of fossil fuels.
- Map opportunities to systematically increase biodiversity and functioning eco-services by, for example, identifying appropriate places for aquatic and/or vegetated corridors and habitats, community farms, etc. This has been done in rare cases.
- Prioritize eco-retrofitting over new development, recognizing that poorly designed infill development can increase the ecological footprint and reduce the physical footprint. This requires up-skilling in creativity and site-specific design.
- Identify ways to intensify rather than 'densify' urban development by increasing public activities, multiple uses and natural systems. More 'dense' development often reduces the intensity of, and public access to, facilities and amenities.
- Recognize that accessible and clean air, energy, food, water and soil resources are essential to resource security. Identify where cities can be made more self-sufficient, while increasing the vitality and quality of the public estate.
- Plans can proactively identify areas in which we can address resource imbalances between cities and regions (eg replace imports, reduce transport). Planning should stimulate ecological revitalization, as well as social, economic and environmental revitalization.

### Planning implementation [Chapter 14]

Planners have traditionally assisted decision-makers in choosing among development options presented by special interests. They could instead help empower the community by exposing and trying to eliminate perverse subsidies, redirecting incentives towards Positive Development, and helping NGOs identify social and ecological needs. NGOs should demand that the biases in planning implementation that militate against good design be removed (such as green buildings penalized by the cost of certification). Planners can work with NGOs, for example, to:

- Advocate the creation of incentives for solarization and/or eco-retrofitting programmes such as performance contracting. Similarly, create systems of credits/awards for positive *off-site* impacts in planning assessment systems.

- Apply 'direct action' principles to planning. For example, invest in making public transport and physical activity convenient, low-cost and attractive, through varied and attractive public environments (instead of congestion to make driving inconvenient).
- Encourage legislation to prohibit food and garden waste in the urban waste stream, so that all such waste is recycled in buildings and urban parks or sent to farms for food production. Planning has undervalued urban soil nutrients and water storage.
- Implement demonstrations of Positive Development through, for example, public–private+community sector partnerships and/or cross-agency task forces (which, again, share risks, profits and benefits to the parties, and roll-over profits into future positive initiatives).
- Specify or negotiate contracts to prevent materials used at each stage of construction from being sent to landfill or incinerated, or favour construction materials that are non-toxic, recyclable, reusable or able to be composted in urban parklands.

### Ecological space (ES) trading [Chapter 11]

ES is the effective ecological area provided by a development. It creates infrastructure for ecosystem services through multiple integrated functions. It measures the interior and/or exterior space devoted to healthy ecosystems per person or square metre. It provides a measure of positive impacts, and enables trading to facilitate an increase in urban eco-services. Current trading systems largely simply offset the harm of future industrial activity, rather that fostering positive improvements to the ecology and public spaces. We can increase the latter by:

- Allowing developers or building owners credit for ES or indoor/outdoor areas that provide for eco-services; this will increase urban sustainability incrementally and at no 'extra' cost (as retrofitting is ongoing in the urban environment).
- Considering new methods, such as 'reverse' transferable development rights that enable people to rent space on their property for the development of eco-services or even energy production. For example, energy contractors could rent space on private roofs for solar cells.
- Creating credits/awards/rebates for – or require the inclusion of – eco-services in development through ES or bioremediation functions that improve the health of air, soil, water, biota and habitats.

## Step 8: Develop Design Goals, Strategies and Processes

The process of designing and creating is more likely to stimulate positive eco-innovations than conventional planning – which has meant defensively preparing for a non-sustainable future. SmartMode aims instead to improve human and environmental health and whole systems efficiency by replacing resource-intensive machines and products with natural systems. During partnering, planning and decision processes, SmartMode looks beyond the site or project objectives to support wider needs. The design process, however, is not meant to be in separate, sequential stages (except for the purposes of this checklist).

### Identify specific initiatives [Chapter 14]

NGOs can use workshops or focus groups to help identify worthwhile developments or innovations for each community, explore local systems design challenges, or oppose negative projects through counterplans (as in advocacy planning). Where possible, NGOs should consult the local community in conducting needs assessments, or ensure urban planners do so, before a design is conceived. Again, ensure workshops move beyond the process of listing problems and impediments and engage people in collective, creative pursuits to:

- Identify wider off-site public needs (eg social, economic, physical and ecological) in relation to the site and brief (eg the local need for childcare facilities). That is, add value to the community (individuals and civil society) not just meet minimalist owner criteria.
- Identify alternative means to satisfy needs and preferences in less resource-intensive ways, rather than focusing on inputs and outputs, such as by including 'dual' community uses (eg evening and weekend uses of facilities).
- Establish needs-assessment processes that can form the basis for identifying specific impediments to be addressed and, more important, ways of value-adding. Impacts and needs should not be discussed in isolation from potential solutions.

## Articulate design objectives [Chapter 6]

Most negative impacts can be avoided early in the design, so the emphasis should be on constructive mechanisms to encourage better collaborative design processes, involving local NGOs and other potential stakeholders. The design process itself should be *demystified* through participation in design, to ensure that clients and stakeholders are aware of the wider consequences of design and the potential for ongoing environmental improvements. Some considerations that pertain to design include:

- Directing attention to the *sources* of energy and materials (eg fossil versus solar resources). Operating costs could be negligible if passive solar design is used, so ecological and embodied waste should be considered.
- Where possible, increasing multiple human and natural use of spaces, such as greenhouse atriums, vertical landscapes or Living Machines, integrating internal and external open space, and providing infrastructure for eco-services.
- Considering increasing the longevity of existing construction by adding Green Scaffolding and double skins to create multiple ecological and human health and security benefits. (This can reduce temperature swings, need for mechanical backup, the urban heat sink, etc.)
- Identifying past ecological damage, harmful materials (eg asbestos and radon), possible quakes or cyclones, or other problems that the design should address. It may be better to 'encase' an old building than ship it to landfill.
- Respecting indigenous and bio-climatic design traditions, and attempting to use materials sourced from the local region. Where appropriate, retrofit the International Style – which has eliminated regional difference – with indigenous design and plants, etc.
- Considering the rebound effect. Where there is a 'rebound effect', there may be no net gain. The solution is an environment where there are a lot of low-impact choices and lifestyles that replace high-impact ones.
- Focusing on positive resource security and safety, rather than 'defensive design' where buildings are conceived of in negative ways (eg as a shelter or bastion from hostile nature). Buildings can be reconceived as 'gardens for living'.

## Design for eco-services [Chapter 6]

The traditional green design method is focused on the building envelope. It does not aim to improve the ecology and community beyond what was originally on the site and surrounds (ie to push the envelope). SmartMode aims to enhance environmental flows through the building, site and region. Currently, design thinking has been colonized by input–output thinking, which tends to limit our view to boundary issues and building envelopes. Drawing boundaries in order to facilitate measurement means we may ignore cumulative, global distributional impacts. By looking at environmental *flows* through an existing site, building or region, we can reverse some past interventions that reduce environmental and ecosystem health. Some design pointers include:

- Think in flows (not inputs and outputs) through the region, site or building. Natural services are longer lasting, lower maintenance and often more easily modified in the event of initial engineering mistakes.
- Enhance environmental flows through development so that air, water, soil and biota come out ecologically healthier than under original pre-construction conditions by, for example, expanding the building envelope so that it becomes an ecosystem (eg the Green Space Wall).
- Allow the landscape to flow through structures where appropriate to avoid lifeless, single-use spaces. Consider opening part of the ground level to increase urban open space, mitigate flooding, revitalize soil and enable nature corridors below buildings.
- In elevated buildings, ensure the bottom floor plan and heights are varied to allow light to reach all the ground during parts of the day to avoid dead spaces under the building and generate eco-services (eg worm farms and mushrooms). Use adequate floor insulation.
- Where prefabricated structures and components are used, ensure they meet ecological and human health needs and reduce net regional material flows. For example, office fit-outs, interiors and other products could be organic and compostable.
- Avoid or question the 'one size fits all' passive solar templates (eg designs involving 'slab on ground' or major earth moving), as these characteristically ignore the ecology. (And, again, do not under-design for solar energy).

## Step 9: Apply Self-Assessment

In the past we have conformed our analyses to what we can easily measure and already have data for. But assessment should consider a wider range of factors: opportunity costs, distributive justice, accessibility, total flows (eg detoxification, decarbonization, dematerialization) and so on. Self-assessment of projects is more important than project review processes by planning authorities, as they are usually too late in the design process. Some tools for self-assessment are reviewed below.

### The eco-design reporting process [Chapter 5]

Development control processes apply where developers seek approval for a project. A more pragmatic development control system would concentrate on creating a positive framework that encourages designers to increase multiple benefits of buildings beyond the site. Assessment would therefore be complementary to creative eco-solutions and equitable processes. The suggested eco-design reporting process would stimulate sustainability innovation and education:

- Instead of outsourcing assessment reports to specialists to predict impacts, or having developers check off the reporting requirements of a proposal, institute an eco-design report to examine the eco-solutions that the proponents investigated in the design process.
- Require a systematic exploration of eco-logical design options in a public eco-design report and enable 'outsiders' to provide feedback. Project proponents should have the burden of showing in writing that net positive technologies were not feasible.
- Eco-design reports should involve input from planners and NGO representatives early in the design process. Ensure future projects can draw upon this innovation effort by making them public as soon as is practicable.

### The sustainability standard [Chapter 5]

Currently, we use complex tools to predict the negative future impacts of projects compared to standard buildings of similar types or functions. Thus standard buildings have been the benchmark for new development, not sustainability. Instead, the pre-existing natural capital, biodiversity and ecosystem services should be the baseline: a project should provide a net gain over original site conditions. By comparing a proposed development to pre-development conditions, and comparing the health of the urban area before and after a new development or retrofit, we will have a better idea of net positive progress. The following initial questions can be asked during the design process.

Will the action expand the ecological base, future options and/or be reversible? In other words, will it:

- Increase natural capital?
- Increase natural security?
- Be reversible, adaptable, diverse?
- Increase and distribute renewable resources?
- Replace fossil with solar resources?

### The Green Optimum rule [Chapter 9]

Tools for 'choosing' among existing courses of action, policies or developments in the existing context are not adequate to bring about systems re-design. Sustainable development requires design: the creation of synergies, syntheses and symbioses. By establishing the basic decision rule that development should try to increase benefits to everyone, we can encourage design that creates positive synergies and off-site benefits. The Green Optimum decision rule aims to overturn the Pareto Optimum. The latter holds that a policy or action is good if it benefits individuals or groups without disadvantaging individuals, which can obscure long-term, widely dispersed externalities. The following initial questions can be asked during the design process.

Will the action expand the public estate and make everyone (the general public) better off? In other words, will it:

- Deliver net positive outcomes?
- Increase participatory democracy and community engagement?
- Provide freedom from harm and protect human rights?
- Foster responsibility and accountability?
- Increase the range of responsible lifestyle and consumer choices?
- Increase the diversity of sustainable pathways and cultural diversity?

## Step 10: Apply External Assessment

### Assessment [Chapter 7]

Although an eco-design report may be prepared, a public environmental impact assessment may still be required for significant projects. In theory, the above self-assessment should make this largely redundant. However, if a decision to approve the project is subject to a sustainability assessment, then ecological waste and opportunity costs should be considered. Unavoidable impacts could be compensated for by remediating other significant aspects of the built environment, but remediation should not justify increased negative impacts. Buying land and not developing it may offset harm, but it is not really net positive. Conversely, if the benefits of projects were weighed against the costs of inaction, Positive Development projects would be favoured. Some considerations include:

- The public value and purpose of the development itself, and how it affects existing development, should be assessed – as development has high opportunity costs (ie removes resources from other potentially better developments).
- Where appropriate, embodied and ecological waste should be assessed and quantified. Compensation for any unavoidable waste could be achieved by adding value to the ecology and generating positive off-site ecological and social impacts.
- Mechanisms for community-based critiques of assessments (or counter-plans) should be established where appropriate. Decision authorities should provide written explanations on significant land-use and resource decisions in terms of their sustainability.
- Developers should demonstrate that there is no built-up area, building or urban dead space that can meet their requirements before green field sites are approved. Eco-retrofitting and recycling opportunities should always be considered.
- If economic benefits are claimed to outweigh ecological factors, assessments should consider the quality, not just the quantity, of jobs that the development will generate. When projects are approved based on job generation, the jobs do not always materialize.
- The waste entailed in existing construction and demolition does not appear in the public balance sheets as they are paid for by developers. They should be considered even if they are not analysed in great detail in the case of a small project.
- Assessments do not usually assess the context before and after a development. They assess the relativity of development options. We should assess the overall positive and negative impacts of existing and proposed development as if neither existed previously.
- While assessments often discuss the 'no development' option, they do not measure the benefits of eco-services provided, or their loss after development, or the irreversibility of possible decisions and losses of future options.

## A hierarchy of eco-innovation [Chapter 14]

There are now myriad innovation tools that are accessible on the internet. However, most 'innovation' processes are oriented towards creating products and then finding a market. Since they are not designed for sustainability, some could have the effect of increasing consumption. Given there is an infinite amount of work that needs to be done, and an infinite number of design opportunities, it can be necessary to prioritize Positive Developments. Designs and implementation strategies should therefore be reviewed to see whether design improvements are possible, according to a hierarchy of solutions from lowest priority to highest:

1   New designs, products or production systems that increase resource flows, but at less negative impact per unit than the norm, only reduce the relative impacts of *future* actions. In general, these should be the last in this list to be publicly supported.

2   Innovations that reduce the impacts of waste from *ongoing* processes or activities, through reuse, recycling or re-assembly, can still involve some waste and a reduction of use value or 'down-cycling'.

3   Innovations that reduce the impacts of *past* development (toxins or waste already in the environment) add economic value, but 'up-cycling' could involve an increase in conspicuous consumption and resource flows.

4   'No-loop' refers to innovations where waste is 'designed out' of an existing, ongoing or future system entirely. This could still create unnecessary products or have a rebound effect, where

the resource savings are spent on harmful activities.

5 Eco-cycling is up-cycling that contributes to human *and* ecological health (ie is net positive) and does not increase total resource flows. However, this may still not increase access to the means of survival and resource security – the public estate.

6 Innovations at the net positive level improve whole systems and increase both the public estate and ecological base. They can be at the building or system level:

- Net Positive *Development* reverses existing impacts and increases the ecological base and public estate beyond pre-development site conditions.
- Net Positive *Systems* innovations create levers for biophysical improvements and social transformation at the 'glocal' scale (eg converting cities from fossil to solar).

## Step 11: Ensure Measurements have Meaning

### Ecological waste (EW) analysis [Chapter 4]

By considering the loss of ecosystems, and the time needed to replace them, planning and design decisions might begin to respect natural systems as living things, not just inputs and outputs. We usually use energy and materials as surrogates for ecology, which encourages us to measure ecosystems as if they were inert substances. To consider the full life-cycle of, say, a forest or fishery, we would need to think in terms of ecological time. Some measurement concepts that have been discussed are:

- Ecological waste – which weighs in the loss of natural ecosystems and the time and cost of replacing them (ie living ecosystems, not dead resources). EW (a negative) is roughly the opposite of the ecological base (a positive).
- Environmental space – which is the available resource per capita (a Friends of the Earth term). The Earth can absorb a certain amount of carbon or produce a certain amount of topsoil, so these amounts, divided by the relevant population, is the allowable consumption rate.
- Negative space – which is the conversion of (public) non-renewable resources and natural capital. It is a measure of the distributional impacts resulting from the alienation of natural capital, land and eco-services to private development.
- Unjust enrichment – which draws attention to the fact that developers or owners can enjoy benefits that are disproportionate to their contribution to the public environment. It could be seen as environmental space 'per capitalist'.

### Opportunity costs [Chapter 7]

We have looked at the cost of inaction in terms of the environmental, economic and social costs of doing nothing to reverse negative impacts. However, we also need to look at the future benefits we are foregoing by acting later rather than sooner. Some pointers in this direction are:

- By identifying the contextual problems in the region surrounding a proposed development, we can draw attention to both the costs of inaction and the serious 'opportunity costs' of conventional land-use, planning and design decisions.
- Free-riders, whose air, water, temperature and vistas are improved by the development at no cost, are not a 'problem' in design. Comfort and happiness are not zero sum. The more people who benefit, the better, especially where a retrofit pays for itself anyway.
- In the future, due to increasing scarcity, the value of nature will increase along with that of its marketable components, such as water. Where appropriate, an 'eco-factor' can be used to reflect this, instead of discounting the future.

## Step 12: Assess Accountability and Performance

NGOs should demand more accountability from local councils, government agencies and politicians generally. Anti-ecological premises, frameworks, operational assumptions and their biases need to be challenged by responsible environmental managers and planners. Instead of managers assessing performance through compliance and reporting activities to functional staff ('downsourcing'), the public should begin to assess management itself.

### Assessing public agencies [Chapter 9]

We should question what *all* government departments are doing to make positive contributions to sustainability. They should not just be reducing the harm of future activity or reporting on trends in the environment. Communities could:

- Make developers more accountable for the public estate, in proportion to the benefits developers draw from it. For example, over time, there should be no need for 'credit' for providing energy efficiency, as this benefits the developer anyway through cost savings.
- Demand direct action. *Indirect* incentives have uncertain consequences due to the possibility of many intervening forces or factors (eg price-based environmental mechanisms can be avoided by moving where cheaper labour can be found).
- Emphasize forms of reporting that focus on management accountability, rather than just measuring changes in the environment. Again, the focus should be on management performance in responding to change, rather than on nature's ability to cope with change.
- Assess results of government programmes in terms of positive impacts, rather than remedial and custodial actions. Goals are usually expressed as trends, which cannot easily be traced directly to causes. More auditing of *existing* development is needed.

### Reporting and post-occupancy evaluation [Chapter 9]

NGOs should ensure that government and industry report on things that are relevant to sustainability. Wider use of genuine progress indicators could help, but they tend to focus on satisfaction, not sustainability. We do not measure and report on the savings that accrue to the public through the actions of environmental managers and planners in government or industry. While these are reported ad hoc, they are seldom reported in direct ways that would encourage effort towards positive change. Reporting should emphasize what is being done to restock the shelves, not to record how fast the shelves are emptying. For example, reporting has:

- Not linked public sector 'performance' closely to *savings* of human and natural resources, or to *progress* towards positive sustainability goals. There needs to be more recognition of the positive and economic value of eliminating externalities.
- Focused on general trends in downstream impacts that are affected by intervening factors, rather than assessing management performance by positive actions or, conversely, measuring the costs of inaction.
- Not ensured ongoing improvement of built environments through active consideration of means such as extended producer responsibility schemes, revolving funds, pre-cycling insurance and performance contracting.
- Not tracked the transfer of resources among classes, sectors, corporations, regions, etc, nor charted progress towards dematerialization, detoxification and decarbonization (instead of predicting how much damage will occur from this point on).
- Not held the whole of government accountable for outcomes of public relations expenses and

costs of inaction (as opposed to environmental agencies only). All agencies should be responsible for achieving sustainability gains.

- Not related outcomes to basic life-support systems using indicators or measures that consider the ecological base, public estate, range of future options and responsible consumer choices.

## Conclusion

Clearly, this is work in progress. However, hopefully it is evident that sustainability will require whole systems re-design to make all people, communities and ecosystems healthier and more secure. This requires new analyses, but also a move from managerial displacement activity to positive thinking and direct action. More fundamentally, a sustainable society will require design *for* nature, as well as *with* nature. Through Positive Development, we can reverse negative resource flows, expand the life-support system, provide more equitable lifestyles, reduce conflict, and increase environmental and human health, biodiversity, social choice and future options. A SmartMode approach would be far easier than what we are doing now, would have better outcomes and would be more fun. Please accept this invitation to engage, with a view to moving from vicious circles to virtuous cycles, at janis.birkeland@qut.edu.au.

# SECTION F: BOXES

## Box I Net Positive Development

This box attempts to represent the idea of expanding the ecological base and public estate to create surplus eco-services and public amenity.

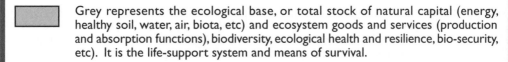 Grey represents the ecological base, or total stock of natural capital (energy, healthy soil, water, air, biota, etc) and ecosystem goods and services (production and absorption functions), biodiversity, ecological health and resilience, bio-security, etc). It is the life-support system and means of survival.

White arrows represents the reduction of the resource stocks and flows (ecological base) in urban and rural development. While partly driven by population, the design of production and construction systems can make a bigger difference to sustainability than population reduction. In other words, people in some regions consume hundreds of times more resources than people in other regions.

Ecologically responsible practices (eco-efficient production, farming, forestry, green building, 'responsible' mining, etc) can mitigate the impacts of development (represented by downward arrows). Design for eco-services can actually increase the ecological base, public estate and carrying capacity (represented by upward arrows) or the 'roof' of the new structure.

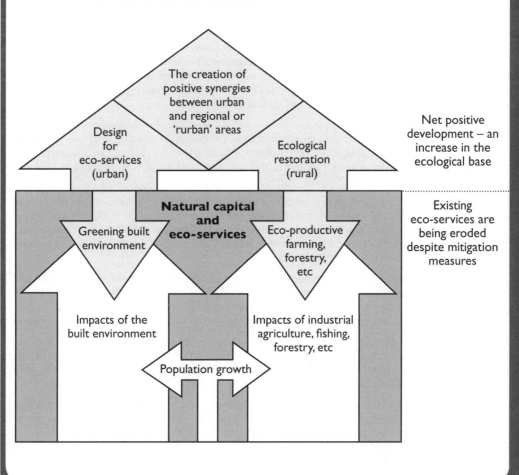

277

## Box 2 Eco-logical Design Defined

Design is a fluid, adaptive and self-generating way of thinking, so it does not lend itself well to rules or prescriptions. Nonetheless, a set of adjectives is provided to describe the nature of design, as used in this book:[1]

**Responsible**: Eco-logical design redefines project goals around issues of basic needs, social equity, environmental justice and ecological sustainability. Eco-logical design involves reconsidering the end uses or purposes served by products, buildings, landscapes and other designed systems. (It does not simply aim to reduce inputs and outputs.)

**Synergistic**: Eco-logical design creates positive feedback loops between different functional elements to foster systems change. Whereas 'pyramidal' design creates negative externalities, eco-logical design creates positive synergies and seeds opportunities for reciprocities and symbioses in other dimensions beyond the specific design 'problem'.

**Contextual**: Eco-logical design involves re-evaluating design conventions and concepts in the context of changing socio-political and economic systems, in order to contribute to positive social transformation. While a design must work within given cultural and political contexts to transform them, it should also contribute to a more eco-sensitive culture. For example, it can help shape consumer demand towards less materialistic aims.

**Holistic**: Eco-logical design takes a life-cycle perspective to ensure that products are low-impact, low-cost and multifunctional on as many levels as possible. Good design inherently often involves collaborative, interdisciplinary work processes, lateral thinking, and the integration of economic, social and environmental parameters.

**Empowering**: Eco-logical design fosters human potential, self-reliance and ecological understanding through the use of appropriate technologies and healthier living environments. Visible technologies can make users more ecologically aware and enhance their ability to interact with, repair and modify their own environments. In contrast, pyramidal design invisibilizes resource transfers and environmental impacts and disempowers users.

**Restorative**: Eco-logical design nurtures and strengthens human and ecosystem health and 'immune systems' and contributes to psychological wellbeing. It can also improve the health of flora and fauna and the integrity of ecosystems, and strengthen their resilience to stress and resistance to illness. It can help reintegrate the social and natural world, heal and re-cultivate a sense of wonder about nature.

**Eco-effective**: Eco-logical design rebalances economics with eco-effectiveness. But it goes further than minimizing inputs of materials and energy or outputs of pollution and waste. Designers should ensure that the design brief is ecologically and socially sound; the project increases eco-efficiency (economy of energy, materials and costs) and also generates positive ecological and social impacts on the region.

**Creative**: Eco-logical design represents a new paradigm that can transcend or bypass the entrenched 'managerialism' often found in academia, business and government. Because design occupies a different sphere – creativity – it is not burdened with the need to justify itself in relation to anachronistic theories. Design can leapfrog over old paradigms and tribal disciplines.

**Visionary**: Eco-logical design focuses on desired outcomes and then selects or invents appropriate methods, tools and processes to achieve them. This involves selecting or designing tools to suit the nature of the specific problems at hand, so that the means fit the ends. In turn, this requires critically reflecting upon existing tools in terms of real world outcomes.

**Multi-dimensional**: Eco-logical design is a multi-layered, multi-dimensional process that accommodates different cultures and personal preferences simultaneously. Eco-logical design can be hard tech, or 'nuts and bolts' (eg polyvalent reactive or digital building envelopes), or soft tech 'nuts and berries' (eg biological water treatment), and on any scale, from natural termite control technologies to bioregional planning.

## Box 3 Examples of Net Positive Development

The aim of net Positive Development is to take affirmative action to make environmental improvements that go *beyond* remediation and restoration. Air, water, soil and people could leave the building in a healthier condition than when they entered it. But this would still be largely 'remediation'. Buildings should also *add* social and ecological value, on- and off-site, to over-compensate for any embodied or ecological waste [Chapter 4]. The following are examples of net positive design concepts that could be scaled up to a whole building, city or regional level.

**Solar ponds**: Solar ponds are salt pools that collect and store solar energy. Solar energy (heat) is absorbed at the bottom of a 2 or 3-metre-deep salt pond. Heat is trapped in the bottom of the pond, where the water is denser than at the surface due to the concentration of salt. The heated water is too heavy to rise and dissipate into the atmosphere. Heat at the bottom of the pond can be over 90 degrees Celsius and can be used for process or space heating, hot water or electricity production. In Australia, which has serious salinity problems, for example, rural land damaged by past mismanagement can be reclaimed in this process. The process can also produce salt as a by-product, and the heat from the solar pond can be used to dry the salt. Solar ponds are beginning to be developed and operated commercially. One in outback Australia will produce salt, process heat and grow brine shrimps for stock feed, while mitigating salination and returning land back into productive use.[1]

**'Reverse' Trombe wall**: Conventional Trombe walls create an air space between a masonry wall and exterior window.[2] Heated air rises to air vents at the top of the air space. When needed, the heated air is circulated through the room by convection (heat rising). The cooled air re-enters the space through vents at the bottom. The high thermal mass wall provides a heat storage bank. Usually a Trombe wall is placed behind what would otherwise be a window. The proposed 'reverse' Trombe wall is more suitable for retrofits [Box 5]. Glass walls could be retrofitted onto existing sun-facing masonry walls of old buildings without sacrificing natural lighting and views. Vents would simply be drilled through the wall. For non-masonry walls, rock stacks (to store heat) could be inserted between the existing wall and new glazing, say in a wire frame (eg a gabion). In summer, the glass would be covered with shadecloths or arbours, and the wall would cool the building by venting hot air to the outside. Simple adjustments to the amount of rocks can be made to adjust the thermal mass.

**Green Space Wall**: This would be a modular space frame wall with a glass exterior and interior, primarily for new structures. This would essentially expand the building envelope into an ecosystem or ecosystems. One module, for example, could have a glass exterior, in-filled with rocks or other media (in a wire frame) to function like the above reverse Trombe wall. This construction system would be 'reversible', as sections could be easily transferred over time if walls or windows needed to be moved. But unlike the reverse Trombe wall, the Green Space Wall modules incorporate a host of other ecological functions [Figure 10]. The building envelopes could also produce compost and soil from organic waste, purify air and water, provide climate control and so on.[3] Horizontal or vertical sections could contain integrated planters for water cleaning functions and temperature mitigation.[4] Some of these sections could be visible from the inside, and even include aquariums, aquaponic food production, terrariums or butterfly breeding cages, which would make an interesting child's room, restaurant wall public foyer.

**Living Machines**: There are many variations on John Todd's Living Machines: a series of vessels containing ecosystems that produce healthy fish or plants at the end of the process. Greywater, organic waste and sewage are increasingly being treated by using series of microbes, mushrooms and earthworms in a series of containers. A careful selection of plants in each container targets specific pollutants. At the end of the biological chain, useful resources are produced, such as healthy food or toxin-free potting soils. Roofs have been retrofitted to support Living Machines in greenhouse that increase usable floor area, thermal insulation and food, reduce the urban heat island and so on [Box 14]. Moreover, heat from roof greenhouses can also be ducted throughout the building (on the inside or outside of the structure).[5] Thus we can create a virtuous cycle where waste, in effect, cleans the air and water and builds soil.

**Fire prevention**: After a fire, we tend to invest our resources on clearing native bushland from around the suburbs, at least in Australia. The bulldozer approach to fire-sensitive landscaping can exacerbate problems of erosion, flooding, siltation, dust, air pollution and so on. A more positive approach would be to add urban environmental amenities that create fire barriers and sprays, and store water in greenbelts for fire fighting. Water stored in recreational ponds or cisterns hidden in the landscape could be linked to gazebos, pavilions, arbours or green space frames that can supply water sprays and/or fountains in time of fire or extreme hot weather. Nothing can stop a firestorm; however, such landscape 'moats' around settlements could stop fires spread by embers and reduce risks to fire fighters and fauna. These structures also support biodiversity habitats as well as social or recreational activities. Urban buildings could also contain external (as well as internal) water sprays for emergency water supplies on hot days or fires and structural support for concealed or sculptural fire escapes. Likewise, 'portable water sculptures' composed of water pipes have been used to facilitate social activity for urban youths while its sprays cool the streets.

**Urban cooling**: Buildings and pavements absorb heat and act as an oven. This 'urban heat island effect' means many cities are several degrees hotter than surrounding areas. This phenomenon is predicted to increase as cities continue to lose net tree cover. US cities have been estimated to have lost over 20 per cent of their trees in 10 years and to have cost the public US$234 Billion according to a study released at the annual National Urban Forest Conference in 2003.[6] By capturing, storing and circulating water in building walls and roofs, a building could support off-site landscaping and nature corridors, while offering some fire protection. Outdoor flyscreens that define spaces can support creepers and provide shade and visual privacy; evaporative cooling of the outdoor space can be achieved by dripping recirculated water along the top of the screen.[7] Cooling sprays recycled through water cisterns could be integrated with sculptures and gardens on roofs, balconies and façades. Exterior retractable shade cloths can be designed to deliver cool air, as well as shade walls, by causing updrafts of cool air from a source such as a shaded pond.

**Fuel cells and thermal chips**: Fuel cells convert the chemical energy of hydrogen fuel directly into electrical energy, with healthy by-products like air and water. Thermal chips can purportedly convert heat directly into electrical energy. These systems can be more or less efficient, depending on their design and application. In the case of fuel cells, obviously, the source of the hydrogen should not be fossil fuel based, or it will militate against the sustainability of the whole system. Thermal chips are a semiconductor device that do not generate emissions, have moving parts, vibration or noise and can operate at any scale.[8] The cooling chip could be used for small light devices such as laptops, but perhaps also on larger-scale applications. The heat source could perhaps be waste heat or solar heat on a roof or wall. So fuel cells and thermal chips can cool or supply electricity to buildings. Fuel cells can also produce water and generate surplus electric power (selling excess power back to the grid). The fuel cell has a low fuel-to-electricity conversion rate. However, the energy not converted into electricity in a building fuel cell could perhaps operate the thermal chips.

**Micro-labourers**: Bacteria are used for many economic and environmental functions. For example, bacteria can be used in the bioremediation of toxic wastes, polluted soils, sewage sludge, petrochemical contamination and oil spills. Oyster mushrooms have been effective in eliminating diesel fuel spills – without toxic oil residues in either the soil or mushrooms.[9] They have been shown to transform other toxic substances into harmless ones, and could provide a substitute for incineration. Non-toxic insecticides can be produced from mushrooms to replace harmful agricultural and domestic poisons. Bacteria are already being used to improve plant growth in desert conditions. Fungi have been used to rehabilitate logging roads to stop siltation. Bacterial 'desert cubes' are now available that can turn conventional (new or existing) urinals into waterless systems.[10] Downstream, these naturally occurring and safe microorganisms can even assist in improving the septic tank or sewage treatment plant. But more exotic uses are being discovered all the time. For example, bacteria have been used to restore deteriorating historic buildings and sculptures, and even produce lighting, energy and oxygen.

## Box 4 Green Scaffolding versus Double Skins

Some of the functions that 'ordinary' building skins *could* serve are to:

- Optimize views
- Collect solar energy
- Generate electricity
- Waterproof walls
- Integrate food gardens
- Support vertical landscaping
- Provide social spaces
- Distribute daylighting
- Circulate fresh air and breezes
- Create microhabitats and nature corridors
- Mitigate storms
- Provide insulation and acoustics
- Collect and treat rainwater
- Increase security and crime prevention

**A typical 'double skin'** building basically just adds double glazing to the exterior wall. Such facades provide solar heating, cooling and ventilating in a variety of ways, like Trombe walls or greenhouse windows. Heat rises due to the thermal stack effect and air movement between the skins. This sucks interior air out of the building and expels it through exterior dampers. External and internal heat loads from office equipment or machinery may require extra high solar stacks. Extraction fans can be powered by solar-powered fans or wind turbines (or mechanical support in extreme conditions). Double skins can also warm the building by trapping warm air between inner and outer skins by closing dampers. The space between the two skins can have louvers which, if close to the outer glass skin, can reduce heat gain by 50 per cent more than internal louvers. Reflectors on louvers can be used to reflect light into the interior on dark days and bounce sunlight away on hot days.

Operating energy savings alone will often not justify retrofitting a building with a double skin. However, it may be economical, where, for example, the building façade needs rehabilitation, or where noise from the exterior (eg the street) or interior (other rooms) is a problem. The type of double skin structure used will depend on particular user needs, building function, the existing building's structural system, and/or priorities such as wind, noise, pollution or security. There are several kinds of double skins, such as:

- The 'window box' type where space is divided by rooms horizontally and vertically, like a bay window. This allows individual control of air intake and extraction as old air is expelled at the top of each window.
- The 'vertical shaft' type, which uses a shaft configuration several storeys high. The used air can be vented into a garden storey for air cleansing.
- The 'horizontal shaft' type, which separates air circulation on each storey. It can be easily combined with balconies. In this case, vents are staggered to avoid bad air entering the next floor.

Unfortunately, the vast majority of double skin buildings increase the heat island effect and create 'dead' spaces that do not have eco-productive or psychological benefits.

**Green Scaffolding**: The proposed Green Scaffolding would provide many additional social, ecological and economic benefits [Box 5]. It would add ecospheres to an existing building while creating the above heating, cooling and ventilating functions. A space-frame-type structure added to the exterior could increase the lifespan of the original building, expand the effective interior space (where codes allow), and support gardens, solar stacks, shading louvers (that also block access by burglars), shower towers, heat and water storage, vertical compost chutes, and light shelves and/or mirrors to bounce light in and prevent glare.

## Box 5 Green Scaffolding Retrofit

Green Scaffolding wraps an ecosystem around an existing building to produce clean energy, air, water, soil and food. The triangular truss supports a vertical greenhouse that can hold continuous vertical wetlands and hanging gardens to clean air and water; shower towers and solar chimneys to cool the building; butterfly and frog breeding habitats (depending on building orientation) and even bird and possum nests to support urban biodiversity, and vertical composters to treat organic waste. Continuous Trombe walls could feed heat into the (old) central heating system, or directly heat and cool rooms. Integrated shading and lighting systems can include louvers, sail cloths, light shelves, blinds, etc. Urban cooling can be achieved on very hot days by sprays from within the pipe truss, fed by water collected on the roof. Some modules could support aquaponic food production systems where fish fertilize water for the hydroponic plant system, accessible through windows. Such mini-biospheres would clip into a vertical triangular truss system. The Green Scaffolding is demountable, flexible and interchangeable, with many possible variations to suit local conditions. The façade can be further articulated by decks, sunspaces or atriums.

## Box 6 Deconstruction

*Neil Seldman*

Souvenir bricks from a university building have sold out at $1 per brick through an innovative programme introduced by Dynasty Deconstruction, a new and fast-growing social enterprise serving the Cleveland Metropolitan Area. In 2 years, the 16 person company has deconstructed no fewer than 75 homes and 2 buildings at Kent State University. The programme is also linking other types of recycling to the culture of higher education, such as end-of-term dorm clean ups. Dynasty Deconstruction is now serving several cities in Ohio. Its expertise in brick recovery and marketing has even brought the company to New Jersey. And the rapid rise of this small business is by no means unique. A non-profit enterprise in Maryland, Second Chance Inc, has grown to 25 workers in just 3 years.

All together, about 300 deconstruction enterprises (both for profit and non-profit) have arisen in the last 5 years. The market for deconstruction grows as the cost of disposing of construction and demolition waste soars. The value of used building materials has similarly increased. Environmental awareness of the need to reduce extraction of virgin materials as an antidote to global warming is driving conscientious businesses to think recovery and recycling. From there they find that this approach improves their bottom lines.

In Massachusetts, there is no choice. Land-filling of construction and demolition waste has been banned since the beginning of 2006. Nationally, about 75 per cent of the estimated 200 million tons of waste is now processed for reuse as aggregate and mulch per year. Innovative equipment, know-how and institutional arrangements have flourished. The annual conferences of the Building Materials Reuse Association feature new nail-removing and wood-planing equipment. The Green Institute in Minneapolis pioneered in the application of tax deductions through deconstruction, an approach expanded and improved upon by Second Chance in Baltimore. Inventory control systems are shared among practitioners as well. Second Chance's contracts for workforce development and deconstruction of public buildings with the city of Baltimore are yet another addition to the techniques replicable in all cities and counties.

Each of these companies is unique. Dynasty Deconstruction, for example, has no resale facility. All sales are made on-site, through word of mouth and newspaper advertising. The company uses hand tools exclusively and partners with demolition companies for demolition services. At the same time, the company is not monopolistic. It has shared information, contacts and offers of joint ventures with others interested in getting in the business. The flow of materials from Dynasty Deconstruction sites is impressive. They include elevators, church pews, birch doors, all makes of furniture, carpets, marble and windows. Many items are reserved for donations to low-income service organizations. Metals are sold to scrap yards and traditional building materials (struts, tresses, flooring and roofing materials) are recovered and sold to local builders.

The company recruits workers locally and provides all training. Ludwig, the founder and CEO, runs a tight ship. If a worker is not seen for 10 minutes on a job an alert goes out for safety and efficiency reasons. In the last 6 months bricks have represented 50 per cent of all materials handled. The buyers send their trucks to pick up cleaned and stacked loads. Ludwig estimates that he has sold over 150,000 bricks in the last year. The immediate next step for the company is to set up, or joint venture with, a resale outlet so that the company can be directly linked to a full service system, and perhaps start local demolition companies. He is also looking for a construction and demolition waste landfill to purchase so that he can recover materials and restore local landfill capacity.

In the UK, social enterprises such as Dynasty Deconstruction can draw on a special national investment fund. Dynasty Deconstruction is self-capitalized and mission driven, even though it is a profit-making enterprise. Thus it joins other private firms such as Urban Ore in Berkeley, California, as a bottom-line oriented company which includes the environment and community as part of its bookkeeping.

## Box 7 Reasons for Not Retrofitting

Despite many efforts to promote eco-retrofitting, and its established financial benefits, there has been little interest or uptake so far.[1] Some of the reasons for this are:

- Lack of means to overcome the belief that 'retrofitting costs too much'. Mechanisms need to be devised to offset the initial design costs of the building with the long-term economic benefits of green design, such as the proposed sustainability standard.
- Lack of 'dark green' retrofitting and demonstration projects that show people how sustainable design can provide more quality of life with less negative environmental and social impacts, at no extra 'inherent' cost (given ongoing refurbishments).
- The 'indirect' approach of encouraging business and/or the community to reduce impacts through market-based or regulatory incentives, rather than through direct design solutions that address whole systems issues (ie 'ecology' as well as the 'environment').
- Lack of public awareness of the issues and potential solutions, such as radical forms of passive solar design, among all sectors that influence the built environment: clients, builders, government, designers, tenants, etc.
- Inadequacy of regulations and incentives to encourage new eco-efficient products, services or processes to counteract the inertia of business as usual; in particular, the lack of government support for eco-retrofitting programmes.
- Fragmentation, segregation and adversarial processes that characterize the building supply chain, and oppositional structural relationships among designers, builders and owners that often lead to zero sum outcomes and tradeoffs.
- Slow adoption of *integrated* design, procurement, construction, commissioning and management processes (such as partnering and quality-based selection), despite widespread acceptance of the fact that they can lead to better outcomes.
- Slow uptake of existing financial mechanisms to reduce the initial costs of retrofitting design, research and development. The focus of planning and environmental management has been on measuring, monitoring and mitigating after the design is conceived.
- Lack of procurement systems to ensure building components (products, materials and equipment) are green and 'appropriately' durable. A design or building is only as good as its weakest link (eg errors that permit mould to grow can destroy a building).
- The concept of 'best practice' being defined by marginal improvements over standard buildings (ie a small reduction over the standard can still obtain a high 'star rating'). Rating tools currently serve to lock in the non-sustainable prototype.
- The influence of the *modus vivendi*, or the tendency for builders and designers to want to continue their customary and comfortable ways of doing things, even when they know capacity-building in retrofitting could lead to increased profits.
- Cultural attitudes that favour new buildings, and the cultural belief that design itself is an added luxury when, in fact, it is a miniscule portion of the cost in the total life cycle of the building. Design is generally devalued, or even regarded with suspicion.
- Risk aversion and the perceived lack of client demand, which cause builders and developers to stick to conventional designs. Light green projects are deemed by the construction industry to be more marketable, but this has not actually been tested.
- Subsidies that favour non-renewable resources (eg fossil fuels reportedly receive $9 billion in subsidies in Australia), which enable highly *inefficient* new buildings to be built and old buildings to continue to operate without improvements.
- The complex, reductionist, prescriptive and retrospective orientation of building codes, assessment and rating tools, which currently favour new construction over retrofitting, and the failure of planning to consider the ongoing costs of existing development generally.

## Box 8 Retrofitting the Suburbs

Many suburbs in developed nations are due for renovation. They may eventually face redevelopment as ecologically insensitve forms of infill. Some of these leaky (old and new) homes guzzle fossil fuels and belch greenhouse gases. In urban areas, the total greenhouse gas emissions and other impacts of buildings can be greater than those of transport. Replacing them would involve extraordinary resource flows and, given current design norms, would entail massive embodied and operating energy.

New, higher-density infill development has sometimes been a curious blend of the worst aspects of consolidation and sprawl. It often reduces biodiversity, solar access, ecosystem services and environmental amenity (ie views and landscaping). It often increases noise, traffic, stormwater runoff and energy consumption. While many advocate reduced interior and exterior living space, new homes in countries like the US and Australia are still growing larger. However, most energy and material flows are not caused by space (which *in itself* does not use or embody energy). Other factors, such as the *source* of energy (ie solar energy or fossil fuels) or the *source* of materials (ie bio-based or extractive/non-renewable), can be more harmful over the building life-cycle.[1]

What matters is the use and design of space. Therefore, a partial material flows analysis was undertaken in Canberra to determine which pattern of housing was preferable from a whole systems and life-cycle perspective:[2]

- Urban 'consolidation' (ie increasing inner-city residential density)
- Replacing dwellings with 'green' infill development
- Green field energy-efficient development
- Renovating the housing stock with energy-efficiency measures

The study indicated that one of the most efficient means of reducing energy consumption and greenhouse gas emissions would be to retrofit the existing housing stock with passive solar design features. Passive solar retrofitting could be achieved more rapidly and with less resource flows and negative impacts than either 'energy-efficient' green field or urban infill. Of course, councils like the new rates and taxes that green field development brings, but they cannot afford to service new areas. While resource autonomous homes would solve this problem, they would cause more green field development. Instead, existing buildings could be retrofitted at net zero cost to homeowners by using financial mechanisms like performance contracting (where contractors recover the cost of construction from the future energy savings of the building).[3] Some local governments have established revolving funds for energy retrofitting for their own buildings. However, given the systemic biases against the eco-retrofitting of existing homes, a positive incentive may be needed.

The study therefore proposed that second storey units be permitted – but only where both dwellings were converted to passive solar heating, cooling and ventilating [Box 9]. This would provide the financial benefits of both rental income and increased capital value. It would also increase suburban density with little increase in land coverage, and without disrupting local communities. The demand on infrastructure would be reduced because the 'resource autonomy' of both dwellings would be required.[4] An eco-retrofitting programme could:

- Reduce greenhouse emissions, waste, resource use and energy consumption while increasing the ecological base.
- Upgrade the housing stock to increase longevity without the extensive demolition and waste that accompany major re-developments.
- Increase residential density, where appropriate, without exceeding the capacity of the existing infrastructure, while generating surplus eco-services.
- Convert suburbs from fossil-fuel dependency and toxic, petrochemical-based materials to clean, safe and healthy passive solar energy systems and compostable materials.
- Provide for responsible lifestyle choices, and preserve the life quality and 'sense of community' that people seek in the suburbs.

## Box 9 Solar Core

The proposed Solar Core is an example of a design concept that would enable existing homes or apartments to be heated, cooled and ventilated with passive solar energy.[1] It works by collecting the solar heat in the attic at the top of a dwelling, storing it in the centre of the structure (in a converted central fireplace or hall closet space). A rock storage container would stabilize the internal building temperature by slow radiation. The hot and cool air can also be distributed as heating and cooling. The Solar Core is essentially a 'solar chimney' (which draws hot air out of the house through a chimney-type structure) combined with a vertical, centrally-located thermal storage container. A frame of, say, galvanized fencing and wire could hold the rocks or used bricks in place in a central closet. This would avoid the disruption of building a masonry structure in an existing home and ensure both adjustability and reversibility.

In winter, the hot air collected in an attic space or collector can be delivered, aided by a solar fan, to the base of the Solar Core through pipes. This hot air heats the thermal mass of rocks as it rises. In summer, cool air can be drawn from below the house, or pool on the shady side in the case of slab-on-ground construction. This would cool the rocks and drive unwanted heat out through the solar chimney. Most heating and cooling would come through slow radiation from the Solar Core. A large surface area generally provides higher comfort levels than a small source (like an electric space heater or air conditioner). Vents and/or fans to the adjacent rooms could aid the circulation of conditioned air.

Using the Solar Core, almost any home could become solar heated and cooled, which, along with solar hot water systems, could eliminate most fossil fuel use (apart from other appliances). Sun-facing windows are not necessary, as any roof could work if not overshadowed by other buildings or tall trees. Where there is not much solar access, a glazed, airtight dormer window or black box amplifier on the roof could be added to collect hot air in winter and to expel hot air in summer (with appropriate attention to insulation and draught-proofing). Where a second floor unit is added, the two dwellings could have adjacent but separate stacks for individual control, but shared thermal mass, or as required to meet code requirements. Where adding an upper unit is prohibited by fire codes, a table-like structure could be constructed to support the new dwelling. The Solar Core could be used with other building configurations such as townhouse or duplex structures (modified to suit structural and firewall provisions).

Allowing the addition of second floor units would provide an investment incentive to encourage higher density and suburban solarization. Unlike the conventional consolidation approach, which either bulldozes existing dwellings or fills in open space, eco-retrofitting with a Solar Core could achieve many simultaneous goals. It would:

- Increase the resource autonomy of the housing stock
- Reduce fossil fuel dependency, and therefore increase 'natural security'
- Cost-effectively reduce greenhouse emissions, waste, resource use and energy
- Upgrade the housing stock without the demolition of existing homes
- Increase density and reduce sprawl, without additional demand on infrastructure
- Provide a positive incentive for homeowners or developers to add dwelling units
- Improve ecological and human health while generating economic growth
- Create more employment, skilled jobs and training in low-cost, constructive work
- Preserve choice in housing arrangements without disrupting existing communities
- Be compatible with any building style, as the roof can be modified
- Reward good design, as only ecologically responsible dwellings would be permitted
- Avoid local conflict caused by current approaches to urban infill development
- Foster the transition to a solar economy

## Box 10 Linear-reductionist Urban Analysis

In urban planning, sustainability is often broken down into factors or categories to facilitate measurement. Targets and indicators are assigned for these factors (usually based on available data).[1] 'Surrogates' for sustainability are used to simplify this process. Consequently, most of the literature on sustainable urban form can be placed somewhere within the following nested sequence of assumptions:

- The urban environment is often taken to be the whole system, as if it could be separated from the bioregion or other systems (eg air transport or cargo containerization).
- Urban environmental 'quality' (eg clean air and water) is often used in place of the broader concept of ecological sustainability (eg health of ecosystems and biodiversity).
- Energy and greenhouse gas emissions are often used as a substitute for the broader concept of environmental quality and then converted to energy for ease of measurement.
- Transport is often regarded as the main cause of greenhouse gas emissions, and other sources are marginalized (yet buildings can be a bigger source than transport).
- The subset of car transport is often taken to represent all transport although, for example, trucks may have greater net environmental impacts than cars.
- Urban population density correlates with reduced car usage, so other factors that influence car ownership and usage are marginalized, such as indirect subsidies to cars.
- Residential 'density' (eg dwellings/hectare) is often used in place of other relevant forms of development 'intensity' (eg energy use per square metre or resource consumption per person).

Increased residential density through compact urban form is thus seen as 'the' solution even if it consumes space less efficiently or uses more energy and water.

Linear-reductionist view of urban form

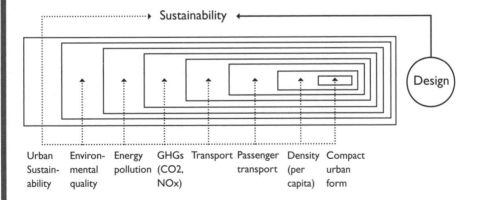

This sequential series of reductions often leads to one narrow solution. Compact urban form (to reduce the land area and discourage car usage) becomes the starting and end point. However, increasing the environmental sustainability of urban areas involves far more than reducing travel distances, car usage or pollution. So far, design templates have been anthropo-centric. A *whole* systems approach in which the ecology and equity would be seen as central, requires front loading design [Chapter 5].

# Box 11 Urban Density, Compactness and Urban Form

*Greg Bamford*

Views of the sustainability of cities often turn on claims about housing densities and overall urban densities, which may seem to be relatively straightforward or independent matters of fact. But how we measure densities depends on how we view cities so caution is needed.

If a city's housing stock consists only or largely of low-density housing types, such as the detached house and garden common in Australia, a low density city is the inevitable result. But the use of higher density housing types (row houses, flats) can produce cities of any density, from high to low, compact or sprawling. Much depends on the extent of open space, both residential and non-residential, in the city and on its urban form.

Unlike the housing stock of Australian cities, that of Copenhagen and Stockholm consists mostly of higher density housing types, yet these cities are not, correspondingly, such higher density cities, because higher density housing types can be used to provide larger open spaces adjacent to dwellings or residential areas, or to deliberately fragment a city without its overall density plummeting.

Although these Scandinavian cities are often praised by compact city advocates they are better understood as dispersed cities whose urban development is compact; they are modern versions of Ebenezer Howard's Social City, a development of his famous Garden City.[1] There is no simple answer to how dense such cities are because of the extent and configuration of their open space. Consequently, estimates of the density of Stockholm, for example, vary from one half to several times that of Sydney.

The measurement of urban density is more problematic than one might at first suppose. Should bodies of water in cities, in the form of rivers, lakes or harbours, be included in the density calculation? What constitutes a gap in an urban fabric? When does an urban area stop being urban and start being rural? As traditional differences between urban and rural settlement patterns or communities change, how do we distinguish 'urban' from 'rural' or 'peri-urban'?

In Howard's Garden City, a rural or green belt, functionally integrated with the town it encircled, was a means of preventing urban spread and the growth of conurbations. Is the density of the Garden City only that of the town, or the town together with its rural belt of farms, woodland etc. in which case its density is much lower? Howard's spatially more complex 'Social City' brings this seemingly academic question to a practical head.

The Social City was to be an urban region, a necklace of six garden cities around a larger 'Central City' intended to carry the urban functions appropriate to a city of the size of the Social City. The seven urban areas of the Social City would be inter-connected by transport corridors but remain separated by wide and continuous rural or green space. The novel form of the Social City would thus produce a density as low as that of any Australian city even though the density of any of its component 'cities', which were quite compact, was several times higher. In a nutshell, then, this is how the variations in estimates of the densities of Stockholm and Copenhagen come about, because of their garden city lineage. We can't decide what constitutes the city in such cases.

Copenhagen nicely illustrates the problem of measuring urban densities without considering urban or city form, and of identifying compactness with density. Rest the palm of your hand flat on a table, with no gaps between your fingers. Then spread your fingers as widely as possible. This is a good approximation of the Copenhagen plan – your fingers are the post-war growth corridors. Notice that your closed hand occupied the same area on the table as your spread hand does. So, by analogy, urban density remains unchanged as your fingers spread (if the space between them is discounted as rural) but the compactness of your hand decreases as your fingers spread (or grow longer).

There is no simple equation of density or compactness with sustainability - much depends on the uses to which open space can be put or the contributions it makes in cities, which these widely admired Scandinavian cities amply demonstrate.

## Box 12 The Social Dimension of Urban Consolidation

*Pat Troy*

A policy of urban consolidation has been pursued by federal and state governments to increase urban density in Australian cities in the belief that it would:

- Reduce environmental stresses because it would lead to reduced energy consumption and reduced water consumption
- Lead to reduced demand for infrastructure investment
- Provide greater choice of housing

None of the governmental propositions which emerged from this policy were based on empirical research, however, and subsequent research has shown that:

1  The per capita consumption of energy is higher for higher density housing compared with traditional housing forms – including for transport energy consumption.
2  The per capita consumption of water of households in higher density housing is not necessarily lower than that of traditional housing. In Sydney, the per capita consumption of water is approximately the same for flat and house dwellers. In Canberra, flat dwellers have virtually the same per capita consumption as those in flats and houses in Sydney, while house dwellers have a significantly higher consumption. Internal household water consumption is more influenced by household composition and behavioural, fashion and social considerations than housing form. Household external consumption of water is more influenced by the annual rainfall and its seasonal distribution, local gardening cultures, and soil conditions in different cities than housing form.
3  The level of infrastructure investment is more dependent on the size and structure of the city than on housing form. Increases in density have not been accompanied by significant savings in infrastructure services.
4  The market response to government encouragement of medium and high density housing has been to constrain the choice of housing so that areas in which consolidation policies have been most actively pursued now have limited opportunities for households seeking accommodation to house the average-sized household. This has led to a loss of diversity in the demographic composition of areas as the smaller-sized dwellings are inappropriate for conventional households. This leads to reduced housing choices in areas throughout the city. Higher density housing also tends to be rented, which in turn means higher proportions of households tend to be transient, with less engagement in the local communities in which the higher density dwellings are located. Moreover, the housing stock is now less flexible than it was and is thus less capable of responding to the changing accommodation needs.

Other consequences of the pursuit of consolidation policies include:

- Reduction in open space, and thus the ability to moderate local micro-climates
- Reduced capacity of the city to produce its own food
- The changed hydrology of local drainage basins leads to increased stormwater runoff, causing local flooding and increased pollution of the rivers, harbours and bays of cities
- Loss of industrial land in the inner suburbs and increased centralization of the city
- The subjection of larger proportions of the population to increased noise levels
- Loss of much independence of households as higher proportions of the housing stock come under the control of bodies corporate that set and manage the rules
- Consolidation projects also tend to be initiated by developers seeking opportunities for profit rather than any interest in the development of communities

In short, consolidation policies are based on a physical determinist approach to urban planning and development, which is not grounded in understanding of the socio-demographic aspects of the behaviour or ambitions of households.

## Box 13 Water and Sewage Management

*Sarah West*

In today's society, nearly every source of water (rainwater, stormwater, snow, floodwaters, groundwater, rivers, lakes, estuaries, wetlands, the oceans, sewage, dams or industrial effluent) is compartmentalized and controlled by different organizations. This has invariably resulted in water from one source polluting another, such as stormwater polluting rivers, or sewage polluting the ocean. Urban water supply and wastewater management schemes in industrialized countries have followed the centralized engineering design established in London and Paris in the late 1800s to protect the public from cholera and other waterborne diseases.

Piping sewage and stormwater away from homes to distant treatment facilities before discharging it to rivers and the sea has protected public health and possibly increased the longevity of many people. However, the design has also affected the environment and degraded the health of aquatic life and ecosystems.[1] Over time the impact has increased in different parts of the world, as more industrial wastes and household pollutants have been added to sewage. Household pollutants primarily occur in the form of pharmaceuticals, hormones, personal care products and cleaning agents.[2] Pollutants in waterways can accumulate and alter the physiology of fish and other aquatic animals, and may affect the health of humans who eat the seafood.

Today, as waterborne diseases have been largely eliminated in developed nations and clean water is in short supply in many countries, we face the challenge of improving the health of waterways and making better use of the water we have. Integrated water management and recycling at the local community and sub-catchment scale can provide a number of long-term benefits, including increased security of water supply and cleaner waterways. Decentralized or distributed water systems are able to efficiently integrate a range of local water sources, including treated sewage effluent, to optimize the variations in seasonal water supplies.

The values and aims that underpin decentralized, integrated water and wastewater management and recycling are resource efficiency, resource maximization, resource recovery, closing the nutrient cycle, closing the water cycle and closing the food loop.[3]

To minimize capital and operational costs, water needs to be captured, stored, used and recycled near its point of origin (approximately 90 per cent of the capital cost of conventional centralized water and sewerage systems is in trenching and installing large pipes over long distances). Current Positive Developments in water management are decentralized household-, cluster- or community-scale integrated water and sewerage systems that incorporate a range of technologies and water qualities 'fit for different purposes'. The design and technologies used will depend on a range of factors, such as local air quality, environmental conditions, cost, ease of management, cultural factors and recycling opportunities. For example, options for household on-site water collection and sewage treatment and recycling systems include:

- Rainwater tanks for drinking, cooking and showering with supplementary water from the reticulated (piped) town supply; a 'wet composting' (vermiculture) system to treat blackwater from the toilet; greywater treated and recycled for toilet flushing, garden irrigation and use in the washing machine.

- Spring, well, dam or river water for drinking, cooking and bathing; rainwater tank for supplementary water supplies; a dry composting toilet; greywater treatment and recycling to garden irrigation.

- Town water supplies for drinking, cooking and hand basins; rainwater into the hot water system for showering and use in the laundry; combined sewage (black and greywater) treated and recycled for toilet flushing and garden irrigation.

- Cluster or neighbourhood sewerage systems incorporating 'effluent sewers' with small diameter watertight pipes, and local sewage treatment and recycling schemes.

The term 'effluent sewer' is used for a system where the household sewage solids separate from the sewage water and settle out in a tank on each lot. The clarified effluent in the tank then either gravitates or is pumped away through a network of watertight pipes to a local sewage treatment plant.[4] When compared to a conventional gravity sewerage system, the benefits of a decentralized watertight effluent sewerage system are:

- No infiltration of stormwater into the sewers
- No need for sewage (plus stormwater) to bypass the treatment plant in wet weather nor be discharged directly to the waterway
- No escape of raw sewage from leaky pipes into the surrounding soil and groundwater
- No sewer-overflow valves that discharge raw sewage into rivers
- Small diameter pipes do not need to be trenched
- Flexible pipes can go around rocks, structures, trees and cultural sites
- Pipes travel short distances within the community area
- As the pipes carry primary treated effluent, and not raw sewage, there is less detrimental impact if a pipe is accidentally broken
- Effluent pumps use minimal electricity, thereby minimizing the generation of greenhouse gases, especially when local sustainable energy is used
- All sewage is treated and beneficially recycled

The treatment component of an effluent sewerage system is a combination of primary treatment (screening and settling) in a household tank and secondary treatment (biological digestion) at the community sewage treatment plant. The benefits of retaining most of the sewage solids in the household tank are:

- The pipes are small because they are not transporting solids
- There is very little likelihood of pipes becoming clogged
- The small pipes are relatively quick and inexpensive to install
- The secondary treatment plant is smaller and cheaper to build and operate, because it does not need to process the majority of the solids

However, household interceptor tanks do need to be de-sludged every 5 to 15 years, depending on the size and characteristics of the wastewater. Through the use of remote monitoring (telemetry), household and decentralized systems can be efficiently and cost-effectively operated and maintained by a centralized management authority.[5]

The design of a local secondary sewage treatment plant for a cluster of homes, neighbourhood or subdivision is based on the reuse opportunities in the surrounding area. Treated effluent can be piped back to homes for garden watering, toilet flushing and use in the washing machine; to community or council land for use on sports fields, golf courses, parks, gardens, road verges, race courses and airfields; to agricultural land for growing pasture, fodder crops, orchards, turf, bamboo, essential oils, herbs, flowers and woodlots; or to mining and industrial sites. Once the recycling opportunities have been identified or created, the sewage treatment system can be designed to achieve the required effluent quality. Effluent recycling opportunities can be created that generate a product for consumption or sale to the community.

Where there are insufficient effluent recycling opportunities in winter or wet weather, the excess can be stored, transported elsewhere or, depending on the soil type, dispersed through the soil profile to groundwater where it later becomes beneficial baseflow in the adjacent rivers. Final effluent from 'best practice' decentralized sewage treatment systems, such as textile filters, sand filters and reed-beds, are safely disposed of through the soil in winter in New Zealand and the US.[6]

Through decentralized local water collection and sewage treatment and recycling systems that are designed to meet the needs of the local community and catchment, we can protect human and aquatic life and live in better balance with our environment.

## Box 14 Advantages of Eco-roofs

*Linda S. Velazquez*

Roof greening is an environmentally friendly technology that produces a living, breathing 'fifth façade'. Green roofs or eco-roofs are simply sloped or flat vegetated rooftops covered in plants and engineered lightweight soil. They are a healthy, responsible and eco-effective alternative to the common hot asphalt, tar and concrete roofs. The vegetation and growing media atop an eco-roof mimic the natural processes of evapotranspiration and photosynthesis found at ground level. Design options run the gamut from naturalistic meadows planted with grassy wildflower drifts to modern, sleek, geometric plans. The two main types of eco-roofs are extensive – a shallow, 1–6 inch lightweight vegetated cover of mostly succulents and herbs not meant for human access – and intensive – a heavier roof garden with 8–12 inch growing media which allows for vegetable gardens, and even trees and human recreation (the roof loading must be engineered accordingly). Eco-roofs offer a huge array of public and private benefits while restoring and revitalizing the environment, our psyche and our pocketbooks.[1] Just some of these benefits are:

**Stormwater management**: Eco-roofs act as sponges on top of buildings by capturing, reducing and slowing down stormwater volumes on-site and serve to alleviate stormwater infrastructure systems. Many large older cities have combined sewer systems where storm drains and sewage pipes come together. Heavy rainfall produces runoff from sealed surfaces, such as rooftops and pavements, which can wreak havoc with already over-burdened systems, contaminating lakes, rivers and other freshwater sources with sewer overflow. Depending on factors such as the depth of the growing media, type of plants and rainfall intensity, eco-roofs can absorb 50–95 per cent of the rain, reducing the peak flow rate and delaying runoff.

**Water quality improvement**: Through evapotranspiration, eco-roofs filter and cool down the water that slowly runs off. Nitrogen, phosphorus and toxins can enter a vegetated stream as dissolved substances. Heavy metals and nutrients found in stormwater are bound in the engineered soil instead of being discharged into the groundwater or streams or rivers. Over 95 per cent of cadmium, copper and lead and 16 per cent of zinc can be taken out of rainwater, and nitrogen levels can also substantially fall.[2] Coastal cities have issues pertaining to the warming of their rivers and bays from the result of heated stormwater, as the temperature change can greatly affect the health of cold water fish populations such as salmon.

**Heat mitigation**: At ground level, vegetative canopy biomass greatly lowers air temperatures, whereas the artificial, altered surfaces found on developed landscapes and rooftops greatly raise them. Average city rooftops can easily reach 65–79°C in the summer. Tightly sealed surfaces, such as asphalt and concrete in parking lots and on rooftops, soak up the heat during the day and reradiate it back into the Earth's atmosphere as thermal infrared radiation after sunset. The temperature in downtown areas is often 5–6°C warmer than the surrounding outlying areas. The added heat contributes to air quality problems and increases the amount of ozone that is produced. Used on a large scale, eco-roof infrastructure reduces the urban heat island effect by lowering ambient air temperatures through the evapotranspiration of the plants and engineered soil. A 2002 Toronto study by Environment Canada estimated that urban temperatures could dip 1–2°C if just 6 per cent of the city's roofs were 'greened'.[3]

**Storm mitigation**: Impervious surfaces not only contribute to the urban heat island effect with significant impact on our health, environment and the cost of utilities, they also amplify storms. Tied to the heat released at night from buildings and roads, heat islands can also affect the local weather by creating damaging convective thunderstorms. These storms create a lot of water runoff, water that does not percolating back into the aquifer.

**Air quality improvement**: Eco-roofs can filter and bind dust particles and naturally filter airborne toxins. Ventilation is sometimes inhibited due to the vertical design of downtown areas, which reduces wind speed and traps heat in air pockets; pollutants can remain suspended for days. But on an eco-roof, atmospheric dust is held in the growing media substrate until rain washes it off. Smog, sulphur dioxide, carbon dioxide and other airborne toxins from the city air are absorbed and filtered through the foliage, naturally cleansing the environment. As a result of urban heat islands, more ozone gas is created – a major contributor to global warming. NASA studies have shown that an increase in ozone levels also affects sufferers of asthma and other breathing conditions.[4]

**Erosion and sedimentation control:** Watersheds and sewer systems are protected because eco-roofs act as erosion barriers through reduced stormwater volumes and assist in the control of sediment transport and overall soil erosion. The combination of plant and media properties such as friction, root absorption and substrate matter can control sediments from entering waterways.

**Wildlife habitat conservation:** Displaced birds, bees, butterflies and other beneficial insects – and, in some cases, endangered species – are offered a healthy vegetative patch in otherwise disturbed urban roofscapes.

**Food production:** Diminishing urban greenspace for gardening at ground level can be achieved on an eco-roof. Herbs and vegetables can be grown and harvested privately for resale or in community roof gardens, and otherwise barren roofs can be productive.

**User benefits:** The glare off a white roof can be blinding at close distances, and a eco-roof creates a soothing alternative for windows overlooking it. An eco-roof can result in noise suppression ranging from 8dB up to 50dB due to the depth of the substrate. The increased amenity space of an eco-roof can be enjoyed by residents and employees, and higher occupancy and rental and increase resale rates can be reaped by owners.

**Increased roof longevity and reduced maintenance costs:** The most vulnerable layer of any roof is the waterproofing course, which degrades over time due to exposure of the elements. Eco-roofs greatly protect these buried membranes from extreme wind, temperature fluctuations, damaging ultra violet rays and mechanical injury. European eco-roofs have been around from 40 to 75 years or more and when properly installed with high quality materials, they can double the roof longevity and functionality. Major eco-roof providers commonly issue a 20-year assembly warranty and performance guarantee.

**Reduced energy consumption and costs:** Thermally insulating eco-roofs offer energy savings through reduced energy usage in varying degrees based on geography, number of storeys, system type and depth of the soil substrate. A 2000 report found that in general savings of up to 50 per cent of cooling costs and 25 per cent of heating costs could be achieved, at least for the floor directly below the eco-roof.[5] A 2003 study found the Seattle Justice Center is saving as much as US$148,000 each year due to its eco-roof.[6]

**Increased developable space:** Eco-roofs can significantly reduce the size of, or even completely eliminate, the costly and unattractive large tracts of land necessary for retention ponds. As a stormwater management measure to offset permeability requirements, some cities extend density bonuses to developers who use eco-roofs (instead of impervious rooftops), resulting in higher floor-to-area development ratios. Currently Portland, Oregon, and Chicago, Illinois, offer developers increased floor area within the Central City, depending on eco-roof coverage in relation to the building's footprint.

**Reduction of stormwater infrastructure:** The need to capture, slow down and then release urban runoff is necessary in every municipality, and eco-roofs are considered to be a low impact development solution since they manage stormwater on-site. If applied on a large scale and treated as a stormwater infrastructure 'best management practice', eco-roofs could feasibly lower the overall costs of stormwater rehabilitation in our cities through reduced replacement of conventional elements such as drains, pipes and sewer lines.

**Reduced local impact fees and increased incentives:** Utility surcharges are often levied against owners of impervious surfaces. European countries such as Germany, The Netherlands, Switzerland and Sweden offer reduced stormwater and impervious cover fees plus energy credits, grants and tax incentives. For example, some German municipalities issue stormwater fee reductions of 50 to 80 per cent for eco-roofs. Portland provides a discount on the stormwater management charge for property owners who manage their stormwater on site. Chicago offers fast tracking permits to developers incorporating eco-roofs and grants to homeowners and small businesses.

## Box 15 Net Positive (Physical) Development Criteria

Positive Development is that which leaves ecological and social conditions better off after construction than before. Assessment criteria would be relative to pre-development conditions, rather than conventional buildings. The following criteria relate mostly to biophysical design. They are also included, together with social criteria, in the SmartMode overview [Chapter 15]. Design for Positive Development would be reversible, and aim to:

- Prioritize the eco-retrofitting of existing cities and suburbs to eliminate the use of fossil fuels and toxic materials, mitigate existing impacts of surrounding development, produce clean air, water and soil, and make humans and ecosystems healthier.

- Exceed 'resource autonomy' (ie self-sufficient energy production, water and waste treatment), through design that *increases* the ecological base and public estate of the site *and* surrounding region (to counteract decreasing carrying capacity and biodiversity).

- Create conditions and support for eco-services and integrate them with development to improve the viability and self-sufficiency of urban areas; in other words provide infrastructure and space in buildings for the production of ecosystem goods, services and ecosystems.

- Actively restore and expand the urban ecology by creating natural habitats, nature corridors and so on to support appropriate biodiversity in urban areas, by designing spaces to accommodate the needs of indigenous and, especially, endangered species.

- Reduce net land coverage of development by combining social functions and natural systems (ie renewable energy, ecosystems and biodiversity) through design for multi-functional use of space (eg green space walls with terrariums and vertical wetlands).

- Weigh in the embodied and ecological waste of development or design decisions, and compensate for any unavoidable waste or resource use by net positive improvements to the urban and/or regional ecology (ie not simply aim to reduce embodied energy and water).

- Increase the 'natural security' and self-sufficiency of urban areas by creating space and infrastructure for food production, in a manner that mitigates the heat island effect of existing development (eg green roofs, balconies, building skins and eco-atriums).

- Identify and correct social, economic and ecological deficiencies of the surrounding urban or rural environment to reduce social inequities and increase accessibility (eg parks and playgrounds that also store water for adjacent landscapes and fire protection).

- Analyse and design for social needs, interpreted broadly to include community, economic, cultural and psychological needs, making places for positive social interaction, communion with nature, sense of community, social security and physical safety.

- Provide training for urban ecosystem managers and facilities managers to plan, design and manage continuous improvements to buildings that proactively improve human and environmental health, as opposed to just reducing toxins in the environment.

- Avoid or replace 'fossil' with 'renewable' resources: that is, wind and solar power and biobased materials (as opposed to fossil-fuel-based electricity, fibres, fuels and processes) to increase available energy while reducing the impact of existing sources.

- Design to *maximize* 'passive' solar design systems, which can be more efficient than energy production in both embodied and operating energy. If under-designed , theydo not realize their potential, and may even require back up systems.

- Explore opportunities to replace resource- and capital-intensive machines with natural micro-organism-powered systems (however, the burden of proof should be on proponents of patented microbes to demonstrated that no natural life form could do the job).

## Box 16 Making Positive Impacts

*Sonia S. Mendoza*

The Ecological Solid Waste Management Act of the Philippines mandates the decentralization of waste management to the barangay level (the smallest unit of government). Each barangay or a cluster of barangay is mandated to establish Materials Recovery Facilities (MRFs) where the segregated waste collected from the point of generation will be managed to keep the community clean and free of disease-causing vermin and micro-organisms.

Mother Earth Foundation (MEF) and other groups in the Ecowaste Coalition conduct training workshops on waste management to the different sectors of society – to barangays, schools, government offices, business establishments, church groups and NGOs. We have helped establish successful sites in cooperation with these sectors and in particular with barangays. We started with pilot barangays and they have achieved waste diversion rates of at least 62 per cent to at most 90 per cent. At present we are working with municipalities, cities and most recently a whole province.

Barangay Bagumbuhay is densely populated and has virtually no land space for composting. It is very clean and is able to divert 62 per cent of waste from landfill. The barangay employed 4 eco-aides at the start of the project in 2003 and now has 14 full-time employees. Income from their Ecowaste programme and incentives from the City Mayor have enabled them to add a conference hall, a session hall for barangay meetings and a lush garden which is an eco-tour site. Residual wastes from sweet wrappers, composite packaging for chips, etc are gathered by about 20 to 25 families. These are cut into small pieces in their homes and sold to the barangay for 6 US cents per kilogram. These pieces are incorporated into their pavement tiles, which are now sold at US$1 per piece. These will supply the sidewalk beautification of a portion of the district where the barangay is located. The barangay boasts a gym and a day-care centre for its residents. The City Health Centre has reported that incidences of diarrhoea, typhoid, cholera and respiratory diseases have gone down in the barangay since the Ecowaste programme was implemented. With another composting unit planned for next year, it will achieve 85 per cent waste diversion.

Barangay Parang in another city in Metro Manila is also an eco-tour site for students, local government units and offices from all over the country. They have a lush garden of herbs, vegetables, ornamental plants and fruit-bearing trees near their composting area, an audiovisual room and a livelihood area where beautiful paper beads are made from glossy magazine pages. The livelihood team could not cope with the local demand for their beads, trays and other products, which are displayed in their souvenir shop. The barangay joins in an annual exhibit along the riverbanks and gets to display their beautiful products from recyclable discards to visitors from the different cities in Metro Manila and the provinces.

The Municipality of Ibaan (south of Manila) has no dumpsite and all its 26 barangays have an MRF where composting (if not done in backyards) and further sorting of clean recyclables is done. They have organic vegetable gardens in the backyards and in the barangay MRFs produce fresh squash, cucumbers, eggplant and okra. There are no rubbish bins along the highway in this municipality. All discards are responsibly addressed in the households or in the barangay MRFs. Colourful lanterns, Christmas decorations and shopping bags have been crafted from the residual waste of 2-litre soft drink bottles, juice packs and plastic straws.

In Caloocan City, 155 out of 188 barangays have established MRFs. The recyclables are collected and stored in mobile MRFs for barangays that have no space. Some of its barangays exchange rice for recyclables brought by their residents, and space allotted for the programme has expanded to three times its original size.

These and many other examples in different parts of the Philippines have become educational tour sites for other local government units and communities. Discards management has sparked community participation and inculcated a sense of pride and belonging among the residents.

## Box 17 Urban Wind Energy

Wind and solar power are essentially 'reversible' and mobile forms of electricity generation because, unlike fossil fuel and nuclear plants, they can be dismantled and relocated. Small wind generators can assist in making buildings energy self-sufficient. Combined wind and solar installations on urban buildings can capture energy virtually year round. Owners can sell energy back to the grid, or rent roof space to energy producers. A diverse range of small and aesthetically pleasing, low embodied energy wind generators is coming onto the market. However, there are still negative myths raising concerns about wind power that have impeded its adoption. Some relatively progressive countries are beginning to address the various finance, regulatory planning and technical standards that are slowing adoption.[1] Some of these concerns, pertaining to both large and small wind generators, are addressed below.[2]

### Can wind turbines be used in urban areas?

There is now a wide range of urban wind turbines on the market. They do not need to be shaped like windmills high above the roof. They can be horizontal elements along the ridgeline of roofs or vertical elements along the corners of façades. They are designed to avoid noise and vibrations. They can be integrated with the architecture, add architectural interest and be retrofitted on older buildings.

### Does wind energy cost more?

Fossil fuels have received far more government subsidies over the last few decades than all forms of green energy together.[3] Currently, it can cost more to construct a new wind power plant than continuing to draw energy from an existing fossil fuel plant (especially offshore plants). However, many predict that energy demand will continue to skyrocket. This makes new wind power plants competitive with *new* fossil fuel plants – especially given the risk of increased fuel prices. If we considered the externality costs of fossil fuel-based production sources, of course, wind energy would be far cheaper already.

### Does wind variability increase the costs of a utility system?

Variability affects the operations of other energy facilities in a system. When these costs are distributed across consumers, however, increases are negligible. Some weak distribution grids could require upgrades, but the amount of wind energy could be limited to the grid's existing capacity. Arguably, the costs of modernization are inevitable anyway, unless we shift to self-sufficient housing. Moreover, integrating wind power into an electric power system could reduce total costs to consumers.[4] In other words, losses from coping with fluctuations will be small compared to overall savings.

### Can rural wind power cooperatives compete with big providers?

There are cases where farmers have formed cooperatives to build and own wind power plants.[5] The success of these independent ventures depends on access to the grid, tax credits, regulations and the like. Small wind plants cost more per megawatt than larger ones but, again, when distributed across all customers, the premium is negligible. There is a clear trend towards willingness to pay more for energy independence and for other benefits to the local community such as the increased employment and tax base that would follow.

## Does wind power need back up with conventional sources?

All electricity sources are subject to outages or need for repairs. Most utility systems are interconnected to backup sources and fluctuations in supply, so reliability is not an issue. The dispersed generation from building integrated systems would reduce the load on the distribution network. So, in most cases, additional backup would not be needed. Typical wind generators produce electricity about 80 per cent of the time. Energy storage systems for wind and solar power (eg graphite) would be easier to develop than, say, nuclear storage, but they have received relatively little funding.[6]

## Will wind energy reduce demand and raise coal power prices?

Energy consumption is increasing to the extent that conventional sources of fuel have no reason to worry about losing their market share. However, if demand for conventional fuels were reduced by wind power, any reduced fuel prices would compensate for the (currently) higher costs of renewable sources. In other words, rates would decrease overall. While energy consumption is increasing, demand for green energy is also rapidly increasing. Wind power still has to compete with existing fossilized plants, but many are willing to pay *extra* for green energy.[7]

## Is wind energy expensive?

Wind is commercially competitive now, despite perverse subsidies, and is the fastest growing energy source. The unit cost of wind energy is being reduced rapidly with economies of scale – over 80 per cent in 25 years. Energy from natural gas is currently cheaper, but gas prices are rising and may continue to do so. Future energy supplies from wind power will be stable, and wind does not increase in price. Wind generators do not have fuel costs or supply risks, are low in operation and maintenances costs, and will benefit from future carbon pricing mechanisms and environmental regulations.

## Is wind energy inefficient?

Wind power plants convert up to 50 per cent of the energy from wind into electricity, while coal power plants convert about 25 per cent of the energy from coal into electricity, and two thirds of this energy is lost in transmission. Operation energy efficiency is not critical in the case of wind, as wind is free and does not produce waste. Coal, on the other hand, contains many highly toxic elements that are released into the air and water. Moreover, the average wind farm pays back its embodied energy in about half the time taken by coal or nuclear power plants.[8]

## Do wind plants kill wildlife?

Studies show that wind generators kill far fewer birds than bird collisions with buildings, cars or power plants. Conventional fossil fuel energy sources do far more harm to animals by destroying their habitat and polluting their environments – not to mention their contribution to climate change. Some have also suggested that the productivity of farm animals could be reduced by wind farms, but research does not back this up.[9] We do not know the genetic impacts of nuclear power. It has been argued that the damage caused by Chernobyl was greatly exaggerated, as there was not a substantial increase in cancers. However, there were reportedly 200,000 coerced abortions in the wake of Chernobyl, so we cannot know how many of those might have had genetic abnormalities.

## Do wind plants tolerate extreme weather?

Wind power turbines can be built to operate from −20 to +50 degrees Celsius. Wind is often highest in the afternoon in summer, when demand is greatest for air conditioning. Conventional coal-based power plants actually increase extreme weather and its impacts (storms, droughts, fires and floods). Wind turbines do not attract lightning as they have built-in lightning protection systems. Fire risks of wind farms are low as flammable parts are high above ground and high-voltage connections are underground.

## Are wind plants noisy and ugly?

The noise of modern large wind generators at about 300 metres overhead is about that of a home refrigerator. They are certainly arguably less ugly and noisy than nuclear or coal-based plants, and the mining that they entail. Some even feel that wind farms add visual interest to the landscape. They can also be built offshore. Legislation can protect sensitive areas from *any* development, and few people will live in sight of wind power plants. In any case, they can eventually be removed with little damage to the environment.

## Will they make any real difference?

Generally, a megawatt hour of wind energy avoids one ton of greenhouse gas emissions. A typical 2MW wind turbine will reduce greenhouse emissions by about 6000 tons per year. Worldwide wind energy capacity is roughly 60,000MW, which is the equivalent of taking 36 million cars off the road each year in terms of greenhouse gas emissions. Like solar energy, the amount of space that wind generators use in relation to their outputs is small compared to mining fossil fuels or uranium.

## Will wind power put people out of business?

All industrial structures, like coal-based and nuclear power plants, have limited life spans. Centralized energy plants are being closed down by environmental and health legislation or obsolescence. Wind power, due to its dispersal, creates jobs in construction and operation and other benefits to regional communities. It can reduce the social dislocation that will result from the inevitable closure of conventional plants. The jobs created are of a higher quality and less dangerous than those associated with coal or uranium.

## What about the up-front costs?

As with other technologies that eventually pay for themselves, performance contracting can be used to cover the initial costs. If the building owner does not have to pay for the installation, energy service providers can eventually recover their costs from the energy savings. They could demand a relatively higher profit, as long as the building owner saves money in the end. Further, there is little evidence that wind power plants affect property values negatively, and some communities earn additional income by showing wind farms to tourists.

## Box 18 Solar Powering the Future

*Keith Lovegrove*

We have been led to believe that solar power is too expensive or incapable of supplying all the needs of society. Not so.

In the more energy intensive societies of the world, such as the US and Australia, fossil fuels are being consumed at a rate of between 15kg and 20kg per day 365 days per year for every man, woman and child. This in turn leads to emissions of carbon dioxide of around 50kg per day per capita. This adds up to a lot of energy, a lot of fossil fuel to provide it and a lot of greenhouse gas emissions. However, at the personal level, 800MJ/day per person is needed, which is the amount of energy falling on 40m$^2$ of the average house roof in Australia. Less sunny parts of the world, such as Europe, would need twice as much area per person to achieve this from solar inputs but, of course, they also benefit from good wind, biomass and hydro, or other renewable energy resources. So powering the future from solar energy is not limited by the amount of solar energy available, yet Australia has been slow to implement this technology.

There are basically two approaches to producing electricity directly from solar radiation:

1    Turning photons to electricity with photovoltaic cells; or
2    Using the radiation to produce high temperature fluids that turn turbines or other power cycles in solar thermal power systems.

Photovoltaic (PV) cells are predominantly made from wafers of silicon, the same stuff that computer chips are made from. In simple terms, individual photons from the sun give individual electrons a kick to a higher energy place and so create a voltage. Solar cells are typically dark blue squares 10–20cm a side, assembled into panels about a metre long. Arrays of such panels can be assembled on house roofs and connected to an inverter. This converts the DC electricity from the panels to the higher voltage AC electricity that household appliances run on. Such inverters can connect into the electricity mains so that a house can import or export electricity to the grid. Houses can run completely autonomously if electric storage batteries are added to store energy for night and cloudy days. PV systems can be installed in large arrays as well, for connection to the electricity grid.

Over the last two decades the photovoltaic industry has been booming, with annual growth rates of over 30 per cent. Worldwide annual sales in 2006 had a capacity to generate electricity at a rate of approximately 2000MW, equivalent to two large coal power stations. Much of the growth has been stimulated by favourable policies in some countries, Germany and Japan in particular. The downside of PV is the high capital cost, considerably higher per unit capacity than a wind farm, for example. New technologies are currently being commercialized that achieve the same results with much thinner layers of silicon and so have considerable potential to bring costs down in the future.

Solar thermal power is best suited to the construction of much larger power systems than the household scale. But with the world increasingly looking for utility scale renewable energy, proponents feel its time may have finally come. Solar thermal power systems work using ordinary glass mirrors to focus radiation onto high temperature receivers, where fluids such as molten salt, heat transfer oil or steam are heated up to provide the heat input for power systems. The vast majority of the world's electricity today is produced from steam turbines provided with steam from either coal or nuclear boilers. Solar thermal power systems have the ability to directly substitute for these heat sources and allow power stations to continue to be built with steam turbines on the same scale. In Southern California, plants with a total capacity of 354MW (enough to power a small city) have been working successfully for 20 years. In 2006, another 200MW of systems were under construction in the US, Spain and Australia. Solar thermal systems also offer the potential for large-scale, cost-effective energy storage through stores of hot fluids or thermo-chemical processes.

## Box 19 E-waste

*Robin Tennant-Wood*

'E-waste', or electronic waste, is toxic waste and is a serious problem worldwide.[1] The components of this waste include glass and plastics, as well as heavy metals and contaminants such as mercury, cadmium and lead. Even if it were not toxic, the sheer quantities of electronic and electrical equipment being discarded would make e-waste a major concern. There are billions of computers, digital cameras, mobile phones, PDAs, iPods and games machines in use and, as technology improves, so too increases the desire to constantly upgrade or replace equipment. In 2005 over 731,000 computers were dumped in landfills in Australia alone, and this number is likely to double in 2006.[2]

There are currently two main regulatory approaches for controlling the dumping of e-waste. First, regulation implemented by local governments banning disposal of electronics in landfill; second, regulation at the international level, represented mainly by the Basel Convention on the Control of Transboundary Movements of Hazardous Wastes and their Disposal (1989). The Basel Convention is essentially an agreement prohibiting global free trade in toxic waste; however, the US neither controls nor prohibits toxic trade and has not ratified it. As a result, vast quantities of hazardous e-waste are shipped from the US to developing countries, in particular Nigeria and China, where computers are stripped for any recyclable materials and the rest dumped in landfills or waterways, or burned in the open air. The environmental and health impacts of this practice are catastrophic and there is no regulatory means of controlling the so-called 'recycling' processes within these countries.

Recycling waste electronic equipment is a highly specialized field. In Europe, waste electronic and electrical equipment (WEEE) disposal plants are being established to deal with the increasing amounts of material.[3] Facilities of this type will become commonplace across the developed world with their associated economic benefits in employment and resource recovery. These facilities also serve to raise community awareness of the waste problem, which might otherwise go unnoticed.

Regulation, resource recovery and recycling, however, are end-of-pipe approaches. There is a need for systemic long-term solutions to the mounting problem of e-waste. While regulatory control is important, it must be supported by a strong policy framework that incorporates not only the economic benefits of resource recovery but controls over the design and manufacture of products. The EU has led the way in the latter area with regulation which, from 1 July 2006, bans the import or manufacture of electronic equipment that does not meet certain standards on limiting use of the two most common brominated flame retardants and on reducing the use of lead, mercury, cadmium and hexavalent chromium.[4] The regulation, known as RoHS (Restriction on the Use of Certain Hazardous Substances in Electrical and Electronic Equipment) applies only to electronics sold in EU countries, but the strength of the combined European market has forced manufacturers to take action on the design and manufacture of products across the board.

Clearly, e-waste is a problem that is not going away. Like all forms of waste, e-waste is highly political and the long-term solution, therefore, will be political. The European Commission is currently adopting a new Regulatory Framework for the Registration, Evaluation and Authorization of Chemicals (REACH). This will tighten the restrictions imposed on the electronics industry through RoHS. Such regulations will enforce changes in design and manufacture and increase producer responsibility. Dealing with waste before it becomes waste is widely recognized as the key to sustainability in waste management. Extended producer responsibility (EPR) ensures manufacturers take responsibility for their products beyond the sale and encourages the production of equipment that complies with environmental standards. Local regulations on the disposal of e-waste are becoming more common, and as well as placing more responsibility on producers, these will ensure that consumers, too, accept greater responsibility for the ultimate destination of the equipment they purchase.

## Box 20 Designing for Successful Failures

*Dr Paul Bannister*

Essentially all buildings are complex, one-off designs filled with a wide range of mechanical and electrical, automated and manual systems that act as valves on the resource consumption of the building. Irrespective of the best intent of all the parties concerned, it is inevitable that these systems break down. As a result, the resource consumption of the building depends critically on how the building responds to such failures.

This can be illustrated by the following simple example of a light switch. If a light switch is not turned off at the end of the day, the light will stay on until the following morning, wasting a great deal of energy. The light switch as a control system can be seen to be a poor solution as one simple (and probable) failure can cause much waste. Furthermore, the waste is potentially difficult to detect, in that it occurs overnight when no-one is in the building to notice the failure. No-one is negatively affected by the failure (except the accountant or owner, and they are unlikely to recognize the existence of the problem), and driving past the building many would assume that someone must be present to justify the lights being on.

Of course, there is a range of methods by which one could reduce the impact of this problem. One could install automatic controls such as a timeclock or occupancy sensor; one could reduce the number of lights serviced by the light switch; one could improve the efficiency of the lighting system so that the energy impact of control failure is reduced; or one could provide an alarm that tells people that the lights were on overnight. Each of these methods has strengths and weaknesses but, together, they can produce a control that is robust to failure.

Given the range of potential failure scenarios associated with a simple light switch, it is small wonder that failures in more complex systems often go unnoticed. Each of these failures reduces the building's efficiency and, in an extreme case, can lead to the performance of the building being worse than average rather than leading edge. To avoid this fate, designers need to consider the following techniques:

- Identify the opportunities for failure. It is worth consulting with building maintenance specialists to establish this.

- Reduce the number of moving parts. Fewer moving parts means fewer opportunities for failure.

- Limit the domain of failure. Ensure that the total amount (kW) of the plant that would be incorrectly operated in the event of a failure is limited. This can be achieved by improving the basic efficiency of this plant, or by reducing the area or number of plant items attached to an individual failure point.

- Remove compensatory mechanisms. Ensure that in the event of a failure there are no energy consuming systems that will operate to hide the failure.

- Provide failure detection. For systems that are likely to fail with energy consequences, provide additional monitoring to alert the building operator to the failure.

- Ensure that all moving components can be inspected and accessed readily. A plant that is difficult to inspect or access will be less likely to be detected and fixed.

- Design buildings with ongoing ecological upgrading and simple passive adjustments in mind.

For any building, there will be a balance of each of these approaches required to achieve a building that is designed to fail successfully. In design, failure is successful if we in fact learn from it.

## Box 21 The Case of Steel-Frame Housing

Despite their impressive advances, there are many examples of life-cycle analyses that take a narrow perspective. A whole systems analysis would look at the life-cycle of products, programmes, buildings and materials – but also at geographically specific ecological factors, such as biodiversity, environmental flows and ecosystem integrity. To take a case in point: steel-frame housing has been advocated on grounds of long life and durability. The Australian Greenhouse Office was promoting steel frame housing at one stage because they discounted the embodied energy of materials. But again, if buildings used passive solar heating, cooling and ventilating, then embodied energy would be the more critical issue.[1] Yet even this 'narrow' life-cycle approach presents unresolved, complex issues:

- A timber-frame house stores almost three times more carbon than a steel-frame house, and production of the steel-frame house releases about five times more $CO_2$ than a timber-frame house. Therefore, energy and pollution reduction through recycling may be less important than a shift from fossil fuels to solar energy and, ultimately, to a 'carbohydrate economy' (ie an industrial system where carbohydrates replace hydrocarbons, that is where vegetables, not minerals, supply factories for fuel and particularly materials).[2] Growing materials may be better for the environment than mining them.

- Steel has at least 20 per cent more embodied energy than timber (the steel industry alone uses as much electricity as the residential sector).[3] A timber-framed building takes six years of operation to consume the same amount of energy as that used in construction, while a steel-framed building takes about nine years. Although steel is increasingly 'recycled', the recycled content is often still small compared to that of 'virgin' ore. Organic materials are generally less harmful to produce than minerals, and can be composted at the end of their life rather than being transported to landfill.

- The longevity of a structure often depends on the least durable *component*. The lifespan of housing is shortened by many factors other than the strength of the steel frame. Steel framing, for example, can be subject to moisture problems in walls. Like timber frames, they are susceptible to mould damage if not properly moisture- and vapour-proofed (although not as vulnerable to termites). Mould damage is a billion dollar issue in San Francisco, for example. In such cases, steel would not be likely to realize its potential lifespan.

- The electromagnetic field implications of steel-frame are still under investigation and could have long-term public health consequences, although some consider this highly debatable. Few take this potential problem seriously, but nor were the effects of radon or microwaves taken seriously at one time.[4] The precautionary principle suggests it is *not* advisable to lock society into a permanent construction system that might have long-term health impacts and lose opportunities for future adaptation and innovation.

- The insulation value of steel framing is around 30 per cent lower than wood construction. Steel members can cause 'thermal bridging', where hot or cold leaks through an insulated wall via a highly conductive material. Materials with better insulative properties are available that are cheaper, locally produced and have lower impacts, such as strawbale or earth construction. These can be combined with steel framing, of course.

- While steel can be designed for disassembly, steel structures also lock us into building systems and aesthetics that might become obsolete or otherwise unsuitable in changing times ('11 September' was hopefully a learning experience for urban designers among others). On a smaller scale, the long spans possible with steel allow internal walls to be easily rearranged to accommodate changing user needs, but timber lattice space frames can also enable high spans.[5]

Some of these issues cannot really be determined by numbers. It is too easy to advocate – or object to – steel framing without a whole systems analysis that takes into account a broad range of criteria and recognizes changing needs, values and contextual factors.[6] The built environment is a complex system, and this is before we try to factor in the ecology.

## Box 22 Green Building Guidelines

General design considerations vary according to climate, topography, annual and diurnal temperature range, wind, humidity, and so on. Generalized notes do not apply in every situation, and those below[1] generally assume a temperate climate. Such green design considerations are for convenience only and should *not* be applied in a 'tick the box' fashion.

### Broader social considerations

- Including public uses like childcare facilities, galleries and restaurants.
- Reflecting traditional design elements that characterize the region, where appropriate.
- Designing for crime prevention through people-friendly design.
- Creating mixed-use development, as in the existing 'urban village' model, to increase access to services with reduced transport.
- Ensuring access and use by the disabled and elderly (usually required by legislation).
- Laying out residential developments to encourage a sense of community by creating communal open space and park areas.
- Respecting the need for privacy and outdoor semi-private space (by the use of patios, porches, conservatories, trellises, etc).
- Providing for public environmental education tours of green buildings if appropriate.

### Broader environmental considerations

- Ensuring adaptability of design for future uses, including future solar technology such as fuel cell heating and cooling systems.
- Rehabilitating existing homes instead of demolishing them, where feasible.
  Ensuring the maintenance of urban biodiversity in infill development.
- Reinstating diversity through landscaping, façade articulation, increased 'edge' and vertical gardens.
- Designing for allowable envelopes of adjacent buildings to ensure *future* solar access.
- Minimizing dependency on urban infrastructure (water, gas, electricity, sewers).
- Considering embodied and ecological waste in all design decisions [Chapter 4].
- Clustering of buildings or units where appropriate to reduce the need for energy and materials etc.
- Conducting an energy efficiency site analysis which details site parameters, microclimate, shade, slope, drainage, wind, relative humidity, diurnal and annual temperature range, etc.
- Avoiding development on green-field sites and geographically or ecologically sensitive areas.
- Ensuring the site is not on a flood plain or landslide area.

### Landscaping considerations

- Laying out the site to take advantage of existing trees, shrubs and slopes to reduce heating and cooling loads (eg deciduous trees can reduce summer cooling needs by 30 per cent).
- Using or creating new microclimates to reduce heating and cooling loads.
- Avoiding lawns, which consume large amounts of water and require pesticide use and energy in mowing. Native grasses that use less water and do not require mowing are available. Or consider perennial groundcovers.
- Minimizing lot coverage for paving, parking and structures.
- Considering permaculture design principles for ease of maintenance, food production and biodiversity.
- Ensuring builders take adequate steps to protect trees during construction.
- Protecting topsoil during site-work and relocating good topsoil that will be covered by buildings.

## Waterscaping considerations

- Providing rainwater tanks for rooftop rainwater collection. Water can be stored under the building or in walls where it provides thermal mass.
- Connecting the water tank to landscaping with drip feeders for water conservation.
- Landscaping for stormwater retention. Excess water can be stored in retaining walls or in landscaped mounds for later use.
- Using water-efficient, low-maintenance landscaping – called xeriscaping.
- Utilizing permeable paving and swales to allow rain and stormwater absorption on site.
- Creating wetlands or reed beds for greywater water treatment where space allows.
- Connecting outflow of water from sinks, showers or clothes washers to landscaping.
- Considering ponds for biodiversity and solar landscaping: breezes over ponds can have a cooling effect in summer and reflect sunlight into the home in winter.

## Windscaping considerations

- Locating fencing, shrubs and trees to block strong winds and channel breezes into buildings.
- Reducing existing and potential urban wind tunnels effects through urban building form.
- Designing building roof shapes, floor plans, locations of windows and doors, etc to protect living areas from winter winds, collect summer breezes and optimize wind effects.

## Firescaping considerations

- Considering flyscreens integrated in pergolas and fences that are moistened with spray irrigation from a watertank to reduce bush fire hazards and provide evaporative cooling.
- Considering a water sprinkler on the roof connected to the rainwater tank for use in case of bush fire. In bushfire prone areas, link to external fire alarm.
- Constructing a brick wall 'fence' around slow combustion fireplace to reduce the risk of fire escaping and to provide thermal storage of heat from the fireplace.
- Follow fire-sensitive design principles for building design and landscaping (eg which reduce places for embers to burn on the building).[2]

## Contact with nature in urban areas considerations

- Providing outdoor open space, seating and plazas for employees and/or the general public.
- Ensuring the possibility of integrated food production on-site (eg roofs, balconies, atria).
- Providing worm or mushroom composting facilities attached to restaurants and tea rooms for on-site gardens.
- Designing building forms to provide areas for indoor plants, ponds and fountains.
- Using solar landscaping (eg trees for shading and ponds/fountains for cooling).
- Allowing private and public areas for gardening (eg roof gardens, balconies and atria).
- Integrating indoor/outdoor work areas with gardens where possible.
- Including visual amenities such as butterfly sanctuaries.
- Creating micro-habitats for flora, fauna and fungi (eg nest areas on solar screens and balconies).

## Atria and sun spaces considerations

- Using atria to bring in light and heat and remove hot and polluted air.
- Opening office spaces onto atriums for fresh air and contact with gardens.
- Designing atria to support plants and moderate the diurnal temperature variation.
- Increasing functions of atria (as corridors, entry spaces and air locks, social spaces, coffee nooks).

## Transportation and global warming considerations

- Avoiding contributing to congestion (eg location of vehicle entry and loading bays).
- Encouraging tele-commuting policies where feasible to reduce employee travel.

- Ensuring building is located to reduce regional transport requirements.
- Selecting products and materials that minimize ozone-depleting or greenhouse gases.
- Accommodating public transport (eg by convenient and safe bus or tram access).
- Using locally-sourced and healthy construction materials and products.
- Using local sub-contractors and labour force in construction where feasible.

## Natural light: Light wells, skylights, light shelves and clerestories considerations

- Maximizing daylighting (electric lighting can amount to 60 per cent of a building's energy costs).
- Considering these design elements to get daylight into interior work spaces and provide for internal gardens.
- Designing daylighting elements to avoid overheating and overcooling and leaking.
- Considering using light wells as sculptural design forms in the building.
- Considering triple glazing for noise control, security, pollution, heating and cooling loads.
- Avoiding glare and heat from windows by orientation, screening, smart windows, etc.
- Integrating sunscreens, light shelves, louvers, shading and energy collection (PVCs).
- Integrating facade with passive solar systems (eg light shelves, trombe walls, trellises).
- Organizing direct user participation in planning and design (as well as user surveys).
- Maximizing natural lighting in interior (eg light shelves, atriums, skylights, mirrors).
- Using shallow floorplates for cross ventilation and daylighting; with wider floor plates consider internal stair wells or skylights for more air and lighting.
- Designing ceilings for both noise prevention and absorption of heat from lights.
- Varying facade design and window treatment according to solar orientation, wind, etc.

## Air quality, health and comfort considerations

- Optimizing natural ventilation using solar stack technology (eg in facades and roofs).
- Reducing or avoiding air-conditioning by cool air intake (over water, underground, etc.).
- Using design of atriums and building mass to moderate climate extremes.
- Avoiding hazardous materials (eg VOCs) in furniture, walls and carpeting.
- Providing plant containers (with natural light and irrigation) to enable plants to grow in every room to reduce indoor air pollution.
- Ensuring adequate air changes (eg 1.5 changes per hour).
- Reducing noise amplification through wall and ceiling articulation, materials, etc.
- Ensuring low-radon materials and design that prevents radon entry into the building if development is in a high radon area.
- Assessing local air quality (eg openable windows in polluted or high crime areas).
- Making windows operable by users (where dirty air is significant consider double skins).
- Applying and positioning moisture and vapour barriers correctly, as mould is a serious problem in many regions, both in terms of occupant health and building longevity.
- Using non-toxic design approaches to termite and other insect-resistant detailing.
- Ensuring air intake is not near kitchens, loading docks, congested streets or garbage areas.

## Floor planning and layout considerations

- Locating services (wires, ducts) in the floor for easy access and upgrading.
- Considering business trends (such as hot-desking or tele-commuting) in floor planning.
- Locating heating loads like office equipment and machines to minimize impact.
- Screening the sun in hot areas with services (eg storage, lifts, corridors to east and west).
- Ensuring that movable partitions cannot disrupt ventilation systems or air registers.
- Optimizing open plan and private workspace opportunities for adaptability.
- Maximizing individual access to green spaces and windows in buildings.
- Ensuring lighting fixtures are easy to access for maintenance.

## Resource and materials conservation considerations

- Using materials and products that have low embodied energy in manufacturing and operation.

- Designing in the capture, storage and reuse of rainwater from roofs.
- Developing a system for collecting, storing and distributing surface water runoff.
- Treating greywater on-site with low-maintenance organic systems (eg Living Machines).
- Dedicating basement space to local organic waste treatment plant.
- Retrofitting an existing building in lieu of new construction.
- Reusing materials of buildings to be demolished nearby, if feasible.
- Using easily replaceable parts and 'design for disassembly'.
- Designing for durability (reusable, compostable, recyclable parts and components).
- Designing for long life and 'loose fit' (flexibility of future use).

## Timber usage considerations

- Avoiding rainforest timbers and native forest timbers or timber from forests with high ecological value.
- Specifying sustainably-managed timber products and biobased material substitutes.
- Specifying timber products with low gaseous emissions during manufacture.
- Using 'woodless' timbers (eg from hemp, bamboo) and engineered timber alternatives.
- Minimizing timber waste (offcuts) through design for generic sizes or correct specification.
- Planting trees to replace those used in the construction.

## Energy and heat conservation considerations

- Designing for local climate – wind, humidity, 'worst case' conditions.
- Considering co-generation (heat from a process used to power/heat another function).
- Using passive solar heating and cooling technologies throughout.
- Considering (partially or totally) underground building for energy conservation.
- Specifying green lights, products and appliances in fit out.
- Ensuring high-efficiency electrical office equipment is used.
- Using double skin walls to expel hot air out of the building or absorb warm air.
- Using service areas for solar shading (lifts, stairs and toilets at the periphery).
- Considering wind scoops to channel wind into interior spaces through ceiling plenums.
- Ensuring structural air-tightness and avoid thermal bridging (breaks in insulation).
- Using optimum insulation serving multi-functions (eg noise and heat control).
- Reducing temperature swings with exposed thermal mass (eg floor slabs, walls).
- Optimizing low embodied energy and thermal storage capacity of building form itself.

## Technology considerations

- Ensuring flexibility, expansion and adaptability for new technology in plan layout.
- Avoiding technical complexity to reduce risks of failure and avoid maintenance costs.
- Considering testing experimental green technologies.
- Designing for future upgrading and downsizing of mechanical equipment.
- Ensuring back-up mechanical equipment (where required) is not over-specified.
- Using automatic windows for night-time chilling of the structure.
- Using smart windows that shade automatically and generate electricity.
- Using photovoltaic cells that are integral to the roof or walls to generate electricity.

## Construction process considerations

- Demanding minimal packaging of materials and products that are delivered to the site.
- Evaluating relative eco-efficiency of on-site/off-site assembly of building components.
- Using performance-based contracting systems to provide incentives for eco-solutions.
- Ensuring that construction processes are eco-efficient, as well as building operation.
- Developing a comprehensive waste management plan for the construction process.
- Ensuring a construction safety plan is developed and implemented.
- Ensuring energy conservation measures are checked and fine-tuned after use.
- Conducting post-occupancy evaluation to ensure equipment operates properly.

## Box 23 Digital Modelling for Sustainability

*Professor Robin Drogemuller and Professor John Frazer*

Digital modelling tools are the next generation of computer aided design (CAD) tools for the construction industry. They allow a designer to build a virtual model of the building project before the building is constructed. This supports a whole range of analyses, and the identification and resolution of problems before they arise on-site, in ways that were previously not feasible.

The current state of digital modelling tools for sustainability reflects the current structure of the construction industry. The CAD systems and analysis tools used by the various design disciplines are not well integrated and do not support whole-of-life analysis for buildings. The flows of information are disjointed and inefficient, and there are large gaps in the information required to design buildings that are sustainable. However, there are indications that the situation is starting to improve. The building construction industry is in the process of moving from two-dimensional drawing to three-dimensional modelling. Three-dimensional (3D) CAD systems have been available for two decades but the uptake within the construction industry has been slow.

Those sectors of the industry that have been using 3D CAD are moving towards 3D modelling. For the present discussion, 3D CAD produces drawings and images that look correct to humans but only contain information on shapes, patterns and textures. There is no embedded information that allows walls to be differentiated from roofs or windows, for example. In 3D modelling systems, the 'type' of an object is defined within the system, along with information on the construction of the component. Modelling systems can also add intelligence by automatically joining walls where they touch each other, cutting openings in walls for windows, etc. This additional intelligence is important in supporting ease of use and also accuracy within the model.

The companies that develop 3D modelling software are following two complementary approaches to improving the flow of information. Some companies are building suites of software that support a range of users and that all share the same data format.[1] Second, there are industry efforts to develop standards for interoperability (seamless information exchange) between software systems from different software companies. Interoperability is important since no one software company will ever have computer programs that cover every possible type of design or analysis problem.

Another parallel development is the emergence of parametric and constraint-driven digital modelling systems. These allow a range of alternative designs to be modelled using key parameters. For example, the number and capacity of lifts in a building could be a function of the number of people who will occupy the building, which can be derived from the area of the building and activities that will occur within it. These parameters can then be varied to move towards an optimal design across the range of design solutions. Recent designs by Frank Gehry using Digital Project show what can be achieved with this type of digital modelling system.

The major technical impediment to sustainable building designs lies in analysing sustainability itself. Some areas of sustainability analysis, such as operational energy performance, are well served by analysis tools and the necessary data to run them. Other areas, such as analysing embodied energy, greenhouse gas emissions, biodiversity, health, etc, are poorly served by analysis tools and data.

Integration of analysis tools with digital models of the buildings would substantially reduce the time required to perform analyses, and would consequently allow sustainability to be considered earlier in the design process. If sustainability analyses can be performed with minimal extra effort and within a reasonable amount of time, then a series of analyses of alternatives could be used to guide design at important stages within the design process.

There are a number of significant technical developments that are needed before digital modelling tools can support design for sustainability in a seamless manner:

- Accurate data for sustainability for those areas of analysis that are poorly supported, such as whole-of-life impact assessment for the full range of materials and components used in buildings, embodied energy, assessing design for deconstruction and re-use, biodiversity, impact of site works, etc.
- A wider range of analysis tools to improve support for areas such as embodied energy, pollutant emissions, and other factors involved in manufacturing, maintenance and recycling. These will need to support the inclusion of individual materials, single components and assemblies of components. These analysis tools will also need to support multiple stages of the design process by allowing 'high'-level descriptions of entire assemblies, such as a timber truss roof with metal deck cladding and plasterboard ceiling and 100mm of fibreglass insulation at the early design stage, through to a full 3D model of the roof framing system with individual members and connectors at the documentation stage of design.
- Libraries of sustainability solutions that can be 'dragged and dropped' into digital modelling environments to allow rapid evaluation of alternatives.
- Better integration of digital modelling and analysis tools to reduce the time required to prepare data for analysis. For example, LCADesign[2] uses a 3D building model as the basis for an eco-efficiency assessment of the building. The user spends between 30 and 60 minutes entering specific data to the standard CAD model and then exports this information as an IFC[3] file. This file is then read in to LCADesign for analysis. Various substitutions can be made within LCADesign, such as changing non-load-bearing wall systems or floor coverings, so that a range of related alternatives can be explored in a few hours. LCADesign does not support major substitutions which have wide ranging implications, however, such as alternative structural systems (eg concrete frame versus load-bearing brickwork) or entire system options (eg ducted-air versus chilled-water air-conditioning systems).

The improvements described above are achievable within the current state of understanding of the building design process and the current capabilities of computer software. If we are to build high performance building optimization tools, it is necessary to link building information modelling with active design tools and generative and evolutionary design and analysis techniques to form an iterative building performance optimization loop.

Currently data and parametric functions and logical operators are all entered manually into a building information model, usually in an unstructured manner lacking any rigorous theoretical basis. This is inefficient and labour intensive. Every building becomes a one-off prototype (a concept unthinkable in, say, the aircraft industry). The lack of structure in the model leads to later difficulties in changing the model or accessing the data efficiently in complicated models.

The output data could be subject to analysis of performance, structure, cost, etc. This can occur inside the system (such as with FEA analysis within Catia), or data can be exported with IFCs and subject to external analysis. But what happens to the results of the analysis? In most cases it requires tedious manual manipulation of the variables of the parametric model followed by a re-iteration of the whole process.

To improve the entire situation it is necessary to provide:

- A theoretical framework which structures the building of the model so that it facilitates later change and improves data access
- A methodology for automating or semi-automating the model building process
- The potential for automatic modification of the parameters on the basis of feedback from the analysis and evaluation step

Of course, having the technology and capability is not enough. The social and commercial imperatives must also exist before the technology is used widely.

## Box 24 Typology of Green Aesthetic Orientations

The following is a highly generalized typology. In practice, such distinctions merge, of course, but it may be useful in exploring and developing one's own views about building design.

| | 'Inside–out' (human-centred) orientation | 'Outside–in' (resource-centred) orientation | A net positive orientation |
|---|---|---|---|
| **Basic goals driving the initial building form** | Needs of individuals: contextual factors affecting individual comfort (eg comfort, lighting, noise, privacy, quiet, views and feelings) | Needs of building: forces of nature and external conditions impacting on the site and building envelope (eg solar access, wind, flood and fire) | Needs of community and life support system: means to increase eco-services and improve human and ecosystem health |
| **Key design aims** | Operational efficiency: reduce energy and water demands of users (outputs) | Resource efficiency: reduce resource demands of the building on environment (inputs) | Increase ecological base and public estate and reduce 'designed waste' (flows) |
| **Spatial criteria and determinants** | Adds space for interior human activities, limited by cost and other constraints | Adds space for public areas, limited by planning constraints etc | Adds (multi-functional) ecological space for humans and nature |
| **Starting point for layout** | Bubble diagram defines linkages and barriers between internal functions | Site diagram defines the linkages and barriers between the envelope and the environment | Map environmental flows through site to restore, capture and create surplus eco-services |
| **Shape of building plan** | Floor plan, based on bubble diagram, is often projected into a three-dimensional shape | Cross section is often projected into a three-dimensional and sculptural shape | Environmental and human health is enhanced by building form |
| **Envelope definition** | Cross-section focuses on environmental forces on the interior | Cross-section focuses on environmental forces on the exterior | Diagrams expanded to include regional factors and environmental flows |
| **Image/brand** | Interior experiential effects on user are created by exciting spaces, art works and quality materials | Exterior art works and/or the sculptural form of the building itself created to impress passers-by | Integration of landscape and building to increase eco-services leads to relative 'invisibility' |
| **Designers perspective** | Through the experience or eye of future users (journey) | Through bird's-eye view (eg conceptual symbols and axes) | Invisibility of building (salience of landscape) |
| **Building services emphasized** | Human services (eg openable windows for individual control) | Building services (eg automatic building management systems) | Ecosystem services created by building to support the urban ecology |
| **Adaptation over time** | Interior that is responsive to changing uses (eg flexible or open plan) | Exterior that is responsive to elements (eg movable shades and louvers) | Adaptable, demountable, expandable and reversible structure |
| **Aesthetic qualities** | Exciting spaces and visual art to enhance the interior experience | Building form itself as art, reflecting the established style of the day | Diversity of green exterior façades, interior walls and atrium spaces |

## Box 25 Solar Design Myth-Conceptions

Even when applied, passive solar design principles have been greatly underutilized. This is partly due to myths that catch hold as a result of trying to replace site-specific design with generalized templates and rules of thumb:

- **'Passive solar design all looks the same'**. The same range of design styles and images are possible with passive solar design as with standard construction. Examples exist that range across the full spectrum from 'nuts and bolts' to 'nuts and berries'. Any construction can be enhanced by passive solar principles, so there is no reason why passive solar design should not accommodate varied aesthetic preferences.
- **'Passive solar means orienting towards the sun (only)'**. Heat gain and glare through windows can make rooms uncomfortable, and curtains need to be closed at night and open during the day. Conservatories, by contrast, allow heat to be collected when it is hot, and emitted into the room when it is cool and the reverse. Heat can be vented into the home directly or delivered to a storage area with high thermal mass inside the home.
- **'Passive solar is more expensive'**. The construction costs, embodied and operating energy, and overall life-cycle costs of passive solar design should be less than that of conventional construction – depending upon the experience of the designers and builders. When they do cost more, it is often because of 'experimental' features and the inertia of conventional practices.
- **'Good solar access depends on the site'**. Poorly laid out subdivisions or difficult sites are often used as an excuse for not applying passive solar design principles. A conservatory can face any direction. It often reduces heat loss through walls by 20 per cent and increases the usable floor space for little cost. Such improvements increase both the capital and use value of a dwelling.
- **'Concrete slabs are necessary in cold climates'**. 'Cut and fill' of the earth to accommodate concrete slabs is not always ecologically appropriate.[1] Concrete slabs, without edge insulation, are not good insulators. Further, slabs have about four times the embodied energy of timber floors. Thus building off the ground with insulation (or underground) and using *vertical* thermal mass should be considered.
- **'It is essential to space houses far apart for solar access'**. Similarly, the idea that houses need to be spaced far apart for solar access has been based on the ostensible need for the sun to hit the wall. Passive solar collection can be separate from the building. As the Solar Core concept demonstrates, the roof itself can be used as a collector or distribution system [Box 9].
- **'The choice of building materials is not important if insulated'**. Conventional building materials have huge impacts during resource extraction and disposal, high embodied energy and greenhouse impacts, and adverse health impacts. Alternative bio-based materials, such as engineered timbers or wheatboard, are good insulators and do not (necessarily) off-gas toxins. Also, the use of local materials greatly reduces transport (greenhouse) impacts.
- **'The impacts of apartments are lower than those of detached dwellings'**. The total material flows, embodied waste and operating energy, and so on can be higher per square metre in apartments than in detached dwellings – depending on design. While apartments have shared walls and plumbing, they can be more difficult to convert to resource autonomy.
- **'Still air is important to achieve thermal comfort'**. Still air stratifies. If the temperature at floor level is cooler than at head level, people tend to get headaches. Warm internal air temperatures near cold walls or windows that draw heat from the body also cause discomfort. Similarly, heat from a small source such as an electric fan heater is less comfortable than from a large warm wall. Fresh air and natural ventilation reduce these air temperature differentials.

## Box 26 Contextual Design (the Case of Plastic)

Design must work into existing systems to change them. This is illustrated by the current debate over which is more ecologically sound: plant-based or fossil fuel-based plastics. The production of plastics involves fossil fuels as a raw material and energy source. Power plants and transport systems use more than 90 per cent of oil, and plastics use most of the remainder. On the one hand, some scientists argue that plants should not be used as a raw material for plastics, but instead should be used as an energy source. Bio-engineered plant production is energy intensive. On the other hand, a firm currently producing plant-based plastics argues that as their technologies develop, energy efficiency will be greatly increased over time. After all, fossil fuel processes have had 200 years of development to improve efficiency.[1] Due to the changing geopolitical and biophysical context, corn-based recycling is already economically competitive.[2] Plastics can be grown in plants via a fermentation process or in the stalks and leaves of bioengineered crops:

- Fermentation process: Typically, the plants are processed for sugar, which is then fermented. In this process, micro-organisms convert the sugar into lactic acid, which is then chemically transformed into plastic.
- Bioengineering process: The fermentation process can be skipped by using bioengineered corn. The plants can be harvested for their corn and the stalks and leaves can then be harvested for plastic. In other words, this means two uses for the corn.

Some advantages of plant-based plastics are that:

- They are biodegradable and compostable (ie reduce landfill and cause less harm to animals); however, this process emits greenhouse gases.
- Their production is far more energy-intensive than conventional petrochemical plastics, but uses far less fossil fuel as a raw material.
- The price of oil is rising, making corn-based plastic economically competitive.
- Burning the carbon in stalks does not increase net carbon dioxide in the atmosphere – assuming crops that absorb the same amount of carbon dioxide replace the plants.
- They cannot easily be separated from bottles made from petroleum without expensive sorting equipment, which is out of reach of many small-scale recyclers.
- They can contaminate the recycling of fossil fuel plastic if they get in the waste stream, and thus undermine the investment in recycling.

Some advantages of fossil fuel-based plastics are that:

- Plastics grown in corn compete with other agricultural uses for land and water.
- Plastics can sequester carbon if buried in landfill.
- They are produced from fossil fuels as a raw material; however, far less fossil fuel (energy and emissions) is required in their production than plant-based plastics.
- A lot of energy is required to grow corn.

The above simplified list of issues suggests apparent tradeoffs:

- Relative value of agricultural land versus use of fossil fuel energy with emissions.
- Relative value of fossil fuels as non-renewable raw material versus using fossil fuels in energy production, which produces greenhouse gases.
- Economic and other values of established recycling industries versus avoiding the transport and machinery entailed in recycling.
- Relative biodegradability versus carbon storage potential for fossil-based plastic.

In either case, the crops are generally grown using mineral fertilizer, which is produced in a very energy-intensive process which uses fossil fuels in the production of energy. If crops are fertilized with compost rather than nitrogen, the environmental impacts are greatly reduced.[3] The debates usually omit the design approach: to consider whether we really need the products and, if so, to consider whether there are better means of meeting the same needs.

**Box 27 Spectrum of Design Approaches**

The following table suggests some distinctions that can be made as we progress along the evolution from conventional to eco-logical design.

| Conventional | Impact reduction | Positive Development |
|---|---|---|
| Fossil fuel dependency | Fossil fuel reduction | Uses only 'solar resources' |
| Depends on established processes in spite of risks | Minimizes known risks and impacts | Applies precautionary principle regarding unknowns |
| Locks in future choices in non-adaptable urban forms | Aims for permanency, despite changing contextual forces | Proactively creates and expands future social options |
| Limited recycling or reuse encouraged | Closed-loop systems (recycling) – waste as resource | Creation of no-loop and regenerative systems |
| Prioritizes operational energy but not whole systems | Counts embodied energy and water in materials | Compensation for ecological as well as embodied waste |
| Substitutes ecosystems with industrial engineering systems | Emulates ecosystem functions in building design | Provides context and conditions for (living) eco-services |
| Analyses predict (untested) impacts of proposed buildings | Analyses relative impact of alternative components | Analyses system performance (adaptation, reversibility) |
| Performs rating calculations for compliance, not design | Makes tradeoffs between various forms of impacts | Seeks design innovations that increase positive impacts |
| Assumes activity can expand up to limits of nature's thresholds | Reduces the relative ecological footprint | Expands ecosystems and hence ecosystem resilience |
| Looks at engineering efficiency of components | Looks at efficiency of systems in whole building | Looks at contribution of building to bioregional systems |
| Looks at inputs and outputs of sequential steps in process | Looks at whole supply chain to find efficiencies | Looks at equity in resource transfers (ie who gets what where) |
| Self-regulation of process by developer or designer | Approved assessment via independent consultant | Accessible and assessable by general public |
| Reduces space for people and each building function | Minimizes land coverage of development | Seeks to increase ecological space (per person or area) |
| Uses 'negative' incentives (eg less approval time or fees) | Gives awards or credits that increase the market value | Gives credit for off-site impact reduction or positive impacts |
| Applies (hence reinforces) standard design templates | Encourages passive solar design principles | Avoids all fossil fuel and improves basic systems health |
| Data collection required is disproportionate to value | Data collection is tailored to relevant impacts | Data collection is subsidiary to a design framework |
| Draws from list of green materials | Selects materials with low life-cycle costs | Seeks to utilize surplus wastes available in region |
| Leaves performance to future owners | Post-occupancy evaluation included | Promotes continuous improvement of building life |
| Focuses on building style and received 'consumer demand' | Focuses on environmental controls in façade and shape | Integrates ecology in living building skin and interior |

## Box 28 Green Building and Product Procurement

*David Baggs*

What is and what is not an environmentally or health-preferred product, material or technology (hereinafter described as 'products') is a major issue for the industry, as manufacturers often either knowingly or unknowingly promote products by the use of 'greenwash' or marketing language that makes products sound as though they provide environmental benefits even though they may actually not deliver all or any of the implied benefits. So how do designers, engineers, specifiers and building practitioners 'cut the wheat from the chaff'? They need a reliable source of verified information. But what is an environmentally preferable product? It is defined (for the purposes of the Ecospecifier tool) as follows:

1  An environmentally preferable product is a commercially available product or material that:

   • Embodies one or more unique environmental attributes or qualities as a result of deliberately eliminating or reducing potential environmental impacts across its life-cycle, compared to other products in its category.
   • Embodies one or more unique health attributes or qualities as a result of deliberately eliminating or reducing potential human heath impacts across its life-cycle, compared to other products in its category.
   • Is a member of a product category that in itself embodies an ecologically- or health-preferred product category (eg photovoltaic panels as a preference to diesel or petrol generators or fossil fuel powered electrical grid energy).

2  It is further characterized by its development and existence being significantly driven or motivated by environmental objectives, as opposed to an existing material that has undergone incremental environmental improvement.

3  It is also preferably distinguished by its accompanying product specifications, brochures and marketing materials, which clearly and explicitly explain and/or promote the relevant environmental attributes.

4  It has been awarded the Good Environmental Choice Australia or other Global Ecolabel Network member ecolabel.

5  It does not contain significant quantities of substances known to have deleterious ecological or health impacts, in particular:

   • Persistent organic pollutants
   • Carcinogenic compounds classified as Group 1 or 2 carcinogens by the IARC
   • Bio-accumulative compounds
   • Hormone disrupting compounds
   • Mutagenic compounds
   • Teratogenic compounds
   • Substances listed in the National Pollutants Inventory (www.dpi.gov.au) as required to be reported as of 2002
   • Substances sourced using processes deleterious to high conservation value and/or remnant natural ecological communities or bio-reserves
   • Materials that create major environmental or health degradation

Only with such a source of reliable, verified information on the ecological and health benefits of products can the industry hope to deliver reliable, forward movement on mitigating the ecological and health impacts of the existing or new built environments.

## Box 29 Tools for Specifying Green Building Products

*David Baggs*

The rapid growth and market impact of green building councils and green building rating schemes in Australia and internationally can be observed in the current dramatic increase in the interest and implementation of more ecologically- and health-benign developments and buildings. In a recent informal media survey by the author across Australia, six out of seven new major commercial office buildings were advertised for lease with Green Star building sustainability ratings. This growth in ecologically sustainable development (ESD) is dependent on designers, engineers, practitioners and specifiers being able to locate ecologically- or health-preferable products with reliable information about their performance.

*Ecospecifier*[1] is a guide to selecting ecologically- and health-preferable products, materials and technologies for the construction sector, specifically targeted at the needs of decision-makers and specifiers by:

- Providing greater clarity about what is and is not 'green'

- Enabling easier identification, specification or location of preferred products

- Facilitating greater understanding of the issues surrounding ecoproducts

- Providing clear, independently assessed, unbiased information

- Providing third party, independent and unbiased assessment of information provided by manufacturers and other sources.

Ecospecifier assesses products using recognized Australian and international standards, codes, ecolabels, life-cycle assessment methodologies, and green building rating schemes. It also reviews independent test data, third party research and/or expert opinion to test manufacturer declarations and claims, and seeks advice from an expert National Product Standards Technical Committee.

### Multi-criteria product search functions

The database contains well over 3000 independently vetted eco- and health-preferable products against approximately 60 common industry categories and 400 subcategories. The database may be searched by industry categories and sub-categories (eg Floors leads to Carpets), by eco-outcomes (eg 'water efficient' or 'low VOC') and keywords. The outcomes search also enables searching by individual ratings tools such as BASIX and Green Stars.

### What it covers

Ecospecifier assesses and presents information on sustainable, healthy materials, products and technology as well as materials relevant to building design construction, fit-out and operational functions relevant to many professionals, including facilities managers:

- Residential – new single- and multi-unit dwellings as well as alterations and additions

- Commercial – offices, retail, hospitality, ecotourism, healthcare, care for the elderly, etc

- Educational facilities

- Industrial and process technology

- Renewable energy generation

Ecospecifier has recently introduced a geographical search function as it expands its vision to include other countries and will continue to expand its product base, rigour and depth of life-cycle assessment, as well as developing further aids to specifiers such as a Green Specification.

## Box 30 Evolution towards Positive Development

The following suggests an evolution in development. Traditional development control systems aim to reduce the collateral damage of development by devices like 'exactions' (fees or offsets) that transfer some of the internalities (public benefits transferred at below cost to a development) back to the community. The green solution at present is to close loops or design systems that are essentially 'no loop' because they draw on natural systems instead of industrial ones. However, we need to design to reverse impacts (ie improve the health of the air, water, soil and people) *and* increase eco-productivity. We also need to go further to support nature and ecosystems as living things.

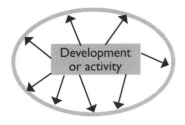

**Externalities**: Conventional design externalizes negative impacts onto nature and society. Externalities are where a development or system imposes collateral damage on society. They are generally created by interventions in natural systems (eg engineering structures) that remove and/or reduce the ecological base.

**Expropriations**: Conventional design also internalizes free resources and benefits from nature and society are where resources are extracted from the public domain at below replacement cost. This results in 'internalities' or even unjust enrichment, where a private business or organization receives inordinate benefits at the expense of the general public.

**Closed loop**: Negative impacts are internalized in closed loop design, not imposed upon nature. Closed loops internalize the impacts of development. They could be 'no loop', which means the design does not produce any waste to begin with (eg buildings that provide natural ventilation versus air conditioning. Closed loop design can achieve relative 'resource autonomy'. However, this can be essentially recycling. It is not re-distributive or net positive in itself.

**Net Positive Development**: Positive off and on site impacts are generated to increase the ecological base and public estate If a development is net positive, the flows through the building contribute back to the natural environment (ie buildings increase natural capital and eco-services). What comes out of a building is healthier than what goes in. In addition, however, the total size and health of the ecology is improved over what existed before.

We need to challenge the planning, management and design legacy that hides or justifies externalities, internalities and expropriations. One way to assist this is to ensure that measurements include the time involved in restoring ecosystem functioning (ie ecological waste) [Chapter 4].

## Box 31 Potential of Flows Analyses

It is important to determine the appropriate method, and appropriate combination of predictive and performance tools before undertaking any planning exercise. While MFA (material flows analysis) provides a different perspective to input–output based analyses, it omits other issues. The list below identifies some of the potential advantages of flows analyses. By determining areas of waste or inefficiency, and tracing these flows to their origins in social, structural, institutional and/or industrial sources, metabolic 'maps' have the potential to assist both the public and private sector in finding sources of eco-innovations.

MFA is useful as a planning support tool to:

- Examine aspects of urban, industrial and agricultural systems as one system
- Identify imbalances in resources and environmental flows at a regional level
- Determine suitable urban, industrial or agricultural systems for particular bioregions
- Find gaps or inconsistencies in input–output data and ways to reconcile them
- Improve trans-disciplinary communication across disciplines involved in sustainability
- Provide early warning systems of health crises (eg build up of toxins in groundwater)

MFA is useful in reporting and public education to:

- Understand the complex interdependencies of natural and human systems
- Make externalities visible to the public (eg toxic runoff)
- Link policies and actions to positive trends such as decarbonization
- Assist public and private sectors in visualizing long-term consequences of decisions
- Reveal where land-use activities transfer wealth out of regions (eg loss of soil fertility)
- Expose the total flows through urban development, not just those in materials per se

MFA is useful as a financial support tool to:

- Find ways to increase regional self-reliance through import substitution
- Identify existing stocks of waste materials and substances for 'resource mining'
- Find leverage points for systems change with relatively small investments
- Support the evaluation of the fit between an innovation, markets and distribution
- Generate quantitative information for improving efficiency and lowering costs
- Improve supply chain efficiencies

Ecological transformation (ET) analysis would facilitate mapping to:

- Help to determine the best ecological use of land
- Find opportunities for increasing eco-services and biodiversity
- Find potential for space optimization (versus space reduction and segregation)
- Reverse negative space (ie privatization of the public estate) and dead space
- Facilitate biomimicry by comparing current and initial indigenous conditions

Resource transfer (RT) analysis would facilitate mapping:

- The inequitable transfer of resources over time (eg from poor to rich, rural to urban)
- The contextual deficiencies and injustices that a new development might help to reverse
- Opportunities to potentially expand future choice through development
- Make externalities , internalities and unjust enrichment visible

Institutional Design (ID) analysis would facilitate mapping:

- Wealth transfers facilitated by economic mechanisms (eg subsidies and discounting).
- Ongoing losses of social options (eg lifestyle and life quality) through planning
- Transfers of power from public to private control (eg privatization) through legislation
- Impact transfers (eg pollution and waste) through design and engineering conventions

MFA analyses cannot really look at ecosystems and living things, as these are reduced to surrogates like energy or substances. Arguably, only design can do this (informed by flows analyses) by creating infrastructure and space for nature to function, expand and diversify.

## Box 32 Tools for Capturing Regional Synergies

*Glen Corder*

Industrial ecology aims to achieve symbiosis, or mutually beneficial co-existence, between industrial production and consumption. In essence, it supports the concept that an industrial system is working with the surrounding systems and not in isolation from them. The concept of industrial ecology leads to regional synergies (also referred to as 'industrial symbiosis') where industry can mimic nature by re-using by-products from one industry in another. These can extend into utility synergies (the shared use of utility infrastructure), for example for energy production, water and wastewater treatment.

In 2004, the Co-operative Research Centre for Sustainable Resource Processing (CSRP) commenced projects on regional synergies with a focus on analysis and innovation across industrial regions.[1] To complement practical facilitation projects in the Kwinana (Western Australia) and Gladstone (Queensland) regions in Australia, the CSRP also initiated a higher-level engineering and technology project with the specific aim of developing an engineering and technology platform for regional resource synergies.

Although the number of examples of regional resource synergies around the world is growing, many of these have largely been opportunistic, rather than through deliberate design. The hypothesis of the project is that deliberate design of regional synergies is, in principle, possible – provided practical tools are developed and trialled for the systematic identification, evaluation and realization of synergy opportunities. Continuing to rely on opportunistic synergy development may mean many potential synergy initiatives are missed. The 'higher-level engineering and technology' project delivered a package of tools to provide a rigorous and systemic approach to identifying and ranking synergy opportunities and associated technologies for new and existing industries within an industrial area. The project adopted a three-pronged project strategy: best practice review and promotion, development and trial of a regional eco-efficiency assessment methodology, and assessment of technology needs and opportunities.

For 'best practice review and promotion', the CSRP produced a status report on the development of regional synergies from around the world.[2] The Global Synergies Database is an effective means of promoting existing regional synergy examples and encouraging other industrial regions to develop similar synergy initiatives.

The 'regional eco-efficiency assessment methodology' provides a targeted process for identifying and evaluating opportunities by using a three-phase process:

1  A 'preliminary assessment tool' provides an extensive list of indicative synergy opportunities based on the pre-loaded input–output streams for specific industries.

2  An 'input–output inventory tool' generates registers of more specific synergy opportunities, based on the preliminary assessment tool outcomes and specific company data, in three main groups: water, energy and materials/by-products. A search engine enables the user to generate specific reports on potential synergy opportunities.

3  A 'screening tool' assesses the potential contribution to sustainable development for the identified synergy opportunities, in terms of their contribution to sustainable development as well as their expected feasibility and ease of implementation.

The 'assessment of technology needs and opportunities' provides an analytical framework to assess the role of technology in the realization of regional resource synergies across three components: capture, recovery and utilization. The framework evaluates the synergy needs in regard to the three components through three specific categories: water, energy/heat and materials. The overall aim of this package of tools is to provide a rigorous and systemic approach to identifying and ranking synergy opportunities and associated technologies for industries within an industrial area.

## Box 33 Enhancing Supply Chain Performance

*Kumar Venkat*

Supply chains are the complex networks behind the scenes that support the world of commerce. Every product that we use begins its life as a disparate collection of raw materials extracted or harvested in different parts of the world. The raw materials make their way through value chains, where a series of processing steps performed by different companies add value to the raw materials. These value chains merge to create complicated products. The production, storage and transportation activities often consume significant resources, making the environmental performance of supply chains an increasingly important issue. The sustainability of global commerce depends on the sustainability of supply chains. 'Green' supply chains have attracted significant interest in recent years. A number of large companies – including Hewlett-Packard, Nike and STMicroelectronics – have focused attention on the manufacturing practices of their suppliers in an attempt to make their supply chains greener. But there is more to it than more efficient manufacturing: how we move materials and goods in a carbon-constrained world will also impact our progress towards a sustainable future.

Supply chains are increasingly vulnerable to energy prices and constraints on greenhouse gas emissions. Supply chains now span long distances and require significant use of fossil fuels and carbon dioxide emissions to manufacture and deliver goods to consumers. Freight transport consumes nearly a quarter of all the petroleum worldwide and accounts for over 10 per cent of the carbon emissions from fossil fuels.[1] At the same time, techniques such as lean manufacturing are keeping inventory levels low and require frequent replenishment throughout the supply chain – which can increase energy use and emissions, depending on the product.[2] The total energy use and emissions in supply chains depend on transport modes, frequency and size of deliveries, and inventory levels.

One way to improve the environmental performance of supply chains is by analysing the whole system and finding leverage points that can be used for performance optimization. The system includes all the production, transportation and storage along supply chains. Transport modes that can deliver larger quantities of a product result in higher inventory levels, while transport modes that deliver smaller quantities more frequently result in lower inventory levels. Larger inventories require more energy to maintain, while larger delivery sizes require less energy per unit product for transportation. This tradeoff exists at every transport link and associated storage in typical supply chains. Our results suggest that significant opportunities exist for improving the energy/emissions footprint of supply chains.

This insight has led to the development of a new software package called the Supply-Chain Environmental Analysis Tool (SEAT). SEAT is an interactive software tool that can be used to quantify and improve the environmental performance of supply chains. SEAT allows users to easily model supply chain elements – including transportation, storage and production – from an energy and carbon dioxide emissions perspective. It then provides powerful methods to analyse, report and explore improvements to supply-chain environmental performance. The analysis includes a comprehensive accounting of energy usage, carbon-dioxide emissions and financial cost. SEAT can be used for detailed analysis of existing supply chains, 'what if' experiments and comparisons of alternative supply chain configurations.

SEAT can be valuable in a variety of applications, such as:

- achieving overall cost savings from reduced energy use in supply chains;
- meeting voluntary or mandatory greenhouse gas emission targets;
- emission calculations for use in offsetting carbon footprints; and
- detailed corporate reporting of energy use and emissions.

The larger lesson and hope from this development effort is that sophisticated software techniques (including those borrowed from entirely unrelated areas) could indeed play a role in analysing and optimizing the resource efficiencies of complex, large-scale systems and networks that have evolved over many decades without any sustainability consideration.

## Box 34 Making Progress

*Richard Eckersley*

To make progress, we have to be able to measure it.[1] How we measure progress depends, in turn, on how we define it. Progress can take many forms: better health and education, greater equality and freedom, more choice and opportunity, less conflict and suffering.

However, progress in the modern era is principally defined in material terms – a rising standard of living – and measured as growth in per capita income, or Gross Domestic Product (GDP). Yet GDP, an aggregate measure of the value of economic production in a nation in a given period, was never intended as a general measure of economic welfare, let alone quality of life. Despite this, growth is pursued in the belief that, overall, it makes life better.

In the late 1980s, the Chilean economist Manfred Max-Neef and his colleagues proposed a threshold hypothesis, which states that for every society there seems to be a period in which economic growth (as conventionally measured) brings about an improvement in quality of life, but only up to a point – the threshold point – beyond which, if there is more economic growth, quality of life may begin to deteriorate.

The threshold hypothesis has been supported in the past decade by the development of indices, such as the Genuine Progress Indicator (GPI), that adjust GDP for a range of social, economic and environmental factors that GDP either ignores or measures inappropriately. These include income distribution, unpaid housework and voluntary work, loss of natural resources, and the costs of unemployment, crime and pollution. These 'GDP analogues' show that trends in GDP and national wellbeing, once moving together, have diverged since about the mid-1970s in all countries for which they have been constructed, including the US, UK and Australia.

Redefining Progress, the American non-profit public-policy organization that developed the GPI, points out that GDP considers every expenditure as an addition to wellbeing, regardless of what that expenditure is for or what effects it has. 'By this reasoning, the nation's economic hero is the terminal cancer patient going through an expensive divorce, whose car is totalled in a 20-car pile-up. The economic villain is the healthy person in a solid marriage who cooks at home, walks to work and doesn't smoke or gamble'. In other words, what economists call 'growth' is not always the same as what most people would consider 'good'.

While national governments are slow to accept this truth about the relationship between economic growth and wellbeing, powerful international bodies have come a long way in the past few years towards embracing it. A 2000 report by the World Bank, *Quality of Growth*,[2] stresses the importance of 'the sources and patterns of growth to development outcomes'. It questions why policymakers continue 'to rely so heavily, and often solely, on the pace of GDP growth as the measure of progress'.

As the Bank's vice president and lead author of the report, Vinod Thomas, said at its launch: 'Just as the quality of people's diet, and not just the quantity of food they eat, influences their health and life expectancy, the way in which growth is generated and distributed has profound implications for people and their quality of life'.

In recent years, this message about growth has been reinforced by a range of subjective measures of progress and wellbeing, including life satisfaction and happiness, and people's perceptions of quality of life and of the future. Trends in self-reported health and a range of chronic health problems such as diabetes and depression also raise questions about the equation of more with better.

Measuring progress is still in an exploratory and developmental phase: some national statistical agencies are collating objective indicators of economic, social and environmental trends; public-interest organizations, which developed the GPI and similar indices, are updating and refining these, applying them at the regional level, and experimenting with different aggregate indicators.

## Box 35 From SoE to Sustainability Reporting for Cities

*Peter W. Newton*

In 2007 we had the twentieth anniversary of the *Brundtland Report*,[1] which launched sustainability as an increasingly powerful driving force for change in thinking across government, industry and community sectors. It encouraged an important shift from the rather narrow environmental thinking and measurement of the 1970s, which focused on individual performance indicators, end-of-pipe solutions and compliance, to an approach now increasingly aligned with systems thinking, solutions linked to understanding of systems performance and innovation in design, science and technology, and creative partnerships (eg public–private or private–community) for delivery of solutions. State of Environment (SoE) reporting represented a first attempt at the application of systems thinking to environmental assessment and reporting via its Pressure–State–Response Model, albeit restricted initially to solely environmental domains.[2] SoE reporting has subsequently been extended to embrace a broader framework, including driving forces, direct pressures, condition (state) implications, responses, effectiveness (monitoring),[3] and the inclusion of the built environment as a key area.[4]

SoE reporting, as currently applied in most contexts, is episodic (every five years in most jurisdictions), is poorly supported from a data perspective, operates primarily within solo domains (eg atmosphere, land or inland waters themes), has little facility for multi-factor analysis, and, as its title suggests, is reporting on current conditions and recent trends rather than exploring future development scenarios and their sustainability. An extended urban metabolism model was devised as a framework for SoE reporting on human settlements in Australia in 1996 and has evolved to the version used in the 2006 Report.[5] It has normative value in being able to articulate key sustainability goals, such as reduced resource use, reduced waste and emissions, greater liveability and human wellbeing, improved urban systems and processes, and improved urban environmental quality. These five key aspirational goals have also found their way into government sustainability action statements for metropolitan development[6] together with more explicit targets and metrics.

The basis for a transition to sustainability reporting is, however, emerging from within individual SoE thematic areas (eg human health impacts modelling in the Atmosphere theme). In the Human Settlements domain, metabolic stocks and flows modelling has now been extended from national[7] to sub-metropolitan scale.[8] This permits exploration of future urban development scenarios associated with a range of alternative populations and land uses, at varying densities, with an ability to assess city 'performance' in terms of key indicators such as conversion of greenspace, consumption of water, energy and building materials, and bio-region impacts (eg quality of receiving waters, urban airshed quality and change in catchment land use). It also provides a platform for exploring the impact on cities of key exogenous pressures such as climate change, peak oil, potential health pandemics and alternative food futures. Additional challenges will revolve around estimating the relative contributions that patterns of household consumption (ie behaviour) versus patterns of urban development (eg housing densities and land use–transport configurations) make to urban sustainability.

The challenge will be to initiate studies on Australian cities with a scope equivalent to that outlined above if we are to begin to match the impact that the Australian Treasury's (2002) Intergenerational Report has had in firstly identifying and then engaging with the challenges facing a Federal Government in relation to its fiscal sustainability – that is, matching future outlays on health, care for the elderly, welfare payments, education and training, environment, etc against sources of future income – all within a context of the nation's future demographic (ageing and migration) and economic (growth, productivity and employment) prospects.[9] At present the domain specific (water, energy, waste, transport, housing, etc) vulnerabilities of Australia's cities as identified in the 2006 SoE Report[10] have not been combined and projected into the future to the extent necessary to define urban sustainability crises of a magnitude to which a national response is required.

## Box 36 Certification and Labelling

*Tim Cadman*

Forest certification should be understood as a process that results in a written quality statement (a certificate) attesting to the origin of raw wood material and its status and/or qualifications following validation by an independent third party.

The *criteria* are to be understood as states or aspects of forest management requiring adherence to a principle of forest certification.

A *principle* is a fundamental rule or aspect of forest management.

*Indicators* are qualitative or quantitative parameters, which are assessed in relation to a criterion.

*Standards* are a set of principles, criteria and indictors that serve as a tool to promote sustainable forest management, as a basis for monitoring and reporting or as a reference for assessment of actual forest management.

### Types of certification

A *process-based* approach is designed to evaluate whether systems are in place that allow forest managers/owners to achieve and review targets they have set. Usually, it is the system itself, and not necessarily the forest, that is assessed to determine the success of the standard (eg the Program for the Endorsement of Forest Certification Schemes – PEFC) and including a *hybrid* with some performance requirements but predominantly systems-based (eg Australian Forestry Standard, a PEFC member):

- 'Quality assurance' useful for markets that require forest products guaranteed to come from legal sources.
- Endorsed by government; but because landowner and industry groups choose which other stakeholders participate, they ultimately control the PEFC.

*Performance-based* management standards are designed to evaluate whether management practices in the forest itself meet specified ecological and social performance measures, and reduce the impacts of logging (eg Forest Stewardship Council).

- 'Eco-label' useful for markets that have clients seeking products from managed forests that exceed government requirements.
- Endorsed by third parties (eg environment groups and indigenous peoples' organisations).
- In contrast to the PEFC, the FSC has equally distributed voting powers between members, who are divided into three equally weighted 'chambers' (economic, social and environmental).

Certification should be seen within the context of an emerging variety of regulatory approaches towards improving forest management, which are encouraging similar developments in other sectors. These are driven by NGOs and industry associations, rather than exclusively by government, and, although voluntary, are becoming increasingly adopted through their linkage to markets and governmental management systems.

Although forest certification can be seen as a governance system for regulating forest management, it is best understood as a system of regulatory law making, with the institutional focus being around developing – and certifying – standards of forest management. Forest certification is a significant indicator of broader trends in the administrative law of global governance, posing the question of how political legitimacy is framed in trans-national regulation: Who is in charge? Is it the state, the private sector, civil society, or all three, and what does this mean for democratic decision-making regarding matters of environmental protection and regulation in an era of globalization?

## Box 37 Ethical Investment

*Konrad Knerr*

There is a strong case for ethical or socially responsible investment in current and future financial markets for investment monies. The main reason for this is that, in the long term, protecting environmental and social capital creates a sustainable economic basis for financial capital to be utilized.

Socially responsible investment represented approximately US$4.55 trillion in 2005. This form of investment will continue to grow, as it accounts for social and environmental capital as well as financial capital. Managed Australian socially responsible investment portfolios grew 56 per cent during the 2005/6 financial year. In the US from 1995 to 2005, socially responsible investment assets grew 4 per cent faster than the entire US universe of managed assets.[1] Recognition of this kind of growth means this kind of investment can work as a strong force for change. Indeed ethical investment can impact financial, environmental and social activity in the market over the long term.

This runs contrary to the dominant short-term view many actors in political and financial circles use to justify actions or motives, regardless of long-term consequences. It is partly because of this that ethical or socially responsible investment is not considered a valid investment alternative to conventional profit-focused investment approaches. This is a mistaken assumption. For example, superannuation or pension funds are generally held in trust by trustees. The responsibilities of trustees of a superannuation fund are set out in the trust deed. Generally money held on behalf of members of a superannuation or pension fund that is not used to cover costs, charges or expenses or for the immediate purposes of the fund is invested. The word 'invest' in this context means the purchase or acquisition of some form of property from which interest or profit is expected. Trustee covenants generally require trustees to formulate an investment strategy with regard to the composition of the entity's investments as a whole, including the extent to which investments are diverse, or involve the entity in being exposed to risks. Hence trustees invest fund monies in the interests of members and the financial interests of members are served by adequate diversification across different asset classes. So choice is exercised across different kinds of alternative investment options in different markets to avoid risk.

There is great interest in the environmental and social impact of business activities for these kinds of investment choices. Financial markets regulate the availability of such funds. However, in financial markets focus is generally on expected future returns, not on past performance. So in competing for finance it is necessary to show potential providers of capital the economic prospects of success and security associated with financial commitments. Any financial negotiations over future expectations and risks that take place in investment markets dictate the flow and direction of financial capital. Hence access to finance can determine the investments in types of production processes, business directions and products themselves, as well as the conditions for these investments.

This is where the idea of ethical or socially responsible investment has potential to change markets. There is no invisible market mechanism that regulates financial flows. Each individual citizen is an actor in the financial market. Each individual influences the market by exercising financial decisions based on considerations that may factor in ethical, environmental or social consequences. So individual citizens as actors in this financial process can influence and shape economic development. Ethical investment can be utilized by business to move capital towards more sustainable (ethically, socially, environmentally beneficial) enterprises, particularly when they demonstrate significant returns against calculable risk. This can create a shift towards new sectors in financial markets and growth in areas of business that may not otherwise receive finance. Thus economy, society and environment are not antagonists in the market; rather, they are dependent on one another. Ethical investment can therefore be very effective in creating change in global financial markets.

## Box 38 Engaging the Public in Sustainability Planning

*David Biggs*

While both computer-based planning tools (eg Geographic Information Systems and Transportation Analysis Models) and public engagement in the planning process have been mainstays in municipal and regional planning agencies, the practice of combining them has been slower to emerge. Increasingly, decision-makers mobilize community support for more sustainable policies and practices by using software as a central part of their long-range planning process. The mantra of 'sustainable cities' has come to represent the need to improve the planning process in three dimensions:

1  **Longer-term planning scenarios**: Cities are increasingly creating 20–50 year plans. While this adds complexity to the traditional 5-year planning horizon, it also has increased awareness of the life-cycle impacts of choices, many of which are masked by shorter-term analysis. For example, municipalities which approve 'sprawling' see their tax base improve in the short term; in the longer term, however, the maintenance costs of roads and pipes rise well above what the residents are willing to pay in taxes.

2  **Triple bottom line and systems thinking**: Sustainability reminds us that we need to juggle ecological, economic and social priorities simultaneously to understand how our cities work as systems. For example, we now realize that investing in a new transit line will have little impact on travel behaviour, and therefore air pollution and congestion, if a small percentage of the population lives and works within 500 metres of a stop. Zoning for compact development near transit requires integrated land-use and transportation plans.

3  **Community support and engagement**: A plan is only useful if it is implemented, and in democracies implementation hinges on public and political support. Public resistance and NIMBYisms are regularly cited as reasons for the failure of forward thinking policies and plans. Cities are seeking innovative ways to engage a large enough portion of the population to mobilize the support that is needed to carry out course-changing plans.

Engaging non-experts in the planning process has been difficult because many lack the expertise and the time required to engage in detailed analysis. Yet community support is necessary for progressive change. Early attempts to use computer models to stimulate public engagement enjoyed limited success. Most were extensions of desktop GIS systems and were designed for more analytical purposes. The University of British Columbia's Sustainable Development Research Institute therefore developed MetroQuest, a 'real life SIM-City'.[1] This allows non-experts to see the consequences of alternative visions for their city played out in 40-year future scenarios on-the-fly. The process brings the community, stakeholder groups and decision-makers together in interactive workshops to collaborate in the creation of a desired future city. A web-based version allows the process to extend even further. So far, the process has been used successfully in cities on four continents, including cities in Canada, Australia, New Zealand, Malaysia, China, India and Mexico.

MetroQuest allows users to experiment with land-use, housing, transportation, economy and resource management scenarios played out in 40-year future periods. They receive feedback on projected impacts on a wide range of priority areas, including air quality, traffic congestion, tax rates, green space, housing, waste management, water conservation, greenhouse gas emissions and ecological footprint. Projects typically engage tens of thousands of participants, sometimes over 100,000, amounting to a politically significant portion of the population. Adopting a growth management plan that, for example, clusters new housing and jobs close to existing transit hubs can save billions of dollars. Savings also extend to many other areas, such as avoiding the costs of traffic congestion, energy and water supply, and waste management. By seeing the results instantly, diverse participants are able to: visualize the impacts of various decisions decades into the future; learn about tradeoffs and synergies between environmental, social and economic priorities; experiment with 'what if' futures; co-create a shared vision for the city; and gain a real sense of ownership over the plan going forward.

## Box 39 Closing Loops between Sectors

Environmental management focused initially on reducing flows (air and water pollution) by pollution regulations and standards. It did not close loops or address causes:

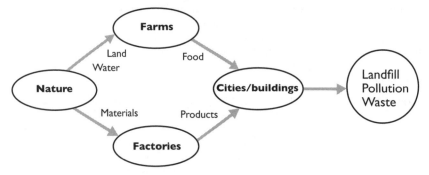

The next stage was closing loops within sectors through recycling and eco-efficiency measures. This is generally labelled 'best practice'. It did not make connections between different sectors:

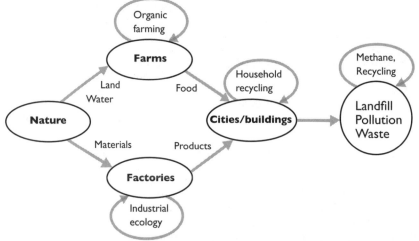

Efforts are now moving towards symbiotic relationships in resource flows between sectors:

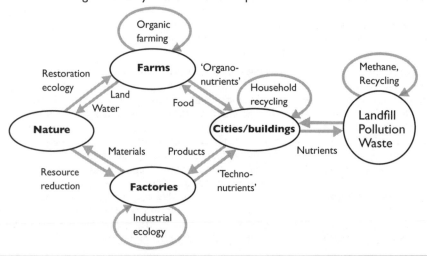

## Box 40 Linking Policies to Outcomes

*Ian Swain*

The world's cities take up less than 2 per cent of the Earth's surface, yet now account for roughly 78 per cent of the carbon emissions from human activities. This suggests that significant environmental gains are possible by improving the way in which cities use the resources available to them. So just how effective has government strategy been in improving the 'metabolism' of fundamental urban resource flows such as energy and water? Analysing the effectiveness of common policy approaches on specific resource flows can provide insight into this issue.

The effectiveness of government sustainability initiatives is made clearer by examining trends in resource metabolism in chronological relation to the implementation of key policy initiatives. Through the processing and conversion of existing data from a range of government and industry sources, it is possible to derive standardized time-series trends for the consumption of various forms of energy. A 'smoothed' line graph display of these trends can then be superimposed with vertical axes representing the temporal distribution of specific policies. In this way, a clear graphical display of the relative effect of a range of sustainability policies can be produced. Sustainability policy applying to the Australian Capital Territory (ACT) over the last ten years typifies common contemporary approaches to resource management, particularly in Australia.

An example of this approach can be demonstrated in relation to a case study of energy consumption in Canberra. These policies are characterized by a fundamental reliance on efficiency gains, supply-side solutions and impact mitigation of new developments. The policies appearing on the graph below are a combination of both local (ACT) and Federal Government schemes.

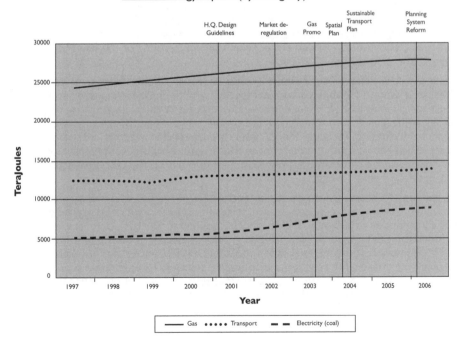

The consumption of electricity can be seen to steadily rise until 2002, after which it continues to increase but at a reduced rate. This change corresponds to a rise in the consumption of gas at around the same time. Transport energy inputs have been rising gradually and uniformly since 2000. The graph below represents the sum energy inputs of the three fuels analysed in the previous graph. When population change is accounted for by dividing the sum of these fuels by total population at each point in time, it is also clear that per capita energy consumption has continued to rise, from approximately 135 GigaJoules to 155 GigaJoules over the last decade.

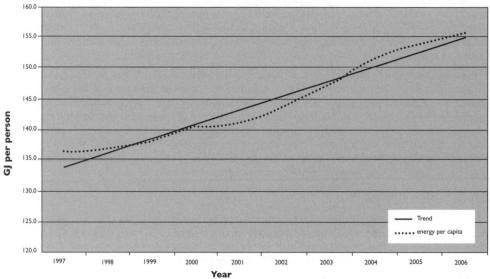

Combined Energy Input per capita

Taken together, the two graphs suggest that increases in total energy metabolism are caused by both population growth and increased per capita consumption. While the rate of increase may have flattened, the direction of change remains undesirable from an ecological standpoint. The apparent ineffectiveness of current policies calls for scrutiny of the key characteristics underlying these approaches.

First, the heavy reliance on efficiency initiatives has proven ineffective for several reasons. Such initiatives are favoured largely due to a compatibility with 'business-as-usual' and society's preference for avoiding lifestyle change. However, increases in efficiency translate to increased affordability, which may in turn actually *increase* overall demand due to 'elasticity' effects. There are also indirect effects of reducing energy costs through efficiency in that consumers are able to afford more products/appliances, or choose more feature-packed, energy-intensive models. Consequently, resource efficiency does not guarantee resource conservation, particularly where affluence is simultaneously rising.

Second, policies to increase the supply of alternative energy sources, as currently implemented, are also limited. As overall supply is increased, prices (or at least price rises) may be dampened, and thus consumption of *all* forms of electricity is supported. Similarly, increases in gas supply and consumption can be seen to only dampen growth in electricity consumption, rather than reducing consumption. Although gas is half as polluting it is less expensive than electricity. This effectively lowers total energy costs, thus encouraging demand. Through these supply-side processes, the urban system is maintained in a perpetual state of exploitation, rather than evolving towards a mature conservation-oriented structure as found in natural ecosystems.

In summary, the analysis points to the urgent need for sustainability policy that focuses on reducing the *need* for resources, rather than providing for increasing demand more efficiently. Efficiency and conservation are clearly different things. Political and capital interests remain major obstacles to achieving the latter, as reflected by a lack of strategic commitment to achieving stated goals.

## Box 41 Eco-service Offsets versus Credits

The following compares typical eco-service trading programs to the alternative approach of giving credits for design for eco-services, in relation to issues that have been raised regarding environmental trading systems.

# Offsets                                              # Credits

### Ensure the use of the right supports for eco-services

| Offsets | Credits |
|---|---|
| Mitigative actions to protect a species can be undone by unexpected changes in context: | Design for eco-services (DES) in urban areas would increase ecosystem resilience: |
| • Fire can change the sequestration value of the forest and web of biodiversity<br>• Small biodiversity areas can be wiped out by disease, cyclones or temperature change | • Fires and floods generally do not wipe out whole cities, so species could escape disasters<br>• DES can moderate even regional climate change and would reduce the urban heat sink |

### Ensure the rights are well defined

| Offsets | Credits |
|---|---|
| Eco-services for trading have been hard to define: | The nature and extent of the DES credit would be straightforward to define: meters allocated to nature ecosystems and services per building floor area, per capita or per lot size. |
| • Wrong ecology: Planting plantations or geo-sequestration could disrupt bio-diversity (as a monoculture) or be in the wrong place<br>• Long-term issues (eg salinity, global warming and groundwater pollution) are unknown and can take decades to manifest<br>• Most offsets are for what we are going to do in the future, not what we have done, so there is no net gain | • DES in urban areas could create a diverse gene pool and not a monocultural approach<br>• Any errors in biodiversity in urban DES are not likely to affect natural areas in the hinterland<br>• DES would add ecosystems to existing cities as well as new buildings for net ecological gain |

### Ensure the rights can be measured and verified

| Offsets | Credits |
|---|---|
| We do not know how to measure biodiversity. For example: | The measurement of increased biodiversity is through the 'surrogate' of space allocated for: |
| • Salinity has complex contributing factors and non-point sources<br>• There is global agreement on measuring tons of $CO_2$ equivalent, but not science on how much carbon soil and vegetation sequesters<br>• Biodiversity varies between ecosystems | • Natural ecosystems (eg roof gardens)<br>• Eco-services (eg vertical wetlands)<br><br>We do not need to know equivalence of $CO_2$ sequestered, as design for eco-services would serve multiple values (eg air and water cleaning and environmental amenity) |

# Offsets

# Credits

## Ensure the proper use of the rights can be enforced

| Offsets | Credits |
|---|---|
| Non-point sources of negative impacts are hard to monitor. For example:<br><br>• In emissions trading schemes, smoke stack detectors could be linked to monitors at the regulatory agency<br>• In eco-service issues, it is difficult to measure negative impacts or their non-point sources | Enforcement of ownership of eco-service credits is no special problem, as it runs with the property:<br><br>• Post-occupancy evaluation is a well-established method for large buildings<br>• If the infrastructure for eco-services has been put in place, there is no reason not to use it for landscaping values |

## Ensure there are enough parties to cover transaction costs

| Offsets | Credits |
|---|---|
| There are lots of fossil fuel industries that emit carbon and need credits, but:<br><br>• There are not many who want to trade in biodiversity<br>• Eco-service trading therefore needs to be subsidized | All urban property owners could take advantage of a DES scheme in retrofitting:<br><br>• Properties sell often, which would enable businesses to 'churn' retrofit projects<br>• Costs can be covered by performance contracts |

## Ensure the transfer of rights involves low transaction costs

| Offsets | Credits |
|---|---|
| If there is not a brokerage agency, firms can spend too much time finding sellers and making transactions:<br><br>• There has to be enough money to support the costs of the private or public operating agency<br>• Selling or trading emissions, sequestration or biodiversity involves complex arrangements | Developers can acquire points for permit approvals by installing ecological space in buildings owned by others:<br><br>• The planning agency needs only to certify that the space is 'planted' (normal building inspection)<br>• The DES could be maintained by others (as in urban gardens) without new legal arrangements |

## Ensure future government decisions will not adversely affect investment

| Offsets | Credits |
|---|---|
| In the case of conventional mitigative trading, new scientific evidence may require changes in policies and programmes:<br><br>• New knowledge could vitiate programmes (eg levels of sequestration in varied ecosystems)<br>• Investors could lose money | Urban amenity and biodiversity is positive and would be unaffected by new science:<br><br>• Ecological space could be easily modified if new science made discoveries about urban biodiversity – as ecological space is not based on specific biota itself<br>• An investment in amenity value is seldom lost |

## Box 42 Economic Valuation of Eco-services

**Cost–benefit framework**: A common view is that government decisions should be based on the same calculus that private business uses, ie cost–benefit analysis (CBA). In fact, many accept CBA (or risk analysis etc) as a universal framework of analysis. CBA is often used by governments to determine the overall benefit to society of an action, policy or programme, or which option has the greatest net benefit in relation to costs. For example, in the US, the proposed economic benefits of environmental regulations must be shown to exceed the economic costs of compliance. When applied to development proposals, CBA, in effect, can translate into tradeoffs. In other words, development is deemed appropriate if the figures indicate that social and economic benefits 'outweigh' the environmental costs.

Assigning monetary values to ecological and health impacts is highly technical yet, simultaneously, necessarily subjective and relative. It assumes costs and benefits can be aggregated and tradeoffs can be made in a context where the overriding issue is still money or efficiency, not ecology. The CBA framework means that inherently risky or harmful activities (eg nuclear) can be justified if compared to something arguably worse (eg coal-fired power stations), or if there is adequate offsetting. Further, CBA does not consider unjust enrichment, where investors or developers profit unreasonably at the expense of the public.

**Environmental valuation**: To obtain figures for CBA frameworks, various forms of valuation can be used as surrogates that reflect environmental qualities, including:

- *Use values*, which do not require actual use and can be 'secondary' uses, like watching a TV show on the Tarkine wilderness in Tasmania, which is currently being destroyed.
- *Option values*, which are what people would pay for preserving options. Even though people themselves may not enjoy something, they have the option to do so, like the Tarkine someday.
- *Bequest value*, which is what people would pay so that future generations can enjoy something. This still has 'use value' to people today if they want their grandchildren to see the Tarkine.
- *Non-use values*, which are what people would pay for something, even though they never expect to enjoy it – just to know it is there (ie the Tarkine has 'existence' value).

**Discounting**: CBA discounts to present values, which means a factor is used to reflect inflation and the idea that people prefer to spend now rather than later. When applied to public goods, such as natural systems, which do not 'depreciate' in value, this makes little sense [Box 43].

**Monetary equivalents**: Various methods can be used to assign a 'value to ecosystem services, so that the environment can be made to fit into a cost–benefit framework. These methods include 'costs avoided', 'market price', 'productivity', 'hedonic pricing', 'travel cost' and 'surveys', as discussed below.

*Costs avoided*: A relatively simple method used to determine the benefits of an ecosystem is to calculate the cost of avoiding damage, substituting the environmental service or restoring the environment. For example, the costs of protecting a watershed or river can be compared to the total cost of dealing with erosion, treating water, dredging sediment, regenerating animal populations, floods, insurance, etc. (This justified the preservation of New York City's Catskill watershed, where a new water filtration plant would have cost four times more than restoration of the watershed and yet still have more maintenance and operating costs.)

*Market price*: Economic value is usually based on 'willingness to pay'. Willingness to pay depends on the ability to pay and thus can favour the preferences of the wealthy. This method could, for instance, support more spending on prolonging the lives of relatively few wealthy elderly than saving children in poor countries from preventable diseases. Some economists have even calculated the lives of people in rich nations to be worth more than those in poor countries. When something is not traded in the market, some economists apply the same reasoning by (indirectly) determining what people would hypothetically be willing to pay. This assumes 'perfect knowledge' on the part of those surveyed about the value of ecosystems to survival and life quality, as well as their capacity to adapt to human interventions. The idea of market value is influenced by marginal analysis: the market value of eco-services, like any other commercial good, is determined by their contribution to the total 'surplus' goods traded in the market. The *total economic surplus* equals the *consumer surplus* + the *producer surplus*. The consumer surplus is the maximum people would pay minus what they do pay (ie how much money the buyers feel they save). The producer surplus is the total revenues from a good, minus total costs of producing it. The surplus is a measure of the changes in quantity or quality of marketed goods, not the total value. So the surplus only counts the marginal value, ie not the total value of eco-services, but the value-added. As Heal argues, this sort of marginal economic thinking cannot really deal with ecosystem collapse or irreversible change.[1] Thus there seems to be some confusion in applying willingness to pay to man-made products versus self-maintaining systems whose value is not marginal but essential. For example, the costs of cleaning up a lake would be measured by effects on total consumer and producer surplus, but not the whole value of the industry – let alone the intrinsic value of nature. It is understood that pollution reduces the quality and quantity of goods like fish or crops, and cleaning pollution imposes costs. However, if the costs were greater than the benefit, the costs of restoring nature would not be seen as economically sound.

*Productivity*: This measures the economic benefits of improved environmental quality. Ecosystems, such as wetlands and forests, can be seen as 'inputs' which increase the amount of 'outputs' produced (clean water, fish, birds, honey, etc). This method only counts resources that are inputs in marketed goods – not the whole system that is required to sustain those resources. It places no value on nature per se.

*Hedonic pricing*: This usually uses property and house values to measure the value that individuals place on environmental quality. A house will be worth more if it has good views, clean air and water, etc. Other variables (eg size, number of rooms) can be statistically eliminated to determine the value of one environmental characteristic, like closeness to open space. While studies may indicate that people are willing to pay to be close to open space, this does not capture the multiple values of nature. They may also assume people have choices, but most cannot really choose where to work. Lifestyle considerations such as 'downshifting' (ie giving up income for more leisure time and life quality) are hard to factor in.

*Travel cost*: This assesses the value of, say, wilderness, mountains or lakes by measuring what people pay in time and money to travel to them. This is an admittedly rough approximation of value, but it has been used to support arguments to protect natural use.

*Survey techniques*: Another means of calculating 'willingness to pay', where eco-services are not traded on the market, is to survey people what they would be willing to pay.

**Contingent valuation**: People are surveyed about what they would be willing to pay for something like an ecosystem – or to be compensated for sacrificing it. 'National' parks, however, need samplings of the whole population of the country, as they belong to all citizens. Such surveys have made decision-makers more aware of the full extent of bequest, existence and option values. They have been used to justify the removal of dams or to increase the environmental flows of (dammed or diverted) rivers. However, they only weigh people's economic values, not the functional values of eco-services. Biases can also be created that can work both ways:

- People will inflate the value that they would actually be willing or able to pay. This is called the 'Halo Effect'. Generally people have said they would pay more for 'clean' products than they actually do.[2]
- It assumes people decide about the economic worth of some aspect of nature without knowing what will happen in the wider environmental context.

**Contingent choice**: These surveys ask people how they would rank two or more actions, policies or programmes. This can also be a means of determining the most politically acceptable among environmentally harmful options.

## Box 43 Problems with Pricing Eco-services

- We cannot measure the ecological base because it represents the whole life support system. Thus its value is infinite. We cannot even measure the eco-services it provides, because these are an inextricable part of the intricate web of nature. Their protection currently relies largely on their relevance to economists' frameworks.
- Prices are a reflection of the 'ability' to pay and thus power relationships. For example, some women in developing nations sell body parts for very small sums of money to feed their children. This does *not* mean that they do not value or need their kidneys. By analogy, ecosystems are the kidneys and lungs of the planet.
- Prices fluctuate according to socio-political variables and other factors that affect supply and demand. Some resource development interests are virtual monopolies or cartels that can limit the availability of raw materials to increase corporate access to public resources through scare campaigns about resource shortages.
- Communities may willingly sell off natural areas despite their recreational or wilderness values, expecting to be able to travel to enjoy other people's forests. The remaining natural areas will eventually be over-used, even if through eco-tourism. Due to their scarcity, charges will be applied to access the public estate, which will exclude the poor.
- Prices cannot register the need for ecosystem integrity. Ecosystems are self-managing only if the area allocated to them is large enough that they can continue to function as an integral system. Smaller areas will not have the ecological resilience to survive due to feral invaders, fires or species extinction triggered by disease.
- Wilderness areas can be too prevalent to have economic value one day, yet become too small to survive when critical ecological thresholds are crossed. The value of resources only needs to exceed the value of the wilderness areas containing them briefly, as in war time, for them to be irreversibly lost (eg dams change ecosystems forever).
- Eco-services go up in value as they become scarce, but so do mineral resources. When these areas are scarce enough to have a high conservation value, the value of the resources they contain (such as minerals and timber), will also go up accordingly.
- Marginal analysis is not contextual (and arguably excludes whole systems issues), so it is inconsistent with design. For example, it cannot deal with larger forces that affect supply and demand, such as global warming or chain reactions to environmental shock.
- Prices cannot reflect the infinite value of the life support system. Market prices can only indicate a small change in ecosystem services, not a total collapse. For example, even if water prices were high, prices could not prevent a global shortage of potable water.
- Discounting allows the value of nature to be reduced over time even though it becomes scarcer. This is contrary to the belief that the market will protect resources because prices will go up as nature becomes scarcer and is therefore more highly valued.

### Value of raw materials relative to ecosystem services

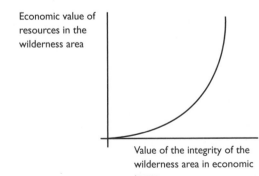

Economic value of resources in the wilderness area

Value of the integrity of the wilderness area in economic terms

Even 'permanently' reserved areas can be renegotiated when there is a (temporary) economic crisis. In the given political economy, resource crises occur periodically in a boom and bust cycle, creating a vicious circle of resource exploitation.

# Box 44 Measuring Living Wall Performance

*Yael Stav*

Living walls are considered a green technology that, like green roofs, provide a multitude of environmental benefits, from energy savings to water and air quality improvement through to wildlife habitat restoration. However, a comprehensive analysis of living walls presents a range of problems. The first set of problems derives from the complexity of the interactions between living walls and their environment: site-specific variables, including building orientation and layout, and thermal capacity, greatly affect measurements of thermal performance. Roof-to-wall and window-to-wall ratios influence living wall performance in terms of stormwater retention and filtration, air quality improvement, food production and wildlife habitat restoration as well as thermal performance. Temperature, humidity, wind, pollution, elevation, radiation and climate all influence the species of plants that can thrive in a specific living wall project.

These in turn influence all the other variables. For example, different roof-to-wall ratios may explain the substantial range of results for energy savings reported by different experimental studies: results range from 0.6 per cent to 75 per cent.[1] Tropical climates are expected to allow a greater improvement in the performance of living walls than cooler climates because vegetation is considered much better at cooling than at reducing heat loss. Also, living walls can mitigate the enormous runoff peak load caused by subtropical rainfall. Unfortunately, the only quantitative measurements of the thermal and hydrological benefits of living walls have been performed in temperate climates, specifically Germany and Canada.[2]

Other examples of variability relate to design decisions. For example, the decision between the use of tap water irrigation, greywater integration, or rainwater retention and filtration can make a difference between a system that requires ongoing resource inputs and a system that is self-maintaining while providing water quality improvement and other hydrological benefits. Design choices that attract indigenous species of flora and fauna can make the difference between a living wall that merely enlarges biomass and a living wall that actually enhances the ecology and provides a platform for local wildlife propagation. The complexity of the interactions between living walls and their environment, and indeed the complexity of the living walls themselves as a system, makes it impossible for us to calculate or simulate the behaviour of these systems. Therefore, we must rely on experimentation.

The second class of problems stems from the fact that very few living wall projects exist and those that do are young. For example, when trying to estimate the extent to which a living wall may protect building exterior surfaces, we find no living wall projects that are both old enough and appropriately documented. Thus we can only assume that the prolonged life of the green roof membrane applies to walls. Green roofs extend the life of a roof by two to four times.[3] Nevertheless, even these estimations are hypothetical as the oldest modern green roofs are 35 years old.

The last class of problems is related to benefits of living walls that can be quantified only partially or cannot be quantified at all. Added psychological value can be measured monetarily, as has been demonstrated by a green roof study [Box 14]. However, this is a narrow aspect of the effect of vegetation on people. A more holistic approach would probably attribute a higher social value to urban vegetation. Benefits such as additional wildlife habitat and living walls' potential as food production platforms are not quantified at all at this time.

In short, in order to get an idea of the effect of the different design parameters and environments on the performance of living walls, many more projects must be taken on and scientifically measured. Moreover, the definition of living wall performance should expand to include those values which are at this time unquantified. Perhaps we will see performance that has thus far been defined as a reduction of negative impacts (energy savings, absorption of pollution, minimizing health problems, etc) changed to the use of a positive and holistic approach, measuring the overall contribution of living walls to the environment.[4]

## Box 45 Decision Trees – Terminal and Reversible

### 1. Traditional decision tree: Choosing 'best' practice or technologies

Pruning process to eliminate risks and achieve maximum industrial growth

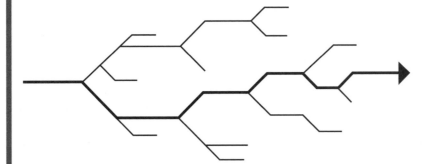

Towards one single future with less and less opportunity to diversify or reverse direction

### 2. Proposed decision tree: Designing wider options for natural security and social choice through a rhizomatic approach

Diversity of social choice and decentralized re-source production

Public Estate

Positive Development transforms negative space into reversible, healthy diverse environments that increase both the public estate and ecological base

Ecological Base

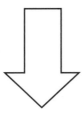

Increased natural security by diversifying pathways, sources of urban food and energy, habitats, etc

## Box 46 Community Management of Ecosystems

*David Eastburn*

Members of many rural communities have a rich knowledge of their landscapes, are highly sensitive to climatic, environmental, market and policy changes, and have a strong interest in a sustainable future. However, only a fraction of their potential to contribute to a sustainable future is realized, as the following case studies demonstrate.

### Lower Murrumbidgee flood country

The Lower Murrumbidgee floodplain, between the towns of Hay and Balranald in southwestern New South Wales, is the largest area of floodplain wetland remaining in the Murrumbidgee Valley (at 217,000ha). It includes the second largest red gum forest in Australia. Layers of alluvium, deposited by silt-laden floodwaters over much of the past 50 million years, allow large-scale organic grain and oilseed production. Floodplain farmers mimic natural flooding by ponding water in spring to store it in the soil profile, minimizing evaporation loss over the hot summer. More than 40 species of waterbird breed on the floodplain. Farmers have set aside habitat areas, and self-imposed rules ensure that environmentally sensitive areas receive first access to any water that flows onto the floodplain.

### Lower Murray Lakes and Coorong Fishery

At a time when fisheries are collapsing globally, there are also valuable lessons to be learned from the Lower Murray Lakes and Coorong fishing community. Commercial fishing has taken place in Lakes Alexandrina and Albert, the Coorong, and the Southern Ocean, around the mouth of the River Murray in South Australia, since 1846. The completion of the Murray Mouth Barrages in 1940 turned the lakes to freshwater, resulting in the loss of 89 per cent of the richest fishing grounds. Only a few resilient families remained. In the late 1980s, the fishers again came under pressure to assess, justify and articulate their activities. It helped to focus the group to reaffirm positive processes and develop additional rules to ensure that their fishery remained sustainable.

### Similarities between the two groups in the studies

- Recognition that healthy ecosystems are crucial to livelihoods.
- The use of local knowledge and vernacular processes, developed over generations of observation and experience, to work in harmony with local ecosystems.
- Vulnerable geographic location. Ecosystems and communities at the bottom ends of rivers 'dying from thirst', as a result of excessive upstream diversions, is a global issue.
- Both bioregions have been seriously impacted by pre-ecological river regulation priorities.
- Adaptive management: a timely response to a situation with scientific and local (sometimes including intergenerational) knowledge.
- Diversity. Neither group is confined to one ecosystem or one product/species for their livelihoods. Fishers can move between freshwater, estuary and the ocean. During droughts, floodplain farmers make a living from forest products.
- Self-imposed rules to improve the sustainability of species and natural habitat.
- Independent accreditation of activities (eg Biological Farmers of Australia and Marine Stewardship Council).
- Recognition of the importance of cooperation for survival through the establishment of industry associations.
- Value-adding to maximize returns while reducing impacts (eg farming organically, operating fish restaurants).
- Appreciation of the importance of ongoing communication with Australian society.

Centralized technocratic bureaucracies can make important but limited progress towards sustainability. Community groups with thorough knowledge of local bioregions must be embraced as authentic partners to fine-tune and accelerate procedures.

## Box 47 Wagga Wagga Eco-industrial Park

*Sharon Stacy*

In 2001, the Laminex factory in regional Wagga Wagga, NSW, Australia, decommissioned and sold its medium-density fibreboard (MDF) plant, leaving 220 employees without immediate employment. Riverina Investments, which was to become a three-way partnership, was incorporated that year for the purpose of acquiring the industrial property, comprising 25,000 square metres of high span buildings situated on approximately 116 hectares on the Bomen Industrial Estate. Although the main role of Riverina Investments was as landlord, it has taken on a secondary role, supporting the tenants to achieve resource efficiencies.

This role followed from an endogenous initiative by existing industries within the region called the Innovative Resource Management Group (IRM). The IRM consisted of multinational industries in collaboration with the local university and local government support. To pursue the original IRM goals, Riverina Investments actively:

- Encourages compatible industries onto the industrial site that 'fit' in terms of resource requirements and by-product opportunities.
- Engages Zero Waste Australia (ZWA), a not-for-profit NGO, to come onto the site and facilitate the efficiency and synergy outcomes across all industries.

At a time when the outsourcing of physical and intellectual labour to China and India was growing in Australia, recycling and sustainable industries were identified as secure future domestic industries. The cost of transport secures these industries on-shore. Examples of the tenants are:

- Specialized Packaging Services, which is developing a new lightweight, recycled plastic pallet and packaging. Its features are the capacity for the 3kg pallet to support a one ton payload; the capacity to stack 100 unused pallets 2.2m high; and alignment with quarantine requirements which prohibit timber that harbours micro and macro organisms.
- Marvel Glass, which applies recycled glass technology to create an alternative to marble, ceramic and stone. The translucence enables lighting from behind, and the hard, non-porous material is a good alternative in chemically active areas such as laboratory benches. Marvel Glass uses a waste product as the primary input and relatively low temperatures in production.
- The Bio-Recycle group of companies, which specializes in creating organic waste recycling solutions. These solutions incorporate a range of processes and technologies built on many years of industry experience. The aim of the group is to design responsible programmes that maximize the return of valuable organics to the earth. It is able to manage many types or organic waste materials from a diverse range of waste producers, serving wool combing, abattoir, food processing and sale yard industries within the eco-industrial park.

Riverina Investments has provided ZWA with an office and support. ZWA is in turn applying its domestic and international networks to synergies. Current activities include:

- Mapping flows to identify resource requirements, waste and by-product streams.
- Creating a network structure across industry at the CEO level and the production management level to identify specific industry needs.
- Networking industries with its consulting directories to stimulate innovation.

A project is under way to treat pre-existing toxic sludge ponds on-site with natural bioconversion systems. The resulting water and fertilizer will be transferred to an adjacent farm. This is a linear system that converts existing waste to a valuable resource, increasing natural capital and natural security.

By 2006, almost all the 220 jobs lost when the factory closed had been re-established and the implementation of sustainable core values continues to expand.

# Box 48 Equity Mapping

*Jason Byrne*

Equity mapping can reveal how patterns of exposure to environmental harm and access to environmental benefits are distributed across urban landscapes. Using geographic information systems (GISs), researchers in the 1990s began to investigate issues of environmental equity within US cities. Researchers wanted to see whether relationships existed between the location of environmental benefits, harms and natural hazards, and the social and demographic characteristics of urban populations (ie 'environmental justice'). What they found is that socioeconomically vulnerable populations – usually people of colour – bore a disproportionately high burden of environmental harm. Why do such patterns exist?

Because poor communities lack financial resources and political power, corporations and governments have targeted these communities for unpopular land uses like hazardous waste incinerators, toxic chemical plants and radioactive waste facilities, without their knowledge or consent. Over the past two decades, detailed empirical research has proven that in the US, people of colour and the poor are more vulnerable to natural hazards (eg living on flood-prone land or in poorly constructed or substandard housing). Hurricane Katrina in New Orleans showed this clearly. Researchers have also found that freeways are often built through impoverished neighbourhoods and that the poorest (and usually non-white) residents are restricted to parts of the city with the worst air quality and least access to good quality, fresh fruit, vegetables and meat.

So what is equity? The concept of equity basically means that society considers a particular situation to be fair and reasonable (eg that all people have access to fresh drinking water). Equity mapping takes into account four basic expressions of equity:

- Equitable distribution – where all members of society have the same access to environmental benefits and the same exposure to environmental harms;
- Compensatory equity – where benefits are redistributed to those most in need and harms are redirected, to offset inequalities created by class, race or gender differences;
- Demand distribution – where the most vocal members of the community are given the most resources; and
- Market-based distribution – where people who can afford to pay for goods or services get the best access to those goods or services.

In a market economy, access to the best food, cleanest water and healthiest jobs is usually financially determined. What equity mapping can reveal is whether or not resource managers like planners should intervene to redistribute environmental risks, harms or benefits more fairly among the broader community. Let us take parks as an example. Some neighbourhoods have a severe lack of parks and green space. People living in certain neighbourhoods may also encounter barriers to park access (eg freeways or railway lines) absent in other neighbourhoods. Equity mapping enables us to see who enjoys access to parks and how public funding for parks is distributed within cities. Recent studies have revealed that neighbourhoods with abundant parks are predominantly wealthy and also receive more park funding. This raises serious concerns about the effectiveness of urban planning, since parks are supposed to be a public good available to everyone.

Recognizing that planners seem unable to fix these problems, some community groups are now performing their own equity mapping. Groups of women with breast cancer, for example, have come together to map cancer-causing land uses within their communities to see if there is a relationship between the incidence of breast cancer and the location of certain land uses. Environmental equity also has global dimensions. Rich nations from the industrialized North are increasingly sending hazardous waste such as old computer components or used batteries to poorer developing countries in the South for recycling or disposal; some non-governmental organizations have begun to use equity mapping to challenge this practice. Thus equity mapping enables people to generate interactive maps that provide an objective basis for challenging the inequities of existing development.

## Box 49 Conventional Approach to Regulation

### Industrial society aims to increase supply and demand

In this conventional world view, it would appear that industry would benefit if:

- Access to natural resource, transport and labour were cheaper and/or
- There were more consumers and/or more consumption per capita

Therefore, policies have sought to increase access to resources and consumption. Sometimes there are efforts to increase demand to balance supply. This results in increased throughput of materials and energy over time and is unsustainable.

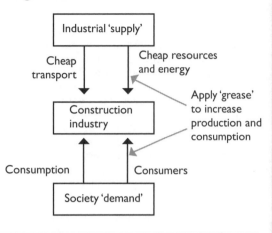

### Environmental regulation aims to reduce supply and demand

When environmentalists and policymakers became aware of environmental issues, they tried to reduce these drivers by creating friction on consumption and production. Thus environmental regulation was shaped by the same (unsustainable) paradigmatic approach. Given this industrial framework, environmental controls try to reduce or tax:

- *Inputs* (resource extraction); or
- *Outputs* (pollution and waste) of industry; or
- *Consumption* by consumers

These environmental controls displease both industry and consumers, because they constrain supply and/or demand. This inevitably leads to ever more conflict.

### A more positive approach

The built environment can drive, rather than just respond to, industrial and social transformation. It can increase production of public goods and establish projects that improve life quality, instead of creating wealth differentials.

We need a rethink of 'supply and demand'. We can design to increase the ecological base and public state without reducing options, choices and basic freedoms.

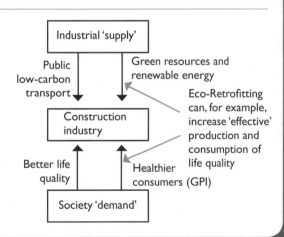

## Box 50 Organic Waste to Farms

*Gerry Gillespie*

Every economy is underpinned by the quality of its soil. Up to 70 per cent of all industrial inputs come from the soil. Yet around the world, soil is being mined in a linear, dead-end process. It takes between 60 to 90 minerals, nutrients and trace elements to grow a plant, and this is removed from the land with every crop. Agriculture is not sustainable, therefore, unless quality organic products – with their nutrients and biology – are returned to the soil to restore the biological activity and nutrients lost through cropping. Values accruing to the farmer by returning quality products to the soil include reduced water and fertilizer costs, soil compaction, and salinity, along with increased productivity, nutrients and carbon. Research, including trials undertaken on behalf of the Department of Environment and Conservation in NSW, Australia, show that dollar values from compost products can be attributed to yield, water savings, nutrient delivery and carbon. There are also a range of community values including carbon sequestration, nitrous oxide reduction and $CO_2$ reduction.

The single largest component of the waste stream, by weight, is organic material. Including non-recycled paper it can be as high as 60 per cent of the total waste stream. This organic material is essential to sustain food production. In typical resource recovery operations, however, this market is the last thing considered. The collection, processing and marketing of organic wastes are undertaken in a segmented, sequential manner. Compost firms take the product, but their true capital gain is only realized when they sell it. But farmers currently do not see compost as adding value to their business. When the cost of transport is combined with the cost of spreading it on the land, the price appears prohibitive.

By looking at the problem from a whole systems perspective, we can create a net positive system that pays for itself, benefits all parties and improves the health of the soil. For example, if the farmer/collector/processor were a single contractual identity – a 'soil cooperative' – the material collection and part of the processing would be paid for up-front by those using the waste. Once collected by the soil cooperative, the product would be transported to the land, where it would be made into a range of solid or fluid products – modified to agronomic standards, depending on local soil and crop applications. A price would then be set for the product by the soil cooperative's members. A low price for members and a low cooperative joining fee should see membership increase rapidly.

To provide security of investment in the return of quality compost products to agriculture, an ongoing stream of material must be guaranteed. The average individual in Australia, for example, produces up to one litre of organic wastes per day, and commercial and agricultural wastes can all contribute to the compost products produced. Security of inputs can be achieved by patenting the collection infrastructure and structure. The proposed soil cooperative will generate 'patient funds' to enable the poorer farmers to stay on the land and to build financial capacity. These funds will make it possible to tolerate slow payment caused by climatic changes and provide drought proofing for its members. It can lift the community capacity of landholders who may be asset rich but financially poor.

This structure also creates the potential for carbon trading. As humic levels rise, so does the carbon sequestration level. Humic compound levels can be registered by the soil cooperative prior to product application. Part of the benefit can be retained by the cooperative and real tradable benefits paid to farm members. Farm credits could be provided for nitrous oxide reduction levels. The Federal Government could match the payments to farmers made by the soil cooperative to meet greenhouse gas targets. This would enable farmers to increase the value of the farm as a tradable entity. Relationships with large corporations requiring carbon credits could be developed as the scheme progresses. At a later stage, the cooperative could trade with large corporate partners both in Australia and overseas, with Zero Waste Australia serving as the certifying body. The cooperative will foster a symbiotic relationship between the urban and rural community, thus linking the economy back to the true producer of community wealth, the farmer.

## Box 51 Precycling Insurance

*James Greyson*

The most daunting global problems, such as climatic change, loss of nature, pollution and resource conflicts, are shaped by market signals that are beyond effective control by existing economic instruments. However, a new instrument, based on insurance, offers hope of reforming capitalism to align self-interest, wealth creation and global survival. Conventional insurance works with localized risks. The value of an insured house is protected by a payout following a disaster such as a fire. However, global problems may not always be reversible so a new form of insurance is needed to encourage the prevention of environmental impacts in the first place.

Global ecological problems are linked to linear patterns of using resources, from nature to products to accumulating wastes. So the key leverage point at which to apply premiums is on the risk of a product ending as waste in the land, air or water. The vast majority of the technosphere can be covered, since chemicals, fuels, equipment, houses, roads and most other human works take part in the economy of products. Even product components are products. Every producer should already know if their product will add to waste levels. 'Is our product recyclable or biodegradable?' 'Have we contributed towards sufficient industrial or ecological processing so that our product can become a new resource for people or nature?'

How could premiums best be spent to reduce the risk of products becoming waste and to prevent additional worsening of global problems? Support is needed for a wide array of activities that build economic, societal and ecological capacity to make resources, not wastes. This goal of 'circular economics' was devised by Kenneth Boulding in 1966. It is now national policy, for example, in China's 11th five year plan (for 2006 to 2010). Sustainable development and circular economics may be implemented in practice by 'precycling': action taken to prepare for current resources to become future resources for people or nature. Premiums charged to producers in proportion to waste-risk would fund precycling. This generalizes the 'recycling insurance' enacted by the European Waste Electronics (WEEE) Directive, which funds recycling to cut the risk of particular products becoming waste. A generalized 'precycling insurance' could support the full range of sustainable development activities:

- Action to cut dependence on substances that unavoidably accumulate as waste (fossil fuels, heavy metals, persistent synthetic compounds).
- Action to give products (any part of the technosphere) a future as a resource.
- Action to expand ecological habitats (that process non-solid emissions).
- Action to use resources efficiently enough to meet more people's basic needs.

Precycling insurance allows market mechanisms to inspire change. The incentive of avoiding premiums would support producer investment in systems which give their products a future as a resource – 'precycled' products. Those who choose to continue making 'prewasted' products would pay a premium and find their products less competitive in a market where alternatives rapidly emerge. Premiums would also influence the market by directly funding solutions which bridge the gap between what is being done and what is needed. Small per-item premiums could add up to large market shifts.

Unresolved global-scale problems are expensive. The prescriptiveness and complexity of governmental constraints on economic activity are expensive. Both these expenses may be tackled by retaining primary responsibility for externalities within the market, leaving government with the more manageable monitoring task. This achieves 'producer responsibility' whilst eliminating inefficient prescriptiveness. A stable climate, for example, does not require mandatory emissions limits. Savings to government would allow some taxes to be phased out (such as value added taxes which have a large point-of-sale burden), while precycling insurance (which does not require any transactions at the point-of-sale) is phased in. A level playing field for all significant producers could be achieved with simultaneous global introduction of obligatory precycling insurance, with insurers accredited by government and web-based information open to public scrutiny. Administrative effort, regulation and long-term prices would be minimized while economic stability and growth would be maximized.

## Box 52 Negative Resource Transfers

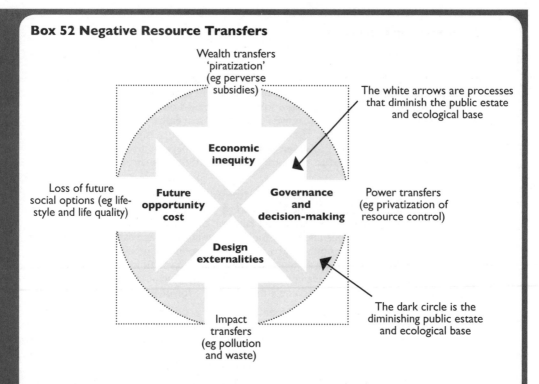

Wealth transfers 'piratization' (eg perverse subsidies)

The white arrows are processes that diminish the public estate and ecological base

**Economic inequity**

Loss of future social options (eg life-style and life quality)

**Future opportunity cost**

**Governance and decision-making**

Power transfers (eg privatization of resource control)

**Design externalities**

The dark circle is the diminishing public estate and ecological base

Impact transfers (eg pollution and waste)

The public estate should not be confused with public control or public property. The public sector does not necessarily make better resource allocation decisions than the private sector. The concept of the public estate, however, conveys the idea that citizens can theoretically take back control of public sector management and decisions. They can do little about corporate power, when it operates above public control. Stockholders in particular corporations will not realistically protect the wider public interest.

Types of negative resource transfers

| Decision sphere | Negative resource transfers | Negative characteristics | Negative mechanisms | Negative consequences |
|---|---|---|---|---|
| **Biophysical (design):**<br><br>**Loss of options** | From future to present generations; opportunity cost | Irreversible designs and developments that cut off future options | Planning; design; environmental management frameworks | Loss of ecological base and meaningful future options |
| **Institutional (state):**<br><br>**Power transfers** | From public to private interests | Legislated standards or processes transfer power | Privatization; deregulation; pareto optimum | Loss of public estate and future meaningful democratic rights |
| **Technical (industrial):**<br><br>**Impact transfers** | From natural environment to 'industrial' development | Substitution of natural capital with financial, manufactured, and built capital | Externalities; internalities | Loss of future human health and life quality and meaningful choice |
| **Economic (market):**<br><br>**Wealth transfers** | From poor to wealthy, 3rd world to 1st world | Indirect and often 'hidden' mechanisms like perverse subsidies | Subsidies to status quo | Loss of opportunities and meaningful choices |

## Box 53 Converting Negatives into Positives

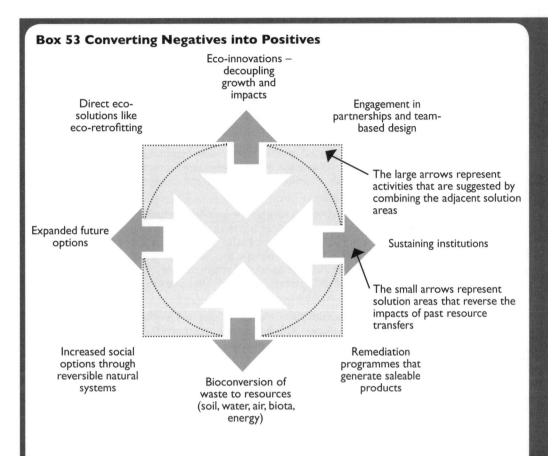

Eco-innovations – decoupling growth and impacts

Direct eco-solutions like eco-retrofitting

Engagement in partnerships and team-based design

The large arrows represent activities that are suggested by combining the adjacent solution areas

Expanded future options

Sustaining institutions

The small arrows represent solution areas that reverse the impacts of past resource transfers

Increased social options through reversible natural systems

Bioconversion of waste to resources (soil, water, air, biota, energy)

Remediation programmes that generate saleable products

Ways to create net positive social and natural capital

| Decision sphere | Reversal of 'negatives' | Potential 'positive' change drivers | 'Positive' decision rules | New 'positive' processes |
|---|---|---|---|---|
| **Biophysical (design):**<br><br>**Expansion of options** | From present to future generations; opportunities for Positive Development | Eco-solutions that increase the ecological base and public estate | Sustainability standard: net positive design | Trans-disciplinary charettes and participatory design teams |
| **Institutional (state):**<br><br>**Power transfers** | Institutions that can create a just and equitable society | Social engagement and open 'participatory democracy' | Green Optimum, constitutional design, and due process | Direct solutions like eco-retrofitting |
| **Technical (industrial):**<br><br>**Impact transfers** | Development that gives back more to nature than it takes | Eco-efficiency and waste mini-mization (waste as a productive resource) | Zero waste or no loop systems that use natural systems | Bioconversion of waste to resources (soil, water, air, biota, energy) |
| **Economic (market):**<br><br>**Wealth transfers** | Decoupling growth and impacts through Positive Development | Businesses or arrangements that address environmental problems equitably | Full cost pricing; partnering; and performance contracting | Offsets for fixing existing damage (not future damage) |

## Box 54 Reversing the Role of Fashion

*Fabia Pryor*

Green fashion challenges political, ideological, economic, cultural and social forces that are embedded in 'consumerism'. The sustainable fashion and textiles sector incorporates environmental and humanitarian concerns into this otherwise individualistic, consumption and appearance-focused sector.

Sustainability in these industries is an achievable target, with economic gains for businesses which invest in it. Numerous examples exist of innovative, entrepreneurial and sustainable fashion and textile businesses which are stimulating widespread change within both the production and the consumption sectors.

The revival of the Cambodian silk industry illustrates the breadth of change that can be achieved by utilizing sustainable textiles as a driver. This is the brainchild of a Japanese silk expert, former refugee worker and UNESCO consultant Kikuo Morimoto. Morimoto founded the Institute for Khmer Traditional Textiles when he saw the once highly valued industry fading away, following decades of civil war and the advent of synthetic fabrics and mass-production technology.[1] Working closely with the community, he set about reviving the Cambodian silk trade, encompassing the entire silk-making process.

Morimoto's vision led to the creation of two new silk villages in Cambodia and is an example of whole system thinking. These villages incorporate schools, farmland, market gardens and livestock breeding areas. The concept also encompasses an established 'self-sustaining forest preserve', the outcome of revegetation which aimed to replant the natural forests, devastated by years of war, from which the silk and dye constituents are sourced.

As Morimoto puts it, 'Rather than a faithful recreation of a silk village, we consider it to be a new model of a village that utilizes traditional wisdom.'[2]

In redeveloping this industry, Morimoto scoured Cambodia in search of the remaining women, or 'silk grandmothers', who had survived the Pol Pot era and still possessed the traditional knowledge of silk-making, handed down over 1200 years.[3] These women have now passed their knowledge down to younger women in the community, ensuring the survival of traditional knowledge and a key component of Khmer cultural heritage. Now custodians of this knowledge, the recently-skilled women are able to generate an income from silk-making, diverting them from paths which may otherwise have led to begging or prostitution.

As well as social benefits, environmental benefits have resulted from the silk industry's revival. Reforestation of native vegetation has increased biodiversity in the region, enhancing natural capital and the self-sufficiency of the local community. The silk project is resourceful, using wastes from the material and dye production as organic fertilizer on the community's farmland.

Morimoto points out that while Cambodia was never rich, it did have a self-sustaining rural economy. "War ruined this," he states, "but too rapid and thoughtless modernization can have the same result over time."[4]

Key to the revived industry's success has been the high acclaim the silk has enjoyed within the mainstream sector, generating increased awareness of the plight of the Khmer people and the Cambodian environment. The revival of the Cambodian silk industry, using traditional knowledge and increasing environmental and social capital, exemplifies the positive effects of incorporating traditional knowledge within a sustainable framework in the textiles and apparel sector. It is just one example of similar initiatives being taken throughout the world in both fashion and textile production.

# Glossary

New terms, and/or terms that in this book are used differently from standard usage, are in **bold**.

*Active solar systems* involve mechanical devices, such as solar cells (photovoltaics), energy storage units, and pumps or fans to operate heating and cooling systems. Active collectors are not part of the building itself. Combined passive and active solar systems can be cost-effective.

*Biodiversity* means the variety of ecologically appropriate and indigenous species and ecosystems. Biodiversity applies to genes, species and ecosystems. Urban areas can provide the habitats for endangered species and conditions required for ecosystem resilience.

*Bioregion* is a region whose often fluid and overlapping boundaries are defined by biophysical and cultural features (eg watersheds, deserts or rainforests). Bioregionalism would align social decision-making systems with regions and cultures, rather than political jurisdictions.

*Bioregional planning* is concerned with aligning economic and political systems around the region's ecology and resources. It involves the community in envisioning and shaping the future. It does not usually involve examining inequitable resource transfers, however.

**Brain waste** refers to the fact that many potential geniuses have suffered brain damage from malnutrition or social deprivation due to maldevelopment. While innovation theories and tools multiply, the creativity of a third of the world's population and their offspring is being lost.

*Built environment* refers to the whole human-made context – infrastructure, landscapes, products, buildings, factories, cities, etc. Its design is reciprocally related to social relations, cultures and personal development, but the focus here is on physical spaces and structures.

*Carbohydrate economy* refers to the conversion to systems of production where carbohydrates replace hydrocarbons; in other words where vegetables – not minerals – supply fuel, materials, food and fibres.

*Carrying capacity* has usually been defined as the population of humans or other species that a natural area can support without reducing its ability to support that species into the future. It is argued here that cities can increase a region's carrying capacity.

*Chain-of-custody*, in the environmental labelling context, is where a product is tracked throughout the supply chain, so that consumers can be assured that all product components, materials or processes used in production meet relevant sustainability standards.

*Charrettes* are increasingly popular means of obtaining wide citizen input and setting goals for a community. Local citizens (with planners, artists, architects, developers, etc) can work together to develop visions and plans for their region or neighbourhood.

*Cleaner production* is the minimization of resource usage and waste (heat, emissions, etc) for maximum material output in industrial processes through a variety of means, including technology, management and the plant itself.

*Compound savings* result where a change in product or building design reduces resource usage and/or waste 'upstream' in the production system as well as in operation (eg a building using passive solar design principles can have a smaller heating plant or none at all).

*Corporatism* is used here in a general way to describe where governments negotiate policies and their implementation with leading business and industry organizations. The term is sometimes used in a derogatory way from both left- and right-wing positions.

**Dead space** refers to space created by built environment design that alienates land from the public and/or excludes nature. Many new buildings, for example, create double skins that improve energy efficiency but increase the urban heat sink effect.

*Decarbonization* is the reduction of the use of fossil fuels in energy, materials, processes, production and products. Currently, despite cleaner production and more efficient design, the carbon in the atmosphere and oceans is increasing.

*Dematerialization* is the reduction in materials (and energy) intensity of industrial production and products. Despite public campaigns to reduce consumption and impressive efficiency gains in some areas, consumerism and material flows through the economy are increasing.

*Design* is a holistic, future-oriented process directed at creating something that has not existed before. It creates synergies, symbioses, syntheses and synchronicity. Eco-logical design is the opposite (and can complement) linear-reductionist thinking [Box 2].

*Design for adaptability* has been developed to ensure access and use of buildings and landscapes by the disabled and elderly (becoming even more important as the population ages). Construction details exist to enable retrofitting to accommodate these people.

*Design for disassembly* ensures that components of a product are easily separated for purposes of recycling to enable producers to 'take back' products more cost effectively after use. The tyre exemplifies a product that was once difficult to deconstruct due to the mix of materials.

**Design for eco-services** refers to the integration of natural systems with the existing built environment to increase the ecological base (life-support functions) – in place of the current target of reducing impacts of development *relative* to standard buildings.

*Design for environment* is design that minimizes part or all of the environmental impacts over a product life-cycle from resource extraction to manufacture, distribution, use or operation, and recycling. It often requires management support to facilitate.

*Designed waste* is the redundancy, disposability, planned obsolescence and wasteful end purposes to which resources are put through design – for example creating a need for lawnmowers, rather than planting native grasses or lawn covers to eliminate mowing.

*Direct action* implements *physical* design solutions as opposed to (indirect) incentive systems that can have unintended consequences. Government agencies tend to be risk-averse, and err in the direction of 'inaction', as they may not obtain recognition for saving resources.

*Down-cycling* is a term for recycling to lower-value uses, such as using sawdust for co-generation or wood chips for paper or as mulch for gardens, instead of higher-value products. It was introduced in the book *Cradle to Cradle*,[1] which advocated closed and 'no-loop' systems.

*Eco-cycling* means adding ecological value, whereas 'up-cycling' can include recycling to a higher economic use (eg high quality furniture from wood pallets). Eco-cycling logically requires the use of natural systems, since industrial systems inevitably generate waste.

*Eco-design reporting* would show how existing eco-technologies, eco-logical design concepts and new innovations were explored and integrated into a design to create positive impacts. When eco-innovations were not used, reasons would be required.

*Eco-efficiency* is the delivery of competitively priced goods and services that satisfy human needs and enhance quality of life, while progressively reducing ecological impacts and resource intensity throughout the life-cycle.[2]

*Eco-governance* refers to decision structures designed explicitly to suit the nature of ecological and sustainability issues. This implies intellectual, institutional and technical systems that protect the underlying ecological and democratic platforms that make sustainability possible.

*Eco-innovation* is an institutional or technological design that improves human and environmental health, wellbeing and equity while reducing resource consumption (ie whole systems efficiency), by utilizing natural systems that replace 'unnecessary' machines or products.

*Ecological base* is an umbrella term for natural capital, biodiversity, ecosystem goods and services, ecological health and resilience, bio-security, etc. It represents the life-support system and 'means of survival'. Those services not under private control represent the 'public estate'.

*Ecological footprint* is the *equivalent* area of land and water needed to produce the supplies from around the world to feed, clothe, house and entertain urban dwellers in a given city. A city's ecological footprint can be many times greater than the geographic footprint.

*Ecological space* is the effective ecological area provided in a development. It is a measure of positive impacts (eg air and water cleaning and natural heating, cooling and ventilating) – in contrast with the 'ecological footprint' (or negative impacts that can only be minimized).

*Ecological transformation analysis* would measure ecological deficiencies by comparing current urban conditions to pre-development (indigenous) conditions, and in order to find ways that a new or retrofitted development can correct on-site and off-site ecological problems.

*Ecological waste* is the loss of ecosystems and encompasses the time and cost of replacing them (of a whole forest ecosystem, for example, and not just the biomass). Ecological waste (a negative measure) is the converse of ecological space (a positive measure).

*Ecologically sustainable development* (ESD) refers to development that meets sustainability goals, but in practice just means 'greener' than average. Development could instead produce more energy than it uses, cleaner air and water than it takes in, and so on.

*Eco-retrofitting* means modifying (and 'greening') urban areas to improve environmental and human health while reducing resource depletion, degradation and pollution. The aim would be to achieve a 'sustainability standard' – net positive improvements over pre-existing conditions.

*Eco-services* is short for the ecosystem services (and ecology) provided by natural systems (air and water decontamination, pollination, flood control, climate stabilization, fertile soil, storm water retention, biodiversity, etc). 'Ecosystem services' tends to have an anthropocentric usage.

*Embodied energy* is the combined energy inputs used in producing a material, product or building. It includes energy used to provide indirect support services or equipment. The energy used in manufacture is often less than the energy used up to that point.

*Embodied waste* refers to the total 'accumulated' waste that occurs at each stage of the whole production/consumption process over the product's life span (eg the percentage of the tree not captured in products). It includes embodied energy, water, materials and other waste.

*End-of-pipe* controls or technologies are those that filter or disperse pollution, instead of changing the materials, processes, fuels or other elements of design that cause the pollution in the first place, or closing loops so that waste is at least used as a resource.

**Expropriation** is where resources are extracted from the public domain at below replacement cost (as in public forestry auctions that cost more to conduct than is received for the timber). It is the transfer of resources by stealth or the exercise of power relationships.

*Extended producer responsibility* is where manufacturers are required to take back products at the end of their useful life for reuse or recycling, or pay others to do so. This is more efficient than encouraging consumers to ensure products are recycled.

*Externality* is an economic concept that refers to the costs and benefits of economic activities that are imposed on people outside the relationship or transaction. The term implies pollution is incidental. However, externalities are intrinsic to the design of the economic system.

*Free-riders* are those who benefit from others' investments, developments or products without paying. Good environmental design benefits 'free-riders' in adjacent areas (eg people whose air, water, views and other amenities are improved by the development at no cost to themselves).

*Front-loading design* refers to putting more time and energy into original planning and design stages, rather than mitigating the impacts of conventional designs. Currently, environmental policies put resources into cleaning up problems afterwards – often at public expense.

*Full cost pricing* would be where the replacement costs of resources were charged for their use. Full cost pricing is supposed to cover externalities, but does not include ecological waste. Although the taxpayer pays for everything in the end, governments prefer paying for incentives.

*Green energy* sometimes means energy purchased from providers that source their electricity from renewable energy. The problem is that citizens are made to 'sign up' and pay more for clean energy than for 'dirty' energy, which runs counter to full cost pricing.

**Green Optimum** is the converse of the Pareto Optimum. The latter holds that a decision is good if it makes someone better off without making others worse off. Thus we neglect opportunities to identify and invest in actions that make everyone better off.

**Green Scaffolding** is a structure retrofitted onto a building which supports many functional and ecological elements in 'ecospheres' (eg vertical landscapes, solar stacks, shower towers, vertical composting systems, decks, Trombe walls, etc).

*Green space frames* are indoor/outdoor structures created in spaces between buildings, on roofs, in parks, etc that are designed to support plants and habitats for indigenous species, while adding value to human activities (eg urban food production or recreation).

*Green space walls* are walls that become ecosystems in themselves and provide eco-services (like Green Scaffolding) as well as social and working spaces. That is, they provide biodiversity support through terrariums, aquaponic systems and microhabitats for indigenous species, etc.

*Heat island effect* is where tightly sealed surfaces in urban areas, such as asphalt and concrete, soak up the heat and re-radiate it back into the atmosphere as thermal infrared radiation. The heat forms a dome of higher temperatures over cities, which are often hotter than nearby areas.

*Hydrogen economy* refers to the use of hydrogen as fuel for large-scale systems and transport. The emissions created by fuel-cell cars would only be water. However, the hydrogen must be produced with non-fossil, non-greenhouse gas energy to be sustainable.

*Industrial ecology* is where industries develop synergistic relations with other industries by, for example, using the by-products from another industry. Industries can share utility infrastructure for energy production, water and wastewater treatment.

*Intensification* is used in different ways. Intensification refers here to urban infill that increases the diversity of land uses as opposed to 'densification' which increases residential population density in urban areas but not necessarily a variety of land uses.

*Internalities* refers to the inordinate benefits that a private business or organization receives at the expense of the general public (economists consider 'free-riders' a problem because they get free benefits from private investment). 'Externalities' only reflect private *costs* imposed on the public.

*Living Machines* are self-contained networks of (solar powered) ecological systems designed to accomplish specific chemical functions that support the micro-organisms that eat toxic wastes. They can also support gardens and fishponds at the end of the remediation chain.

*Metabolic analysis* applies the concept of 'metabolism' as a model for analysing material flows through urban and industrial systems. In biology, metabolism refers to the chemical reactions by which an organism or ecosystem interacts with its environment.

*Negative space* is a measure of the natural capital and land alienated from the public to private land use and control. Instead of just looking at the rate of decrease in natural capital stocks, it provides a measure of inaccessible resources and natural capital (means of survival).

*Offsets* are actions to compensate for environmental impacts elsewhere, such as activities that absorb carbon after it is emitted. Some projects are called 'carbon neutral' simply because they plant trees or purchase 'green energy' as offsets to reduce net impacts.

*Passive solar energy* is where the building itself collects and stores heat, and circulates warm and cool air without the support of mechanical equipment, using the natural movement of heat (using conduction, convection, radiation and evaporation).

*Performance contracting* (PC) is where private businesses provide energy efficiency services at little or no cost to clients, and recover their costs and make profits from the reduced energy, water or sewage bills. Thus retrofitting can be 'free' to the building owner.

*Piratization* is where de facto or direct control over public resources is given to special (public or private) interests as in bio-piracy (eg there are cases where impoverished people must now pay for local water that is 'managed' by international corporations).

*Planting walls* are walls, room dividers or screens that provide space for plants in their structure for air-cleaning functions, visual amenity and so on. Their design can accommodate windows or openings and they can be structural or temporary, indoor or outdoor.

**Positive Development** would meet established ecologically sustainable development criteria – but also reverse the impacts of *current* systems of development, increase the ecological base and public estate, and improve human life quality; that is, enhance the ecology and equity.

*Precautionary principle* refers to the idea that we should not use a lack of scientific evidence as an excuse for inaction in addressing an environmental problem. It does not say we should take affirmative action to improve conditions whether there is a threat or not.

*Primary industries*, such as mining, fishing, agriculture and forestry, were addressed by environmental laws. Because construction was seen as 'secondary', pollution controls have not addressed the *demand* for harmful materials caused by built environment design.

**Public estate** refers to accessible means of survival. As civilians lose access to the means of survival, they also effectively lose basic democratic rights and autonomy. Ownership per se is not at issue (eg nature conservancies protect land for future generations).

*Rebound effect* is where a more energy-efficient product reduces the costs of production or operation, but leads to an increased use of that product (such as efficient cars that are driven more miles) or the money saved being spent on other products or services with greater impacts.

*Resource autonomous* homes or buildings are largely self-sufficient. They produce their own energy, clean the air, grey water and sewage on site, and use healthy materials (eg rammed earth instead of fired brick). They aim to be impact neutral (not net positive).

**Resource transfer analysis** would map inequitable transfers of resources over time in a region (eg from poor to rich, rural to urban or public to private), in order to determine inequities that a new development might help to reverse or compensate for.

**'Reverse' TDR (transferable development rights)** are where people or businesses acquire the right to develop part of their property (eg yard or roof) for, say, urban food production purposes or other eco-productive activity through purchase or a percentage of profits.

**'Reverse' Trombe wall** operates like a conventional Trombe wall (see below), but glass is added to the exterior of masonry walls of old buildings to avoid sacrificing natural light and views. (Usually windows are sacrificed when Trombe walls or greenhouse windows are added.)

*Rhizomatic approach* refers to the opposite of a non-hierarchical, reductionist, linear approach. It is based on an analogy to rhizomes, the underground portion of the plant from which roots and shoots grow, through the interaction of bacteria with the plant.

*Solar resources* refer to organic materials and renewable energy power from the sun. The term 'solar' is a misnomer as fossil fuels ultimately derive from the sun, and wave power is mostly driven by the moon. In any case, the term 'solar resource' excludes nuclear and fossil fuels.

*Sunk costs* are those costs already incurred and which cannot be retrieved. According to mainstream economic theory, it is not rational to continue to invest in unprofitable or inefficient systems. The idea is that decisions should be based on where one is now.

**Sustainability** means that all future generations will inherit substantive environmental and democratic rights – control over the means of survival, an increased ecological base, and genuine social choice (not 'substituted' by manufactured capital).

*Sustainability ombudsman* is an individual or group representing the interests of the natural environment (and other species and future generations) in the planning and decision-making process, as opposed to the short-term interests of immediate stakeholders).

**Sustainability standard** requires an improvement in human *and* ecological health over what would have been the case if the development was not built. This means the ecological base would be more extensive and resilient than before development occurred on the site.

**Systemic corruption** is where individuals or agents use public funds or resources to serve their own special interests. The public pays for everything in the end, in effect, so corporations, public agencies and politicians should be obliged to put the public interest over special interests.

**Systems mapping** is a generic term for tracing the flows and transformations of energy and materials in, out and through a system, such as an urban area, farm, region or factory. It has tended to focus on negatives, rather than potential value-adding, however.

**Systems re-design** means changing the basic functions and forms of development systems. The term systems design often only refers to efficiency, without considering the whole system (ie fossil fuel versus free solar energy).

*Transferable development rights* are used in city planning regulations to allow developers to exceed the allowable floor area or height limits on another property as compensation when their development rights are restricted by a new regulation (eg to create a historic district).

*Triple bottom line* or 'TBL' framework is one that includes social, economic and environmental considerations. However, in practice, it generally means that positive impacts in one category can in effect be traded off for negative impacts in another. 'TBL + 1' includes governance.

*Trombe wall* is a structure creating an air space between a glass panel and a wall with high thermal mass. The air, heated by the sun, rises to air vents at the top of the wall, circulates through the room by convection and re-enters the space through vents at the bottom.

**True zero waste** is where all waste generated in the supply chain is prevented or reused. This is to differentiate 'zero waste', which usually means 'zero waste to landfill'. Generally, less than 10 per cent of materials consumed in production are captured in a product.

**Unjust enrichment** is a legal remedy or measure of damages (ie it is not a misdemeanour in itself). Unjust enrichment can be a measure of what we can call 'internalities': excessive private benefits extracted from the public estate.

*Urban consolidation* or 'compact cities' generally means increasing residential 'density' (less floor area per person or more people per hectare). It can eliminate space for conservatories, composting, rainwater tanks, plants to clean and cool the air, 'living technologies', and so on.

*Vertical wetlands* are series of containers of plants, soil and rocks suspended from ceilings or hung on walls, through which water collected from the roof or greywater from the building passes. These 'hanging gardens' filter the water, clean the air and provide visual amenity.

# Notes

## Introduction

1    Weizsacker, E. van, A. Lovins and H. Lovins (1977) *Factor 4: Doubling Wealth – Halving Resource Use*, Earthscan, London; Hawken, P., A. Lovins and H. Lovins (1999) *Natural Capitalism: Creating the Next Industrial Revolution*, Earthscan, London; Hargroves, C. and M. H. Smith (2005) *The Natural Advantage of Nations*, Earthscan, London.

2    For a different mapping of sustainable development, see Hopwood, B., M. Mellor and G. O'Brien (2005) 'Sustainable development: Mapping different approaches', *Sustainable Development*, vol 13, pp38–52.

3    For a good overview, see Beder, S. (2006) *Environmental Principles and Policies: An Interdisciplinary Introduction*, Earthscan, London.

4    IUCN/UNEP/WWF (1991) *Caring for the Earth: A Strategy for Sustainable Living*, IUCN (The World Conservation Union)/UNEP (United Nations Environment Programme)/WWF (World Wide Fund for Nature), Earthscan, London.

5    World Commission on Environment and Development (1987) *Our Common Future*, report of the Brundtland Commission, Oxford University Press, Oxford.

6    UNEP (2005) 'Millennium ecosystem assessment: Strengthening capacity to manage ecosystems sustainably for human wellbeing', download from http://ma.caudillweb.com/en/about.overview.aspx.

7    World Commission on Environment and Development (1987) *Our Common Future*, Oxford University Press, Oxford, p45.

8    See, for example, Markandya, A. and S. Pedroso-Galinato (2007) 'How substitutable is natural capital?', *Environmental and Resource Economics*, vol 37, no 1, pp297–312.

9    Richard, S. (1993) *Is Brundtland's Model of Sustainability a Case of Having Our Cake and Eating it Too?*, Proceedings of the Ecopolitics VII Conference, Griffith University, Queensland, Australia, pp133–137.

10  This is the definition I have used for decades as it seems self-evident; however, see Norton, B. G. (2005) *Sustainability: A Philosophy of Adaptive Ecosystem Management*, University of Chicago Press, Chicago, IL, for an in-depth discussion on this concept.

11  See Wall, D. (1994) *Green History: A Reader in Environmental Literature, Philosophy and Politics*, Routledge, London.

12  Corporatism is used here in a very general way to describe where governments negotiate policies and their implementation with peak business and industry organizations that represent vested interest groups; see http://en.wikipedia.org/wiki/Corporatism.

13  Ninety-five per cent of our calories come from only 30 varieties of plants; the FAO estimates that 75 per cent of agricultural genetic diversity has been lost in the past century.

14  It is strange that, in a world where political censorship is a fact of life, pornography and violence pervade all forms of entertainment and expression – on the grounds that restrictions would lead to political censorship.

15  See www.who.int/ceh/en/; for statistics on these environmental issues, see Worldwatch Institute, www.worldwatch.org/, and World Resources Institute (2007) 'EarthTrends: Environmental information, available at http://earthtrends.wri.org.

16  Fennerty, H. (2006) 'Standards, technology and sustainability', *Environmentalist*, vol 26, no 2, pp93–98.

17  For lots of examples and data, see Myers, N. and J. Kent (2001) *Perverse Subsidies: How Tax Dollars Can Undercut the Environment and the Economy*, Island Press, Washington, DC.

18  For further information, see www.who.int/topics/water/en/.

19  de Moor, A. P. G. 'Perverse incentives: Subsidies and sustainable development', Institute for Research on Public Expenditure, The Netherlands, www.worldpolicy.org/globalrights/ecoindex.html (commissioned by the Earth Council).

20  Kimbrell, A. (ed) (2002) *Fatal Harvest: The Tragedy of Industrial Agriculture*, Island Press, Washington, DC.

21  See Emergency Management Australia disaster database, www.ema.gov.au/.

22  Birkeland, J. (1995) 'Cultures of institutional corruption', in J. Bessant, K. Carrington and S. Cook (eds) *Cultures of Crime and Violence: The Australian Experience*, LaTrobe University Press, Melbourne, Australia, pp199–212.

23  There is a tendency to think of vibrant downtown shopping districts rather than the many square miles of desolate, dirty and dreary urban areas surrounding them; see Kaika, M. (2005) *City of Flows: Modernity, Nature and the City*, Routledge, New York, for a discussion of how cities are perceived differently over time.

24  For an example of the perspective that suggests cities cannot be ecologically sustainable and therefore should be given dispensation, see Bithas, K. and M. Christofakis (2006) 'Environmentally sustainable cities: Critical review and operational conditions', *Sustainable Development*, vol 14, pp177–189.

25  As argued by Philip Sutton, see www.green-innovations.asn.au/greenleap.htm.

26  Daly, H. E. and J. B. Cobb, Jr (1989) *For the Common Good: Redirecting the Economy Toward Community, the Environment and a Sustainable Future*, Beacon Press, Boston, MA; Hamilton, C. (1994) *The Mystic Economist*, Willow Park Press, Canberra, Australia.

27  Peter Costello, speech to the Press Club in Canberra, 2 April 2007.

28  The metabolism of cities is increasing per capita with respect to wastewater, energy materials and water; see Kennedy, C., J. Cuddihy and J. Engel-Yan (2007) 'The changing metabolism of cities', *Journal of Industrial Ecology*, vol 11, no 2, pp43–59.

29  Girardet, H. (1996) *The Gaia Atlas of Cities: New directions for Sustainable Urban Living* (second

edition), Gaia Books, London.

30 Birkeland, J. (2002) 'Legislative environmental controls', in *Design for Sustainability: A Sourcebook of Eco-logical Solutions*, Earthscan, London, pp210–214.

## Chapter 1

1 IFRC (International Federation of Red Cross and Red Crescent Societies)(2004) *World Disasters Report 2004*, chapter 2 summary, available at www.ifrc.org/publicat/wdr2004/chapter2.asp.

2 van de Ryn, S. and S. Cowan (1996) *Ecological Design*, Island Press, Washington, DC.

3 Todd, J. (2002) 'Environmental management tools', in J. Birkeland (ed) *Design for Sustainability: A Sourcebook of Integrated Eco-logical Solutions*, Earthscan, London.

4 Williams, K. and C. Dair (2006) 'What is stopping sustainable building in England? Barriers experienced by stakeholders in delivering sustainable developments', *Sustainable Development*, vol 15, pp135–147.

5 The sorcerer's apprentice is a traditional story about how a little learning is a dangerous thing. The apprentice tried to stop a broken water pipe using a mop. Misapplying his limited knowledge of magic, the mops began to multiply. He ran around in 'vicious circles' trying to control the mops.

6 Moore, R. (2002) 'Adaptable housing', in J. Birkeland (ed) *Design for Sustainability: A Sourcebook of Integrated Eco-logical Solutions*, Earthscan, London, p124.

7 Birkeland, J. (2002) 'Construction ecology', in *Design for Sustainability: A Sourcebook of Integrated Eco-logical Solutions*, Earthscan, London.

8 See Poirrier, A. M. (2002) 'Beyond the chemical barrier', in J. Birkeland (ed) *Design for Sustainability: A Sourcebook of Integrated Eco-logical Solutions*, Earthscan, London, pp148–152.

9 Indoor air pollution is one of the top four health hazards and contributes to many other health conditions. Levels of indoor air pollution can be 10 times greater than those of outdoor air, because indoor air not only concentrates outdoor air pollution, but also contributes toxins from modern materials that off-gas volatile organic compounds, formaldehyde and other toxic substances.

10 Terry A. 2002, 'Indoor air quality in buildings', in J. Birkeland *Design for Sustainability: A Sourcebook of Eco-logical Solutions*, Earthscan, London, pp143–147.

11 See Creighton, S. H. (2002) 'Air quality problems in buildings', in J. Birkeland (ed) *Design for Sustainability: A Sourcebook of Integrated Eco-logical Solutions*, Earthscan, London, p153.

12 Poirrier, A. M. (2002) 'Beyond the chemical barrier', in J. Birkeland (ed) *Design for Sustainability: A Sourcebook of Integrated Eco-logical Solutions*, Earthscan, London, pp148–152.

13 Mould can grow inside walls and can be toxic.

14 Danenburg, J. (2002) 'Hemp architecture', in J. Birkeland (ed) *Design for Sustainability: A Sourcebook of Integrated Eco-logical Solutions*, Earthscan, London, pp205–208.

15 Marmot, M. (2004) *Status Syndrome: How Your Social Standing Directly Affects Your Health and Life Expectancy*, Bloomsbury and Henry Holt, New York.

16 Ibid.

17 The IPCC suggest that buildings could provide the largest single contribution to reduction targets of $CO_2$ emissions – of up to 60 per cent.

18 Buildings are now being lit up with LEDs to create, in effect, giant electronic billboards; see http://english.chosun.com/w21data/html/news/200701/200701250009.html.

19 For a short eco-efficiency checklist see WBCSD (World Business Council for Sustainable

Development) with DeSimone, L. D. and F. Popoff (2002) 'Eco-efficiency checklist', in J. Birkeland (ed) *Design for Sustainability: A Sourcebook of Integrated Eco-logical Solutions*, Earthscan, London, pp62–63.

20  The built environment uses 3 billion tons per annum or over 40 per cent of materials worldwide; Roodman, D. M. and N. Lenssen (1995) 'A building revolution: How ecology and health concerns are transforming construction', Worldwatch Paper 124, Worldwatch Institute, Washington, DC.

21  The OECD agrees that the operation of buildings accounts for 25–40 per cent of final energy consumption in the OECD area. This does not even count the energy consumed for manufacturing building materials, which is roughly equal to operational energy; Takahiko Hasegawa (2002) 'Sustainable buildings', *OECD Observer*, OECD Territorial Development Service, www.oecdobserver.org/news/printpage.php/aid/765/Sustainable_buildings.html.

22  World military spending was estimated at around $1 trillion by Reuters, of which almost half was spent by the US; see www.usatoday.com/news/world/2005-06-07-world-military_x.htm; www.globalsecurity.org/military/world/spending.htm.

23  Esty, D. C. and A. S. Wilston (2006) *Green to Gold: How Smart Companies Use Environmental Strategy to Innovate, Create Value and Build Competitive Advantage*, Yale University Press, New Haven, CT, and London.

24  See Environmental Australia (2002) 'Implementing design for environment', in J. Birkeland (ed) *Design for Sustainability: A Sourcebook of Integrated Eco-logical Solutions*, Earthscan, London, pp186–187.

25  Key sources for eco-efficiency include van Weizsacker, E., A. Lovins and H. Lovins (1977) *Factor 4: Doubling Wealth – Halving Resource Use*, Earthscan, London; Hawken, P., A. Lovins and H. Lovins (1999) *Natural Capitalism: Creating the Next Industrial Revolution*, Earthscan, London; Hargroves, C. and M. H. Smith (2005) *The Natural Advantage of Nations*, Earthscan, London.

26  Hawken, P., A. Lovins and H. Lovins (1999) *Natural Capitalism: Creating the Next Industrial Revolution*, Earthscan, London.

27  Jayne, M. (2006) *Cities and Consumption*, Routledge, New York.

28  See Hamilton, C. (2003) *Growth Fetish*, Allen & Unwin, Crow's Nest, Australia; Hamilton, C. and R. Denniss (2005) *Affluenza: When Too Much Is Never Enough*, Allen & Unwin, Crow's Nest, Australia.

29  The 1998 Human Development Report by the United Nations Development Programme noted that "Americans spend more on cosmetics ($8 billion annually) and Europeans on ice cream ($11 billion) than the estimated cost of providing basic education ($6 billion) or water and sanitation ($9 billion) to the more than 2 billion people worldwide who are forced to go without schools and toilets."

30  Birkeland, J. (2002) 'Construction ecology', in *Design for Sustainability: A Sourcebook of Integrated Eco-logical Solutions*, Earthscan, London, pp64–68.

31  Editors of *The Ecologist* (1994) 'Whose common future: Reclaiming the commons', *Environment and Urbanization*, vol 6, no 1, pp106–130.

32  Ridgeway, J. (2004) *It's All for Sale: The Control of Global Resources*, Duke University Press, Durham and London, UK.

33  Birkeland, J. (2002) 'Construction ecology', in *Design for Sustainability: A Sourcebook of Integrated Eco-logical Solutions*, Earthscan, London, pp64–68.

34  Myers, N. (1996) *The Ultimate Security: The Environmental Basis of Political Stability*, Island Press, Washington, DC.

35  Todd, N. J. and J. Todd (2002) 'Living technologies', in Birkeland, J. (ed) *Design for Sustainability: A Sourcebook of Integrated Eco-logical Solutions*, Earthscan, London; Todd, N. J. and J. Todd (1994)

*From Eco-Cities to Living Machines*, N. Atlantic Books, Berkeley, CA.

36 BBC News, Saturday, 20 May 2006, http://news.bbc.co.uk/2/hi/asia-pacific/5000092.stm.

37 For further discussion, see Hargroves, C. and M. H. Smith (2005) *The Natural Advantage of Nations*, Earthscan, London, pp66–67.

38 UNEP (2005) 'Millennium ecosystem assessment: Strengthening capacity to manage ecosystems sustainably for human wellbeing', download from http://ma.caudillweb.com/en/about.overview. aspx.

39 Ibid.

40 Ibid.

41 See books by Ken Yeang, including Yeang, K. (1999) *The Green Skyscraper: The Basis for Designing Sustainable Intensive Buildings*, Prestel Verlag, Munich, Germany; Yeang, K. (2006) *Ecodesign: A Manual of Ecological Design*, Wiley, London.

42 Schnieders, E. and A. Hermelink (2006) 'CEPHEUS results: Measurements and occupants' satisfaction provide evidence for passive houses being an option for sustainable building', *Energy Policy*, vol 34, no 2, pp151–171.

43 Vale, R. and B. Vale (2002) 'Autonomous servicing', in J. Birkeland (ed) *Design for Sustainability: A Sourcebook of Ecological Solutions*, Earthscan, London, pp182–185; Mobbs, M. (1998) *Sustainable House*, Choice Books, Sydney, Australia.

44 See *Environmental Building News* (www.buildinggreen.com/ecommerce/ebn.cfm), a periodical running since the early 1990s, for an overview of the evolution of green building.

45 Crawford, R. and G. Treloar (2005) 'An assessment of the energy and water embodied in commercial building construction', paper presented at Fourth Australian LCA Conference, Sydney, Australia.

46 Edge has been developed as a permaculture concept; see Mollison, B. (1996) *Permaculture: A Designers' Manual* (fifth edition), Tagari Publications, Tyalgum, NSW, Australia.

47 Osmond, P. (2002), 'The sustainable landscape', in Birkeland, J. (ed) *Design for Sustainability: A Sourcebook of Integrated Eco-logical Solutions*, Earthscan, London, p200.

48 For early precedents see McHarg, I. (1969) *Design with Nature*, Natural History Press, Garden City, NY.

49 See www.melbourne.vic.gov.au/info.cfm?top=171&pg=1933.

50 Benyus, J. (2002) *Biomimicry: Innovation Inspired by Nature*, William Morrow, New York; Beattie, A. and P. Ehrlich (2004) *Wildsolutions* (second edition), Yale University Press, New Haven, CT; Daily, G. and K. Ellison (2002) *The New Economy of Nature*, Island Press, Washington, DC.

51 Benyus J. (2002) *Biomimicry: Innovation Inspired by Nature*, William Morrow, New York, NY.

52 See Waterhouse, G. (2002) 'The bionic method in industrial design', in J. Birkeland (ed) *Design for Sustainability: A Sourcebook of Integrated Eco-logical Solutions*, Earthscan, London, pp84–88

53 Failing that, existing skyscrapers may have the height to help eject bacteria into the air where it can seed clouds (W. Jehne, personal communication).

54 For example, the CRC for weeds was reportedly not continued because although it saved the taxpayers substantial sums it did not lead to much commercialization.

55 One cannot help but wonder if such technocratic interventions suggest the testosterone imbalance.

56 Anderson, J. (2005) 'Blueprint for a greener city: Growth need not cost the Earth', *Water Science and Technology*, vol 52, no 9, pp61–67.

57 See Birkeland, J. (1995) 'Cultures of institutional corruption', in J. Bessant, K. Carrington and S. Cook (eds) *Cultures of Crime and Violence: The Australian Experience*, LaTrobe University Press, Melbourne, Australia, pp199–212.

58  Ridgeway, J. (2004) *It's All for Sale: The Control of Global Resources*, Duke University Press, Durham and London, UK.

59  Birkeland, J. (1996) 'Ethics-based planning', *Australian Planner*, vol 33, no 1, pp47–49.

60  Shiva, B. (1997) *Biopiracy: The Plunder of Nature and Knowledge*, South End Press, Cambridge, MA

61  Barlow, M. and T. Clarke (2003) *Blue Gold: The Battle against Corporate Theft of the World's Water*, Earthscan, London.

62  The sustainability of built environment and civil infrastructure systems will best be achieved through inter- and intra-industry collaboration with the support of public policymakers; Hartshorn, J., M. Maher, J. Crooks, R. Stahl and Z. Bond (2005) 'Creative destruction: Building toward sustainability', *Canadian Journal of Civil Engineering*, vol 32, no 1, pp170–180.

63  See Wheeler, S. (2000) 'Planning for metropolitan sustainability', *Journal of Planning Education and Research*, vol 20, no 2, pp133–145.

## Chapter 2

1  Part of this chapter was published in Birkeland, J. (2005) 'The case for eco-retrofitting', *Solar Progress*, vol 26, no 2, pp7–9.

2  The additional first costs associated with green buildings were about 2 per cent, while the financial benefits are 10 times as large, but this is reportedly changing rapidly in the US, due to capacity building; see Kats, G. (2003) *The Costs and Financial Benefits of Green Buildings: A Report to California's Sustainable Building Task Force*, CSBTF, San Francisco, CA.

3  Lucuik, M. (2005) *A Business Case for Green Buildings in Canada*; RICS (2005) *Green Value – Green Buildings, Growing Assets*, UK; GBCA (2006) *The Dollars and Sense of Green Buildings: Building the Business Case for Green Commercial Buildings in Australia*, GBCA, Sydney, Australia.

4  Edwards, B. (1998) *Green Buildings Pay*, Spon Press, London.

5  Esty, D. C. and A. S. Wilston (2006) *Green to Gold: How Smart Companies Use Environmental Strategy to Innovate, Create Value and Build Competitive Advantage*, Yale University Press, New Haven, CT, and London.

6  The Australian National Sustainability Centre has explored ways in which the public partnership model can be expanded into a new form of public–private+community model in order to develop a sustainability centre.

7  Birkeland, J. (2002) 'Legislative environmental controls', in *Design for Sustainability: A Sourcebook of Integrated Eco-logical Solutions*, Earthscan, London, pp210–214.

8  Romm, J. (1999) *Cool Companies: How the Best Businesses Boost Profits and Productivity by Cutting Greenhouse-Gas Emissions*, Island Press, Washington, DC, p55.

9  Books on passive solar design have been available for a long time; see, for example, Anderson, B. (1976) *The Solar Home Book: Heating, Cooling and Designing with the Sun*, Brick House Publishing, Harrisville, NH; AIA Research Corporation (1976) *Solar Dwelling Design Concepts*, US Department of Housing and Urban Development, Washington, DC; Shurcliff, W. A. (c. 1979) *Solar Heated Buildings of North America: 120 Outstanding Examples*, Brick House Publishing, Harrisville, NH.

10  One of the exceptions is the NABERS tool for assessing existing homes and buildings; see www.nabers.com.au/ and www.deh.gov.au/industry/construction/nabers. Others are under development.

11  There have been few studies of the sustainability costs and benefits of retrofitting versus rebuilding,

but see Dong, B., C. Kennedy and K. Pressnail (2005) 'Comparing life-cycle implications of building retrofit and replacement options', *Canadian Journal of Civil Engineering*, vol 32, no 6, pp1051–1063.

12  McGray, D. (2007) 'Pop-up cities: China builds a bright green metropolis', *Wired Magazine*, issue 15.05, www.wired.com/wired/archive/15.05/feat_popup.html.

13  Woollard, R. F. and A. S. Ostry (2000) *Fatal Consumption: Rethinking Sustainable Development*, UBC Press, Vancouver, BC, Canada.

14  Eckersley, R. (2002) 'Redefining progress', in J. Birkeland (ed) *Design for Sustainability: A Sourcebook of Integrated Eco-logical Solutions*, Earthscan, London, pp38–41; Hamilton, C. (1997) 'The genuine progress indicator: A new index of changes in wellbeing', Australia Institute Discussion Paper 14, The Australia Institute, Canberra.

15  I have been advocating ecological retrofitting for many years in many circles but with little response, even though it is win–win–win.

16  Birkeland, J. (2002) 'Economic instruments', in *Design for Sustainability: A Sourcebook of Integrated Eco-logical Solutions*, Earthscan, London, pp215–219.

17  Storey, J. (2002) 'Designing for durability', in J. Birkeland (ed) *Design for Sustainability: A Sourcebook of Integrated Eco-logical Solutions*, Earthscan, London, pp46–49.

18  Browning, W. and J. Romm (2002) 'Greening the workplace', in J. Birkeland (ed) *Design for Sustainability: A Sourcebook of Integrated Ecological Solutions*, Earthscan, London, pp154–57; Romm, J. (1999) *Cool Companies: How the Best Businesses Boost Profits and Productivity by Cutting Greenhouse-Gas Emissions*, Island Press, Washington, DC., p55.

19  Terry, A. (2002) 'Indoor air quality in buildings', in J. Birkeland (ed) *Design for Sustainability: A Sourcebook of Integrated Eco-logical Solutions*, Earthscan, London, pp143–146.

20  EBN (2004) 'Productivity and green buildings', *Environmental Building News*, vol 13, no 10.

21  Bell, J. et al (2008) *Productivity and Health in Commercial Office Buildings: Guidelines and Benchmarks for Facilities Management*, Queensland University of Technology, Brisbane, Australia.

22  Romm, J. (1999) *Cool Companies: How the Best Businesses Boost Profits and Productivity by Cutting Greenhouse-Gas Emissions*, Island Press, Washington, DC., p79.

23  EBN (1999) 'Productivity and green buildings', *Environmental Building News*, vol 8, no 9.

24  See www.cbpd.arc.cmu,edu/bidstrial.

25  EBN (1999) 'Productivity and green buildings', *Environmental Building News*, vol 8, no 9.

26  Kats, G. 2003 *The Costs and Financial Benefits of Green Buildings: A Report to California's Sustainable Building Task Force*, CSBTF, San Francisco, CA.

27  Roughly, a square metre of plants provides enough vegetables for a person each year.

28  Urban farms vary from futuristic to practical. See www.dpi.nsw.gov.au/aboutus/news/agriculture-today/november-2007/urban-farm.

29  See Building Materials and Reuse Association, www.buildingreuse.org/resources/articles/?article_id=42.

30  For example, the commercial office market in Australia is 19.5 million square metres or about 1 square metre per head of population; see GBCA (2006) *The Dollars and Sense of Green Buildings: Building the Business Case for Green Commercial Buildings in Australia*, GBCA, Sydney, Australia.

31  Vale, R. and B. Vale (2002) 'Autonomous servicing', in J. Birkeland (ed) *Design for Sustainability: A Sourcebook of Integrated Eco-logical Solutions*, Earthscan, London, pp182–185; Vale, R. and B. Vale (2000) *The New Autonomous House: Design and Planning for Sustainability*, Thames and Hudson, NY.

32  See Todd, N. and J. Todd (2002) 'Living technologies', in Birkeland, J. (ed) *Design for Sustainability: A Sourcebook of Integrated Eco-logical Solutions*, Earthscan, London. 'Living Machines' are cylinders containing ecological systems that support micro-organisms that perform specific chemical functions, like eating toxins.

33  Current tools do not attempt to institutionalize sustainable models; see Crabtree, L. (2005) 'Sustainable housing development in urban Australia: Exploring obstacles to and opportunities for ecocity efforts', *Australian Geographer*, vol 36, no 3, pp333–350.

34  Heede, R. et al (1995) *Homemade Money*, Rocky Mountain Institute with Brick House Publishing, Harrisville, NH.

35  Birkeland, J. and J. Schooneveldt (2002) 'ACT Sustainability Audit: A material flows analysis of the residential sector of Canberra', report for PALM, Sustainability Science Team, Canberra.

36  When a house in the ACT is sold, the energy rating must be disclosed; www.houseenergyrating. com/process_act.html.

37  Proposed in Birkeland, J. and J. Schooneveldt (2002) 'ACT Sustainability Audit: A material flows analysis of the residential sector of Canberra', report for PALM, Sustainability Science Team, Canberra. See also Birkeland, J. (2004) 'The Solar Core', *Solar Progress*, vol 25, no 3, pp 26–28; another version with diagram can be found in Hargroves, K. and M. H. Smith (2005) *The Natural Edge of Nations*, Earthscan, London, p367.

38  Heede, R. et al (1995) *Homemade Money*, Rocky Mountain Institute with Brick House Publishing, Harrisville, NH.

39  EPA (1998) *Market Values for Home Energy Efficiency* (study by Nevin and Watson), EPA, Washington, DC.

40  A study by Energy Partners, Canberra, ACT, see www.enerstrat.com.au/energypart.html.

41  When I have told even solar power advocates that I have solar cells on my roof, they usually criticize my decisions because the payback period is long.

42  The Australasian Energy Performance Contracting Association is formed from ESCO's, State Government Departments and private companies interested in the performance contracting process, see www.aepca.asn.au.

43  Birkeland, J. (1995) 'Priorities for environmental professionals', paper presented at 'Linking and Prioritizing Environmental Criteria', CIB TG-8 Workshop, Ontario, 25–26 November, CIB, Rotterdam, The Netherlands, pp27–34.

44  Yik, F. and W. Lee (2004) 'Partnership in building energy performance contracting', *Building Research and Information*, vol 32, no 3, pp235–243.

45  Birkeland, J. (2003) 'Beyond zero waste', *Societies for a Sustainable Future*, Third UKM-UC International Conference, UKM-UC, University of Canberra, Australia.

46  Stephenson, A. (2000) *Alliance Contracting, Partnering, Co-operative Contracting: Risks, Avoidance or Risk Creation*, Clayton Utz, Canberra, Australia.

47  Eilenberg, I. (2002) *Dispute Resolution in Construction Management*, UNSW Press, Sydney, Australia.

48  Personal communication (1993) from D. McLagan, University of Canberra, about research conducted comparing two similar college buildings in Canberra, one constructed by partnering, the other not.

49  Eilenberg, I. (2002) *Dispute Resolution in Construction Management*, UNSW Press, Sydney, Australia.

50  Hood, D. (2004) 'Implementing energy efficiency and ESD from a development perspective', in *Environmental Design Guide*, GEN 60, RAIA, Melbourne, Australia, p1.

51  Esty, D. C. and A. S. Wilston (2006) *Green to Gold: How Smart Companies Use Environmental*

*Strategy to Innovate, Create Value, and Build Competitive Advantage*, Yale University Press, New Haven, CT, and London.

52 Birkeland, J. (1995) 'Rethinking pollution', *Turning Growth into ESD – Economically*, 1995 EIA National Conference, Brisbane, 26–27 October, EIA, Brisbane, Queensland, Australia.

53 My foray into Australian Federal Government made this palpable for me.

54 The new Melbourne City Hall 2 project has gained the Council worldwide recognition (even though errors were made in green elements); see www.melbourne.vic.gov.au/rsrc/PDFs/CH2/CH2FactSheet.pdf.

55 This is not new. See Birkeland, J. (2002) 'Pollution prevention by design', in *Design for Sustainability: A Sourcebook of Integrated Eco-logical Solutions*, Earthscan, London, pp69–72.

56 For a discussion on supply chains generally, see Tsoulfas, G. T. and C. P. Pappis (2006) 'Environmental principles applicable to supply chains design and operation', *Journal of Cleaner Production*, vol 14, no 18, pp1593–1602.

57 House of Representatives Standing Committee on Environment and Heritage (2005) *Sustainable Cities*, Australian Government, Canberra, Australia.

58 Berkeley Cohousing, www.mccamant-durrett.com/project-details.cfm?select=16&cat=cohousing; see also McCamant, K. and C. Durrett (1994), *Cohousing: A Contemporary Approach to Housing Ourselves* (revised edition), Ten Speed Press, Berkeley, CA.

59 Trainer, T. (2002) 'Limits to growth and design of settlements', in J. Birkeland (ed) *Design for Sustainability: A Sourcebook of Integrated Eco-logical Solutions*, Earthscan, London, pp33–36; Trainer, F. E. (1995) *The Conserver Society: Alternatives for Sustainability*, Zed Books, London.

60 Canberra instituted free household audits to encourage retrofits.

61 A leading effort to establish an eco-village is the Currumbin development in Queensland, Australia; see www.theecovillage.com.au/.

62 Hood, D. (2004) 'Implementing energy efficiency and ESD from a development perspective, in *Environmental Design Guide*, GEN 60, RAIA, Melbourne, p1.

63 See Nabers (National Australia Built Environment Rating System), www.nabers.com.au/; see AGBR (Australian Greenhouse Building Rating), www.abgr.com.au/.

## Chapter 3

1 Portions of this chapter were presented at the 2004 Ecopolitics Conference, Macquarie University, North Ryde, NSW, Australia.

2 Birkeland, J. and J. Schooneveldt (2002) *ACT Sustainability Audit: A Material Flows Analysis of the Residential Sector of Canberra*, Report for PALM, Sustainability Science Team, Canberra.

3 Office of Sustainability (2004) *Measuring our Progress: Canberra's Journey to Sustainability, Volume 2: Our Core Dimensions*, ACT Government, Canberra.

4 Masnavi, M. R. (2007) 'Measuring urban sustainability: Developing a conceptual framework for bridging the gap between theoretical levels and operational levels', *International Journal of Environmental Research*, vol. 1, no 2, pp188–197.

5 Wellman, K. (2002) 'Complexity and the urban environment', in J. Birkeland (ed) *Design for Sustainability: A Sourcebook of Integrated Eco-logical Solutions*, Earthscan, London, pp74–77.

6 Rounsefell, V. (2002) 'Unified human community ecology', in J. Birkeland (ed) *Design for Sustainability: A Sourcebook of Integrated Eco-logical Solutions*, Earthscan, London, pp78–83.

7 Kaufman, P. (2002) 'Place, community values and planning', in J. Birkeland (ed) *Design for Sustainability: A Sourcebook of Integrated Eco-logical Solutions*, Earthscan, London, pp105–108.

8   Williams, K., E. Burton and M. Jenks, (eds) (2000) *Achieving Sustainable Urban Form*, E&FN Spon, London and Melbourne, p2; Jenks, M., E. Burton and K. Williams (eds) (1996) *The Compact City: A Sustainable Urban Form*, E&FN Spon, London and Melbourne.

9   For a summary of the problems of cars, see Newman, P. (2002) 'ESD and urban transport infrastructure', in J. Birkeland (ed) *Design for Sustainability: A Sourcebook of Integrated Eco-logical Solutions*, Earthscan, London, p82; see also, Newman, P. and J. Kenworthy (1999) *Sustainability and Cities: Overcoming Automobile Dependence*, Island Press. Washington, DC.

10  The third International Ecocity and Ecovillage Conference was held in Yoff, Senegal; see Register, R. and B. Peeks (1979) *Village Wisdom/Future Cities*, Ecocity Builders, Berkeley, CA.

11  Halweil, B. and D. Neirenberg (2007) 'Farming the cities', in *State of the World 2007: Our Urban Future*, World Watch Institute, Washington, DC. p52.

12  Dovey, K. (1999) *Framing Places: Mediating Power in Built Form*, Routledge, London.

13  Editors of *The Ecologist* (1994) 'Whose common future: Reclaiming the commons', *Environment and Urbanization*, vol 6, no 1, pp106–130.

14  See Wener, R., and H. Carmalt (2006) 'Environmental psychology and sustainability in high-rise structures', *Technology in Society*, vol. 28, nos 1–2, pp157–167.

15  In Forde, ACT, allotments are as small as 290 square metres with rear garages.

16  Ambrose, P. (1994) *Urban Process and Power*, Routledge, London.

17  Imrie, R. (2004) 'The role of the building regulations in achieving housing quality', *Environment and Planning B*, vol 31, no 3, pp419–437.

18  Jenks, M. E. Burton and K. Williams (eds) (1996) *The Compact City: A Sustainable Urban Form?*, E&FN Spon, London and Melbourne.

19  Diesendorf, M. (2007) *Greenhouse Solutions with Sustainable Energy*, University of New South Wales Press, Sydney, Australia, p291.

20  In Australia, with about 5 TV channels, the morning shows have almost exactly the same guests, segments, and discussion topics and content. At times, all five channels have sport on.

21  Birkeland, J. (2002) 'Legislative Environmental Controls', in *Design for Sustainability: A Sourcebook of Integrated Eco-logical Solutions*, Earthscan, London, pp210–214.

22  Lukaszyk, J. P. (2002) 'Sample dwellings', Appendix 3, in Birkeland, J. and J. Schooneveldt *ACT Sustainability Audit: A Material Flows Analysis of the Residential Sector of Canberra*, Report for PALM, Sustainability Science Team, Canberra.

23  Birkeland, J. and J. Schooneveldt (2002) *ACT Sustainability Audit: A Material Flows Analysis of the Residential Sector of Canberra*, Report for PALM, Sustainability Science Team, Canberra.

24  In many places, the approach is to eliminate downtown parking without providing adequate bus services (eg in Canberra).

25  Cotgrove, R. (2002) 'Sustainable personal urban transport', in J. Birkeland (ed) *Design for Sustainability: A Sourcebook of Integrated Eco-logical Solutions*, Earthscan, London, pp158–162.

26  See Troy, P. (ed) (1999) *Australian Cities: Issues, Strategies and Policies for Urban Australia in the 1990s (Reshaping Australian Institutions)*, Cambridge University Press, London.

27  See Troy, P. (1996) *Perils of Urban Consolidation*, Federation Press, Annandale, NSW, Australia.

28  Thackara, J. (2006) *In the Bubble: Designing in a Complex World*, MIT Press, Boston, MA.

29  Droege, P. (2006) *Renewable City: A Comprehensive Guide to an Urban Revolution*, John Wiley, Chichester, UK.

30  Scheer, H. (2004) *The Solar Economy*, Earthscan, London.

31  See Newman, P. and J. Kenworthy (1999) *Sustainability and Cities: Overcoming Automobile Dependence*, Island Press, Washington, DC; see also www.worldcarfree.net/resources/freesources/ad_myths.pdf.

32  In the ACT, for example, $18 million of the $70 million spent on the bus system was recouped through fares.

33  See www.earthtrack.net for further information on perverse subsidies.

34  For example, an average household produces 15 tons of greenhouse gas each year. The residential sector in Canberra accounts for over 46 per cent of Canberra's greenhouse gas emissions, while transport fuels account for 26 per cent: Office of Sustainability (2006) *Avoid, Abate, Adapt: A Discussion Paper for an ACT Climate Change Strategy*, ACT Office of Sustainability, Canberra, Australia, March, p16.

35  See Troy, P. (1996) *Perils of Urban Consolidation*, Federation Press, Annandale, NSW, Australia.

36  See Odum, H. T. (1981) *Energy Basis for Man and Nature*, McGraw Hill, New York, NY; Odum, H. T. (1971), *Environment, Power and Society*, John Wiley, Hoboken, NJ.

37  Halweil, B. and D. Neirenberg (2007) 'Farming the cities', in *State of the World 2007: Our Urban Future*, World Watch Institute, Washington, DC.

38  Romm, J. (2005) *The Hype about Hydrogen: Fact and Fiction in the Race to Save the Planet*, Island Press, Washington, DC.

39  Birkeland, J. (2002) 'Construction ecology', in *Design for Sustainability: A Sourcebook of Integrated Eco-logical Solutions*, Earthscan, London, pp64–68.

40  Half of the energy goes into building as a general rule.

41  Brylawski, M. and Rocky Mountain Institute (2002) 'The "hypercar" concept', in J. Birkeland (ed), *Design for Sustainability: A Sourcebook of Integrated Eco-logical Solutions*, Earthscan, London, p163

42  Hoyle, C. and P. Downton (2002) 'From sub-urbanism to eco-cities', in J. Birkeland (ed) *Design for Sustainability: A Sourcebook of Integrated Eco-logical Solutions*, Earthscan, London, pp164–167.

43  The public cost of cars in the US, for example, was calculated at $464 billion annually (medical costs, road maintenance, etc).

44  See Trust for Public Land, www.tpl.org/.

45  See Holmgren, D. (2002) *Permaculture: Principles and Pathways Beyond Sustainability*, Holmgren Design Services, Hepburn, VIC, Australia; Mollison, B. (1996) *Permaculture: A Designers' Manual* (fifth edition), Tagari Publications, Tyalgum, NSW, Australia. For an excerpt, see Mollison, B. (2002) 'Permaculture: Functional analysis of the chicken', in J. Birkeland (ed) *Design for Sustainability: A Sourcebook of Integrated Eco-logical Solutions*, Earthscan, London, p172.

46  Lovegrove, K., A. Luzzi, I. Soldiani and H. Kreetz (2001) *Developing Ammonia-Based Thermochemical Energy-Storage for Dish Power Plants*, Centre for Sustainable Energy Systems, Australian National University, Canberra, ACT, Australia.

47  The SunBall is a solar collector for homes that refracts the sunlight through a wide lens onto solar cells. The circular hemispherical design also tracks the sun. See www.abc.net.au/tv/newinventors/txt/s1487858.htm.

48  Franklin, E. and A. Blakers (no date) *Sliver® Cells for Concentrator Systems*, Centre for Sustainable Energy Systems, The Australian National University, Canberra, ACT, Australia, solar.anu.edu.au/level_1/pubs/papers/sliver_concentrators.pdf.

49  Scheer, H. (2004) *The Solar Economy*, Earthscan, London.

50  Fibre-optic lighting can send light into a building: www.fiber-optics.info/fiber-history.htm.

51  The Twin Towers were arguably not designed well for such contingencies as extreme fire. See for example www.civil.usyd.edu.au/wtc.shtml.

52  See New Inventors at www.abc.net.au/tv/newinventors/txt/s1699340.htm.

53  Birkeland, J. (2002) 'Urban forms and the dominant paradigm', in *Design for Sustainability: A Sourcebook of Integrated Eco-logical Solutions*, Earthscan, London, pp114–117.

54　Birkeland, J. (1995) 'A critique of ecological architecture', in *Protecting the Future – ESD in Action*, University of Wollongong, NSW, Australia, 7 December, pp397–402.

55　Davidson, S. (2002) 'Marketing-led design', in J. Birkeland (ed) *Design for Sustainability: A Sourcebook of Integrated Eco-logical Solutions*, Earthscan, London, pp125–128.

56　Marmot, M. (2004) *Status Syndrome: How Your Social Standing Directly Affects Your Health and Life Expectancy*, Bloomsbury and Henry Holt, New York.

57　Meltzer, G. (2002) 'ESD and sense of community', in J. Birkeland (ed) *Design for Sustainability: A Sourcebook of Integrated Eco-logical Solutions*, Earthscan, London, pp134–137.

58　Jenks, M., E. Burton and K. Williams (eds) (1996) *The Compact City: A Sustainable Urban Form?*, E&FN Spon, London and Melbourne.

59　See books by Ken Yeang, including Yeang, K. (1999) *The Green Skyscraper: The Basis for Designing Sustainable Intensive Buildings*, Prestel Verlag, Munich, Germany.

60　In the San Francisco Department of City Planning, for example, we 'encouraged' green roofs on new buildings.

61　Hirst, A. (2002) 'Urban forms and the dominant paradigm', in J. Birkeland (ed) *Design for Sustainability: A Sourcebook of Integrated Eco-logical Solutions*, Earthscan, London, pp95–98.

62　Some scientists have argued for greater interactions among researchers, managers and decision-makers, which also requires cultural change among ecologists. See Palmer et al (2005) 'Ecological science and sustainability for the 21st century', *Frontiers in Ecology and the Environment*, vol 3, no 1, pp4–11.

## Chapter 4

1　See Lapinski, A. M. Horman and D. Riley (2006) 'Lean processes for sustainable project delivery', *Journal of Construction Engineering and Management*, vol 132, no 10, pp1083–1091.

2　Hill, G. (2002) 'Designing waste', in J. Birkeland (ed) *Design for Sustainability: A Sourcebook of Integrated Eco-logical Solutions*, Earthscan, London, pp43–45.

3　See Klang, A., P. Vikman and H. Brateebo (2003) 'Sustainable management of demolition waste – an integrated model for the evaluation of environmental, economic and social aspects', *Resources Conservation and Recycling*, vol 38, no 4, pp317–334.

4　Roodman, D. M. and N. Lenssen (1995) 'A building revolution: How ecology and health concerns are transforming construction', Worldwatch Paper 124, Worldwatch Institute, Washington, DC.

5　CSIRO (1998) 'Smart buildings to deliver huge savings', media release, ref 98/48, 5 March, available at www.csiro.au/files/mediarelease/mr1998/SmartBuildingsToDeliverHuge.htm.

6　Santana, M. E. (2002) 'Timber waste minimization by design', in J. Birkeland (ed) *Design for Sustainability: A Sourcebook of Eco-logical Solutions*, Earthscan, London, pp188–191.

7　McDonough, W. and M. Braungart (2002) *Cradle to Cradle: Remaking the Way we Make Things*, North Point Press, New York.

8　Roodman and Lenssen (1995), op. cit.

9　*Building Industry News* (2006) 'Construction waste to be halved by 2012', www.azobuild.com/news.asp?newsID.

10　Yost, P. (1999) 'Construction and demolition waste: Innovative assessment and management', in C. J. Kibert (ed) *Reshaping the Built Environment: Ecology, Ethics and Economics*, Island Press, Washington, DC.

11　Wann, D. (1996) *Deep Design: Pathways to a Liveable Future*, Island Press, Washington, DC.; Hill, G. (2002) 'Designing waste' in J. Birkeland (ed) *Design for Sustainability: A Sourcebook of*

*Integrated Ecological Solutions*, Earthscan, London, pp43–45.

12   Tibbs, H. (2002) 'Industrial ecology' in J. Birkeland (ed) *Design for Sustainability: A Sourcebook of Integrated Ecological Solutions*, Earthscan, London, pp52–56.

13   HM Treasury (2006) *Stern Review: The Economics of Climate Change*, UK Government, downloadable from www.hm-treasury.gov.uk/contact/contact_index.cfm.

14   Hawken, P. (1993) *The Ecology of Commerce*, HarperCollins, New York.

15   IWMB (2005) *Recycling: Good for the Environment, Good for the Economy*, Publication 410-04-002, Integrated Waste Management Board, San Francisco, CA, downloadable from www.ciwmb.ca.gov/Publications/Economics/41004002.pdf.

16   IPPR and Green Alliance (2006) *A Zero Waste UK*, Institute for Public Policy Research and Green Alliance, London, UK.

17   Bell, N. (2003) 'Waste minimization and resource recovery', in *BEDP Environmental Design Guide*, GEN 21, RAIA, Melbourne, Australia; Forsythe, P. and P. K. Marsden (2004) 'GEN 30: A model for formulating a project waste management plan based on costing and quantifying construction waste', in *BEDP Environmental Design Guide*, RAIA, Melbourne, Australia; Graham, P. (2002) 'TEC 1: Waste minimization – Resource reduction', in *BEDP Environmental Design Guide*, RAIA, Melbourne, Australia; Nolan, P. (2004) 'GEN 29: Waste minimization and building design professionals', in *BEDP Environmental Design Guide*, RAIA, Melbourne, Australia; Bell, N. (2002) 'Waste reduction checklist', in J. Birkeland (ed) *Design for Sustainability: A Sourcebook of Integrated Ecological Solutions*, Earthscan, London, pp50–51.

18   Schmidheiny, S. with the BCSD (1992) *Changing Course: A Global Business Perspective on Development and the Environment*, MIT Press, Cambridge, MA; WBCSD (World Business Council for Sustainable Development), L. DeSimone and F. Popoff (1997) *Eco-Efficiency: The Business Link to Sustainable Development*, MIT Press, Cambridge, MA.

19   Crowther, P. (2005) 'DES 31: Design for disassembly – Themes and principles', in BEDP *Environmental Design Guide*, RAIA, Melbourne, Australia; Environment Australia (2001) *Product Innovation: The Green Advantage*, Australian Department of the Environment and Heritage, Canberra.

20   Thorpe, B., I. Kruszewska and A. McPherson (2004) 'Extended producer responsibility', Clean Production Action, www.cleanproduction.org.

21   Greyson, J. (2007) 'An economic instrument for zero waste, economic growth and sustainability', *Journal of Cleaner Production*, vol 15, pp1382–1390; see also www.blindspot.org.uk.

22   WCED (World Commission on Environment and Development) (1987) *Our Common Future*, Oxford University Press, Oxford.

23   Esty, D. C. and A. S. Wilston (2006) *Green to Gold: How Smart Companies Use Environmental Strategy to Innovate, Create Value, and Build Competitive Advantage*, Yale University Press, New Haven, CT, and London, p47.

24   Ridgeway, J. (2004) *It's All for Sale: The Control of Global Resources*, Duke University Press, Durham and London.

25   The CSIRO is Australia's federal research organization, the Commonwealth Scientific and Industrial Research Organization, www.csiro.au/.

26   For a discussion on views of nature and cities, see Kaika, M. (2005) *City of Flows: Modernity, Nature and the City*, Routledge, New York.

27   Hill, G. (2002) 'Designing waste', in J. Birkeland (ed) *Design for Sustainability: A Sourcebook of Integrated Ecological Solutions*, Earthscan, London, pp43–45.

28   Boyden, S., S. Millar, K. Newcombe and B. O'Neill (1981) *The Ecology of a City and its People: The Case of Hong Kong*, Australian National University Press, Canberra.

29  See Ayres, R. U. and U. E. Simonis (eds) (1994) *Industrial Metabolism: Restructuring for Sustainable Development*, UN University Press, Tokyo, NY; Graedel, T. E. and B. R. Allenby (1995) *Industrial Ecology*, Prentice Hall, Englewood Cliffs, NJ.

30  Graedel, T. E. and B. R. Allenby (1995) *Industrial Ecology*, Prentice Hall, Englewood Cliffs, NJ; Ayres, R. U. and U. E. Simonis (eds) (1994) *Industrial Metabolism: Restructuring for Sustainable Development*, UN University Press, Tokyo, New York.

31  A range of issues concerning industrial ecology are explored in Korhonen, J. (2005) 'Industrial ecology for sustainable development: Six controversies in theory building', *Environmental Values*, vol 14, no 1, pp83–112.

32  See www.c4cs.curtin.edu.au; www.csrp.com.au.

33  Bossilkov, A., D. van Beers and R. van Berkel (2005) *Industrial Symbiosis as an Integrative Business Practice in the Kwinana Industrial Area: Lessons Learnt and Ways Forward*, 11th International Sustainable development Research Conference, Helsinki, Finland.

34  For example, see Singh, A., H. H. Lou, C. L. Yaws, J. R. Hopper and R. W. Pike (2007) 'Environmental impact assessment of different design schemes of an industrial ecosystem', *Resources, Conservation and Recycling*, vol 51, no 2, pp294–313.

35  Droege, P. (2006) *Renewable City: A Comprehensive Guide to an Urban Revolution*, John Wiley, Chichester, UK.

36  Personal communication, Keith Lovegrove, physicist, Australian National University.

37  Ridgeway, J. (2004) *It's All for Sale: The Control of Global Resources*, Duke University Press, Durham and London.

38  Esty, D. C. and A. S. Wilston (2006) *Green to Gold: How Smart Companies Use Environmental Strategy to Innovate, Create Value, and Build Competitive Advantage*, Yale University Press, New Haven, CT, and London, p47.

39  The 60L building is the headquarters and project of the Australian Conservation Foundation, www.acfonline.org.au/articles/news.asp?news_id=524&c=251553.

40  The author is working on a demonstration of net Positive Development with the Australian National Sustainability Centre.

41  Kerans, G. (2002) 'Housing wastewater solutions', in J. Birkeland (ed) *Design for Sustainability: A Sourcebook of Integrated Eco-logical Solutions*, Earthscan, London, pp7–12.

42  McQuaid, M. (2006), *Shigeru Ban*, Phaidon Press, London.

43  Dunnett, N. and N. Kingsbury (2004) *Planting Green Roofs and Living Walls*, Timber Press, Portland, OR.

44  For a short summary, see Todd, N. J. and J. Todd (2002) 'Principles for designing living machines' in J. Birkeland (ed) *Design for Sustainability: A Sourcebook of Integrated Eco-logical Solutions*, Earthscan, London, p181; see also Todd, N. J. and J. Todd (1994) *From Eco-Cities to Living Machines*, N. Atlantic Books, Berkeley, CA.

45  See www.oceanarks.org.

46  Ibid.

47  See Kibert, C. J., J. Sendzimir and G. Bradley (2002) *Construction Ecology: Nature as the Basis for Green Buildings*, Spon Press, London.

48  Graham, P. (2004) 'GEN 31: Education for the next industrial revolution – Teaching resource efficiency and resource effectiveness as aspects of environmental literacy', *BDP Environmental Design Guide*, RAIA, Melbourne, Australia.

49  Hargroves, C. and M. H. Smith (2005) *The Natural Advantage of Nations*, Earthscan, London; Hawken, P. A. Lovins and H. Lovins (1999) *Natural Capitalism: Creating the Next Industrial Revolution*, Earthscan, London; van Weizsacker, E., A. Lovins and H. Lovins (1977) *Factor 4:*

*Doubling Wealth – Halving Resource Use*, Earthscan, London.

50  Davidson, S. (2002) 'Marketing-led design', in J. Birkeland (ed) *Design for Sustainability: A Sourcebook of Integrated Eco-logical Solutions*, Earthscan, London, pp125–128.

51  Harrison, D., A. M. Chalkley and E. Billet (2002) 'The rebound effect', in J. Birkeland (ed) *Design for Sustainability: A Sourcebook of Integrated Eco-logical Solutions*, Earthscan, London, p129.

52  See Birkeland, J. (2002a) 'Education for eco-innovation', in *Design for Sustainability: A Sourcebook of Integrated Eco-logical Solutions*, Earthscan, London, pp7–12.

53  Davidson, S. (2002) 'Marketing-led design', in *Design for Sustainability: A Sourcebook of Integrated Ecological Solutions*, Earthscan, London, pp125–128.

54  Norton, B. G. (2005 ) *Sustainability: A Philosophy of Adaptive Ecosystem Management*, University of Chicago Press, Chicago, IL.

55  Beattie, A. and P. Ehrlich (2004) *Wildsolutions* (second edition), Yale University Press, New Haven, CT; Benyus, J. (2002) *Biomimicry: Innovation Inspired by Nature*, William Morrow, New York; Daily, G. and K. Ellison (2002) *The New Economy of Nature*, Island Press, Washington, DC.

56  Ferguson, I. (2007) 'Integrating wood production within sustainable forest management: An Australian viewpoint', *Journal of Sustainable Forestry*, vol 24, no 1, pp19–40.

57  Eckersley, R. (2002) 'Redefining progress', in J. Birkeland (ed) *Design for Sustainability: A Sourcebook of Integrated Eco-logical Solutions*, Earthscan, London, pp38–41; Hamilton, C. (1997) 'The genuine progress indicator: A new index of changes in wellbeing', Australia Institute Discussion Paper 14, The Australia Institute, Canberra.

58  Jungk, R. (1976) *The Nuclear State*, translated by Eric Mobacher, J. Calder, London.

## Chapter 5

1  There are many dozens of assessment and rating tools.  For example: NABERS (Australia), Green Star (Australia), BASIX Building Sustainability Index (NSW, Australia), ABGR Australian Building Greenhouse Rating (Australia), NatHERS/Accurate (Australia), EcoSpecifier (Australia), GBTool (international), BREEAM (UK), LEED (US), ATHENA (Canada), BEES (US).

2  Esty, D. C. and A. S. Wilston (2006) *Green to Gold: How Smart Companies Use Environmental Strategy to Innovate, Create Value, and Build Competitive Advantage*, Yale University Press, New Haven, CT, and London.

3  First presented in a talk to Brisbane City Council, 14 October 2004.  A similar message was delivered at the Planning Institute Australia Conference, Yeppoon, Queensland, on 14 July 2005.

4  For an overview of some rating tools, see www.knoxadv.com.au/docs/sustainability_tools_pathway.pdf.

5  See, for example, Kohler, N. and T. Lutzkendorf (2002) 'Integrated life-cycle analysis', *Building Research and Information*, vol 30, no 5, pp338–348.  Measuring sustainability values does not measure potential ecological improvements.

6  An attempt to rationalize these instruments is found in Warnock, A. C. (2007) 'An overview of integrating instruments to achieve sustainable construction and buildings', *Management of Environmental Quality*, vol 18, no. 4, pp427–441.  See also Hassan, O. A. B. (2006) 'An integrated management approach to designing sustainable buildings', *Journal of Environmental Assessment Policy and Management*, vol 8, no 2, pp223–251.

7  How to begin moving from 'green' to 'sustainable' is discussed in Luetzkendorf, T. and D. Lorenz (2006) 'Using an integrated performance approach in building assessment tools', *Building Research*

*and Information*, vol 34, no 4, pp334–356.

8   Personal communication (2006) with Peter Hickson, an earth builder with decades of experience who has had a leadership role in earth building organizations.

9   Even a NSW state government tool that is mandatory (BASIX) is 'black boxed' so users cannot be sure what assumptions lie behind it.

10  O'Brien, M. (2000) *Making Better Environmental Decisions: An Alternative to Risk Assessment*, MIT Press, Cambridge, MA.

11  Post-occupancy evaluations can assess either the mechanical equipment or the occupants' subjective experience of the indoor environment. The latter is context-dependent and varies with time; see Nicol, F. and S. Roaf (2005) 'Post-occupancy evaluation and field studies of thermal comfort', *Building Research and Information*, vol 33, no 4, pp338–346.

12  The ability of building assessment tools to deal with sustainability issues is discussed in Cole, R. (2005) 'Building environmental assessment methods: Redefining intentions and roles', *Building Research and Information*, vol 33, no 5, pp455–467.

13  Currently, in Australia, efforts are being made to find ways to award green star points for living walls.

14  According to the lead designer of the CH2 building in Melbourne, even a costly two week charrette paid dividends because the parties understood the project aims.

15  Studies show that occupants evaluate different qualities of a building (eg thermal comfort and lighting) on different scales, so it may be advisable to rely on a combined index; see Humphreys, M. (2005) 'Quantifying occupant comfort: Are combined indices of the indoor environment practicable?', *Building Research and Information*, vol 33, no 4, pp317–325.

16  RAIA seminar on AccuRate in Canberra.

17  For a discussion on integrating LCA concepts into one methodology, see Erlandsson, M. and M. Borg (2003) 'Generic LCA-methodology applicable for buildings, constructions and operation services', *Building and Environment*, vol 38, no 7, pp919–938.

18  See Diesendorf, M. (2007) *Greenhouse Solutions with Sustainable Energy*, University of New South Wales Press, Sydney, Australia, p290.

19  See www.alp.org.au/download/now/national_clean_coal_initiative_factsheet_campaign_launch. pdf.

20  Japan's Shigeru Ban and Germany's Otto Friei have worked in production of large space wooden roofs; see Japan Pavilion, EXPO 2000, Hanover, Germany, www.designboom.com/history/ban_ expo.html.

21  Roaf, S., M. Fuentes and S. Thomas (2003) *Ecohouse 2: A Design Guide*, Architectural Press, Burlington, MA.

22  Birkeland, J. (1996) 'Improving the design review process', in *CIB Commission Conference*, Royal Melbourne Institute of Technology, Melbourne, Australia, 16 February, pp150–155.

23  For example, Greenstar barely mentions embodied energy. A participant in the development of Greenstar informed me that they had considered embodied energy but decided it was too hard.

24  For whole system costs of fossil fuels, see Scheer, H. (2004) *The Solar Economy*, Earthscan, London.

25  As advocated by the US-based Institute for Local Self-reliance, www.ilsr.org/.

## Chapter 6

1   Henderson, K. (2002) 'Green theory in the construction fields', in J. Birkeland (ed) *Design for Sustainability: A Sourcebook of Integrated Eco-logical Solutions*, Earthscan, London, pp89–92.

2   See BedZed project, a zero energy development in London, which applies the standard passive solar design template to row houses: www.bioregional.com/programme_projects/ecohous_prog/bedzed/bedzed_hpg.htm. See also the Aurora project, which applies basic green design principles to conventional suburban homes: www.rmit.edu.au/re-imagining/.

3   Corbett, J. and M. Corbett (1999) 'Toward better neighbourhood design', College of Human Ecology, Michigan State University, www.lgc.org/freepub/land_use/articles/energy_betterdsgn.html.

4   There are many prefabricated 'green' home plans that can be purchased off the web; see, for example, www.builditsolar.com/Projects/SolarHomes/plansps.htm; www.builderonline.com/industry-news.asp?sectionID=26&articleID=572447.

5   For food for thought, see Hendriks, L. and K. van der Linden (2003) 'Building envelopes are part of a whole: Reconsidering traditional approaches', *Building and Environment*, vol 38, no 2, pp309–318.

6   For a discussion on tacit design assumptions, see Yevenes, K. (2002) 'Gender and produce semantics', in J. Birkeland (ed) *Design for Sustainability: A Sourcebook of Integrated Eco-logical Solutions*, Earthscan, London, pp130–132.

7   Under the auspices of a grant from AusIndustry via Sustainability Science, coordinated by Rolf von Behrens.

8   See eco-logical design principles developed by W. McDonough (Hannover Principles) and S. van der Ryn and S. Cowan, summarized in 'Eco-logical design principles' in J. Birkeland (ed) (2002) *Design for Sustainability: A Sourcebook of Integrated Eco-logical Solutions*, Earthscan, London, p25. See also, van der Ryn, S. and S. Cowan (2002) 'Conventional and eco-logical design compared', in J. Birkeland (ed) *Design for Sustainability: A Sourcebook of Integrated Eco-logical Solutions*, Earthscan, London, pp18–19.

9   See Diesendorf, M. (2007) *Greenhouse Solutions with Sustainable Energy*, University of New South Wales Press, Sydney, Australia.

10  For further information, see www.adobe.com/education/pdf/aac/inside_bauhaus.pdf.

11  A Corbu house was tested and did very badly on an energy rating test.

12  James, l. and J. Birkeland (2002) 'Models of ecological housing', in J. Birkeland (ed) *Design for Sustainability: A Sourcebook of Integrated Eco-logical Solutions*, Earthscan, London, pp119–123.

13  The ING Bank building in Amsterdam, see www.rmi.org/sitepages/pid102.php.

14  Ross, H. (2002) 'Sustainability and aboriginal housing', in J. Birkeland (ed) *Design for Sustainability: A Sourcebook of Integrated Eco-logical Solutions*, Earthscan, London, pp138–141; see also Ross, H. (2002) 'Aboriginal dwellings, in J. Birkeland (ed) *Design for Sustainability: A Sourcebook of Integrated Eco-logical Solutions*, Earthscan, London, p142.

15  Birkeland, J. and J. Schooneveldt (2002) *ACT sustainability Audit: A Material Flows Analysis of the Residential Sector of Canberra*, Report for PALM, Canberra.

16  Strawbale is fire and insect resistant, of course: see St. Jacques, L. (2002) 'Strawbale construction', in J. Birkeland (ed) *Design for Sustainability: A Sourcebook of Integrated Eco-Logical Solutions*, Earthscan UK, pp197–199.

17  See www.bioregional.com/programme_projects/ecohous_prog/bedzed/bedzed_hpg.htm.

18  Jenks, M., E. Burton and K. Williams (eds) (1996) *The Compact City: A Sustainable Urban Form?*, E&FN Spon, London and Melbourne.

19  The cost of tree loss in urban areas in the US was $234 million.

20  Means of identifying vacant urban land for development is discussed in Myers, D. and P. Wyatt (2004) 'Rethinking urban capacity: Identifying and appraising vacant buildings', *Building Research and Information*, vol 32, no 4, pp285–292.

21  See books by Ken Yeang, including Yeang, K. (1999) *The Green Skyscraper: The Basis for Designing Sustainable Intensive Buildings*, Prestel Verlag, Munich, Germany, and Yeang, K. (2006) *Ecodesign: A Manual of Ecological Design*, Wiley, London.

22  Osmond, P. (2002) 'The sustainable landscape', in J. Birkeland (ed) *Design for Sustainability: A Sourcebook of Integrated Eco-logical Solutions*, Earthscan, London, p200.

23  Trainer, T. (2002) 'Limits to growth and design of settlements', in J. Birkeland (ed) *Design for Sustainability: A Sourcebook of Integrated Eco-logical Solutions*, Earthscan, London, pp33–36.

24  For a discussion on durability and sustainability, see Mora, E. P. (2007) 'Life-cycle, sustainability and the transcendent quality of building materials', *Building and Environment*, vol 42, no 3, pp1329–1334.

25  It is recognized that these issues are complex, of course. See Schmidt, A., A. Jensen, A. Clausen, O. Kamstrup and D. Pastlehwaite (2004) 'A comparative life-cycle assessment of building insulation products made of stone wool, paper wool and flax', *International Journal of Life-Cycle Assessment*, vol 9, no 1, pp53–66.

26  Burroughs, S. (2002) 'Earth building', in J. Birkeland (ed) *Design for Sustainability: A Sourcebook of Integrated Eco-logical Solutions*, Earthscan, London, pp193–196.

27  Danenburg, J. (2002) 'Hemp architecture', in J. Birkeland (ed) *Design for Sustainability: A Sourcebook of Integrated Eco-logical Solutions*, Earthscan, London, pp205–208.

28  Storey, J. (2002) 'Designing for durability', in J. Birkeland (ed) *Design for Sustainability: A Sourcebook of Integrated Eco-logical Solutions*, Earthscan, London, pp46–47.

29  St Jacques, L. (2002) 'Strawbale construction', in J. Birkeland (ed) *Design for Sustainability: A Sourcebook of Integrated Eco-logical Solutions*, Earthscan, London, pp197–199.

30  Hawken, P., A. Lovins and H. Lovins (1999) *Natural Capitalism: Creating the Next Industrial Revolution*, Earthscan, London.

31  Fuad-Luke, A. (2002) *Eco-Design: The Sourcebook*, Chronicle Books, San Francisco, CA; Walker, S. (2006) *Sustainable by Design*, Earthscan, London; Poole, B. (ed) (2006) *Green Design*, Mark Batty Publisher, New York.

32  'Green scaffolding' was presented on the Australian TV show 'The New Inventors. Special: Future Thinking' on Wednesday 3 Oct 2007.

33  See Sudin, R. and N. Swamy (2006) 'Bamboo and wood fibre cement composites for sustainable infrastructure regeneration', *Journal of Materials Science*, vol 41, no 21, pp6917–6924.

34  For a discussion on health impact assessment (HIA), see Greig, S, N. Parry and B. Rimmington (2004) 'Promoting sustainable regeneration: Learning from a case study in participatory HIA', *Environmental Impact Assessment Review*, vol 24, no 2, pp255–267.

35  Personal communication from Graham Treloar. See also Crawford, R. and G. Treloar (2005) 'An assessment of the energy and water embodied in commercial building construction', *4th Australian LCA Conference*, Australian Life Cycle Assessment Society (ALCAS), Sydney, Australia.

36  Means of reducing radon in buildings are available on the web: for example www.ccohs.ca/oshanswers/phys_agents/radon.html; www.doh.state.fl.us/environment/community/radon/dcastdrd.htm.

37  Crowley, M. (1995) 'Homes for the Earth: site sourcing of building materials', in J. Birkeland (ed) *Catalyst 95: Rethinking the Built Environment*, conference proceedings, University of Canberra, Canberra.

38  Cusack, V. and L. Yiping (2002) 'Bamboo as a building resource', in J. Birkeland (ed) *Design for Sustainability: A Sourcebook of Integrated Eco-logical Solutions*, Earthscan, London, pp201–204.

39  Monocultural farming systems can use more energy to produce food than the food itself provides (it can take ten calories to produce one calorie of food). Monocultural systems can also deplete topsoil at an alarming rate (it takes two kilograms of topsoil to produce one kilogram of corn). See Kimbrell, A. (ed) (2002) *Fatal Harvest: The Tragedy of Industrial Agriculture*, Island Press, Washington, DC.

40  The world mines 139 million tons of phosphate rock and 26 million tons of potash a year.

41  For more on organic materials studies, see Harris, C. and P. Borer (2005) *Whole House Book: Ecological Building Design and Materials* (second edition), Centre for Alternative technology, Machynlleth, UK; Berge, B. (2002) *Ecology of Building Materials*, translated from Norwegian by Filip Henley with Howard Liddell, Architectural Press, Oxford, UK.

42  Johnson, C. (2004) *Homes Dot Com: Architecture for All*, Government Architects Publications, Sydney, Australia.

43  Brylawski, M. and Rocky Mountain Institute (2002) 'The hypercar concept', in J. Birkeland (ed) *Design for Sustainability: A Sourcebook of Integrated Eco-logical Solutions*, Earthscan, London, p163.

44  Ibid.

45  The architect, M. Safdie, hoped that his idea would become widespread. However his other attempts to build similar structures all failed to be funded. For more information on Habitat 2 Montreal, see www.pushpullbar.com/forums/showthread.php?t=3295.

46  One of the main books on design is Broadbent, G. (1973) *Design in Architecture: Architecture and the Human Sciences*, John Wiley and Sons, Hoboken, NJ. See also Lawson, B. (1980) *How Designers Think*, The Architectural Press, London.

47  For example, take the building known as 'The Gherkin', 30 St Mary Axe, London, see www.architectureweek.com/2000/0920/news_1-2.html, or the 'Glass Egg', London City Hall, see http://kambiz.aminus3.com/image/2007-11-04.html.

48  Green, B. (2002) 'Ergonomics or human-centred design', in J. Birkeland (ed) *Design for Sustainability: A Sourcebook of Integrated Eco-logical Solutions*, Earthscan, London, p133.

49  In either approach, of course, there is a competing tendency to shape the envelope into a preconceived 'brand' or style that the firm or designer is establishing, or current fashion dictated by design journals.

50  Mclennan, J. F. (2004) *The Philosophy of Sustainable Design*, Ecotone Publishing, Kansas City, MO.

51  Todd, J. (1995) 'Judging the judges: Are environment and energy issues adequately covered in architectural awards?', in *Catalyst 95 Conference: Rethinking the Built Environment*, University of Canberra, Canberra, Australia.

## Chapter 7

1  See development assessment forum, www.daf.gov.au/.

2  When the author moved to Australia 26 years ago, planners were notably uninterested in sharing information about respective planning systems. Environmental management and planning has become internationalized.

3  See, generally, Birkeland, J. (2002) 'Limits of environmental impact assessment', in *Design for Sustainability: A Sourcebook of Integrated Eco-logical Solutions*, Earthscan, London, pp247–250.

4    Doelle, M. and A. J. Sinclair (2006) 'Time for a new approach to public participation in EA: Promoting cooperation and consensus for sustainability', *Environmental Impact Assessment Review*, vol 26, no 2, pp185–205.

5    In Australia, the response to the likelihood of rising oil crises was to set up a body of nuclear experts to determine that nuclear plants should be built in Australia. This has been superseded by a recent federal election.

6    When in San Francisco, MacDonald's Corporation approached the author to find out if neighbourhood groups were 'active' in an area they were considering building a fast food facility. Based on that information they did not proceed with planning for a MacDonald's on the proposed site.

7    Esty, D. C. and A. S. Wilston (2006) *Green to Gold: How Smart Companies Use Environmental Strategy to Innovate, Create Value and Build Competitive Advantage*, Yale University Press, New Haven, CT, and London.

8    The author has heard more than one reputedly 'green' architect boast that they can obtain green building awards for adding pelmets to windows, without knowing anything about energy-efficient design.

9    O'Brien, M. (2000) *Making Better Environmental Decisions: An Alternative to Risk Assessment*, MIT Press, Cambridge, MA.

10   This is not new, just not widely applied. The process was performed by the San Francisco City Planning Department in the 1970s when they felt a site was 'ripe' for development.

11   For a discussion of contemporary issues in sustainability assessment, see Pope, J. and W. Grace (2006) 'Sustainability assessment in context: Issues of process, policy and governance', *Journal of Environmental Assessment Policy and Management*, vol 8, no 3, pp373–398; Gibson, R., S. Hassan, S. Holtz, J. Tansey and G. Whitelaw (2005) *Sustainability Assessment: Criteria, Processes and Applications*, Earthscan, London.

12   See Birkeland, J. (2002) 'Mini debates on EIAs', in *Design for Sustainability: A Sourcebook of Integrated Eco-logical Solutions*, Earthscan, London, p251.

13   Gibson, R., S. Hassan, S. Holtz, J. Tansey and G. Whitelaw (2005) *Sustainability Assessment: Criteria, Processes and Applications*, Earthscan, London.

14   Alshuwaikhat, H. M. and I. Abubakar (2007) 'Towards a sustainable urban environmental management approach (SUEMA): Incorporating environmental management with strategic environmental assessment (SEA)', *Journal of Environmental Planning and Management*, vol 50, no 2, pp257–270.

15   Birkeland, J. (2002) 'Planning for ecological sustainability', in *Design for Sustainability: A Sourcebook of Integrated Eco-logical Solutions*, Earthscan, London, pp231–234.

16   This was the approach used by the Project Review Section at the San Francisco City Planning Department when the author headed the section in the 1970s.

17   I drafted policies for eco-industrial parks that shift the burden of proof to developers for the Natural Edge Project.

18   Gibson, R., S. Hassan, S. Holtz, J. Tansey and G. Whitelaw (2005) *Sustainability Assessment: Criteria, Processes and Applications*, Earthscan, London.

19   The tragedy of the commons refers to where unlimited access to resources leads to resource exhaustion as those that exploit the resource are able to externalize the impacts. See Hardin, G. (1968) 'The tragedy of the commons', *Science*, vol 162, pp1243–1248.

20   See Trust for Public Land, www.tpl.org/.

21   See material by Paul Downton and Cheryl Hoyle at www.urbanecology.org.au/christiewalk/.

22   In the Australian island state of Tasmania, where the author lived for 13 years, the forest industries

appeared to be deliberately trying to wipe out ecologically sensitive areas before they could be preserved.

23   When in charge of major project review, the author was politely told not to interfere in a big project where the planning decisions were made directly by politicians and developers.

24   See Forester J. (1989) *Planning in the Face of Power*, University of California Press, Berkeley, CA.

25   HM Treasury (2006) *Stern Review: The Economics of Climate Change*, UK Government, London, downloadable from www.hm-treasury.gov.uk/contact/contact_index.cfm.

26   Myers, N. and J. Kent (2001) *Perverse Subsidies: How Tax Dollars Can Undercut the Environment and the Economy*, Island Press, Washington, DC.

27   Wackernagel, M. and W. E. Rees (1996) *Our Ecological Footprint: Reducing the Human Impact on the Earth*, New Society Publishers, Gabriola Island, BC, Canada, and New Haven, CT.

28   See Lash, J. et al (2000) *The Weight of Nations*, World Resources Institute, Washington, DC; Foran, B. and F. Poldy (2002) *Dilemmas Distilled: Options to 2050 for Australia's Population, Technology, Resources and Environment: A Summary and Guide to the CSIRO Technical Report*, Commonwealth of Australia, ACT, Australia.

29   Institutional analyses of this sort exist, of course, but seem to have gone underground with the demise of socialism.

## Chapter 8

1   For a brief discussion, see Birkeland, J. and J. Schooneveldt (2002) 'Regional sustainability audits', in J. Birkeland *Design for Sustainability: A Sourcebook of Integrated Eco-logical Solutions*, Earthscan, London, p246.

2   To illustrate, the author applied this legal concept when an uphill neighbour chopped trees on my property to enhance his view. Several lawyers said one could only get the value of the wood (a few hundred dollars at most), but with the threat to sue for the increased value in his property (in proportion to the inflation in the respective properties), the neighbour's insurance company settled for $30,000 (1981 dollars).

3   For a one-page introduction, see Rees, W. E. (2002) 'Eco-footprints and eco-logical design', in J. Birkeland (ed) *Design for Sustainability: A Sourcebook of Integrated Eco-logical Solutions*, Earthscan, London, p73.

4   Wackernagel, M. and W. E. Rees (1996) *Our Ecological Footprint: Reducing the Human Impact on the Earth*, New Society Publishers, Gabriola Island, BC, Canada, and New Haven, CT.

5   Hunter, C. and J. Shaw (2007 'The ecological footprint as a key indicator of sustainable tourism', *Tourism Management*, vol 28, no 1, pp46–57.

6   World Bank (2006) *The Little Green Data Book 2006*, World Bank, Washington, DC; World Bank (2006a) *World Development Indicators*, World Bank, Washington, DC; Daly, H. E. and K. N. Townsend (eds) (1992) *Valuing the Earth: Economics, Ecology, Ethics*, MIT Press, Boston, MA.

7   Barlow, M. and T. Clarke (2003) *Blue Gold: The Battle against Corporate Theft of the World's Water*, Earthscan, London.

8   ABC (Australian Broadcasting Commission), 'Protest turns violent at APEC', ABC News, article posted 18 November 2005, viewed August 2007, www.abc.net.au/news/stories/2005/11/18/1510 311.htm.

9   Lecture by Peter Cock of Monash University at Students for Sustainability Conference, Latrobe University, Melbourne, Australia, July 2004.

10  Food mile labelling indicates carbon content, in particular associated with how far the food has come, and therefore indicates its carbon footprint.

11  See www.gci.org.uk.

12  As environmentalists have long argued, birth rates go down when people do not need large numbers of children as 'old age insurance'.

13  Personal communication from physicist Richard Meuller.

14  See Pearce, F. (2002) 'Green foundations', *NewScientist*, 13 July, pp39–40.

15  See Ecoforestry Institute, British Columbia, http://ecoforestry.ca/default.htm.

16  See Lifset, R. (2004) 'Probing metabolism', *Journal of Industrial Ecology*, vol 8, no 3, pp1–3, and other articles at www.mitpressjournals.org.

17  Brunner, P. H. and H. Rechberger (2004) *Practical Handbook of Material Flow Analysis*, Lewis Publishers, Stockport, UK.

18  Lash, J. et al (2000) *The Weight of Nations*, World Resources Institute, Washington, DC.

19  Boyden, S., S. Millar, K. Newcombe and B. O'Neill (1981) *The Ecology of a City and its People: The Case of Hong Kong*, Australian National University Press, Canberra.

20  Vermeulen, W. J. V. and P. J. Ras (2006) 'The challenge of greening global product chains: Meeting both ends', *Sustainable Development*, vol 14, pp245–256.

21  See Birkeland, J. and J. Schooneveldt (2002) *Mapping Regional Metabolism: A Decision-Support Tool for Natural Resource Management*, Land and Water Australia (first published as a report in 2002), Canberra.

22  Birkeland, J. (2002) 'Education for eco-innovation', in *Design for Sustainability: A Sourcebook of Integrated Eco-logical Solutions*, Earthscan, London, pp7–11.

23  See Birkeland, J. and J. Schooneveldt (2002) *Mapping Regional Metabolism: A Decision-Support Tool for Natural Resource Management*, Land and Water Australia (first published as a report in 2002), Canberra.

24  Birkeland, J. (2002) 'Responsible design', in *Design for Sustainability: A Sourcebook of Integrated Eco-logical Solutions*, Earthscan, London, pp26–30.

25  For further information, see www.ilsr.org/index.html.

26  Birkeland, J. (2002) 'Centrality of design', in *Design for Sustainability: A Sourcebook of Integrated Eco-logical Solutions*, Earthscan, London, pp13–17.

27  Bamford, G. (2002) 'Density, environment and the city', in J. Birkeland (ed) *Design for Sustainability: A Sourcebook of Integrated Eco-logical Solutions*, Earthscan, London, pp168–171.

28  For the case of Cornelia Rau, see www.aph.gov.au/library/pubs/rb/2004-05/05rb14.pdf.

29  See Diesendorf, M. (2007) *Greenhouse Solutions with Sustainable Energy*, University of New South Wales Press, Sydney, Australia.

30  The field of environmental justice goes into this in depth. See, for example, Camacho, D. E. (ed) (1989) *Environmental Injustices, Political Struggles: Race, Class and the Environment*, Duke University Press, Durham and London; Bryant, B. (ed) (1995) *Environmental Justice: Issues, Policies, and Solutions*, Island Press, Washington, DC.

31  Before becoming a lawyer, the author applied this legal concept when an uphill neighbour chopped trees to enhance his view. Several lawyers said one could only get the value of the wood (a few hundred dollars at most), but the insurance company settled for US $30,000 (in 1981 dollars), which was the increased value of his property in proportion to inflation since the respective properties were purchased.

32  Diamond, J. (1999) *Guns, Germs and Steel: The Fates of Human Societies*, W. W. Norton and Co, New York.

33  Birkeland, J. (1972) *The Value and Limitations of Advocacy Planning*, Report, University of

California, Berkeley, CA.

34  Urban Services and ACTPLA (2003) 'Draft Sustainable Transport Plan for the ACT', ACT Government, Canberra.

35  For example, the Chinese Three Gorges Dam project relocated thousands, which could not happen in a rich nation as the costs of relocation would be too high.

## Chapter 9

1   For an example or overview of public environmental reporting, see Environment Australia (2003) *Triple Bottom Line Reporting in Australia: A Guide to Reporting against Environmental Indicators*, Department of Environment and Heritage, Canberra.

2   Maclean, R. and K. Rebernak (2007) 'Closing the credibility gap: The challenges of corporate responsibility reporting', *Environmental Quality Management*, vol 16, no 4, pp1–6.

3   Dummett, K. (2006) 'Drivers for corporate environmental responsibility (CER)', *Environment, Development and Sustainability*, vol 8, no 3, pp375–389.

4   Sheu, H-J. and S-F. Lo (2005) 'A new conceptual framework integrating environment into corporate performance evaluation', *Sustainable Development*, vol 13, pp79–90.

5   For an example of a report, see Office of Sustainability (2004) 'Measuring our progress: Canberra's journey to sustainability, Volume 1: Our story', ACT Government, Canberra; Office of Sustainability (2004), 'Measuring our progress: Canberra's journey to sustainability, Volume 2: Our core dimensions', ACT Government, Canberra.

6   See, for example, Olwilwe, N. (2006) 'Environmental sustainability for urban areas: The role of natural capital indicators', *Cities*, vol 23, no 3, pp184–195.

7   The final plan was somewhat improved: www.actpla.act.gov.au/__data/assets/pdf_file/0016/2581/wtc-masterplan2004.pdf.

8   See Barrett, P. (Auditor-General for Australia) (2004) 'Public sector reporting and triple bottom line', Department of the Environment and Heritage at www.anao.gov.au/uploads/documents/Public_Sector_Reporting_and_Triple_Bottom_Line.pdf. For an example of a triple bottom line report see Australian Government Department of Family and Community Services (2003) at www.facs.gov.au/triplebottomline/2003/_lib/pdf/tbl02_03.pdf.

9   See Parris, T. and R. Kates (2003) 'Characterizing and measuring sustainable development', *Annual Review of Environment and Resources*, vol 28, pp559–586.

10  The Australian Federal Government recently announced that it intends to spend hundreds of thousands of dollars 'explaining' the virtues of nuclear power to the citizenry.

11  Birkeland, J. and R. Lubanga (2002) 'Environmental quality indicators', in J. Birkeland (ed) *Design for Sustainability: A Sourcebook of Integrated Eco-logical Solutions*, Earthscan, London, p224.

12  Birkeland, J. and J. Schooneveldt (2002) 'Design criteria and indicators', in J. Birkeland (ed) *Design for Sustainability: A Sourcebook of Integrated Eco-logical Solutions*, Earthscan, London, p320.

13  This comment is based on first-hand experience in government.

14  See Hallen, P. (1989) 'Careful of science: A feminist critique of science', *The Trumpeter*, vol 6, no 1, pp3–8.

15  The proportion of scientists paid at least indirectly by the military has been put at over 70 per cent.

16  Birkeland, J. (1995) 'Cultures of institutional corruption', in J. Bessant, K. Carrington and S. Cook (eds) *Cultures of Crime and Violence: The Australian Experience*, LaTrobe University Press, Melbourne, Australia, pp199–212.

17  Birkeland, J. (1993) *Planning for a Sustainable Society: Institutional Reform and Social Transformation*, University of Tasmania, Hobart, Tasmania.

18  The cargo cult represents the belief that spiritual agents will deliver manufactured products to the cult members if they perform the right rituals; see http://en.wikipedia.org/wiki/Cargo_cult.

19  See, for example, Daly, H. E. and J. B. Cobb Jr (1989) *For the Common Good: Redirecting the Economy toward Community, the Environment and a Sustainable Future*, Beacon Press, Boston, MA; Ekins, P. (ed) (1986) *The Living Economy: A New Economics in the Making*, Routledge, London; Ekins, P., M. Hillman and R. Hutchinson (1992) *Wealth Beyond Measure: An Atlas of New Economics*, Gaia Books, London.

20  See Hamilton, C. (1994) *The Mystic Economist*, Willow Park Press, Canberra, Australia.

21  See Hamilton, C. (2002) 'Genuine progress indicators', in J. Birkeland (ed) *Design for Sustainability: A Sourcebook of Integrated Eco-logical Solutions*, Earthscan, London, p42.

22  Marmot, M. (2004) *Status Syndrome: How Your Social Standing Directly Affects Your Health and Life Expectancy*, Bloomsbury and Henry Holt, New York.

23  Bhutan developed the concept of Gross National Happiness (GNH) in 1972 to prioritize the wellbeing of individuals as part of the national development agenda.

24  Hamilton, C. (1997) 'The genuine progress indicator: A new index of changes in wellbeing', Australia Institute Discussion Paper 14, The Australia Institute, Canberra. For a discussion of biases in national accounting systems, see Waring, M. (1998) *Counting for Nothing: What Men Value and What Women are Worth*, Bridget Williams Books, Wellington, New Zealand.

25  Term from Mark Taylor, Queensland University of Technology.

26  NABERS (the National Australian Built Environment Rating System) is a performance-based rating system for existing buildings. NABERS rates a building on the basis of its measured operational impacts on the environment, including the ecology. For an overview of some rating tools, see www.knoxadv.com.au/docs/sustainability_tools_pathway.pdf.

27  The Green Lights programme, a voluntary energy-efficiency programme in the US, encouraged savings from energy efficiency to be rolled over to fund larger projects.

## Chapter 10

1  For futures tools, see www.innovationtools.com/. For an overview of types of tools, see http://en.wikipedia.org/wiki/Futures_techniques.

2  Along similar lines, PERT (programme evaluation and review technique) charts and CPM (critical path method) have been used in complex construction projects, as well as in manufacturing and commercialization, for decades.

3  Gordon, T. J. (2004) 'Science and technology road mapping', in *Futures Research Methodology*, AC/UNU Millennium Project, World Federation of UN Associations, Washington, DC. See www.millennium-project.org/.

4  Ibid.

5  For example the EMRET (Mandated Renewable Energy Target) in Australia, although it was set at a low level; see www.greenhouse.gov.au/markets/mret/.

6  Deranged people can attain political power; they can also rise to the top of corporations. See Clarke, J. (2005) *Working with Monsters*, Random House, North Sydney, Australia.

7  Department of Energy (1999) *Carbon Sequestration: A Third Approach to Carbon Management*, US Department of Energy, Washington, DC.

8  Scheer, H. (2004) *The Solar Economy*, Earthscan, London.

9   Estimates by the former Australian Chief Scientist of the costs per ton of $CO_2$ sequestered by geosequestration were far off the mark; see www.abc.net.au/7.30/content/2003/s1006343.htm and www.bobbrown.org.au/files/campaigns/extras/Chief%20Scientist%20report.pdf.

10  To compare approaches, see www.isf.uts.edu.au/publications/ISF_Water_Article.pdf and Australian Water Industry Roadmap Project at www.bartongroup.org.au/pdf/Chapter%201. pdf.

11  Glenn, Jerome C. (2004) *The Futures Wheel*, AC/UNU Millennium Project, World Federation of UN Associations, Washington, DC.  See www.millennium-project.org.

12  Sarkissian, W. (2002) 'Pros and cons of design charrettes', in J. Birkeland (ed) *Design for Sustainability: A Sourcebook of Integrated Eco-logical Solutions*, Earthscan, London, p113.

13  Register, R. (1987) *Eco-city Berkeley: Building Cities for a Healthy Future*, North Atlantic Books, Berkeley, CA.

14  Birkeland, J. and J. Schooneveldt (2003) *Mapping Regional Metabolism: A Decision-Support Tool for Natural Resource Management*, Land and Water Australia (first published as a report in 2002), Canberra.

15  Berg, Per G. (1996) 'Sustainable exchange of nutrients between townscapes and landscapes', in M. Rolen (ed) *Urban Development in an Ecocycles-Adapted Industrial Society*, Swedish Council for Planning and Coordination of Research, Stockholm.

16  Diagram from Birkeland, J. and J. Schooneveldt (2003) *Mapping Regional Metabolism: A Decision-Support Tool for Natural Resource Management*, Land and Water Australia (first published as a report in 2002), Canberra.

17  Further information can be obtained from Zero Waste Australia, www.zerowasteaustralia.org/.

18  Glenn, Jerome C. (2004) *Scenarios*, AC/UNU Millennium Project, World Federation of UN Associations, Washington, DC.  See www.millennium-project.org.

19  Meadows, D. H. et al (1972) *The Limits to Growth: A Report for the Club of Rome*, Universe Books, New York; Meadows, D. H., D. Randers and D. L. Meadows (2004) *Limits to Growth: The 30 Year Update*, Earthscan, London.

20  However, psychological profiling seems to be used to provoke self-destructive action on the part of foreign leaders rather than introspection.

21  Birkeland, J. and J. Schooneveldt (2003), *Mapping Regional Metabolism: A Decision-Support Tool for Natural Resource Management*, Land and Water Australia (first published as a report in 2002), Canberra.

22  See http://en.wikipedia.org/wiki/Futures_techniques.

## Chapter 11

1   A short version was published as Birkeland, J. (2006) 'Carbon trading: Business as usual', *Solar Progress*, vol 27, no 1.

2   Roxburgh, S. H., S. W. Wood, B. G. Mackey, G. Woldendorp and P. Gibbons (2006) 'Assessing the carbon sequestration potential of managed forests: A case study from temperate Australia', *Journal of Applied Ecology*, vol 43, pp1149–1159.

3   Costanza, R. et al (1997) 'The value of the world's ecosystem services and natural capital', *Nature*, vol 387, pp253–260.

4   Calculations were based on the value of 17 kinds of services (eg pollination, waste treatment) in 16 types of ecosystems (eg deserts, lakes) to get an average dollar value per hectare.  This was multiplied by the total area that each ecosystem type occupies on Earth.

5   Toman, M. A. (1998) 'Why not calculate the value of the world's ecosystem services and natural capital', *Ecological Economics*, vol 25, pp57–60; Heal, G. (2000) *Nature and the Marketplace: Capturing the Value of Ecosystem Services*, Island Press, Washington, DC.

6   In the New Orleans flood of 1927, the dykes in the poor areas were deliberately breached to minimize the impacts on the wealthy areas.

7   Eg Landcare, Waterwatch and Wastewise programmes in Australia.

8   HM Treasury (2006) *Stern Review: The Economics of Climate Change*, UK Government, London, downloadable from www.hm-treasury.gov.uk/contact/contact_index.cfm.

9   Heal, G. (2000) *Nature and the Marketplace: Capturing the Value of Ecosystem Services*, Island Press, Washington, DC.

10  Daily, G. and K. Ellison (2002) *The New Economy of Nature*, Island Press, Washington, DC.

11  This was the case in Tasmania, for example.

12  Ridgeway, J. (2004) *It's All for Sale: The Control of Global Resources*, Duke University Press, Durham and London.

13  Ibid.

14  For example, some are designed to flush out mosquitoes.

15  Recently land was sold by Aboriginals for uranium mining in Australia.

16  Birkeland, J. and S. Baird (2002) 'Carbon storage', in J. Birkeland (ed) *Design for Sustainability: A Sourcebook of Integrated Eco-logical Solutions*, Earthscan, London, p209.

17  Kapambwe, M. C. (2006) 'Wood use and carbon sequestration in housing', PhD thesis, University of Melbourne, Victoria, Australia.

18  Roxburgh, S. H., S. W. Wood, B. G. Mackey, G. Woldendorp and P. Gibbons (2006) 'Assessing the carbon sequestration potential of managed forests: A case study from temperate Australia', *Journal of Applied Ecology*, vol 43, pp1149–1159.

19  Adger, N. and K. Brown (1994) *Land Use and the Causes of Global Warming*, John Wiley, New York.

20  This seems to have been attempted unsuccessfully in post-Cold War Russia.

21  Ecological restoration for offsets is happening in the US, but apparently to offset increased development in urban areas. See Noon, K. (2007) 'Wetlands mitigation banking', presented at 'Environmental trading: The essentials', seminar at the Institute for Sustainable Resources, Queensland University of Technology, Brisbane, 22 November.

22  Recently the Australian Federal Government took a form of 'direct action' to stop endemic aboriginal child abuse. Regardless of the merits of this action, it is not what is meant in this book by 'direct action', which is used to mean physical solutions that improve the ecological base and public estate.

23  Birkeland, J. (2002) 'Pollution prevention by design', in *Design for Sustainability: A Sourcebook of Integrated Eco-logical Solutions*, Earthscan, London, pp69–72.

24  www.bioacoustics.info/index.html

25  As a law school exercise in the 1970s, the author developed an incentive scheme whereby homeowners or developers could build beyond the allowable development envelope for greenhouse windows that served environmental functions, such as heating, cooling and ventilating or providing plants for food and air cleaning. A version of this proposal was adopted by the City Planning Department.

26  Some banks offer favourable mortgage terms that reflect the fact that the costs of living will be lower in green and centrally located homes.

27  See www.fao.org/AG/AGL/agll/carbonsequestration/Activities.stm.

# Chapter 12

1    In a planning conference in the 1990s, my proposed talk on 'sustainability' was not seen as relevant to the conference and I was asked to speak on another subject. Likewise, at an environmental conference in the 1990s my proposed talk on 'planning' was not seen as relevant to the conference and I was asked to speak on another subject.

2    Popper, K. (1959, original 1934) *The Logic of Scientific Discovery*, Routledge, Abingdon, UK.

3    Birkeland, J. (1993) *Planning for a Sustainable Society: Institutional Reform and Social Transformation*, University of Tasmania, Hobart, Tasmania.

4    Davidoff, P. (1965) 'Advocacy and pluralism in planning', *American Institute of Planning Journal*, vol 31, pp331–338.

5    Rittel, H. and M. Webber (1973) 'Dilemmas in a general theory of planning', *Policy Sciences*, vol 4, pp155–169.

6    Daly, H. E. and J. B. Cobb Jr (1989) *For the Common Good: Redirecting the Economy toward Community, the Environment and a Sustainable Future*, Beacon Press, Boston, MA.

7    Harding, R. and E. Fisher (1999) *Perspectives on the Precautionary Principle*, Federation Press, Sydney, Australia; Deville, A. and R. Harding (1997) *Applying the Precautionary Principle*, Federation Press, Sydney, Australia.

8    Birkeland, J. (2002) 'Green philosophy', in *Design for Sustainability: A Sourcebook of Integrated Eco-logical Solutions*, Earthscan, London, pp20–24.

9    Birkeland, J. (1995) 'The relevance of ecofeminism to the environmental professions', *The Environmental Professional*, vol 17, pp55–71.

10   Davidoff, P. (1965) 'Advocacy and pluralism in planning', *American Institute of Planning Journal*, vol 31, pp331–338.

11   Rittel, H. and M. Webber (1973) 'Dilemmas in a general theory of planning', *Policy Sciences*, vol 4, pp155–169.

12   See Checkland, P. and J. Scholes (1990) *Soft Systems Methodology in Action*, John Wiley, Hoboken, NJ.

13   Norton attributes adaptive management to Aldo Leopold: Norton, B. G. (2005) *Sustainability: A Philosophy of Adaptive Ecosystem Management*, University of Chicago Press, Chicago, IL.

14   Moynihan, D. (1969) *Maximum Feasible Misunderstanding*, The Free Press, New York.

15   Birkeland, J. (1988) 'Redefining the environmental problem', *Environmental and Planning Law Journal*, vol 5, no 2, pp109–133.

16   For a discussion on NGOs and partnerships, see Sanyal, P. (2006) 'Capacity-building through partnership: Intermediary non-governmental organizations as local and global actors', in *Nonprofit and Voluntary Sector Quarterly*, vol 35, no 1, pp66–82.

17   There was a board game in the 1960s called Blacks and Whites. The game was set up so that no matter who did what, the blacks would lose.

18   Birkeland, J. (1995) 'Ecophilosophy and the built environment', in *Pacific Vision: Ecopolitics VIII Conference Proceedings*, Lincoln University, Canterbury, New Zealand.

19   An overview of systems thinking can be found in Bosch, O., C. King, J. Herbohn, I. Russell and C. Smith (2007) 'Getting the big picture in natural resource management – Systems thinking as "method" for scientists, policymakers and other stakeholders', *Systems Research and Behavioral Science*, vol 24, pp217–232.

20   Lake, L. M. (ed) (1980) *Environmental Mediation: The Search for Consensus*, Westview Press, Boulder, CO. See also, for example, www.ecodirections.com/pdf/Mediation_Booklet_Sept2003.pdf.

21  See Townsend, M. (2006) 'Feel blue? Touch green! Participation in forest/woodland management as a treatment for depression', *Urban Forestry and Urban Greening*, vol 5, no 3, pp111–120.

22  Birkeland, J. (1994) 'Ecofeminist playgardens', *International Play Journal*, vol 2, pp49–59.

23  Alinsky, S. (1972) *Rules for Radicals*, Vantage Books, New York; Dean, A. O. (1976) 'Community design centres: Practising "social architecture"', *American Institute of Architects Journal*, January.

24  For example, when the author was working at the Community Design Centre, it partnered with the city and EDAW, a landscape architecture firm.

25  Toker, Z. (2007) 'Participatory design', *Design Studies*, vol 28, no 3, pp309–323.

26  Satisficing was coined by Herb Simon to describe what many decision-makers actually do, which is decide on something that is 'good enough'.

27  Corporatist processes are the merger of government and corporate power.

28  Birkeland, J. (1993) *Planning for a Sustainable Society: Institutional Reform and Social Transformation*, University of Tasmania, Hobart, Tasmania.

29  Aberley, D. (ed) (1994) *Futures by Design: The Practice of Ecological Planning*, New Society Publishers, Philadelphia, PA; Brunckhorst, D. J. (2000) *Bioregional Planning: Resource Management Beyond the New Millennium*, Harwood Academic Publishers, Amsterdam.

30  Birkeland, J. and C. Walker (2002) 'Bioregional planning', in J. Birkeland (ed) *Design for Sustainability: A Sourcebook of Integrated Eco-logical Solutions*, Earthscan, London, pp236–240.

31  McGinnis, M. (ed) (1999) *Bioregionalism*, Routledge, London.

32  Traina, F. and S. Darley-Hill (1995) *Perspectives in Bioregional Education*, North American Association for Environmental Education, Troy, OH; Andruss, V. et al (1990) *Home! A Bioregional Reader*, New Society Publishers, Cabriola Island, BC, Canada.

33  Sarkissian, W., A. Cook and K. Walsh (2002) 'Pros and cons of design charrettes', in J. Birkeland (ed) *Design for Sustainability: A Sourcebook of Integrated Eco-logical Solutions*, Earthscan, London, p113.

34  Department of the Environment, Sports and Territories (1995) 'Approaches to bioregional planning conference', Biodiversity Series, Paper No 10, Biodiversity Group, Department of the Environment, Sports and Territories (now Environment Australia), Melbourne.

35  A term from Amory Lovins.

36  See Birkeland, J. (2002) 'Education for sustainability principles', in *Design for Sustainability: A Sourcebook of Integrated Eco-logical Solutions*, Earthscan, London, p12.

37  Birkeland, J. with K. Uddin (1999) 'Applications of GIS in bioregional planning', paper presented at GIS 99 Conference, Vancouver, Canada, 4 March.

38  Ibid.

39  Birkeland, J. (2002) 'Bioregional boundaries', in *Design for Sustainability: A Sourcebook of Integrated Eco-logical Solutions*, Earthscan, London, p241.

40  Dodge, J. (1981) 'Living by life: Some bioregional theory and practice', *CoEvolution Quarterly*, vol 32, pp6–12.

41  Birkeland, J. (2002) 'Bioregional boundaries', in *Design for Sustainability: A Sourcebook of Integrated Eco-logical Solutions*, Earthscan, London, p241.

42  Sale, K. (1985) *Dwellers in the Land*, Sierra Club Books, San Francisco, CA.

43  See Land and Water Australia, http://audit.ea.gov.au/ANRA/docs/final_report/final_report_land_and_water.cfm.

44  Noon, K. (2007) 'Wetlands mitigation banking', paper presented at 'Environmental trading: The essentials', Seminar at the Institute for Sustainable Resources, QUT, Brisbane, 22 November.

45  See 'The business of saving water' at www.napswq.gov.au/publications/books/pratt-water/pubs/

pratt-water-main.pdf.

46  Barlow, M. and T. Clarke (2003) *Blue Gold: The Battle Against Corporate Theft of the World's Water*, Earthscan, London.

47  Ibid.

48  See www.naturalsequencefarming.com/.

49  McHarg, I. (1969) *Design With Nature*, Natural History Press, Garden City, NY.

50  A paint company in Tasmania found it was cheaper to move interstate and rebuild, rather than clean up the pollution.

## Chapter 13

1   Birkeland, J. (1991) 'An ecofeminist critique of mainstream planning', *Trumpeter*, vol 8, no 2.

2   This chapter is largely drawn from Birkeland, J. (1993) *Planning for a Sustainable Society: Institutional Reform and Social Transformation*, University of Tasmania, Hobart, Tasmania.

3   Norton, B. G. (2005) *Sustainability: A Philosophy of Adaptive Ecosystem Management*, University of Chicago Press, Chicago, IL.

4   Birkeland, J. (1995) 'The relevance of ecofeminism to the environmental professions', *The Environmental Professional*, vol 17, pp55–71.

5   Ibid.

6   Enloe, C. (1989) *Bananas, Beaches and Bases: Making Feminist Sense of International Politics*, University of California Press, Berkeley, CA.

7   For example, the impact study of a Camalco plant in Tasmania said it would create far more jobs than it in fact did.

8   Ridgeway, J. (2004) *It's All for Sale: The Control of Global Resources*, Duke University Press, Durham and London.

9   Birkeland, J. (1993) *Planning for a Sustainable Society: Institutional Reform and Social Transformation*, University of Tasmania, Hobart, Tasmania.

10  Nash, R. (1967) *Wilderness and the American Mind*, Yale University Press, New Haven, CT, and London.

11  After all, torture is not sanctioned within US borders.

12  Henderson, K. (2002) 'Green theory in the construction fields', in J. Birkeland (ed) *Design for Sustainability: A Sourcebook of Integrated Eco-logical Solutions*, Earthscan, London, pp89–91.

13  See www.earthcharter.org; Birkeland, J. (2002) 'The Earth Charter', in *Design for Sustainability: A Sourcebook of Integrated Eco-logical Solutions*, Earthscan, London, p235.

14  Australia does not have a Bill of Rights.

15  John Locke believed that ownership of *property* is created by *labour*. Property precedes government so government cannot take land arbitrarily. Property mean goods as well as land.

16  Interestingly, Australia has more democratic electoral processes than America: preferential voting as opposed to electoral colleges.

17  Some more modern constitutions, such as Japan's, purport to protect environmental rights.

18  Repetto, R. C. and M. Gillis (1988) *Public Policies and the Misuse of Forest Resources*, Cambridge University Press, Cambridge, UK.

19  Myers, N. and J. Kent (2001) *Perverse Subsidies: How Tax Dollars Can Undercut the Environment and the Economy*, Island Press, Washington, DC.

20  Scheer, H. (2004) *The Solar Economy*, Earthscan, London.

21  Birkeland, J. (1995) 'Cultures of institutional corruption', in J. Bessant, K. Carrington and S.

Cook (eds) *Cultures of Crime and Violence: The Australian Experience*, LaTrobe University Press, Melbourne, Australia, pp199–212.

22  Ferguson, R. 'The devil and the disappearing sea: A true story about the Aral Sea catastrophe', www.goodreports.net/reviews/thedevilandthedisappearingsea.htm.

23  Barriaux, M. (2007) 'How capitalism got a conscience', *The Guardian*, Wednesday 15 July, http://business.guardian.co.uk/print/.

24  Birkeland, J. (1994) 'Green history: A reader in environmental literature, philosophy and politics', *Environmental Politics*, vol 3, no 4, pp259–260.

25  Birkeland, J. (1993) *Planning for a Sustainable Society: Institutional Reform and Social Transformation*, University of Tasmania, Hobart, Tasmania.

26  Birkeland, J. (1996) 'Ecological government: Redesigning democratic institutions', *Technology and Society*, vol 15, no 2, pp21–28.

27  Birkeland, J. (1993) 'Towards a new system of environmental governance', *The Environmentalist*, vol 13, no 1 pp19–32.

28  See Esty, D. C. and A. S. Wilston (2006) *Green to Gold: How Smart Companies Use Environmental Strategy to Innovate, Create Value, and Build Competitive Advantage*, Yale University Press, New Haven, CT, and London.  More generally, see Brown, L. (2001) *Eco-Economy: Building an Economy for the Earth*, W. W. Norton and Co, New York.

29  For futures tools, see www.innovationtools.com/.  For an overview of types of tools, see http://en.wikipedia.org/wiki/Futures_techniques.

30  For discussion of this point, see Hudson, R. (2005) 'Towards sustainable economic practices, flows and spaces: Or is the necessary impossible and the impossible necessary?', *Sustainable Development*, vol 13, pp239–252.

31  Birkeland, J. (2002) 'Legislative environmental controls', in *Design for Sustainability: A Sourcebook of Integrated Eco-logical Solutions*, Earthscan, London, pp210–214.

## Chapter 14

1  Hawken, P., A. Lovins and H. Lovins (1999) *Natural Capitalism: Creating the Next Industrial Revolution*, Earthscan, London.

2  It has been estimated that 70 per cent of water is now used in agriculture, and that in Australia available water is likely to be reduced by 25 per cent over the next few years due to global warming.

3  Some years ago, it was discovered that waste management firms in New York were dumping garbage off the continental shelf.  The waste management industry in Australia has been a lobby group against change.

4  Harris, S. M. (2007) 'Does sustainability sell? Market responses to sustainability certification', *Management of Environmental Quality*, vol 18, no 1, pp50–60.

5  Cadman, T. (2002) 'Timber certification and labelling', in J. Birkeland (ed) *Design for Sustainability: A Sourcebook of Integrated Eco-logical Solutions*, Earthscan, London, p192.

6  See Raynolds, L. T., D. Murray and A. Heller (2007) 'Regulating sustainability in the coffee sector: A comparative analysis of third-party environmental and social certification initiatives', *Agriculture and Human Values*, vol 24, no 2, pp147–163.

7  For another approach, see Palm, E. and S. O. Hansson (2006) 'The case for ethical technology assessment (ETA)', *Technological Forecasting and Social Change*, vol 73, no 5, pp543–558.

8  McDonough and Braungart coined the terms up-cycling and down-cycling, to which I am adding

eco-cycling; see McDonough, W. and M. Braungart (2002) *Cradle to Cradle: Remaking the Way We Make Things*, North Point Press, New York.

9   Ibid.

10   See www.molectra.com.au/default.aspx.

11   See www.oceanarks.org.

12   See Birkeland, J. (1999) 'Community participation in urban project assessment', in B. Martin (ed) *Technology and Public Participation*, University of Wollongong, NSW, Australia.

13   Reich, C. A. (1991) 'The endangered individual', *California Lawyer*, July, p116.

14   See www.non-gm-farmers.com/news_details.asp?ID=652.

15   In the US, for example, the assumption is that one should not be able to challenge the *constitutionality* of a law unless one can demonstrate one will be harmed by it. The eventual loss of democracy or fairness to others is not harm.

16   A spokesman of the nuclear industry once claimed on TV that they had never killed anyone, only shortened some life spans.

17   Initially, the company claimed it was a natural phenomenon, but they are now being pressured to pay compensation.

18   Planners have said this to me often. This is more typical in Australia, which has a Benthamite legacy (black letter law), rather than a natural justice heritage of the US.

19   Recently in Australia, the Prime Minister coincidentally commissioned a huge 'public' study to advocate nuclear power, five days after meeting with three powerful resource magnates who had formed a business to develop nuclear power. It was effectively a free business plan.

20   Recent energy legislation in both the US and Australia provided as many benefits for the fossil fuel industries as for renewable energy (to 'strike a balance' between sustainability and anti-sustainability).

21   The first project was reputedly in Urbana, Illinois, as part of a prairie restoration project, adding value to an adjacent public park and retirement home.

22   'Natural sequence farming' restores farmland using natural systems, somewhat similar to permaculture. It was developed by Peter Andrews in Australia.

23   Yunus, M. (2007) *Creating a World Without Poverty: Social Business and the Future of Capitalism*, Public Affairs Books, New York.

## Boxes

### Box 2

1   Adapted from material in Birkeland, J. (2002) *Design for Sustainability*, Earthscan, London.

### Box 3

1   For information on the solar pond, see www.publish.csiro.au/?act=view_file&file_id=EC117p8.pdf, accessed August 2007.

2   See Anderson, B. (1976) *The Solar Home Book: Heating, Cooling and Designing with the Sun*, Brick House Publishing Co, Harrisville, NH, and the AIA Research Corporation (1976) *Solar Dwelling Design Concepts*, US Department of Housing and Urban Development, Washington, DC.

3   See McLennan, J. F. (2004) *The Philosophy of Sustainable Design*, Ecotone Publishing, Kansas City, MO.

4   Duffy, K. (2004) 'NASA studies how to cool area as heat builds up', *Atlanta Journal Constitution*,

18 April.

5   Todd, N. J. and J. Todd (1994) *From Eco-Cities to Living Machines*, N. Atlantic Books, Berkeley, CA.

6   www.planetark.org/avantgo/dailynewsstory.cfm?newsid=22281.

7   Holmgren, D. (1992) *The Flywire House: A Case Study in Design Against Bushfire*, Nascimanere Pry Ltd, Maleny, Queensland.

8   www.eneco.com/technology.html.

9   Stamets, P. (2005) *Mycelium Running: How Mushrooms Can Help Save the World*, Ten Speed Press, Berkeley, CA.

10  See Ecospecifier.org. for information on the desert cube.

### Box 7

1   The '60L' building in Melbourne utilized a Living Machine in the central atrium – see www.60lgreenbuilding.com.  The '40 Albert Road' building was the first retrofit in Australia to receive a 5 star Australian Green Building Rating (AGBR) commitment – see www.cfcl.com. au/Assets/Files/Smart_Power_Newsletter_06-02.pdf.

### Box 8

1   For information on new green bio-based materials, see Mohanty, A., M. Misra and L. Drzal (2002) 'Bio-composites from renewable resources: Opportunities and challenges in the green materials world', *Journal of Polymers and the Environment*, vol 10, nos 1–2, pp19–26.

2   Birkeland, J. and J. Schooneveldt (2002) 'ACT sustainability audit: A material flows analysis of the residential sector of Canberra', report for PALM, sustainability Science Team, Canberra.

3   Birkeland, J. (1995) 'Rethinking pollution', paper presented at 'Turning Growth into ESD – Economically', 1995 EIA National Conference, Brisbane, Australia, 26–27 October.

4   For an example of a process to assist in retrofitting urban development generally, see Bentivegna, V. et al (2002) 'A vision and methodology for integrated sustainable urban development: BEQUEST', *Building Research and Information*, vol 30, no 2, pp83–94.

### Box 9

1   For diagrams of the Solar Core, see Chapter 18 in Hargroves, C. and M. Smith (2005) *The Natural Edge of Nations*, Earthscan, London.

### Box 10

1   The need to rationalize sustainability indicators is discussed in Parris, T. and R. Kates (2003), 'Characterizing and measuring sustainable development', *Annual Review of Environment and Resources*, vol 28, pp559–586.

### Box 11

1   Howard, E. (1946) *Garden Cities of Tomorrow*, Faber and Faber, London, UK.

### Box 13

1   Colborn, T. et al (1997) *Our Stolen Future: How We Are Threatening our Fertility, Intelligence and Survival*, Penguin Books, New York; see www.ourstolenfuture.org.

2   Ternes, T. and J. Adriano (eds) (2006) *Human Pharmaceuticals, Hormones and Fragrances: The Challenge of Micropollutants in Urban Water Management*, IWA Publishing, London (www. iwapublishing.com).

3    Werner, C. et al (2004) 'Ecosan – Closing the loop', in *Proceedings of the 2nd International Symposium on Ecological Sanitation*, April 2003, Luebeck, Germany.

4    Crites, R. and G. Tchobanoglous (1998) *Small and Decentralized Wastewater Management Systems*, WCB McGraw-Hill, Boston, MA.

5    West, S. (2003) 'Innovative on-site and decentralized sewage treatment, reuse and management systems in northern Europe and the US', www.clearwater.asn.au.

6    Ibid.

### Box 14

1    See www.greenroofs.com.

2    Johnston, J. and J. Newton (1993) *Building Green: A Guide to Using Plants on Roofs, Walls and Pavements*, The London Ecology Unit, London.

3    National Research Council (2002) 'Government of Canada reveals major greenhouse gas reductions and air quality benefits from widespread use of "greenroofs"', *Canadian Corporate News*, 9 October.

4    Kevin Duffy (2004) 'NASA studies how to cool area as heat builds up', *Atlanta Journal Constitution*, 18 April.

5    WESTON (2000) 'Urban Heat Island Initiative pilot project', energy study for the City of Chicago.

6    Steinbrueck, P. (2005) 'Putting a green cap atop the Emerald City', *The Seattle Times*, 13 January, referring to a study commissioned by Seattle's Office of Sustainability and the Environment.

### Box 17

1    Dayan, E. (2005) 'Small scale, building integrated, wind power systems', information paper, BRE Centre for Sustainable Development, UK, www.bre.co.uk.

2    Ross, A. (2006) 'Debunking the myths', *Refocus*, May/June 2006, pp40–42; see www.eere.energy. gov/windandhydro/windpoweringamerica/pdfs/wpa/34600_misconceptions.pdf and http://www. bwea.com/energy/myths.html.

3    www.earthtrack.net.

4    www.nyserda.org/publications/wind_integration_report.pdf.

5    There are community-owned wind generators in Denmark, and Australia is developing its first community wind power facility.

6    Zhang, Z. and X. Fang ( 2006) 'Study on paraffin/expanded graphite composite phase change thermal energy storage material', *Energy Conversion and Management*, vol 47, no 3, February, pp303–310.

7    In Australia, people can pay extra for Green Power.  Users of brown coal pay less as a reward for not investing in renewable energy.

8    See Diesendorf, M. (2007) *Greenhouse Solutions with Sustainabile Energy*, University of New South Wales Press, Sydney, Australia.

9    Ibid.

### Box 19

1    In 2005, there were 1 billion sales of personal computers worldwide; the number of used computers requiring management was 100 million; the number of computers landfilled was 75million; over 2 million tons of e-waste was sent to landfill; and over 780,000 tons of hazardous materials was recovered from end-of-life computers that will require management. *Source:* Environment

Victoria (2005) 'Environmental report card on computers 2005 – Computer waste in Australia and the case for producer responsibility', Environment Victoria, Melbourne, Australia.

2   Australian Bureau of Statistics (2006) www.abs.gov.au/AUSSTATS/abs@.nsf/ mediareleasesbyCatalogue/FB2F33C170E4987DCA2572210077D0FA?OpenDocument#.

3   Grossman, E. (2006) *High Tech Trash: Digital Devices, Hidden Toxics and Human Health*, Island Press, Washington, DC.

4   European Commission (2006) http://ec.europa.eu/environment/chemicals/reach/reach_intro. htm.

## Box 21

1   For a recent comparison of wood and steel reinforced concrete, see Gerilla, G. P., K. Teknomo and K. Hokao (2007) 'An environmental assessment of wood and steel reinforced concrete housing construction', *Building and Environment*, vol 42, no 7, pp2778–2784. They note that using solar energy in building operation amounts to a 73 per cent reduction in total life-cycle carbon emissions.

2   Morris, D. (2002) ' A carbohydrate economy', in J. Birkeland (ed) *Design for Sustainability: A Sourcebook of Eco-logical Design Solutions*, Earthscan, London, p200.

3   See Lawson, B. (2002) 'Assessing building materials' in J. Birkeland (ed) *Design for Sustainability: A Sourcebook of Eco-logical Design Solutions*, Earthscan, London, pp225–229.

4   Hildyard, N. (1983) *Coverup: The Facts They Don't Want You To Know*, New English Library, Kent, UK.

5   McQuaid, M. (2006) *Shigeru Ban*, Phaidon Press, London.

6   For a steel industry perspective, see Burgan, B. A. and M. R. Sansom 'Sustainable steel construction', *Journal of Constructional Steel Research*, vol 62, no 11, pp1178–1211.

## Box 22

1   Adapted from material in Birkeland, J. (2002) *Design for Sustainability*, Earthscan, London.

2   Ramsay, C. and L. Rudolph (2003) *Landscape and Building Design for Bushfire Areas*, CSIRO publishing, Victoria, Australia.

## Box 23

1   The Revit suite (Architectural, Structural, MEP) from Autodesk and the Triforma (Architecture, Structural, etc) suite from Bentley are two examples of this trend.

2   See www.construction-innovation.info/images/pdfs/Brochures/LCADesign_brochure.pdf.

3   See www.iai-international.org/Model/IFC(ifcXML)Specs.html.

## Box 25

1   Flooring can account for 30–40 per cent of a building's thermal mass, while the wall material can be 60–70 per cent.

## Box 26

1   Cargill Dow Company, a leader in plastics made from corn, has argued this.

2   The argument has been made that the transition to a carbohydrate economy should be done in a way that does not disrupt or destroy existing recycling infrastructures; see http://maryland. sierraclub.org/newsletter/archives/2007/03/a_008.asp.

3   Butterworth, B. (2006) 'Biofuels from waste', *Refocus*, May/June, pp60–61.

## Box 29

1    Further information available at www.ecospecifier.org.

## Box 32

1     www.csrp.com.au.
2    Bossilkov, A., R. van Berkel and G. D. Corder (2005) 'Regional synergies for sustainable resource processing: A status report', www.csrp.com.au/_media/pdf/3A1StatusReportJune2005Final, accessed 21 November 2005.

## Box 33

1    *Scientific American*, September 2006, pp55–61.
2    Venkat, K. and W. Wakeland (2006) 'Is lean necessarily green?', Conference of the International Society for the Systems Sciences, www.suryatech.com/pages/ISSS06-IsLeanNecessarilyGreen.pdf.

## Box 34

1    Eckersley, R. (2005) 'Redefining progress', in J. Birkeland (ed) *Design for Sustainability: A Sourcebook of Eco-logical Design Solutions*, Earthscan, London, pp38–41; see also Eckersley, R. (2005) *Well and Good: Morality, Meaning and Happiness*, Text Publishing, Melbourne, Australia.
2    World Bank (2000) *Quality of Growth*, World Bank, Washington, DC, www.worldbank.org/wbi/qualityofgrowth/overview.pdf

## Box 35

1    WCED (World Commission on Environment and Development) (1987) *Our Common Future*, Oxford University Press, Oxford.
2    OECD (1994) *Environmental Indicators. Core Set*, Organization for Economic Cooperation and Development, Paris.
3    Yenken, D. and D. Wilkinson (2000) *Resetting the Compass. Australia's Journey Towards Sustainability*, CSIRO Publishing, Melbourne, Australia.
4    Newton, P. W. (2003) '2001 Australia state of the environment: Human settlements', Environment Design Guide No 11, Australian Council of Building Design Professions, Melbourne; see also www.deh.gov.au/soe.
5    Newton, P. W. (2006) 'Australia state of the environment: Human settlements', theme paper, www.deh.gov.au/soe.
6    See www.dse.vic.gov.au/ourenvironment-ourfuture.
7    Foran, B. and F. Poldy (2002) *Future Dilemmas: Options to 2050 for Australia's Population, Technology Resources and Environment*, Department of Immigration and Multicultural Affairs, Canberra.
8    Lennox, J. A. and G. M. Turner (2005) 'State of the Environment Report on Human Settlements: Stocks and flows indicators', www.deh.gov.au/soe.
9    The Australian Government Treasury (2002) 'Intergenerational Report 2002/3' and 'Budget Paper No 5', Australian Government Treasury, Canberra.
10   See www.deh.gov.au/soe.

## Box 37

1    For further information see www.eia.org.au/files/PF5QGPZHO2/SRI%20Benchmarking%202006%20EIA.pdf (Australia), www.eurosif.org/publications/sri_studies (Europe) and www.socialinvest.org/areas/research (US).

## Box 38

1    Further information available at www.QuestForTheFuture.com.

## Box 42

1    Heal, G. (2000) *Nature and the Marketplace: Capturing the Value of Ecosystem Services*, Island Press, Washington, DC.
2    Frankel, C. (1998) *In Earth's Company: Business, Environment and the Challenge of Sustainability*, New Society Publishers, Gabriola Island, British Columbia.

## Box 44

1    Wong, N. et al (2003) 'The effect of rooftop garden on energy consumption of a commercial building in Singapore', *Energy and Buildings*, vol 35, no 4, pp353–364; E. Oberndorfer, Lundholm, J., Bass, B., Coffman, R. R., Doshi, H. et al (2007) *Green Roofs as Urban Ecosystems: Ecological Structures, Functions, and Services, BioScience*, vol 57, no 10, pp823–833.
2    Schmidt, M. (2006) 'The evapotranpiration of greened roofs and facades', *Greening Rooftops for Sustainable Communities, Fourth Annual International Greening Rooftops for Sustainable Communities,* GRHC and the City of Boston, Boston, MA, see http://www.greenroofs.org/boston/index.php; Bass, B.and B. Baskaran (2003) Evaluating Rooftop and Vertical Gardens as an Adaptation Strategy for Urban Areas, Institute for Research and Construction, *CCAF Impacts and Adaptation Progress Report*, National Research Council, Ottawa, Canada.
3    Porsche, U. and M. Köhler (2003) 'Life-cycle costs of green roofs – A comparison of Germany, USA and Brazil', presented at RIO 3 – World Climate and Energy Event, Rio de Janeiro, Brazil; Saiz, S. et al (2006) 'Comparative life-cycle assessment of standard and green roofs', *Environmental Science and Technology*, vol 40, no 13, pp4312–4316.
4    Birkeland, J. (2007) 'GEN 4: Positive Development: Design for eco-services', *Environmental Design Guide*, The Royal Australian Institute of Architects, Canberra, ACT

## Box 54

1    Further information on the Institute for Khmer Traditional Textiles available at http://iktt.esprit-libre.org/en/.
2    Cribb, J. (2006) 'Silk road to new hope', *Canberra Times: Times 2*, 10 January, pp4–5.
3    Ibid.
4    See www.rolexawards.com/laureates/pdf/laureate0080.pdf.


## Glossary

1    McDonough, W. and M. Braungart (2002) *Cradle to Cradle: Remaking the Way We Make Things*, North Point Press, New York.
2    Schmidheiny, S. with the BCSD (Business Council for Sustainable Development) (1992) *Changing Course: A Global Business Perspective on Development and the Environment*, MIT Press, Cambridge, MA; WBCSD (World Business Council for Sustainable Development), L. DeSimone and F. Popoff (1997) *Eco-Efficiency: The Business Link to Sustainable Development*, MIT Press, Cambridge, MA.

# Biographies of Contributors

**David Baggs**, FRAIA, alongside Mary-Lou Kelly, leads the team of Ecospecifier, a division of Natural Integrated Living Pty Ltd (NIL). NIL has nearly 50 years' combined experience in delivering sustainable built environments to the commercial and residential sectors throughout Australia. As eco-materials consultants, green building architects, sustainability facilitators consultants and educators, NIL specializes in facilitating high-level ESD performance in products, supply-chain design, construction, interior design, healthy built environments and renewable technology to some of Australia's most internationally recognized 'green' projects. There is also a dedicated team keeping subscribers and manufacturers up to date with product information and communications.

**Greg Bamford** is a senior lecturer in architecture at The University of Queensland. He holds a PhD in philosophy on aspects of rationality and the scientific method, with publications on the philosophy of science and design. His current research interests include the relations between housing and urban densities and the social and environmental aspects of housing and neighbourhood design and housing with shared facilities and spaces. He teaches design studies and people/environment studies in architecture.

**Paul Bannister** is Managing Director of Exergy Australia, one of the country's leading energy-efficiency consultancies. He specializes in commercial and institutional building energy-efficiency in both new and existing buildings, and has worked on hundreds of projects throughout the sector. He has a particular interest in the question of how buildings achieve efficient performance, having extensive experience of how buildings fail to work in practice. Paul is also the primary technical author of the Australian Building Greenhouse Rating Scheme.

**Dave Biggs** has been both personally and professionally devoted to creating sustainable cities since the term 'sustainable development' was coined in 1987. He has been a pioneer in the development and use of computer tools to engage stakeholders in planning for sustainable futures. As a co-founder of Envision Sustainability Tools, Dave has led over 100 cities around the globe in their efforts to create

40- to 100-year sustainability plans in partnership with their citizens. Dave is an internationally recognized consultant, speaker and workshop facilitator and has written several books and papers on sustainability and the role of scenario tools in inspiring positive change.

**Janis Birkeland** is Professor of Architecture at the Queensland University of Technology. She is known for developing the concept of Positive Development and design for eco-services, where development itself can become a sustainability solution. She has taught this new approach to sustainable development and ecological architecture for 15 years and has set up new courses in sustainable systems in 3 universities. She has written over 100 publications and over 100 conference talks pertaining to sustainability and built environment design, including *Design for Sustainability: A Sourcebook of Integrated, Eco-logical Solutions* (Earthscan, 2002). She worked consecutively as artist, advocacy planner, architect (registered), urban designer, city planner and attorney (registered) in San Francisco before entering academia in Australia.

**Jason Byrne** is currently completing his PhD in geography at the University of Southern California (USC). He is investigating issues of park equity through the theoretical perspective of urban political ecology. Jason is a research fellow with the Johns Hopkins University's Institute for Policy Studies and with USC's Center for Sustainable Cities. He has recently co-authored academic papers on the political ecology of parks and has authored a report for the US National Park Service on recreational trail use in the Santa Monica Mountains. Jason previously worked as an environmental planner in Western Australia.

**Tim Cadman**, MA, is currently completing a PhD in the School of Government, University of Tasmania and has 15 years' background in forest conservation and certification. He was the country representative of the Forest Stewardship Council in Australia for 3 years, and served on the technical reference group of the Australian Forestry Standard. 650,000 hectares of timber resources in Australia have been certified under the FSC system, and a similar amount under the AFS.

**Glen Corder** is a senior research project manager at the Centre for Social Responsibility in Mining at the University of Queensland, Australia. He is a chemical engineer and holds a BSc (Hons) and an MSc in engineering from the University of Queensland and a PhD from the University of Cambridge. He has over 15 years' experience in the minerals industry, predominantly in the areas of mineral processing and process control. More recently, his research has focused on industrial synergies, which has resulted in collaborative research with Curtin University of Technology's Centre of Excellence in Cleaner Production.

**Robin Drogemuller** is Professor of Digital Design at the Faculty of Built Environment and Engineering at Queensland University of Technology (QUT) in Brisbane, Australia. Prior to joining QUT in 2007 he was a team leader for the Urban Informatics/Integrated Design Systems team within CSIRO, the Australian Government's national research organization. Prior to this he worked as an academic at James Cook University of North Queensland, Townsville, and the Northern Territory University, Darwin. Before entering academia he worked as an architect in the public sector in the Northern Territory and in the private sector in South Australia.

**David Eastburn** holds a Master in Applied Science in environmental education and has more than 35 years' experience of working mainly with rural communities in Australia and the Pacific on community capacity realization, education and sustainability communication projects. He spent a decade in Papua New Guinea. He has worked with communities in rural New South Wales on projects to help address rural 'identity crises'. As Director of Communication with the Murray–Darling

Basin Commission he was responsible for the development and implementation of a major multi-faceted sustainability communication programme. He is currently working with landholders and the Murrumbidgee Catchment Management Authority to develop a natural resources management plan to assist with an agro-ecological future for a 300,000 hectare wetland-based bioregion in southwest New South Wales.

**Richard Eckersley**'s work explores issues to do with progress and wellbeing, and whether life is getting better or worse. It includes measures of progress; the relationships between economic growth, quality of life and ecological sustainability; the social and cultural determinants of health and happiness; visions of the future; and young people and their world. He is a founding director of Australia 21, a non-profit, public-interest research company established to promote interdisciplinary and cross-institutional networks on important challenges facing Australia this century, and a visiting fellow at the National Centre for Epidemiology and Population Health at the Australian National University in Canberra.

**John Frazer** is Professor and Head of School of Design at the Queensland University of Technology. Previously he was International Research Co-ordinator for the Gehry Technologies Digital Practice Ecosystem. His research is on the application of advanced digital design tools to the sustainability agenda. Previously he pioneered the development of intelligent and interactive building design systems and generative evolutionary design computation. Trained as an architect at the Architectural Association, he then taught at Cambridge University, was Professor and Head of School at the University of Ulster and then Swire Chair and Head of School of Design in the Hong Kong Polytechnic University. His book *An Evolutionary Architecture* presents a generative approach to sustainable design. He is founding chair of the d_city research network to develop dynamic digital data designs for cities (dcityresearch.net).

**Gerry Gillespie** is currently Chair of Zero Waste Australia. He entered the recycling industry publishing books for local governments in New South Wales in 1988, and was involved in the ACT Government's 'No Waste by 2010' strategy in 1996, the world's first official zero waste strategy. He then became the founding Manager of the Zero Waste New Zealand Trust in 1997. The objective was to have New Zealand become the first country to have zero waste to landfill as its strategy – this has since occurred. More than 30 New Zealand councils now have zero waste to landfill as their strategic direction. He also currently holds the position of Coordinator for the Zero Waste International Alliance – a global support network of communities and businesses with zero waste as their long-term goal.

**James Greyson** is an independent sustainability analyst and researcher based in England. He is interested in the use of systems thinking to design small interventions with the potential for large-scale rapid improvements to the toughest global problems. James is an active member of the UK Sustainable Development Panel and a driving force behind several websites: www.blindspot.org.uk; www.grosspeacefulproduct.org.uk; www.frontofpipe.net.

**Konrad Knerr** is the Company Secretary of the Centre for Australian Ethical Research (CAER). He has an honours degree in European Studies from the Australian National University in Canberra. From 2000 he worked for the ASX-listed funds management company Australian Ethical Investment Limited, before helping to establish the not-for-profit Centre for Australian Ethical Research Pty Ltd in 2002. He is a member of the Australian Ethical Sustainability Committee and a finance committee member of a local community association.

**Sonia Sales Mendoza** resides in Quezon City, Metro Manila, the Philippines. Sonia was a founding member of the Mother Earth Foundation and is now its Chairman. She was the first NGO Commissioner to the National Solid Waste Management Commission (2001 to 2005). She serves as a resource person on ecological waste management and advocate for Environmental Health and Justice, and was one of three Zero Waste Fellows in the first Berkeley Ecology Center Zero Waste Fellowship in Berkeley, California. She coordinates with local government officials (governors, mayors and *barangay* captains) for their zero waste programmes. Sonia campaigns actively with the Global Alliance for Incinerator Alternatives (GAIA) and the Ecowaste Coalition for Environmental Health and Justice, and dreams of the conservation of biodiversity and a sustainable environment for the Philippines.

**Peter W. Newton** is Professor of Urban and Regional Development at Swinburne University of Technology in Melbourne. Prior to 2007 he was Chief Research Scientist at the Commonwealth Scientific and Industrial Research Organisation (CSIRO), where he held several key leadership roles, including Chief Scientist, Deputy Chief and Science Director (Sustainable Built Environment Technologies). He is author of the 2006 *Australia State of Environment Report: Human Settlements*.

**Fabia Pryor** holds a combined Bachelor of Arts/Sciences degree from the Australian National University. She has studied development studies, international relations, geography and sustainability studies and has combined this breadth of interest into a particular focus on sustainable textiles. As an honours pathway project she undertook an independent research project investigating the role of sustainable textiles as a driver of whole system change, particularly focusing on 'developing' countries. Fabia intends to pursue postgraduate studies in this area, in preparation for which she is travelling to South America to undertake further research.

**Neil Seldman** was co-founder (in 1974) and is President of the Institute for Local Self-Reliance in Washington, DC. His expertise is in recycling and economic development. For over 30 years he has helped start and expand small businesses that generate little or no waste. Currently, he is focused on zero waste industrial parks, deconstruction and recovery of building materials which have a dramatic impact on global climate change, and local training and employment. Neil trained in the history of ideas and was a university lecturer in political science. He has also been a manufacturer in New York City, where he was born.

**Sharon Stacy**, BSc, began as an adventure tour operator before moving into teaching environmental studies. It was a natural transition from there to the development and trial of the Ecotour Curriculum for the Australian tourism industry. Married to a fifth-generation sheep and cattle producer, she is privileged to look across five generations of land management and apply the informal daily lessons of primary production towards understanding sustainability. She came to understand that primary producers could not bear the burden alone. This was when she began to look at the secondary sector and the role it can play in establishing a sustainable economy.

**Yael Stav** has an interdisciplinary background in computer science and design. Her studio, Invivo Design, focuses on the integration of living plants into household and office products. As director of design in the Plantware initiative, she is responsible for the design and prototyping of products made of living trees using unique horticultural techniques. Her current research, at the Queensland University of Technology, involves Living Walls and their potential to increase urban environment sustainability, as well as the integration of computer-based tools in the building-integrated vegetation design process.

**Ian Swain** has completed an MSc in environmental science at the Australian National University, focusing on sustainable planning and design. His other qualifications include a graduate diploma in resource and environmental management and BA and BSc degrees. His main interest is in the application of ecological principles to the understanding and improvement of human–environmental systems. He has experience in both government organizations and private environmental consulting firms, as well as with various local land-management and conservation groups. Ian is currently teaching research skills and information literacy at the ANU.

**Dr Robin Tennant-Wood** is Director of the Canberra Environment and Sustainability Resource Centre at the Australian National University. She has a background in local government, having served a term as Councillor on the Snowy River Shire Council, and in waste and environment policy. She chaired the New South Wales Government's South East Waste Board, is a member of the ACT Government's Sustainability Expert Reference Group and Urban Services Community Advisory Group, and is a member of the board of the Australian National Sustainability Initiative. Robin has researched extensively on the political and social aspects of waste generation and management.

**Patrick Nicol Troy**, is driven by a strong sense of social equity as well as a passion for sustainability. He has published on urban planning, housing and transport in Australian cities and is currently working on water policy, the vulnerability of the city, the construction of energy, water profiles for Australian cities and the suburbanization of Australian cities. He was a founding member of the Australian National University's Urban Research Unit and is currently Emeritus Professor and Visiting Fellow at the Centre for Resource and Environmental Studies at the Australian National University, Adjunct Professor of the Urban Research Program at Griffith University, and Visiting Professor at the City Futures Research Centre of the Faculty of Built Environment at the University of New South Wales.

**Linda S. Velazquez** holds a Bachelor's Degree in landscape architecture from the University of Georgia. She is founder and publisher of Greenroofs.com, the international greenroof industry's resource and online information portal, and publisher of *The Greenroof Directory of Manufacturers, Suppliers, Professional Services, Organizations and Green Resources*. Greenroofs.com serves as a clearinghouse for news, upcoming events and organizations, and includes contributing editor columns, guest features, forums and the global Greenroof Projects Database. As principal of Sky Gardens Design and a LEED-Accredited Professional, Linda designs, consults and presents on greenroofs. She has written and reported extensively about greenroofs, including in her occasional column entitled 'SkyGardens – Travels in Landscape Architecture' on Greenroofs.com.

**Kumar Venkat** has spent over 20 years developing complex computer hardware and software products. For the last 10 years, he has been an independent software developer providing analysis and optimization software to the semiconductor industry for integrated circuit design. He is currently working on applying a similarly rigorous approach to solving problems in environmental sustainability using innovative software tools. Kumar holds an MSc in electrical and computer engineering and a graduate certificate in computer modelling and simulation. He has published widely and has received two engineering patents (see www.suryatech.com).

**Sarah West** gained a BSc and a Master's Degree in environmental management after an earlier career in health and education. In 2000, and again in 2004, she conducted extensive research into sustainable small-scale sewage treatment and recycling systems and ecovillages in Europe and the US. Sarah has worked for Sydney Water, a private consultancy firm, and the Environmental

Protection Agency in Victoria, assessing the benefits, risks and costs associated with installing and managing innovative sewerage and recycling schemes for unsewered towns and green field sites. These experiences have deepened Sarah's conviction that community-scale integrated rainwater, stormwater, reclaimed water and local energy systems are an important model for regional prosperity, security and sustainability.

# Index

# B

# C

# E

# F

# N

## Q

## R